The
Complete
Bible
Companion

D1707555

The Complete Bible Companion

BARBOUR
PUBLISHING

Published by Barbour Publishing, Inc., P.O. Box 719, Uhrichsville, Ohio 44683, www.barbourbooks.com

Our mission is to publish and distribute inspirational products offering exceptional value and biblical encouragement to the masses.

Member of the
Evangelical Christian
Publishers Association

Printed in the United States of America.

Contents/
How to Use This Book

Here's a single-volume library of study helps, especially for the everyday reader—*The Complete Bible Companion*, a perfect resource for laypeople of all ages and backgrounds. When you're interested in better knowing God's Word, this is the book to consult.

In the pages to follow, you'll find eight sections designed to improve your comfort with the scripture—whether in specific areas such as names and dates or in your handling of Bible reading and study:

Time Lines (beginning on page 7): You may find it helpful to begin here, to familiarize yourself with some of the chronology of important events and names in the Bible story.

Bible Handbook (beginning on page 11): This section, the largest in *The Complete Bible Companion,* provides helpful explanations for every passage of the sixty-six books of scripture. Here you'll find background information on the Bible books and their authors, commentary on the historical and literary context of each passage, and other helpful clarification on your Bible reading.

Dictionary/Concordance (beginning on page 257): If you are seeking information on a particular name, word, or topic, you'll find more than one thousand definitions along with references to key Bible verses.

Complete List of Individuals Named in Scripture (beginning on page 379): Additional information on the fascinating people of the Bible—more than 3,100 individuals—can be found here. Key references are provided for each, as well as brief biographies for more prominent characters.

Archaeological Evidences for the Bible (beginning on page 537): This section shares further information on many of the people, places, and things already mentioned, showing how perfectly their stories mesh with scientific discoveries of the near and more distant past.

Maps of Bible Lands and Events (beginning on page 591): Thirty-six information-rich maps show locations of key Bible towns and cities, rivers and lakes, and other geographical features, as well as the movements of important Bible characters.

How to Study the Bible (beginning on page 629): A bestselling guide that provides clear direction on the various types, tools, and techniques of Bible study, along with step-by-step Bible study practice to help you on your learning journey.

Bible Reading Plan (beginning on page 691): A 365-day program to help you read the entirety of God's Word in a year, with an Old Testament, New Testament, and "Wisdom Book" (Psalms or Proverbs) passage each day.

We hope this volume is helpful to you in your study of the "powerful" (Hebrews 4:12) Word of God, which provides a "light unto [our] path" (Psalm 119:105).

THE EDITORS

Time Lines

This section of *The Complete Bible Companion* provides an overview of the chronology of the entire Bible. It may be helpful to review the following names, events, and dates, since scripture's sixty-six books do not always follow a chronological order.

Most dates in the following time lines, and throughout *The Complete Bible Companion*, are approximate. Though a few dates can be specified according to outside, non-Bible sources, most are estimates based on the best guesses of conservative scholars.

Additional information on many of the people and places in the following section can be found in the "Dictionary/Concordance of Key Bible Names, Places, Terms, and Topics" beginning on page 257 and in the "Complete List of Individuals Named in Scripture" beginning on page 379. An extensive section of maps begins on page 591.

Early Old Testament History

2100–1500 BC: Age of the patriarchs (Middle Bronze Age)
c. 1950 BC: Amorites conquer Mesopotamia
1500–1200 BC: The Exodus and conquest of the Promised Land (Late Bronze Age)
c. 1469–c. 1211 BC: Possible dates for the Exodus
1200–900 BC: Establishment of Israel (Early Iron Age)
c. 1050 BC: The Philistines settle in southern Palestine

Ancient Empires

Assyrian Empire 1100–609 BC
859–824 BC: Reign of King Shalmaneser III
855–625 BC: Assyrian influence on Palestine
783–773 BC: Reign of King Shalmaneser IV
744–727 BC: Reign of King Tiglath-pileser III
c. 732–612 BC: Israel and Judah subject to Assyria
727–722 BC: Fall of Israel to Assyria; Samaria destroyed
722 BC: Reign of King Shalmaneser V
705–681: BC Reign of King Sennacherib
612 BC: Fall of Nineveh to Neo-Babylonian (Chaldean) Empire
609 BC: Chaldeans defeat Assyria

Neo-Babylonian (Chaldean) Empire 605–538 BC
c. 626 BC: Start of Neo-Babylonian (Chaldean) Empire
586 BC: Fall of Jerusalem to the Chaldeans; temple destroyed
539 BC: Fall of Neo-Babylonian Empire

Persian Empire 538–331 BC
538 BC: Cyrus conquers Babylon (Chaldea) and establishes Persian Empire
522–485 BC: Reign of King Darius I
486–465 BC: Reign of King Ahasuerus (Xerxes) of Persia
c. 479 BC: Esther made queen of Persia
465–423 BC: Reign of King Artaxerxes I of Persia
333 BC: End of Persian control of Palestine
331 BC: End of Persian Empire

Macedonian Empire 336–168 BC
336–323 BC: Rule of Alexander the Great
333 BC: Alexander the Great gains control of Palestine
331 BC: Alexander the Great conquers Persian Empire

Seleucid rule 312–83 BC
175–163 BC: Rule of Syrian king Antiochus IV (Epiphanes)

Roman Empire 27 BC–AD 476
63 BC: Roman Empire takes control of Judaea
37–4 BC: Reign of Herod the Great, king of Judaea

Israel/Judah

Prophets

770–750 BC: Ministry of the prophet Jonah in
  Assyria
763–750 BC: Ministry of the prophet Amos in
  Israel
750–722 BC: Ministry of the prophet Hosea
  in Israel
742–687 BC: Ministry of the prophet Micah
  in Judah
740–700 BC: Ministry of the prophet Isaiah in
  Judah
640–621 BC: Ministry of the prophet
  Zephaniah in Judah
627–586 BC: Ministry of the prophet Jeremiah
  in Judah
612–588 BC: Ministry of the prophet
  Habakkuk in Judah
c. 605–536 BC: Ministry of the prophet Daniel
  in Babylon
593–571 BC: Ministry of the prophet Ezekiel
  in Babylon
c. 586 BC: Book of Obadiah written to Judah
520 BC: Book of Haggai written to Judah
520–518 BC: Ministry of the prophet Zechariah
  in Judah
440–430 BC: Ministry of the prophet Malachi
  in Judah

Rulers

United Israel

1050–1010 BC: Reign of King Saul of Israel
1023 BC: Samuel anoints David king of Israel
1010–970 BC: Reign of King David of Israel
970–930 BC: Reign of King Solomon of Israel
c. 966–959 BC: King Solomon builds the
  temple

Divided Israel

930 BC: Start of Divided Kingdom (separate
  states of Israel and Judah)

Judah

930–913 BC: Reign of King Rehoboam
913–910 BC: Reign of King Abijam
910–872 BC: Reign of King Asa
872–853 BC: Reign of King Jehoshaphat
853–841 BC: Reign of King Jehoram
841 BC: Reign of King Ahaziah
841–835 BC: Reign of Queen Athaliah
835–796 BC: Reign of King Joash

796–792 BC: Reign of King Amaziah
792–750 BC: Reign of King Azariah (Uzziah)
750–735 BC: Reign of King Jotham
735–715 BC: Reign of King Ahaz
715–697 BC: Reign of King Hezekiah
697–642 BC: Reign of King Manasseh
642–640 BC: Reign of King Amon
640–609 BC: Reign of King Josiah
609 BC: Reign of King Jehoahaz
609–598 BC: Reign of King Jehoiakim
598–597 BC: Reign of King Jehoiachin
597–586 BC: Reign of King Zedekiah

Northern Israel

930–909 BC: Reign of King Jeroboam I
909–908 BC: Reign of King Nadab
908–886 BC: Reign of King Baasha
886–885 BC: Reign of King Elah
885–874 BC: Reign of King Omri
874–853 BC: Reign of King Ahab
853–852 BC: Reign of King Ahaziah
852–841 BC: Reign of King Joram (Jehoram)
841–814 BC: Reign of King Jehu
814–798 BC: Reign of King Jehoahaz
798–793 BC: Reign of King Jehoash
793–753 BC: Reign of King Jeroboam II
753–752 BC: Reign of King Zechariah
752 BC: Reign of King Shallum
752–742 BC: Reign of King Menahem
742–740 BC: Reign of King Pekahiah
740–732 BC: Reign of King Pekah
732–722 BC: Reign of King Hoshea
586 BC: Babylonian Empire conquers Judah and
  destroys Jerusalem and Solomon's
  temple
538 BC: The first exiles return to Jerusalem
c. 516 BC: Second temple completed
457 BC: Ezra returns to Judah with more exiles
c. 445 BC: Nehemiah leads Jews back to
  Jerusalem
432 BC: Nehemiah's second visit to Jerusalem
152–37 BC: Rule of the Maccabees

New Testament

c. 6 BC: Birth of Jesus

4 BC–AD 6: Rule of Herod Archelaus,
ethnarch of Judaea, Samaria, and
Idumea

4 BC– AD 39: Rule of Herod Antipas, tetrarch
of Galilee and Perea

4 BC– AD 34: Rule of Herod Philip, tetrarch
of Iturea and Trachonitis

AD 26: Jesus' public ministry begins

AD 30: Jesus' death and resurrection

AD 47–49: Paul's first missionary journey

AD 49: Roman emperor Claudius expels Jews
from Rome; church holds Council
of Jerusalem

AD 50–52: Paul's second missionary journey

c. AD 52–56: Paul's third missionary journey

AD 59: Paul's first Roman imprisonment
begins

AD 67–68: Paul's final imprisonment and
death in Rome

AD 70: Herod's temple destroyed

Bible
Handbook

This section of *The Complete Bible Companion* is designed to provide you with a simple, yet meaningful overview of each book of the Bible. It is intended for students of all ages and evangelical denominational backgrounds.

For each of the Bible's sixty-six books, you'll find

- An introduction that gives critical background information, including details on the author, occasion and purpose of the book, and key themes in the larger Bible story.
- Passage-by-passage commentary focusing on the logical flow of the book as well as the historical and literary context for each section of scripture.
- Explanatory sidebars that explain puzzling Biblical customs or difficult Bible passages, or provide critical observations you can apply to your life today.

Additional information on many of the people and places in the following section can be found in the "Dictionary/Concordance of Key Bible Names, Places, Terms, and Topics" beginning on page 257 and in the "Complete List of Individuals Named in Scripture" beginning on page 379. An extensive section of maps begins on page 591.

Genesis
Introduction to Genesis

The first eleven chapters of Genesis trace events such as Creation, the Fall, the Flood, and the establishing of the nations. The accounts of four great people complete the book in chapters 12–50: Abraham, Isaac, Jacob, and Joseph.

Genesis comes from the Greek word *geneseos*, meaning "origin, source, generation, or beginning." Geneseos is a translation of the Hebrew word *toledot* ("generations").

Author
Although Genesis does not directly name its author, Jesus and the writers of scripture clearly believed that Moses was the author of the Pentateuch (the first five books of the Bible, often referred to in the New Testament as "the Law," Mark 10:5; Luke 24:44).

Occasion/Purpose
Genesis spans more time than any other book in the Bible. In fact, it covers more than all the other sixty-five books of the Bible put together (approximately 2,400 years). The total duration is from the time of creation to the time when the Israelites arrive in Egypt and grow into a nation (about 1800 BC). The date of Genesis is sometime after the Exodus, during the fifteenth century BC.

Themes
God's choice of a nation through which He would bless all nations is a theme throughout Genesis. It is the passing on of blessings from one generation to another.

Background & Context
The setting of Genesis divides neatly into three geographical areas:

1. The Fertile Crescent (1–11)
2. Canaan (12–36)
3. Egypt (37–50)

The setting of the first eleven chapters changes rapidly and spans more than 2,000 years and 1,500 miles. The middle section of Genesis spans about 200 years and moves from the Fertile Crescent to the land of Canaan. The final setting in Genesis is found in Egypt, where God transports the seventy souls.

Creation (1:1–2:25)
The initial recipients of this story are the Israelites of Moses' day. Because it is written to the people of God, not as an apologetic to convince those who do not believe, Genesis is much more of a declaration than a defense. These chapters are not intended to give an account of the Creation that would answer all of the scientific problems and phenomenon. Rather, there is an air of mystery that permeates these two chapters,

and within that mystery is the fact that God created this world and it exists within His control.

The Summary of Creation:
God Formed the Earth
God Filled the Earth
    Day 1: Light (1:3–5)
    Day 2: Air (1:6–8)
    Day 2: Water (1:6–8)
    Day 3: Land (1:9–13)
    Day 3: Plants (1:9–13)
    Day 4: Lights (1:14–19)
    Day 5: Birds (1:20–23)
    Day 5: Fish (1:20–23)
    Day 6: Animals (1:24–31)
    Day 6: Man (1:24–31)

Background & Context

In 2:8-9, God's care is made evident by His provision of a garden paradise with two trees—the Tree of Life and the Tree of the Knowledge of Good and Evil. Verses 10-14 describe the boundaries of this garden. Of the four rivers mentioned, the Pishon and Gihon are unknown in the modern world (though the land of Havilah is probably an area of southwestern Arabia). The Tigris and Euphrates are now in Babylonia. The name Eden means "delight, pleasure." This rather extensive description sets the stage for Adam and Eve's expulsion from the garden in 3:24. It also probably signifies to the Israelites an anticipation of the Promised Land. Two of these rivers are exactly the ones that God uses to explain to Abraham where the Promised Land will be (15:18).

The Fall of Humanity (3:1–5:32)

This passage reveals how sin enters the world and how sin can be overcome. At the end of Genesis 2, life seems ideal—paradise. Then the events described in this section forever change the world. Fear and shame enter and judgment begins. But the seeds of redemption can be found as well.

The Flood (6:1–9:29)

Genesis 6–8 covers a lot of ground. These chapters document the degradation of society, Noah's great flood, and the beginnings of life beyond the Flood with Noah's three sons, Shem, Ham, and Japheth.

Background & Context

How could Noah's ark potentially hold over a billion species of animals (6:19-21)? Keep in mind that the modern concept of species is not the same as a "kind" in the Bible. There were probably only several hundred different kinds of land animals that would have to be taken into the ark. The sea animals stayed in the sea, and many species could have survived in egg form. Also, Noah could have taken younger varieties of some larger animals. And finally, the ark was a huge structure—the size of a modern ocean liner three stories high.

Noah's Descendants (10:1–11:32)

Chapters 10–11 track the repopulation of the earth from Noah's sons and the separation of the nations into individual cultures.

The genealogies in Genesis 10 include reference to the separation of nations (10:5, 20, 31) that occurs at the Tower of Babel, which is described in chapter 11. This interspersed narrative (11:1–9) separates the two genealogies of Shem (10:21–31; 11:10–26), paving the way for the link between the Terah (father of Abraham) clan and Shem's lineage (11:27).

Abraham (12:1–20:18)

Chapter 11 describes the third time in Genesis that humanity strikes out—first in Eden, then with the Flood, and finally at Babel. Beginning with chapter 12, we at last see the foundation God is laying for a solution. Through Abram, God promises a descendant who will eventually bring salvation. This is an act of grace. God is certainly a God of justice and judgment, but in His economy, grace always prevails.

Isaac (21:1–25:18)

Chapters 21–25 offer the accounts of Isaac's birth and Abraham's death. This period of time is the beginning of the fulfillment of God's promise that Abraham would father a nation.

Isaac's Family (25:19–36:43)

The entire book of Genesis emphasizes the sovereignty of God and the wisdom of His "delays." Chapters 26–36 trace this sovereignty through the generation following Isaac. The struggles that Jacob and Esau face, as described in retrospect in Genesis, reveal God's plan rising to the surface against the odds.

Jacob's Sons (37:1–50:26)

For the final time, Genesis introduces a new series of generations. This marks the final section in the book of Genesis. The storyline of the last fourteen chapters focuses on Jacob's sons. Of those twelve sons, most of the focus is on Joseph. This whole section reveals how God's plan for His people triumphs over human frailties to guide and strengthen those who follow Him.

Background & Context

What is the birthright, and why does Jacob want it so badly (25:32–33)? Deuteronomy 21:17 and 1 Chronicles 5:1–2 tell us the birthright involves both a material and a spiritual blessing. The son of the birthright receives a double portion of the inheritance, and he also becomes head of the family and the spiritual leader upon the passing of the father (Genesis 43:33). And, in the case of this family, the birthright determines who will inherit the covenant God made with Abraham—the covenant of a land, a nation, and the Messiah.

Exodus
Introduction to Exodus

Exodus tells the story of the birth of the nation of Israel through their deliverance from bondage in Egypt and the receiving of God's instructions, based on His covenant, for building their nation to honor Him.

Author
Though there is debate among scholars about the authorship of Exodus, Moses is considered the author by most evangelical scholars.

Occasion/Purpose
The main purpose of the book of Exodus is to describe God's rescue of His enslaved people and His making them a nation. This book chronicles God's faithfulness to His people—in spite of their sin.

The book of Genesis closes with the family of Israel making a home in Egypt under the leadership of Joseph. Exodus picks up centuries later in Egypt after the family of Israel has grown into the nation of Israel. While Joseph had saved the Egyptians from starvation, his family's descendants had become slaves. Exodus follows the story of God's people from the birth of Moses, the leader of Israel during this period in their history, through their deliverance from bondage, the giving of the law, and the construction of the tabernacle in the desert.

Themes
Exodus is rich in themes that will recur in the Old and New Testaments—the burden of bondage to sin, God's faithfulness and deliverance in spite of stubbornness, and the radical vision that He has for His people.

Contribution to the Bible
In many ways, Exodus expands on what Genesis teaches us about God's character and His intentions for creation. We witness both His judgment in the plagues on the Egyptians and His mercy in the deliverance of the Israelites from slavery. The Exodus

introduces the Law of the Lord, which will bring both blessing and suffering to the nation of Israel until it is fulfilled by the work and person of Jesus Christ. Exodus establishes how Israel is going to be set up, and much of the rest of the Old Testament recounts their struggle to meet God's requirements. The book also describes God dwelling with His people in the tabernacle, which is ultimately an image for the kingdom of heaven. It is rich in relevance to the New Testament with its many symbols of the sacrificial lamb, the holiness of God, and the fatal consequences of people's failure to keep His commandments.

Pharaoh's Fears and Israel's Faith (1:1–22)
There are times when God is there, but He is, at least from our perspective, silent. The period of time depicted in the first chapter of Exodus is a time when, from all appearances, God is silent. Nevertheless, God is present, and His hand is at work in the lives of His children.

Moses: Israel's Deliverer (2:1–25)
Few stories in the Bible are more familiar than that of Moses set afloat in the waters of the Nile and his rescue by the daughter of Pharaoh. Exodus 2 shows how God's hand is at work in the history of Israel, preserving the life of one child who will become Israel's deliverer.

Background & Context
The deliverance of Moses is significant in that it is a beautiful illustration of the truth declared in Ephesians 3:20-21. Not only was Moses spared and protected by Pharaoh's daughter's love, but his parents were allowed to keep him for a time, train him in the ways of their God, and then, in addition to all these blessings, they were paid for it. Now, in the palace of the Pharaoh whose orders were, "Throw them in the water!" there is a Hebrew boy whose name means "Taken from the water." Once again, God providentially preserved and prospered His people. Not only was Moses spared, but now there is a Hebrew living in the palace, part of the royal family. What a challenge to the limits of our faith! What a gracious God we serve!

The Burning Bush (3:1–22)
Chapter 3 introduces a significant change in the drama of the deliverance of God's people from Egypt. From God's providential dealings in the life of the nation of Israel, we move to God's direct intervention through Moses and the miracles He performs. We move from the silence of God over the past four hundred years to God's speaking directly to Moses from the bush, and later on, from the same mountain.

Background & Context

Attempts to explain the burning bush as something other than miraculous abound. Some of the most common include that it was a natural phenomenon called "St. Elmo's fire," which is a discharge of electricity that causes a kind of glow, or firebrands of light that often occur in dry lands with an abundance of storms. Others suggest that it may have been a volcanic phenomenon, or simply that this account is a myth, like other ancient accounts of burning objects that were not consumed. Still others say that it may have been a beam of sunlight piercing through a crack in the mountain, or a purely psychological experience. The author (Moses) himself, however, provides a wholly supernatural explanation—the burning bush that would not be consumed was aglow with the angel of the Lord (Genesis 16:7; 22:11; Exodus 3:2; Judges 6:11; 13:3), the preincarnate manifestation of the second person of the Godhead.

Beating Around the Burning Bush (4:1–31)

Moses seeks to prove that he is not the man for the task that God has given him. The essence of Moses' argument is, "Send someone else!"

The Reality of Bondage (5:1–6:13)

After Moses has met with God, he returns to Egypt where his fears that Pharaoh would resist God's demands to let the Israelites go are realized.

God's People: Moses and Aaron (6:14–7:13)

God often uses genealogies to testify to His faithfulness and work across generations in space and time.

The Finger of God (7:14–10:29)

The plagues God brings upon the Egyptians are a unique kind of tragedy—part of God's judgment of Pharaoh and his people for their oppression of the Israelites (see Genesis 15:13–14; Deuteronomy 11:1–4; Psalm 78:44–52).

Background & Context

Frogs were also regarded as having divine power. In the Egyptian pantheon, the goddess Heqet had the form of a woman with a frog's head. From her nostrils, it was believed, came the breath of life that animated the bodies of those created by her husband, the great god Khnum, from the dust of the earth. Therefore frogs were not to be killed.

The Passover and the Plague on the Firstborn (11:1–13:16)
The slaughter of the firstborn of the Egyptians raises tremendous moral issues. God uses the tenth plague as the means to release His people from slavery. This text insists that we examine and accept the meaning and application of God's judgment at work in His creation and in the lives of His people.

Background & Context
For the Israelites, the Passover and the tenth plague serve as a judgment on the gods of Egypt, whom the Israelites had worshipped (Joshua 24:14), and as evidence of the grace of God in the lives of His people. The plagues point out the sin of the Egyptians and their need to repent and believe in the God of Israel.

The firstborn of Israel are not spared because they are more worthy or more righteous than the Egyptians, but because of the grace of God alone. God made provision for non-Israelites to partake of the Passover if they were circumcised (acknowledging their faith in the Abrahamic Covenant; see Genesis 17:9–14; Exodus 12:48–49). Since there were many non-Israelites who left Egypt with Israel (Exodus 12:38), it is likely that a number were converted and physically spared from death through the process of the plagues and the provision of the Passover.

The Red Sea: Israel's Deliverance and Egypt's Defeat (13:17–14:31)
This text portrays the hardness of humanity's heart, which leads ultimately to destruction. The sea that destroyed the Egyptians is the instrument of God's wrath, but it is also the instrument of Israel's deliverance.

The Song of the Sea (15:1–27)
Israel's first great affirmation of faith is expressed in a song. Some have titled this song the "Song of the Sea." The mood of the song is triumphant. The structure has two parts: what God has done for Israel at the Red Sea and what God will surely do for Israel in the future (15:11–21).

Obedience Boot Camp (16:1–36)
In the passage, Israel is guilty of two sins: greed and grumbling. Both of these sins are symptomatic of an even more serious underlying sin. Exodus 15:26 provides the background for God's provision of manna for His people. God's instructions regulating the gathering and use of the manna serve as a test of Israel's faith and obedience.

God's Grace to Israel (17:1–16)
Leaving the Desert of Sin, where the provision of manna had commenced (Exodus 16), the Israelites went from place to place as the Lord directed them. While Israel's later wandering in the wilderness is the result of their sin at Kadesh Barnea

(Numbers 13–14), the wanderings in this chapter are designed to serve as Israel's "boot camp" experiences.

The Tyranny of the Urgent (18:1–27)
Moses' father-in-law, Jethro, having heard of God's protection and deliverance of the Israelites, comes to visit in order to reunite Moses with his wife and children. The first half of the chapter reveals several symptoms of a serious problem in Moses' life, which prompts not only Jethro's arrival, but also his advice about achieving balance.

The Preamble to Israel's Constitution (19:1–25)
Chapter 19 serves as a preamble to the commandments given by God to Israel. It reveals the purpose of the commandments, as well as the perspective we should have toward them.

The Ten Commandments (20:1–26)
The Decalogue, also called the Ten Commandments, is one of the keys to understanding the Old Testament. It is the central core of the lengthy Mosaic Law.

Beyond the Ten Commandments (21:1–23:33)
The Ten Commandments set out in broad strokes God's law for His people, outlining how we are to relate to Him and honor His image in others. The Mosaic Law continues for two more chapters in Exodus, outlining God's design for protecting servants, persons, and property, and further explaining the role of social responsibility, mercy, and justice in the nation of Israel.

The Magnificent Meal on Mount Sinai (24:1–18)
Centuries before the scenes described in this text, God promised Abraham a seed (a son, which would become a great nation), a land (the land of Canaan), and the promise that this nation would be blessed and be a blessing to all nations (Genesis 12:1–3). The promises God made were ratified as a covenant between Himself and Abraham in Genesis 15. Now the Mosaic Covenant, which has been spelled out in the Ten Commandments, is formally imposed upon Israel by the God who has delivered her out of Egypt.

Background & Context
Covenants had several common elements. Usually they involved promises or commitments to which the parties bound themselves. Often a sacrifice was made, followed by a meal, which included some of the sacrifice. Also a memorial, some kind of physical token of the oath, served to remind the parties of their commitments. A curse was attached to the one who broke the covenant he had made. A sense of solemnity prevailed in the making of a covenant, for it was a serious step of commitment.

A Place to Worship (25:1–31:18)
Now that Israel has been delivered from Egypt, they need a place where they can worship their God, a place where He can be present among them. Once God gives Moses the law, He follows with specific instructions for such a place—the tabernacle.

The Rejection of God and the Revelation of Man (32:1–35)
In the story of the golden calf, Israel is guilty of impatience for God's manifestation in the tabernacle, but it is her idolatry that condemns her.

The Presence of God with His People (33:1–34:9)
Because of Israel's sin, God deals with His people from a distance as they travel through the wilderness. The grace of God is seen even in God's threat to remove Himself from Israel's midst. God states that the purpose for keeping a distance between Himself and the Israelites as they travel on toward the Promised Land is that their sinfulness would require Him to destroy them. The threatened consequence for Israel's idolatry is losing God's intimate presence among them. God's grace is evident as well in the provision of Moses as the mediator for the people. In the midst of Israel's sin, and the threat of God withholding His presence, God provides a tent where not only Moses, but all the people, can go to seek God. This provides the people a means of worshipping God and offers them a hope for a future fellowship with God.

A New Beginning (34:10–35)
Moses returns from the mountain with a radiantly beaming face, a reflection of the glory of God. Every time he speaks to God face-to-face, the radiance will be renewed. Every time he speaks to Israel with his beaming face, the people know that God is speaking to them through Moses, giving him credentials that they dare not ignore.

Israel's Offerings (35:1–36:7)
Chapters 35–40 conclude by describing the construction of the tabernacle, and climax at God's descent into the midst of the camp. The theme of this section is the presence of God in the midst of His people.

The Tabernacle, the Dwelling Place of God (36:8–39:43)
The description of the tabernacle provides the first biblical revelation as to how God dwells among His people, and what this suggests for the church today.

The Consecration of the Tabernacle and the Presence of God (40:1–38)
This is the climax of the story of Exodus: The tabernacle is completed, and the glory of God descends upon it. It is also an introduction to Leviticus. God commands the anointing of the priesthood, who will dominate the next story in the history of the Israelites and receive God's instructions regarding the use of the carefully constructed tabernacle.

Leviticus
Introduction to Leviticus

Though many see Leviticus as a book addressing the priests of Israel, the information here was actually written for the people, yet includes specific instructions for the priests. The laws relate to the entire nation of Israel, but it was the priests who were to teach others how to live as God's holy people and to regulate worship in the tabernacle (also called *sanctuary*, or *tent of meeting*), where God's holy presence dwelled.

Author
Moses is generally ascribed as the author of the first five books of the Old Testament, or the Pentateuch (which means "five books" or "five scrolls"). These books are also known as the Law of Moses, or Mosaic Law. It is most likely that Moses wrote during the time when Israel was wandering and intermittently camping in the desert for forty years during the second half of the fifteenth century BC.

Occasion/Purpose
In the Hebrew text, the first word of the book of Leviticus, translated "and He called," serves as the title of the book, though its English title means "of the Levites." The book served as a handbook for the priests God put in place after the institution of the Mosaic Covenant at Mount Sinai. The specific details are many, and this preciseness was to ensure the Israelites that the continuing presence of God was with them. The laws on both ceremonial holiness and personal holiness were supposed to teach the Israelites about their holy God and how to live set apart as His people. Not only does God tell the Israelites how to worship, but He gives them practical ways to live out holiness in everyday life.

Themes
The book of Leviticus is comprised of twenty-seven chapters, including many regulations and guidelines. The rules are not arbitrary, though. Each of the seemingly minute details in Leviticus deals with the main theme of holiness.

The phrase that is repeated most often in Leviticus is a variation of God's command, "Be holy, for I am holy." During this time, Israel was a new nation. God's laws were designed to teach them how to become set apart—holy people who imitated God's character.

The tent of meeting was built by the Israelites as a holy place to house the presence of a holy God. Sinful people could not approach their God, though, because He was the essence of holiness. The rituals and offerings detailed in Leviticus are God's compassionate design to allow His people to find atonement so that they could approach Him in worship and experience a covenant relationship with Him.

Leviticus can be divided into two major sections, separated by chapter 16, which deals with the annual Day of Atonement. Chapters 1–15 deal with what we might call priestly holiness, by giving instructions about sacrifices and rituals that relate to one's holiness. Chapters 17–27 deal more with what we could call practical holiness—that which is worked out in daily life.

Contribution to the Bible

The book of Leviticus is quoted or referred to in the New Testament at least forty times (more than any other book in the Bible). Many of Jesus' teachings, particularly those on the Great Commandment, come from Leviticus (19:18). New Testament teachings on holiness tie directly to Levitical teachings (1 Peter 2).

The greatest theological contribution of Leviticus is an introduction to atonement. The sacrificial system detailed in Leviticus reveals human sinfulness and introduces atonement through a substitutionary blood sacrifice. To fully understand the reason for and importance of Jesus' ultimate sacrifice, a student of the Bible would need to understand the Old Testament system's purpose and flaws.

The Burnt Offering (1:1–17)

In Exodus, God gives Moses instruction for how to build the tabernacle (2:1–8; 38:1–7). In Leviticus, He gives Moses instruction for how to offer sacrifices at the tabernacle. The burnt offering illustrates God's principle of atonement, where humanity's sin is answered through a sacrificial shedding of blood.

Background & Context

During the writing of Leviticus, the Israelites were camped at the base of Mount Sinai in the desert after their deliverance from Egypt and before their entrance into the land of Canaan. It was at Mount Sinai that God entered into a covenant relationship with the Israelites. He would be their God, and they would be His people. God communicated to His people through their leader, Moses, how they should live out their covenant responsibilities.

Leviticus is the third book in the Pentateuch. It is closely connected with the book of Exodus and often repeats or expands on instructions God gave through Moses there. Exodus records God's detailed instructions to the Israelites for how to build His holy tabernacle. Leviticus follows up with regulations God communicated from that tabernacle. The laws of Leviticus did not initiate sacrificial offerings, but they did serve to regulate them.

The Grain Offering (2:1–16)

The second offering explained in Leviticus is the grain offering. This name *grain offering* refers to the material most often used, but the Hebrew name for this offering indicates its primary function, which is "gift." At this time, the Israelites were camped in the desert, where they could not grow grain, so this offering (most likely wheat or barley) was a great sacrifice. To sacrifice this seed to God was an act of faith because they would have to depend on God to provide more.

The Peace Offering (3:1–17)

The burnt offering focuses on God's righteousness and an individual's atonement through an animal sacrifice. The grain offering focuses on the Israelite's dependence on God. The peace offering is made on top of the burnt offering (3:5) and focuses on the Israelites' peace with God—the peace of mind and wholeness that comes with knowing God is at peace with us. There is also a strong element of fellowship signified by the sharing of the meal together. This is why some translations translate it "fellowship offering."

Three principle passages in Leviticus deal with the peace offering: 3:1–17 (the mechanics of the sacrifice); 7:11–34 (the meaning of the sacrifice); and 19:5–8 (the law of leftovers).

Background & Context

Some Bible versions have translated *peace offering* as *fellowship offering*. Both *peace* and *fellowship* are appropriate. The word *peace* has the connotation of "wholeness" or "completeness." The Israelites became whole when they were accepted by God in worship (19:5). The meal that the offerer enjoyed, along with fellow Israelites, signified the peace that the sacrifice brought about. Today, through Christ's death, we can have peace and fellowship with God and peace and fellowship with others.

The Sin Offering (4:1–35)

Offerings in Leviticus 1–3 are organized by sacrificial animal. The sin offering in chapter 4 is organized by categories of people: high priest (4:3–12); congregation of Israel (4:13–21); leader (4:22–26); and individual Israelite (4:27–35). The sin offering is for a specific sin, as opposed to a state of sinfulness addressed by the burnt offering. Also, while chapters 1–3 are concerned with the process of sacrifice, chapters 4–6 emphasize result of the process: forgiveness. (The sin offering is further explained in 5:1–13 and 6:24–30.)

Sin and Guilt Offerings (5:1–19)

Leviticus 5:1–13 continues to explain the sin offering (see chapter 4) and begins to address sins specifically. In verses 14–19, the sin offering and the guilt offering are combined.

More Offering Rules (6:1–30)

Chapter 6 flows directly out of chapter 5, including additional details related to the guilt offering, burnt offering, grain offering, and sin offering.

Even More Rules (7:1–38)

After a few more rules about the guilt offering, the majority of chapter 7 gives additional regulations for the peace offering, including the grain offerings that should accompany it and how to handle the leftovers.

Principles of Priesthood: Ordination (8:1–36)

Leviticus 8 describes the origin and ordination of the Aaronic priesthood. This chapter portrays the fulfillment of God's commands pertaining to the ordination of Aaron and his sons, as detailed in Exodus 29.

Principles of Priesthood: Ministry (9:1–24)

Leviticus 9 turns the focus from Moses to Aaron. Aaron and his sons are now commanded to offer sacrifices, first for their own sins and then for the sins of the nation.

Principles of Priesthood: A Dangerous Job (10:1–20)

At the end of chapter 9, fire consumes what is left of the people's sacrifice, and at the beginning of chapter 10, fire comes from God's presence, consuming two of Israel's priests. Nadab and Abihu are sons of Aaron who die because they exercise their priestly duties in a way that dishonors God. The priesthood was an exceedingly dangerous job, for those who drew near to God in service dared not do so casually or irreverently.

Clean and Unclean, Part 1: Food Rules (11:1–47)

The third major section of Leviticus (chapters 11–15) defines what is clean and unclean. The label *clean* and its counterpoint *unclean* comprise a prominent theme in Leviticus. The importance of distinctions between the holy and the profane is introduced in 10:10. To get a good grasp on Leviticus, it is important to understand what clean and unclean mean and how they relate to holiness.

Clean and Unclean, Part 2: Mothers Only (12:1–8)

Chapters 12–15 continue to define what is unclean, along with the process of purification. Chapters 12 and 15 address uncleanness related to sexual reproduction, and chapters 13 and 14 address skin ailments.

Clean and Unclean, Part 3: Problem Skin, Mildew (13:1–59)

The laws in chapters 13 and 14 declare that serious skin disease (physical evidence of decay) make an individual unacceptable before a holy God and unacceptable within the Israelite community. Chapter 13 in particular helps the priests identify these skin disorders.

Background & Context

The term *leprosy*, used in many Bible translations, is most likely not used to describe the disease we know as leprosy. It is more likely a generic term referring to a number of skin disorders rather than a specific disease. The New International Version better translates the original term as "infectious skin disease."

Clean and Unclean, Part 4: Cleaning Infections and Mildew (14:1–57)
The laws in chapters 13 and 14 declare that serious skin ailments make an individual unacceptable before a holy God and even within the Israelite community. Chapter 14 in particular outlines the purification process.

Clean and Unclean Discharges (15:1–32)
Chapter 15 picks up where chapter 12 leaves off, declaring certain discharges as unclean. Both men and women have what might be called normal (15:16–18, 19–24) and abnormal discharges (15:2–15, 25–30). Aside from practical hygienic concerns, the laws once again address the subject of holiness.

The Day of Atonement (16:1–34)
Chapter 16 serves in part as a kind of addendum to chapters 8–10, as it addresses the expectations of the Aaronic priesthood. It opens with instructions God gives Moses to give to Aaron after the death of Aaron's two sons in chapter 10. The focus of these regulations is to make the people of Israel clean (a topic explained in detail in chapters 11–15). The chapter ends with a command for the high priest to make atonement for all the sins of Israel once a year. This is the introduction of the annual Day of Atonement.

Precious Is the Blood (17:1–16)
Leviticus 17 is a transitional chapter. It concludes the previous 16 chapters, which focus on the sacrificial process, by applying the value of blood to the daily practices of the Israelites. It also introduces the following chapters that deal with the practice of holiness in the everyday life of the Israelites. If the first 16 chapters of Leviticus were addressed primarily to the priests of Israel, this chapter is addressed mainly to the people of Israel. If the previous chapters dealt with the sacred—the tabernacle, the sacrifices, and the priests—this chapter deals with the secular—the normal course of life for the Israelite.

Living as Holy People (18:1–30)
The Israelites had been the slaves of Pharaoh. The Exodus freed the Israelites from bondage to Egypt, but it also brought them under the yoke of their God, who had delivered them. These people were to live under a new order, spelled out in the covenant that God made with them. God spells out clearly what kind of behavior He expects from His people. This chapter begins a new section of Leviticus that offers practical guidelines for how the Israelites are to live as a holy people.

Holy, Holy, Holy (19:1–37)
The Mosaic Covenant was established so Israel would be a holy nation (Exodus 19:6), set apart as God's people. Leviticus hammers home the importance of holiness for the Israelites. The book provides instructions for holiness involved with special ceremonies, holy days, and how to approach the tabernacle. Chapter 19 provides detailed, specific ways to practice everyday holiness that includes respect for God and for others.

Background & Context

Leviticus 19 is important because of the prominence of its teaching in the New Testament. Both our Lord (Matthew 5:43; 19:19; 22:39; Mark 12:31, 33; Luke 10:27) and the apostles (Romans 13:9; Galatians 5:14; James 2:8; 1 Peter 1:16) make a great deal of the two great commandments that are given here: "Ye shall be holy, for I the LORD your God am holy" (Leviticus 19:2), and "Thou shalt love thy neighbour as thyself" (19:18). In the context of this chapter, it becomes clear that the Israelites' enemies are included in the broad category of "neighbor," something Jesus also taught (Matthew 5:44-48).

Capital Crimes (20:1–27)

Chapter 20 falls into the broader context of chapters 18–20, which stress practical holiness in the everyday life of the Israelite. Chapter 18 has focused primarily on the family, chapter 19 instructs Israel to love their neighbor, and chapter 20 follows up by detailing the capital punishment for serious sins forbidden in the previous chapters. The actions highlighted become crimes as well as sins.

Background & Context

These capital crimes are violations of God's covenant with Israel. The crimes in Leviticus that call for a death penalty are all crimes against God's covenant, which emphasizes that God set Israel apart from the surrounding nations to distinguish them by means of holiness as His people (Exodus 19:5-6). The Mosaic Covenant is the definition of the holiness that God requires in order for Him to dwell among His people and for them to be His holy nation.

Holiness: True/False, Part 1 (21:1–24)

Chapters 17–20 are addressed to the Israelites in general, defining how holiness is to be practiced in the everyday activities of life. Chapters 21 and 22 return to addressing the Aaronic priesthood. Of particular importance is how they are to avoid being defiled and to remain holy. Each section is marked by the statement, in slightly modified forms, "I am the LORD, who sanctifies you" (21:8, 15, 23; 22:9, 16, 32).

Holiness: True/False, Part 2 (22:1–32)

As with chapter 21, chapter 22 addresses the Aaronic priesthood with a continued emphasis on how to avoid being defiled and how to remain holy. Each section is marked by the same statement, in one form or another, "I the LORD, which sanctifies you, am holy" (21:8, 15, 23; 22:9, 16, 32).

Background & Context

Aaron's position as high priest did not make him holier than others, though it did hold him to a higher standard. God chose Aaron and his descendants, just as God chose the Israelites. A look at Aaron's life reveals that neither he (Exodus 32) nor his sons (Leviticus 10) were holy by their own merit. Even though a priest was ceremonially pure, he still could approach God only by means of sacrifice and atoning blood.

All in Good Time (23:1–44)

The Lord's appointed times are festivals and holy days that commemorate significant times and events in Israel's history. The commemorative holidays show truths of God's salvation, love, and plans. The appointed times create a sacred rhythm in the lives of the Israelites.

Background & Context

The Jewish calendar is based on the relative motion of both the moon and the sun. Each month is defined by phases of the moon. The first of every month coincides with a new moon, and the fifteenth of every month coincides with a full moon. The calendar keeps the months and their respective seasons together by inserting a leap month, meaning most years have twelve months, but some have thirteen. The primary markers in the calendar are the sacred holidays.

Lamp, Loaves, and Loudmouth (24:1–23)

Leviticus 24 addresses how the Israelites should care for the dwelling place of God and how they should deal with someone who blasphemes God's name. The first 9 verses concern the ritual of maintaining the lamp and the loaves. Justice is also to become a matter of consistency (24:10–33). In all three sections, the element of continuity in ritual is present.

Background & Context

God's instructions to the Israelites relating to blasphemy are such that justice would be carried out consistently, without variation, without deviation, and without cessation. The principle of equality in punishment is consistently taught in the Old Testament. In Deuteronomy 17:2 and 17:7, the principle of equality in punishment is applied to men and women. It is most clearly taught in the book of Numbers (Numbers 15:13-16; Deuteronomy 29:10-13; 31:11-12).

God then gives general rules for how to deal with blasphemy. God's holiness is emphasized by the severe punishment prescribed for someone who blasphemes. The other rules in verses 17–22 show that the punishment provided should match the crime committed.

Super Sabbath (25:1–34)

Leviticus 25 reveals God's compassion for the poor and oppressed. The Sabbath year and the Year of Jubilee are part of God's gracious provisions for all His people. The two events are interrelated, so they are dealt with at the same time. Verses 1–34 lay down God's law pertaining to the land, while verses 35–55 apply to people.

Background & Context

The "laws of the land" were designed to hinder greed by keeping in check those who would try to accumulate vast land holdings at the expense of others.

A Welcome Warning (26:1–46)

Leviticus 26 is one of the clearest warnings in the Pentateuch (and is reiterated more emphatically in Deuteronomy 28). God's standards for Israel's conduct and the results of obedience or disobedience are given well in advance of punishment or blessing. This chapter does not contain just words of warning, though. It also reveals some of the greatest words of hope found in the Bible.

Background & Context

A number of passages are parallel to Leviticus 26. Exodus 23:22–33 is the first recording of the promise of blessings and curses, based upon Israel's obedience to the Mosaic Covenant. In Deuteronomy 28, the blessings and curses are repeated in greater detail for the second generation of Israelites who are about to possess the land of Canaan. Joshua 24:20 is a brief summation of the warnings of this chapter, and the writings of the prophets reveal some direct dependence on it (Isaiah 49:1; Ezekiel 34:25–30; 37:21–28). Leviticus 26 is key to understanding the history of Israel.

The Value of a Vow (27:1–34)

The key to the structure of chapter 27 is found by the categories of things that are vowed as offerings to God. In a systematic way, this chapter deals with the various kinds of things that men and women may promise to dedicate to God. Regulations appropriate to each are then specified. The vows of Leviticus 27 are voluntary promises to offer a particular gift to God. But God, knowing human nature, makes provisions for vows that are made irresponsibly.

Numbers
Introduction to Numbers

The book of Numbers derives its name from the two censuses taken of the nation of Israel at the beginning and the end of this book. Before being referred to as *Numbers*, this writing had also been known as *In the Desert* (or *Wilderness*), referring to the fact that the Israelites spent forty years in the desert.

Author
Many evangelical scholars consider Moses the author of Numbers. Additional support for Moses as the author is found in the fact that Jesus calls the first five books of the Bible "the book of Moses" (Luke 24:27, 44).

Occasion/Purpose
The instructions included in the book of Numbers are intended to prepare the people to travel to Canaan. The families are counted and they are organized. Numbers accounts for the forty years the Israelites wandered in the wilderness and moves from the judgment that fell on the first generation that left Egypt to the hope of the second generation who would see God's promise come true.

This book covers a history of thirty-nine years in the travels of the Israelites from Mount Sinai to the border of the Promised Land. Throughout this book, Israel is sometimes seen as a complaining and rebellious nation, often needing God to intervene with discipline. In the midst of His discipline, however, this book also clearly establishes the reality that God will still keep His covenant and will continue to provide for the needs of His people. Thus, Numbers does not end with failure but with a generation ready to enter the Promised Land because of God's mercy and grace.

Themes
Numbers highlights certain critical theological themes, including God's covenant with Abraham and His power to deliver. Along with that is the essential theme of the obedience (or disobedience) of the people. In addition, many of the laws that are described in Exodus are either restated or expanded upon in Numbers.

Contribution to the Bible
Numbers is an important part of the first five books of the Old Testament. It links the book of Exodus to the book of Deuteronomy. Exodus shows the movement of Israel from Egypt to the early years of Sinai. Numbers picks up the next forty years, taking the Israelites from Sinai to the plains of Moab. Then Deuteronomy picks the story up in the plains of Moab and the final preparations to enter Canaan.

Israel at Sinai and the Journey to Kadesh (1:1–2:34)
The book of Numbers opens with a census, a counting of the people. The nation of Israel is organized by tribes. This census prepares the tribes for their march,

identifying those who will be fit for battle once the people enter the land. As a number of scholars have pointed out, this number is really more of a military registration than a simple census.

Verse 1 gives us a telling reference point. This census takes place in the second month of the second year after the Israelites have left Egypt. The Passover described in Numbers 9:1 was to have happened in the *first* month of the second year. So, while the facts and figures are included at the beginning of the book of Numbers, the census actually happens after the first Passover feast is commemorated.

The Responsibilities of the Levites (3:1–4:49)
The Levites are given the care of the tabernacle. Once the people enter Canaan, the Levites will have no specific piece of land. Instead, they will be scattered throughout the land and will live off a portion of the offerings brought by the people.

Cleansing the Camp (5:1–31)
As the Israelites prepare to go on the move, they must purify themselves. This pursuit of purity is meant to impact all their social interactions. In this chapter, God focuses the attention of the nation on dealing with three specific issues: physical impurities, moral impurities, and marital impurities.

Background & Context
The test for infidelity described in verses 11–31 seems like a double standard to the contemporary mind. Where was the man with whom the woman was unfaithful? What if the woman suspected her husband of infidelity? The hard truth is that in this tribal culture, women were not given the same rights as men. No demands seem to be made, for instance, on the husband who falsely accuses his wife. Elements of this practice, however foreign it sounds to us, did serve to protect women to a certain point.

In reality, the point of this test is to protect paternity rights so that a child by another man does not inherit the estate of the husband. That is why the negative consequences involve the shriveling of the "thigh" (a euphemism for the womb), which would result in a miscarriage.

The Dedication of the Tabernacle (7:1–89)
Chapters 7–9 describe the dedication of the tabernacle. The events of chapters 7–9 actually precede the events described in chapters 1–6.

Numbers 7 is the second longest chapter in the Bible. It describes the twelve-day festival in which the people bring gifts to be used in the tabernacle. Each day different tribes send a representative to offer the gifts. There is much repetition, but to the original readers of Numbers, this repetition is understood as an emphasis.

God's Instructions (8:1–26)

In verses 1–4, God gives instructions regarding the lampstands. They are to be mounted so their light falls forward, resembling a tree. This symbolizes the fact that God is the giver of life to humankind. It also may symbolize the fact that Israel is to be a light to the world. The light from this lamp also shines brightly upon the showbread, which symbolizes the daily provision of God.

Verses 5–26 prescribe how the whole Levite workforce (in place of the first-born Israelites; 3:40–51) is dedicated and purified for their work, and how those who retire at age fifty may continue to help the younger Levites as guards in the tabernacle. The male members of the Levites are to be set apart by being cleansed by water and shaving their hair; washing their clothes; offering burnt, sin, wave, and grain offerings. Without being made clean through an offering and a spiritual washing, the Levites could not serve God.

Observance of the Passover (9:1–10:10)

In Numbers 9:1–10:10 three very important aspects of life in Israel are established—the Passover celebration, the presence of God in the cloud covering the tabernacle, and the silver trumpets that function as a kind of public address system.

Background & Context

Ethnic purity was an important issue in ancient Israel, but only in the protection of religious purity. This is evidenced in the instructions of Ezra to his countrymen to separate themselves from their pagan foreign wives before they could lead their husbands into idolatry.

Throughout the law of the Old Testament, however, are explicit instructions that there is one code of law for both the native Israelites and the sojourning foreigners in the land. In Numbers 9:14, aliens living among the Israelites can celebrate the Passover if they do so according to the statutes. So while Miriam and Aaron's charge against Moses has some foundation, it isn't entirely valid.

Dissension in the Ranks (11:1–35)

The people have now become frustrated with their circumstances. The inconveniences and sacrifices required of them are great, and they begin to complain. They have lost sight of God's promises and have become focused on their immediate suffering.

From Dissension to Treason (12:1–16)

In Hebrews, the grammar of the opening verses of chapter 12 suggests that Miriam is the one leading the attack against Moses, but she is backed by her brother Aaron. This conflict is bigger than a family squabble. Miriam and Aaron have national religious positions of leadership, and they are challenging the leadership of Moses as sole mediator between God and Israel. Though the question seems to be about Moses' wife's ethnicity, it is really Moses' right to lead that is at the heart of the issue.

Israel Delayed at Kadesh and the Journey to Moab (13:1–14:45)
The events recorded here take place while Israel is camped at Kadesh. The sending of the spies and all that come from this event become engraved on the corporate memory of God's people. Later writers refer back to these incidents with a sense of painful disappointment (see Deuteronomy 1:26–46; Psalm 95:10–11).

Background & Context
The test described here involves offering incense because this was one of the most holy responsibilities of the priests. The fatal disaster of Nadab and Abihu, priests who died by offering strange fire, seems to confirm this (Leviticus 10:1-3).

Renewing Worship (15:1–41)
Though we often think of the book of Numbers as the Israelites' journey across the wilderness, Numbers 15 marks the beginning of the only five chapters of this book that provide narratives of that journey (15–19).

This chapter also marks the first set of instructions for the people who now know they will wander in this wilderness until their deaths. Notice that this section begins with the reaffirmation of worship. The first thing God does after the pronouncement of the consequences of Israel's sin is reestablish the worship He wants from His people.

The Rebellion of Korah (16:1–50)
This chapter marks the fifth complaint of the Israelites in the desert, this time against the authority of Aaron and his priestly line. In verses 1–3, the chief rebel is Korah, who descended from Levi through his son Kohath. As a Kohathite, he has high duties at the tabernacle—but he isn't a priest. Just as Korah wants more power, so do Dathan, Abiram, and On (who is not mentioned again). The rebels rise up against Moses and Aaron with 250 leaders of the community. The heart of their accusation is Moses' arrogance in claiming a special relationship with God. These rebels want the same privilege.

Aaron's Rod—God's Affirmation of His Men (17:1–13)
The story of Aaron's rod is the third in a series that demonstrates the divine sanction of the priestly leadership of Aaron and the Levites. This incident, though, is inverted in structure compared with the first two (Korah's rebellion and the plagues at the end of chapter 16). Rather than people's complaints precipitating the threat of destruction, here God seeks to prove Aaron's call once and for all, and the people end up crying out to God for fear of destruction.

Renewed Commitment to the Levitical Order (18:1–32)

Israel's high priests (Aaron's family line) and the Levites in general, as guardians of the tabernacle, are called to a dangerous and crucial task. After affirming their position to the Israelites, God now spells out to Aaron the Levites' roles, responsibilities, regulations, and rewards.

Background & Context

Numbers 18:19 restates the fact that the tribute from Israel is a gift from God for the priestly families, both male and female. God calls it "an everlasting covenant of salt" (NIV). Though the origin of this covenant is unknown, the function of salt in ancient Near Eastern society included the concepts of preservation and permanence.

Though the Levites receive no land, God is their inheritance. This is not to say that the priests and Levites somehow owned God (18:20–24). Instead, what physically accrued to God from the territorial inheritance of the Israelites would belong to them. These gifts become the Levites' birthright instead of territorial grant.

Purification (19:1–22)

Numbers 19 offers the cleansing process for those who have been in contact with a dead body. This is an important ceremony for the Israelites, because the nation will encounter many deaths on a daily basis for several decades. Thus, they must be prepared as to how they are going to remain ceremonially clean after dealing with a dead body.

A Sad Day (20:1–29)

In Numbers 20, Moses faces a series of sad events, beginning with the death of his sister, Miriam. This chapter highlights the seriousness with which we must treat the Word of God. In addition, it shows how God is faithful to Israel in allowing a next generation to emerge so that His work might continue.

Background & Context

Chapter 20 opens with the death of Miriam and closes with the death of Aaron (20:22-29). When the Israelites come to Mount Hor, near the border of Edom, Moses, in obedience to God, takes Aaron and his son, Eleazar, up the mountain. (Scholars are not certain where Mount Hor is located, despite an early tradition identifying it with Jebel Nebi Harun near Petra.) There he gives Aaron's garments to Eleazar, and Aaron dies. When Moses places Aaron's vestments on Eleazar's shoulders, he is also transferring his responsibilities as Israel's high priest, the supreme mediator between God and Israel. The people mourn for Aaron for thirty days.

This point in the lives of the Israelites seems to be the lowest so far. Yet, God is allowing the next generation to take over, to carry on the work. God is still working and preparing the next generation to live in Canaan.

So Near, Yet So Far: Lessons along the Way (21:1–35)

After Aaron's death, Moses alone leads the Israelites closer to Canaan. Moving northward, the king of Arad attacks them and takes captives (21:1–3). This is an important first battle because it establishes a pattern. God will do the winning. The Israelites acknowledge that unless God gives their foes into their hands, they will not have any success.

Balaam's Story (22:1–24:25)

The deceptively simple but profound story of Balaam and his donkey begins a period in which the Israelites—poised on the border of the Promised Land—encamp for an apparently lengthy time at the foot of the mountains of Moab, not unlike their encampment four decades prior at Sinai.

These accounts are humorous as well as somber. Some characters are stupid and stubborn, and there is more spiritual awareness in the donkey than in the humans. Structurally, watch for threes: the donkey avoids the angel three times, Balaam arranges for three sets of sacrifices, he has three encounters with God, and so on. The narrative itself extends over six days, through Numbers 24.

Background & Context

Some scholars portray Balaam as a saintly seer; others as a money-hungry heathen sham. In the beginning of the story, he appears positive, intent on listening to God. Other Bible passages aren't so flattering, for instance Deuteronomy 23:4-5; 2 Peter 2:15; Jude 11; and Revelation 2:14.

The Threat from Within (25:1–18)

After Balaam goes home, a new and more subtle assault on Israel spreads through the immense population. And, as we find out later (31:8, 16), Balaam is tied to it.

This strategy uses Moabite women—possible temple prostitutes—to seduce the men of Israel and lead the whole nation to ruin through idolatry. God hates sexual immorality, especially when it is tied to idol worship. Therefore, if Moab could not take down Israel through a curse from Balaam, it hoped to use the lust of the flesh.

Preparations Begin (26:1–65)

Preparations are now beginning for the Israelites to take the land. The first thing that must take place is a census, in which men age twenty and older within each tribe are counted.

The counting of the people provides several things for the Israelites:

- It confirms the reality of God's promise of the land in Genesis 12:7. God makes good on His promises.
- It focuses the people on the step before them. They are going to get land that will be big enough for their clan, but they are going to have to fight for it. Thus, numbering the men for war makes that point abundantly clear.
- It reaffirms God's faithfulness to Israel. Even though people from every tribe rebelled against God, He did not wipe out every tribe. Therefore, this walk down memory lane reminds the people that God is trustworthy, just, kind, and reliable.

Resolving the Issues (27:1–23)
The first issue is one of inheritance among the daughters of Zelophehad (27:11). These five women approach the Tent of Meeting to implore Moses, an unprecedented act of courage and conviction.

Patterns for Worship (28:1–29:40)
The Lord prescribes specific daily and yearly observances for the sons of Israel to keep when they enter into the land. The entire calendar for the nation is to be governed by worship.

The Lord commands Moses to be careful to present the various offerings at their appointed times, not as rote actions, but as prayers of dependence.

Vows (30:1–16)
Vows are commitments made to God that are over and above what is required by the law. Moses introduces the topic in 30:1–2, by reminding the leaders of Israel that vows obligate us to follow through.

God Vindicated (31:1–54)
This chapter is a call to war. The Israelites are to go to war with the Midianites. The Midianites were the principle instigators of the wicked scheme of seduction in Numbers 25, in which they planned to entrap the Israelites into the double crime of idolatry and licentiousness. The Lord tells Moses that he is to treat the Midianites as enemies and to kill them. Now is the time for their destruction.

An Interesting Twist (32:1–42)
As the entire nation looks across the river to the Promised Land (32:1–5), two tribes, Reuben and Gad, see that the land in the Transjordan region will be suitable for their numerous livestock. They request that they be allowed to settle in this region rather than going across the Jordan.

A Review of God's Faithfulness (33:1–56)
Before the Israelites take the Promised Land, Moses reviews the hand of God in leading the children of Israel out of Egypt to Canaan.

In the first four chapters of Numbers, we see how many of the generation that is entering the Promised Land were babies when the Lord delivered the Israelites from Egypt. They would not have remembered the great miracle of the Lord delivering them from their bondage, the most powerful event in the entire forty-year period. (Time and time again God refers to Himself as "I am the God who delivered you out of Egypt." One of the main ways God wants to be defined is as the God *who delivers*.)

Distribution of the Land (34:1–29)

Throughout Numbers, God has reiterated in multiple ways His promise that the people would reach Canaan (see 13:2; 14:8, 16, 23, 30; 15:2, 18; 27:12; 32:7, 9, 11). Now, the children of Israel are about to hear what portions of the land will be assigned to each tribe. This continues to affirm the certainty of this promise. God will distribute the land before they take it, because it is a sure thing that they will have the land.

Special Land Provisions (35:1–34)

The Levites are to be given a portion of each tribe's inheritance (35:1–8). This is because the Levites are to devote their lives to the worship of God. The Levites are not to be given just one specific area of land; instead, they are allocated forty-eight towns with pastureland around them. The surrounding land extends around the city 500 yards (1,000 cubits) and extends 1,000 yards (2,000 cubits) around the city walls.

Future Ownership of the Land (36:1–13)

In Numbers 27:1–11, there is land that is to be distributed to the daughters of Zelophehad, who had died without sons. The daughters want to know if they will get land since there are no men left in their family. God says they will. Now the question arises, what happens if these girls marry? Do they lose their land?

This brought up a question about marriage and land being inherited by other families. Could one family begin to marry women in another family and thus begin to amass a giant amount of land? It would be a very natural way of thinking for individuals to become self-centered and try to acquire wealth and take from others, to their own determent.

Background & Context

After just receiving the history of their people, they must not take lightly this command found in verses 50-56. God calls His people to be separated from the world in order to be a light to the world about His great plan of salvation. Thus, the Israelites must be called out from these people, and they must ensure that the idolatry is cleared completely from the land. God makes it clear that He will do to Israel what He plans on doing to the idolaters if they do not drive them from the land. The consequences will be great if they fail to take God seriously.

When they take possession of the land, they must do it by lot, assigning to each tribe their portion as the Lord delineates. God is going to give each tribe what He determines they need. Even though the land is God's gift to the people, they still need to distribute the land according to lots so that there is impartial distribution. No doubt high levels of emotion would surface if they all had to pick their own land. God is going to give the land to the nation exactly in a manner that He wants so that all will be able to worship God for what He has provided.

Deuteronomy
Introduction to Deuteronomy

Deuteronomy might be called the Romans of the Old Testament. It is chock-full of the great themes of scripture. It is a wonderfully down-to-earth and practical book that provides counsel about both the large and small issues and questions of life. It addresses itself both to private matters such as the inner conflicts of the believing soul, the way of faith under trial, marriage and family, and to such public and corporate issues such as worship and the proper stewardship of the environment.

Author
Moses is clearly identified as the author of Deuteronomy in verse 1. Moses' authorship is claimed throughout Deuteronomy (1:5, 9; 5:1; 27:8; 29:2; 31:1, 30) as well as in other Old Testament books (1 Kings 2:3; 8:53; 2 Kings 14:6; 18:6, 12). Jesus also identified Moses as the author of Deuteronomy (Matthew 19:7–8; Mark 10:3–5; John 5:46–47), as did Peter (Acts 3:22), Stephen (Acts 7:37–38), and Paul (Romans 10:19; 1 Corinthians 9:9).

The final chapter, recording Moses' death and burial (34:1–12), was added by another writer after Moses' death.

Occasion/Purpose
The title *Deuteronomy* means "second law." In this book, Moses reiterates and expands on the laws God has already given Israel and calls them to renew their covenant with God by pledging their obedience.

The book of Deuteronomy records Moses' last words to the people of Israel as they are poised to enter the Promised Land after forty years of wandering in the wilderness. Moses reminds the people of all that the Lord has done for them to this point and calls them to a life of faithful obedience in the land they are to receive.

Themes
Some of the most prominent themes in Deuteronomy include the obedience of the law, and being God-fearing. Deuteronomy may seem full of specific rules and laws, but it also showcases the theme of faith before works, or obedience. Deuteronomy

outlines the grace of a faithful God to his people, and how to live holy lives before God. Some other major themes in this book are consequences and blessings. If we obey God's laws and love Him, we will be blessed beyond belief. On the other hand, failing to obey God's laws results in consequences as well.

These themes are specifically shown in Deuteronomy with the example of Moses and the disobedience of God's people. Israel's constant foolishness and God's constant faithfulness are prominent throughout the book, and while Moses' leadership ends in Deuteronomy, God's faithfulness never does.

Faith Before Works (1:1–46)

When Deuteronomy commences, Israel as a nation is poised on the eastern bank of the Jordan River opposite Jericho. Two months later, she will cross the river, on dry land, into the Promised Land for the first time. It is at this juncture in her history that God initiates a renewal of the covenant He had established with the Israelites when they were camped at Sinai (Exodus 19–24). Chapter 1 records the preamble to this renewal and the beginning of a lengthy review of God's dealings with Israel. The historical prologue, which begins here in chapter 1, serves to provide a rationale for obedience to the commandments that occupy the largest part of the book.

Background & Context

Most ancient Middle Eastern treaties were "suzerainty treaties," or treaties of sovereignty of a stronger king over a weaker one. The Lord had given Moses this covenantal revelation in the form drawn from the custom of ancient Middle Eastern diplomacy. It provides a wonderful example of God's condescension, of His employing a literary form that would have been easily appreciated and understood in Moses' day. He wanted to be understood and wanted His covenant to be kept.

From Wandering to Conquest (2:1–37)

Moses, at the end of the forty years of desert wanderings, is recalling for the people their history. Chapter 1 ends with the Lord's decree that the generation who left Egypt will not enter the Promised Land of Canaan. Chapter 2 begins the saga of Israel's forty-year sojourn in the wilderness.

Background & Context

Why would a holy God condone such annihilation? Such destruction is a judgment on the wickedness of the people destroyed (see 9:4). Keep in mind that God has already given the nations ample time to repent. In fact, He delayed Israel's conquest for some four hundred years for this reason (Genesis 15:16). In the end, however, Israel was not spiritually strong enough to withstand the influence of pagan nations, and judgment fell (see Deuteronomy 20:17-18).

Moses' Last Battle (3:1–29)

Chapter 3 continues the historical prologue that precedes the covenant laws and decrees that make up the bulk of Deuteronomy. The Israelites' desert wanderings have come to an end, and they are engaged in the business of conquering and claiming the land.

Background & Context

Leaving no survivors was not always the outcome of an Israelite conquest. Outside of Canaan (the land the Israelites were in inhabiting), the women and children were spared. The men (who would serve as warriors against the Israelites) were killed. Inside Canaan, all were destroyed; but keep in mind that even in those situations, should the people surrender, they were spared (see 20:10–15).

Laws and Orders (4:1–49)

The first three chapters of Deuteronomy recall God's faithfulness and power. Now Moses begins to lay out the commandments that God calls Israel to obey in response to what He has already done.

Background & Context

The peoples of the ancient Middle Eastern world made and worshipped idols of every kind. Gods and goddesses were represented as animals—fish, bulls, calves, and the like—or as human beings in figurine form, or as poles and pillars. What is more, as indicated in Deuteronomy 4:19, they not only worshipped gods through images that represented them, but they also actually considered heavenly bodies as gods themselves. Idolatry was a universal institution and a part of the fabric of life for all of these people, save one: Israel herself.

Despite God's clear command, Israel drifts toward idol worship over and over again. Indeed, while Moses is still at the top of Mount Sinai, receiving the law from the hand of God, Israel is at the foot of the mountain cavorting before a golden calf, with bitter consequences, as Moses reminds them (4:21–22).

Love, Fear, and Obedience (5:1–33)

The book of Deuteronomy follows the pattern of ancient Near Eastern treaties. The preamble in chapter 1:1–5 gives the historical and geographical setting. The historical prologue in chapters 1:6–4:49 comprises a lengthy review of God's dealings with Israel and serves to provide a rationale for obedience. In chapter 5, we begin the particular stipulations of the covenant: the commandments that occupy the largest part of the book.

Background & Context

The Ten Commandments are not simply ten of the many laws that God gave His people; they are not even the ten most important of those laws. The Ten Commandments are a summary of the *entire* law of God. All the rest of the commandments in God's Word are applications or elaborations of these fundamental duties. Their character as a general summary is further indicated by the fact that both in the Old and the New Testaments these ten can be further summarized by only two commandments: to love God with all your heart and soul and to love your neighbor as yourself (see, for example, Deuteronomy 6:5; Luke 10:27).

God-Fearing Children (6:1–25)

Deuteronomy 5 looked to the previous generation and emphasized how essential it was for the current generation to inhabit as their own the covenant made with their parents and grandparents. Deuteronomy 6 takes a forward view to the next generation. In it we read of God's exhortations for parents to nurture their children in the faith of the covenant God.

Background & Context

Many observant Jews take literally the injunctions in Deuteronomy 6:8-9. They bind small, scripture-filled leather cases, called *tefillin*, on their arms and foreheads, and post small cases containing the words of Deuteronomy 6:4-9, called *mezuzahs*, on their doorframes.

Gifts and Rewards (7:1–26)

Some refer to the book of Deuteronomy as the Romans of the Old Testament. Well, then, we should not be at all surprised to find in it such a strong statement of the doctrine of divine election, the very doctrine to which Paul devotes such considerable and famous attention in his letter to the Romans.

Background & Context

While chapter 7 was being written, Israel was poised on the brink of entering the Promised Land. But Canaan was not only a fertile and beautiful land that God had given His people; it also represented their spiritual inheritance, the blessings of the eternal Promised Land. A great point of this is made in the New Testament letter to the Hebrews, especially in chapter 11. There we read that Canaan was never as significant as a piece of real estate as it was as a figure, an enacted prophecy of the heavenly country to which God's people, by faith, were headed. The promise of great blessing for covenantal faithfulness is also true in the sense that it will eventually be perfectly fulfilled, in even the most literal way, in the life of God's faithful people in the world to come.

Forget Not All His Benefits (8:1–20)

You would think that Israel's escape from Egypt and desert wanderings would have been so indelibly printed on every Israelite heart that forgetting it would be nearly impossible. But Moses knew human nature too well to think that. He knew that when they entered the lush and fruitful land that God was giving them, and settled down into their new homes and began enjoying their wealth and prosperity, it would be entirely natural for them to forget all about the desert and all that God had done for them, even forget that the new land and prosperity was His gift to them. Moses knew full well what the human heart is capable of, and how it can so quickly begin to take credit itself for the Lord's achievements.

Background & Context

While the land of Canaan may not seem like a fertile land by North American standards, it was more fertile and verdant in antiquity especially before the land was raped by the Ottomans. Also keep in mind that the Israelites were seeing the land compared to desert, where Israel had wandered for forty years, and to Egypt, which depended on irrigation. It was indeed a good land (8:7-8).

Unrighteousness (9:1–29)

Interestingly, all of the examples Moses uses to demonstrate how unworthy Israel is of the gift she is about to receive are from the life of the previous generation, not this generation about to cross into the Promised Land. Those who aroused the Lord's anger at Mount Sinai, who cavorted before the golden calf, and then who later rebelled at Kadesh Barnea—they all lie dead and buried back in the wilderness. They had forfeited the Promised Land by their faithlessness. But, with that sense of family solidarity that is so common to the Bible, the present generation is addressed as if they, too, had been at Horeb, they, too, had worshipped the golden calf, they, too, had participated in the cowardly refusal to enter the Promised Land at Kadesh Barnea.

Background & Context

It is significant that Moses assures the people they will conquer the Anakites. These are the very people that terrified the Israelites so much that they refused to enter the land forty years earlier (see Numbers 13:26–33). The Anakites were very tall and very strong, and some thought they were descended from a race of giants.

A Faithless People; A Faithful God (10:1–22)

The Bible was written in largest part not to the world but to the people of God. Most of its contents, both in the Old Testament and the New Testament, are directly addressed to the church and the people of God. And for that reason one of its greatest themes is the possibility and the temptation, and the frequent reality and danger, of formalism in the Christian faith—of a faith that is not a matter of the heart.

The tragic story of the Old Testament is of a people who were religious in an outward way but whose hearts were far from God. Moses has repeated some of that history to the people; now he calls them specifically to give their whole hearts to God.

Background & Context

Circumcision was the original sign of God's covenant with Abraham and Abraham's descendants (Genesis 17). It was an outward, physical sign, but the command in Deuteronomy to circumcise one's heart indicates that circumcision was always intended to reflect an internal reality, not merely external obedience.

Love and Obedience (11:1–32)

It is imperative that the Israelites understand that the key to staying in the land is to obey God. All obedience to God starts with love. A person who does not love God cannot obey God. For this reason, Moses reiterates the call to love.

Background & Context

Moses was very clear that love and obedience are intrinsically connected (6:5–6; 7:9; 10:12–13; 11:13, 22; 19:9; 30:6, 8, 16, 20). In Hebrew, the command to love the Lord carries with it something more than just a feeling; it carries the idea that a person will follow God in a very personal and intimate relationship and then express that desire to follow in obedience to His revealed will. Thus, it means more than just a close relationship; it is a relationship that causes one to be united with God in intent and purpose.

Form and Freedom in Worship (12:1–32)

This chapter opens the next major section of Deuteronomy. The first four chapters are a historical introduction, or prologue, an account of the previous relationship between the Lord and His people Israel. Chapters 5–11 set out the general commandments or stipulations of the covenant with repeated exhortations to Israel to keep the covenant that God made with her. Chapter 12 begins the third and longest section of the book, stretching from 12:1 to 26:15. These chapters contain the specific stipulations, or legislation, covering matters as diverse as worship and the management of criminal cases in court.

Background & Context

Unfortunately, not all of God's people listened to these warnings. No sooner had Israel settled in the Promised Land than there were people attracted and lured into Canaanite worship. It was this problem, this running after Canaanite worship, that finally ruined the faith of Israel in the Old Testament. In chasing after the worldly way, they finally stopped worshipping God altogether and began to worship only themselves and false gods—though still claiming to be true Israelites.

Contend or Die (13:1–18)

Deuteronomy 13 continues the warnings about worshipping other gods. Here, however, the source of temptation is not the Canaanites, as in chapter 12, but rather people among the Israelites themselves.

A Holy, Giving People (14:1–29)

Deuteronomy, in its recapitulation of the commandments about clean and unclean animals, gives but a brief account of the laws of cleanliness. This paragraph in Deuteronomy 14 should be understood as representing the much longer legislation touching ceremonial cleanliness in Leviticus 11–15.

Holy Extravagance (15:1–23)

Deuteronomy 15 flows thematically from the previous chapter. Deuteronomy 14 concludes with a concern for the poor and the tithe as a means of providing for the poor. Deuteronomy 15 continues the concern for the disadvantaged—in this case, those in debt and those who have to sell themselves as servants.

Background & Context

Debts were to be canceled every seventh year. The number seven was significant among many ancient Near Eastern peoples—possibly having to do with the cycles of the moon. But for the Israelites, the number seven stood for something that was complete—reflecting the seven days of creation.

The God of Holidays (16:1–17)

The chapter gives only a summary statement on the three great yearly feasts of the Israelite calendar. More complete legislation is found in Exodus 12; 23:14–17; Leviticus 23; and Numbers 28:16–31.

Background & Context

The three feasts described here (Passover, the Feast of Weeks, and the Feast of Tabernacles) are still celebrated by observant Jews today. Passover begins on the fifteenth day of the month of Nisan on the Israelite calendar—sometime in March or April of the Gregorian calendar. The Feast of Weeks begins on the sixth of Sivan (in May or June), and the Feast of Tabernacles on the fifteenth of Tishri (late September through October).

Under Authority (16:18–17:13)

In this section, God is saying that His people must be under His authority and live their lives under that authority. These verses are about judges, trials, and punishment, but that is all to demonstrate that God requires His will be done in the community of His people. All of this instruction is to that end and purpose.

Background & Context

The Hebrew word for "feast" used in these verses is *Hag*, which reminds us of the Muslim annual pilgrimage to Mecca, the Haj. The idea of pilgrimage belongs to the Hebrew word as well.

The Three Offices (17:14–18:22)

Deuteronomy 17:14–18:22 is a highly interesting passage of scripture for the way in which it places together the three great offices of the Old Testament religious structure. God communicates His presence directly to the hearts of His people by His Spirit, and He also uses people as instruments of His presence. He speaks to His people through prophets, He grants forgiveness of sins and maintains fellowship with them through priests, and He rules over them through kings.

Lest Innocent Blood Be Shed (19:1–21)

The apparent subject of the chapter is the laws governing murder and its punishment. But, really, the subject of the chapter is the purpose of all of these laws, which is stated in Deuteronomy 19:10—that innocent blood not be shed in the land. This is the purpose of all that we read in this chapter.

Background & Context

The law of retaliation in verse 21 is also found in Exodus 21:23-25 and Leviticus 24:17-20.

The principle of justice by equity is stated in Deuteronomy 19:21—punishments are to be, as far as possible, the exact equivalent of the crime. An eye for an eye, a hand for a hand, and a life for a life means that justice requires a murderer forfeit his own life. Anything less or more is not retribution in proportion to the crime. Other ancient Near Eastern law codes (famously, the Code of Hammurabi) sometimes insisted on excessive punishments, so the guidelines here function to guard from that excess.

The Commands of God Are Not a Burden (20:1–20)
Chapter 20 begins a section of the book of Deuteronomy devoted to particular laws addressing many different issues. In certain cases, they reiterate points that have already been made in previous chapters. This chapter, for example, recapitulates some of what was already stated in chapter 7: laws governing the conduct of war.

Laws for Difficult Situations (21:1–23)
This chapter gives laws that govern three sets of issues. The first is what to do on the discovery of a murdered body when there is no way to ascertain who committed the crime. The second set of laws governs family life, and the third set of laws governs how to handle the remains of a person who has been executed for a crime.

Background & Context
It is important to note that Deuteronomy 21:14 is not endorsing divorce. Jesus says (in Mark 10:5) that these laws are in place to protect the women, not to endorse a behavior. The laws were in place so that a woman would be treated in a respectable manner even if her husband chose to send her away.

The reality is, because of the sinful nature of humanity, not all relationships will be successful. The husband could therefore end the marriage by simply releasing his wife to go wherever she wished. He was forbidden to sell her as property or regard her as a slave.

Laws about Love and Sex (22:1–30)
The laws here deal with the sixth and seventh of the Ten Commandments and the themes that lie beneath them—the sanctity of life and marriage.

Background & Context
Engagement in ancient Israel was more like marriage than engagements in Western cultures today. The engaged woman described in Deuteronomy 21:23–27 is also referred to as her fiancé's wife (21:24). Unfaithfulness to her betrothed received the same penalty

as adultery—death. Likewise, a man who had intercourse with a woman engaged to another man—whether consensually or by rape—was also accounted an adulterer.

Various Laws (23:1–25)
Chapter 23 continues the laying out of laws relating to a variety of situations.

Background & Context
The key to understanding the laws about exclusion from the assembly is that they dealt with the ceremonial aspects of worship. These were not laws excluding people from believing in God, loving God, or having eternal life. These laws were in place to govern the ceremonial worship for the nation of Israel. Since that worship dealt with Israel's sin and redemption, it had to be done in a way that was according to the holiness of God.

Various Laws, Continued (24:1–22)
Deuteronomy 24 continues the rather lengthy section devoted to various laws touching many different aspects of life. There is no clearly discernible principle of organization in these chapters. The laws are not even grouped together according to theme, as is clear from the English versions that use paragraph titles such as "Various Laws" and "Miscellaneous Laws."

Background & Context
Jesus' interpretation of Deuteronomy 24:1-4 indicates that divorce (like polygamy) goes against the divine ideal for marriage (see Matthew 19:3-9).

Marriage is held in high honor. Thus the nation is to allow a man to get settled into his new relationship after marriage. It is considered cruel to send a recently married man to war (20:7; 24:5). If he is killed in combat, he will probably have no children to preserve his name in Israel. A newly married man is also to be free of other responsibilities in order to have time to adjust and bring happiness to his wife.

Living Before the Holy God (25:1–19)
All of the details of the laws in Deuteronomy 25 point to two important things: God is holy and He is everywhere. Thus these laws highlight the incredible detail with which God's holiness should be taken and how much every person should recognize God's presence every day and everywhere.

Presentations (26:1–19)

The book of Deuteronomy is a reiteration of the law for the children of those who were brought out of Egypt and allowed to enter into the Promised Land. Since all that is said here is a reiteration of the law for those entering the land, it is stated in its simplest form. Chapter 26 describes some of the rituals that are to be followed as soon as they enter the land.

Background & Context

Tithing and giving firstfruits were not unfamiliar requirements for the Israelites. Legislation regarding firstfruits and the tithe had already been given in Deuteronomy (14:28-29; 18:3-5). What is unique in this passage, however, is the declaration ritual for each offering (26:3, 5, 13). It seems that these declarations were meant to be practiced only once: for the firstfruits after Israel's first harvest and for the tithe after being in the land three years. They were given in order to celebrate Israel's transition from a nomadic existence to a settled community through the power of the Lord.

Blessings and Curses, Part 1 (27:1–26)

Deuteronomy 27 begins a new section in the ancient Near Eastern treaty form that structures the book. Following the opening preamble (1:1–5), historical introduction (1:6–4:49), and the particular stipulations of the treaty (chapters 5–26), chapter 27 opens the section of blessings and curses that will result from keeping or breaking the treaty.

Background & Context

The writing of laws on large stones coated with plaster was a common practice in Egypt. It was a way of preserving the words of important documents for generations.

The stones are to be set up on Mount Ebal (27:4-6), at the base of which lies the city of Shechem. The altar will commemorate God's faithfulness in giving them the land. There are two possible reasons for not using any iron tools (27:5). Because the nation probably did not have any access to iron, they had to get it from the surrounding nations. This would put them into contact with the nations and might cause them to stumble. A second reason could be that the altar should not have any human additions that would cause humans to get the glory.

Blessings and Curses, Part 2 (28:1–68)

In this chapter, Moses sets before Israel the blessings and curses of the covenant they are renewing. The curses section (28:15–68) is about four times longer than the blessings section (28:1–14). This underscores the importance of obedience. God is making the point that if you fail to obey, there is no such thing as success; every area of life will be impacted in a great way. This commitment is intended to make a strong point—they should obey God.

An Appeal to Obey (29:1–29)
Chapter 29 opens with the conclusion of the reiteration of the covenant. At this point, Moses begins to unfold a summary of the covenant to highlight what the Israelites should keep foremost in their minds.

Background & Context
The two places mentioned in verse 1 are significant. Horeb is the same location as Mount Sinai, where God gave the Ten Commandments at the beginning of the Israelite journey. Here, in Moab, the people are at the end of the journey, almost to their destination.

Blessings for Obedience (30:1–20)
In chapter 29, the language seems to assume the reality that the people of Israel will fall into exile because of their tendency toward idolatry. Chapter 30, then, is the good news—they will eventually be brought out of exile. God will not abandon His people, even in the midst of the worst punishment—that of losing the land they believe God had promised them.

Transitions (31:1–29)
Here, at the end of their journey through the wilderness and at the doorstep of the conquest, Moses prepares to step out of the way. He is now going to transfer leadership from himself to Joshua. Moses' priority is ensuring that the next generation places a priority on their relationship with God.

Background & Context
The reading of the law every seven years was important for two reasons. First, not everyone had a copy of the entire law in their homes. Therefore, it would be a time for the whole nation to hear the entire law read in its context.

Second, the celebration of the Feast of Tabernacles (with its tradition of the Israelites leaving their homes) would remind them of the exodus from Egypt and the forty years of wandering their ancestors experienced. This event is central to the theology of Israel as well as her history. Because of this, the people would hear the law within the context of God's deliverance.

The Song of Moses (31:30–32:52)
Deuteronomy 31:19–21 tells us that Moses' song is to be used to remind Israel of God's law within the context of God's deliverance. It will remind the people of their sin and rebellion and of the fact that their hearts are far from God.

Background & Context
A true understanding of Moses' song must come within the context of Deuteronomy 30:6, a verse of hope in the midst of disappointing news. This verse tells that God is going to show the people of Israel their sin so that they can embrace the salvation that the Messiah is going to bring.

The Blessing of Moses on the Tribes (33:1–29)
The blessing of Moses given here, just before his death, is very important and common for that day. It was typical for a father to impart a blessing just before his death. Moses, leader of the Exodus and mediator of the covenant, served in a fatherly capacity for the nation. As they were being birthed into a nation, Moses was there to provide the earthly fathering that they needed.

Background & Context
The giving of this law was more than just a moment when the glory of God shined upon the world; it was also a moment of love. This moment served to be the time when God's love came to the earth in the form of the revelation of His will and His heart. Thus, the response of all the followers of God was a response to this love.

The proclamation of the Lord's kingship over *Jeshurun* (a name for Israel; 32:15; 33:26) is a reference back to the nation's deliverance from Egypt and the giving of the law (when the leaders and the tribes assembled to receive God's commands). When God brought the law to the people, they gathered under His rule, and He became their official king. The giving of the law was then the event that ratified His kingship over the nation.

The Death of Moses (34:1–12)
At the close of the book of Deuteronomy, Moses ascends to Mount Nebo as the Lord told him to do. Though Moses is not to lead the people into the land, God allows Moses to see the land.

Joshua
Introduction to Joshua

For centuries, the descendants of Abraham had anticipated possessing the land God had promised to the patriarch in the Abrahamic Covenant (Genesis 12:1–3; 15:5–8) and then reiterated to Isaac and Jacob. Joshua is the compelling history of the fulfillment of that promise.

Author
There is some tradition that claims Joshua as the author of this book. But the author is unknown, as is the date of writing.

Occasion/Purpose
This is an account written to reveal God's faithfulness and how, by faith in God's promises, God's people can overcome and experience His life-changing deliverance.

The book of Joshua describes the conquest and possession of the land of Canaan. This is the land God had promised Israel through Abraham, Isaac, and Jacob. Here God fulfills that promise, though not exhaustively, since there still remains a rest for the people of God. Joshua describes the military triumph of God's people through faith and obedience. However, unlike most military histories, Joshua's focus is on the commander's Commander, the Captain of the Lord's host (5:15). Repeatedly, as Joshua's name illustrates ("Yahweh saves"), the book demonstrates that Israel's victories are due to God's power and intervention.

Themes
The primary theme of the book of Joshua is God's faithfulness to His promises, that He has done for Israel exactly what He promised (Genesis 15:18; Joshua 1:2–6; 21:43–45). The events recorded in Joshua set forth God's special intervention on behalf of His people against all kinds of tremendous odds. The fulfillment of God's promises, as is evident in the birth of Isaac to Abraham and Sarah (Genesis 17:19–21; 21:1–5) and in possessing the land with its fortified cities, is the work of God, which cannot be accomplished without God's blessing no matter how hard one tries (see Romans 4).

Contribution to the Bible
God's Word continually shows our need of deliverance that only God can provide. This story reminds us of the absolute necessity of looking to God for salvation. The Israelites were brought into the Promised Land, which was an image of the eternal inheritance we now claim in the saving work of Jesus Christ. The book of Joshua portrays the rest that comes to the believer who experiences the blessings of salvation through a faith that overcomes the various trials, temptations, and difficulties of life that are faced in our three enemies: the world, the flesh, and the devil. The battle belongs to the Lord.

The Commissioning of Joshua (1:1–18)

In Joshua, we are introduced to the leadership of Moses' successor. Joshua is first mentioned in Exodus as a military leader fighting the Amalekites (Exodus 17:9–13). The book of Numbers reveals that he served as Moses' aide (Numbers 11:28). What better preparation could there be to lead the Israelites? Israel's preparation for taking control of the Promised Land proceeds out of God's commission and charge. Here we see God's people behaving well, responding to His revelation according to His will.

Background & Context

Jericho lay just five miles on the other side of the Jordan and was one of the most formidable fortresses in the land. Conquering this city would not only give them a strong foothold into the land, but it would literally split the forces of the Canaanites by hindering their communication and supply lines. This would have a further demoralizing effect on the rest of the inhabitants.

Faithful Preparations (2:1–24)

Joshua and the people are called to accomplishments far beyond their ability. Regardless of these obstacles, Joshua, believing the promises of God, courageously moves ahead, preparing to lead the Israelites into the Promised Land.

Background & Context

The king may have assumed that the spies were staying with Rahab, but he would have had reason to expect that she would do her patriotic duty and turn the spies in. The ancient law code of Hammurabi contained a provision for putting prostitutes who harbored felons to death. And yet Rahab had faith in God's ability to deliver her against all odds.

Crossing the Jordan (3:1–17)

Life in a fallen world necessitates our need for strength from above, even for God's chosen people. The battle is really the Lord's, and this is what Israel is being taught in this chapter. With their hopes high, they prepare to confront the challenges ahead.

Background & Context

Joshua is the history of Israel's conquest of the land of Canaan in fulfillment of God's promises for the people of Israel. In Joshua, the nation of Israel crossed over Jordan and took possession of the land

God had promised them. If Moses is the symbol of deliverance, then Joshua is the symbol of victory. Joshua teaches us that faith is the victory that overcomes the world (1 John 5:4).

Lest We Forget (4:1–24)

God is often wisely concerned over our proneness to forget His faithfulness. Here we see His reminder for the Israelites by building a physical monument to their crossing of the Jordan.

Background & Context

The name *Gilgal* means "a circle of stones." Every time Israel returns to Gilgal, they will see the circles of stones and remember what God has done to roll away the waters of the Jordan. The very site of the stones was to be an encouragement, but also a reminder of the sovereign power of the Lord over nations and creation so they might fear the Lord forever and remain faithful to their purpose in the plan of God.

Consecrating the People (5:1–15)

This chapter bridges the crossing of the Jordan and the beginning of the military campaigns. Israel needed a preparation of heart and willingness to submit to God's directions that they might experience His power and overcome the enemy.

Victory at Jericho (6:1–27)

God guides the Israelites into a miraculous victory with an unlikely strategy.

Background & Context

The number seven is used eleven times in this chapter. Seven signifies perfection or completion, which reminds us that God's plan is always perfect and cannot be improved upon (Romans 11:33-36; 12:2; 1 Corinthians 1:18). Further, the number seven shows that the conquest is part of a spiritual exercise designed to set the people apart (sanctify them) for the Lord as a holy people who belong to a holy God.

Because of the significance of the number seven to creation and the Sabbath, and the fact they were entering into their inheritance, it also signifies the beginning of a new order and the land as a picture of the believer's rest in the Lord (Hebrews 4).

The Agony of Defeat (7:1–26)

The distance between a great victory and a terrible defeat is one step and often a short one at that. Ai is the next objective in the path of conquest because of its strategic location.

Background & Context

The defeat at Ai demoralizes God's people. It creates misgivings and a lack of hope in the Lord. Rather than examine their own lives as the source of their defeat, they begin to doubt the Lord. People are quick to blame, make excuses, and hide, but they often fail to honestly examine their own lives.

Victory at Ai (8:1–35)

Often God engineers defeat before He engineers victory. Sometimes success comes through the back door of failure. In this chapter we again see the grace of God and the truth of restoration. Defeat never has to be the end.

Background & Context

The place where Joshua led the people had outstanding acoustical properties, kind of like a natural amphitheater, and one person standing on one mountain could be easily heard by someone standing on the other mountain. Mount Ebal stood for cursing, and Gerizim stood for blessing. These mountains formed a huge object lesson. What happened to the Israelites in the land was going to depend on where they lived, as it were—on Mount Ebal, in disobedience and under the curses, or on Mount Gerizim, in obedience and under God's blessing.

The Peril of Walking by Sight (9:1–27)

This passage describes the danger of failing to commit to the Lord, the peril of prayerlessness, and the peril of walking by sight—making decisions on the basis of how things appear rather than trusting in God for guidance. As we have seen, Israel's failure at Ai was to a large degree the result of failing to consult the Lord.

Destruction of the Coalition (10:1–43)

During Israel's campaign and victory over the southern portion of Canaan, something miraculous happens that provides Joshua with a great military opportunity for a quick victory over a number of enemies at once.

Background & Context

Obviously, this was a unique day in the history of creation. Views concerning this phenomenon fall into two categories. The first assumes a slowing or suspending of the normal rotation of the earth so that there were extra hours that day. God did this so that Joshua's forces could complete their victory before the enemy had a night for rest and regrouping. The Hebrew for *stood still* (10:13) is a verb of motion, indicating a slowing or stopping of the rotation of the earth on its axis. The second category includes views that assume no irregularity in the rotation of the earth. One view argues for the prolonging of daylight by some sort of unusual refraction of the sun's rays. While the details of how it took place are not described in scripture, what is made clear is that God did something completely amazing to give the Israelite armies a complete and decisive victory.

The Conquest of the North (11:1–23)

Joshua has a decisive victory over the south of Canaan. Now the rulers of the cities in the north have become scared. Although earthly rulers are quick to devise plans to stop Israel, they underestimate the power of God being on one's side. The victory He promised Israel will be realized, even if the battle is long and grueling.

Background & Context

Josephus, a Jewish historian of the first century AD, estimated that this northern alliance included 300,000 infantry soldiers, 10,000 cavalry troops, and 20,000 chariots. With such a huge army, it would appear from outside observation that Joshua and his army had good reason for fear.

Kings Conquered (12:1–24)

The list in this chapter is the only complete list of the kings Israel conquered. This list is a testimony to the power of God to accomplish His purposes, overcome earthly powers, and provide for His people in a magnificent manner.

Background & Context

In addition to the significance of the list of names, Joshua calls out the land itself. While the geography of this region is not something many of us have experienced firsthand, the Promised Land had been traversed by the nation of Israel. When Joshua mentions the hill country, the western foothills, the Arabah, the mountain slopes, the desert, and the Negev, the people had literally walked over those various areas and they could picture precisely what God's provision included. Indeed, this land is the backdrop for their nation's history. These are the same hills and valleys that Jesus and His disciples will travel through, the same territory that Rome will conquer, and later still, the Muslims. It is a setting that has significance not just to the generation of Israelites that fought alongside Joshua, but for all generations to come.

These kinds of lists remind the people that their victory in the Lord does not come without tremendous cost—indeed thirty-one conquered kings represent a vast swath of humanity whose lives were completely interrupted and destroyed so that Israel might be given the inheritance the Lord had promised to Abraham. This list reminds the people of a crucial truth: There is no one more powerful than God, and no one can stand in His way.

The Division of the Land (13:1–33)
This chapter deals with an exciting time for the Israelites—the distribution of the land. After four hundred years in bondage in Egypt, forty years of wandering in the desert, and years of long hard fighting, they now are able to enjoy and possess the Promised Land.

Caleb's Portion (14:1–15)
This chapter describes the process by which the land is distributed to the rest of the nine-and-a-half tribes. The first inheritance is given to Caleb. This is fitting because Caleb, along with Joshua, is one of the only two left from those who were freed from Egypt, and they had been the only two who believed all along that God was powerful enough to give the land to Israel. Here, Caleb gets his reward.

Background & Context
After the Israelites first escaped Egypt, they traveled across the desert to the border of Canaan and sent twelve spies (one from each of the twelve tribes) across the border to do reconnaissance. Caleb and Joshua were two of the twelve spies and were the only two who brought back a good report. Rather than being fearful of the task ahead, Joshua and Caleb encouraged the people to believe that God would help them conquer the land.

Unfortunately, the people were not convinced, and because of their lack of faith they wandered for forty more years before reapproaching the border for entry. During that forty years, the generation that originally left Egypt died out except for Joshua and Caleb, the only two who made it across the border (Numbers 13:1–14:38).

Land for the Tribe of Judah (15:1–63)

After Caleb's allotment, Joshua now turns to the distribution of the land for the tribe of Judah. Judah receives the largest portion because they are the largest tribe. In the distribution of the land to Judah, there are some things already spoken by Jacob that have a remarkable bearing on this tribe.

Ephraim and Manasseh (16:1–17:18)

Years before, while Joseph was away in Egypt, he had two sons: Ephraim and Manasseh. When his father Jacob discovered Joseph was not dead (Genesis 48:21), he included these two children in the blessing of the Promised Land. In his joy, Jacob brought Ephraim and Manasseh into his direct inheritance. Thus, they were considered heads of tribes with their uncles (Joseph's brothers).

The Allotment of the Rest of the Land (18:1–28)

The context of chapter 18 is very simple. There are still seven tribes that need to receive their allotment. The story now reaches a turning point in the land distribution lists for the nation of Israel. The nation is now moving to Shiloh. It is at this new location that the Tent of Meeting is mentioned for the first time in the book. The Tent of Meeting is going to be set up in a place where the presence of God will be close to the center of the entire nation.

Background & Context

To begin the process of dividing the rest of the land, Joshua instructs that three men from each of the seven remaining tribes be appointed as surveyors. The role of these surveyors will be to travel throughout the land and record its description (18:4). They are to write down their findings. This is highlighted three times (18:4, 6, 8); God is making sure that all generations will know the land division.

The previous allotments are reviewed to remind the remaining people how God has provided for all the people of Israel (18:5-7). The Lord was with the nation, not only in the tabernacle, but also in the casting of lots for the remaining allotments. The Levites' special inheritance is important, so Joshua mentions it again. He will make sure that those set apart for God's service are cared for and given everything they need.

The Rest of the Land (19:1–51)

Joshua is now ready to allot the rest of the land to the remaining tribes. God deals with each tribe according to their lot.

Cities of Refuge (20:1–9)

God knows that all murder should not be treated in the same manner; thus He commands the Israelites to set up cities of refuge for people who have accidentally killed another person.

Cities for the Levites (21:1–45)

The Levites are not to possess land but are to be given cities and pasturelands to raise their families and care for their cattle (Numbers 35:1–8). They are to be set apart to the Lord for the service to God.

Home to the East (22:1–34)

As the eastern tribes returned home and got settled, something occurred that almost disrupted the unity of the nation. The eastern tribes acted so inappropriately that a civil war almost overtook the newly formed nation. In the midst of this tension, God protected the nation and taught them some serious lessons about true worship.

Joshua's Charge (23:1–16)

Joshua ends with his farewell address. His parting words express his deep concern for a potential danger emerging in Israel—a growing complacency on the part of Israel toward the remnants of the Canaanites. Joshua feels compelled to warn the people that obedience to God is essential to His blessing, including enjoying all the fruits of the land.

The Covenant Renewed (24:1–33)

Joshua's last meeting with the people takes place at Shechem. In this significant city, Israel's covenant with God is renewed.

Background & Context

The location is one of importance, because this spot symbolizes the covenant that God made with Israel. Consider what would be in this location: The stones on which the law had been written were still there reminding people of their theological heritage and that their calling as a nation serves something higher than just being a nation. They serve the one true God to whom all the glory for their victory is owed. This place had been dedicated as the spot for worshipping the Lord and remembering His holiness.

Judges
Introduction to Judges

The book of Judges gets its name from its main characters: the people God graciously selected to save ancient Israel from itself. It tells the stories of colorful and imperfect individuals with charismatic qualities God uses to break the yoke of oppression that Israel experienced, time after time, as a result of its own sinfulness. Through these types of saviors, God calls His children back to Himself.

Author
Although Samuel was traditionally thought to be the author of Judges, no one knows who put it together. Experts say it could have been a single author, because the material is well-shaped into a coherent whole; or there may have been more than one compiler.

Occasion/Purpose
Judges is a compilation of selected independent stories, mostly centered on one individual. But there is one overall message: Israel's repetitive cycle of sin, and God's consistent and merciful response.

Themes
In Judges we see Israel's continual cycle of unfaithfulness:

1. Obedience to the law of God
2. Moral complacency
3. Moral compromise as a result of their complacency
4. A falling away from their faith and religious roots
5. Oppression from other nations as their weakening faith results in a weakened nation
6. Deliverance from these consequences and a temporary return to faith

It is in the deliverance that God provides at the turn of each cycle that reveals His righteousness, mercy, and long-suffering nature. The individuals God chooses, though certainly imperfect deliverers, can be seen as temporary models of the great deliverance that will one day come through Jesus, the perfect and permanent deliverer of the people of God.

Background & Context
Judges is known as one of the books of the "former prophets," and it reveals God working throughout the history of His people. The book covers approximately 350 years, from the time of Joshua's death until the rise of Samuel, the last judge before the kings of Israel begin to lead as the formal monarchy is established.

The era that Judges recounts is a period of transition—from the conquest of Canaan in the latter part of the thirteenth century to the beginning of the monarchy with King Saul, perhaps in 1020 BC. There is a direct correlation between the decisions Israel makes during these centuries and her downfall later.

After Joshua (1:1–36)

The era in Israel's history described in this book occurs after Joshua, Moses' successor, had led the Israelites into Canaan and begun the process of conquering the land assigned to each of the twelve tribes that make up the nation of Israel. Judges then describes the occupation of Canaan. The accounts here track the growing consequences of the people's compromises as they fail to obey God faithfully and completely in this process.

Background & Context

The lessons of the book of Judges are taught not through a systematic recounting of theology, but through stories. These stories teach us about a purity of faith in the midst of a culture that is often in opposition to that faith. They also teach us that victory has nothing to do with the size of the enemy, but rather with the size of our faith in the promises of God.

Vicious Cycle (2:1–3:6)

At this point, though God had commanded them to enter the land and drive out any peoples there that refused to follow Yahweh, the Israelites are convinced that their half attempts and compromised efforts in claiming their territories are justified and, in fact, represent practical victories. They are at least in the Promised Land, and they are settling down. The story of the Exodus, the mission the people set out upon, and the amazing works God performed seem to be a distant memory.

Background & Context

The judges were deliverers of Israel. This was their life's work. Their position was not hereditary, in most circumstances. While some believe the judges had legislative authority, much like elected officials today, there is not strong evidence that this is the case. Their special work was to act as avengers for Israel—being anointed to destroy God's enemies and deliver His people. In this way, they foreshadowed the redemptive work of Jesus Christ.

Othniel and Ehud (3:7–31)

We now turn to the first of two stories of exemplary judges: Othniel and Ehud. The story of Othniel is given to us without much detail. In this simple story, we see the sovereign goodness and grace of God in both His chastisements and in His deliverance. The story of Ehud is a violent comedy, but also in some ways a picture of the Gospel.

Deborah and Jael (4:1–24)

In the account described in this section, a woman raises a man to lead an army against the enemy of Israel. Then a second woman completes the victory by crushing a wicked leader.

Background & Context

The image of trees is a significant one in the Bible. Trees were a source of comfort and shade. They provided not only shelter, but sometimes food as well. They are often included in important biblical events and images. Humanity was first judged at a tree, and that judgment is paid by a Savior who hangs on a tree. The tabernacle is pitched under a great tree where the Book of the Law of God was kept (Joshua 24:26). It was a place that represented a gate to heaven, a place of righteousness and justice, and (later) a place of healing and food (Revelation 22:2). In this chapter, Deborah judges under the Palm of Deborah, and Jael's husband moves away from the Lord and pitches a tent under a great tree.

The Song of Deborah (5:1–31)

In chapter 5, Deborah and Barak praise God for His victorious strength. They exalt those who keep their word and serve the Lord in battle, and chastise those who fall back in their comfortable religion. They contrast the true and living God with Baal, the false god, and mince no words in describing the violent victory of the righteous and the violent debauchery of the fallen.

The Call to Gideon (6:1–40)

The cycle of falling away from faith, becoming oppressed, and then praying for deliverance starts again. This section begins the literary center of Judges, involving Gideon and his idolatrous son, Abimelech; and it emphasizes the central issues: the worship of Baal and the Lord's kingship over His covenant people.

Background & Context

The Midianites have a long history with the Israelites. Where did they come from? This people group actually descended from Abraham (like the Israelites), but the Israelites were descended from Isaac, Abraham and Sarah's son. The Midianites were descended from Abraham and his second wife Keturah.

It was the Midianites who bought Joseph from his brothers and sold him as a slave in Egypt. Generations later, Moses married a woman who was a Kenite, a subset of the Midianites. Her Kenite father was Moses' father-in-law and adviser.

The Midianites were severely routed under Moses in Numbers 31. Here in Judges, some two hundred years later, the tables are turned. God is now using the Midianites as a judgment upon Israel.

Gideon's Battles (7:1–8:17)

The theme of weakness in people and strength in God is paramount to the story of Gideon's battle over the Midianites, foreshadowing what the apostle Paul taught in 2 Corinthians 12:9–11: that God's strength is made perfect in our weakness.

Shadows on Gideon (8:18–32)

Gideon is a man of faith. He is listed in the "hall of faith" in Hebrews 11. He has the kind of faith we are to imitate, the kind of faith that perseveres to the end. But there are other lessons to learn from Gideon. God does not give us stories like fairy tales, where the good prince goes off and lives happily ever after. In fact, one of the greatest lessons to learn from the end of Gideon's life is that we must never rest on our laurels or think that we are no longer susceptible to temptation. We must learn the importance of finishing well and the incredible covenantal connection between us and future generations.

Gideon's Evil son (8:33–9:57)

Following Gideon's forty years of peace, the consequences of sin and compromise weave a web of great judgment upon the next generation. The story of Abimelech is a warning.

Return to Apostasy (10:1–18)

Following the accounts of Gideon and Abimelech, passages like 10:1–5 (and 12:8–15, at the end of this section) seem to be filled with minor details, but that is not always the case. Consider their placement in light of the greater passages and the whole book to make sense of what they offer.

Background & Context

What we can see in this opening description, as with the account of Gideon, is the struggle to establish a dynasty. Keep in mind that there was not a prohibition against having many wives in the Old Testament, and having many children was a sign of blessing. This is why the count of children is significant here.

Jephthah (11:1–12:15)

The beginning of the story of Jephthah is full of comparisons and contrasts. First, notice that Jephthah looks a lot like Abimelech. Both are sons of a mix representing faithfulness and unfaithfulness. Both are surrounded by worthless men. But Jephthah is listed as a believer, a man of great faith (Hebrews 11:32), a mighty man of valor (Judges 11:1), one who speaks with and worships the Lord (11:11). In addition, this part of the story (Gilead and Jephthah) closely parallels the exact situation of Israel and the Lord.

Samson's Parents (13:1–25)

Over a thousand years before the birth of Jesus, an angel appeared to a woman. He told her that she would conceive in a miraculous way and give birth to a son. He said that her son would be set apart for the Lord from his birth on and that he would start to save his people from their enemies. We have learned from our study in Judges that these are not simply coincidences. The background of the birth of Samson reveals that this unintentional deliverer is a gift from God.

Samson (14:1–20)

The account of Samson is one of the strangest stories in the book of Judges. He is surprising in his actions and in his strength. At first it doesn't seem that Samson is acting as a judge but rather just doing his own thing. But we are told that the Lord raised up Samson to begin to deliver Israel (13:5) and that the Spirit of the Lord had begun to move upon him (13:25). To understand the stories of Samson, we should keep in mind three things: first, Samson's association with Philistine women; second, Samson's Nazirite vow; and third, Samson's ministry of stirring up a sleeping Israel and his work of beginning a deliverance from the Philistines.

Samson's Battles (15:1–20)

Holy violence sounds like an oxymoron and brings to some an image of religious fanaticism. The story of Samson is neither for the squeamish pacifist nor the Victorian prude. But the story is for the people of God, that they might fear a mighty and holy God and rest alone in the life, provision, and vengeance of the Savior.

Background & Context

Over and over, Judah and Israel turn their back on the deliverers God sends to them. Even in the first century, Jesus' rejection and His trial and execution are an extension of this same pattern (John 11:49-52).

Samson and Delilah (16:1–31)

There are many literary parallels between Judges 14–15 and Judges 16. In both, a woman is approached by Samson, she obtains and betrays a secret, Samson is bound, and there is a great slaughter of Philistines. But there is a significant contrast. Three times in Judges 14–15 the Spirit of the Lord comes upon Samson. In Judges 16, amidst Samson's sin, the Spirit is not mentioned and then later is mentioned as having departed.

False Priests (17:1–13)

The book of Judges begins with two introductory passages and concludes with two appendices. The accounts in chapters 17–21 most likely took place before the first judges came upon the scene. Moses' grandson is mentioned in Judges 18:30 and Aaron's grandson in Judges 20:27–28. Their placement here at the end of the book is to emphasize what went wrong in Israel and why she fell into idolatry so often. The first appendix is contained in chapters 17–18.

Some see Judges 17 and 18 as a parody of the story of Moses. Moses delivered the people of Israel, and through him God established a house of worship, a priesthood, and the promise of conquest of a land. Judges 17 perverts this history of an established worship and priesthood, and Judges 18 will pervert the story of the conquest. This parody displays for us why Israel falls into such apostasy time and time again throughout the following generations (described in the first 16 chapters of Judges) and is told through the life of the priest who is the grandson of the same Moses.

Background & Context

Part of the role of the Levites in Israel's history was as a substitution for the firstborn of Israel. By the laws of God given to these ancients, the firstborn always belonged to God, as well as the firstfruits of a crop. This practice carries over today in the practice of offering a tithe or offering to God first from our income.

In this substitutionary role, the Levites gave up certain freedoms. They lived in appointed cities because they had no land, and they also served in the towns of Israel, more or less like pastors of synagogues. The Levites were to reveal God's truth and lead true worship. Unfortunately, in the first 16 chapters of Judges, the Levites are conspicuously absent.

Dan's Deceit (18:1–31)

In the days of Moses and the Exodus, the Lord led His people out of Egypt, established His priesthood, sent His spies, and conquered the land, burning the first city, Jericho. This section is similar to that story but is more of a distorted parody. This account reveals how the people of Israel, during the times of the judges, continue to miss the mark, fall into the sin of idolatry, and find themselves under God's wrath. Their story is a reminder of the importance of walking in faithfulness.

The account here gives the details of the Danites' compromise, something that has already been mentioned in Judges 1:34 and even in the account of Joshua, the first Israelite leader in the land of Canaan (Joshua 19:47).

The Levite's Concubine (19:1–30)

This section includes one of the most shocking stories in the Bible, a horror story of sorts. But God has a purpose in it for us. One structure that has been applied to these appendices is this:

- Chapters 17–18 show us that the Levites fail to protect the people from idolatry.
- Chapters 19–21 show us that the Levites fail to protect the people from immorality.

In the Bible, idolatry leads to immorality. If we don't love God exclusively, we will not love others.

Background & Context

It's important to understand the account of the Levite in a broader context. When the Israelites entered Canaan to claim it as their inheritance from the Lord, each tribe was assigned a territory. It was that tribe's responsibility to conquer the territory and drive out all those who would threaten the faithful worship of the Israelites. The Benjamites had failed to trust God and follow Him to battle against the Canaanites. They never conquered the land or claimed it for their religion. By this point in their history, they have come to live like Canaanites rather than forcing the Canaanites to adopt the Israelite way of life.

Responding to the Crime (20:1–48)

At the close of chapter 19, a Levite responds to the brutal death of his concubine, or second wife, by cutting her corpse into twelve pieces and sending each piece to a tribe of Israel. Judges 20 records the response of the tribes of Israel against the tribe of Benjamin on behalf of the crime committed against the Levite and his concubine.

Some consider the Levite's decision to act in this way to be a picture of Israel that is torn apart by sin and unfaithfulness.

Background & Context

Sometimes in reading a biblical account, the details provided in one book reveal context for the information in another book. Verse 28 is such a case, where the mention of Phinehas, son of Eleazar, helps to put this event in a historical context. Phinehas is mentioned in Numbers 25:10-13.

The Rebellion of Benjamin (21:1–25)
As we end this story of the rebellion of Benjamin, we see the grace of God in this final chapter. The Levites have been unable to protect the people from idolatry and immorality, and thus the judgment of the Lord falls hard upon the house of the Lord in chapter 20. The tribe of Benjamin is dead. And God, in His extraordinary and unpredictable ways, resurrects the tribe.

Ruth
Introduction to Ruth

Ruth is a small book, only four chapters, that reveals God's work of providence in the details of people's lives.

Author
Even though there has been speculation about possible authors, no one knows who wrote the book of Ruth. We do believe, however, that the book was written during the time of King David. This seems reasonable because of the genealogy included at the end of the book, a genealogy that includes David's ancestors.

Occasion/Purpose
One option for the purpose of this book is to reveal how a Moabite—a non-Jew—can become a faithful follower of Yahweh, Israel's God. Another option is that it is meant to be a contribution to the genealogy of David, an ancestor to Jesus. Just as likely, however, the primary purpose of the book of Ruth is to illustrate how simple, obedient people can be saved by God's providence and become part of His larger plan.

It's unclear when the book of Ruth was written, though it likely was written during King David's reign, thus the genealogy at the end of the book. In the English Old Testament, it comes right after the book of Judges. This placement may allow Ruth to provide a stark contrast to the greed and disobedience displayed by God's people during the time of the judges. In the Hebrew Old Testament, this book follows Proverbs, displaying Ruth as an example of the virtuous woman described in Proverbs 31.

Themes
The book of Ruth focuses on divine providence. Through obedience and lovingkindness, God's people continue in His plan even in the face of obstacles and mistakes.

Background & Context
Throughout Christian history, the book of Ruth has been considered part of the historical record of God's people. In addition to a story about love and obedience, Ruth reveals the workings of religious laws

related to widowhood, as well as a part of the genealogy of Christ—
even through a Moabite woman.

The Journey (1:1–22)

This chapter has a poignant lesson: God's providence is certain and He makes
no mistakes. As He unfolds the intricacies of His divine purpose in our lives, He
does so with a goal in mind. We also see how the saving purposes of God often
begin in the sometimes dark periods in someone's life.

The Couple (2:1–23)

In discovering how Naomi and Ruth are to survive, we are introduced to Old
Testament laws of gleaning, which were meant to provide for the poor and for
the widow.

Background & Context

The national religious laws of Israel stated that after harvesting a field,
a certain amount had to be left on the side of the field and in the
corners of the field for the poor and for those who could not provide
for themselves (Leviticus 19:9-10; Deuteronomy 24:19-22). Often women
and widows used this provision to find sufficient grain to make food
for one, two, or even three days, but no more than that. To survive only
from the grain gleaned from a harvested field was a menial and difficult
existence.

In addition to the law of gleaning, the Hebrew people also operated
under the law of the kinsman redeemer: If a woman was left as a widow
and childless, the nearest relative would take her as his wife, yet any
children that she bore would be considered the heirs of her previous
husband (Deuteronomy 25:5-6). In this way, the kinsman redeemer was
helping continue that family line rather than his own. Naomi may have
been already hoping that this kinsman's kind treatment of Ruth would
lead to a marriage.

When Ruth tells Naomi that Boaz instructed her to work with
his servants until the end of the harvest (2:21), Naomi supports this
instruction. Several times in the book of Ruth, the narrator hints that
the harvest fields can be a dangerous place for women. Harvest time
could also be a time of drinking and celebration, intensifying the risk
for vulnerable workers. Thus, Naomi agrees that staying near Boaz's
servants would decrease the risk of someone attacking or mistreating
Ruth (2:22-23).

The Agreement (3:1–18)

The narrative of the book of Ruth is clearly leading to Ruth and Boaz's marriage, which will fulfill God's plan for the line of David, leading to the birth of Jesus. Also of note is the setting of daytime and nighttime. Chapter 3 begins in daytime, then moves to night, and ends in daytime again. In the middle of the night, the greatest risk occurs.

The Legacy (4:1–22)

In chapter 4, the fulfillment of God's plan is evident not only for Naomi and Ruth, but also for the beginning of the line of David. Boaz has fallen in love, but he's not the nearest kinsman.

Background & Context

In ancient times, the city gate was the place where justice was administered. If you had a case that needed to be resolved in some way, you would go to the city gate and call upon the elders to make a judgment.

1 Samuel
Introduction to 1 Samuel

The book of 1 Samuel is best understood after a thorough review of the book of Judges. This was a dark era of history for the nation of Israel. God had delivered the Israelites from slavery in Egypt to the Promised Land in Canaan. The transition had not been a smooth one, yet under the leadership of Joshua the people had done reasonably well. However, after the death of Joshua, Israel went through repeated cycles of blessing and discipline—the result of their obedience or rebellion. Judges ends with the bleak statement: "In those days Israel had no king; everyone did as he saw fit" (Judges 21:25 NIV). That is the situation as 1 Samuel begins.

Author

What we know is 1 Samuel and 2 Samuel were originally a single book (along with 1 and 2 Kings in its final form), and Jewish tradition credits Samuel as the author. But since Samuel's death is included halfway through the (combined) book, other sources clearly were involved. Several resources were available to other authors at that time, which are mentioned in Samuel and related passages (1 Samuel 10:25; 2 Samuel 1:18; 1 Chronicles 29:29). Even assuming that Samuel made a major contribution to the book that bears his name, no one can state with certainty who authored the other portions. The date of writing is also questioned. Some suggest that since David's death is not included in 1 or 2 Samuel, the writing may have been concluded prior to that time. Others believe

Samuel could have been written considerably later—after the kingdom was divided (based on clues such as "kings of Judah" in 1 Samuel 27:6).

Occasion/Purpose

The books of Samuel deal with the transition between Israel's judges and their kings. This was a period when word from the Lord was rare (1 Samuel 3:1). Samuel was just the leader the nation needed to remind them of their spiritual commitments and help them move forward. Even though they would eventually reject Samuel's advice regarding their leadership, he continued to faithfully mediate between the people and the Lord.

The books of 1 and 2 Samuel were recorded to provide historical accounts of a crucial period of Israel's past. The book of 1 Samuel spans Samuel's life from birth to death, chronicles Saul's entire reign as the first king of Israel, and reveals the lengthy transition David underwent from shepherd boy to heir to the throne.

Themes

Numerous times throughout 1 Samuel, the significance of *obedience* is emphasized, as are the consequences of disobedience. The Israelites would reject both Eli's sons and Samuel's sons as leaders because they did not obey God. We are also shown Saul's recurring tendency to be almost, but not quite, obedient. Closely related is the issue of *receiving guidance from God.* Some of the improper methods attempted include using the ark of God like a good luck charm (4:1–11) and seeking spiritual advice through a medium (28:4–25). In contrast, we see Hannah's fervent prayer (1:1–20), Samuel's ability to discern God's voice (3:1–21), the use of the priestly ephod with the Urim and Thummim, and other methods not fully explained (14:18–19).

Contribution to the Bible

The book of 1 Samuel contains some of the favorite stories familiar to children's Sunday schools and Bible story books: Hannah and the boy Samuel, Samuel hearing God speaking to him, Israel's first king, and David and Goliath, to name a few. It is also enlightening to reflect on the stories of people who come into contact with the ark of the covenant when it is not in its traditional location in the tabernacle (or temple). Both the Philistines and the Israelites learn some hard lessons about misusing the holy things of God in this book. Additionally, it is in 1 Samuel where we find an explanation of the cryptic line in the older versions of the hymn, "Come Thou Fount of Every Blessing." When we sing, "Here I raise my Ebenezer," it is a reference to 1 Samuel 7:12–13.

The Son and the Psalm of Hannah (1:1–2:10)

The book of 1 Samuel is known for its grand accounts of Samuel (the great prophet, priest, and judge), Saul (Israel's first king), and the rise of the great King David. But it begins with the story of a humble and burdened young woman. Hannah's story is a model of the value of ongoing faithfulness and prayer, even when life's circumstances seem overwhelming.

Background & Context
The previous era of Israel's judges had been a downward spiritual spiral as Israel's numerous enemies dominated them until the people repented and God responded with a leader who would free them, at least temporarily. As the people moved from judges to kings, the reign of Saul wouldn't be much better. The rules of David and Solomon were, in part, bright spots of repentance, spiritual renewal, and prosperity. But the series of kings, with only a few exceptions, would soon drift away from God, resulting in eventual capture and captivity for Israel and Judah.

The Rise of Samuel (2:11–4:22)
After the birth of Samuel, it doesn't take long for Eli and the people of Israel to see that he is a special person with a rare (in those days) call from God. As Samuel moves into the office of the priesthood and the role of a prophet, his spiritual integrity is clearly evident in contrast to those around him.

The Philistines Encounter Israel's God (5:1–7:17)
The Israelites appear to be in a bleak situation. The Philistines have just routed the army, with thirty thousand casualties. Their priests are among the dead. Worst of all, the ark of the covenant was captured. But as will become evident in this section, God is still in control and remains active on behalf of His people.

Background & Context
After the Israelites chase the fleeing Philistines, Samuel erects a stone between Mizpah and Shen. He calls it *Ebenezer* ("stone, rock of my help"). It served as a lasting commemoration that the battle had been won with God's help.

After the battle, the Philistine domination over Israel ends for a while. Peace is also established between the Israelites and Amorites, all largely because of the influence of Samuel. From his home in Ramah, he will travel throughout Israel as a kind of circuit rider, fulfilling the roles of priest, prophet, and judge.

Israel Insists on a King (8:1–11:13)
In spite of Israel's recurring tendency to fall away from God, He has faithfully called a series of judges to free them from the oppression of various enemies. Now, even though the people have been pleased with the leadership of Samuel, they want to have a king like the nations around them. Samuel will be specific about the potential drawbacks, but the people are insistent.

Renewing the Kingdom (11:14–12:25)

The Israelites have asked for a king in spite of Samuel's clear warning about what their request would eventually entail. In essence, the people are rejecting the leadership of both Samuel and God. As Saul assumes leadership of the nation, Samuel gives his farewell address and offers a final challenge for the Israelites.

The Beginning of the End for Saul (13:1–23)

Most of what has been written about Saul so far has been quite complimentary. He has displayed physical strength, spiritual experience, and military skill. He has the full support of the people. But soon things begin to go wrong for Saul— not in major ways, but in numerous little situations where he doesn't quite obey God as he should.

Jonathan's Display of Faith (14:1–52)

Outnumbered and without a plan of action, the Israelites are facing the Philistines. Driven by desperation and self-interest, Saul has made an offering to God, and Samuel has rebuked him and left. But Saul isn't the only leader of Israel's army. His son, Jonathan, is also in charge of some troops. In this section the emphasis shifts to him.

The Consequences of Partial Obedience (15:1–35)

Saul got off to a pretty good start as Israel's first king. But as time passed, he began to make some poor decisions, including issuing a foolish oath that almost resulted in the death of his son, Jonathan, and overseeing an offering that Samuel should have made. In this section he again is given some specific instructions to follow, but he doesn't quite obey them fully. The results will be worse than he ever anticipated.

Background & Context

Israel already had a lengthy history with the Amalekites. In addition to the conflict that took place under Moses' leadership (Exodus 17:8-13; Numbers 14:25, 43, 45), the Midianites and Amalekites had joined forces to plunder Israel during the time of Gideon (Judges 6:3, 33; 7:12). Later they would create problems for David as well (1 Samuel 27:8; 30:1, 18; 2 Samuel 1:1).

God's instructions to Saul appear harsh to modern sensibilities. But Saul, and anyone familiar with the history of Israel, would have had a different perspective. The law provided the reasoning behind the intentional deaths of entire nations, and even their cattle (Leviticus 27:28-29). Joshua had the same instructions as Saul after the walls of Jericho fell. Not long afterward, as a result of failing to fully eliminate the inhabitants of the Promised Land, the Israelites found themselves regularly in subjection to other powers.

When a predominantly sinful nation is not totally destroyed, the native peoples would usually teach the Israelites their sinful ways and thus bring them under divine condemnation. In cases such as this one with the Amalekites, the annihilation is retribution for not only the sinful condition of the current generation, but also for their predecessors who had sinned greatly (1 Samuel 15:18, 33). Those who cursed Israel were to receive a curse in return (Genesis 12:1–3). The Amalekites had already been singled out to perish (Numbers 24:20). God had not forgotten what the Amalekites had done, and Israel was not to forget either (Deuteronomy 25:17–19). If we are unsettled by the just wrath of God, we should also note that God takes no pleasure in meting out punishment (Jonah 4:9–11).

The Rise of Saul's Successor (16:1–17:58)
In the previous section, Samuel walks away from Saul, never to visit him again. But it isn't long until God sends Samuel on another assignment, this time to anoint Saul's replacement as king of Israel. Samuel will follow God's instructions, but this time he isn't told in advance exactly who the person will be. And although it isn't emphasized, this section begins with a lot of fear and nervous tension.

David among Saul's Family (18:1–20:42)
David's courageous defeat of Goliath is an impressive moment that changes the course of Israel's history as well as the dynamic within Saul's family. David's instant fame creates jealousy in Saul, even as his display of faith cements a bond between David and Saul's son, Jonathan. After David becomes a member of Saul's family, loyalties change and rivalries intensify.

David the Fugitive (21:1–23:14)
At one time, Saul had felt very warmly toward David, but the closeness ends soon after David's victory over Goliath. Saul's jealousy of David's instant fame creates a rift between David and Saul. Envy soon gives rise to outright hostility, with Saul attempting to kill David a number of times. David has become a fugitive, and this section describes a number of events that take place as Saul pursues him, still hoping to end his life.

A Fugitive Models Mercy, Patience, and Forgiveness (23:15–26:25)
David has been hiding from Saul, moving from place to place to avoid being killed. People are beginning to support his leadership, and he has already freed one city from a threatening Philistine presence. In this section, we see David's faith in God demonstrated in a number of difficult situations. His dependence on God allows him to show forgiveness to those who offend him and repeated mercy to the person who is most eager to see him dead—King Saul.

The Final Days of King Saul (27:1–31:13)
After Saul is told his kingdom is being removed by God and given to another, a considerable amount of time passes before the prediction is fulfilled. In the meantime, David has already been anointed to take Saul's place. Although Saul is trying hard to put David to death, David has twice had Saul's life in his hands and refused to harm him. But after long months of conflict and turbulence, Saul finally runs out of time—seemingly farther away from God than ever. The book of 1 Samuel concludes with his death and burial.

2 Samuel
Introduction to 2 Samuel

Author
There is no mention of the author in the book of Samuel, though Jewish tradition states that Samuel wrote the first twenty-four chapters of what was originally one book of Samuel. In fact, 1 and 2 Samuel and 1 and 2 Kings are thought to be a single historical work edited by the same theological circle during the exile.

Occasion/Purpose
This book tells the story of how David sets out to establish his throne with God's blessing following King Saul's death. David is a man after God's own heart, but he is still simply a man with real shortcomings, and his sin with Bathsheba has a myriad of truly tragic consequences. The text recounts the events of the second half of King David's life during which his reign unites Israel and testifies to God's faithfulness to His servant David and to all His children.

The book of 1 Samuel ends tragically, with King Saul a virtual madman. He turns against David, his loyal servant and friend, and seeks to kill David as though he is a traitor. He fails to obey God's Word, and so brings about his own downfall and demise. Saul even goes so far as to consult with a medium. The closing chapter of 1 Samuel is the account of his death at the hand of the Philistines and his own hand as well. As sad as it is, we breathe a sigh of relief, for now David's days of fleeing from Saul as a fugitive are over. Second Samuel starts immediately afterward to tell how David will reign in Saul's place.

Themes
Second Samuel is a study in contrasts—of the blessing and curse of power, of the sinfulness that is present even in God's greatest servants, and of the power that temptation, lust, and covetousness have against even the mightiest kings. In this book we are reminded of how even a man of God can fail in major ways, including adultery and murder. And yet, we are struck again and again by God's forgiveness and grace even in the midst of some harsh consequences from David's sinfulness. The resounding theme of 2 Samuel is that even the greatest world leaders must remember that the kingdom, the power, and the glory belong to the Lord alone.

Contribution to the Bible

Second Samuel leaves us with an appreciation for the greatness of David and also a realization of his human weaknesses. If there is to be a king who will dwell forever on the throne of David (2 Samuel 7:12–14), it must be one who is greater than David. If David is the best king who ever ruled over Israel, then God will have to provide a better king. And so He will; Jesus is the perfect king that David cannot be.

The Death of a Mentor and a Friend (1:1–27)

David and his men are certainly grateful for the defeat of the Amalekites and the recovery of their families and possessions. But this victory must be overshadowed by David's concern for what is taking place in Israel. When David left Achish to return to Ziklag, the Philistines had mounted a massive fighting force to attack Israel. David knows very well how awesome this military effort is, because he and his men marched in review at the end of the procession. On his third day back in Ziklag, a young man approaches David with news of Israel's defeat.

Background & Context

Israel is divided when David first comes to power, thanks to the intrigue of men like Abner and Joab. This division is a foreshadowing of future times for the nation of Israel. It is not without some challenge that David becomes king of all Israel.

David Becomes King (2:1–32)

Now that the grieving is over, it is time for David to take his rightful place as king of Israel. Yet there are some obstacles that still remain in his way, as the next several chapters reveal.

Background & Context

Abner is the commander of Saul's army, but even more important, he is Saul's cousin. As Abner has much to gain from Saul's appointment as Israel's king, he also has much to lose if Saul is removed. Abner knows that David is the one Samuel anointed as Saul's replacement. Once Saul is dead, Abner is the one who actively resists David's appointment as king in Saul's place. It would not be a stretch to assume Abner fed Saul false information—information that made David look like an adversary who must be hunted down and put to death. Abner is no friend of David's, nor is he a good friend to his cousin Saul.

King David's House (3:1–39)

The conflict between Abner and Joab continues, and David is forced to wait on the Lord to reunite Israel.

Waiting on the Lord (4:1–12)

As the conflict continues to sort itself out, David exemplifies patience during a tough time of transitioning power.

Background & Context

David waits fifteen years from the time he is first anointed by Samuel to the time he becomes king over Judah. Even after David is anointed as king of Judah, he must wait a full seven years to be anointed king of all Israel. This means David waited more than twenty years of his life to be made king. How David handled this two-decade delay is the subject of this message. As David waits on the Lord, the divisions around him splinter and crackle relationships even among his closest friends and family. This is a reoccurring theme in his life—how sin can come between even the closest allies to make them enemies. David has gone through many different experiences, all of which will make him a better king for having endured them. He is now much better prepared to reign as Israel's king (5:4-6).

The promise God made to Israel and to David took a long time being fulfilled. David becomes king of Israel after a considerable delay and with a great deal of adversity. This is typical of the way God brings about His promises and purposes. God is not in a hurry. It is in times of waiting for God that many have failed in their faith and obedience. Waiting tests our faith and endurance. Like David, waiting is a significant part of each of our lives, and God will reward us if we are patient and faithful as we await His blessing.

David: King of Israel (5:1–25)

Ish-bosheth has just been murdered in what concludes a bloody and difficult phase of David's coming to power as king of Israel. Now God has new lessons for the king to learn as he takes over Jerusalem and meets with an old enemy, the Philistines.

God Rained on David's Parade (6:1–23)

Some days, no matter how carefully we plan and orchestrate events, things just have a way of going wrong. And sometimes even the most well-intentioned actions can inflict the wrath of God.

Background & Context

The ark had accompanied the Israelites wherever they went while they were in the wilderness. It went before the Israelites when they crossed the Jordan River (Joshua 3:14-17). We find the ark mentioned quite often in 1 and 2 Samuel. Samuel sleeps near the ark as a child (1

Samuel 3:3). When the Israelites are being beaten by the Philistines, they unwisely take the ark into battle with them as a kind of magic charm. They not only lose the battle, they lose the ark as well (1 Samuel 4). The next two chapters (5-6) of 1 Samuel are the account of how God plagues the Philistines, and how they finally decide they do not want the ark among them. In Exodus 25, God tells Moses He will meet with him and speak to him from above the ark, between the cherubim (Exodus 25:22). God chose to manifest His presence in the tabernacle, specifically from the ark. When God's glory first filled the tabernacle, even Moses was not able to enter (Exodus 40:34-35). Sinful men cannot get too close to a holy God.

Building God's House (7:1–29)
David begins to formulate a plan to build a house for God. However, Nathan reveals that God will build for David, and it surpasses the temple-house David wants to build for God.

War and Peace (8:1–10:19)
David uses his newfound power at war with the enemies of Israel in chapters 8 and 10. In chapter 9, we learn of how David's kindness toward Mephibosheth allows him to use his power to fulfill his covenant commitment to his beloved friend, Jonathan, and his promise to Saul.

Background & Context
At this time, when one king prevailed over another by winning in battle, he would cut off the thumbs and the big toes of his opponent, and then keep them as a kind of showpiece. These incapacitated kings would sit under the table of the victorious king, getting the scraps, like dogs. These defeated kings were not honored guests; they were trophies of war. David would have none of this with regard to Mephibosheth. He does not want him at his table as a subjected foe, but as an honored guest, the son of his beloved friend, Jonathan. It is an amazing act of grace (9:7-13).

David Commits Adultery (11:1–27)
The picture of David at the pinnacle of his success in chapters 8–10 sets the scene for David's fall to the depths in chapters 11–12. David's experience is proof that spiritual highs do not assure that we cannot fall, but may in some ways prepare us for a fall.

David and God (12:1–31)
In this section God sends the prophet Nathan to confront David about his sin.

Tragedy in the Royal Family (13:1–15:12)

God gives King David power, riches, and prosperity, not because of David's greatness, but because of God's grace. Following the death of David's first son with Bathsheba, David's family continues to experience serious tragedies and trials as a consequence of his sin. Soon, David's sin will divide the nation and deprive David of his throne for a time.

Trail of Tears (15:13–16:19)

Word comes to David that the people's allegiance has turned to Absalom and that a full-scale rebellion is about to occur. It is at this point that David decides to flee from Jerusalem, along with many of his followers. Those who will be numbered among his followers (and who will remain behind in Jerusalem) will be determined by whether or not they are true friends of David.

Darkest Days (16:20–19:8)

This passage is filled with intrigue and drama and more tragedy for David. David is overwhelmed by sorrow and suffering. Still, there is deliverance and hope for David in these dark hours as he passes through the valley of the shadow of death (Psalm 23).

Return to Jerusalem (19:9–20:26)

David is about to return to Jerusalem to resume his reign over the nation of Israel. To win the favor of the people (and perhaps to remove a thorn in his own flesh), David removes Joab as commander of his armed forces, replacing him with Amasa.

Promise Breakers and Keepers (21:1–22)

King Saul had violated a covenant with the Gibeonites that was more than four centuries old. His actions with regard to the Gibeonites bring a famine upon the land of Israel sometime after he dies. Now David must deal with Saul's covenant breaking and make things right.

Background & Context

This passage emphasizes the importance of covenants. Throughout Old Testament history, God deals with people through covenants (Genesis 9:1-17; 12:1-3; 17:1-22; Exodus 19–20; 31:12-17; Deuteronomy 5; 2 Samuel 7:12-17). Then, in the New Testament, He ushers in the New Covenant by the Lord Jesus Christ through the shedding of His blood (Jeremiah 31:31-34; Luke 22:20; 1 Corinthians 11:25; 2 Corinthians 3:6; Hebrews 9:11-22). God has not dealt with His people capriciously; He has always dealt with them in accordance with a covenant. David's dealing with the Gibeonites, at its roots, is a matter of keeping covenants. Israel had made a covenant with the Gibeonites. Even though this covenant is four hundred years old, it is still to be honored. No matter how good Saul's intentions might have been, the covenant must be kept. The breaking of that covenant had serious consequences.

Not only does it remind us that God relates to His people by means of His covenants, but it speaks to us particularly of the New Covenant. Saul's sins had to be atoned for or God's blessings could not be enjoyed. Saul's sin brought adversity in the form of a famine. Money could not atone for this sin—only the shedding of blood. It is the shedding of this blood that brings about atonement and appeases both God and the Gibeonites. The story of Saul, David, and the Gibeonites reminds us not only that sin must be atoned for by the shedding of blood, but that there is a payday, according to God's timing, for sin.

David's Song of Salvation (22:1–51)
This passage records David's reflections, penned at the outset of his reign as Israel's king. The text is virtually identical to (and possibly quoting) Psalm 18.

Epilogue (23:1–24:25)
As David continues to reflect on his time as king of Israel, we are reminded to celebrate the greatness of other people.

1 Kings
Introduction to 1 Kings

First Kings was originally joined with 2 Kings in one book. The narrative covers almost five hundred years, tracing the history of Israel and Judah from the last days of the monarchy under David to the disintegration and capture of the divided kingdoms.

Author
The author of this book is unknown. While there is a Jewish tradition that points to the prophet Jeremiah as the author, there is more evidence that the book evolved over a long period of time.

Occasion/Purpose
The purpose of 1 Kings is not explicitly stated. However, the fact that Kings doesn't mention the return of the exiles to Jerusalem suggests that the book is written in order to answer the question, "Why are we in exile?" This book serves as a kind of warning about the consequences of falling away from faith and the practice of that faith. In the same way, it serves as an encouragement toward consistent obedience.

Many scholars believe that the exilic author(s) of Kings is looking at the history of Israel and Judah through the prism of Deuteronomy. They are evaluating how well they have observed the law, and of course the answer is not well at all.

Themes
There is no single theme in 1 Kings. It instead offers historical events and theological commentary that continues biblical themes consistent with earlier books. For example:

- God in history as sovereign Lord
- God in judgment
- God as deliverer
- God's promise to David
- God's prophecy

Background & Context
While today 1 and 2 Kings appear as two separate yet related books in the Bible, it is important to remember that they are actually two parts of the same book. The date of both should be considered at the same time. The last event mentioned in 2 Kings 25 is the release of Jehoiachin from Babylonian prison during the reign of Evil-Merodach (Amel-Marduk) who reigned from 562-560 BC, thus the book had to be completed in its final form between this date and the end of the exile (which is not mentioned in the book of Kings) in 539 BC.

Solomon Becomes King (1:1–53)
The first section begins dramatically in the twilight of King David's glorious reign, with the question of his successor hanging in the air. His oldest living son, Adonijah, wants to reign. But the throne of Israel will not be left to the rules of hereditary succession; God will determine the next king.

Background & Context
The mule in ancient Israel was rare and expensive. It had to be imported and was ridden only by royalty. Everyone else rode donkeys.
    No one could use anything owned by royalty without permission. Thus Solomon riding on David's mule was a sign that David had appointed him his successor.

The Securing of Solomon's Throne (2:1–46)
After his father, King David, bids farewell with final instructions, Solomon takes care of old business as a way to secure his reign.

Solomon Is Given Great Wisdom (3:1–28)

God gives Solomon the opportunity to ask for anything, and Solomon wisely asks for wisdom, even after unwisely bringing a new Egyptian wife into his court. He then famously uses his godly wisdom to decide a conflict between two mothers claiming one baby.

Background & Context

Marrying a foreign woman was not against the Law of Moses—if she became a convert to the God of Israel. Ruth was an example of this. A Moabite, she returned to Bethlehem with her mother-in-law Naomi and adopted Naomi's faith. Ruth then married into Naomi's family (Ruth 1-4).

Solomon eventually collects a thousand foreign wives and concubines, which makes him more than just a bad example. They ruined his spiritual life. First Kings 11:4 says Solomon turns away from the Lord when he is old, but the pattern is set with this first marriage to the Egyptian princess. It perhaps makes political sense, but not spiritual sense.

Solomon's Administration (4:1–34)

Solomon's leadership is organized, creative, and, initially at least, non-oppressive, perpetuating the prosperity established by his father David.

Preparations to Build the Temple (5:1–18)

Solomon nurtures his father's friendship with the king of neighboring Tyre, who helps supply him with needed materials and manpower for the building of the temple.

The Construction of the Temple (6:1–38)

Solomon begins to build the temple four hundred years after the Israelites began worshipping God at His tabernacle. Solomon uses only the very best skills, men, and materials of his day.

Solomon's Palace and the Temple Furnishings (7:1–51)

Solomon may have taken seven years to build the temple, but he puts almost twice that into building his palace. Meanwhile, a skilled bronze worker crafts the temple's furnishings.

The Dedication of the Temple (8:1–66)

In what must have been a celebration on the scale of our modern installation of a new pope, Solomon assembles the elders of Israel, the heads of the tribe, and the chiefs of the families for the dedication of the temple.

God's Warning to Solomon (9:1–28)

God again visits Solomon and gives him a promise and a warning. Meanwhile, the king negotiates with his old friend and neighbor, King Hiram of Tyre, and we are told of the forced labor for his other major projects.

The Queen of Sheba Visits Solomon (10:1–29)

The queen of Sheba travels thousands of miles to see Solomon's riches and wisdom for herself, and indeed the reader of 1 Kings 10 is given a taste of his vast wealth and possessions.

Solomon's Decline and Death (11:1–43)

Solomon's love of foreign women leads to his downfall, and adversaries begin to rise as he approaches death.

Rehoboam and Jeroboam (12:1–33)

Solomon's son, Rehoboam, is made king and opens the door for the breakup of the kingdom. His opponent, Jeroboam, begins his idolatrous rule over the northern kingdom.

Background & Context

Shechem is a city with a rich history. Abraham worshipped there (Genesis 12:6). Jacob built an altar and purchased land there (Genesis 33:18-20). Joseph was buried there (Joshua 24:32). It was also the geographical center of the northern tribes. Having to meet the ten northern tribes on *their* territory instead of demanding that representatives come to Jerusalem is a weak start for Rehoboam.

The Man of God from Judah (13:1–34)

A prophet comes up from Judah to prophesy against Jeroboam, and then he himself becomes an object of God's judgment.

The End of Jeroboam and Rehoboam (14:1–31)

In this section we see the end of both Jeroboam and Rehoboam. One started as a populist with a shining prophecy of success and ended terribly, the other governed as a tyrant but humbled himself toward the end (2 Chronicles 12:6–7).

Abijam, Asa, Nadab, and Baasha (15:1–34)

Of the four next kings of Judah and Israel, only Asa does right before God, and God grants him a long reign.

Five Successive Kings of Israel (16:1–34)

Sinful kings come to power in Israel, culminating in Ahab and his wicked wife, Jezebel.

The Early Ministry of Elijah (17:1–24)

The prophet Elijah comes on the scene, challenges Ahab, and then encounters a widow with a dying son.

Background & Context

The name *Elijah* means, "Yahweh is my God." In the days when Ahab's government officially supported the worship of Baal and other gods, even the name of this prophet told the truth.

Elijah's Victory at Carmel (18:1–46)

Elijah returns to Israel and meets faithful Obadiah in Ahab's court. He arranges the dramatic confrontation on Mount Carmel between Baal's prophets and Elijah, the prophet of the true God.

God Encourages Elijah (19:1–21)

In this famous chapter, we see Elijah go from the high point of winning a contest with the prophets of Baal to the low point of post-traumatic depression. God ministers to him, though, and sends him to anoint a new king and his own successor, Elisha.

Israel's Victories over Syria (20:1–43)

God gives Israel two victories over the attacking Syrians to the north, and Ahab is condemned for letting the ruler Ben-hadad go free.

The Murder of Naboth (21:1–29)

Ahab and Jezebel arrange the death of Naboth to obtain his land. Elijah strongly condemns the murder.

The Death of Ahab (22:1–53)

The book of 1 Kings ends with Ahab's death and Jehoshaphat's reign in Judah.

2 Kings
Introduction to 2 Kings

The books of 1 and 2 Kings were originally joined in one book. The narrative covers almost five hundred years, tracing the history of Israel and Judah from the last days of the monarchy under David to the disintegration and capture of the divided kingdoms.

Author
The author of this book is unknown. While a Jewish tradition points to the prophet Jeremiah as the author, there is more evidence that the book evolved over a long period of time.

Occasion/Purpose
The books of 1 and 2 Kings were written to the people of the southern kingdom of Judah to explain that the fall of the northern kingdom of Israel was God's judgment on their idolatry, to call the southern kingdom to repentance for following Israel's example, and to remind them of the hope promised through the royal—and ultimately messianic—line of David.

Themes
The book of 2 Kings repeatedly demonstrates the judgment that results from unfaithfulness and idolatry. Over and over, kings and commoners are charged with worshipping false gods or worshipping the true God in false ways.

The book also highlights the way God uses other nations to execute His judgment: Israel falls to Assyria in 722 BC, and Judah falls to the Babylonians in 586 BC.

Along with God's judgment, however, 2 Kings underscores God's patience. He sends prophets to call His people to repentance, warns them over and over of the consequences of disobedience, and hears the prayers of faithful people.

Background & Context
The compilation of 1 and 2 Kings began before Babylon invaded Judah in 586 BC, but since the final chapters tell of events that occurred midway through the Babylonian captivity, obviously the book could not have been completed until then.

Ahaziah and Elijah (1:1–18)
The book of 1 Kings ends with King Ahab's death and his son Ahaziah's ascension to the throne. The reign of Ahab had been a spiritual disaster for Israel, the northern kingdom, but it was a time of political security and economic prosperity. Moab, the land just south of Israel and west of the Dead Sea, had been under Israelite domination since the days of David (2 Samuel 8:2, 11–12). After Ahab's death, the kingdom of Moab finds a good opportunity to remove their

nation from the domination of Israel. This is where the book of 2 Kings picks up the story.

Background & Context
Identifying Elijah by his clothes also connects him to the ministry of John the Baptist, who dressed in hairy skins from animals (Matthew 3:4). When the priests and Levites saw him they asked, "Are you Elijah?" (John 1:19-21).

Elijah's Ascension (2:1–25)
Chapter 1 of 2 Kings relates Elijah's confrontation with King Ahaziah and concludes with Ahaziah's death. Chapter 2 picks up the story at the end of Elijah's ministry and tells the account of his miraculous departure in a whirlwind and of Elisha's succession as prophet.

War against Moab (3:1–27)
King Ahab dies, leaving the throne of the northern kingdom of Israel to his son Ahaziah. When Ahaziah dies without a son, his brother Jehoram (or Joram) succeeds him. There has also been a change in the prophets: Elisha succeeded Elijah after Elijah is carried to heaven in a whirlwind.

God Works Miracles through Elisha (4:1–44)
We are not told precisely when the events recorded in chapter 4 occurred. In contrast to the faithlessness of King Ahaziah and King Jehoram described in 2 Kings 1–3, here we read of simple people with profound faith.

Naaman the Leper (5:1–27)
The miracle recounted here in 2 Kings 5 does not occur chronologically between the events described in chapter 4 and those in chapter 6. Rather, this account, grouped with other miracles that Elisha performs, demonstrates his credibility as a prophet of God.

Background & Context
The disease called *leprosy* at this time began as small, red spots on the skin. Before too long the spots got bigger and started to turn white, with sort of a shiny or scaly appearance. Pretty soon the spots spread over the whole body and hair began to fall out—first from the head, then even from the eyebrows. As things got worse, fingernails and toenails became loose, started to rot, and eventually fell off. Then the joints of fingers and toes began to rot and fall off piece by piece. Gums began to shrink until they couldn't hold the teeth anymore, so each tooth was lost. Leprosy ate away at the face until literally the nose, the

palate, and even the eyes rotted—and the victim wasted away until death.

God's Protection of Elisha (6:1–33)

Chapter 6 of 2 Kings deals with needs both great and small. The recovery of a lost ax head is a miracle of provision. The miracle of protection from the Samarian army is a dramatic demonstration of God's invisible but very real power. Chapter 6 concludes with a situation even graver: a siege that threatens to destroy the population of an entire city.

Background & Context

Horses and chariots were the most sophisticated and mighty military instruments of the day. But the invisible army of God had literally more firepower than the horses and chariots of the Syrians. The spiritual army had chariots of fire all around Elisha.

The Syrian soldiers could not see the spiritual army, so they do not hesitate to approach Elisha. But just as he previously prayed that God would give sight to his servant, he now asks God to strike this people with blindness. God answers this prayer, just as He previously answered the prayer to give perception to the servant (6:18).

When Elisha tells the army to follow him, he tells a technical truth but certainly intends to deceive. He does in fact bring them to the man whom they seek (when their eyes are opened, Elisha is there with them). However, he leads them back to Samaria—the capital city of the kingdom of Israel and an unfriendly place for a group of Syrian soldiers (6:19–20).

Elisha commands the king of Israel to treat the soldiers with kindness and generosity (6:21–22). This practice of answering evil with good successfully changes the policy of freelance raiders from Syria, and the bands of Syrian raiders no longer invade the land of Israel (6:23).

God's Miraculous Provision for Samaria (7:1–20)

Chapter 7 of 2 Kings picks up the account of the Syrian's siege of Israel's capital, Samaria.

New Kings in Syria and Judah (8:1–29)

The story of the kings of Judah pauses at 1 Kings 22:50, where Jehoshaphat the son of Asa ends his twenty-five-year reign and his son Jehoram comes to the throne. This chapter picks up the story of Jehoram again. But first we read of the king of Israel and the assassination of Ben-hadad, king of Syria.

Jehu Takes the Throne of Israel (9:1–37)

After the account of kings Jehoram and Ahaziah of Judah in chapter 8, the story shifts back to the northern kingdom of Israel in chapter 9. Joram, the king of Israel identified in 2 Kings 3, is king at the time the events of this chapter take place.

The Reforms of Jehu (10:1–36)

Jehu, anointed king of Israel at God's command, has executed the wicked queen mother, Jezebel, her son, Joram, who is Israel's king, and her son-in-law, Ahaziah, who is Judah's king—all in fulfillment of the judgment the Lord had sworn against them. But seventy sons of King Ahab, the patriarch of this idolatrous family, remain alive.

The Young King Joash (11:1–21)

King Ahaziah of Judah has been executed by Jehu, as recorded in 2 Kings 9:27–29. We don't know how many sons he leaves as heirs, but Ahaziah's mother has plans of her own for the throne of Judah.

The Reign of King Joash Over Judah (12:1–21)

Chapter 12 of 2 Kings chronicles the reign of King Joash, who comes to the throne at the age of seven (2 Kings 11). The Hebrew text uses the variant spelling Jehoash. Some translations use this spelling, while others use the name Joash. Both refer to the young king introduced in 2 Kings 11.

The Death of Elisha (13:1–25)

When Jehoahaz, the king who opens this chapter, comes to the throne, it is the beginning of the fulfillment of a promise made to Jehu, recorded in 2 Kings 10:30. God promised him that his descendants would sit on the throne of Israel to the fourth generation. This dynasty—though founded on a violent overthrow of the previous royal house—continues because Jehu came to the throne doing the will of God.

Background & Context

In the general history of this time, the Assyrian Empire kept the Syrians weak and unable to expand their domain into Israel. But there was a period when internal problems made the Assyrians bring back their troops from the frontiers of their empire, and the Syrians took advantage of this time of Assyrian distraction.

The Reigns of Amaziah and Jeroboam II (14:1–29)

The parallel and intersecting histories of the southern kingdom of Judah and the northern kingdom of Israel continue in this chapter. Chapter 12 of 2 Kings outlined the reign of Joash in Judah; chapter 13 highlighted the reigns of first Jehoahaz, then Jehoash in Israel. The next chapters relate the reigns of their successors.

Unstable Monarchy in Israel (15:1–38)

This section of 2 Kings 15 begins the story of five kings over Israel and anticipates the final dissolution of the northern kingdom. The kings, families, and dynasties ruling Israel change quickly during this period. Yet there is an amazing continuity of evil through these dynasties. Each is evil and each continues the state-sponsored idolatry in Israel.

The Compromise of Ahaz (16:1–20)

Chapter 15 closes with an account of King Jotham of Judah. Chapter 16 is devoted entirely to the reign of Jotham's son, Ahaz. Ahaz may well have been the worst king of a nation ruled by bad kings.

The Fall of Israel (17:1–41)

Two hundred years and nineteen kings after the time of Solomon (the last king over a united Israel), the northern kingdom of Israel falls. It is not because the God of Israel is unable to help them, but because they have so forsaken God and ignored His guidance and correction that He finally stops actively protecting them and allows them to degrade according to their desire.

Background & Context

When the Assyrians depopulate and exile a conquered community, they lead the captives away on journeys of hundreds of miles, with the captives naked and attached to one another with a system of strings and fishhooks pierced through their lower lips. (See also Amos 4:2-3.)

Hezekiah's Reign; Assyria's Threat (18:1–37)

Hezekiah, the subject of chapter 18, comes to the throne of Judah at the very end of the kingdom of Israel. Three years after the start of his reign, the Assyrian armies lay siege to Samaria, and three years after that the northern kingdom is conquered. The sad fate of the northern kingdom is a valuable lesson to Hezekiah. He sees firsthand what happens when the people of God reject their God and His Word and worship other gods.

God Delivers Jerusalem from Assyria (19:1–37)

Hezekiah's response to the current national crisis reveals a king who was wise enough to seek God's guidance.

God Extends Hezekiah's Life (20:1–21)

Chapter 20 is set at the time of the Assyrian invasion of Judah; Jerusalem has not been delivered from the Assyrian threat yet (20:6). The events of this chapter are also recorded in Isaiah 38.

The Wicked Reigns of Manasseh and Amon (21:1–26)

After the death of Hezekiah (2 Kings 20), Manasseh takes the throne in Judah. This is about twenty-five years after the fall of the northern kingdom of Israel. The kingdom of Judah will survive one hundred more years, but already an unfaithfulness like that of Israel's is apparent.

King Josiah Finds the Book of the Law (22:1–20)

With the death of King Amon, Josiah becomes king in Judah. He is one of the few kings who is obedient to the Lord throughout his reign.

The Reforms of Josiah (23:1–37)

Chapter 22 recounts the finding of the Law and Josiah's response to it. Chapter 23 highlights some of the outcomes of Josiah's convictions.

Judah Subjected under Babylon (24:1–20)

As the book of 2 Kings comes to a close, this chapter recounts the reigns of the last three kings of Judah before Judah is taken into exile.

The Fall of Jerusalem and the Captivity of Judah (25:1–30)

The book of 2 Kings opens with Elijah being carried to heaven. It ends with the people of Judah being driven into exile. God's judgment has fallen on His disobedient people.

Background & Context

The final words of the book of 2 Kings describe small kindnesses and blessings given in the worst circumstances. Judah is still depopulated, the people of God are still exiled, and the king of Judah is still a prisoner in Babylon. Yet, looking for even small notes of grace and mercy as evidences of the returning favor of God, the divine historian notes that King Jehoiachin begins to receive better treatment in Babylon. This is small, but evidence nonetheless that God is not done blessing and restoring His people, foreshadowing even greater blessing and restoration to come.

---

1 Chronicles
Introduction to 1 Chronicles

In the Hebrew, 1 and 2 Chronicles are one single book. The title means "the events of the times." The book of 1 Chronicles covers the same time period and many of the same events as portions of 1 and 2 Samuel and the first chapters of 1 Kings, but has a unique perspective. While the books of Samuel and Kings focus more on the political history of Israel and Judah, the Chronicles dwell more on the religious history and stay focused primarily on Judah. The information included in the Chronicles helps the people of Judah understand their history so they can live well in the present.

Author

Many scholars believe that Ezra wrote 1 and 2 Chronicles, which is quite possible. The book of 2 Chronicles flows smoothly into the book of Ezra, and the time frame (450 to 430 BC) is reasonable. However, the author's identity cannot be proven beyond reasonable doubt, so it has become traditional to refer to him as "the Chronicler."

Occasion/Purpose

In Jewish thought, genealogies were extremely important. The firstborn of each family was entitled to a double portion of the inheritance. The land was portioned out first by tribe, and then by family, and would never permanently leave that family. Levites had to prove their family credentials in order to serve in the temple. Priests had to show they were descendants of Aaron. Jewish people would consult these genealogies frequently, for various reasons. Genealogies were particularly important to post-exilic Judeans returning from exile after a disruption of their cultural history.

The Chronicler focuses his genealogies on the tribe of Judah, which eventually leads to the reign of David. Late in life, David is promised a "house" in which one of his offspring will reign forever (17:10–14). The Chronicler realizes the importance of such a promise and verifies the line of Judah both before and after David. For an audience who no longer has a temple or a Davidic king, 1 Chronicles is both a reminder of God's faithfulness in their past and an optimistic look toward the future.

The Israelites are captives of a powerful foreign empire, but some of the citizens are being allowed to return home. Their current status seems uncertain, so the Chronicler goes back to Adam (1:1) and reviews their history up to the current time (2 Chronicles 26:23). In doing so, he supports his outlook with various citations from the books of law, the Psalms, the prophetic books, and other sources. His repeated emphasis is on the covenants, the temple, and other reminders of how God has always provided for and delivered His people. As they look to return home and rebuild the temple that the Babylonians left in ruins, the Chronicler wants to assure them that God will continue to be with them.

Themes

The Chronicler is fond of the term *all Israel*, and he uses it frequently, downplaying the divided kingdom of Israel/Judah, while highlighting the perspective that the kingdom is indeed intended to be a single nation. Associated with Israel are the temple, priests, and Levites—all ongoing concerns of the author.

Most of 1 Chronicles, aside from a lengthy series of opening genealogies, focuses on David as God's chosen king over the united nation. In conjunction is the prominence of Judah over the northern tribes.

Contribution to the Bible

One of the interesting aspects of Chronicles is not so much what it adds to scripture but what it leaves out. (The translators of the Septuagint titled the book "the things omitted.") While covering much of the same content as 1 and 2 Samuel, the author streamlines the story to make it a targeted look at God's ongoing involvement in honoring the covenants He had made with Abraham and David. The Chronicler has a distinct perspective. While the books of Samuel and Kings were written during the exile and answer the question "What did we do to deserve the exile?" Chronicles addresses the questions, "What do we do now?" and "What is our connection with the past?"

There are a few things unique to 1 Chronicles involving some of the names in genealogies (much of 23–27, for example) and a number of orations found nowhere else. The Chronicler identifies a Shalleketh Gate of the temple (26:16) that is mentioned nowhere else in scripture. And the Jabez who sparked a best-selling book in the early 2000s is not mentioned anywhere else in the Bible except 1 Chronicles 4:9–10.

Background & Context

The Chronicles were written for a Hebrew audience no longer completely in control of their lives. They have recently undergone captivity at the hands of the Babylonians, but control has quickly shifted to the Persians. It is a time of uncertainty, if not despair, for the Jews, who have always taken for granted that they are God's chosen people. The book of 1 Chronicles, therefore, is a review of the best of their past history: the beginning of the kings, David's eventual rise to power, his desire and plans to build a temple for God, and the transition from his reign to that of Solomon.

Important Family Histories (1:1–7:40)

The first nine chapters of 1 Chronicles cover a number of genealogies going all the way back to Adam. While such lists of family histories are sometimes perceived to be insignificant (or even boring) to modern readers, the Hebrew mindset was quite different. Such lists helped define who they were as a people and were a reminder of the blessings of their past. In particular for this group of exiles returning home, the genealogies grounded them in their history. This section contains family lines for Noah, Abraham, and Israel.

Background & Context

When Jacob was blessing his sons, he made a somewhat cryptic statement that the scepter would not depart from Judah and that there would not cease to be a lawgiver until Shiloh comes (Genesis 49:10). The reference to the *scepter* brings to mind a king with the right to execute capital punishment. (Perhaps the best-known biblical example is King Xerxes in the book of Esther [see Esther 4:10-11].)

The Jewish nation eventually loses the right to govern themselves as they always had, which is why the Jewish leaders appeal to Pilate to have Jesus put to death. After the Romans deny Israel the right to pass a death sentence, rabbis walk through the streets of Jerusalem in sackcloth and ashes. They perceive that the scepter had been taken away before the Messiah had come, and they weep because they believe the Word of God has been broken. They do not realize that some seventy miles to the north, in a town called Nazareth, a young boy is working in his father's carpenter shop. The Messiah *has* come before the scepter departed, but He is not yet revealed to them.

The Beginning and End of the Era of Kings (8:1–10:14)

The lengthy opening list of genealogies in 1 Chronicles concludes in this section with an account of some of the people who return to Judah after being released from captivity. The author then backtracks to the first king of Israel and explains why, in spite of all his potential, King Saul falls far short of what God wants him to be.

Background & Context

The Chronicler adds an editorial note about Saul's life that isn't included in Samuel (10:13-14). The author of Samuel implies that Saul's consultation with a medium is entirely inappropriate. But here (10:13-14) the author provides three specific reasons why Saul falls short of what God wants him to be:

1. *Saul is unfaithful to God.* The Lord had instructed Saul to wipe out the Amalekites, but Saul uses his own discretion to determine who and what should be spared (1 Samuel 15:1-26).
2. *Saul disregards God's Word.* Only priests were permitted to sacrifice animals to God. Yet in a moment of desperation and panic, Saul makes an offering himself without waiting for Samuel, as he had been instructed (1 Samuel 13:5-14).
3. *Saul fails to seek God properly.* After the death of Samuel, Saul no longer receives direction from God. Again motivated by fear, he seeks counsel from a medium where he learns of his impending death (1 Samuel 28:4-25).

The Rise of David (11:1–12:40)

After providing all the opening genealogies and the brief account of King Saul, the Chronicler in this section turns his attention to the primary focus of this portion of his writing: the life story of King David. We need to remember that 1 and 2 Chronicles were originally a single book; the rest of what we know as 1 Chronicles (11–29) will be about David, concluding with his death.

David and the Ark of the Covenant (13:1–16:43)
Once anointed the next king of Israel, David had already waited a decade or so until God had determined King Saul's reign should come to an end. Saul tried persistently to capture and kill David, but it was Saul who died on the battlefield after drifting away from God. David was initially the king of Judah alone, but he eventually won over all the Israelites and received their endorsement as king. This section describes some of his early acts in his official leadership role.

David the Warrior (17:1–20:8)
David has become king, united the nation, moved the ark to Jerusalem, and built his palace. He is becoming a popular leader, respected by the people. Now he has a desire to provide a more permanent and fitting home for the ark. It sounds like a good idea at first, but God has other plans.

Background & Context
Why does the Chronicler omit such a significant story as David's affair with Bathsheba? A couple of good reasons have been suggested. First, the focus of Chronicles is different than that of Samuel and Kings. And a second reason is simply that the people would have been well aware of David's story from the previous writings, and the repetition was not necessary. The Chronicler certainly isn't trying to gloss over or minimize the sins of David. He has already pointed out David's frustration while moving the ark (13:9-13) and his many wives (14:3-6), and he will soon detail an even more grievous sin (21:1–22:1).

David's sin has already been duly (and thoroughly) described in scripture. The Chronicler is not inspired to repeat it. Like a parent talking about a child, he chooses to dwell primarily on the positive qualities of his subject. David had sinned, repented, and confessed. God had forgiven him and no longer held his sin against him.

The Significance of the Temple Site (21:1–22:19)
With only a few exceptions, everything the Chronicler has said about David so far has been positive and uplifting. He chose to omit the story of David's affair with Bathsheba and subsequent murder of her husband—the sin that most people appear to be familiar with. But David has another serious breach of faith that puts his nation at risk, and that event is included in this section.

Organizing People to Serve in the Kingdom (23:1–27:34)
By this point in David's life, he is old and preparing to turn the kingdom over to

Solomon. As plans for the temple construction are being completed, the human staffing is yet to be organized. In this section, David turns his attention to that job. While much of the content of 1 Chronicles has a corresponding version in Samuel or Kings, most of the content of this section is not found elsewhere.

David's Final Days (28:1–29:30)

David has put much thought and work into his organization of labor for the temple. In this section he is approaching the end of his life, so he calls together all the leaders he has appointed to gather their support for his son and Israel's next king, Solomon.

2 Chronicles
Introduction to 2 Chronicles

The books of 1 and 2 Chronicles were originally written not as two books but as one continuous history. The majority of 2 Chronicles describes the history of Israel after Solomon's reign as the kingdom divided into northern Israel and southern Judah. This is not a history written as it was happening, however. Instead, it is a history written long after the fact to remind the people of Judah of the journey of their ancestors.

Author

The author of the books of 1 and 2 Chronicles is not explicitly stated in the text. Many scholars ascribe the work to Ezra, citing a unified authorship of the Chronicles and the books of Ezra and Nehemiah. However, parts of the book are obvious additions and expansions on the original work, and it is difficult to date the entire book within Ezra's lifetime. The author was a wise and God-fearing person, writing with tremendous knowledge and insight into the significance of the community of God's people during this period.

Occasion/Purpose

The book of 2 Chronicles is more of a commentary on a period of Israel's history than an exhaustive, chronological account of the events that took place during that time. The book is written to guide the remnant of God's people as they seek to reestablish their lives in the Promised Land.

While the accounts recorded in 2 Chronicles describe Israel's history during Solomon's reign and the fall of Israel afterward, the occasion of the writing is much later. It was written after the Jews had been exiled away from their homeland and had been given permission to return again. Therefore, it begins with Solomon, but it ends with Cyrus's decree that allowed the people passage back to Jerusalem.

Themes

Beginning with the account of Solomon, and throughout this book, the

Chronicler describes the dangers of religious compromise and demonstrates the vanity of seeking or serving anything besides God. He writes in order to help Jews returning to Jerusalem to know how they are connected to the past and how they should now live in light of their history. This is why negative stories about Israel are minimized here. The themes revolve around the temple, Judah, those who seek God, and a connection with past national history.

Contribution to the Bible

This book is often considered one of the most unreadable of the Old Testament and therefore has been largely neglected and overlooked. Still, although at times the details seem mundane, the material supplements the stories told in Samuel and Kings and illuminates what was a very complicated and confusing period of Israel's history. From a broader biblical perspective, it emphasizes the continuance of the community of God and outlines how the Israelites are to interpret their history as a consistent reminder of God's faithfulness and love. The book also reminds them of the consequences of straying from the religious institutions God had established in order to help them honor Him and live well with one another.

Wisdom and Wealth (1:1–17)

Following the end of King David's reign over Israel, his son, Solomon, begins his reign seeking and receiving God's blessing with boldness.

Background & Context

The burnt offering was given totally to the Lord, burned completely up, symbolizing the offerer's consecration to Him. On the other hand, the peace offering, also referred to in Leviticus 3 as the fellowship offering, was partly given to the Lord and partly eaten by those making the offering. It symbolized communion with the Lord. Historically, in this part of the world, when a person ate with someone, they formed an intimate relationship in a sense. Thus the connection between the names—peace and fellowship.

Preparations for the Temple (2:1–18)

Solomon almost immediately begins an elaborate and extensive building project constructing his own palace and the temple of the Lord.

Temple Building Begins (3:1–4:22)

Solomon begins construction on his temple at the site David had purchased for this very purpose (1 Chronicles 22:5).

The Ark Arrives (5:1–14)

With the help of a foreign king and a massive conscripted labor force, Solomon has completed the construction of the temple. Now it is time to bring the ark of the covenant into the new temple of the Lord.

Temple Dedication (6:1–42)
The glory of the Lord has just filled the temple, and in response, Solomon speaks to the people and to the Lord. The account here parallels 2 Kings 8:14–21.

Temple Dedication Continues (7:1–22)
The Chronicler parallels 1 Kings 8:54, 62–66 in this section, but he changes the focus. Here, he emphasizes the glory of God rather than the people's blessing (the focus of the 1 Kings passage).

Fleeting Glory (8:1–9:31)
Following God's conditional blessing of the work Solomon had accomplished, Solomon continues to build Israel's infrastructure, even receiving praise from the Queen of Sheba. And yet in the final analysis, despite his tremendous achievement and wealth, Solomon is destined to join his father in the grave.

Power Shift (10:1–11:23)
Solomon has died, and his son Rehoboam reigns in his place. But the people are overburdened by taxes and stand ready to challenge their new leadership. The events described in this section propel Israel into a permanent state as a divided kingdom.

Further Trouble (12:1–16)
In the first three years of his reign, Rehoboam walks in the way of David and Solomon, and the southern kingdom is strengthened.

Changing Times (13:1–14:15)
Even as Israel experiences turmoil, power shifts, and civil war, God still works with them to restore the nation. This chapter tracks history in both the southern and the northern kingdoms of Israel.

Judah's Godly Kings (15:1–17:19)
Asa, too, eventually becomes prideful and pursues his own desires. This does not go unnoticed by God. As the seer declares, "The eyes of the Lord run to and fro throughout the whole earth, to give strong support to those whose heart is blameless toward him" (16:9 ESV). Jehoshaphat picks up his father Asa's legacy and reigns in the fear of the Lord (17:3).

Seek God (18:1–19:11)
Jehoshaphat allows his son Jehoram to marry the daughter of Ahab and Jezebel, the famously wicked duo of the Old Testament. As we read about the consequences of this and other choices made by Israel's leaders, we are reminded of how important it is to seek God in all our decisions.

The Battle Is the Lord's (20:1–37)

This chapter describes how three nations rise up against the southern kingdom of Judah. This battle is not described in Kings, which parallels the same period of Israel's history. It is a powerful story distinctive to the Chronicles.

Turning from God (21:1–28:27)

This section marks the end of two generations of spiritual reform in the southern kingdom of Judah under Asa and his son, Jehoshaphat, and the beginning of a period of turning from God.

Hezekiah: A Good King (29:1–32:33)

Judah never fully recovers from Ahaz's negative influence, and judgment in the form of the Babylonian captivity is looming a mere 110 years down the road. Even a good king like Hezekiah cannot reverse their path away from the Lord.

Background & Context

During the feast of Passover you were to take your own lamb, without spot or blemish, and sacrifice it yourself (Deuteronomy 16:16–17). The problem was that many of the people had not ceremonially cleansed themselves, and so the Levites sacrificed the lambs for those who were unclean. These people were seeking God, and thus, they just came as they were. Hezekiah understood that it is not the religious ritual that makes one acceptable to God; it is a matter of the heart (2 Chronicles 30:13–20).

Rapid Decline (33:1–36:23)

The account of Manasseh in 2 Kings 21:1–18 is harsher than this one. The writer of Chronicles wants to emphasize to his audience that even the worst sinner can be forgiven and restored through repentance and faith. However, we also witness Israel's rapid decline before their eventual defeat at the hands of the Babylonians.

Ezra
Introduction to Ezra

The book of Ezra is a chronicle of hope and restoration. Originally, Ezra and Nehemiah were together as one book, recording the stories about a remnant of God's chosen people who had been taken captive by the Babylonians after the destruction of Jerusalem and who were returning to the Promised Land to rebuild their nation.

The dramatic narrative starts in 538 BC and revolves around three epic tales. First is the struggle to rebuild the temple in Jerusalem under Zerubbabel (chapters 1–6). Next is the second expedition from Babylon sixty years later, led by Ezra, a scribe and scholar, whose task it is to reestablish the Law of Moses (chapters 7–10).

Third is the work of Nehemiah, the appointed governor leading the rebuilding of Jerusalem until around 433 BC.

Author

Bible experts have long suggested that the author of Ezra also wrote 1 and 2 Chronicles and Nehemiah, referring to the writer as "the Chronicler." But recent scholars question this assumption and conclude both Ezra and Nehemiah were not written by the Chronicler. As to who wrote Ezra and Nehemiah, there is support for the Jewish tradition that teaches Ezra was the writer of both books. It's interesting to note that the narration switches from third person to first person after Ezra appears in the story (chapter 7).

The book was likely written between 460 and 440 BC, but there are competing views regarding the date.

Occasion/Purpose

Ezra, with Nehemiah, tells the story of God's faithfulness to His promises regarding His chosen people, restoring them to their land after seventy years of captivity.

Three views dominate regarding the date of Ezra's return to Jerusalem. If the Artaxerxes mentioned is Artaxerxes I, Ezra returned in 458 BC, in the seventh year of the king's reign. About thirteen years later, Nehemiah begins rebuilding the walls of Jerusalem. During the dozen years Nehemiah is building, Ezra returns again, and the two work together in shaping the nation. This view is the most plausible, but there are a few issues with it. For one, Nehemiah is not mentioned in Ezra. Also, Ezra is only mentioned once in Nehemiah, with nothing said of his reforms earlier in 458 BC.

Another view suggests Ezra actually returns to Jerusalem under Artaxerxes II, in 398 BC, after Nehemiah. This would fit better, for example, with the issue of marrying foreign wives. (Ezra battles the trend, so why would it still be a pervasive problem thirteen years later when Nehemiah arrives?) Yet Nehemiah 8:2 suggests Nehemiah and Ezra are contemporaries.

Third, Ezra may have returned in the thirty-seventh year of Artaxerxes I, during Nehemiah's second term (428 BC). This view is willing to say the text has been corrupted, with the seventh year actually meaning thirty-seventh. There is no evidence to support this position.

Themes

Ezra, with Nehemiah, relates historical events that communicate the love and power of a God active in the world. Some themes include God's sovereignty, God's covenant with His people, and God's grace.

Background & Context

Ezra covers the period following 539 BC, well into the time in biblical history called the post-exilic period. The exile of Judah occurred under

Nebuchadnezzar, who deported the remnant of Israel to Babylon in 587 and 586 BC. But on October 29, 539 BC, Babylon surrendered to the Persians, and the policies of a new emperor, Cyrus II, came into place. This was good news for the Jews because Persians were known for being temperate in their treatment of captors. In general, they did not deport and relocate captive peoples. They also were ecumenical in their religious policy. They encouraged subject peoples to worship their own gods and goddesses. And, perhaps most importantly, they encouraged exiles to return to their homelands.

God Moves History (1:1–11)

Israel was not a major player in the days of Ezra and Nehemiah. The big powers were first Babylon, then Persia. No one cared about the postage-stamp size kingdom in the political backwater of the Ancient Near East or about the people who used to live there. But God did indeed still care about the Israelites. He had made promises to them and would see to it they were fulfilled.

Background & Context

Here is a list of Persia's most prominent leaders, most of whom you'll meet in Ezra and its companion book, Nehemiah:

- Cyrus II, also known as Cyrus the Great (539-530 BC)
- Cambyses II (530-522 BC), son of Cyrus
- Darius I (521-486 BC)
- Xerxes I, also known in the Bible as Ahasuerus (486-464 BC), the king in the book of Esther
- Artaxerxes I (464-423 BC)
- Darius II (423-404 BC)
- Artaxerxes II (404-359 BC)

What You Can Discover on the Church Roll (2:1–69)

Most of Ezra 2 is instructional more than entertaining. It shows what is—or should be—characteristic of the people of God. Ezra 2 includes a list of returnees in 538 BC, the first group led by Zerubbabel—years before Ezra comes on the scene. There's a parallel passage in Nehemiah 7.

God's People in Gray Times (3:1–13)

A less-than-enthusiastic attitude toward life typifies the Jewish remnant around 538 BC. Life is hard and times are tough. But Ezra 3 shows that God's people can live through bleak times.

Let the Troubles Begin (4:1–24)

The returnees from exile proceed to work on the rebuilding of the temple. But not everyone is excited about the project.

God Is the Ruler Yet (5:1–6:22)

At the end of Ezra 4, the work on the temple had stopped. About fifteen years have passed. Chapters 5–6 consist of the inquiry of Tattenai and the favorable response of the Persian court.

The Strong Hand of God (7:1–8:36)

Ezra 7 introduces the scribe Ezra himself into the narrative. It's now 458 BC, decades after the first group of returnees returned from Babylonian captivity under Zerubbabel. Ezra 7 summarizes that King Artaxerxes authorizes Ezra to lead another, smaller group to Judea. Ezra 8 gives the details. A thematic element that binds these chapters together is the repeated reference to the hand of God.

Background & Context

In Ezra 7:10 we're given a clue as to why the hand of God is on Ezra. The Hebrew text includes the initial *ki* ("because"). God prospers the venture because of Ezra's purpose. Ezra has set his heart to study the law, practice it, and teach it.

Trouble in Covenant City (9:1–15)

Ezra and his group of exiles have been in Jerusalem about four and a half months when the problem of intermarrying, and therefore rejection of the law and its demand for spiritual purity, is brought to his attention.

Making Confession (10:1–44)

Ezra and his leaders respond to a large outpouring of exiles motivated by Ezra's lamentations to repent of their sin of intermarriage and make things right with God.

Nehemiah
Introduction to Nehemiah

The book of Nehemiah is one of the Old Testament's historical books. Until the fifteenth century AD, Ezra and Nehemiah were considered to be one book, and we see evidence of this with Ezra's abrupt ending. The events of Nehemiah pick up naturally where Ezra leaves off, with the continual rebuilding of Jerusalem and the return of the final group of exiles from Babylon in 445 BC.

Author

Nehemiah is believed by some scholars to have written the majority of the text—much of the book of Nehemiah is written in the first person, and Nehemiah 1:1 identifies the speaker as Nehemiah, son of Hacaliah, an exiled Jew who served as the cupbearer to the Persian king, Artaxerxes I. Yet Jewish tradition holds that Ezra authored the books of Ezra and Nehemiah. Because Ezra and Nehemiah were one book, Nehemiah may have been edited by Ezra, or the two may have been combined by a historical chronicler. No one knows for certain.

Occasion/Purpose

The book of Nehemiah has two primary purposes—to provide a historical account of the rebuilding of the wall of Jerusalem and to document the reformation of the post-exilic Israelites who returned to the city and renewed their covenant with Yahweh. Through these two main purposes, God's continuous provision for His chosen people is revealed.

The events recorded in the book of Nehemiah are dated from circa 445 to 431–432 BC. It begins with Nehemiah returning to Jerusalem in the twentieth year of the reign of King Artaxerxes I of Persia (1:1), approximately thirteen years after Ezra returned with the second group of exiled Jews. Nehemiah leaves Jerusalem for a brief period of time in the thirty-second year of the reign of Artaxerxes I and returns shortly thereafter (13:6–7), dating the events at the end of the book around 432 BC.

Themes

Revival is one of the main themes of the book of Nehemiah. Nehemiah leads in the rebuilding of the wall, and he also makes sure the Jewish practices are reestablished so that temple worship is also revived.

This book also focuses heavily on the importance of godly leadership. Nehemiah seeks wisdom from the Lord.

Adversity is another theme evident throughout the book, as Nehemiah faces opposition to his rebuilding plan, conflict among the people working on the wall, and specific instances of the covenantal law being broken by the people. Despite the various adversities Nehemiah and the Israelites face, the wall is rebuilt and temple worship resumes, at least for a time.

Contribution to the Bible

Nehemiah's memoir provides a genealogy of a third specific group of Israelites to return to Jerusalem. More than a history of the people and the rebuilding of the wall, Nehemiah also provides a historical account of the rejuvenation of the holy city. With the rebuilding of Jerusalem and its wall complete, it is once again the holy city of God.

Background & Context

While there were surely other groups of Jews returning from Babylon, those who return with Nehemiah to rebuild the wall mark the third group described specifically in the Old Testament. Of the specific accounts offered in Ezra and Nehemiah, Zerubbabel led the first group home in 538 BC (Ezra 1:1-6:22), and Ezra returns with the second group in 458 BC (Ezra 7:1-10:44). The first group is tasked with the rebuilding of the temple, a work that couldn't truly be celebrated until the wall that protected the city and the temple was also complete. Nehemiah brings closure to the events recorded in Ezra and the aftermath of the Babylonian exile.

Prayer in the Palace (1:1–11)
Nehemiah introduces himself and his times in Nehemiah 1:1–3. The reference to the twentieth year (1:1) is to the year of Artaxerxes I, or 445 BC. Comparing Ezra 7:7, we note that this is thirteen years after Ezra's coming. The month of Chislev is November–December. Susa was in what is now southwest Iran, in the alluvial plain 150 miles north of the Persian Gulf. It serves as a winter palace for the Persian kings.

Background & Context
The position of cupbearer was one of great responsibility and influence. Kings wanted a cupbearer they could trust. When Nehemiah makes his cupbearer remark, he is recognizing that Yahweh's providence has been at work long before this moment. He was high up in the civil service with access to the king, and therefore, in a favorable position to seek good for the people of Judah.

From Court to City (2:1–20)
Nehemiah doesn't act hastily on his desire to return to Jerusalem and lead in the rebuilding of the walls. Following his prayer in chapter 1, he waits four months before taking the first step toward returning—asking King Artaxerxes's permission to leave.

Blessed Builders (3:1–32)
Chapter 3 is Nehemiah's detailed account of the rebuilding of Jerusalem's walls. The description starts at the Sheep Gate in the northeast corner and works its way counterclockwise.

Threats against God's Work (4:1–23)
Having chronicled the building efforts in chapter 3, here, in chapter 4, we return to Nehemiah's memoirs. The last verse of chapter 2 reflects on the success God will grant to those in the rebuilding efforts (2:20), so it is not surprising that shortly thereafter an enemy's voice speaks out.

Background & Context

How are we to view Nehemiah's prayer? It is a prayer for justice against sin. As such, it is a prayer for God to act. Nehemiah is not presuming to take vengeance into his own hands; he commits that to God. These are not personal enemies but enemies of God's kingdom. There is no indication that Sanballat, Tobiah, and their men seek repentance. There is a high cost to mocking the people of God, implicit in Nehemiah's prayer in verses 4-5.

Folly among God's People (5:1–19)

While the threat of external assault is the fear in chapter 4, here in chapter 5, internal dissension begins to take place.

Stratagems against God's Servant (6:1–19)

The schemes recorded in this chapter are directed toward Nehemiah, either to eliminate him or at least to discredit him. Undoubtedly his enemies want to bring trouble to his exemplary leadership. Note the emphasis on fear throughout the chapter (6:9, 13–14, 19).

The Exiles Who Returned (7:1–73)

The rebuilding of the wall, Nehemiah's original task, is now complete. But his work in rebuilding Jerusalem and the morale of the Israelites is far from over. This chapter begins the shift in focus from the wall to the securing and populating of the city.

The Foundation of Reformation (8:1–18)

Now that the wall is rebuilt, Nehemiah moves on to the rebuilding of people's lives. The rest of the book of Nehemiah will deal with the reformation of the people, beginning with the reading of God's Law.

The Preparation for Reformation (9:1–38)

The reading of the Word of God is a catalyst for the Israelites' reformation. Having been away from the temple and the daily worship practices, the scripture they hear reminds them that a change on their part is necessary.

The Structure for Reformation (10:1–39)

Here we find the response to the prayer of chapter 9, or perhaps better stated, the consequence of the prayer. In light of the ongoing history of apostasy and infidelity, what can Judah do but repent? Covenant is the vehicle of repentance.

The Order of the People of the Lord (11:1–36)

Although Jerusalem had been a city with little structure and little to offer its residents, the completion of the wall and the city's increased morale make it a more appealing place to live. This section lays out Nehemiah's plan for encouraging the Jews to populate the city.

The Celebration in the Joy of the Lord (12:1–43)

This next section is the account of the dedication of the newly rebuilt wall of Jerusalem. We are not sure how long after the completion of the wall this dedication occurred. One has the impression that the dedication takes place after the events of Nehemiah 7–11. It is not something to be neglected, but there may have been other, more pressing concerns at the time when the wall was finished.

The Perseverance in the Worship of the Lord (12:44–13:3)

The dedication of the wall in Jerusalem marks a fully restored city, and as the holy city this means that the religious community is fully restored. Once again the temple functions as it once had, as the center of worship for a spiritually strong people. The Israelites have not had such a sense of security since before the exile, so to the very last detail they ensure worship will resume as it once had.

The Ongoing Perils of the Church (13:4–31)

The final chapter of the book of Nehemiah includes a closing series of reforms Nehemiah enacts among the people. Each reform covers an area of the covenantal law that the Israelites are guilty of breaking.

Esther
Introduction to Esther

The book of Esther is a good complement to the books of Ezra and Nehemiah. While those books describe the trials and challenges of the Jewish exiles who were finally allowed to return to their homeland, Esther shows the plight of the Jewish people in Persia during the same period of time. Some people uphold Esther and Mordecai as heroic figures, yet others question whether they were actually godly individuals. God is not once mentioned by name in this book, yet it is a testament to divine providence.

Author
The author is unknown yet certainly appears to be a Jewish individual who had remained in Persia after other Jews had departed.

Occasion/Purpose
Esther and Mordecai have become role models for their courage and perseverance. Yet their success requires the reader to acknowledge God's work in postexilic Persia—even though God is never *specifically* acknowledged.

The account of Esther is a magnificent work purely on the grounds of literature: character, plot, conflict, and so on. But it was probably written to provide the background and setting for the creation of the Jewish holiday of Purim.

Themes

Much of the action of Esther takes place during banquets. Many significant meals are mentioned in this short book (1:3, 5, 9; 2:18; 3:15; 5:4, 8; 7:1; 8:17; 9:17–18). But perhaps more significant are the themes that *aren't* mentioned: God, prayer, Jerusalem/Judah, and worship (other than fasting).

Contribution to the Bible

Along with Ezra and Nehemiah, Esther offers a look into Jewish life under the rule of the Persians. Esther's distinction is an insider's look from within the Persian Empire. The book also provides the only mention of Purim, a Jewish feast, in the Bible. More than anything, this book shows how God's providence preserves His people.

Background & Context

Esther would be near the end of the Old Testament if the books were positioned chronologically. As God had forewarned, His disobedient people had been carried off into captivity, many to Babylon. But by the time Esther was written, the Persians had already conquered the Babylonians.

A New Queen in Susa (1:1–2:18)

Due to their disobedience and pursuit of idols and other gods, the people of Israel and Judah have been carried into captivity by Assyria and Babylon. The Babylonians, in turn, are conquered by the Medes and Persians, so the group of Jews who originally went to Babylon is now under Persian rule. It is a trying time, but the story of Esther demonstrates how God's people obtain not only a voice but also an advocate in the king of Persia himself.

Background & Context

The actions and direction of God are evident throughout the story of Esther, even though the name of God is never mentioned in the book. However, some hold the perspective that the book of Esther even more so reflects the struggles of Jewish exiles who became too attached to the land of their captivity, and thus dishonored God by not returning to their homeland when they were able to. From this perspective, God's providential care for the Jews in Persia was accomplished not because of their faithfulness but in spite of their unfaithfulness.

The Influence of Mordecai (2:19–4:17)

With Esther as queen, Mordecai has an ally at the highest level of government—

and he will need it. He so alienates a villain named Haman that Haman determines to destroy not only Mordecai but all Jewish people. Because Esther has chosen not to reveal her ethnic identity, few people in Susa are aware that she is of Jewish descent. And that secret tends to complicate Esther's desire to help Mordecai.

Two Banquets and a Hanging (5:1–7:10)

Esther has been chosen to be queen by Ahasuerus, the king of Persia, but he still is not aware of her Jewish ties. Meanwhile, her cousin/stepfather Mordecai has made a powerful enemy of Haman, the king's second-in-command. Haman has secured the king's permission to annihilate all the Jews. Mordecai has enlisted Esther's help, but by approaching Ahasuerus without being summoned, she places her life at risk.

A New Feast Is Established (8:1–10:3)

After discovering Haman's plot against all the Jews throughout the Persian Empire, Queen Esther has risked her life to approach the king for help. He is more than sympathetic to her request, to the point of having Haman immediately executed. Yet Haman's official message has already gone out, so Esther and Mordecai now turn their attention to preventing the potential damage that could be done.

Job
Introduction to Job

Many people who read the book of Job miss the God-centered message because they are focused on the human-centered problems. Why the righteous suffer is never really answered in this book. As God shows Job, knowing the answers to life's problems is not as important as knowing and understanding the awesomeness of God and how wise He is.

Author

The author of the book of Job is unknown. Most likely, he was an Israelite, because he uses the Israelite covenant name for God (*Yahweh*, or the LORD).

Occasion/Purpose

We do not know when Job was written, though the account describes history around the time of Abraham—that is, around 2000 BC. The first eleven chapters of Genesis pre-date the story of Job, but they were not written down in a book form until the time of Moses, around 1500 BC.

Themes

One of the most obvious themes in the book of Job is suffering. Or more specifically, God's wisdom in the face of human suffering. Every possible thing that could go wrong in Job's life has indeed gone wrong, and mirrors an often-asked question by many: why do bad things happen to good people? The book of Job addresses God's ultimate presence and wisdom in even the bleakest of situations.

Contribution to the Bible
The book of Job is one of the five Wisdom Books, comprising Job, Psalms, Proverbs, Ecclesiastes, and Song of Solomon. Much of these books is poetic, but in the Hebrew sense. While much of western poetry is associated with rhyme and meter, Hebrew poetry is associated with contrasting thoughts or parallel thoughts set against each other.

The Story Begins (1:1–22)
The book of Job has been called a masterpiece that is unequaled in all literature. The meaning of the name *Job* is "enemy" or "to be hostile toward." While this does not seem to typify Job's character, it does reflect his experience. When we look at Job's circumstances, we see his faith lived out in his life—he practices what he believes.

Background & Context
Job was likely a contemporary with Abraham, around three hundred years or so after the Flood. The reasons for placing Job in this period of time are as follows:

- *Long life*: Job lives another 140 years after the events of this book (42:16), which makes him around 200 years old at his death. After the Flood, human life span progressively decreased. Terah, Abraham's father, was 205. Abraham was 175. Isaac, 180. Jacob, 147. So Job fits in nicely around the time of Abraham.
- *No law*: There is no mention of the Ten Commandments or any of the Mosaic Laws in the book of Job.
- *Sacrifices*: Before the Mosaic Law, the patriarchal head of each family would offer sacrifices, just as Job does (see 1:5).
- *Wealth*: Job's wealth is listed in terms of livestock and not money, as was the practice during the time of Abraham (see Genesis 12:16).

More Trials (2:1–13)
Chapter 2 opens with another board meeting in heaven, as the angelic hosts come before the Lord, and Satan also comes to renew his charges against Job. Many people have a hard time understanding why God allows this to continue, but Satan is serving the purposes of God at this time.

Job Speaks (3:1–26)

The events of chapter 3 come on the heels of some tragic events in Job's life. In one day, Job, one of the wealthiest men in the area, loses all his material possessions. Not only that, but his ten children, who he loves very much, are all killed on the same day as well. And yet, in all this tragedy, Job is still able to worship God. Sometime after these events, Job's health is taken away. He develops boils from the top of his head to the tips of his toes. And yet in all this, Job does not charge God foolishly. Job's friends Eliphaz, Bildad, and Zophar have gathered around him, mourning silently for seven days. And now Job is going to speak from his heart.

Eliphaz Speaks (4:1–5:27)

Job has broken a seven-day silence to wish he had never been born. Now, after all these words from Job, Eliphaz wants to interject some of his own thoughts regarding this situation.

Background & Context

The point of this book is that Job did not deserve the suffering he received. Thus, this book is associated with the question, "Why do bad things happen to good people?" While the Bible teaches that none of us is actually good (Romans 3:10-18), the question is still a relevant one. Keep in mind, however, that the book of Job does not carry the responsibility of answering that age-old question. We can extrapolate our own reasoning about how Job's story reveals some purpose to suffering, but our best reasoning does not lead us to God's truth. Instead we need to understand what the scripture does teach—God's purposes continue even in our suffering. There is a bigger story happening outside of our own circumstances. And certainly elsewhere in scripture we find the truth that even in our suffering God's presence continues as well.

Job Replies (6:1–7:21)

After sitting with his friends in silence for seven days (4:11–13), Job pours out his anger and despair in a monologue (chapter 3), to which his friend Eliphaz feels compelled to reply (chapters 4–5). Eliphaz, after suggesting that Job has brought his troubles on himself through his own sin, suggests that Job plead his case (and presumably repent) before God. Chapters 6 and 7 contain Job's response.

Bildad Speaks (8:1–22)

Job has poured out his complaints to God, and his friend Bildad is shocked that Job dares to speak to God in this way. Here he takes Job to task.

Background & Context
Job and his friends lived around the time of Abraham, which was only
250 to 300 years after the Flood. When Bildad refers to what previous
generations learned, he is probably thinking of how God destroyed
all the wicked by a flood. Now Job, presumably because of his sin, is
being wiped out as if by a flood.

Job Replies to Bildad (9:1–10:22)
Job's friend Bildad has taken Job to task for questioning God. He has declared
that God sends punishment to the wicked and brings blessing to the righteous,
with the implication that Job will again be blessed if he lives righteously. This
prompts Job to reflect on what it means to be righteous in God's sight.

Zophar Speaks (11:1–20)
Eliphaz was eloquent with his words, but they were not encouraging, only judgmental. Bildad was brutal as he accused Job of not being as innocent as he tried
to make others believe. And now Job's third friend, Zophar, comes on the scene
and blasts Job with stinging sarcasm.

Job Replies to Zophar (12:1–14:22)
In response to Zophar's oration (chapter 11), Job again speaks.

Eliphaz's Second Speech (15:1–35)
Each of Job's three friends has had his say. Now Eliphaz begins round two with
his second speech.

Job's Second Response to Eliphaz (16:1–17:16)
Eliphaz has enumerated the bad things that happen to wicked people—things
that are now happening to Job. The implication is clear: Job is a wicked person.
Now Job replies, addressing Bildad and Zophar as well as Eliphaz.

Bildad's Second Speech (18:1–21)
After hearing Job's complaint in chapters 16 and 17, Bildad steps up to the plate to
have a second try at arguing Job into agreeing with his friends and their theology.

Job's Second Response to Bildad (19:1–29)
Job responds to Bildad's poetic discourse on the fate of the wicked—and by implication, the fate of Job—with some well-chosen words of his own.

Zophar's Second Speech (20:1–29)
As we move into Job chapter 20, we are closing out round two of this verbal
tongue-lashing that Job is receiving from his three friends. Zophar is going to
respond to what Job has just said. Job accuses his friends of speaking lies and

making up stories to prove their neatly packaged theology. They are accusing Job of hiding sin in his life and that is why all this calamity has come upon him. But Job tells them to be afraid of being judged themselves. He turns the tables on them now, and it is to this that Zophar is going to respond.

Job's Second Response to Zophar (21:1–34)
Not willing to let Zophar have the last word, Job responds to Zophar's speech.

Eliphaz's Third Speech (22:1–30)
The third round of this three-on-one conversation between Job's friends and Job now begins, with Eliphaz, as in the previous two rounds, taking the lead and speaking first.

Job's Third Response to Eliphaz (23:1–24:25)
Eliphaz has exhorted Job to return to God (22:23). Job replies that that is just what he wants to do—not because he has wickedness to confess but because he wants to present his case to God.

Bildad's Third Speech (25:1–6)
We are in round three of the verbal tongue-lashing given to Job by his friends Eliphaz, Bildad, and Zophar. As Bildad begins to speak, he doesn't have a lot to say. It seems that he is running out of material with which to condemn Job. This may also be the reason that Zophar does not speak for a third time; we would expect him to take his turn after Bildad, but there is really nothing left to say; it has all been said before. Chapter 25 records the shortest speech in the book of Job, but it will lead to the longest speech in the book—from chapter 26 through chapter 31.

Job's Final Response (26:1–31:40)
Job's three friends seem to have run out of steam. After two or three rounds of arguing with Job, they have little left to say—as evidenced by how short Bildad's final speech is (chapter 25). Job, on the other hand, is just getting warmed up. What follows is his longest speech in the book.

Elihu Speaks (32:1–37:24)
Job's three friends Eliphaz, Bildad, and Zophar have run out of gas. They have nothing left to say, for they have said more than enough to Job already. By this time a crowd has gathered to watch the confrontation—a confrontation that is loud and animated. And in this crowd is Elihu, a young man who has heard all these words and now has something to say.

The Lord Speaks with Job (38:1–42:6)
As Elihu is finishing his words against Job, a huge storm is forming in the distance. Elihu draws some illustrations from this storm and relates them to God. For some thirty-five chapters, Job and his friends have spoken, but now it is time

for God to speak. For thirty-five chapters humankind has attempted to understand the how's and why's of God with finite minds—and no one has come to an understanding of these things. Now God is going to speak out.

What is interesting in this section is that God does not explain to Job—or us—exactly why He has done these things to Job. In fact, He asks Job a series of some seventy questions, and in the end, God's *answer* is far more important than an understanding of His *ways*. Simply speaking, God gives Himself as the answer.

Background & Context

God uses the elements of nature to bring about His will. Remember in Judges 5, Barak defeats the army of Sisera when God causes a torrential rainfall, causing their chariots to be stuck in the mud so that they have to flee on foot. God causes hailstones to fall from the sky, destroying the Amorites in Joshua 10. And in 1 Samuel 7, God uses thunder to confuse the Philistines, giving Israel the victory.

God reminds Job that He waters the wilderness, causing the vegetation to grow (38:25-27). He did not just create life and sit back and watch what happens, as the deists believe (38:28-30); He is actively involved in sustaining His work.

Epilogue (42:7–17)

God's dialogue with Job is concluded, but God has two more things to do before the case is closed. First, He has a few things to say to Job's three friends. And second, He restores justice to Job.

Psalms
Introduction to Psalms

The book of Psalms has been called the "hymnbook" of the Old Testament. Depending on one's perception of a hymnal, the title can be misleading, or it can be quite accurate. Sometimes the modern church approaches hymns lightly—singing one before the "real" worship service begins and another before going home. Or perhaps old hymns are disregarded altogether. But anyone who closely examines a traditional hymnal and reads the words of Martin Luther, Charles Wesley, Fanny Crosby, and others will find a wealth of biblical truth and weighty theological tenets. The fact that the words are rhymed and set to music may actually disguise their importance to modern ears.

This is the case with the book of Psalms as well. Its poetic format tends to diminish its importance for some people. They turn to Psalms for comfort or for light reading, yet many fail to approach the psalms with the same reverence as other portions of scripture. Yet for those who read closely, the psalms reveal much about God and the impact of His presence during the joys and struggles of human life.

And just as a modern hymnal may contain hymns with updated language in places, or perhaps a newer hymn set to an old familiar tune, so too the book of Psalms has revisions. It is believed that in certain instances, psalmists from the exile or later may have adapted much earlier psalms to apply to Israel's current situation.

Author

The psalms have a variety of authors. Some psalms identify the writer, and others don't. Yet even the people acknowledged as authors may not have actually written the psalm. A psalm attributed to David may have been written *by* David or possibly written *for* David. Or it could have been another psalmist's attempt to write in the style of David. One of the writers, Asaph, was a contemporary of David's, yet some of the psalms of Asaph refer to events of the exile that occurred long after his death. Therefore it is sometimes a challenge to verify authors. Other times the content of the psalm provides a clear indication of the author. In cases where the writer is uncertain (or not identified), it is traditional to refer to "the psalmist" as the author.

Almost half of the psalms (seventy-three) are attributed to David. Asaph (including his descendants, one of the clans of Levites assigned to oversee the music ministry of the temple) is credited with twelve psalms. Another music ministry clan, the sons of Korah, is identified with eleven psalms (although Psalm 43, which is unattributed, may have originally been an extension of Psalm 42 and therefore added to the total). Two psalms are assigned to Solomon. One each is assigned to Moses, Heman, and Ethan. That leaves forty-nine psalms with no designated author.

Occasion/Purpose

The Hebrew title for the book means "praises." (The word *psalm* comes from the Greek translation rather than the original Hebrew.) Overall, the content of the book is intended for prayer and praise, although there is much variety within those broad categories. Some of the psalms were written as individual laments, some as community laments, some as thanksgiving hymns. Some are classified as penitential—confessional psalms asking God's forgiveness. Others were written as laments that cried for God's mercy on the psalmist and retribution on his enemies. Some were intended as regal celebrations when a new king was crowned.

Some psalms celebrate special occasions in the community, such as annual pilgrimages to Jerusalem, the coronation of a king, and liturgical ceremonies. Other psalms are written in regard to personal experiences. (Of David's seventy-three psalms, fourteen of the introductions refer to specific events in his life.) Yet the poetic nature of the psalms leads to their use on many occasions. Jesus and numerous New Testament writers naturally referred to the psalms to emphasize what they were trying to say. Jesus even quoted from the psalms as He hung on the cross (see Psalm 22:1 and Matthew 27:46; Psalm 31:5 and Luke 23:46).

Themes

Unlike most of the biblical books that precede it, Psalms is not written in chronological order or any linear fashion. It is a collection of poetry written by numerous people over a long period of time. Yet regardless of the author, time period, or specific situation, the author invariably acknowledges the presence of—and humanity's total dependence on—God. Whether describing the wonders of creation, expressing a personal and painful trauma, recounting the history of the nation, bemoaning life in exile, or detailing any other experience, the psalmist's words are directed toward God. Some psalms express more faith than others, but they all appeal to God's strength, mercy, forgiveness, deliverance, and other qualities that are exclusively His.

Contribution to the Bible

No collection of ancient lyrical poetry is more extensive than the book of Psalms. Hebrew poetry was not known for rhyme and meter but rather for repetition of thoughts and a style of parallelism that reemphasized or contrasted a concept in adjoining lines. The psalms also introduce some words that have never been clearly defined—words such as *sheminith* (Psalms 6, 12), *shiggaion* (Psalm 7), *gittith* (Psalm 8, 81, 84), *alamoth* (Psalm 46), *mahalath* (Psalm 53), *mahalath leannoth* (Psalm 88), *miktam* and *maskil* (various psalms), and *selah* (found seventy-one times in thirty-nine psalms). Most are believed to be musical or perhaps historical references.

Psalms 1–19

The first "book" within Psalms is the earliest of the five compilations. It is widely associated with David's life and reign. This section contains the first nineteen (of forty-one) psalms from the first book.

Background & Context

With one psalm attributed to Moses and others to psalmists during and after the exile, the content of the psalms covers centuries of Israel's history. The scope of the psalms covers times when individuals and the nation were close to God and basking in His blessings as well as times when the people had drifted away from the will of God, and they were suffering as a result. In addition, some of the psalms have messianic applications, so the context is future as well as past and present.

Psalms 20–41

This section continues and completes Book I, the compilation that opens the biblical book of Psalms. Essentially all of the psalms in this section are attributed to David. It is the section that contains perhaps the most beloved and widely known psalm: Psalm 23.

Background & Context

Several times within Psalm 37 "the land" is mentioned as a reward for the faithful. After God delivered Israel from Egypt and slavery, He guided them to the land that had been promised to Abraham. Under David's rule, the boundaries of that land continued to expand. The people's homes and surroundings were the result of God's direct blessing. And God's previous faithfulness in escorting them to the land was an assurance of His ongoing presence and involvement among them.

Psalms 42–57

As Book II of the biblical book of Psalms begins, new authors begin to be identified. In Book I, all but four of the psalms are attributed to David, and those four have no designated author. David will continue to contribute to the book of Psalms, but his name will be joined by several others from here on.

Background & Context

Throughout the first book within Psalms, the word used for God is almost always *Yahweh*. In the second book, however, the preferred word changes to *Elohim*. Despite all the similarities between Psalms 14 and 53, the word used to refer to God is changed.

Psalms 58–72

This section continues and concludes the psalms found in Book II of the biblical book of Psalms. Most in this section are psalms of David. Some continue to have superscriptions that refer to specific events in the psalmist's life.

Psalms 73–89

Book III of Psalms contains seventeen psalms, eleven of which are attributed to Asaph. However, several of the psalms contain references to events in Israel's history that would have been later than Asaph's lifetime, so there is good reason to believe that some of these psalms were penned by his descendants.

Psalms 90–106

This section contains the compilation of psalms comprising Book IV of the biblical book of Psalms. In this portion of Psalms, the introductory superscriptions are less specific than previous ones, and several psalms lack introductions altogether. Only three of the seventeen psalms in this section identify the writer, so there is more mystery and speculation as to authors and dates.

Background & Context

In most cases when a psalm refers to a *trumpet*, the word indicates an instrument made from a ram's horn. But verse 6 refers to the trumpets used at the temple—the only such mention in the book of Psalms. The official trumpets were long and straight, and made of hammered silver. They were used to assemble the community and to celebrate special feasts and festivals (Numbers 10:1-10).

People and nature alike are to respond with joy to the work of God. According to verse 1, He has already done incredible things, but His work is not finished. The whole world can look forward to the day when He will come as judge, bringing righteousness and justice. In anticipation of that day, joy and singing are quite appropriate (98:7-9).

Psalms 107–134

This section begins the last of the five books contained within the biblical book of Psalms. It is likely the final book compiled chronologically, so along with some additional psalms of David are other songs that contain references to events later in Israel's history. This first half of the final book contains the shortest psalm, the longest psalm, and the series of fifteen psalms known as the Songs of Ascents.

Background & Context

The idols of this time period and location were usually carved of wood and then overlaid with thin sheets of gold or silver. They have been discovered in assorted shapes and sizes, including some that were life-sized. The carvings weren't believed to be actual gods, but the foreign deities were thought to use the idols to make known their desires. Some cultures took great care of their idols, going to the point of dressing and washing them each day, and even "feeding" them with sacrifices of food.

Psalms 135–150

This section finishes up Book V, and therefore the biblical book of Psalms as well. Of the sixteen psalms that remain, half of them comprise a series attributed to David. The remaining ones are anonymous.

Proverbs
Introduction to Proverbs

As the preface to the book states, Proverbs is about wisdom. On one level, wisdom is a skill of living, a practical knowledge. Wise people know how to say the right thing at the right time and to do the right thing at the right time. They live in a way that maximizes blessing for themselves and others in the world that God created.

But at a deeper level, wisdom is more profound than an ability to navigate life well. Indeed, it begins with a proper attitude toward God characterized by "fear." This is not the type of fear that makes someone run away, but it is more than respect. It is the awe that a person should feel when in the presence of the sovereign Creator of the universe.

Proverbs is a book about wisdom, and it intends to make its reader wise.

Author
The book of Proverbs is associated with Solomon, Israel's wisest king. His writings—or his teachings put into writing by a scribe—form most of the book. It was revealed in 1 Kings 4:32 that Solomon spoke three thousand proverbs, and it is good to have the book of Proverbs to see what he was teaching. A few additional short sections come from other contributors: anonymous writers (22:17–24:22), Agur (chapter 30), and Lemuel (chapter 31).

Occasion/Purpose
The purpose of the book of Proverbs is stated in 1:2–3: to provide wisdom that, when applied, will lead to a godly life. Solomon seemed especially eager for his son to learn and apply the principles in this book, but they are general enough (and simple enough) for everyone to benefit from.

Themes
The theme that runs throughout Proverbs is the value of wisdom, particularly in contrast to folly in its various forms. Wisdom should permeate one's life in personal attitudes and behaviors, family relationships, business dealings, worship, and every other aspect of the human experience. The fact that such teachings are associated with the wealthiest king in Israel's history gives them added weight.

Contribution to the Bible
Proverbs belongs to the collection of Old Testament books called Wisdom Literature, which comprises the books of Job, Psalms, Proverbs, Ecclesiastes, and Song of Songs (also known as Song of Solomon). These books are all concerned with ordinary life and how to live it well.

The book of Proverbs has two major parts. In chapters 1–9, the reader encounters speeches. Mostly, they are the speeches of a father to a son (see 1:8–19), but occasionally a figure named Wisdom speaks to all the young men (1:20–33).

The second part of the book is filled with proverbs proper, short observations, warnings, and encouragements that are typically very practical.

A proverb is a very important literary device that played a prominent role in Israel and also the Middle East. A proverb is a short saying that combines knowledge with action. It is a truth that is applied to real life.

Look at Proverbs 13:3: *Whoever guards his mouth preserves his life; he who opens wide his lips comes to ruin* (ESV). This is a truth being put into real life. A person who speaks without thinking, and thus speaks things that are hurtful or harmful, will in the end hurt himself. A person who takes responsibility for his thoughts, guards his heart, and thus watches what he says, will not suffer the fate of the careless. This proverb deals with the issue of a person's heart (there is the lofty principle)—what we are thinking about and what we are focusing on—and offers a practical application of how to guard the heart.

Fatherly Wisdom (1:1–9:18)
The book of Proverbs is not just a grouping of pithy sayings but rather the application of the knowledge of God to real life. This is true wisdom. When we acquire such wisdom, we have more than just good advice; we have the key that unlocks the door to instruction, moral discernment, guidance, and spiritual insight.

The book of Proverbs does not begin with a long set of instructions as to how we are to live our lives. It begins by telling us the great value of wisdom and that the first step in gaining wisdom is to fear God.

Solomon's Wisdom, Part 1 (10:1–15:33)
This chapter marks a change in the way the book of Proverbs is written. Chapter 10 begins the part of Proverbs that most people think of when they encounter this book: short pithy statements of wisdom.

Background & Context
The tree of life is first mentioned in Genesis 2:9. Adam and Eve's sin puts the tree of life out of reach; they are banished from the garden where it grows. The book of Revelation tells of regaining the right to eat from the tree of life (Revelation 2:7; 22:14). Proverbs is the only other book of the Bible in which the tree of life is mentioned (Proverbs 3:18; 11:30; 13:12; 15:4).

Solomon's Wisdom, Part 2 (16:1–22:16)
In this ongoing segment of the proverbs of Solomon (10:1–22:16), this particular section begins a minor shift. Chapters 10 through 15 made a lot of contrasts between righteous and unrighteous behavior. Chapters 16 through 22:16 contain fewer contrasts and instead begin to focus more on the value of righteous behavior.

Sayings of the Wise (22:17–24:34)
Proverbs 10:1–22:16 contains proverbs of Solomon, and more follow in 25–29.

But this section is made up of "Sayings of the Wise." The unknown writer lets his readers know that he has provided thirty sayings of counsel and knowledge. Like Solomon, he is focused on the perfect wisdom of God that brings nothing but the best results for those who find it.

Solomon's Wisdom, Part 3 (25:1–29:27)
Chapter 25 begins a new section of the book of Proverbs. Chapters 1–9 provide a more narrative approach to the value of wisdom and the importance of shunning evil. Chapters 10–22:16 present the first collection of the words of Solomon. Chapter 22:17 through chapter 24 contain another section of Proverbs that was probably added later. Chapters 25–29 return to the wisdom of Solomon with a series of unrelated proverbs.

Background & Context
The proverbs in chapters 25 through 29 may have been locked away some two hundred years after Solomon's reign, when King Ahaz closed the temple (see 2 Chronicles 28). When Hezekiah succeeded Ahaz as king, he reopened the temple and recovered many of the temple objects (2 Chronicles 29). Quite possibly these proverbs were among them (see Proverbs 25:1).

Wisdom from the Massaites (30:1–31:31)
Chapter 30 marks the beginning of the final section of the book of Proverbs: the sayings of the Massaites. Massa was a clan from the line of Ishmael that lived in north Arabia. The two men whose wisdom is recorded here were contemporaries of either Solomon or Hezekiah and probably were influenced greatly by the theology of Israel. Some have speculated that Agur (chapter 30) was a leader of the Massaites and that Lemuel (chapter 31) was probably the king of that region.

Background & Context
Because women were not permitted to buy land at the time Proverbs was written, some have concluded that verse 16 shows that the poem is not about a woman but about the personification of wisdom. However, a wife, even though she might not be the one actually buying and selling, could just as easily give the instructions for the purchase.

Ecclesiastes
Introduction to Ecclesiastes

The book of Ecclesiastes is considered part of the Wisdom Literature of the Old Testament. Contained within its verses are proverbs, teachings, stories, reflections, and warnings about a myriad of topics. But the underlying pursuit of the book as a whole is the meaning of life. The author explores the purpose of life and, more importantly, asks what humanity's purpose is as a creation of a sovereign God. Verse by verse through the book of Ecclesiastes, the author answers that question. The purpose of life, meaningless though it may feel, is to fear God and obey His commands.

Author

The question of authorship of Ecclesiastes is a debated subject. The author does not directly identify himself, but he does state that he is the son of David and king in Jerusalem. Traditional scholarly opinion is that Solomon is the writer of the book, and early church testimony supports this view. A few passages that support this view internally include 1:1, 12; 2:4–9; and 12:9. Solomon was known for his wisdom and dedicated most of his life to its pursuit. He also wrote most of the books of Proverbs and Song of Songs. With Solomon in mind as the author, many of the teachings of the book seem to have a direct correlation to the events of his life.

It wasn't until the 1700s that Solomon's authorship came into question. The chief argument against Solomonic authorship is rooted largely in debates over the original Hebrew, which is a different dialect than that of Solomon's other writings and seems to reflect a later version of Hebrew. Furthermore, the writer refers to himself as *Qohelet*, or *the teacher*, a pseudonym that scholars argue would be unnecessary for the king. As far as internal evidence against Solomon's authorship is concerned, in 1:12 the writer seems to allude to a time when Solomon was alive following his reign, but no such time exists. It should also be noted that after chapter 3, the references to Solomon taper off, and many of the proverbs and teachings that follow seem to contradict those in Proverbs.

Within this commentary are included some of the opposing views and relevant points that support each view, and the author will be referred to by the generic title *Qohelet*. It should also be noted that there is an unmistakable narrator present in 1:1–11 and 12:8–13, who is likely the author of the book. For those who favor Solomonic authorship, this is an elder Solomon reflecting back on the pursuits and teachings of much of his life—the body of the work within the frame. Those who take a non-Solomonic view, however, believe this to be the voice of the author. The switch to first-person in 1:12, then, begins the quotation of the unidentified Qohelet.

Occasion/Purpose

The main purpose of the book of Ecclesiastes is threefold. First, it paints a picture of a sovereign God who controls everything in the world. Second, Qohelet's teachings highlight the meaninglessness of life apart from fearing and obeying the sovereign God. And last, the book provides wisdom and counsel for future generations rooted in the things Qohelet learned throughout his life's pursuit of meaning.

The date of Ecclesiastes depends heavily on which view of authorship one holds. Most scholars who deny Solomonic authorship agree that Ecclesiastes should have a date in Israel's late history, anywhere from 450–250 BC. Because the book doesn't contain any direct internal evidence that helps date it, the date is based largely on the style of the Hebrew it is written in, which most agree is similar to a later Hebrew style. On the other hand, for those scholars who hold to Solomon's writing, the book must have been written during his reign, which covers a span anywhere from 971 BC to 931 BC.

Themes
Ecclesiastes contains several proverbs and teachings, but they all center on just a few main themes. These themes include: wisdom, the sovereignty of God, the limitations of humanity, and death. Throughout the author's quest for meaning in life, he returns again and again to the meaninglessness of everything, a reality based on humanity's smallness in the face of God's great sovereignty and control.

Contribution to the Bible
Many of Qohelet's teachings seem to contradict teachings in other parts of the Bible. However, one cannot deny that Qohelet's reflections on life paint one of the most realistic pictures of the fallen world in which we live and humanity's purpose within that world. As God's sovereignty is acknowledged again and again throughout the book, one can't help but look forward to the coming of Jesus Christ and His redemptive work on the cross. Ecclesiastes paints a picture of a fallen world and the impact of sin, but knowing the promises that have been fulfilled post-Christ make the realities of this world bearable. Christ is the meaning to all the meaningless Qohelet observes, and the death that he fears takes on a new hope for all who believe in Christ.

Everything Is Futile (1:1–2:23)
Verse 12 notes the shift from the narrator's voice to the voice of Qohelet, who will be the speaker through 12:7. While the narrator (or the elder Solomon) establishes the tone and theme in the prologue, it is Qohelet's first-person reflections that form the bulk of the book.

God's Purpose and Timing (2:24–3:22)
Having presented his initial observations of life and its futility, Qohelet now shifts gears—be it ever so slightly—from reflection to instruction. In the following verses, Qohelet presents the reader with advice gleaned from his life's pursuit.

The Burdens of Life (4:1–12)
Qohelet's search for purpose moves from the role of justice in the world to the

heavily burdened people he has seen around him, including the oppressed, those who labor in vain, and the friendless. For each he concludes the same thing—this, too, is meaningless.

Everything Is Futile (4:13–6:9)

Having paused to voice his thoughts on the predetermined structure of time and those who live burdened lives, Qohelet returns once again to his subject of futility. While the meaninglessness remains the foundation for his conclusions, verse 13 picks up where 2:23 ends.

Qohelet's Wise Counsel (6:10–12:7)

These two brief verses (6:10–12) are a pivotal point in Ecclesiastes. Now, halfway through his discourse, Qohelet turns his attention from his observations to wise counsel for how others should live.

Song of Songs
Introduction to Song of Songs

Song of Songs (or Song of Solomon), for the most part, is a book of poems about romantic love.

Author

The title "Song of Songs" suggests that it is the greatest of all songs. There is disagreement among scholars as to whether Solomon wrote Song of Songs, but he is mentioned in the book and many credit him with part of its authorship, if not all.

Occasion/Purpose

The Song celebrates sexuality in its proper context. While some apply it as an allegory of spiritual truths (for example, the relationship of God and Israel or of Christ and the church), here it is treated as poetry that describes a love relationship between two people.

The Song of Songs represents the courtship of a man and a woman, both young, probably just coming to maturity. In ancient Israel, marriage took place in the early or mid-teen years. Many define the major sections of the book as courtship (1:2–3:5), wedding and honeymoon (3:6–5:1), and lasting marriage (5:2–8:4). Others, however, consider this book a collection of love poems that don't occur in any chronological kind of order.

Themes

Song of Songs is a poetic book of the Bible that centers around the theme of love. It celebrates all facets of love and intimacy in its proper setting.

The Transformations of Love (1:1–2:17)
In this first section of the Song of Songs, we learn about the joys and difficulties of love.

Background & Context
The mention of a veil in verse 7 highlights the fact that the Israelite women didn't always wear veils. They were for special occasions, such as weddings. Some attribute the veil to the clothing of a prostitute, but there is nothing else here that points to any kind of impropriety. If anything, she may not wish to be mistaken as a prostitute.

The Joy of Love (3:1–5:1)
The opening of chapter 3 is a poem about yearning. Absence and longing always lead to search and discovery in the Song.

The Endurance of Love (5:2–8:14)
The remainder of chapter 5 makes up a poem that actually spans through verse 3 of chapter 6. Rather than the symbolic language as in the poems of chapter 4, the woman seems to be telling the women of Jerusalem about an actual experience.

Isaiah
Introduction to Isaiah

The book of Isaiah is a potentially intimidating challenge for novice Bible readers, but it is a rich and rewarding pursuit for those willing to delve into it. Its sixty-six chapters comprise the fifth longest book of the Bible in terms of word count. But even more daunting than its sheer length is the prophetic nature of the writing. The author (or perhaps authors) writes of events that cover centuries, and it can be difficult in places to tell if he speaks of the present, the near future, or the long-range future. Yet while the prophet's narrative can be a bit confusing in places, large portions are quite clear in presenting a merciful God who does not give up on His people even though they have been repeatedly rebellious and wayward.

Author
The name *Isaiah*, "Salvation of Yahweh," is closely related to that of *Joshua* ("Yahweh is salvation"), which is the Old Testament equivalent of *Jesus*. However, not much is known about the prophet other than what he reveals in his book. He is identified as "the son of Amoz" thirteen times. He also writes that he has a wife and two children (7:3; 8:3). Little more is known about his personal life. Justin Martyr recorded the tradition that Isaiah died a martyr's death at the hands of King Manasseh, sawed in two (possibly the source of the reference in Hebrews 11:37).

A debate has raged for more than a century now as to whether the book of Isaiah was written by a single person or more than one author. Most scholars agree the book has distinctive sections. Chapters 1–39 comprise one unit and chapters 40–66 another. (Many purport that 40–55 should be a second unit and 56–66 a third, and that a different Isaiah wrote each section. Still others suggest the existence of an Isaiah "school," where disciples carried on the work of the original Isaiah.) If a single author wrote the entire book, he was given extremely precise insight into Judah's future, including the name of the ruler who would release the people after their captivity (44:28–45:1). Yet Cyrus wouldn't come to power for more than a century, after the Medes conquered Babylon, which was the rise of Babylon and fall of Assyria. However, the oldest available scrolls have no breaks between the different sections, recording Isaiah as a single book. And numerous New Testament figures, including Jesus Himself, quote from various portions of Isaiah as if the writing is from a single author. So the debate will continue, but for purposes of this commentary, references to the author throughout the entire book will be, simply, "Isaiah."

Occasion/Purpose

Isaiah's purpose in writing is described during a vision in which he receives his calling from God (6:6–10). He is instructed to speak to his people, even though most are spiritually rebellious and disobedient and will not listen to him. (Jesus later quotes this very passage to explain why He uses parables to teach the people [Matthew 13:13–15].) Isaiah faithfully brings God's word to the people, warning anyone who will listen of what is to come.

Themes

God's sovereignty is evident throughout Isaiah. The Lord maneuvers great empires to accomplish His will, including the chastisement of His people, and then brings those "powers" to nothing in judgment of their arrogance and sin. He allows His people to be dispersed throughout the world but then promises to call them back to Jerusalem, bringing their captors with them to worship together. Even in the turbulence and violence of the ancient world, the supremacy of God was always certain.

The book of Isaiah repeatedly emphasizes the sinfulness of humanity as well as the holiness, mercy, and grace of God, creating an overarching theme of redemption. In one section are four "Servant Songs" that describe a special servant God will provide to suffer for and deliver His people.

Contribution to the Bible

Isaiah is sometimes called the evangelist of the Old Testament (or even "the Paul of the Old Testament"). The influence of his writing is reflected by its frequent citations in the New Testament. (Isaiah is quoted more than all the other prophets combined.) The prophet is identified by name twenty-one times and is cited in numerous other places without direct attribution.

Background & Context

During Isaiah's lifetime in the eighth century BC, the Near East was already a political miasma. Nations continually struggled for dominance. Egypt was still a major power, yet she could no longer hold her own against a more recent contender: Assyria. As the surrounding nations grew in power, thus jostling to control more and more territory, the small nation of Judah was caught in a crossfire. Assyria conquered the northern kingdom of Israel in 721 BC. It appeared that Judah would follow quickly, but Isaiah assured the people that Assyria would not, in fact, take Judah. Jerusalem and the southern kingdom stand until 586 BC, when Nebuchadnezzar's Babylonian forces destroy the city and carry away most of the productive population. The people remain in Babylon for seventy years until the empire falls to the Persians, who allow the Jewish people to return to their homeland. Isaiah covers this entire span of history in his writing.

An Ominous Introduction (1:1–5:30)

It can be disheartening to read the opening of Isaiah without context, yet even providing the historical background doesn't help much. Israel and Judah, having deserted God for the gods and customs of surrounding nations, find themselves powerless pawns in an international struggle. Assyria, Babylon, and Egypt are all attempting to establish and/or maintain empires. Israel's and Judah's loyalties, which should have been to God, have been bouncing from one power to another in an attempt to persevere. But Israel will soon fall to Assyria, followed more than a century later by Judah's overthrow at the hands of Babylon.

Background & Context

Vineyards were important commodities in ancient Judah. When someone went to the trouble of planting a vineyard, he expected to eventually reap fruit from his labor. So the song of the vineyard in Isaiah 5:1-7 is a prophetic parable, and there is no doubt as to its meaning.

Verse 7 clarifies that the vineyard of the Lord represents the house of Israel. God has taken great care of His vineyard. He has done all He can, but still the vineyard does not yield fruit as it should. God looks for the fruit of justice but finds bloodshed. He desires righteousness but hears instead an outcry from the oppressed, poor, and powerless. Therefore, God will remove His protection, and what had once been a beautiful vineyard will be trampled and destroyed. With no further blessing (rains) or cultivation, it will become a wasteland.

Isaiah's Call, God's Sign, and Israel's Failure (6:1–12:6)

In this section Isaiah describes his distinct calling and begins to provide some hope-inspiring prophecies about Immanuel. The people certainly need hope because of conflict with the Assyrians that is devastating their nation. It is a desperate and miserable time, so the anticipation of God's Messiah is especially welcome.

Prophecies against Other Nations (13:1–23:18)

For the next several chapters, Isaiah presents a number of judgments concerning the nations around Israel and Judah. He has already been writing about Assyria and the crown jewel of its empire: Babylon. Eventually Babylon overtakes Assyria to form an empire of its own. In this section, Isaiah addresses Babylon and a number of other countries, delivering messages from God.

Background & Context

The superpowers of Isaiah's day were the Assyrians and the Persians. There was not always a clear succession of one empire falling and being replaced by the next. Rather, various nations coexisted for periods and had numerous coalitions and conflicts. For example, there was an alliance between the Medes and Babylonians in the late 600s BC, but about fifty years later the Medes were absorbed by the Persians, who then conquered Babylon. Various opinions exist, but it is likely that Isaiah's reference in 13:17 is to an early conquest of Babylon by the Assyrians in 689 BC rather than its more notable defeat by the Persians in 539 BC.

There is general agreement that the *Babylon* in verse 19 refers to the city rather than the empire. The people's arrogance and sense of immortality will be shattered. After centuries of existence and influence, Babylon will come to an inglorious end. History confirms that Babylon does indeed become a ghost town by the seventh century AD, confirming Isaiah's prophecy in 13:19-22.

Yet for the time being, Babylon is one of the biggest threats to Israel and Judah. What a surprise and comfort it must have been to hear Isaiah's prediction that one day, thanks to God's great compassion, He will reestablish Israel and people will flock there from all nations (14:1-2). Israel will have the last word with Babylon. God will lift up His people even as their enemies are falling (14:3-23).

The World Struggles, but God Reigns Supreme (24:1–35:10)

After delivering a series of judgments against numerous nations (chapters 13–23), Isaiah expands his focus to the world as a whole. Isaiah 24–27 is frequently called Isaiah's Apocalypse, although many argue that the term is a bit strong. The remaining chapters in this section (28–35) are more specific and develop a historical perspective for the reader, although they do so with a series of woes.

A Historical Verification (36:1–39:8)

This section of Isaiah is quite different from what precedes and follows it. For a few chapters, Isaiah provides a historical narrative with specific dates, names, and events.

Good News in Bad Times (40:1–44:23)

This section begins a shift in tone and focus in the book of Isaiah, so much so that many believe it must have been written by someone other than the author of Isaiah 1–39. The regularity of judgmental pronouncements diminishes, as much more is written about salvation and restoration. The previous chapters present Assyria as the dominant threat; the following ones jump ahead to anticipate the end of the Babylonian captivity. (After the fall of Israel to Assyria, Judah remains as a nation for more than a century, and their exile in Babylon lasts another seventy years before they are able to return to their homeland.) But regardless of one's opinion of whether or not a second "Isaiah" takes up the writing of the original prophet at this point, this section contains some of the more optimistic looks toward the future in all the Old Testament.

Background & Context

The observation that the threat from the East moved on unfamiliar ground (41:3) suggests that Isaiah is no longer talking about Assyria. The new power in the East is most likely Cyrus, the Persian leader whom the prophet will soon identify by name (44:28–45:1). In addition, Isaiah has already said that the Medes will conquer Babylon (13:17–19). A later reference to Cyrus speaks of him coming from the north (41:25) because that is the site of his Babylonian conquests. Worldly powers will continue to shift, but God remains in control of them all.

Israel, Babylon, and Cyrus (44:24–48:22)

Isaiah has been attempting to help his people understand that they will certainly be conquered by Babylon and taken into exile. Here, however, he moves ahead to write of the fall of Babylon and the end of their captivity, predicting a benefactor that Israel might not have counted on: a foreign leader named Cyrus.

The Work of God's Servant (49:1–55:13)

The first of four songs for God's servant is found in Isaiah 42:1–4 (or possibly 42:1–7 or 42:1–9). The other three songs are found in this section: 49:1–6 (possibly 49:1–7 or 49:1–13); 50:4–9 (possibly 50:4–11); and 52:13–53:12. These songs and the surrounding material foretell a servant of God who will be a deliverer not just of Israel but of all the nations as well. In fact, the emphasis of Isaiah's writing shifts to the point that neither Babylon nor Cyrus is mentioned again. The people of God are still in a captivity of sorts, but it is less the harsh physical captivity of specific nations and more of a spiritual bondage that only a special agent of God can remedy.

Promises for (and Previous Failures of) God's People (56:1–59:21)

Isaiah has been writing about a rather optimistic future for the people of God. But the spiritual strength of their future will be largely dependent on their willingness to take action in the present and correct the things they are doing wrong. The invitation of salvation is being extended to those outside of Israel, and God's people need to start taking an honest look at their own spiritual actions and attitudes.

The Glory of the Lord (60:1–62:12)

This section is a bright respite coming after a number of dark and sometimes even disturbing passages. Israel's recent past has been one of drifting away from God. Their immediate future will involve God's judgment on them as well as on numerous other nations. But their long-range future is something to look forward to. Isaiah has already written of God's servant who will make possible such a future. In this section he describes a number of wonderful outcomes that result from the work of the servant.

Looking ahead with Hope (63:1–66:24)

As the book of Isaiah concludes with this section, the prophet reviews several of his ongoing themes, including God's vengeance, judgment, salvation, and redemption. But throughout it all is the assurance that Israel's future will be much better than its recent past, or even its present state. The Lord is in control of everything that is taking place, and His ultimate plan is to restore His people and renew close fellowship with them.

Jeremiah
Introduction to Jeremiah

The Old Testament book of Jeremiah is considered one of the canon's major prophets and is named after the book's author, the prophet Jeremiah. By word count, Jeremiah is actually the longest book of the Bible, with even more words than Psalms. It follows the work of another major prophet, the book of Isaiah, and precedes the short poetic work Lamentations.

Author

The book of Jeremiah is highly autobiographical, and more can be learned about the prophet from his work than from any other historical source. Jeremiah was a Judean, from the town of Anathoth, located about three miles outside of Judah's capital city, Jerusalem. We don't know when he was born, but he probably died in Egypt after the exile of 586 BC. His call to prophecy came around 627 BC. Jeremiah was assisted in compiling the book of Jeremiah by his scribe, Baruch, who is referenced several times in the work and accompanies Jeremiah on many of his journeys.

Jeremiah's writing is permeated with his personal feelings and the emotional turmoil he experiences as he ministers to the people of Judah. These are his fellow countrymen, and he is deeply burdened for their spiritual state. It is from the emotional overtones and many recorded laments that Jeremiah receives the nickname "the weeping prophet." The prophet is chosen by God to speak judgment to a people who have turned their backs on Him. For his troubles, Jeremiah is beaten, thrown in pits, placed in stocks, and publicly ridiculed. His own townspeople put out a contract on his life. Even his family members become his enemies. God had instructed Jeremiah to not take a wife—his ministry was to be too difficult to sustain a marriage and the coming judgment so severe as to preclude having a family. Jeremiah lives a life of loneliness and depression, and he certainly earns his nickname of "weeping prophet."

Occasion/Purpose

As a prophet of God, Jeremiah is tasked with communicating God's message of coming judgment to the people of Judah, the southern kingdom, and more specifically the city of Jerusalem. The people had fallen into a pattern of idolatry, and it was going to destroy the nation if they did not soon repent of their sins and turn back to God. Jeremiah preaches a message of hope and repentance until it becomes evident that the people have no intention of repenting. Then his message becomes one of warning about God's coming judgment as he prophesies the invasion by a nation from the north that will destroy Jerusalem. Jeremiah's prophecies target all people groups in Judah: kings, priests, prophets, and ordinary townspeople. The book also includes a series of oracles to foreign nations, in which God voices judgment on them for their sins as well. It should be noted, however, that Jeremiah saw beyond the judgment to the restoration after the judgment. Chapters 30–33, in particular, reveal this restoration as a part of Jeremiah's task.

The book of Jeremiah is composed of writings and preachings throughout Jeremiah's ministry, which began in approximately 627 BC. The precise date the final work was compiled is unknown, but it can be estimated to be sometime after the last historical reference in the book, which extends beyond the release of King Jehoiachin from Babylonian captivity in 561 BC (52:31–34) and into the return of the Jewish exiles to Jerusalem after 586 BC in chapters 40–44. It is important to note that the events recorded in the book of Jeremiah do not unfold in chronological order. Jeremiah's prophecy takes place during the reigns of Judah's last five kings: Josiah, Jehoahaz, Jehoiakim, Jehoiachin, and Zedekiah. This is the time leading up to the Babylonian invasion of 586 BC, when Jerusalem falls. The historical events surrounding Jeremiah's prophecies are recorded in 2 Kings 21–25 and 2 Chronicles 33–36.

Themes

A few main themes make up the bulk of Jeremiah's prophetic work. Chief among these is God's personal involvement with His people. Jeremiah's role as prophet is to communicate God's words to His people on His behalf. The reason such communication is necessary is because of the sin of idolatry the people have made a habit in their lives, the second main theme of the book. By sinning in such a manner, the people are guilty of breaking their covenant with God, established just after the Exodus. Another theme in Jeremiah's prophecies is the nation's repentance, or turning from idolatry back to God. Many of Jeremiah's prophecies also cover the theme of God's judgment, which was what the people could expect if they failed to repent and continued down the path of idolatry away from God. Ultimately, Jeremiah includes the theme of God's restoration of His people.

Contribution to the Bible

As part of the biblical canon, Jeremiah is considered one of the three major prophetic books. Although it is largely a prophetic work, the book of Jeremiah contains a wide variety of literary elements in addition to prophecy, including history, poetry, and narrative. The presence of all of these elements makes Jeremiah's work arguably one of the most compelling books of the canon. The book of Jeremiah has also been referred to as an anthology of Jeremiah's prophecies and an autobiographical account of the prophet's life.

Background & Context

The superscription to the book of Jeremiah dates his prophecies from 627 BC (the thirteenth year of Josiah's reign) to 586 BC (the eleventh year of Zedekiah's reign), with chapters 39–44 extending beyond this time frame into the exilic period. Jeremiah's contemporary prophets were Ezekiel, Daniel, Zephaniah, and Habakkuk. The two national superpowers at that time were Egypt to the south and Assyria to the north. The northern kingdom, Israel, had been infiltrated and dispersed about one hundred years earlier, but Judah had survived through the faith of Hezekiah and Isaiah.

In 640 BC, Josiah becomes king of Judah at the age of eight and eventually begins to purge his country of idolatry, about the time that Jeremiah begins his ministry. In 622 BC, Josiah finds part of the Mosaic Law in the temple. These writings had not been seen or read for many years. Assyria was too distracted with her enemies, the Babylonians and the Medes, to control Josiah's reform. Later, in 609 BC, Josiah is defeated and killed when he tries to stop the Egyptians at Megiddo. He is succeeded by Jehoiakim and Zedekiah, his sons, and Zedekiah rules until the fall of Jerusalem in 586 BC.

Much of the prophecy of Jeremiah has to do with this political and spiritual climate. Judah was like a pawn in this major political upheaval, a mere buffer between Egypt and Assyria, and later between Egypt and Babylon. A major part of this book deals with Judah making unwise treaties with these nations to gain protection and deliverance. In the midst of this tumultuous time, God announces judgment, but He is still reaching out to save His people. During the ministry of Jeremiah, Babylon to the east begins its ascent and is on its way to becoming the next world power, replacing Assyria. Babylon becomes the invader from the north, mentioned several times in Jeremiah's prophecy. In 586 BC, Jeremiah's prophecy of Judah's downfall and the people's exile comes true when Babylon, under the reign of King Nebuchadnezzar, destroys Jerusalem.

Jeremiah's Call and Purpose (1:1–6:30)

The book of Jeremiah begins with an introduction of the prophet and his call to prophesy to his own people as well as all nations. In the first section, which includes chapters 1–6, God sends His prophet to the people with a warning of impending judgment and punishment because of their lifestyle of sin. This judgment is based on the covenant God made with this nation and the consequences that would come to them if they failed to follow God's laws.

Background & Context

The people's sins against God aren't limited to Judah. Israel has been treating God with irreverence and apathy for some time. As verse 12 notes, one of the lies spread by people from both the northern and southern kingdoms is that God won't judge them, even though He has proven otherwise in the lives of their ancestors. And as if that isn't bad enough, some of God's own prophets had taken on the same complacent spirit and no longer feared Him (5:13). But Jeremiah, a prophet who continues to speak God's truth, is quick to remind them that no one can escape God's judgment.

Hypocrisy and Wrong Religion (7:1–10:25)

This section of the book of Jeremiah continues with the prophet's warnings to the nation. In this portion of prophecies, the warnings are more specifically geared toward the sins of hypocrisy and practicing false religion, and the consequences of those sins.

Judah's Breaking of God's Covenant (11:1–13:27)

Chapters 11–13 of Jeremiah detail the consequences in store for Judah as a result of having broken God's covenant. The covenant being referred to is the Mosaic Covenant, in which God promised to bless the Israelites if they obeyed Him. Their idolatry is a severe disobedience and breach of the covenant. This section also includes two of Jeremiah's laments about the gravity of the nation's sin and God's pending judgment.

God's Warnings (14:1–20:18)

The next section of Jeremiah begins with a detailed prophecy of the drought and famine that will accompany the coming invasions. From there, it moves into a series of confessions from Jeremiah about his personal hardships as they relate to his ministry among the people of Judah, followed by another section of metaphors symbolizing the nation's relationship with God. This section ends with an example of the persecution Jeremiah faces because of the message he delivers. Interspersed throughout are additional warnings against Judah's idolatry and their need to repent to avoid the coming judgment.

Messages about Leaders and Captivity (21:1–25:38)

Previously in the book of Jeremiah, the prophet delivered a series of prophecies detailing the future judgment by God on the nation of Judah. In chapter 21, Jeremiah transitions into more specific prophecies directed at Judah's kings and spiritual leaders. This section of prophecies culminates in the prophecy of the seventy years of Babylonian captivity (Jeremiah 25).

Background & Context

The following is a brief review of Judah's kings during Jeremiah's prophetic reign. King Josiah began his reign over Judah in 640 BC, when he was only eight years old. His rule ended in 609 BC, following his death in a battle with the Egyptians. During this great king's reign, a part of the law was found in the temple, and Josiah led a reform movement to encourage his people to turn back to God. Josiah and Jeremiah, partners in this endeavor, sought to restore true worship in Judah. Following the death of Josiah, things quickly deteriorated. Prior to the fall of Jerusalem, Josiah was succeeded by four kings: Jehoahaz, Jehoiakim, Jehoiachin, and Zedekiah. However, none of these kings sought the Lord with all their heart. Zedekiah was installed as a puppet king by Nebuchadnezzar, king of Babylon, in 597 BC. Zedekiah continually tried to overthrow the rule of Babylon, leading to the destruction of Jerusalem in 587 BC.

Jeremiah and Judah Dialogue (26:1–29:32)

The central theme of chapters 26–29 is dealing with the false prophets who continue to speak lies in the name of God. The focus shifts from what Jeremiah is proclaiming to how the people react to his prophecies. Jeremiah represents the genuine prophet, and the false prophets are contrasted to him and his message.

The Book of Consolation (30:1–33:26)

Hundreds of years after enslavement in Egypt, the children of God are once again experiencing captivity in another land. As Judah braces itself for seventy years of anguish, the God of comfort wants His children to know that there is hope. Chapters 30–33 include text that reiterates the hope of a coming day when normal life will return for God's people—Judah and Israel—and they will return to activities like building and planting. While in exile, Judah can read these words and find comfort in the midst of barrenness. This is why Jeremiah 30–33 is often referred to as the Book of Comfort.

Incidents Surrounding the Fall of Jerusalem (34:1–45:5)

Chapters 30–33, referred to previously as the Book of Consolation, provide a series of hope-centered prophecies for the nations of Judah and Israel in the midst of much suffering and struggle. The four chapters also serve as an intermission from Jeremiah's prophetic messages of God's judgment against His sinful people. Chapter 34, however, resumes where 29 leaves off—with a description of Jerusalem just prior to its captivity and fall.

Prophecies and the Nations (46:1–51:64)

Chapters 46–51 chronicle Jeremiah's prophecies concerning the nations (46:1). Such prophecies are not unique to Jeremiah. All of the prophetical books of the Bible contain a similar collection of prophecies, with the exception of the book of Hosea. The themes of this section include God's judgment for idol worship and misplaced trust; the punishment that comes as a consequence of such sins; and the continuing theme that God either won't destroy completely or will destroy now but restore later, which can be seen as evidence of God's amazing mercy. The geographical catalog of nations moves from west to east.

Background & Context

The territory of Moab was a mountainous plateau on the eastern side of the Dead Sea, in modern-day Jordan. The Moabites were descendants of Lot, Abraham's nephew, who reportedly fathered Moab by his oldest daughter (Genesis 19:30-38). Perhaps the best-known resident of Moab was Ruth, who left her home country to embrace the land and culture of Israel. The Moabites received protection from the Egyptians in return for their allegiance to pagan gods.

Conclusion of the Book of Jeremiah (52:1–34)

In this section, the reader gets an overview of how all of Jeremiah's prophecies look from a historical perspective. This section is almost exactly like 2 Kings 24:18–25:21. Most importantly, though, is the inclusion of the fall of Jerusalem as the final chapter of this book of Jeremiah's prophecies, revealing that the city's destruction happens just as Jeremiah said it would—validating Jeremiah's prophecies.

Lamentations
Introduction to Lamentations

Wedged between two of the major prophet works—the books of Jeremiah and Ezekiel—is the short, five-chapter poem titled Lamentations. The book's name reveals what it is—a poem of lament. It records in grave detail and sorrow the aftermath of one of the lowest points in the history of the Israelites. But it also provides one of the greatest testimonies of God's justice and mercy.

Author
There is a tradition that the prophet Jeremiah wrote this book, and thus it has its place in the Bible following the book of Jeremiah. However, no author is named in this specific book itself, and there is no place in the rest of the Bible where this writing is attributed to Jeremiah.

Occasion/Purpose
Lamentations is a poem that reflects on the nation of Judah's suffering. The author witnessed the fall of Jerusalem and the exile of many Israelites, and in this work he is grieving the nation's fall and the demise of his people. God punished His people for their unfaithfulness to Him and His covenant, and the author and poet who wrote this poem wrote it from that place of suffering as both a reflection on the people's sins and its consequences, and a prayer to God for His mercy and redemption.

Lamentations was most likely written soon after 586 BC, shortly after the fall of Jerusalem at the hands of the Babylonians. The author is reflecting on what he sees around him, making it most likely that the city's fall was recent at the time the book was written. In this work he alludes to the future redemption God promised His people, but that redemption has not happened yet, and the wounds of their sins and consequences are still fresh.

Themes
The themes of the book include the following: sorrow and grief, as evidenced by the book's title; the consequences of sin; and God's judgment, mercy, and sovereignty. However, the strongest theme, which is largely unexpected based on the historical context of the book and its genre, is that of hope. Hope in God and His mercy is the foundation on which the author's lamenting takes place.

Contribution to the Bible
Lamentations is one of the poetic books of the Bible. Chapters 1–4 are written in the very specific literary structure of an acrostic, with each verse beginning with progressive letters of the twenty-two-letter Hebrew alphabet. Chapters 1, 2, 4, and 5 have twenty-two verses, and chapter 3 has sixty-six. Each Hebrew letter is used in three verses in chapter 3.

The Elements of Godly Grief (1:1–22)

The introductory chapter to the book of Lamentations focuses on the depth of the author's grief over Jerusalem's destruction. The fall of the city marked the fulfillment of what had been prophesied for years—that eventually the people's idolatry would be their downfall.

Background & Context

In 586 BC, the Babylonian army under the command of King Nebuchadnezzar attacked the city of Jerusalem, Judah's capital and the holy city that housed the temple of God. The city and temple were destroyed, and the people who weren't killed were exiled to Babylon. These events are recorded in 2 Kings 25 and 2 Chronicles 36. The people would remain in exile for almost fifty years. The author witnessed the city's fall and wrote this book shortly thereafter.

Jerusalem's Suffering (2:1–22)

The second chapter of Lamentations describes God's anger at the sin of His people. For too long, the people of Judah have lived in a state of continual sin through the idolatry they both practiced and tolerated.

Hope (3:1–66)

Because of the faithlessness of the people of Jerusalem, this holy city has been destroyed. The people who survived the attack were taken off into Babylonian captivity. Their situation is one of complete hopelessness. But God is a faithful God. It is in this truth that hope for the nation of Judah rests.

Evidence of Jerusalem's Destruction (4:1–22)

Lamentations reaches its climax in chapter 3, when the author responds to God's unwavering mercy, goodness, faithfulness, and control. In chapter 4, he looks more closely at what caused God to judge Judah in this manner by comparing the state of the city of Jerusalem before and after the Babylonian attack.

The Poet's Prayer (5:1–22)

Having grieved for the suffering of the nation, cataloged the related tragedies, voiced words of hope and a reminder of God's mercy, and prophesied an end to the suffering and the downfall of the enemy, Lamentations closes with a prayer for God's swift mercy.

Ezekiel
Introduction to Ezekiel

Ezekiel was a prophet caught up in the turmoil of his time. He was among ten thousand exiles carried off to Babylon in the second of three deportations from Judea (2 Kings 24:14). He and his wife settled in a Judean community established near Nippur, on the Kebar Canal. God's people needed a prophet in Babylon because, with some wonderful exceptions, they carried all the spiritual baggage from the years of idolatry and apostasy that began their ruin.

Author
Ezekiel was a priest, and his priestly orientation comes through in his prophecies. More than any other prophet, he depicts the consummation of the kingdom of God in terms of a new temple and revitalized worship. His prophetic call came at age thirty, which would have made him a young eyewitness to the spiritual reforms during the reign of King Josiah. Unable to serve as priest in a traditional capacity due to his relocation (and subsequent destruction of Jerusalem's temple), his spiritual preparations are still put to use as God calls him to be a prophet during a crucial time of Israel's history.

Occasion/Purpose
Ezekiel has a clear voice from God during a difficult time. He prophesies several years in Babylon before the Babylonians actually destroy the temple and the city of Jerusalem, warning his people of what will happen. He then continues to minister several years afterward to assure them of God's continued sovereignty throughout their bleak circumstances.

God's people were caught in the maw of conflict between world powers Egypt and Babylon. International tensions overshadowed the circumstances of many smaller states and turned the lives of countless individuals and families upside down. Ezekiel's world was turbulent, which makes his message surprisingly relevant for today.

Themes
Ezekiel's book contains a number of themes:

- *Visions.* No other Old Testament prophet is given as many visions as Ezekiel, and no other Old Testament book devotes so much space to visions.
- "*Then you will know that I am the LORD.*" This phrase is found again and again throughout Ezekiel's writing. Israel has forgotten the Lord her God. Ezekiel repeatedly passes along God's reminder to assure the people that God is still at work to put Israel's culpable ignorance right.
- *Individual responsibility.* The people tended to blame their problems on their ancestors or circumstances beyond their

control. Ezekiel stresses the importance of one's individual relationship with the Lord.

- *God using Ezekiel as a sign.* Many other prophets were orators, and Ezekiel did his share of preaching. Yet he is distinctive in how frequently God uses the prophet himself as a sign. Much like Jeremiah, Ezekiel acts out or symbolizes what he is saying on several occasions.

Contribution to the Bible

Much of what Ezekiel teaches is similar to the writings of Jeremiah or other prophets. But unique to his writing is the fascinating vision of the valley of dry bones (37:1–14) and his vision of a temple unlike anything that has yet been constructed (chapters 40–48).

Background & Context

When Ezekiel began his prophetic work, Babylon had gained the upper hand and was holding sway over the entire ancient Near East. Judah's King Jehoiakim had first submitted to Babylon, but—with the encouragement of the Egyptians, but against the advice of Jeremiah—later rebelled. As a result the Babylonian leader, King Nebuchadnezzar, dragged him to Babylon in shackles where he was apparently executed. Jehoiakim's eighteen-year-old son, Jehoiachin, succeeded him as the Babylonian appointee, but he, too, was summoned to Babylon a few months later.

The Call of a Prophet (1:1–3:27)

The first section of Ezekiel (chapters 1–24) is devoted to prophecies of judgment and divine wrath to befall the citizens still remaining in Judea and Jerusalem. The first subsection of this large division concerns the call of Ezekiel.

Background & Context

The description of these cherubim may have appeared less bizarre to Ezekiel's original audience than to modern ears. The iconography of the ancient Near East included figures that had more than one head, multiple sets of wings, human bodies with animal heads, etc. However, no symbols have been discovered that exactly match Ezekiel's depiction.

Lessons in Divine Judgment (4:1–7:27)

The people of Judah are being taken in large groups to Babylon where they will live in captivity. Ezekiel was among one of the earlier groups, and while in

Babylon, God called him to a prophetic ministry. He appeared to be initially reluctant, but in this section he begins to respond to God's instructions, even though many of his actions must have seemed quite strange to onlookers.

A Vision of Jerusalem's Temple (8:1–11:25)

Ezekiel has been delivering some hard-to-hear messages to the Israelites who have already been deported to Babylon. The city of Jerusalem will soon be conquered and the temple destroyed. In this section, Ezekiel is given a vision that makes evident the source of God's displeasure in regard to the temple.

Ezekiel Speaks Out (12:1–14:23)

Having been shown the deplorable spiritual condition of Jerusalem in a vision, Ezekiel is now told to enact the exile of all those remaining there—or more accurately, the exile of the few who will survive the destruction of the city. He is also told to confront other so-called prophets who are telling the exiles only what they want to hear.

Background & Context

Idolatry was the standard form of religion and religious practice in Babylon and surrounding areas at the time. People believed that any depiction of a god, however crude, partook of the essence of the god himself or herself. Anything offered to the image was thus offered to the god. It was also believed that the gods appreciated gifts and would respond in kind. They were relatively easily pleased; and the more generous the worshipper, the more prosperity he or she would receive from the gods.

Three Allegories to Describe Israel (15:1–17:24)

As Ezekiel continues to address the spiritually defiant exiles in Babylon, passing along God's judgment for their recurring rejection of the Lord and pursuit of idolatry, he is given three allegories that illustrate Israel's condition. In each case the meaning is clear because the interpretation is provided.

A Retired Proverb, a Lament, and More Warning (18:1–21:32)

Ezekiel 18 is one of the better-known sections of this mostly unfamiliar book. In this section, the prophet clarifies God's attitude toward sin and who is responsible. Afterward, Ezekiel returns to his message of judgment on Judah and Jerusalem.

Some Final Words for Judah (22:1–24:27)

With this section, Ezekiel completes the first of three major sections of his book. He will finish his message of judgment directed to Judah/Jerusalem, after which he will begin to address other nations. But as he concludes this portion, his words will be punctuated with symbolic actions, even in regard to the death of his wife.

Impending Judgment against the Nations (25:1–32:32)
After completing his six-year ministry of preparing the exiles for the fall of Jerusalem, Ezekiel next turns his attention to God's judgment on a number of surrounding nations. Babylon is not included because, at this time, Babylon is the instrument of God's judgment. In fact, this section provides a wider sense of the impact of Babylon's imperial designs on the nations of the ancient world.

After God's Judgment of Judah (33:1–36:38)
This section begins the third and final segment of Ezekiel's writings. Most of what he has said so far has been somber. The first section (chapters 1–24) dealt with God's judgment on Judah. The second section (chapters 25–32) covered the judgment of Judah's enemies. With those matters behind, however, his look to the future is hopeful and positive. In the final chapters of his book, he foresees Israel's restoration and prosperity as they again receive the blessings of God.

Dry Bones and New Life (37:1–39:29)
This section contains one of the few passages from the long book of Ezekiel that might be somewhat familiar to the average person. As Ezekiel continues his message of God's redemption of Israel, he is shown in a most emphatic way God's immense power to restore His people. Ezekiel also alerts the people of a king to come who will unite them again, and he delivers a prophecy against the land of Gog.

A New Temple (40:1–46:24)
The final nine chapters of the book of Ezekiel, beginning with this section, are a great vision of the future of Jerusalem and Israel presented in terms of an idealized temple and Promised Land.

The River Measured and the Territory Divided (47:1–48:35)
As Ezekiel finishes describing his vision of a future temple, he also concludes his lengthy book. In this section he depicts the river flowing out of the temple and explains how the land is to be divided among the tribes.

Daniel
Introduction to Daniel

The book of Daniel contains some of the best-known stories in the Bible, but it also provides some of the most challenging and intriguing passages to attempt to comprehend. Some of the prophets had sent warning of a judgment of God's people to come; others are present at the end of the captivity to help encourage and empower the beleaguered exiles. But Daniel goes into exile along with his countrymen and provides an insider's view of Judah's experiences in the faraway land of Babylon.

Author
Daniel came from a royal family. He is compared with Noah and Job in terms of faithfulness to God and righteousness (see Ezekiel 14:14). Daniel also demonstrates great wisdom, always giving God complete credit. Unlike Solomon, who started life strong as a young man but strayed from God as an adult, Daniel's faith and wisdom are consistent and evident throughout his long lifetime.

Occasion/Purpose
Daniel describes events that occur during one of the worst situations the people of God ever experienced. The nation of Israel had fallen to the Assyrians more than one hundred years earlier, but Judah survived. Yet Judah continues to refuse to heed God's warning and soon faces humiliating defeat themselves. The Babylonians breach the walls of Jerusalem, ransack the temple, and carry off most of the population in a series of deportations. Daniel is among the first group taken. His writing offers much assurance in that even though circumstances are bad, God is still with His people.

Themes
From start to finish, the theme of the book of Daniel is the sovereignty of God. This theme is detected in the way the Lord interacts with individuals, controls nations, and shares with Daniel plans for the long-range future of His people.

Contribution to the Bible
In addition to some of the Bible's most beloved stories (including the fiery furnace and the lions' den), the book of Daniel is an invaluable source of information concerning various events of future history. Coupled with John's writing in Revelation, many of the symbols of the apocalyptic literature begin to cohere and make sense. Certainly, there are numerous ways to interpret the same information, and it can be difficult to do more than speculate in many places. However, Jesus quotes Daniel as a source for what to look for in the future (see Matthew 24:15–16), giving the prophet's writing the highest degree of credibility.

Background & Context

Babylon was considered to be one of the most glorious and powerful kingdoms of the world at the time that Daniel was written. The palace and gardens are listed among the seven wonders of the ancient world. God uses Babylon's strong armies to conquer Judah after the people refuse to serve Him. In the process, the Babylonians kill many Judeans and take many into captivity. Yet by the end of Daniel, the Babylonian Empire has already fallen to Cyrus, leader of the Medes and Persians.

Daniel Taken to Babylon (1:1–21)

The book of Daniel describes some of the same era as 2 Kings and 2 Chronicles, yet Daniel describes this era from within the Babylonian exile. Due to persistent disregard for God's laws and other sins throughout Judah, the Lord had allowed His people to be conquered. The Babylonian armies had shown little mercy as they marched into Judah, laid siege to Jerusalem, and eventually left the city and the surrounding territory in ruins. Many people died while fighting; many others starved to death. Most of those who survived were deported to Babylon—Daniel among them. The people feel as though God has deserted them. However, Daniel repeatedly attests to the power of the one true God at work, even while His people are exiled in the idolatrous land of Babylon.

Background & Context

For modern readers with New Testament awareness, it may sound peculiar to read that Daniel refers to Nebuchadnezzar as "king of kings" (2:36-37). Literally, the phrase refers to a king that all other kings are subject to, which is why it becomes such a meaningful messianic title for Jesus. But Daniel uses the term to affirm that Nebuchadnezzar is a dominant figure. From Babylon's inception (Genesis 10:8-12), it had always stood for defiance of God. In time, the kingdom of Nebuchadnezzar came to symbolize the kingdom of this world. So in a literal sense, Nebuchadnezzar is indeed king of kings over those who are opposed to God.

Daniel Interprets Nebuchadnezzar's Dream (2:1–49)

After going through Nebuchadnezzar's three-year training period and excelling among his fellow participants (1:3–5, 18–20), Daniel is soon put to the test. In an account that demonstrates how eccentric and brutal Babylonian leadership could be at times, the king makes a demand of his advisers that seems impossible, yet their failure will result in their deaths. As the Lord had done previously, He again provides a way out for Daniel—an act that delivers not only Daniel but also spares the entire group of Nebuchadnezzar's advisers.

The Fiery Furnace and God's Deliverance (3:1–30)

Four men of Judah are mentioned by name as being taken from Judah to Babylon to be trained to serve King Nebuchadnezzar (1:6–7). The primary focus so far has been on Daniel. In this section, however, the attention is placed on his three friends, better known by their Babylonian names: Shadrach, Meshach, and Abednego.

Nebuchadnezzar's Humbling Experience (4:1–37)

The previous two chapters of Daniel have shown how God is dealing with the pride of King Nebuchadnezzar, first through Daniel and then through Shadrach, Meshach, and Abednego. This section is the final segment concerning Nebuchadnezzar, as the king recounts what he has learned. Even Nebuchadnezzar has come to realize that God is the Lord of the universe, and he opens and closes the section with a declaration about the sovereign power and glory of God.

Daniel and Belshazzar (5:1–31)

At least six years have passed between the previous section and this one. In that time, King Nebuchadnezzar has been replaced by Belshazzar. It appears that Daniel's high-profile position in the king's court has also come to an end. Although the previous section highlights a public letter from Nebuchadnezzar warning his fellow Babylonian leaders what can happen if they defy the God of Judah, Belshazzar is either oblivious or defiant. Either way, he will suffer for it.

Daniel and Darius (6:1–28)

The previous section ends with the demise of Babylonian King Belshazzar and his replacement by Darius the Mede. This section continues with the establishment of Darius as king and how he comes to experience the power of Daniel's God.

Daniel's First Vision (7:1–28)

The first half of the book of Daniel (chapters 1–6) is a mostly chronological narrative of Daniel's service to various kings of Babylon and Medo-Persia. The second half (chapters 7–12) contains more personal accounts of some of Daniel's dreams and visions.

Background & Context

For those living in the Middle East, the only great sea they knew was the Mediterranean Sea. It was the territory that all the kingdoms of the world sought to control. The Mediterranean provided a path for international shipping, sustenance for living, and protection from invading forces. It was both literally and figuratively a "great sea."

Daniel's Second Vision (8:1–27)

This section follows the previous one as another account from the private life of Daniel, in contrast to his interactions with various kings in chapters 1–6. This vision of Daniel's is also filled with symbols, as is his dream in chapter 7.

Background & Context

The geographic spread of the Medo-Persian Empire was one step in preparation for the Roman Empire to eventually unite diverse areas in language and customs. In the first century AD, the Gospel will be taken throughout the world with great efficiency. In this way, the unity formed (forced) by the Persians could be seen as laying the foundation for the early church.

Daniel's Third Vision (9:1–27)

Continuing his record of various divine revelations he has received, Daniel describes a prayer for which he is given a most emphatic response. During his prayer, he is visited by the angel Gabriel, who tells Daniel what to expect in the future, although the symbolism used is challenging and difficult to properly interpret and understand.

Background & Context

Jerusalem was an integral part of worship for the Jewish people. It symbolized the land God had given to His people, and the temple represented the presence of God among them. With the temple destroyed and the people scattered, Jerusalem was desolate at the time of Daniel's writing.

Daniel's Fourth Vision (10:1–12:13)

Daniel has recorded three visions so far: one of the destruction of human kingdoms and establishment of the kingdom of God (chapter 7), one of the punishment that will be inflicted on God's people because of their sin and rejection of God (chapter 8), and one of the coming Messiah who will conquer sin and provide a way of everlasting righteousness (chapter 9). In the rest of his book, Daniel records one final vision that encompasses, integrates, and further explains much of what he has already witnessed.

Hosea
Introduction to Hosea

In our present age, fixed truths, moral absolutes, divine imperatives, sure hope, and life-transforming power often seem to be overshadowed by uncertainty, insecurity, and subjectivism. Yet in the story of Hosea, we are confronted with the truth about God's persistent and unlikely love for an unfaithful people, the Israelites, even as we marvel at the tragic and remarkable beauty of one prophet's unconditional love for his faithless wife that exemplifies the love story between God and humanity.

Author

Hosea's prophecy may have existed first simply in spoken form, then later it may have been gathered together in written form by disciples or scribes. Still, this work is traditionally attributed to Hosea, the son of Beeri (1:1). We don't know much about the prophet's life except for the little that we learn from chapters 1 and 3.

Occasion/Purpose

The purpose of the book of Hosea is to remind God's people of their unfaithfulness and of the judgment that will come because of that unfaithfulness. Hosea teaches that, in spite of their unfaithfulness, it is impossible to escape the love of God, who is ultimately their only hope of salvation from themselves.

When Hosea is called to serve as God's prophet, the nation of Israel is in a state of rebellion. Based on the kings reigning during his prophecy (1:1), we know that the nation of Israel has been split by civil war (1 Kings 12) and that Hosea is sent to the northern kingdom of Israel, which is characterized by corrupt kings, crime, and compromised morality (Hosea 4:1–2).

Themes

Both themes of love and judgment run through Hosea's prophecy. God's saving love is faithful even in the face of unfaithfulness. Yet the consequence of that unfaithfulness will be faced. Hosea's ministry is meant to awaken the Israelites to their own unfaithfulness to God and to call their adulterous hearts back to Him.

Background & Context

God called Hosea to the northern kingdom, or Israel, at a time when the nation was in a position of strength and wealth, probably during the later years of Jeroboam II's reign. Hosea was a contemporary of other Old Testament prophets: Amos, Isaiah, Jonah, and Micah. Already on the horizon was the Assyrian menace, and within thirty years, Israel had fallen in defeat.

An Unusual Calling (1:1–2:1)
God calls Hosea to an unlikely method of ministry: Hosea becomes an example of God's message to a rebellious and unfaithful people.

Punishment and Restoration (2:2–23)
Hosea describes God's coming punishment of Israel for her sin, telling of God's wrath and anger and, ultimately, His saving love that brings about the restoration of His people.

Reconciliation (3:1–5)
Hosea is called to reconcile with his wife despite her adultery. God draws a parallel between the story of Hosea's love for his wife and God's love for unfaithful Israel.

The Case against Israel (4:1–19)
Hosea lays out God's charges against Israel, describing the people's sinfulness and God's holiness.

The Judgment (5:1–15)
One of the solemn messages Hosea and other Old Testament prophets are called to deliver is the terrible seriousness of rebellion against God. Not only will God's people someday have to give an account for their unfaithfulness, but there will also be immediate consequences for their rebellion.

Israel Refuses to Repent (6:1–11)
Most of Hosea's prophecy focuses on proving how Israel betrayed the Lord and His covenant and enumerating the curses that God is about to visit upon His people for their faithlessness and apostasy. Hosea also proclaims that after God is finished with His judgment, He will return to bless a future generation of His chosen people.

Israel's Great Challenge (7:1–16)
Hosea dwells on Israel's complete, final, and irreversible failure of faith. The people continue to be religious and call upon the Lord, but all the while they do not really put their trust completely in Him. God longs to redeem His people, but they persist in their sin. The great challenge for Israel is to admit that she has lost her faith and to return to God's truth.

Reap the Whirlwind (8:1–14)
Hosea's prophecy continues to describe how Israel is about to reap the whirlwind of God's judgment for their unfaithfulness. His manner is serious and somber and sets the tone for the punishment to come in the chapters ahead.

Punishment to Arrive (9:1–10:15)

Israel tried to be like other nations by seeking to become wealthy by the same means that the nations used: the fertility cult. But Israel isn't like the other nations; Israelites are God's children, and God will not bless them to operate with this level of harlotry. When Israel embraces these pagan religious practices, they are acting in a way that is inconsistent with their own identity and calling.

Background & Context

Memphis (9:6) is the Greek name for the Egyptian Mamphta, which is the capital of Egypt at this time (Isaiah 19:13; Jeremiah 2:16; 44:1; 46:14; Ezekiel 30:13). Its name means "the dwelling of Phta," the Greek Vulcan. In it is the well-known court of Apis. There, in the home of the idol to whom the rebellious Israelites look for refuge, they will be gathered to be buried. This place is a favorite burial place of the Egyptians. Hence the place of their refuge is the place of their destruction.

God's Displeasure (11:1–12)

This chapter draws heavily on two components of Israel's history: the Exodus and the destruction of Sodom and Gomorrah.

Background & Context

If you look at the history of Israel, you see how through the centuries the people disregarded the prophets' messages. The more God spoke, the more they rebelled. The more God revealed Himself, the more they ran from Him. From the moment they left Egypt, they were fighting against the will and plan of God, seeking to do things their own way. The text continues to reflect upon what God did for Israel to care for the people. God cared for the needs of the nation—describing Israel as His child and His animal. Yahweh fed Israel throughout the Exodus (11:2–4). Hosea warns that the Exodus will be undone and Israel will return to its former condition of slavery. Yet this time the captivity will not be in Egypt but in Assyria (11:5).

Lessons from History (12:1–13:16)

Hosea continues his meditation on the history of Israel's relationship to God—tracing the nation's sin and how it has provoked God's judgment.

Blessing from Repentance (14:1–9)

Following the total disaster and judgment described in the previous chapter, Hosea ends with the blessing and hope that his own story—of loving restoration of his unfaithful wife Gomer—parallels. Hosea's vision of Israel's restoration is partial.

Joel
Introduction to Joel

The book of Joel is an intriguing book, beginning with the fact that we know little about the author, his historical time frame, or even whether he was writing to the northern kingdom of Israel or the southern kingdom of Judah. We are left, then, with the words themselves—the brute force of the message of the divine author.

We may be unaware of the specifics of Joel's personal information or the audience to whom he writes, yet he delivers the message of God with boldness and clarity.

Author

Joel (meaning "Jehovah is God") is a popular name in the Old Testament, with a dozen other men bearing the same name. However, little is known about the prophet Joel.

Occasion/Purpose

Joel writes in response to a devastating attack by locusts. But the destructive insects are described as an invading army, symbolizing the potentially greater destruction awaiting those who do not heed the words of the prophet and repent. Then, beyond the immediate situation in the land, Joel writes of the Day of the Lord, when judgment will come to the enemies of God's people and Israel will eventually be restored.

Themes

The Day of the Lord—a time, known only to God, when He will exact judgment on the nations—is a key theme throughout Joel. The concept encompasses other related themes, including the need for repentance, the certainty of coming judgment, and eventual redemption and restoration for the people of God.

Contribution to the Bible

Perhaps the most well-known use of Joel's prophecies is on Peter's lips on the Day of Pentecost, when the Holy Spirit comes upon the church. Joel's insight into the fresh manner in which God's Spirit will interact with human beings is a tremendous contribution to scripture (2:28–32; Acts 2:14–21).

Background & Context

Without any references to specific events, it is difficult to put Joel's message into a specific historical context. Some people cite the enemies of Judah that are listed (Egypt, Edom, Philistia, and Phoenicia [3:4, 19]) and suggest an early, pre-exilic date for the book. But with no mention of the northern kingdom and a specific reference to Greece (3:6), others feel the book must have been written much later—and was perhaps the last of all the Old Testament prophetic books. So, proposed dates of writing can vary by as much as six or seven centuries.

Destruction: Present and Future (1:1–2:11)

The terrible arrival of a swarm of locusts is the catalyst for Joel's writing. In his opening section, he responds to the great destruction, calling on the people to mourn. Such a sobering event should also remind them that an even worse time of suffering is in store for those who refuse to humble themselves before God.

Background & Context

It is rather common in scripture (as well as in other ancient literature) to read of invading armies described as swarms of locusts. In Joel's case, it appears he has reversed the imagery. He describes a literal invasion of locusts in terms of a human army attacking (1:6–7). As far as the effects on an agrarian society, locusts could be every bit as merciless and cruel as enemy soldiers.

Surviving the Destruction (2:12–32)

After a rather distressing section pertaining to a current plague of locusts and an even worse similar scourge to come, in this section Joel at last offers some hope to the readers and listeners. Yes, the coming Day of the Lord will be dreadful, but there are things the people can do to avoid its potentially terrifying consequences.

The Coming Judgment (3:1–21)

Up to this point, Joel has primarily dealt with God's message to His own people. In this section, after God has just promised redemption and restoration of Israel, the Lord turns His attention to the judgment of other nations that have treated His people badly throughout history. Their relentless cruelty has not been overlooked. Their judgment will be harsh indeed, and although Israel had been guilty of much wrongdoing in the past, they will experience God's great forgiveness.

Amos
Introduction to Amos

The prophet Amos was a contemporary of Old Testament prophets Hosea and Isaiah. He stood for justice in an era of Israel's history in which the nation was politically strong but spiritually weak.

Author

The first verse of this book attributes the writing to a man named Amos. Though his prophecy is directed to Israel, the northern kingdom, Amos himself is from Tekoa, a town in Judah, five miles south of Bethlehem. His work as a shepherd and gardener implies he belongs to the working class until the Lord commissions him to be one of His prophets.

Occasion/Purpose

Amos's prophecy condemns the powerful, self-satisfied, wealthy upper class that had developed in Samaria, the capital of Israel.

Amos's ministry falls in the first half of the eighth century BC, during the last half of the reign of Jeroboam II (793–753 BC). Israel is enjoying a measure of domestic affluence and international power that she has not known since the reign of Solomon. Israel and Judah have expanded to the point that they nearly encompass all the land that David and Solomon controlled two centuries before. It is a time of military conquest and economic prosperity. It is also a time of moral darkness.

Themes

Themes in the prophecy of Amos include God's sovereign power, the covenant agreement between God and Israel, and the day of the Lord's judgment.

The Coming Lion (1:1–2:3)

The opening section of Amos is a series of oracles of judgment pronounced against Israel's neighbors: Syria (Aram), Philistia, Tyre (a city in Phoenicia), and so on. In each case, these nations are condemned not for their false religion and worship but for their various crimes against humanity. They have violated principles of morality that are universally recognized by human beings. But Amos does not preach these oracles to these nations themselves. They are rather part of Amos's sermon against Israel—Israel being, as we learn in 1:1, the focus of Amos's preaching and prophecy. The point of these oracles of judgment is that if these foreign nations cannot escape God's wrath on account of their sins, Israel most assuredly will not escape it for her similar sins.

The Path to Apostasy (2:4–16)

The two oracles of judgment in chapter 2—against Judah and Israel—show the progress of apostasy. Things are not as bad in Judah during Amos's ministry as they are in Israel, but eventually Judah will be guilty of all the sins that Amos accuses Israel of in verses 6–12.

Within but Without (3:1–15)

In this section, the indictment that Amos has drawn up against Israel in 2:6–16 is expanded, clarified, and proved. Israel believes she, as Yahweh's people, was delivered from bondage in Egypt on eagles' wings, but her rebellion, disobedience, and unbelief render her the object of God's wrath, not His care and protection.

The Point of No Return (4:1–13)
Chapter 4 begins a new indictment against Israel that opens with a call to the upper-class women.

Repentance and the Day of the Lord (5:1–27)
This book begins by condemning the nations that surround Israel for their sins and with a promise of God's judgment. If these other nations will not escape God's wrath, how much more judgment must Israel face, a nation who has sinned against God's grace? Chapter 5 is an eloquent plea addressed to the nation of Israel, in hopes that at least some of her people will hear it and respond.

A Hard Truth (6:1–14)
Amos continues to focus on the northern kingdom in this section. The influential and the rich who live and work in the capital cities are the target of Amos's condemnation. Both their complacency and their coming judgment are described.

The Contest for the Truth in the Church (7:1–17)
While the prophecy thus far has included accusations and condemnations, this chapter marks a change. Here, Amos begins to describe a series of visions. Much of the rest of his prophecy will follow this same form.

Too Late (8:1–14)
Chapter 8 opens with a basket of ripe fruit. While Amos may be seeing a physical bowl of fruit, he is likely seeing a vision. Significant to this scene is that the fruit is ripe. In this way, the fruit is an image of Israel.

Future Blessing (9:1–15)
The theme of this conclusion is that no one can escape God's wrath. God punishes unfaithfulness, and no person can get in His way.

Obadiah
Introduction to Obadiah

The book of Obadiah is the shortest of the Old Testament, yet its brief message has numerous applications far beyond its relevance to Edom. Obadiah provides a warning to anyone who mistakenly believes that sin will go unnoticed (and unpunished), but he also offers confidence that for those who continue to seek God, the Lord is able to both forgive and deliver.

Author
Personal facts are scarce concerning the prophet Obadiah. He provides no family references or pertinent locations that enlighten the reader as to his biography. Even his name (meaning "worshiper of the Lord") was a common one in his day. At least a dozen Old Testament men are named Obadiah.

Occasion/Purpose
Obadiah has a single purpose in writing: to bring God's message of judgment to the people of Edom. The nation's deeply rooted sense of pride will result in its certain downfall.

Themes
Obadiah highlights the problems that arise from unbridled arrogance and self-centeredness. Edom (the descendants of Esau) has family ties to Israel (the descendants of Jacob), so Edom's sadistic glee in response to the previous troubles of the Israelites does not go unnoticed; they will be judged for their actions.

Contribution to the Bible
Obadiah is a seldom-quoted book. Even the New Testament writers, who cited many of the Old Testament prophetic writings, are silent in regard to Obadiah. Yet the message of this short writing has practical applications that make it a significant contribution to scripture.

Background & Context
With so few clues provided, it is difficult to determine a precise date for the writing of Obadiah. But the conflict between Edom and Israel was ongoing and had existed throughout their entire histories. If the event referred to in verses 11–14 is the Babylonian destruction of Jerusalem (586 BC), then Obadiah was most likely written during the exile.

The Problem with Taking Joy in the Suffering of One's Enemies (1–21)
The concise writing of Obadiah is a pointed accusation against the nation of Edom, whose people had survived while they saw Judah fall to powerful enemies. More than that, Edom had taken perverse pleasure in seeing their enemies suffer and had even acted aggressively against Judah during a vulnerable time. What Edom didn't realize, however, was that Judah's fall was a result of God's judgment on His people. Obadiah now reveals that God will certainly judge Edom as well and that judgment will be severe.

Background & Context
Israel had requested permission to travel through Edom during their exodus from Egypt, but the Edomites had marched out with a large and powerful army to deny them passage (Numbers 20:14-21). Later, when Israel was an established nation of its own, the Edomites waited until other people attacked Israel and then invaded and took prisoners (2 Chronicles 28:16-21). And when Jerusalem eventually fell to the Babylonians, the Edomites cheered and celebrated (Psalm 137:7-8).

Jonah
Introduction to Jonah

Jonah is the only prophet who is recorded as having run away from God. In this way, Jonah is not known for his piety but for his prodigality. Jonah, in his rebellion, disobedience, and hardness of heart, is a man who typifies the rebellion of Israel as described by other prophets. Ironically, the name *Jonah* means "dove," a bird often associated with peace.

Author
Very little is said of the prophet Jonah outside of the book of Jonah itself. It does seem safe to conclude that the Jonah in 2 Kings 14:25 is the same person who is the subject of the book of Jonah, especially since both are identified as the son of Amittai.

The book of Jonah does not name its author. While it is about Jonah, there is no specific claim as to whether Jonah actually wrote it.

Occasion/Purpose
The book stood to reveal to Israel the possibility of repentance, even for those whom Israel would have considered the most wicked. The point was, if repentance is a possibility for the most wicked, then repentance is a real possibility for Israel herself as well.

Jonah is a prophet in the northern kingdom of Israel during the first half of the eighth century BC. His predecessors are Elijah and Elisha. The ministries of Hosea and Amos immediately follow that of Jonah.

Themes
Throughout the book of Jonah runs the theme of second chances, worked out through opportunities for repentance, some taken and some wasted. Hand in hand runs the theme of those who choose to obey God and those who don't.

Contribution to the Bible
In the New Testament, Jesus mentions Jonah (Matthew 12:39–41; 16:4; Luke 11:29–32). When asked for a sign, Jesus refers the religious leaders to the sign of Jonah that already exists. He points out the parallel of Jonah's three days in the fish and the Son of Man's three days in the heart of the earth.

Jonah and the Sailors (1:1–17)
At the opening of Jonah's story, he is given a divine commission to go to the great city of Nineveh, capital city of Assyria and a potential threat to Israel (see Genesis 10:8–11).

Background & Context

Jonah is associated in 2 Kings 14:25 with the reign of King Jeroboam, a time of prosperity for Israel. Assyria, whose capital city is Jonah's target of Nineveh, has already begun to exercise her dominance in the Near East, but for a time her control will wane, allowing Israel to expand her borders. Israel's empowerment at this time may have been a factor in her lack of repentance. This makes the story of Jonah all the more pointed, in that a nation Israel considered to be wicked repents before God when His own people won't.

Jonah and His Psalm (2:1–10)

Jonah 2:1 picks up the story from under the sea. Verses 2–9 present Jonah's prayer in psalm format.

Jonah and the City (3:1–10)

In chapters 1 and 2, Jonah's sin is apparent yet still somewhat subtle and passive. But this changes in chapters 3 and 4, for Jonah's preaching and the repentance of Nineveh reveal his sinfulness in its ugliest dimensions. In the following chapters, all appearances of piety vanish in the account of the prodigal prophet.

Jonah and the Shade (4:1–11)

Had Jonah been any other prophet in the history of Israel, he would have been overjoyed with the results of his ministry—the repentance of the great city of Nineveh. In chapter 4, Jonah blurts out his reasons for rebelling against the command of the Lord. The events in this chapter reveal Jonah's sin.

Micah
Introduction to Micah

Sometimes called the prophet of the poor, Micah is a contemporary of Isaiah and speaks a similar message, though, as recorded in the Bible, shorter. King Hezekiah initiates sweeping spiritual and moral reforms in Judah in response to the preaching of Micah and Isaiah, but unfortunately these reforms are short-lived.

Author

The first verse of this book ascribes the authorship to Micah, a prophet about whom we know very little outside of what is revealed through this prophecy. The prophet is mentioned in only one other place in the Bible, in Jeremiah 26:17–19. In this account, Micah is described as a prophet during the reign of King Hezekiah. When Micah prophesied a bad end for Jerusalem, the king repented, saving Jerusalem from the destruction Micah had prophesied.

Occasion/Purpose

Micah prophesies to stir his readers to action. His writing takes the form of three oracles of judgment. This judgment falls on his countrymen, who act as oppressors, as well as on his society in general, which is filled with corruption. Micah also reminds his people of God's restoration (as do other Old Testament prophets), which awaits them in the future.

The first verse of this prophecy identifies the monarchies under which Micah prophesies—Jotham, Ahaz, and Hezekiah. This places Micah in the eighth century BC. The prophecy references the destruction of Samaria and the invasion of Sennacherib in 701 BC, which would agree with that chronology.

Themes

While Micah's prophecy is not a theological treatise, running through it are the themes of God's sovereignty, His consistency of nature, and the destiny of the remnant of the faithful.

The Judgment to Come (1:1–16)

Micah begins with the announcement of judgment because of sins against God and unfaithfulness to God's covenant. This is a major theme of the prophets, leading up to the destruction of the northern kingdom in 722 BC and the devastation and exile of the southern kingdom some 150 years later. This lesson also reveals the nature of God's divine justice, the ferocity of divine wrath, and the final and conclusive judgment of all people at the end of the world.

From Oppression to Hope (2:1–13)

This next oracle is a pronouncement of judgment against the leadership of Judah. But it goes beyond simply promising judgment against the northern kingdom (1:6–7) and the southern kingdom (1:8–16). This oracle specifically identifies one of the sins for which Israel will be judged.

Judgment on the Leadership (3:1–12)

Chapter 3 contains three oracles of judgment of equal length and identical in form, with the same theme in every case—corrupt leadership.

Zion's Future (4:1–13)

While Jerusalem is still being addressed in chapter 4, the mood of the message changes. Micah 4–5 contains the first of the oracles of salvation. These are oracles of an eventual deliverance, unlike the apparent near-terms deliverance described in 2:12–13. These oracles describe a new epoch that lies beyond the judgment that Micah is prophesying for Israel and Judah in the near future.

The Coming Champion (5:1–15)

The first verse of chapter 5 actually completes the closing thought from chapter 4. With verse 2, then, Micah begins a hopeful oracle regarding a champion who will come from Bethlehem. Verses 2–4 discuss the rule and triumph of the Messiah

Himself, and verses 5–6 describe those who rule in His name. The ideal king of the ancient Near East is a shepherd king, one who provides for and cares for his people. The Messiah will be such a king.

More Accusations (6:1–16)
The first oracle in chapter 6 is a kind of lawsuit God brings against the people. Then the chapter closes with a pronouncement of Israel's sentence.

Background & Context
In the Old Testament, a call to remember carries the idea of participation (6:5). In remembering, the people are reliving and reclaiming events of the past. This is very much the same thing that is involved, or is to be involved, in the Lord's Supper when we are told to "do this in memory of the Lord." We are to bring what He did into our present experience.

Eventual Hope (7:1–20)
While Micah's prophecy is full of solemn accusations and bleak acknowledgments, it ends with a sense of triumph. It is Micah's statement of faith.

Nahum
Introduction to Nahum

Nahum is a book that calls into reckoning Judah's enemy, Nineveh. A careful reading of this book reveals that the author has a high view of God and His Word; he preaches against idolatry, immorality, injustice, and all manner of sin.

Author
We don't know many facts about Nahum, but there is no reason to doubt he is the primary author of the material that bears his name. From his writing style we can assume he was born into a family with enough means to provide him literary training.

Occasion/Purpose
Nahum writes his short prophecy (1) to announce the doom of Nineveh and the demise of the mighty Assyrian Empire and (2) to bring a message of consolation to an oppressed Judah.

Nahum witnessed the reduction of his nation to vassalage during the early campaigns of Assyria. These events, a prelude and a means to the judgment of both Judah and Nineveh, are part of the process that accomplishes the restoration of God's people.

Themes

The most basic theological perspective of Nahum is that of God's sovereignty. God is seen as supreme over nature and nations. He moves in just judgment against His foes but with saving concern for those who put their trust in Him. God is shown to be jealous and to abhor sin, but He is also long-suffering and has distinct purposes for His redeemed people.

Background & Context

The origin and setting of Nahum's prophecy can be deduced from the earliest and latest events mentioned: the fall of Thebes (663 BC) in Nahum 3:8 and the fall of Nineveh (612 BC), an event that is predicted throughout the book. The book of Nahum is intimately bound up with this period of dramatic change.

The Doom of Nineveh Declared (1:1–15)

Nahum begins his prophecy with a notice of its central focus—Nineveh (1:1)—and then turns his attention to a description of Nineveh's certain doom (1:2–15). Throughout the book, Nahum's prophecies deal with Nineveh's doom, its eventual defeat, and its destruction. In the opening section, doom is declared to be certain, because it has been decreed by the sovereign and just Judge of the world, who deals equitably with all.

The Doom of Nineveh Described (2:1–13)

Having declared Nineveh's certain doom and Judah's sure relief, Nahum turns to the chief consideration of his prophecy: the fall of Nineveh. The whole section is filled with the book's basic thesis: God will punish wicked Nineveh and restore His own people. This theme is developed with regard to Nineveh by means of a long narrative section (2:3–10) and a woe oracle (3:1–7).

The Doom of Nineveh Detailed (3:1–19)

With the completion of the first description of Nineveh's doom, capped by a taunt song castigating the discredited city (2:3–13), the demise of Nineveh is rehearsed again, this time underlining the reasons for the devastation (3:1–7). Nahum will build upon that description with another taunt song, which will occupy the greater portion of the third chapter (3:8–19).

Habakkuk
Introduction to Habakkuk

Like Nahum, Habakkuk begins by referring to his message as an *oracle*, or a message placed upon his heart by God. Like Nahum, Habakkuk assures his readers that what he is about to relate is not from his own ingenuity but is from God.

Unlike Nahum, however, Habakkuk does not state that his message is specifically directed at any one individual or group of people, though he will devote a great deal of space to a denunciation of the Chaldeans, which is a representation of the Babylonians.

Author

We don't know anything more about Habakkuk than what can be gleaned from this book. We do know, however, that his authorship of this message was accepted from very early on.

Occasion/Purpose

The book of Habakkuk is less of a prophet preaching to his people and more of a prophet speaking to his God. Habakkuk asks probing questions that lead from the current state of Judah to the eventual future of the kingdom.

While Habakkuk may differ from the other prophets in terms of whom he addresses in his message, he is similar in that he is troubled by the disobedience of his people. In Habakkuk's case, however, rather than pleading with God for more time or with the people for more attention, he questions why God's judgment hasn't already fallen on his nation.

Themes

While judgment and the eventual vindication of Israel is a part of Habakkuk's message, as with other Old Testament prophets, he also addresses themes such as faith in God's sovereignty.

The Prophet's Perplexities (1:1–17)

Habakkuk plunges into a rehearsal of his spiritual wrestling with God. In so doing, he tells his readers of his perplexities as to the divine working and of God's answers to his questions (1:2–2:20). This chapter will consider Habakkuk's superscription, his two questions, and God's answer to the first.

Background & Context

The term *Chaldea* is used in reference to the tribes that lived in southernmost Mesopotamia. They made up the biggest part of Babylonia. By at least 705 BC, Chaldean king Merodach-Baladan took the title "King of Babylon," with the result that the terms *Chaldean* and *Babylonian* became used interchangeably in the Old Testament.

God's Sovereignty (2:1–20)

Habakkuk offers God's reply to his complaint, communicates an essential and timeless message about faith for all people, provides insight into the operations of divine government, and reveals the ultimate fate that will befall the wicked Chaldeans.

The Prophet's Prayer and God's Exaltation (3:1–19)
A perplexed prophet had awaited and received God's instructions in chapter 2. In humble response, Habakkuk turns in prayer and praise to God.

Zephaniah
Introduction to Zephaniah

Zephaniah denounced the materialism and greed that exploited the poor. He was aware of world conditions and announced God's judgment on the nations for their sins. Above all, God's prophet had a deep concern for God's reputation and for the well-being of all who humbly trust in Him.

Author
Although some concern has been raised with regard to many passages in the book that bears his name, Zephaniah has generally been accepted as the author of most of this book. Zephaniah traces his patrilineage four generations to a certain Hezekiah. Jewish and Christian commentators alike have commonly identified this Hezekiah with the king by that name, though this is not conclusive.

Occasion/Purpose
Zephaniah speaks out for God and against wickedness. He writes to inform and warn his people of God's coming judgment, not only against all the world, but also against Judah and Jerusalem. Zephaniah also writes to give the people details of the fearsome events of the Day of the Lord that must come because of sin and because of the Lord's undying concern for His people who have humble and contrite hearts.

The occasion for Zephaniah's prophecy lies in the deplorable spiritual and moral condition of Judah in the early days of Josiah's reign. Taking the throne as an eight-year-old, Josiah finds himself the head of an immoral society. As Zephaniah writes, he is cognizant of the conditions that will surely spell the end of Judah itself (2 Kings 23:26–27).

Themes
Zephaniah is best remembered for his presentation of God as the sovereign and just judge of all. It is He who punishes the wickedness of people and nations, particularly those who have opposed His people.

Background & Context
Few scholars have failed to accept that this book's author, as the first verse states, prophesied during the reign of Josiah (640-609 BC). Most discussions about the setting of the book of Zephaniah concern which period of Josiah's reign provides the backdrop, though many favor Josiah's early reign, because many of the problems that

Zephaniah describes in his nation would have been corrected in Josiah's reforms.

The Announcement of the Day of the Lord (1:1–18)
Zephaniah begins his prophecy with notices of his reception of the word of the Lord, his ancestry, and the time of his ministry (1:1). He then announces the coming of God's worldwide judgment and supplies important details concerning the devastation of that coming Day of the Lord (1:14–18).

Details Concerning the Day of the Lord (2:1–15)
In light of the horrifying spectacle of the judgment of the Day of the Lord, Zephaniah presses his fellow countrymen to gather in repentance and humility before God. Utilizing images drawn from the process of separating straw from chaff, Zephaniah gives them a spiritual message designed to achieve the safety and deliverance of those who repent and put their trust in the Lord.

Final Words (3:1–20)
Although the judgments in Zephaniah's prophecy and the pronouncement of woe upon Jerusalem at the opening of this chapter are not encouraging, the prophet's message is not yet complete. Before the final word has been said, his readers will come to understand that the day of the Lord's judgment, however dark, is but the path to a brighter day.

Haggai
Introduction to Haggai

Haggai's message, so effective in shaking the Jews of 520 BC from their lethargy, has an abiding relevance for all who fail to seek first the kingdom of God and His righteousness. The book of Haggai consists of four addresses.

Author
We know very little about Haggai outside of the four months of ministry described in this writing. He is mentioned in the book of Ezra.

Occasion/Purpose
Haggai's purpose is clear. The exiles who returned to Jerusalem after their captivity in Babylonia have failed to complete the temple. Haggai calls these citizens to repentance and to action.

Haggai dates his first recorded revelation to the first day of the sixth month of the second year of the Persian king Darius Hystaspes (522–486 BC). Haggai's ministry falls between the sixth and eleventh months of Darius's second year. After years of exile in what was first Babylonia and then Persia, some of the Jewish exiles are allowed to return home. Their city is in ruins as is the temple, their center for worship. Throughout their history, the spiritual well-being of these people has been typified by the state of their place of worship. There is much in need of repair.

Themes
Themes in Haggai include those familiar to other prophets—repentance, obedience, and worship. In Haggai's writings, however, these themes are built around the temple and all it means to the community of Jews.

Background & Context
In a day of profound discouragement and misplaced priorities after the Jews' return from Babylonian exile, the prophet Haggai sounds a call of rebuke, exhortation, and encouragement to his contemporaries. They have begun to rebuild their homes and businesses and to establish their statehood as a Jewish community but have been derelict in tending to the construction of the temple and making the Lord the central focus of all their hopes and dreams.

The prophets Haggai and Zechariah were contemporaries in Jerusalem at the end of the sixth century BC. This setting can be precisely identified; no other biblical author, with the exception of Ezekiel, ties his ministries and messages more closely to a chronological framework.

Rebuilding the Temple (1:1–15)
The opening superscription provides the setting for the first oracle of the prophet (1:2–11) and identifies him and the immediate recipients of his message.

Haggai, whose name means something like "festive" or "festival," appears (apart from self-references in this treatise) only in Ezra 5:1 and 6:14. Since the oracle is transmitted on the first day of the month, a festival day (Numbers 10:10; 28:11), the prophet's name itself is revelatory of the occasion.

Looking Ahead (2:1–23)
In this chapter comes the message that the unpromising beginning of a second temple will someday give way to one whose magnificence and glory far transcends that of Solomon's. Yahweh is with His people and will, in line with His ancient covenant promises, reenact the Exodus and restoration to such a degree that the temple will become a place of pilgrimage from all nations. Yahweh will bring in the day of peace.

Zechariah
Introduction to Zechariah

The books of Haggai, Zechariah, and Malachi were composed in the postexilic period of Israel's history to offer hope to a people whose national and personal lives had been shattered by the Babylonian destruction of Jerusalem and captivity of the people. Zechariah goes beyond Haggai's burden for the immediate, earthly situation of the postexilic community and sees, through a vision and dream, the unfolding of divine purpose for all of God's people and for all the ages to come.

Author
At least thirty people mentioned in the Bible bear the name *Zechariah*, which means "the Lord remembers." The prophet and author of this book, however, is further identified as being the son of Berekiah and grandson of Iddo (1:1). He was born during Judah's captivity in Babylon and returned to Jerusalem with a group led by Zerubbabel. Iddo was a priest during that time (Nehemiah 12:1–7), and Zechariah eventually succeeds his grandfather in that role.

Some people propose that the latter portion of Zechariah (chapters 9–14) likely has a different author. They cite a variation in writing style and the author's inclusion of historical events that span beyond a single lifetime. Yet those variations are not evidence enough to sway the beliefs of other scholars, who continue to maintain that the book has a single author.

Occasion/Purpose
After about seventy years of exile in a foreign land, God's people are released to return to their homeland, only to discover that the walls and temple of Jerusalem have been demolished. Projects are planned for reconstruction, but the people need much encouragement and faith during this period. As both prophet and priest, Zechariah brings assurance of God's faithfulness and hope for the future of His people.

Themes
Zechariah adopts an already existent apocalyptic tradition of writing from which he draws heavily and to which he makes a significant contribution. The apocalyptic format receives immeasurable momentum from the trauma of the exile, a calamity that not only shook the social and political structures of Judah but also threatened to undermine the covenant faith itself. So Zechariah shifts the focus from the present to the future, from the local to the universal, and from the earthly to the cosmic and heavenly.

Contribution to the Bible
Rich in apocalyptic imagery and packed with messianic prediction and allusion, Zechariah's writings become a favorite of the New Testament evangelists and apostles. No minor prophet excels Zechariah in the clarity and triumph by which he looks to the fulfillment of God's program of redemption.

Zechariah's Night Visions, Part 1 (1:1–3:10)

The overall message of Zechariah, though occasionally obscure, is largely clear and plain. The prophet seeks to comfort his discouraged and pessimistic compatriots, who are in the process of rebuilding their temple and restructuring their community, yet who view their efforts as making little difference in the present and offering no hope for the future. Zechariah challenges members of the restored remnant to work confidently and to fully expect that what they do will be crowned with success when God, true to His Word, will bring to pass the fulfillment of His ancient promises to their forefathers. This section introduces the book and covers the first four of eight visions the prophet sees in a single night.

Background & Context

Early Jerusalem housed only six thousand to eight thousand inhabitants. One estimate of the city's population in 700 BC is twenty-four thousand. And it is unlikely that pre-exilic Jerusalem ever contained as many as forty thousand people. Yet the people who returned from exile in 538 BC numbered 42,360 Jewish citizens, 7,337 slaves, and 200 singers (Ezra 2:64-65). Add to that crowd of people a group of animals exceeding eight thousand (Ezra 2:66-67). Admittedly, not all of them would have settled within the city limits of Jerusalem, but it seems that many did (Ezra 2:70; 4:4).

Zechariah's Night Visions, Part 2 (4:1–6:15)

This section continues to present the visions of Zechariah. This opening series of visions helps provide a basis for understanding the prophet's writings that follow them.

Zechariah's Oracles (7:1–14:21)

A clear break exists between the content of Zechariah 7 and the material that precedes it. Based on the dates Zechariah provides (1:7; 7:1), the oracles of this section begin about twenty-two months later. Unfortunately, the biblical record is silent about the impact of Zechariah's previous visions. Apart from the tantalizingly brief historical references here, there is very little that can be known at all about that period of time. Still, Zechariah has much more relevant information to record.

Background & Context

The release of the people of Judah was in conjunction with the overthrow of the Babylonians by the Medes and Persians. Zechariah begins his ministry in the eighth month of the second year of the Persian king Darius (1:1)—520 BC. Zechariah's final chronological reference (7:1) is to the ninth month of the fourth year of Darius (518

BC). If one accepts that Zechariah is the sole author of the book, the latter date presumably marks the occasion for all the oracles and other messages of chapters 7–14.

The opposition to the rebuilding projects in Judah occurs prior to Darius, and serious antagonism of the Jewish people does not arise again until Xerxes (486 BC). It is safe to assume, therefore, that work on restoring the temple goes unimpeded during the two years of Zechariah's ministry.

Malachi
Introduction to Malachi

The book of Malachi is a summons to repentance and revival. In six disputations, the prophet summons the people to forsake their spiritual doldrums and halfhearted commitment to the Lord and return to an active faith and the practice of devotion to God.

Author

Some have wondered if Malachi's name, which means "my messenger," could be a title rather than a name. But there is no reason to believe that Malachi is written by anyone other than Malachi himself.

Occasion/Purpose

Malachi addresses his people—the small group of exiled Jews who return from Babylonia. He confronts his people for keeping the best for themselves and leaving their leftovers for God. He calls his people back to their commitment and faith, particularly in light of the future judgment awaiting those who do not repent.

The concerns raised by Ezra and Nehemiah in their work of reformation are some of the same that Malachi mentions: spiritually mixed marriages, the neglect of tithing, disregard for keeping the Sabbath, the corruption of the priesthood, and social injustice. Some scholars suggest that it is likely Malachi preached before the reforms of Ezra and Nehemiah, preparing the way for them.

Themes

Malachi uses the disputation form: Certain people raise a point, which is then contradicted by the prophet or, better, by the Lord speaking through the prophet. Malachi is not the only prophet to use this device. We find it in one form or another in Amos, Micah, and Ezekiel, as well as in Isaiah and Jeremiah. But only Malachi raises it to the organizing principle of his prophecy.

The covenant that God made with His people in the Pentateuch is fundamental to the message of Malachi. Malachi presumes this covenant is to establish a living relationship between the Lord and His people. Beginning in 1:1, Malachi uses the name *Israel* for the people of God. The covenant name has been applied to what remains of the people of God. The northern tribes, who were specifically referred to as Israel during the days of the divided kingdom, are no more, but Israel lives on in the remnant of the entire nation that returns from exile, primarily the descendants of the tribes of Judah and Benjamin.

Background & Context

A small company of Jews returns to Jerusalem from Babylon after the exile. The city is still largely in ruins from its destruction fifty years before. By Malachi's time, any enthusiasm and hopefulness has faded. The people are past believing that God is going to do anything grand on their behalf. It is now a time of spiritual discouragement, complaining, and a growing indifference to God's law of perfunctory worship.

So the situation Malachi faces is the same situation faced by Ezra when he came to Jerusalem in 458 BC, eighty years after the first return of exiles from Babylon, and by Nehemiah when he came to Jerusalem in 445 BC.

Israel and the Priests (1:1–2:9)

Malachi opens with a statement about nations rather than individuals. The Israelites, descendants of Jacob, are God's people, as opposed to the Edomites, descendants of Jacob's brother, Esau.

The Sins of the People (2:10–3:5)

Malachi's third disputation returns to the sins of the people, specifically the marital unfaithfulness among the people of God. The same format is followed as in the previous disputations: The Lord asserts through His prophet that His people have violated the covenant (2:10–13). This is followed by the people's questioning reply, the Lord's response (2:14), and the implication (2:15–16).

The Futility of the People (3:6–4:6)

This section contains Malachi's final two disputations. The first one addresses the people's failure to give ample offerings to God. The second one involves the promise of vindication for those who have put their faith in God.

Matthew
Introduction to Matthew

Although this is a commentary on the Gospel of Matthew, and this Gospel can stand alone as an independent witness to Jesus, it is helpful to our understanding of it to see it in relation to the other Gospels, especially Mark and Luke. Matthew, Mark, and Luke are referred to as the *synoptic Gospels* because they are similar accounts and see the story of Jesus "through the same eyes." The Gospel of John had a unique view or approach to the Gospel story.

Although Mark's Gospel appeared first and was early accepted by the church, Matthew soon became the church's favored Gospel. For a number of reasons, throughout the centuries Matthew has continued to be the most prominent of the three synoptic Gospels. Here are some possible reasons:

- It is commonly believed to have been written by one of the original apostles.
- It is more comprehensive than Mark, containing messianic genealogy, birth narratives, and a considerable amount of Jesus' teaching material.
- It contains more than 90 percent of Mark's Gospel since Matthew used Mark as a basis for his Gospel.
- Its incorporation of large blocks of Jesus' teaching material, especially the Sermon on the Mount, has met the educational and liturgical needs of the church through the centuries.

Author

Our earliest records claim that the apostle Matthew wrote this Gospel. Early church tradition was almost unanimous in this regard. While there remains some continuing discussion about Matthew's authorship, the Gospel itself was accepted without question by the early church and incorporated into the New Testament canon.

Occasion/Purpose

It is obvious that Matthew's Gospel was addressed to a Jewish-Christian audience or community. Matthew presented Jesus to this audience as God's messianic King.

Themes

Several characteristics of Matthew's Gospel are immediately apparent:

- A strong Jewish interest. Matthew used a number of literary devices that indicate a Jewish audience.
- A strong sense of messianic expectation and fulfillment in Matthew. Matthew made much of fulfilled prophecy in his narrative. Quoting heavily from the Old Testament, Matthew claimed that fifteen Old Testament prophecies were fulfilled in Jesus' ministry. He showed great interest in Jesus' teaching on the Law of Moses. Jesus' statement that He came to fulfill the law rather than abolish it is found exclusively in Matthew (5:17–20).
- Universalism and missions. Although Matthew wrote for a Jewish community, he was not a Jewish zealot. He saw Christianity reaching beyond the Jewish nation to the Gentiles. (Note his condemnation of the Jewish leadership in Matthew 23 and the Great Commission in 28:18–20.)

Complete Bible Companion

- Pastoral and ecclesiastical interest. Matthew is, in every sense of the word, a church Gospel:
  - It is the only Gospel to include the term ekklesia, meaning "church" (16:18; 18:17).
  - Matthew was interested in the church's corporate life and the issues of living in a close-knit body (18:15–20).
  - Matthew emphasized Jesus' role as an authoritative teacher (7:29).
  - Matthew emphasized Jesus' instruction regarding the kingdom (chapter 13).
- Messianic kingdom interests. From the first paragraph of the Gospel, Matthew was concerned with Jesus as the Messiah, the King of God's kingdom. His purpose was to show that Jesus was the long-expected Messiah.
- Eschatological interests. Matthew manifested significant interest in the final age of history, the end times. He included several parables that had themes relating to the final judgment, including:
  - The parable of the tares (13:24–30)
  - The parable of the ten virgins (25:1–13)
  - The parable of the talents (25:14–30)

Matthew described the destruction of Jerusalem in much greater detail than Mark and Luke. In Matthew, three chapters are devoted to the destruction of Jerusalem and the confusion of the disciples over the final end of the age (23–25). Mark and Luke used only one chapter for this discussion (Mark 13; Luke 21).

Background & Context
Some scholars date Matthew after AD 70, sometime after the destruction of Jerusalem, while others date it earlier, in the 60s.
    In this commentary we will follow the view that Matthew's community was a group of Jewish Christians or Jewish church communities who had escaped Jerusalem between AD 66 and the destruction of Jerusalem in AD 70. Needing to know that their faith should not be focused on Jerusalem and the temple, which was now destroyed, but on Jesus the Messiah, Matthew wrote for these dislodged Jewish Christian communities who needed to refocus their faith and discipleship.

Narrative 1: Preparation for Ministry (1:1–4:25)
This first block of narrative in Matthew is sometimes overlooked in the misconception that it's not quite as important to the Gospel as, say, the Sermon on the Mount of Matthew 5–7 or the great Kingdom Parables of Matthew 13. It may be seen as simply the backdrop or story setup. However, it actually presents one of the most striking and significant theological emphases of the Gospel. This narrative lays the foundation for Matthew's arguments regarding the messiahship of Jesus.

Discourse 1: The Sermon on the Mount (5:1–7:29)

To fully understand The Sermon on the Mount, it's best to know the context of the theology of Matthew and the discourse that grows out of his first narrative (Matthew 2–4). Matthew's theology is that Jesus is the Messiah, the King of God's kingdom, that He does the works of the Messiah, and that He calls disciples to follow Him and make disciples of all nations.

At the conclusion of the first narrative, Jesus has called disciples to follow Him. In Matthew 4:17 Jesus passes from His preparation for ministry into His public ministry.

The Sermon on the Mount picks up from the calling of the disciples and offers the called disciples information about what kind of person a disciple must be—character development. A key thought is that disciples are different in righteousness, piety, and ambition from the scribes and Pharisees (Jewish religious leaders), and from the Gentiles (non-Jews).

The Sermon can be broken down into six sections:

1. Matthew 5:1–12: The Disciples' Character—The Beatitudes
2. Matthew 5:13–16: The Disciples' Influence—Salt and Light
3. Matthew 5:17–48: The Disciples' Righteousness—To Exceed That of the Scribes and Pharisees
4. Matthew 6:1–18: The Disciples' Piety—Deeds of Righteousness
5. Matthew 6:19–34: The Disciples' Ambition
6. Matthew 7:1–27: The Disciples' Pitfalls

Narrative 2: The Authority of the Messiah (8:1–9:38)

In this section we move from one miracle to the next as we see Jesus performing the works expected of the Messiah. The focus here is on the messianic deeds Jesus performs. Matthew follows Mark in recording a string of Jesus' miracles, with a few observations included by Matthew. As in Mark, Matthew demonstrates Jesus' power over physical illnesses of all types, the demon world, as well as His power over the physical world of nature. The miracles of restoration and healing recorded here also indicate the presence of the kingdom of God (Isaiah 29:22–24; 35:3–10).

While Jesus continues to do the powerful works expected of the Messiah, He is not accepted by the scribes and Pharisees.

Discourse 2: The Limited Commission (10:1–42)

In the second narrative (Matthew 8–9), Matthew paralleled Mark's basic narrative of Jesus' powerful messianic ministry as He went from place to place, performing the powerful works expected of the Messiah. At the conclusion of this narrative, Jesus encouraged the disciples to pray that the Lord of the harvest would send laborers.

At this point, Mathew's narrative takes a dramatic turn, for the laborers sent out into the harvest turn out to be the disciples themselves. Here, Matthew discusses the commissioning of the twelve apostles in greater detail than do Mark and Luke (Mark 6:7–13; Luke 9:1–6).

We call this section "the limited commission" because Jesus limits the scope of the effort to the Jews. The disciples are told not to preach to the Gentiles or the Samaritans at this stage, but only to Israel. Later, in Matthew 28:19–20, Jesus charges His followers to make disciples of all nations—that passage is often referred to as the Great Commission.

Mark and Luke also record this commission (Mark 6:7–13; Luke 9:1–6), but neither of them limit the commission to only Israel. Since Mark and Luke are writing to Gentile audiences, the point is not as relevant, particularly in light of the later, greater commission. However, Matthew is writing to a Jewish audience who should have been able to understand that the Gospel is intended first for their nation, who were to be God's special people and a light of revelation for the Gentiles (Isaiah 49:6).

Narrative 3: Opposition Rejected (11:1–12:50)
Jesus continues the powerful works expected of the Messiah but receives increasing opposition from the Jewish leaders. The events of these chapters are somewhat paralleled by those described in John's Gospel at the time when many disciples were leaving Jesus because He did not meet their expectation of a militant messiah who would lead them to freedom from Rome (John 6:60–69). Also, there is an increasing emphasis on the kingdom of God and its glory.

Discourse 3: The True Nature of the Kingdom (13:1–58)
The previous narrative was about the opposition and controversy to Jesus' identity and message. The events described came approximately at the same time as the events described in John 6, when many of the disciples were leaving Jesus, disappointed with His claims of messiahship. They did not understand the nature of the kingdom of God and had anticipated more of a political physical kingdom, whereas Jesus' kingdom was a spiritual relationship with God. Jesus asks His closest disciples whether they, too, are about to leave Him. Peter has answered that there is nowhere else to go because Jesus alone has the words of eternal life (John 6:68).

Narrative 4: Final Days of Preparation of Disciples (14:1–17:27)
A report of John's death is found in all three synoptic Gospels (Matthew, Mark, and Luke), but briefer in Luke. Luke gives none of the details described in Matthew and Mark. Mark includes the sending out of the twelve disciples, which Matthew has included earlier in his Gospel (Mark 6:7–13).

While John's death is described here, chronologically his death actually occurred earlier on the time line. His imprisonment is mentioned in Matthew 4:12. The details given here are in light of the connection made by Herod about the possible return of John the Baptist. It was a common perception that some of the prophets would return to introduce the end of the age.

Discourse 4: Community—Humility and Forgiveness (18:1–35)
This discourse covers several topics vital to successful church community life. It is introduced by the topic of the previous narrative in which Jesus focuses His attention on the disciples, preparing them for His death and resurrection. In this discourse

Matthew takes the preparation of the disciples one step beyond the Resurrection, namely, on how they will live in a Christian community after Jesus is gone.

This discourse would have been essential for Matthew's readers in the late first century. They, as a community, had established themselves in new territory. In the same way, this discourse is also essential for churches today.

Narrative 5: Toward Jerusalem—The Final Week (19:1–22:46)
In the final week of Jesus' ministry, He continues to prepare His disciples for His death. His conflict with the Jewish leaders sharpens, leading up to exasperation and judgment on the scribes and Pharisees and on Jerusalem and the temple.

Discourse 5: The Apocalyptic Discourse (23:1–25:46)
There are four components to this discourse:
1. Jesus' Condemnation of the Scribes and Pharisees
2. The Destruction of Jerusalem Predicted by Jesus
3. Comments Regarding the End of the Age, or the End of the World
4. Warnings to Be Prepared for the Final End

Background & Context
Originally a talent was a measure of weight, but when applied to silver coinage it became an amount of money. One talent was equal to 6,000 denarii or 6,000 days' wages. Thus one talent was a considerable amount of money.

Narrative 6: The Messiah's Final Week (26:1–27:66)
This final narrative offers the account of the final days of Jesus' life, but also the climax of the Gospel—the passion (death, burial, and resurrection) of Jesus. In fact, some have described the substance of the Gospels as this upcoming passion narrative and the preceding chapters as simply an extended introduction to this narrative. Here you find the fulfillment of God's plan of salvation for humankind.

The Empty Tomb and Resurrection of Jesus (28:1–20)
Matthew 28 focuses chiefly on the final aspect of the Gospel narrative—the resurrection of Jesus. This is the climax of the Gospel story—Jesus' resurrection and His triumph over death and sin.

The narrative does not describe the actual resurrection of Jesus, only the results of the resurrection, namely

- The empty tomb and appearances of Jesus to the two women named Mary
- The narrative of the bribing of the Roman soldiers
- The appearance of Jesus before the disciples in Galilee and the giving of the Great Commission

Mark
Introduction to Mark

The book of Mark is the shortest of the four Gospels and is considered by many to be the oldest. It may well have served as a source for the Gospels of Matthew and Luke. Numerous church leaders (Papias, Irenaeus, Clement of Alexandria, Origen, Jerome, and others) associated this Gospel with John Mark, the disciple of Peter. It was the opinion of the early church that Mark recorded the Gospel that Peter preached.

Author

The writer of Mark never identifies himself, yet no serious suggestion of an author other than Mark has been put forward. John Mark was a young disciple who had traveled with Paul and Barnabas on their first missionary journey (Acts 13–14) but deserted them. His actions later caused such a rift between the two missionaries that they went their separate ways (Acts 15:36–41). Yet Mark's subsequent spiritual growth and faithfulness eventually earned Paul's trust once more (2 Timothy 4:11).

Occasion/Purpose

Mark probably wrote from Rome to an audience comprised primarily of Gentile Christians to provide them with a defense of the Gospel and encourage them in their faith. The content of the Gospel contains several indications of Mark's Roman and Gentile audience. He used ten Latin words, some of which are found nowhere else in scripture; he made a point to explain Jewish traditions; no genealogy is found for Jesus, as in Matthew and Luke; and he doesn't go into geographic or historic detail because his audience would not have been familiar with such Palestinian matters.

Themes

Several themes and emphases can be seen in Mark's Gospel, but foremost among them are Mark's positioning of Jesus as both Son of God and Son of Man.

- Son of God—Some scholars suggest that Mark 1:1 serves as a title to Mark's Gospel: "The beginning of the gospel of Jesus Christ, the Son of God" (esv). As soon as Jesus is mentioned, He is identified as the Son of God. Throughout His life, others confirm this fact about Jesus (1:11; 3:11; 9:7; 15:39). The title alone, however, would not have meant much to a Roman audience unless Jesus also displayed the power of God. So Mark wastes no time getting to the ministry of Jesus and His performance of many amazing miracles.
- Son of Man—Jesus never denied that He was the Son of God and the Messiah (Christ). However, His emphasis was not on power or politics, but on servanthood and suffering. So His preferred term of self-description was "Son of Man." Mark uses this title for Jesus

fourteen times—mostly while quoting Jesus Himself.

- "Son of Man" was a far less politically heated term, though certainly messianic, originating from Daniel's prophecy (Daniel 7:13–14). The Jewish people had been anticipating the arrival of a Messiah for centuries, but they were looking for a military figure to set them free from Roman domination. Throughout His ministry, Jesus slowly reinterpreted His Messianic ministry. He certainly had power, yet He refused to use His power against those in control. And His arrival did indeed bring freedom—not immediate victory over Roman rule, but spiritual triumph over fear and death available only through the suffering and sacrifice of the Son of Man. Half of Mark's Gospel (beginning with 8:31) is dedicated to Jesus' suffering, death, and resurrection.

Contribution to the Bible

About 95 percent of Mark is found in either Matthew or Luke. Yet Mark's Gospel has a fresh and immediate tone not to be missed. His writing has a fast flow of action, moving rapidly from story to story. He records details not found in the other Gospel accounts that make the events more vivid. For example, he frequently notes the emotional reactions and gestures of Jesus. Only two discourses of Jesus are provided (4:1–32 and 13:1–37) and only four parables (Matthew recorded eighteen parables, and Luke, nineteen). Yet Mark contains eighteen of Jesus' miracles—about the same number as Matthew and Luke. So Mark's Gospel gives us a bold, concise, action-filled look at Jesus' life.

Background & Context

The date of Mark's writing is debated. Some people have estimated that his Gospel could have been written as early as AD 45. Most, however, agree that it was written no later than AD 60 to 70.

Not long after the death of Jesus, persecution began to intensify for His followers. For a while the Roman authorities had paid little attention, assuming Christianity was just an offshoot of Judaism, which they had under control. But as the early church began to grow and spread out, believers experienced more and more conflicts with the Roman Empire. By the time of Mark's writing, persecution had become an ongoing concern, so he presented the life of Jesus to illustrate His willingness to suffer and sacrifice.

In the early to mid-60s (AD) the letters of Paul were beginning to circulate to the churches. It was also the time of Nero's reign, which brought more targeted persecution to believers. A horrendous, destructive fire broke out in Rome in AD 64, suspected to have been ordered by Nero himself, and further rumored to have been blamed on the Christians as a cover-up. In the wave of persecution that followed, Peter was among those martyred for their faith (AD 64 or 67).

Preparing for Something New (1:1–13)

Mark quickly moves from the appearance of Jesus on earth to His adult ministry. After eight verses about John the Baptist, Jesus is baptized and sets to work, calling disciples and healing.

Background & Context

People of Jesus' day would expect a messenger to precede the arrival of any important person. It was the messenger's job to: (1) ensure the roads were in proper repair; (2) arrange for food, lodging, and a proper reception of the dignitary; and (3) announce the arrival of the important person. John the Baptist performed the role of messenger prior to the appearance of Jesus.

Jesus' Ministry Begins (1:14–45)

As Mark begins his account of Jesus' ministry, he maintains a focus on Jesus' proclamation and demonstration of the nearness of the kingdom of God. Jesus proclaimed by teaching and preaching; He demonstrated by performing miracles. Mark wants his readers to see that Jesus is more than a prophet—He is the Messiah and the Son of God. As such, His ministry is powerful.

Background & Context

Synagogues may have originated during the Babylonian exile when the Jewish people had no access to the temple. A synagogue was not a place for sacrifice, but rather for reading the scriptures, praying, and worshipping God. The services were led by laymen, supervised by a board of elders, and presided over by a ruler. A synagogue could be organized anywhere there were ten or more Jewish men above the age of twelve.

A Ministry to the "Sick" (2:1–17)

Mark has wasted no time describing the immense popularity of Jesus as He begins His public ministry. But now Jesus does something that many cannot understand: Rather than associating with only the elite of the culture, He instead chooses to hang around with the outcasts of His society. He even selects members of this group to be included among His closest companions.

Conflict Intensifies (2:18–3:6)

In this section of his Gospel, Mark has collected five accounts to chronicle the growing conflict Jesus experienced with the religious leaders of Israel. We have already seen two: their reluctance to accept Jesus' authority to forgive the sin of the paralyzed man (2:1–12) and their disgust at his association with tax collectors and "sinners" (2:15–17). Now we look at three more conflicts and see how quickly the conflict escalated.

Fame and Followers (3:7–19)
Much of what Mark has already introduced is continued in this section. Crowds continue to vie for Jesus' attention as He continues to assemble a team of disciples to assist Him in His ministry. Yet Mark provides new bits of information with each new story.

Family and Foes (3:20–35)
Jesus' teachings were unlike anything the people of Israel had ever heard, and the reactions of the crowds toward Him were frequently unpredictable. Even those closest to Him didn't know what to think. In this section we see that, at times, Jesus' human family didn't respond to Him much differently than those who strongly opposed Him. Mark is here setting up his theme that while many of Jesus' own reject Him, outsiders and outcasts accept Him (John 1:11).

This is the first time Mark uses the literary device common to his Gospel called bracketing or sandwiching. In this section, Mark sandwiches one account in the middle of another. He brings two stories together to support the same point. In this case, it is to show that no one—not the religious leaders and not His own family—truly understood who Jesus was and what He came to do. Other examples of Mark's sandwiching in the Gospel are 4:1–20; 5:21–43; 6:7–29; 11:12–26; 14:1–11; 14:53–72.

The Parable of the Sower (4:1–25)
To this point, Mark has been providing a narrative account of Jesus' public ministry. Here, however, he inserts a series of Jesus' parables, the first being the Parable of the Sower. Mark's point is to announce the Gospel of Jesus Christ and to help explain why Jesus' message will receive mixed reviews.

More Parables about Seeds (4:26–34)
Mark follows Jesus' Parable of the Sower (4:1–25) with two more related parables about seeds. Both are short, yet each one provides a bit more information about the kingdom of God.

Jesus' Actions Verify His Teachings (4:35–5:20)
Mark follows three parables about the kingdom of God (the Sower, the Growing Seed, and the Mustard Seed) with accounts of four miracles of Jesus. The miracles are signs that the kingdom of God is near, revealing the power of Jesus as the Son of God. It would take a long time for people to truly understand, but from the beginning, Jesus' works vindicated His words.

Background & Context
The Sea of Galilee was—and still is—infamous for sudden squalls. Surrounded by mountains at most points, the waters swirl violently when a strong wind bears down. A storm can swell up with little advance warning.

A Planned and an Impromptu Miracle (5:21–43)

Mark has been presenting Jesus as the Son of God, and as such, the only way to salvation. He has just shown Jesus' power over nature (4:35–41) and over demons (5:1–20). He continues now by emphasizing Jesus' power over sickness and death.

Here is another example of Mark's sandwiching technique. In this case, he interposes the story of the woman with the bleeding disorder into the story of the healing of Jairus's daughter. (See note in Family and Foes above.)

Rejection Increases (6:1–30)

As more and more people who witnessed Jesus' ministry struggled with their faith, it was natural to expect a degree of rejection. We have seen that the Gentiles responded to Him in fear, the disciples are running hot and cold, and the Jews see Him as a miracle worker but are slow to respond in obedience and faith. This passage will provide some additional instances of rejection—a preview of what will become an increasing trend.

This section includes yet one more example of Mark's tendency to sandwich one story into another in order to make a point. In this case, both episodes—the news about John's death in the midst of the sending out of the disciples—demonstrate the role of a true disciple.

Background & Context

The Herod of this account was Herod Antipas, the tetrarch of Galilee and Perea from 4 BC to AD 39 (Luke 3:1). He should be distinguished from Herod the Great, his father, who was the Roman client-king of all Palestine from 40 BC to 4 BC and from Herod Agrippa I, who was client-king from AD 41–44. Herod is called "king" (Mark 6:14), but the title is a token of respect. Technically, Herod was only the regional governor.

An Unusual Stroll after an Unusual Meal (6:31–56)

Mark has just reported on the death of John the Baptist and the sending out of the apostles. Now he returns to focus on Jesus. With two more amazing miracles, Jesus is still trying to teach His disciples who He really is, yet they are still slow to comprehend.

Clarifying Some Twisted Laws (7:1–23)

Mark has just described a phenomenal response to Jesus' healing ministry (6:54–56). The stir concerning Jesus has led to the hope—if not outright belief—that the Messiah had arrived. But the ruling religious authorities would never support anyone who did not believe exactly as they did. The things Jesus did were always within the law God had given Moses, yet they did not always conform to the numerous laws that had been tacked on over the centuries. Consequently, a perpetual state of conflict resulted.

Overwhelmed with Amazement (7:24–37)

After Jesus' debate with the religious leaders over the issue of "clean" versus "unclean," Mark follows with two accounts of miracles in Gentile territory. Jesus is teaching that purity has more to do with the condition of one's heart than the adherence to legal rules and ceremonies. This concept will become clearer as a ministry to the Gentiles is initiated.

Repeat Performances (8:1–26)

Mark 8 includes events similar to those he's already recorded. Mark wanted the reader to see and understand that Jesus was more than a good teacher and was indeed the Lord of the universe. As the disciples witnessed repetition of His miracles, this truth was being reinforced in their lives.

The Beginning of the End (8:27–9:1)

This section of Mark records a significant transition. To this point, Jesus' disciples have witnessed (and even initiated) a number of miracles. They have not only heard Jesus teach, but have also been privy to His interpretation of parables and other private instruction. Yet Jesus has repeatedly pointed out their inability to comprehend exactly who He was and what He was doing. They haven't acted in faith when given the opportunity. But here they begin to understand. As they do, Jesus reveals more of what they can expect ahead of them.

The Uniqueness of the Christ (9:2–29)

Context is always important in Mark's Gospel. In the previous passage Jesus has been quite frank about His impending death. Yet from the beginning of his writing, Mark's goal has been to show that Jesus is the Son of God, and death would not be the end. Ultimately, Jesus would be glorified, and we see a preview of that in this section.

Greatness: An Example and Some Obstacles (9:30–50)

At this point, Mark indicates that Jesus' public ministry in Galilee is over. This trip through Galilee will be the first leg of His journey to Jerusalem and the cross.

The Heart of the Matter (10:1–31)

Every story in Mark 10 deals with the heart of a person (or group) who comes into contact with Jesus. Some hearts are filled with arrogance and self-interest, while others contain childlike faith and eagerness to serve God and His kingdom. This passage (Mark 10:1–31) covers three stories; the following passage (10:32–52) will examine two more.

Learning to See Straight (10:32–52)

As he did in the previous section (10:1–31), Mark continues to provide his readers with stories that reveal what is in the hearts of those who surrounded Jesus. While Jesus appears to know what people want from Him, He still encourages them to verbalize their desires before He responds.

Jesus' Final Trip to Jerusalem (11:1–10)

For a while now, Mark has emphasized that Jesus was deliberately moving toward Jerusalem, where He would suffer and die. In this section, He arrives on what will become the original Palm Sunday. The focus of Mark's Gospel is on the humility of Jesus during His entry into the city. In Jesus' humility, we begin to see the foundation for victory in our own Christian lives.

A Nonproductive Fig Tree and a Disrespectful Temple (11:11–26)

Upon reaching Jerusalem, it doesn't take Jesus long to begin to address things that need attention and correction. The improprieties He witnesses in the temple cause His immediate response, and His cursing of a fig tree serves to symbolize the unfruitful spiritual state of the religious leaders of His day.

This section includes yet one more example of Mark's tendency to sandwich or bracket one story into another in order to make a point. In this case, He first tells of Jesus cursing the fig tree, then moves on to His experience in the temple. Then Mark again returns to Jesus at the fig tree, stacking the image of the fruitless fig tree against the image of the fruitless religion found in the temple.

Controversies in the Temple, Part 1 (11:27–12:17)

This section begins a series of seven conflicts between Jesus and the religious authorities. (Three will be examined in this segment; four in the next one.) These stories show how Jesus refutes the errors of the Jewish leaders and why they reject Him. The accounts were also helpful for first-century readers in seeing how Jesus faced opposition to His teachings, something the early church had to do as well.

Controversies in the Temple, Part 2 (12:18–44)

The conflict between Jesus and those hoping to destroy His credibility continues in this section of Mark. The previous section (11:27–12:17) contained three separate controversies. But in the four that follow, we find a few positive examples amid the attempts to discredit Jesus.

Watch and Wait (13:1–13)

Mark 13 has been given a variety of names, including the eschatological discourse, the prophetic discourse, the Olivet discourse (since it was given on the Mount of Olives), and the "Little Apocalypse." Jesus foretells God's judgment, a great cataclysm in the world, and Jesus' eventual return. This passage is the longer of two of Jesus' extended discourses found in Mark's Gospel (the other being 4:1–34). At this point in Mark's account, Jesus begins to reveal to the disciples some of the specifics of what will happen as the ministry of the church begins to unfold in the world.

The End of the Age (13:14–37)

Whenever the return of Jesus is discussed, it's not unusual to find a number of different opinions. Mark reports what Jesus has to say, but it is interpreted in different ways by different people. This passage almost certainly refers to the coming siege of Jerusalem in AD 70. Even so, it's a debated passage that looks far ahead into our future.

A Final Meal Together (14:1–26)
Two days before the annual celebration of Passover and the Feast of Unleavened Bread, the opponents of Jesus are still looking for an opportunity to arrest and kill Jesus—and finally come up with a workable plan. Yet others are beginning to recognize who He is, acknowledging Him in verbal and more emphatic ways.

Arrested and Charged (14:27–72)
After all the predictions and preparations by Jesus, the time has finally come for His arrest and trial. The whole process, including His death and resurrection, will only take a weekend. Yet the emotional toll of dread, denial, betrayal, physical abuse, and everything else will be horrendous.

Jesus' Roman Trial (15:1–20)
Jesus has just been arrested, tried, and sentenced to death. Judas has betrayed Him, Peter has already denied Him three times, and the rest of His friends have deserted Him. That was the treatment He received from His own people. Now He has the Romans to deal with.

Jesus' Crucifixion, Death, and Burial (15:21–47)
The plot to have Jesus put to death is finally implemented. After a number of debates, disagreements, and outright conflicts with Jesus, the Jewish religious leaders finally get what they want. Yet even in His death, there is additional evidence that Jesus is who He claimed to be—the Messiah and the Son of God.

Between Death and Resurrection (16:1–8)
We are accustomed to moving quickly from any consideration of Jesus' death to the joy and certainty of His resurrection. But for His first-century disciples, the emotions following the death of their leader are dark and severe indeed. It is these emotions that help to put the significance of His resurrection into a clearer perspective.

An Addendum to the Gospel of Mark (16:9–20)
Most Bible scholars feel that the Gospel of Mark ended at 16:8 and that verses 9–20 were added considerably later to smooth out the abrupt ending. Although these closing verses are not considered to be part of the scriptures to the extent of the rest of Mark's Gospel, they are an honest attempt to complete the story of Jesus.

Luke
Introduction to Luke

As author of this Gospel and its sequel, the book of Acts, Luke is responsible for over a fourth of the content of the Greek New Testament. He brings a distinctive perspective to the writing as well. While many of Jesus' followers had the reputation of "unschooled, ordinary men" (Acts 4:13 NIV), Luke's writing in his opening paragraph displays the sophisticated style of Greek historians, and then he moves into smooth, everyday vernacular. His eye for detail is evident in numerous places.

Author

Luke doesn't identify himself in either of the books he wrote, but there has been little dispute that he was the author of both. He was a physician (Colossians 4:14) and notes specifics in several of Jesus' healings that other writers do not. Aside from the Colossians reference, Luke is mentioned only two other times in the New Testament (2 Timothy 4:11; Philemon 24). People have theorized that he might have been Lucius of Cyrene (Acts 13:1), one of the seventy-two disciples sent out by Jesus (Luke 10:1–17), one of the Greeks mentioned in John 12:20, or even the other disciple with Cleopas on the road to Emmaus (Luke 24:13–35). But there is no biblical or historic evidence for any of these speculations.

More reliable is the assumption that Luke knew Jesus' mother, Mary. Therefore, his Gospel includes the wonderful account of the shepherds visiting the manger, the story of Elizabeth and Zechariah and the birth of John the Baptist, the mention of Simeon and Anna when Jesus was presented in the temple, and the story of Jesus questioning the religious leaders in the temple at age twelve (Luke 1–2).

Luke also traveled on some of Paul's journeys, which is evident from passages in the book of Acts that switch from third person to first person. And he must have been more than a mere acquaintance because Paul refers to him as a dear friend (Colossians 4:14).

Occasion/Purpose

Evidence points to Luke being a Gentile believer who wrote for a Gentile audience. The primary recipient of both his books was "most excellent Theophilus" (Luke 1:3 NIV; Acts 1:1), a title that suggests someone of wealth and authority—perhaps a ranking official. Luke tended to give details about Jewish locations that wouldn't have been necessary for Jewish readers. These and other clues suggest that Luke's intent was explaining the story of Jesus to Gentiles.

Theophilus may have been a financial backer for Luke's travels and/or writing. However, while he may have been the first recipient of Luke's words about Jesus, it isn't likely he was intended to be the sole reader. Theophilus had already heard about Jesus; Luke was writing to confirm the authenticity and validity of the Gospel. Luke began with eyewitness accounts and then personally investigated them to ensure accuracy (1:1–4). He showed that the faith of Theophilus—and all those who believed in Jesus Christ—had a strong foundation.

Themes

In his concern for Gentiles, Luke's portrayal of the Gospel is more encompassing than that of the other Gospel writers. He stresses an individual's privilege and ability to repent and be forgiven—and the joy that results from each such decision (15:7, 10, 32).

Numerous Samaritans, women, children, Roman officials, and other traditional outsiders are shown in positive light, providing a natural segue into his book of Acts and the worldwide mission of the church. Luke alone tells of the thief on the cross who repents and is promised a place in paradise with Jesus (23:39–43).

Luke had a high regard for women, as seen in stories such as the faith of Elizabeth (1:5–80), Anna in the temple (2:36–38), and the dilemma between Mary and Martha (10:38–42). He records Jesus' gentle words toward women of faith (7:13; 8:48; 13:12, 15–16; 23:28–31), and he credits the women who traveled with Jesus and supported Him (8:1–3). In doing so, Luke introduces his readers to thirteen women who appear nowhere else in scripture.

Luke has much to say about money. More accurately, he records much of what Jesus had to say about wealth that other writers didn't include. For example, Luke is the only source for Jesus' Parable of the Rich Man and Lazarus (16:19–31). He also tells of how first the twelve disciples, and then another seventy-two, were sent out with no provisions in order to see for themselves that God would provide (9:1–6; 10:1–17). And the theme of money is carried throughout the Gospel, as he notes attitudes toward the poor as well as toward the rich.

Though he doesn't usually elaborate, Luke also highlights the prayer habits of Jesus (3:21–22; 5:16; 6:12; 22:41–44; etc.). Because of His example, Jesus' disciples began to ask about improving their own prayer habits (11:1).

Contribution to the Bible

Over half of Luke's Gospel contains content found nowhere else in scripture. In addition to what has already been mentioned (Elizabeth and Zechariah, the Nativity stories, Jesus at age twelve, the repentant thief on the cross, the Rich Man and Lazarus, etc.), Luke includes seven miracles of Jesus and nineteen of His parables that are unique to this Gospel.

Were it not for Luke's Gospel, we would miss out on many of the most-read and appreciated portions of scripture: the parables of the Good Samaritan (10:30–37) and the Prodigal Son (15:11–32), Jesus' visit to see Zacchaeus (19:1–10), one of the accounts of a resurrection from the dead (7:11–17), the healing of the ten lepers (17:12–19), the two disciples on the road to Emmaus after Jesus' resurrection (24:13–35), Jesus' "Father forgive them" prayer from the cross (23:34), and more.

On a related note, Luke tended to notice and record the artistic, poetic expressions of the people he researched. He alone includes the songs of Elizabeth (1:41–45), Mary (1:46–55), Zechariah (1:67–79), Simeon (2:29–32), and even the angels announcing Jesus' birth (2:13–14).

A Miracle Birth—Before Jesus' (1:1–80)

Luke begins his Gospel of Jesus not with the account of Jesus' birth, but with the announcement of the miraculous, approaching birth of John the Baptist. The Jewish people had been told to expect the coming of Elijah prior to the arrival of their Messiah (Malachi 4:5–6). John the Baptist would fulfill the Elijah role of preparing for and announcing the coming of Jesus (Matthew 11:11–14). And Zechariah and Elizabeth prove to be dedicated and influential parents just as Mary and Joseph were.

Background & Context

Luke establishes times within his Gospel by citing rulers of the period (1:5; 2:1-2; 3:1; etc.). However, the actual date of his writing is difficult to determine. Neither of his books makes reference to the fall of Jerusalem (AD 70) or even Nero's persecution of the early Christians (AD 64). It is commonly estimated that Luke was written after Mark, which was probably written in the mid to late 60s.

The Arrival of the Messiah (2:1–52)

Luke interweaves the birth stories of Jesus and John the Baptist. In the previous passage he provided the angelic foretelling of both miraculous births, and provided the story of John's birth. In this passage, he moves on to the details of Jesus' birth and early life.

Luke 2 has three major sections. Verses 1–20 depict the birth of Jesus and the worship and witness of the shepherds. Verses 21–40 feature an account of the presentation of Jesus at Jerusalem, and the inspired testimony of Simeon and Anna. Verses 41–52 describe Jesus' visit to the temple, His Father's house, busy with His Father's business.

Two Ministries Begin (3:1–38)

The first four chapters of Luke's Gospel intertwine the accounts of the birth of both John and Jesus, along with significant childhood events. Thus, when we come to the ministry of John the Baptist in chapter 3, we are finding John in the spotlight, as he has been before, as the forerunner of the Messiah. In fact, all four Gospels begin Jesus' public ministry with the ministry of John the Baptist.

Background & Context

A "winnowing fork" (3:17 NIV) was a shovel-like tool used to toss grain into the air so the outer chaff would either fall and be burned or blow away in the wind and only the good wheat would remain. This was a familiar process in an agrarian community of the first century.

Temptation, Rejection, and Healing (4:1–44)

After Jesus' baptism (3:21–22), He is tempted by the devil for a period of forty days. There are several reasons why the temptation accounts are of importance to us. From the standpoint of Jesus' ministry and calling, His mission is contingent upon His victory over every temptation of Satan. Also, by studying the temptation of our Lord by Satan, we learn a great deal about our adversary, Satan, and the means by which we can withstand his attacks.

Afterward Jesus begins a public ministry of teaching and healing, and quickly becomes a well-known and popular figure. . .except in Nazareth, where He had been raised.

Choosing Disciples and Defining Disciplines (5:1–6:11)

If Luke chapter 4 focused on the ministry of Jesus to the masses, chapter 5 begins to focus on the ministry of Jesus with respect to the leadership of Israel. So far in Luke's account, Jesus has been portrayed as a solitary teacher moving from place to place, teaching in the synagogues. In this passage He begins to call disciples to travel with Him in His ministry of teaching and healing. But when He and His disciples don't conform to established norms, they soon encounter opposition.

Background & Context

Tax collectors such as Levi were not only often dishonest, but they were a painful reminder of the fact that Israel was not a free nation, but subject to Roman rule and authority.

A Different Way of Seeing the World (6:12–49)

This passage contains Luke's parallel to Matthew's Sermon on the Mount. The two versions contain many similarities but more than a few distinct differences. Luke has recently provided a number of accounts of Jesus' encounters with the Pharisees and has shown how legalistic attitudes had twisted the intended meaning of the Gospel. Here Jesus provides His own outlook on how people should live.

It's important to read Jesus' words in terms of the principles of the law, not just specific actions. For instance, Jesus' teaching on "turning the other cheek" is not simply a mechanical kind of response to a right cross punch, but a principle that should govern our relationships with our enemies. We honor the sermon best when we apply it in the broad strokes of our lives.

Saving Faith and a Faithful Savior (7:1–50)

At this point in Luke's narrative, Jesus has been in public ministry for a while. Yet He is still coming across people who stand out from others in the crowd. A Roman centurion displays faith greater than any witnessed in Israel. A woman recognizes the significance of Jesus and anoints Him. And Jesus gives tribute to the faithful ministry of John the Baptist.

Parables, Miracles, and Family Matters (8:1–56)

Jesus' ministry has become very active. He is teaching the crowds, training His disciples, healing all kinds of diseases, casting out evil spirits, and even performing an occasional phenomenal miracle or resurrection of the dead. In this passage Luke records a bit of each of these aspects of Jesus' ministry, along with brief mentions of His supporters and family.

As we look more closely at the description of the ministry of Jesus in the Gospels, we discover that very soon the party that accompanies our Lord becomes quite large. One of the few texts that informs us about this large group is Luke 8. In addition, Luke informs us about the vital role a large number of women play in supporting the ministry of Jesus and His disciples.

Highs and Lows of Ministry (9:1–62)

Any business or ministry that undergoes rapid growth will almost always experience corresponding problems. Jesus' ministry is no exception. In this passage the apostles are given more responsibility, resulting in some successes as well as some failures. Some of them are beginning to see Jesus for who He really is, yet argue about which of them is the greatest. Jesus is still popular with crowds, but now has Herod's attention as well. Meanwhile, His miracles continue.

Seventy-Two Missionaries, a Good Samaritan, and Sibling Rivalry (10:1–42)

Luke chapter 9 is the immediate backdrop for our text in chapter 10. It began with the sending out of the twelve disciples. The report of Herod's concern with the identity of Jesus is followed by the feeding of the five thousand. After this, Peter's great confession is recorded, followed immediately by the transfiguration of Jesus.

The first words of verse 1 in chapter 10 ("After this. . .") show the close link between the sending out of the seventy and the preceding context. The sending out of the seventy disciples is thus related both to the sending out of the Twelve (9:1–6) and the Lord's instruction on discipleship (9:37–62).

Just as Jesus has sent out the Twelve in pairs to experience firsthand ministry (9:1–6), He now sends out seventy-two more. They are thrilled with what they learned from this teaching method. Jesus also teaches an expert of the Law with a classic parable and teaches two sisters an important lesson on priorities.

Prayer, Demons, Signs, and Woes (11:1–54)

People are beginning to respond to Jesus' ministry in various ways. He has preached and healed, but has also taught by personal example. Now His disciples begin to ask about how to pray. Onlookers speculate as to how He casts out demons. People start to expect fantastic signs from Him. And the Pharisees increase their opposition to Him.

Up to this point, the emphasis of Luke has fallen on the prayer life of Jesus. But here a certain unnamed disciple sees the Lord's practice as a pattern, one that each disciple should follow, and thus Jesus is asked to teach the disciples to pray as well. The prayer life that characterizes our Lord will, in the book of Acts, characterize the disciples as well. Luke is paving the way, laying the foundation for that constant communion with God in prayer.

Warnings and Assurances (12:1–59)

After having just publicly confronted the Pharisees and teachers of the Law, Luke moves to an instance where Jesus gives specific instructions to His apostles about the problems of hypocrisy. He also addresses proper stewardship of the Gospel, possessions, and the use of our time.

Clearing Up Some Misconceptions (13:1–35)

In this passage Luke describes Jesus in a number of settings. He is still healing and teaching, but the tone of His message has changed. He speaks of punishment, weeping, gnashing of teeth, and the coming desolation of Jerusalem. Yet He also tells of God's patience and the ongoing opportunities for people to participate in God's rapidly growing kingdom.

Banquet Etiquette (14:1–35)

In recent passages, Jesus has been teaching some difficult lessons, and He continues in this one—once at a dinner and again while beset by crowds as He travels. Much of what He says is easy to understand, even though His listeners might be reluctant to acknowledge it. Some of His teachings are, and have always been, a bit difficult to comprehend without considerable thought and reflection.

Lost and Found—Times Three (15:1–32)

Jesus' debate with the Pharisees continues in this passage. They cite a complaint, and Jesus responds by telling three seemingly related parables, including what has become known as the Parable of the Prodigal Son. But on closer examination, the three parables—each of which describes the finding of a lost item, and each of which describes the joy and celebration that resulted—aren't as similar as they first appear.

Two Challenging Parables (16:1–31)

The entire 16th chapter of Luke revolves around one's attitude toward and use of material possessions. This subject is one that Luke has been speaking to throughout this Gospel. What we find in chapter 16 is not the final word on the subject, but it is more specific in its application than previous references.

Jesus continues to teach His disciples, aware that the Pharisees are listening in on everything He is saying. The Pharisees are lovers of money, so Jesus tells two parables about rich men. One man has a crooked employee he is about to fire, and the other finds himself suffering in hell after a lifetime of selfish luxury.

Faith, Service, and Expectation (17:1–37)

At first this passage may not seem to have much coherence between the topics:

- Not causing your brother or sister to sin—17:1–2
- What to do when your brother or sister sins—17:3–4
- Faith and the disciple—17:5–10
- The healing of the ten lepers and the gratitude of one—17:11–19
- The coming of the kingdom of God— 17:20–37

It takes some effort to determine what the relationship is between these "parts" of the whole. Yet, in the context of Jesus' recent debates and confrontations with the Pharisees, it is likely that His teaching and healing is being done here in full awareness of their prying eyes and listening ears. So what He says and does can be interpreted in light of increasing opposition from Israel's religious leaders.

Persistence and Penitence (18:1–43)
In this section Jesus continues teaching His disciples about the kingdom of God. He uses a number of contrasts to teach some important lessons. He contrasts a persistent widow with a self-centered judge, a Pharisee and a tax collector, little children and annoyed adults, and the priorities of the kingdom of God with those of a wealthy young man. He also continues to heal the sick as He approaches Jerusalem to face His death.

Last Journey to Jerusalem (19:1–48)
Not even halfway through his Gospel, Luke wrote: "As the time approached for him to be taken up to heaven, Jesus resolutely set out for Jerusalem" (9:51 NIV). All the events of Luke 10–18 have occurred along the way.

The subject of the coming kingdom of God has been in view since the Pharisees first asked in chapter 17 about when it would come. In chapter 18, the focus changed from the timing and circumstances of the coming kingdom to who would enter into it. Jesus taught that those who would enter His kingdom would not be those who expected to enter. And so the self-righteous Pharisee is not justified, but the penitent tax collector is (18:9–14). Jesus taught His disciples that while the rich young ruler, and those like him, would have much difficulty getting into the kingdom (18:18–27), those who were childlike would possess it (18:15–17).

And in this section, Jesus finally arrives in Jerusalem. As the time of His death nears, His teachings and actions seem to become more intentional and direct.

Questions of Authority (20:1–47)
Jesus has arrived in Jerusalem to spend the final week of His human life. He has, by His actions, announced His identity as Israel's Messiah. He possessed the donkey (19:29–34), the praises of the people (19:35–44), and finally His temple (19:45–48).

Up to this point, the principle source of opposition to Jesus has been from the party of the Pharisees, who seem to have been dogging the heels of the Savior from very early on in His ministry (see 5:21 and following). Both the Pharisees and Sadducees (teachers of the law or scribes) were political/religious parties, and members from both groups served on the Sanhedrin (the official leadership of Israel). The Sadducees had their primary powerbase in Jerusalem and among the priestly hierarchy, and the Pharisees appear to have been more influential among the synagogue communities, but both were present in Jerusalem.

It is at the Lord's possession of His temple in Luke 19:45 that we see the torch of opposition to Jesus being passed from the Pharisee party to the priests, the scribes, and the elders (20:1). The Jerusalem leaders may not have been overly concerned with Jesus' ministry and influence in the outlying parts of Israel, but became threatened when Jesus invaded their turf. They wanted to stop Him, but the Lord's popularity with the masses was too great to ignore or to challenge (19:48). Thus, they waited for their chance. Their first attack came in the form of an official challenge to the authority by which Jesus did the things He had done (20:2).

The issue that underlies this entire section of scripture is that of authority.

Background & Context

This is Luke's first mention of the Sadducees, a priestly aristocracy who focused more on political matters than religious ones. In addition to not believing in resurrection of the dead, they downplayed the existence of angels and spirits, and they only viewed as authoritative the books of Moses (the first five books of the Old Testament). The traditions and interpretations of the Pharisees meant little to them. Because of their refusal to believe in resurrection, we hear more about them in the book of Acts—*after* the death and resurrection of Jesus. We also hear about them more in Acts because their power base was in Jerusalem, where the church was established, rather than Galilee, where most of Jesus' early ministry was conducted.

The Future: Indications and Instructions (21:1–38)

Jesus and His disciples have arrived in Jerusalem, and Jesus has begun to teach at the temple every day. His time is short, and He is trying to give special attention to His followers. Yet each day large numbers of people arise early and show up at the temple to hear what He has to say.

It seems these four verses are placed here by Luke in contrast to the Pharisees, to show how God's ways differ so greatly from those of men. The Pharisees loved riches, and they viewed wealth as an evidence of piety. God, in their minds, would be impressed by the wealthy, and would be especially pleased by the size of their contributions.

Background & Context

Herod's temple was not only a magnificent work of architecture but it was also built to accommodate Jewish sensitivities. Since only priests were allowed in certain parts of the interior, one thousand of them were trained to do the masonry and carpentry in those portions. Temple service was never interrupted from the beginning of construction in 20-19 BC through the completion of the surrounding buildings and courts in AD 64. Yet all that beautiful white marble fell in ruins in AD 70.

Betrayal, Denial, Arrest, and Anguish (22:1–65)
Luke's Gospel moves abruptly from Jesus' teaching in the temple after His triumphal entry to the events leading to His crucifixion. Remember the broader setting in which the Last Supper is found. The Jewish religious leaders in Jerusalem have already determined that Jesus must die. After He cleansed the temple, the sparks really began to fly, with the religious leaders making every effort to discredit Him or to get Him into trouble with the Roman authorities (Luke 20:19–20). When these efforts, as well as their attempts to penetrate the ranks of our Lord's disciples, miserably failed, the chief priests were delighted to have Judas approach them with his offer. It was only a matter now of waiting for the right chance.

Jesus' Trials and Crucifixion (22:66–23:56)
After Jesus' betrayal by Judas, arrest in Gethsemane, and denial by Peter, He undergoes a series of trials where He is rejected by both the Jews and the Gentiles. It seems that Pilate tries, but fails, to spare His life.

He is crucified between two thieves and buried in a borrowed tomb. The events surrounding the death of our Lord, as described by Luke, fall into several distinct sections. The first of these is the Via Dolorosa ("Way of Sorrow"), the way to the cross, described in verses 26–32. The second is the actual crucifixion scene, the events surrounding the execution of our Lord, taking place on Calvary, in verses 33–43. The final section, in verses 44–49, is the account of the death of our Lord, along with Luke's description of the impact of these events on some of those who witnessed it—namely, the centurion, the crowd, and the women who had accompanied Jesus from Galilee.

Resurrection and Second Chances (24:1–53)
After the bleakness and despair of Jesus' horrid crucifixion, His followers have an assortment of amazing epiphanies. The women discover an empty tomb and angelic messengers announcing His resurrection. Two disciples on the road have a conversation that causes their hearts to "burn" before they realize their fellow traveler is Jesus Himself. And finally the apostles get to see Jesus and hear His explanation for everything that had happened. Consequently, even the absence of Jesus' physical presence would not deter their worship and praise of God.

John
Introduction to John

While the Gospels of Matthew, Mark, and Luke are identified together as the *synoptic* Gospels because of their similarities, the Gospel of John stands apart in style and in content. John's style is simple in vocabulary, yet it is profound and even sometimes poetic. As for content, he records events that the synoptic Gospels don't. Jesus' teaching also has a different focus. In the synoptic Gospels, Jesus' teaching focuses on the kingdom of God, but in John His teaching centers more on His own identity and how His presence manifests God the Father.

Author
The author of this Gospel does not identify himself by name, though he is referred to as the disciple "whom Jesus loved." Through the years, a variety of possible authors have been proposed, yet the apostle John, of the original twelve disciples, still seems the most likely candidate.

Occasion/Purpose
John states his purpose for writing in the Gospel's closing (see 20:30–31). The central theme of this Gospel is Jesus' revelation of God the Father and the connection that revelation enables between humanity and God. This Gospel is a call to faith as well as an encouragement to those continuing in their faith.

Themes
The book of John addresses the theme of who Jesus really is. Jesus' authority and power as deity are expanded upon and "proved" by witnesses of his awesome power. John also touches on themes of man's corruption and spiritual ignorance. This book draws on the two areas of Jesus' ministry as well: his public ministry of speaking to the masses, and his private ministry to followers such as Lazarus and his sisters.

The Prologue or Introduction to the Gospel of John (1:1–18)
This first chapter of John is a summary of the message of the entire Gospel—Jesus has come as the light of the world, and some reject and others accept. The first eighteen verses of chapter 1 offer an outline of his letter. Each topic that John will show us about Christ is introduced in these first verses.
1. The Deity of Christ (1:1–5)
2. The Forerunner of Christ (1:6–8)
3. The Rejection of Christ (1:9–11)
4. The Acceptance of Christ (1:12–13)
5. The Incarnation of Christ (1:14–18)

These topics represent the foundation of Christianity.

The Witnesses (1:19–51)
This first account begins with John the Baptist and the inquisition of the

religious establishment. It introduces the first of many question-and-answer times with the Jewish leadership.

Background & Context
Throughout history, before a great move of God, the people were to consecrate themselves (cleansing and setting themselves apart from sin) so they would be prepared. For John the Baptist, the cleansing was accomplished through repentance. The setting apart was accomplished through baptism.

The Public Ministry of Jesus (2:1–25)
Chapter 1 focused on the words of testimony about Jesus. Now Jesus' actual works witness to the truth that He is the Messiah:

- Seven miracles—all of which show the glory of God dwelling in Jesus' body
- Seven "I Am" statements—which are Jesus' declaration of Himself
- Four interviews—in which Jesus discusses with people about Himself
- Various discourses—in which Jesus explains the Gospel to individuals

All of this is given to provide a testimony that Jesus Christ is the self-revelation of God.

Background & Context
Weddings in first-century Judea were big affairs. Generally they lasted about a week, even longer if the family was wealthy. Every night there was a party, and every night they would parade the couple around town in their wedding clothes. Usually, in the middle of the week, the couple would actually have the ceremony and then spend the rest of the week with the family before they could be alone.

A wedding was an important part of life, for it was the time when the family members of the groom would establish themselves by the type of party that they would throw. If people had a bad time at the wedding—if they did not get enough food to eat or wine to drink—it would reflect poorly on the family. Poorly enough for even the bride's family to think, *What kind of family did we just release our daughter into?*

Running out of wine was a critical situation (2:3) at a first-century wedding. Notice that Mary alerts Jesus to the problem. This might mean that the family was related to Mary, so she was "in the know" on a problem like this.

A Meeting at Night (3:1–36)

This passage of scripture includes some of the most popular verses in the Christian world. John 3 is the most quoted chapter from the New Testament, and holds within it one of the first verses ever memorized by many American Sunday school children, John 3:16.

This text is popular not only because it sets forth for us the great love of God for humanity, but also because it lays out, in very direct terms, the Gospel message. Therefore, it is a treasured chapter in the scriptures for its concise teaching of the nature of humanity, the need for regeneration, and the nature of the Messiah and His great love and work for humanity. We find here a very clear presentation of the Gospel and the essentials of salvation and faith.

A Meeting by the Well (4:1–54)

The Gospel writer John is continuing to show us that Jesus is the revelation of God the Father, and in this text, he uses Christ's conversation with a Samaritan woman.

The Position of Jesus (5:1–47)

The struggle that we experience individually as we seek to surrender ourselves to God's will is similar to what plagued Jesus' relationship with the religious leaders of His day. As He exercised His authority as God, the religious leaders became increasingly angry—not wanting to believe Him to be God or to have authority over them—and desired to kill Him. They did not want a new leader to work outside of their system. They didn't want a new way of doing things. Therefore, when Jesus required them to submit to Him, they rejected Him. This conflict became the source of the anger that built in the Pharisees and caused them to seek to kill Jesus.

Revealing Himself (6:1–71)

Chapter 6 continues within the ministry of Jesus in Galilee, and it provides the same basic structure as chapter 5. In chapter 5 we see Jesus performing a miracle and using that miracle to proclaim His deity as Lord of the Sabbath. In chapter 6 we see Jesus performing a miracle and then using that miracle as a platform to proclaim His deity as the Bread of life.

Challenges to Respond To (7:1–8:11)

From chapter 7 of the Gospel of John, the focus is more on the reaction of the people to Jesus. A theme from this point on will be people's inability to understand who Jesus is.

Another theme that runs throughout this Gospel is Jesus' divine timetable. John will show that Jesus' will only happens at God's appointed time.

Jesus Is the Messiah (8:12–59)

For eight chapters John has been detailing the claims of Jesus Christ. Jesus has given sufficient evidence that He is the Messiah. He has declared Himself the object of the Passover, the object of the Feast of Tabernacles, the source of light, the source of life, the source of eternal life, and the only way to heaven. Jesus has backed up His claims with the miracles that the scriptures said would accompany the Messiah.

How have the Jews responded? The crowds have seemed motivated to follow Jesus as long as He fed them and healed them. Unfortunately, in the following chapters, what has started as a hope that Jesus is the Messiah, will, by the end of chapter 8, turn to an attempt to murder Jesus.

At this point, Jesus changes from a public presentation of Himself to a public condemnation of Israel. This is a turning point in the Gospel of John. Israel is being chastised for her rejection of the Messiah.

The Blind Man (9:1–41)
Chapter 9 is a key chapter in the Gospel of John because it serves two purposes. First, it serves as a theological summary of the entire Gospel of John. Second, it is a transition between Jesus' public ministry to Israel and His public condemnation of Israel. Because the leaders reject Jesus as God and the Messiah, Jesus will condemn them. Because they failed to honor Jesus as Lord and Messiah, they will suffer the consequences.

In this section of John's Gospel, made up of seven signs or miracles, the healing of the man born blind is the sixth sign.

Jesus Confronts the Leadership (10:1–42)
Jesus is continuing to answer the question that was asked by the Pharisees in 9:40. They wanted to know if they were blind, and they are. And because they are blind, chapter 10 goes on to explain, they are not the true shepherds of Israel. Instead, they are false shepherds that harm the sheep.

Verse 22 marks the end of a very important part of the life of Jesus. In the last part of this chapter, Jesus will end His public ministry to the leaders of Israel, and begin His private ministry to the disciples.

Though this is the last in a series of confrontations between Jesus and the leaders of Israel, the same theme emerges: The leaders question Jesus, and Jesus declares that He is God. The dialogue will cover the same ground covered in the past several chapters, yet the religious leaders remain unconvinced.

The Private Ministry of Jesus (11:1–57)
The issue here is faith. As a group of people struggle with death, the ultimate conqueror, will they believe that Jesus is even more powerful than death? The disciples believe that Jesus is going to die when He goes back to Judea. The sisters of Lazarus believe that death has conquered their brother. It seems it has not yet occurred to anyone that Jesus' power is greater than death.

The Faithless and the Faithful (12:1–50)
In the previous chapter Jesus raised Lazarus from the dead, revealing Himself to be the resurrection and the life. This miracle created a lot of attention for Jesus,

which increased the anxiety of the religious leaders over Jesus' ministry.

This passage begins with a contrast of a faithful heart, Mary, and a deceitful heart, Judas.

Final Words (13:1–38)

Chapter 13 begins a very concentrated description of the love of God as seen through the sacrifice of Jesus.

The Passover was a celebration that pointed in two directions. It pointed backward to the great exodus from Egypt, God's deliverance. But it also pointed forward to God's final salvation. Isaiah and other Old Testament prophets described a new and greater exodus that God will accomplish when He delivers His people and establishes His kingdom (Isaiah 11:10–16; 40:1–5).

Jesus is that once-for-all Passover Lamb who will accomplish this new exodus. Jesus knows that He is about to die and become the fulfillment of what the Passover meal pointed to. John tells us that Jesus is fully aware of what is taking place (13:1).

Background & Context

In that day people usually wore sandals. Walking on dusty, sometimes filthy, roads would make their feet dirty. It was the role of the lowest slave to actually clean the feet of the guests as they arrived. At the home the disciples used for this meal, there were no servants, and therefore, their feet did not get washed.

In verse 10, Jesus responds to Peter's request for a bath (13:8-9) with a principle of forgiveness. If a person has taken a bath before he goes to a gathering at someone's house, when he arrives he does not need to get an entire bath again. All he needs is to have the dust of his feet washed off. The rest of his body is already clean. The point—you do not need to go beyond what Jesus offers for salvation. His work is enough for a lifetime. That is why it is a perfect love.

The point of Jesus' explanation of the foot washing is for these men to understand their roles in a new way (13:12-17). The example that Jesus has set is that of humility. True love is an enduring love that seeks to serve others at expense to self. The only way for the world to see what Jesus did to save humankind is for His followers to model before the world that kind of humility.

Hope for the Discouraged (14:1–31)

Jesus is giving His final address before His death. Some have compared His words to Moses' last address to his people before his death (Deuteronomy 31–33).

In this passage, Jesus offers some very specific encouragement regarding the Spirit of God, and the role He will play in the lives of the disciples. Then, in the following chapters (15–16), He offers instructions on how He wants them to act, and speaks of the persecution they are to expect from this point on.

Final Instructions (15:1–27)

Central to the heart of Jesus' message, and especially clear in the Gospel of John, is the fact that Jesus declares that He is what the Old Testament longed for. Jesus is the resolution. He is the one promised as early as Genesis 3:15, the great redeemer of humanity.

Chapter 15 moves from Jesus' first discourse of encouragement to His second discourse of instruction.

A Helper for Difficult Days (16:1–33)

In the last several chapters, Jesus has warned the disciples about the difficulties they will face. John 16 continues on this same topic. This way, when these men face the persecution Jesus has described, they will not be surprised. In fact, it could confirm their faith.

Jesus' Prayer (17:1–26)

This chapter offers a pre-cross preview of the post-cross work of Jesus: the work of intercession—praying on behalf of believers. Jesus prays for Himself, for His disciples, and for believers of every age and every generation. His prayers reveal even more about the beautiful relationship between Jesus and the Father.

Jesus' Trials (18:1–40)

Chapters 18–21 make up the final section of the Gospel of John—the death and resurrection of Jesus. John's focus in this account remains true to the rest of the Gospel—even in the account of the crucifixion, Jesus reveals the Father. This is not the picture of a weak and feeble man who is being taken by surprise by the events. Instead, the point here is that Jesus is actually in control of all of the events that are going on.

This is Jesus' moment. It is God's plan and not the plan of the Jews. The death of Jesus was ultimately the will of God—John's Gospel makes this clear.

Jesus' Death (19:1–42)

Pilate will try over and over again to get rid of Jesus. He has already tried in chapter 18. He put Jesus up against a real insurrectionist named Barabbas, but the accusers chose Barabbas. Therefore, Pilate will attempt to avoid having to face Jesus and having to come to a point of action concerning Him.

Jesus Conquers Death (20:1–31)

Jesus controlled death; death did not control Jesus. He died in humanity's place and then rose from the dead, conquering the bondage of death. John's Gospel offers evidence that Jesus rose from the dead and, therefore, if we believe in the person and work of Jesus, we will have life.

Epilogue (21:1–25)

Chapter 21 is the epilogue of this great Gospel. Jesus gives His disciples a living illustration that He is their provider, and that He is the sovereign Lord of the universe.

In Peter's restoration, we learn what it means to love Jesus and what it means to follow Jesus. This becomes a fitting conclusion of the Gospel of John.

John offers this final account of one of Jesus' post-resurrection appearances to not only confirm the resurrection of Jesus, but to also illustrate one last time the fact that Jesus is truly the manifestation of God.

Acts
Introduction to Acts

One of the earliest titles for this book of the Bible was simply "Acts," with other early titles being "Acts of Apostles," "Acts of the Holy Apostles," and the popular "The Acts of the Apostles," which wasn't really accurate. The acts of Peter and Paul are highlighted in this book, yet many of the other apostles are hardly mentioned. A more accurate title might be "The Acts of the Holy Spirit," but many modern Bibles have reverted to simply using "Acts" as the title.

Author
As was the case with his Gospel, Luke doesn't identify himself as the writer of Acts, though his authorship is seldom questioned. The information he provided in the book of Luke was a result of his research to verify the testimony of eyewitnesses (Luke 1:1–4). His involvement in Acts is even more personal. Much of this book, like Luke's Gospel, is written in the third person. But certain sections (16:10–17; 20:5–15; 21:1–18; 27:1–28:16) switch to first person. It is evident that Luke accompanied Paul on various legs of his missionary journeys.

Luke was a doctor (Colossians 4:14) who had an eye for detail. He seems particularly interested in seafaring, and he provides vivid descriptions as he narrates. Many of his first-person accounts are when Paul is traveling by ship.

Occasion/Purpose
Like his Gospel, Luke's book of Acts is addressed to Theophilus (1:1). The purpose of the Gospel account was "so that you may know the exact truth about the things you have been taught" (Luke 1:4 NASB). With his follow-up book of Acts, Luke is sending his primary recipient (and perhaps his financial sponsor) a well-researched account of the spread of Christianity throughout both Jewish and Gentile communities. Since Luke was personally involved in the growth of the church, he was able to provide both an insightful historical overview and a corresponding apologetic emphasis.

Each of the four Gospel accounts provides a distinctive look at the life, death, and resurrection of Jesus. But none deal with what happened to Jesus' followers after He ascended into heaven and returned to His Father. In Luke's Gospel, we are told only that the disciples stayed at the temple, praising God (Luke 24:53).

The book of Acts picks up at that point to describe the coming of the Holy Spirit on the Day of Pentecost and records the growth, challenges, and miraculous happenings in the early church. Jesus had commanded His followers to make disciples of all nations (Matthew 28:19). Acts details the work of the Holy Spirit and the spread of the Gospel "to the ends of the earth" (Acts 1:8). The offer of God's forgiveness and salvation is extended to the Gentiles, and new opportunities open up for mission.

God's Word went out in ever-widening circles from Jerusalem. Even as the book of Acts concludes, Paul had just arrived in Rome to speak before the emperor there. Though beset by relentless opposition and persecution, the followers of Jesus persevered and continued to carry the Gospel wherever they went.

Themes
From start to finish, the book of Acts emphasizes the work of the Holy Spirit. The Spirit was first evident in the lives of Jewish believers in Jerusalem on the Day of Pentecost, but later was evidence that Gentiles, too, were experiencing the forgiveness and salvation of God.

The establishment and expansion of the church is Luke's ongoing concern in Acts. The followers of Jesus first congregate in a single group and create a unique and exemplary model of community. As they increase in number and persecution pushes them out of Jerusalem, they gather in various other locations, led by pastors and elders. And rather than each body seeing itself as independent, the churches look after one another's needs, financially and spiritually.

The persecution of believers is repeated throughout Acts as well. It was persecution that drove the church out of Jerusalem into surrounding areas. Paul was regularly persecuted during his travels. And at times when Paul could not be located, his associates were persecuted instead. More intense and organized persecution would come later, but Luke describes many of the initial attacks against the early church.

Luke also records a number of impassioned speeches throughout the book of Acts. Many are presentations of the Gospel by church leaders such as Peter, Stephen, and Paul. Every episode contributes in some way to the central theme of the book: the expansion of the church from Jerusalem to the ends of the earth, and from a Jewish beginning to a Gentile expansion.

Contribution to the Bible
The book of Acts holds a distinctive place in scripture. It is the only follow-up provided for the Gospels and provides a revealing look at the interaction, blessings, and problems of the believers in the early church. The Gospels highlight the ministry of Jesus; Acts highlights the ministry of the Holy Spirit. Only when viewed together do readers get the complete picture of God's plan, and how He chose to include humankind in the work of His kingdom.

More importantly, Acts shows how the expansion of the church from Jerusalem to Rome and from Jews to Gentiles was the work of God and part of His plan of salvation. The accounts of this time period provided by secular historians are helpful, to be sure, but they were written by people outside the church, looking in. Luke's account as a participant and believer gives us a trustworthy report that emphasizes things important to those who share his faith. His book of Acts provides much information that amplifies our understanding of other portions of scripture.

In addition, Luke's mostly chronological account of Paul's travels is invaluable in establishing dates for and better comprehension of his Epistles. By combining Paul's references in his letters with Luke's in Acts, the details of Paul's ministry become much clearer.

Making a Big Transition (1:1–26)

The book of Acts picks up where the Gospel of Luke ends. Jesus has been making occasional post-resurrection appearances, but He is about to depart for good. He leaves His followers final instructions, and while they await the promised Holy Spirit, they try to attend to some business.

Background & Context

Since Luke's coverage of world events makes no mention of Nero's persecution of Christians (AD 64 and following), the destruction of Jerusalem in AD 70, or Paul's death in AD 68, many scholars believe he wrote the book of Acts around AD 60-62. He had traveled with Paul to Rome at this time, and may have been writing Acts while Paul was writing his Prison Epistles.

The Arrival of the Holy Spirit (2:1–47)

Prior to His crucifixion, Jesus had tried to tell His followers that the Holy Spirit would come to replace Him after His departure (John 14:15–27; 16:5–16). After His resurrection, just prior to His ascension into the heavens, He instructed them to go to Jerusalem and await the Holy Spirit. He hadn't set a time frame, but their wait was only about ten days. The coming of the Holy Spirit was an unmistakable event that transformed the believers and initiated the establishment of the church.

Persecution Begins (3:1–4:31)

As the early church is formed, Peter quickly emerges as the prominent leader. After making an impassioned and persuasive speech to a large crowd (2:14–36), he soon begins to demonstrate spiritual power and authority similar to what Jesus had modeled. In this section he heals a beggar who had been crippled from birth. And as had been the case with Jesus, the healing didn't go unnoticed by the Jewish religious leaders, who respond with a show of their own power.

New Problems for the New Church (4:32–5:42)

Led by the Holy Spirit, and inspired by recent positive results after an encounter with the Jewish authorities, the newly forming church is a model of unity and mutual sacrifice. So when the first threat to that unity is exposed, the consequences are severe indeed. Yet the believers get past that problem and continue to teach, heal, and share with one another. Meanwhile, opponents continue to intensify their persecution of the believers, which only strengthens the faith of Jesus' followers.

The Church's First Casualty (6:1–8:3)

To this point the commentary on the new and growing church has been over-whelmingly positive, even though problems are beginning to arise. The apostles have been imprisoned and flogged. Two members have died dramatic deaths as a result of lying to God. And this section describes another problem from within: discrimination. Yet the church does such a good job of resolving the problem that one of the people chosen to help attracts too much outside attention and becomes the church's first martyr.

Background & Context

"Grecian Jews" (NIV) or better, "Hellenistic Jews" (TNIV; *Hellenistai*), were Jews who had at one time lived outside of Palestine. They spoke Greek as their primary language and were culturally and socially distinct from the Hebraic Jews (*Hebraioi*). These latter had never left Palestine and spoke Aramaic as their native tongue. The tension between these two groups is understandable, but it prevented the complete unity of the church (6:1).

From Jerusalem to Samaria to Ethiopia (8:4–40)

Jesus had told His followers that they would be His witnesses in Jerusalem, Judea, and Samaria, and to the ends of the world (1:8). Until the stoning of Stephen, they had remained in Jerusalem with an idyllic unity and spirit of fellowship. In this section, however, persecution will drive them out of Jerusalem into the surrounding territories of Judea and Samaria.

The Surprise Conversion of Saul (9:1–31)

After the arrival of the Holy Spirit, shortly after Jesus' ascension, the followers of Jesus were in for a lot of surprises. The apostles stopped cowering in seclusion and began to speak boldly in the streets and temple courts—even at risk of arrest and imprisonment. Priests and Samaritans were among those adding to the number of believers. But the biggest surprise yet is found in this section, where one of the foremost among Christian persecutors has a dramatic encounter with Jesus and becomes one of the foremost among New Testament evangelists.

Inclusion of the "Unclean" (9:32–11:30)

The early chapters of Acts show Peter as the primary leader of the church. He will soon fade from prominence as Saul (Paul) begins his ministry. And the previous section made clear that Saul was chosen to go to the Gentiles. However, in this section we discover that God also called Peter to a ministry that included Gentiles as well as Jews. Male or female, slave or free, Jew or Gentile—anyone who believes in Jesus can be included in His church.

Peter's Prison Break (12:1–24)
Aside from the death of Stephen and a bit of persecution from Jewish authorities, Luke's history of the early church has been very positive so far in the book of Acts. However, the conclusion of the previous chapter hinted at a famine and some monetary need in Jerusalem (11:27–30). This section continues to report increasing problems for the church—in this case, intensified persecution. And while God continues to provide for some of the believers in miraculous ways, others are beginning to be imprisoned and even killed for their beliefs.

The Gospel Moves Outward (12:25–13:52)
Up to this point, any contact between the believers in Jesus and the Gentile community has been quite one-sided. In each case, the contact was clearly God-directed, where Jewish believers were approached by curious Gentiles. But in this section, that will change. The church at Antioch begins to see the opportunity of approaching the Gentiles with the good news of the Gospel. So its leaders designate a pair of proven disciples to travel, preach, and build up churches that have begun in various faraway places.

Completion of the First Missionary Journey (14:1–28)
As Paul and Barnabas take the Gospel into areas where it has not been heard, they continue to encounter a wide variety of problems. They have met resistance that will graduate into full-scale violent persecution in places. Yet the message they present and their ability to convey their ideas are so persuasive that the crowds sometimes go overboard in enthusiasm, creating an entirely different kind of problem. In this section, they complete their first journey and return to the church in Antioch.

The Council in Jerusalem (15:1–35)
Acts 15 begins the second half of the book. It also stands as a pivotal passage in the history of the church. Until this point, the believers in the new church were primarily Jewish, although Gentiles were being converted. But the church had a decision to make. Was it okay to simply express one's belief in Jesus and be included in full fellowship? Or shouldn't Gentiles be expected to adhere to the same high standards as the Jewish believers? Was circumcision and keeping the Law of Moses necessary for salvation? And just as noteworthy as what was decided was how the church leaders arrived at their decision.

A Second Journey, a Different Partner (15:36–16:40)
Little by little the church has been becoming more accepting of the inclusion of Gentile believers. Paul and Barnabas, still in Antioch where many such converts lived, both had a heart for going out into Gentile territory and spreading the good news about Jesus. So when a disagreement kept them from traveling together, they paired up with other people and doubled their outreach. Paul and his new traveling companion, Silas, prepare to revisit the churches previously ministered to, and they end up widening the scope of their ministry considerably.

Moving through Greece (17:1–34)

After Paul and Silas paired up to go back to the churches that Paul and Barnabas had previously visited, God's Spirit then directed them to travel through new territory with the good news of Jesus. Along the way they have been joined by Timothy, who is still with them, and Luke, who has remained in Philippi. This leg of the journey will take them south again, through Thessalonica, Berea, and Athens—and they get quite a different reception in each location.

Background & Context

Epicureans were followers of Epicurus, a Greek philosopher (341-270 BC). He taught that nothing exists but matter and space, so the chief purpose of humankind should be to achieve happiness and pleasure. For a philosopher, that joy was gained through intellectual challenge and growth, but his followers over the years had found pleasure through physical, sensual fulfillment. So what had begun as a philosophy of the highest standards had quickly acquired a bad reputation.

Stoics believed that the true essence of life was the capacity to understand the rational order veiled by natural phenomena. Freedom and joy were the result of detaching from the outer world and mastering one's reactions to his environment. Stoicism didn't allow for sympathy, pardon, or genuine expression of feeling. Famous Stoics included Zeno, Seneca, Cicero, and Marcus Aurelius.

Wrapping Up the Second Missionary Journey (18:1–22)

Paul and Silas have set out on a second missionary journey, picking up Timothy along the way. But after being pursued from city to city by some troublemakers who would do Paul harm, he had gone ahead of the others into Athens while they stayed awhile with the believers in Berea. Paul spoke to a group of philosophers in Athens but didn't get a particularly enthusiastic reception. So he moves on to the next town: Corinth.

The Third Missionary Journey Begins (18:23–19:41)

Paul has spent a number of years traveling from place to place, preaching the Gospel and establishing and building up churches. He made one journey with Barnabas and a second with Silas. In this section he sets out on his third trip, and his emphasis is in Ephesus, a city where he was unable to spend much time previously.

A Forlorn Farewell (20:1–38)

Paul is on his third missionary journey and has never spent as much time in one place as he has in Ephesus. But his desire to collect an offering for the church in Jerusalem and start out for Rome has led to his decision to leave. This time his parting is particularly sad because he realized he might never see the Ephesians again. Yet God continues to do great things through Paul's ministry.

Expecting Trouble, but Moving Ahead (21:1–26)

The majority of the content of Acts 13–20 has been about Paul and his companions' journeys in taking the Gospel out of Jerusalem and Antioch into other parts of the world. In this section he heads back toward Jerusalem after his third trip. Although he has faced various hardships throughout his travels, he is warned specifically of trouble ahead if he continues. Yet he is not deterred.

Trouble in Jerusalem—as Predicted (21:27–22:29)

In this section, Paul finally arrives in Jerusalem after his third journey. From the moment he planned to come, he was aware that it would be a perilous and threatening trip for him. His first few days were nothing but positive as he shared his exploits with the elders of the church and heard how God had been active in Jerusalem as well. But it didn't take long for trouble to start, and it would be a long while before he would get the matter settled.

Paul's Trial Begins (22:30–23:35)

After the completion of his third missionary journey, Paul has returned to Jerusalem. He had been participating in a purification ceremony when he was dragged from the temple by an angry group of Jews who thought his work with the Gentiles involved advocating the rejection of all Jewish customs and traditions. The mob tried to kill him but was stopped by Roman authorities. In this section, the Romans call together the Sanhedrin to help them figure out exactly what is going on.

Paul's Trial Before Felix (24:1–21)

In this section, Paul must defend himself before the Roman governor of Judea, Felix. But things could be worse. The Roman commander in Jerusalem has already taken Paul into protective custody to prevent zealous Jewish traditionalists from killing him. And when an elaborate plot was discovered that involved more than forty assassins sworn to murder Paul in Jerusalem, the Romans initiated a change of venue by leaving during the night to escort him to Caesarea. He is being held in the palace of Herod, awaiting his trial.

A Second Trial in Caesarea (25:1–26:32)

For two years, Paul has been under arrest in Caesarea, the victim of the bureaucracy of the Roman Empire. Charged by a group of Jews in Jerusalem and the target of an assassination plot, he had been brought to Caesarea for trial. The case against him had been weak, yet the governor (Felix) would not pardon him, attempting to endear himself to his Jewish constituents. Felix has just lost his position, leaving his successor, Festus, the problem of what to do with Paul.

Problems on the Way to Rome (27:1–44)

Paul, the prominent figure in the book of Acts, has spent the last two years under guard in Caesarea, waiting for the governor to try him. Felix never got around to it because he was hoping for a bribe. But when Festus, the new governor, arrived,

Paul immediately received his trial. Festus didn't fully understand the intricacies of the case and would not make a decision. In response, Paul appealed his case to a higher court—before Caesar himself. If he hadn't done that, he would have been released (26:32). But Paul was eager to go to Rome, and begins his journey in this passage.

Rome at Last (28:1–31)

Paul's numerous missionary trips had created within him the desire to one day reach Rome and preach there. After a number of legal trials and two years of imprisonment while waiting, he had at last set out on his way—but still as a prisoner. In addition, his ship had encountered a violent storm and wrecked just off the shore of Malta. But he had Jesus' promise that he would arrive in Rome, and in this closing section of Acts he finally gets there.

Romans
Introduction to Romans

It is easy to forget that the epistle to the Romans is a letter and not a theological treatise. It is so often used in doctrinal studies and pursuits that we may miss the heartfelt passion that the author, Paul, had for his readers, many of whom he had never met. It isn't the first of Paul's letters chronologically, though it is placed first among his epistles in the New Testament.

Author
Paul is the writer of this Epistle. Skeptics have challenged the authenticity of some of Paul's other Epistles, but Romans has never seriously been questioned.

Occasion/Purpose
Paul considered himself an apostle to the Gentiles (11:13), yet he had never been to Rome, the center of the secular Roman Empire. He was planning a visit on his way to Spain (15:23–24, 28), and was writing in anticipation of his arrival. Yet his epistle is far more than a casual letter. He laid out a fresh and clear explanation of God's plan of salvation for both Jews and Gentiles—one that has continued to inspire and motivate Bible readers for centuries.

Paul was probably writing from Corinth on his third missionary journey, preparing to return to Jerusalem with a financial gift he had collected from the churches in Greece (15:25–29). But he was already making plans for a fourth missionary journey and hoped to include Rome. So while in Corinth (or near there), he wrote his epistle to inform the church of his plans. As it turned out, he would arrive in Rome as a prisoner (Acts 28:16) but was given a lot of freedom to minister and eventually was released.

Themes

The themes that permeate the epistle to the Romans are righteousness from God and justification by faith. Through faith in Jesus Christ, God's righteousness is imparted to human beings. It was how Abraham was justified before God prior to the giving of the Mosaic Law. And it was how Gentiles were able to come to God without being required to be circumcised or to observe all the Jewish dietary restrictions and feast days.

Contribution to the Bible

The book of Romans has been called the Constitution of the Bible. The privileges and freedoms it describes are good news not only for the Gentiles, who came to God with little knowledge and no traditions, but also for the Jews, who had drifted away from the genuine worship of God and had rejected Jesus. God's love, mercy, and grace are abundant enough for everyone to experience His forgiveness. The realization that people are justified by faith alone has been an eye-opening and life-changing reality for Martin Luther, John Wesley, and other church leaders.

Acting on What We Believe (1:1–32)

Paul wrote his letter to the Romans before ever visiting Rome, yet his heartfelt concern for the believers there is clearly evident throughout this Epistle. After a short salutation and brief personal comments, Paul begins what has become a masterpiece on the topic of righteousness. In this section, he emphasizes the absence of righteousness in humankind, which he will later contrast to the righteousness of God.

Background & Context

We know little about the origins of the church in Rome. It is likely that Jewish pilgrims in Jerusalem had become believers on the Day of Pentecost, returned home, and started the church. When Paul finally got to visit (during the early portion of Nero's reign), a group of believers traveled many miles to meet him along the way and escort him back to Rome (Acts 28:14–16).

God Has No Favorites (2:1–29)

Paul has just presented a somewhat scathing description of the behavior of humans when they reject God and live according to their sinful desires and natural lusts (1:24–32). It isn't a pretty picture. And neither is his next description of people who feel they have their lives together enough to pass judgment on others. Paul is about to point out that no one—Jew or Gentile—is righteous and law-abiding enough to avoid God's wrath on his or her own merit.

At this point in history, the Jews considered (and called) Gentiles "dogs." The Jewish air of spiritual superiority had created a great animosity and antagonism that had resulted in racial conflict. The Jews had been called by God to be a light to the Gentiles, but rather than witnessing God's love, all the Gentiles were seeing was spiritual snobbery, prejudice, and pride.

Bad News and Good News (3:1–31)

Paul continues his evaluation of Jewish religious beliefs and points out that God's righteousness cannot be achieved merely through one's commitment to the law and the practice of circumcision. While knowledge of the scriptures and obedience to their teaching is an excellent start, more is necessary. So first, Paul lays out the bad news of the impossibility of achieving righteousness, but he then follows with the good news of God's plan that overcomes that difficulty.

Justification before the Law Existed (4:1–25)

Paul has been writing about a most significant topic: the fact that salvation is by faith in Jesus alone, and does not require observance of the Mosaic Law or the sign of circumcision. He realizes many of his Jewish readers will find this hard to accept, so in this section he makes an argument using an example out of the greatest hero of their faith: Abraham.

The Fruits of Salvation (5:1–21)

So far in his letter to the Romans, Paul has been explaining the Christian doctrine of justification by faith. He began by describing our need for salvation (1:18–3:20) and followed with the way of salvation (3:21–4:25). In this section, he begins a lengthy examination of the fruits of salvation—the effect salvation has on believers.

Dead to Sin, Alive to God (6:1–23)

In Romans 5, Paul wrote about the doctrine of original sin and defined the root problem as the sinful human condition that exists within everyone. The reason Jesus died on the cross was to reverse the problem of sin that Adam brought into the world, providing the possibility of new life and a right relationship with God. Now Paul wants to ensure that his readers don't misapply what he has been saying. If the abundance of sin resulted in an even greater abundance of God's grace (5:20), why not try to sin so God can continue to lavish us with His grace?

Background & Context
From an American viewpoint, the very word *slavery* brings to mind racism, forced subjection, and harsh treatment. When Rome conquered other nations, their prisoners could face similar treatment.

But the Romans also had volunteer slavery. For example, people in extreme poverty could offer themselves as slaves to someone in exchange for food and housing. During the first century, the Roman Empire had as many as six million slaves, so Paul's imagery of being enslaved would have been quite clear to his readers. He admitted later, though, that slavery wasn't the perfect analogy to symbolize one's relationship with God (6:19).

The Lingering Influence of Sin (7:1–25)
In anticipation of a personal visit to Rome, Paul is writing to the Roman believers. He has been outlining the message of the Gospel, and has just taught that every person has a master. People are either slaves to sin or slaves to righteousness. In this section, he will continue with that theme as he takes up the subject of God's law and its purpose for the Christian.

Assurance and Reassurance (8:1–39)
Paul's epistle to the Romans has been an ongoing defense of justification by faith alone. He has shown that righteousness is the result of one's relationship with God through faith, and not due to adherence to the Mosaic Law, circumcision, or any other external standard. So if believers are not to rely so heavily on such things, what *should* they rely on? Paul's answer in this passage has become one of the most beloved portions of scripture.

Sovereignty, Election, and Love (9:1–33)
Paul has been writing about God's sovereignty over death (Romans 5), over sin (Romans 6–7), and over struggles, persecution, and hardship (Romans 8). In this section, he turns his attention to God's sovereignty in regard to salvation. The Jews had always felt they were God's chosen people. Now that the church was growing into an institution, people were asking how God could be faithful to His promises if the majority of His chosen people—the Jews—were failing to respond to the Gospel. Paul answers that question here by using familiar stories to remind them of God's sovereign choices throughout their history.

Explaining Israel's Rejection (10:1–21)
Paul has had much to say about justification by faith so far in Romans. At the end of chapter 9, he had just returned to his running theme of righteousness. As he continues in this passage, he moves from the past to the present and from the aspect of God's sovereignty to individual accountability.

Good News for Israel (11:1–36)
In Paul's ongoing treatise on righteousness and justification by faith alone, he has just finished a rather frank commentary, explaining that many of the Jewish people had rejected God and missed the significance of Jesus, the Messiah. Even the Gentiles had better spiritual insight. Now Paul asks a different question: Since

the Jews had opted to seek self-righteousness rather than God's justification, had God given up on them?

Radical Transformation (12:1–21)
For eleven chapters in Romans Paul has written at length about the mercy of God. When people were lost in their sin and enemies of God, He opened a way of salvation to them through the gift of His Son. Christ died on the cross, taking their place and paying the penalty for the sins of their lives. It is in light of this awesome mercy of God that Paul now urges his readers to live a life worthy of their calling in Christ Jesus.

The Believer's Place in the World (13:1–14)
Chapter 12 marked a turning point in Romans, where Paul shifted from a theological presentation to a personal appeal for spiritual transformation and love. He listed a number of spiritual gifts and other admirable behaviors for believers to adopt as they related to one another. In this section, he continues with his treatise on practical living and begins to consider relationships with those outside the church.

Weak and Strong Believers (14:1–15:13)
As Paul continues the practical application section of his letter to the Romans, he deals with conflicts that can arise between people who have different levels of spiritual maturity. What may seem completely appropriate to those in one group can appear wrong (if not outright sinful) to those in another. His exhortation to love one another (13:8) still applies as fellow believers learn to respect one another's opinions.

Personal Comments (15:14–33)
Paul has just finished with the "business" of his letter to the Romans after calling on all the believers to accept one another and not let their differences get in the way of spiritual growth. He has completed his thorough explanation of justification by faith and other doctrinal matters. As he begins to close his letter, he turns his attention to some personal matters, including another affirmation of his genuine concern for the believers in Rome.

Paul's Fellow Ministers (16:1–27)
As Paul concludes his lengthy letter to the Romans, he personally acknowledges dozens of people who were working for God. It is a personal and intimate conclusion to his epistle, and was surely an encouragement to those who might have felt unnoticed.

1 Corinthians
Introduction to 1 Corinthians

Corinth was a Roman colony and capital of the province of Achaia. Its population probably reached as many as two hundred thousand free citizens, with close to half a million slaves. The city had been in existence since the Bronze Age. It was located in a most strategic position, midway along a five-mile stretch of land between the Saronic Gulf and the Corinthian Gulf. The city would therefore get all the travelers going to the isthmus at the south of Greece, or north to the continent. Additionally, the hazards of sea travel made it advisable for ships to dock, unload, and transfer their cargo to another ship across the isthmus, east to west or vice versa. Small ships would be dragged across the land bridge while still fully loaded.

With all the people and money going through Corinth, it was naturally an influential city. And along with the crowds and wealth came immorality. The city had a reputation for both idolatry and prostitution. The city's less-than-stellar reputation is mentioned in numerous ancient writings. Paul had started a church there during his second missionary journey (Acts 18:1–18). This epistle to the Corinthian believers alludes to many of the aspects of social life in the city.

Author

The Epistle of 1 Corinthians both begins and ends with an identification of Paul as the author (1:1; 16:21). The early church was quick to affirm his authorship, and few modern scholars dispute it.

Occasion/Purpose

During his second missionary journey, Paul remained in Corinth for about eighteen months (about AD 51–52), teaching and establishing the church there. He then returned to his home base at Antioch, and subsequently set off on his third missionary journey. He traveled to Ephesus, the key city in the Roman province of Asia, where he remained for three years, establishing churches there and in the surrounding regions.

While in Ephesus, Paul began to hear of troubles in the young church at Corinth. One of these problems was related to sexual sin, and Paul seems to have written a short letter (now lost) to correct it (5:9). The church was also suffering from division (1:12). In response to the problems in this immature church, Paul wrote this letter, known to us as 1 Corinthians (about AD 55).

Shortly before writing the letter, a delegation from Corinth (Stephanas, Fortunatus, and Achaicus [16:17]) came to Paul with a financial gift from the church. They probably also brought a list of questions from the church, since Paul answers these questions in his letter (7:1). The report of these three men, along with a report from members of the household of a woman named Chloe (1:11), and perhaps a report from his fellow missionary Apollos (1:12; 16:12), prompted Paul to write the letter.

Paul was planning another trip to Corinth. His letter was an attempt to correct some of the problems in the church before he arrived (4:18–21). He also was collecting gifts for the church in Jerusalem because its members were facing tough times, and he wanted the Corinthians to be ready to give (16:1–4).

Paul considered himself the spiritual father of the Corinthian church (4:14–15). It was his love for the believers that motivated him to confront them so directly concerning spiritual and moral issues. Personally, he had experienced weakness, fear, and trembling in his previous association with the church (2:3), but Paul knew it was the power of God that would sustain both him as the messenger and the Corinthian believers as a body.

Themes

Because of the many ongoing disputes in the church, one of the continuing themes of 1 Corinthians is unity. Paul repeatedly challenges the believers to resolve their conflicts, dissolve their factions, and let God's love rule in the church to bring them together as one body.

Related to unity is the work of the Holy Spirit, especially in regard to spiritual gifts. It is the Holy Spirit who provides the needed wisdom and equips the believers in various ways to minister to one another and the world outside the church.

The sanctification of believers, therefore, is also stressed throughout Paul's letter. Whether supporting their church leaders, addressing sexual sin, foregoing lawsuits against one another, feeling gratitude for their spiritual gifts, or living in anticipation of the resurrection, believers need wisdom from God and the maturity of personal discipline. God has sanctified His people, and in response they are to live accordingly.

Contribution to the Bible

The first letter to the Corinthians is a good example of the importance of integrity within the local church. Much of the focus of scripture is frequently applied to the worldwide church, but here we find a call for each individual body of believers to attend to its own spiritual life and growth.

Paul writes about spiritual gifts in various places, yet his comprehensive explanation in 1 Corinthians 12, using his analogy of the human body, is perhaps his best. The "one body" concept is a universally understood image of the church.

In addition, 1 Corinthians 13 is one of the best-known passages of scripture. Paul's description of love has become a classic piece of literature throughout the centuries since the church at Corinth first read it.

A Church Divided (1:1–2:5)

The church at Corinth was undergoing a number of problems. Paul begins by addressing the main source of trouble: division among church members. This issue was evident in a number of specific ways, which Paul will get to in subsequent chapters. But here he deals with the matter from a broader perspective.

The Holy Spirit's Role in Wisdom (2:6–16)

Paul begins this letter to the Corinthian church by contrasting human wisdom with the wisdom of God. Those who value their own wisdom too highly tend to think that the truth of the Gospel is foolishness. Paul continues his clarification in this section, where he explains how the Holy Spirit contributes to a believer's genuine wisdom.

A Plea for Cooperation Rather Than Competition (3:1–23)

In this section, Paul continues his appeal to the Corinthians to quit dividing into factions based on their personal preference of church leadership. As long as jealousy and arguments continued, the church would never unite. And in addition to the church as a whole, Paul speaks to the importance of individual commitment and work for God.

Proper Regard for Church Leaders (4:1–21)

In the previous section, Paul had explained to the Corinthian believers some of the wrong ways to respond to their church leaders. He challenged them to quit boasting about human leaders (3:21) and to quit allowing their leadership to create jealousy and quarreling among the church members (3:3–4). In this section, he continues to explain how the church should properly respond to and support its leaders.

Background & Context

When a Roman general won a great victory, he would parade his triumphant army through the streets of the city, displaying all the spoils of their conquest. Following at the end of the parade was a group of people who had been taken captive. Soon this group would be taken to the arena to fight against wild animals or armed gladiators, where most would die. This is the image Paul uses, describing the proud Corinthians as victorious kings and the church leaders as the doomed prisoners.

Dealing with Sin in the Church (5:1–13)

To this point, Paul has addressed the problems in the Corinthian church in general terms. But here he gets quite specific. He cites a particular—and particularly offensive—problem, and then provides instructions for how to deal with it. This is the first in a series of specific issues Paul will deal with throughout his letter to the Corinthian believers.

Litigation and Licentiousness (6:1–20)

Paul had begun to respond to specific problems in the Corinthian church he had learned about through correspondence with the believers there. He continues to address their issues in this section, writing about two issues that continue to be problems in many churches today: lawsuits and sexual immorality.

Background & Context

When there was a dispute in ancient Athens, the first attempt to settle the matter was through private arbitration. One arbitrator was chosen by each party, and the two agreed on a third arbitrator to serve as an impartial judge. If that failed to settle the problem, it went to a court known as The Forty. This court referred the matter to public arbitration by Athenian citizens. And if this group couldn't reach agreement, the case went to a jury court that consisted of 201 citizens for small matters and 401 citizens for major issues. Jurors had to be at least thirty years old. Records exist of some cases where the juries numbered in the thousands.

The Jews, on the other hand, had always avoided the public courts. They tended to settle disputes before the leaders of the community or elders in the synagogue. Justice was a matter best left to the spiritual community. So Paul is especially distressed to hear of the Corinthian believers' willingness to allow secular courts to settle their disagreements (6:1-6).

Guidelines for Married and Single Believers (7:1–40)

Paul had just answered questions concerning sexual behavior. So it was only natural that he would follow by discussing the believers' questions on marriage. He rebukes their improper attitudes, but spends considerably more time prescribing positive behavior.

Questions of Christian Freedom (8:1–13)

Paul has been answering questions from a previous letter from Corinth. He has just responded to questions about marriage (7:1) and singleness (7:25). Now he turns to a topic that was a major problem in Corinth, yet not a concern in most modern Western cultures. Still, Paul's approach to the issue provides insight for how to deal with a number of contemporary spiritual problems.

An Apostle's Rights (9:1–27)

Paul has just encouraged the Corinthians to willingly forego their Christian rights if by doing so they could prevent more immature believers from stumbling. In this section, Paul gives a personal example of how he had sacrificed his rights for the good of others. By doing so, he also addresses some underlying resentment from a portion of the Corinthian church.

Temptation and Freedom (10:1–11:1)

In this section, Paul continues to follow up on the issue of eating food sacrificed to idols. He had previously stated that since idols were nothing of substance, it didn't matter if believers ate meat that had been sacrificed to them (8:4). But he had added warnings to avoid anything that would create spiritual difficulties for immature and growing Christians, and had provided an extensive argument for voluntarily suspending the exercise of Christian freedom for the good of others. As he now continues his train of thought, he warns of the danger of temptation for those who take too much pride in their freedom.

Guidelines for Worship (11:2–34)
After a comprehensive response to the Corinthians' question about eating meat sacrificed to idols (chapters 8–10), Paul moves on to another topic in this section. For the next several chapters he will address various issues of church propriety. In this passage, he addresses gender issues and provides clear instructions for the observance of the Lord's Supper.

Understanding Spiritual Gifts (12:1–31)
In this section of Paul's Epistle, he continues to respond to a number of problems that have been creating divisions in the church at Corinth. In the previous section, he addressed some women who were disrupting worship services with the way they prayed and prophesied. He also dealt with the terrible things the Corinthian church members were doing to demean the Lord's Supper. Now he turns his attention to the topic of spiritual gifts—yet another part of church life meant to bring people closer together, but was having the opposite result.

The Difference Love Makes (13:1–13)
Paul has just finished a rather harsh scolding of the Corinthians—first for their self-centered and unacceptable behavior during the Lord's Supper (11:17–22) and then for the arguments they were having over spiritual gifts (chapter 12). Throughout his epistle, Paul has tried to emphasize the importance of love in dealing with the various problems of the church. In this passage, he offers a definition of love, and his words have become a cherished portion of scripture as well as a classic piece of literature.

The Proper Use of Spiritual Gifts (14:1–40)
In 1 Corinthians 12, Paul listed a number of spiritual gifts and challenged the believers to use them for the benefit of the church as a whole. He followed in 1 Corinthians 13 with the importance of love in connection with the exercise of gifts. In this section, he returns to a discussion of spiritual gifts and provides some specific guidelines for how they should be properly exercised in a church context.

Resurrection and Expectation (15:1–58)
In the previous section, Paul concluded a rather extensive passage examining spiritual gifts and their proper place in worship. He had addressed the Corinthians' past behavior and provided instructions for the current state of the church. In this passage, he turns their attention to the future as he writes of what they can expect at resurrection and beyond.

On the basis of a "dualistic" worldview that viewed the physical world as evil and only the spirit world as good, some of the Corinthian believers were evidently claiming that there would be no resurrection of the body. Paul responds by affirming both the certainty of Christ's bodily resurrection and the centrality of the resurrection for the Christian faith. He also discusses the nature of our glorified bodies.

Giving and Greeting (16:1–24)
Paul is wrapping up his lengthy letter to the Corinthians. Before ending, he has one more matter of business to address, and he wants to convey a number of personal greetings and make a few final requests.

2 Corinthians
Introduction to 2 Corinthians

This epistle from Paul to the Corinthian church is a follow-up letter to 1 Corinthians. The topics he discusses are similar, particularly the concern with the false teachers who continued to plague them. Though Paul addresses both general principles and issues specific to the Corinthian community, there is much here for the church today.

Author
Paul not only identifies himself as the author of 2 Corinthians (1:1; 10:1) but also provides more autobiographical information than in any of his other letters.

Occasion/Purpose
Although many Corinthian believers had acknowledged and respected the apostolic authority of Paul, there were others who hadn't. A number of self-designated church leaders had appeared in Corinth and set out to undermine Paul. They accused him of being bold in his letters but weak in person. They said that since he didn't charge the Corinthian church for his service to them, his ministry must essentially be worthless. And as they continued attempts to erode Paul's integrity, they began to attract followers from among the Corinthian Christians. Therefore, throughout this epistle, Paul tends to defend his ministry more than usual. He remains highly supportive and encouraging toward the Corinthian believers, yet targets the troublemakers and rebuts their accusations.

In addition to responding to these criticisms about his apostolic credentials, he needed to ask them to forgive someone who was seeking to restore fellowship with them (2:5–11), and to prompt them to prepare their offering for the church in Jerusalem (chapters 8–9).

After establishing a church at Corinth (Acts 18:1–11), Paul continued to correspond with the believers there. Some of the correspondence between them has never been discovered (1 Corinthians 5:9; 7:1; 2 Corinthians 2:4; 7:8). In 1 Corinthians, Paul had addressed specific issues that had been raised in previous communications. He firmly advised the church how to handle its problems.

Sometime later, while Paul was ministering in Ephesus, he took a trip to

Corinth to correct some of the problems that his first letter had not resolved. This was an unsuccessful mission, and Paul was hurt and embarrassed by his reception at Corinth (2:1; 12:14, 21; 13:1–2). In response, he returned to Ephesus and wrote a severe and sorrowful letter (now lost, but referred to in 2:4; 7:8) to the Corinthians, calling them to repent of their disobedience. He sent this letter to Corinth with Titus (7:8–13).

Paul then traveled north from Ephesus to Troas (in modern northwest Turkey), expecting to meet up with Titus and to learn about the response of the Corinthian church. But Titus was not there, so Paul moved on to Macedonia in northern Greece (Acts 20:1; 2 Corinthians 7:5). There he finally met up with Titus, who brought the good news that many in the Corinthian church had repented and were greatly appreciative of his ministry. Paul sat down and wrote 2 Corinthians to express his great joy and to encourage the believers further in their faith.

Themes

Paul's appeal to the Corinthians reveals his vulnerability. Even during times of dire distress and deep disappointment, Paul demonstrates the value of trust in "the Father of mercies" and "the God of all comfort" (1:3 NASB).

His writing also reflects ongoing encouragement. Throughout this letter, when Paul had every reason to be offended, he instead focuses on the encouragement and comfort he received not only from God, but from the Corinthians as well.

And as Paul provides a reluctant, but necessary, defense of his ministry, he writes of authenticity. His work for God is based on genuine love for others and commitment to his calling, as contrasted to the self-serving and manipulative tactics of the false apostles in Corinth.

Contribution to the Bible

Second Corinthians is a valuable book because it reveals not only the trials and tribulations, but also the joy and fulfillment that come from Christian ministry. Paul's directness, his "tough love," his encouragement, and his compassion, had initiated the repentance of many of the believers at Corinth.

In defending his ministry, we see Paul at his most human. In many of his writings, Paul's tremendous zeal and devotion seem almost unreal and unattainable for most people. Yet all believers can identify with the personal sufferings and frustrations Paul expresses in this letter.

Setting the Record Straight (1:1–2:11)

Paul writes this letter with mixed emotions. Although he knows of some problems in the church at Corinth, he also feels a sense of great relief. He had been hoping to receive word from the Corinthians in response to his previous letter (2:4; 7:8) but was unable to locate the messenger, Titus, for a while (2:13). Later, in Macedonia, Titus catches up to Paul and tells him of the Corinthians' repentance and love for Paul (7:5–7). So even though Paul writes of trials and suffering, he does so out of a heart filled with joy.

Background & Context

Corinth was a much-traveled city and heavily influenced by Greek culture, including its idolatry and sexual promiscuity. Not surprisingly, the church had to deal with members affected by such temptations. Additionally, enough time had passed since the death of Jesus and introduction of the Gospel for false teachers to begin to infiltrate the churches. This problem was particularly evident in the Corinthian church.

Paul's Confidence (2:12–4:18)

Paul here starts to describe what happened when he finally met up with Titus after sending his severe letter to the Corinthians (2:4). He had come to Troas, where he had successful ministry. But he could not find Titus and so was still distraught, wondering how the Corinthians had responded to his stern message (2:12–13). Yet as Paul remembers his anguish, he also recalls the joy he experienced when he finally met up with Titus in Macedonia and learned that the Corinthians had repented. At this thought he breaks into joyful praise to God: "But thanks be to God. . ." (2:14). Paul seems to lose himself in this joy now, launching into an extended discussion of the joys and victory of the Christian ministry (2:14–7:1). He won't resume his discussion of the circumstances of the letter for five more chapters! In chapter 7 he will pick up with, "For when we came into Macedonia, this body of ours had no rest. . ." (7:5 NIV)—exactly where he left off at 2:13! Second Corinthians 2:14–7:1 is therefore an extended parentheses in Paul's letter, a masterful celebration of the trials and joys of the Christian ministry.

New Dwellings, New Creations, and New Attitudes (5:1–7:1)

Paul is writing to the Corinthians, fully aware that some of them are actively opposing his authority. He is defending himself and his ministry, to some extent, even while addressing his concerns for the genuine believers. In this section, he continues to emphasize the impermanence of human life as he turns his readers' attention to eternal things yet to come.

Grieving and Giving (7:2–9:15)

Earlier in this letter to the Corinthians, Paul had written about the circumstances he was facing (2:12–13). In the midst of that discussion, however, he suddenly launched into an extended discussion of the joys and challenges of Christian ministry (2:14–7:1). In this section he returns to where he left off, writing about his joy at the church's repentance and his reconciliation with them.

Ministry: Genuine and Otherwise (10:1–11:33)

So far in this letter, Paul's writing has been authoritative, but rather gentle. After Titus's report from Corinth, Paul must have discovered that he had a lot of support from the believers there. Still, his critics were outspoken, so here he begins to defend himself more emphatically—letting his readers know he feels no shame or regret for his methods or other aspects of ministry.

Inexpressible Glory and Unavoidable Thorns (12:1–13:14)
Paul has turned up the heat in his defense against the accusations of his critics, coming on stronger as he boasts in what God has done through him. As he closes the letter, he provides some additional proof of the authenticity of his ministry. He also shares a personal problem, but one that further verifies his role as an apostle.

Galatians
Introduction to Galatians

The book of Galatians is a centerpiece of New Testament theology that had a great influence during the Protestant Reformation. (Martin Luther's *Commentary on Galatians* ranks with the most influential books to come out of the Reformation.) Galatians is the only one of Paul's letters addressed to a group of churches rather than a single location. The epistle has been called a spiritual Magna Carta, due to its masterful explanation and defense of justification by faith alone.

Author
The style of writing and method of thinking is so true to that of Paul that few scholars throughout the centuries have questioned his authorship. The early church held a strong and unwavering belief that Paul was the writer.

Occasion/Purpose
The epistle to the Galatians was written to emphasize the complete sufficiency of justification by faith alone in one's relationship with God. The Galatian churches (where many new believers were Gentiles) were being strongly influenced to add traditional Jewish beliefs and practices to their newfound faith. While it was quite natural for Jewish believers to continue to worship as they always had in the past, to require the same for Gentiles was, to Paul, tantamount to promoting a different Gospel (1:6).

Paul had established a number of churches in Galatia during his missionary travels (1:8, 11; 4:13–14, 19–20; Acts 13–14). When he left, the believers were holding up under suffering (3:4) and doing well (5:7). But not long afterward, Paul had received word that they were being influenced by a group requiring circumcision for salvation, and he was disturbed and dismayed to hear how quickly the Galatians had forsaken his teaching of salvation by faith through grace (1:6–9; Acts 15:1). So Paul wrote this letter to circulate through the churches and call the believers back to the truth of the Gospel of Christ.

Themes
In Galatians, Paul doesn't move from topic to topic as he does in some of his other letters. His focus is on a single theme throughout: Faith in Christ *alone* is all that is necessary for one's justification before God. It had been true for Abraham,

and has been God's plan all along. While the law has its purpose, attempting to require *anything* for salvation other than by God's grace through faith in Christ is a serious distortion of the Gospel.

Contribution to the Bible

The epistle to the Galatians should be perceived as each believer's emancipation proclamation. For all the attempts of others to impose a yoke (5:1) of some kind in regard to church practice, Galatians insists that faith is the only instrument needed to free us.

And while spiritually oppressed believers can find great freedom in the teachings of Galatians, it doesn't take much reading between the lines to see that the people attempting to restrict freedom were those who believed themselves to be more mature spiritually. Paul both exposes their error and points out the potential of sin to affect the most devoted believers—even Peter and Barnabas (2:11–13). Galatians reminds us that *no one* should ever presume to be beyond the effects of sin and the danger of losing sight of the wonderful grace of God.

Along these lines, as Paul contrasts the actions of the human, sinful nature with the qualities provided by God, he lists the fruit of the Spirit (5:22–23), and assures his readers that the exercise of such characteristics will never oppose any spiritual law.

The Threat of a Different Gospel (1:1–24)

Paul's epistles have a standard opening that usually include a note of thanksgiving for those reading the letter. However, those complimentary words are absent from his letter to the Galatian churches. The epistle to the Galatians has a sense of urgency. Paul gets right to the point: His readers are facing serious problems.

Background & Context

A centuries-long debate has taken place as to whether Paul was writing to churches in the northern part of the province of Galatia, or to those in the south. The different options allow for different dates for the letter. We know from the book of Acts that Paul took his first missionary journey through southern Galatia, establishing churches in Pisidian Antioch, Iconium, Lystra, and Derbe, before returning to his home base in Antioch, Syria (Acts 13–14). According to the South Galatia theory, Paul wrote his letter to these churches that were established on his first missionary journey. After this journey, Paul attended the Council in Jerusalem (Acts 15:1–35), and then went on a second missionary journey that included the regions of "Phrygia and Galatia" (Acts 16:6). According to the North Galatia theory, on this journey Paul established churches in northern Galatia, and it is to these he is writing his letter. Unfortunately, no specific cities in north Galatia are named in the account in Acts, and no details of events are provided.

A greater number of modern scholars favor the South Galatia option for various reasons: (1) The southern churches are named (Pisidian Antioch, Iconium, Lystra, and Derbe), while the northern are not; (2) Those southern churches were on a route that would have taken Paul through Tarsus, his hometown (Acts 15:41); (3) Paul writes about Barnabas without introducing him (Galatians 2:9, 13), and they had only traveled together on Paul's first journey; and (4) It seems unlikely that the Judaizers would have ignored the more prominent southern cities to go to the north instead.

The various options make it difficult to establish a date for the writing of Galatians. Proponents of the North Galatia theory suggest it was written during Paul's third journey, around AD 53 to 57. And those who hold to the South Galatia theory aren't agreed as to the date of the epistle. If written before the Council of Jerusalem, as some believe, the date could be as early as AD 48–49, making it one of the New Testament's earliest books. Others feel a more accurate date is AD 51 to 53.

The Difficulty of Living in Freedom (2:1–21)

Paul has been dealing with a charge by his critics that he is out of step with the Jerusalem apostles as he promotes Gentile freedom without requiring adherence to Jewish ceremonies. Paul's opponents have suggested that his apostleship was derived from those in Jerusalem and should be subordinate to the other apostles, yet his critics accused him of teaching the Gentiles something entirely different. So far Paul has emphatically shown that his Gospel and his commission to preach came directly from Jesus, and not from the other apostles.

A Closer Look at the Law (3:1–25)

Paul has been making the case that the Gospel of grace and justification by faith alone is, in fact, the true and only Gospel. In this section he will begin to demonstrate his point using a biblical, theological argument. As he does, we need to keep in mind that when he makes references to the scriptures, he is referring to what we know as the Old Testament. When he speaks of grace, freedom, and righteousness, he does not present them as new ideas, but as concepts that should have been evident to anyone who was familiar with the law and the prophets.

Children of God (3:26–4:31)

Up to this point, Paul has been stating that from the beginning, the message of the Gospel has been the promise of righteousness before God through faith in Christ (Abraham's "seed"). Justification never had anything to do with good works or obedience to the law. The law, in fact, is a servant of the promise as it exposes people's sin and guilt and points them to the righteousness that God provides as a free gift through faith in Christ.

Background & Context
A common morning prayer among Jewish men included thanks to
God that they had not been born a Gentile, a slave, or a woman.
The reason was not necessarily to demean the other groups, but an
acknowledgement that those people didn't have all the same rights
and privileges available to free Jewish males. Paul's choice of terms in
verse 28 was probably intentional to precisely counter the viewpoint
of the Judaizers.

True Freedom and Spiritual Fruit (5:1–26)
Paul continues the ongoing argument he has been making to refute the restric-
tive and destructive philosophies of the Judaizers. He has just made a contrast
between slavery and freedom, and now continues with a call to the freedom that
only Christ can provide. He will also explain how the Holy Spirit influences the
lives of believers in a way that no law can possibly countermand or contradict.

Doing Good without Becoming Weary (6:1–18)
Paul, in a section about the challenges and benefits of Christian freedom, has just
made a thought-provoking contrast between the acts of the sinful human nature
and the fruit of the Holy Spirit. Clearly, his readers knew the preferable choice,
yet Paul was also aware of the power of sin and the grip it could have on people.
So as he continues, he provides practical advice for how to deal with existing sin
in the church.

Ephesians
Introduction to Ephesians

The book of Ephesians is a powerful and uplifting contribution to the canon of
scripture. Lacking any specific rebuttals of false doctrines, and addressed primarily to Gentile believers, it has long been beloved by seekers and new believers. Its
doctrinal foundation has made it a favorite of Bible scholars as well.

Author
Paul's authorship was not questioned until the early nineteenth century, at which
time certain Bible scholars began to speculate that Ephesians was historically,
theologically, and stylistically inconsistent with Paul's other writings. Paul had
spent much time in Ephesus (Acts 19:1, 8–10), yet his letter to the Ephesians
is impersonal. The discrepancy is easily explained if Paul were addressing a different group of Gentile believers (perhaps newer ones he hadn't yet met), or if
he intended the letter to be circulated to different churches. As for theology,
Paul never even refers to justification in Ephesians, and his references to reconciliation pertain more to unity between Jews and Gentiles than humankind

and God. Yet simply because he emphasizes a different aspect of God's grace in Ephesians is no proof that Paul didn't write the epistle. Any opposition to Paul's authorship is subjective and speculative. Indeed, the logic, the structure of the book, the emphasis on the grace of God, and the full acceptance of Gentile believers are distinct indications that Ephesians was written by the apostle Paul.

Occasion/Purpose

Although some of Paul's epistles address specific problems within a particular church, Ephesians doesn't. Rather, it challenges the reader to set a higher standard for living—the imitation of God (5:1). Paul was writing to a prominently Gentile church, and makes clear that its members have been fully reconciled to God and are entitled to every spiritual blessing that He offers (1:3; 3:16–19).

Paul was a prisoner when he wrote this letter—most likely under house arrest in Rome, awaiting trial before Caesar (Nero). If so, his had been a long, arduous journey, including false arrest in Jerusalem, a series of trials (with ongoing imprisonment) for more than two years, a harrowing shipwreck on the way to Rome, and the current uncertainty of what would happen to him. Yet his letter is filled with enthusiasm, faith, and confidence.

Themes

A number of topics are repeated with some frequency in this Epistle. One is the *Trinity* of God the Father, Jesus Christ the Son, and the Holy Spirit. Where Paul mentions one member of the Trinity, many times he will specify the others as well.

The *mystery* of God is mentioned throughout the letter. Paul explains that, at his writing, it is a revealed mystery—a reference to the Gospel of Jesus Christ that can now be understood even though its full meaning had been hidden for centuries.

Ephesians has much to say about the *heavenly realms*, as Paul regularly shifts his readers' attention from their personal, earthly concerns to the spiritual conflict they are involved in.

And Paul's focus remains on the *church*. Although he provides both a theological basis for how to live and practical applications for what to do, his intent is to build up the body of Christ—not a random assortment of spiritually mature Christians.

Contribution to the Bible

Ephesians in its entirety is a grand epistle of spiritual richness. Yet several of its components have been singled out as favorites of Bible students. One such passage is Ephesians 2:8–9, Paul's clear and concise affirmation of the absolute sufficiency of salvation by grace through faith—and nothing else.

Another favorite selection for memory verses comes at the end of Ephesians 3, where Paul uses physical measurements (wide and long and high and deep) to describe the love of Jesus, and follows that with the assurance that Christ can do immeasurably more than people can ask or imagine.

The submission teachings of Ephesians (5:22–6:9) have generated much discussion throughout the centuries since they were first written. And the closing description of spiritual qualities as the armor of God (6:10–18) is another often-cited section of this epistle.

The All-Sufficiency of Christ (1:1–23)

Paul's letter to the Ephesians has long been considered a masterwork of doctrine and critical thinking. In this epistle, Paul does not address specific problem areas, but directs the thoughts of his readers toward the things God has done for them, and then to what they should do in response. This section will remind believers of many things for which they should be thankful.

Background & Context

Ephesus was a major city in the Roman Empire. The book of Acts details a number of events that took place there, including passionate opposition to Paul by silversmiths who made their living from the great number of visitors to the temple of Artemis (Acts 19). In spite of the heavy influence of idolatry and sexual promiscuity connected with the temple and the culture, a predominately Gentile church had arisen. Although Paul has nothing bad to say of the church there, John would later report that it had forsaken its first love (Christ) and needed to repent (Revelation 2:1-7).

Dead in Sin, Alive in Christ (2:1–22)

After a magnificent opening section reminding his readers of the work of God the Father, Jesus Christ, and the Holy Spirit, Paul critiques the believers in Ephesus and explains how they have come to connect with such a holy God. He describes their transformation as a move from death to life, and his intention is to be more literal than symbolic. His words to the first-century Ephesians are just as relevant for the church today.

Revealed Mystery and Glorious Riches (3:1–21)

Paul has been reminding the predominantly Gentile body of believers in Ephesus of the spiritual blessings that have been provided for them, and he continues to do so in this passage. After just completing a section about how God had brought together Jews and Gentiles, in Christ, into one body, Paul's thoughts seem to turn to the "mystery" of God that had become much clearer in light of the life, death, and resurrection of Jesus.

A Good Walk (4:1–32)

The first three chapters of Ephesians have been theologically based. In this section, Paul turns from theology to ethics. From this point onward in his letter, Paul will focus on the Christian walk. Now that he has shown what God has done on behalf of believers, he addresses practical ways in which believers should respond.

Living Carefully (5:1–33)

In the previous section, Paul had shifted from a theological perspective of spiritual life to writing about applicable and relevant ways that such a perspective plays out in everyday life. In this section, he continues his instruction concerning daily living, including guidelines for sexual propriety, speech, drinking, and marriage.

Standing Firm (6:1–24)

As Paul concludes this insightful letter, he has some very important things left to say before signing off. Having just addressed the relationship between husbands and wives, he now turns to parents and children, and slaves and masters. Then he will explain how all Christians are engaged in spiritual warfare, and instructs them on what they need to do to stand firm and emerge victoriously.

Background & Context

It may seem strange that Paul would use the weapons and dress of war to enumerate qualities befitting a Christian—someone called to be a peacemaker. However, it should be noted that Paul was under arrest in Rome when he wrote this letter. He would have been very familiar with the appearance of a Roman legionnaire. It is not unrealistic to think he might have looked up at his own guards as he was writing this passage, noting their uniform piece by piece, and comparing each component to a believer's spiritual armor.

Philippians
Introduction to Philippians

Paul's letter to the church in Philippi is remembered for its joyful tone of gratitude against the stark background of the fact that Paul was in prison while writing. Paul writes about the peace, joy, and contentment he finds in Christ, no matter what his situation or circumstances.

Author

According to Philippians 1:1, the apostle Paul is the writer of this letter. The theology and personal comments fit with what we know of Paul from other writings in the New Testament. Early church fathers and historians also affirmed Paul's authorship.

Occasion/Purpose

When Epaphroditus visited Paul, he also brought news of troubles in the Philippian church: The Judaizing threat had appeared (Jewish Christians claiming Gentiles must first become Jews in order to be saved), financial troubles and other problems were creating doubts about the Philippians' newfound faith, and discord had surfaced in the church. Knowing they were in need of help, they asked Paul to send them Timothy, but he could not come immediately. However, Paul sent back with Epaphroditus this letter full of thanksgiving and encouragement, instruction and correction, and doctrine and exhortation.

Paul wrote this letter while in prison (1:7, 13, 19). The place of Paul's imprisonment is not clear from the letter, but the ambiguity doesn't affect the interpretation of the book. Some have suggested that this imprisonment was in Caesarea (Acts 23:33; 24:27) or Ephesus (1 Corinthians 4:9–13; 15:32; 2 Corinthians 1:8–10; 4:8–12; 6:4–11), but the evidence points most strongly to Rome. Paul refers to the "praetorian guard" (1:13 NASB)—Caesar's personal guard—and sends greetings from "those of Caesar's household" (4:22 NASB).

Paul was arrested in Jerusalem after completing his third missionary journey (Acts 21–22). He spent two years in a prison in Caesarea before he made his appeal to the emperor and was sent to Rome (Acts 23–28). The year was AD 59 or 60. Most believe that the Philippians heard Paul was in prison in Rome and, wanting more specific information about him and desiring to help, they again raised a large gift and dispatched Epaphroditus to Rome with the money. Because Epaphroditus experienced a substantial delay, Paul had been in Roman prison approximately one year when he arrived. The sacrificial gift touched Paul deeply.

Themes

Philippians includes themes such as joy, humility, self-sacrifice, unity, and Christian living. Partnership in the Gospel is a theme and nucleus of the letter. This partnership includes the fellowship of the church with the Spirit (2:1) and the fellowship of the believers with Christ's suffering (3:10–11).

Background & Context

Philippi was a city in Macedonia (northern Greece), ten miles from the Aegean Sea. The city was named for Philip II of Macedon, father of Alexander the Great. Though a relatively small city, Philippi was a Roman colony, which meant it received special rights and privileges equivalent to those given to the cities of Italy. Many retired Roman military and other colonists from Rome lived there, creating a sense of prestige and civic pride. When Paul says our true "citizenship is in heaven" (3:20 NIV), this meant something in a place where citizenship was of great value.

The story of the founding of the church in Philippi appears in Acts 16. On Paul's second missionary journey he had a vision in Troas, which prompted him to cross the Aegean Sea (Acts 16:8-12). Philippi was the first town in which Paul preached after he crossed the Aegean Sea, making this the birthplace of European Christianity. Paul's normal pattern was to preach first in the Jewish synagogue, but Philippi had few Jewish residents and no synagogue. So Paul began his ministry at a place of prayer beside the river (Acts 16:13). There he met Lydia, a merchant in purple cloth, who became the first convert in the city (together with her household). Lydia subsequently gave Paul and his missionary companions (Silas, Timothy, and Luke) hospitality and a place to stay (16:15). It was also in Philippi that Paul cast out a demon from a fortune-telling slave girl. This provoked the anger of the girl's owners, who were making a tidy profit from her gifts, and they had Paul and Silas arrested, beaten, and imprisoned as troublemakers. That evening an earthquake miraculously opened the prison doors, and Paul led his Philippian jailer to Christ (Acts 16:12-40). In this way, the church at Philippi was founded (about AD 51).

Opening Words (1:1–26)

Paul opens his letter to the Philippian church with heartfelt words of gratitude and rich blessings. It is in this section that Paul introduces a main theme of Philippians—partnership in the Gospel.

Background & Context

When Paul wrote his letter to the Philippians, he was under arrest in Rome. We know little of the precise details of his imprisonment, but there is reason to believe that by this time Paul was reasonably confident he would eventually be released. In those days, one could never count on a just outcome—Paul had certainly not done anything remotely deserving of Roman punishment, but he was hopeful nonetheless. He would be released and enjoy several more years of ministry before being arrested again and executed in Rome, almost certainly during the reign of the emperor Nero, sometime in the mid-60s, perhaps as early as AD 64.

Family Business (1:27–2:30)

This section marks the beginning of the body of Paul's letter. Greetings and personal information out of the way for now, Paul begins his exhortation about the kind of lifestyle the Philippian Christians are called to live.

Knowing Christ (3:1–4:1)

It seems as though Paul is approaching the conclusion of his letter, but one thought leads to another and two more chapters are recorded. In any case, Paul indicates that the Philippians have heard his advice about rejoicing before, but it bears repeating (3:1).

Paul warns the Philippians about dogs. Today, calling someone a dog can be an insult (3:2). But in this first-century context, the term was often used by the Jews to discriminate against the Gentiles. Here, though, Paul twists that usage, referring to the Judaizers who tried to make all new converts live according to Jewish law rather than by simply following in the ways of Christ.

The evil men, or "evil/bad workers" (3:2), Paul refers to is a reference to the Judaizers' emphasis on doing the works of the law. They were demanding circumcision of the new converts to Christianity, thus the reference to mutilation of the body.

Best and Worst Practices (4:2–23)

The previous section of warning and exhortation ends with verse 1 of chapter 4. What follows is a concluding series of more general exhortations quite typical of Paul's letters. He begins here with somewhat of a rebuke, which is unusually personal for Paul's letters.

Colossians
Introduction to Colossians

The New Testament letter to the Colossians presents the person and work of Jesus Christ as the Savior, the Creator, and the Sustainer of the universe and the total solution for humanity's needs, both for time and eternity.

Author

The author of this letter identifies himself as the apostle Paul (1:1; 4:18). Some modern scholars have questioned this, claiming differences in vocabulary, style, and theology. These differences are minor, however, and are best accounted for by the unique topics covered in the letter. Furthermore, the letter is closely connected to the letter to Philemon, which is widely accepted as authentic, and the two letters were probably sent together—the same town, same letter carrier; many of the same companions of Paul are named. No challenges to Paul's authorship were expressed in the early church. We can confidently assert that Paul was the author.

Occasion/Purpose

Paul's purpose in writing Colossians was threefold: (1) to express his personal interest in the Colossians (1:3–4; 2:1–3); (2) to warn them against reverting to their old pagan vices (3:5 and following); and (3) to counteract a particular theological heresy that was being promoted within the church at Colossae (2:4–23). The Colossian heresy wore the mask of Christianity, but it was false.

Several years after the church was established, around AD 61–62, Epaphras traveled to Rome to visit Paul during his first Roman imprisonment. While Epaphras brought some good news regarding the Colossian assembly (1:4, 7–8; 2:5), it appears his primary purpose for visiting was to solicit Paul's help against a certain heresy (or heresies) that was eating its way into the Colossian church.

Paul wrote this letter to counter this false teaching. The epistle was sent to the Colossians by the hand of Tychicus (4:7). In the meantime, Epaphras stayed with Paul, perhaps forced to because of his own imprisonment (4:12; Philemon 23), but surely also for instruction and encouragement from Paul.

Themes

The main theme of the book of Colossians is the supremacy of Christ and the power of the Gospel message. Christ is the object of the Christian's faith because He is God's Son, the Redeemer, the very image of God, the Lord of creation, and the head of the church (1:13–18). It is through Him and because of new life in Him that we are to put away our old manner of life and live according to His grace.

Background & Context

Colossae is located about one hundred miles east of Ephesus. At one time the city had been large and populous, but when Paul wrote to the Colossian church, it had become a small town in comparison to its nearest neighbors, Hierapolis and Laodicea (4:13). Though small, Colossae of Paul's day was still a cosmopolitan city with different cultural and religious elements that were mingled together. For the most part, the inhabitants of the area were Gentiles, but there was a considerable quantity of Jews among them.

As far as we know, Paul never visited Colossae, at least not by the time he wrote this epistle (1:4, 9; 2:1). Nevertheless, the community of faith there was a product of his ministry in nearby Ephesus. A young man named Epaphras, who went to Ephesus and evidently heard the Gospel from Paul there, is credited with taking the message to Colossae. He was trained and prepared by Paul to go back and plant a church in his hometown (1:7; 4:12).

Though there was a significant Jewish population in the Lycus Valley, the Colossian epistle suggests that the membership of the church was primarily Gentile. Within the letter to the Colossians, there are not many Old Testament references and almost no reference to the reconciliation of Jews and Gentiles that is found in Ephesians.

The Person and Work of Jesus (1:1–2:3)

The apostle Paul follows the customary form of greeting for first-century letters. He first identifies himself as the author, with his associate Timothy, and then identifies his recipients, followed by a brief greeting. However, he seasons the greeting with terms that focus on the letter's distinctively Christian character. These first fourteen verses prepare the Colossian readers for the words of warning and the exhortations that will follow. At the same time, these introductory words provide today's readers with insight into the church at Colossae and their growth in Christ.

The Heresy (2:4–23)

In this passage, Paul addresses the issue of the false teachers among the Colossians. His arguments, however, are never far removed from the doctrinal truth regarding the person and work of Christ. With the exhortation regarding the methods of the false teachers (2:4–5), Paul sets forth the dangers facing the Co-lossians. With the exhortation to progress in the faith (2:6–7), he sets forth the means of protection: living in Christ. Finally, with the exhortation regarding the philosophy of the false teachers (2:8), his warning focuses on the danger of being tricked by empty philosophy.

The Way to Live Like Jesus (3:1–4:1)
Paul now shifts gears from the negative to the positive. He tells the Colossians how they are to experience true spirituality in this world. Rather than subjecting themselves to the bondage of the false teachers, they are to understand who they are in Christ, and experience the true freedom that comes from that knowledge. Instead of thinking that the flesh must be contained by human philosophy, religious legalism, or spiritual mysticism, they are to understand that in Christ, the flesh has been killed on the cross. They must think of themselves as dead to sin and alive to God.

In Conclusion (4:2–18)
In this final section of scripture on being raised up in Christ, Paul draws the Co-lossians' attention outward—to their responsibility to make Christ known, both by praying for those who are actively involved in sharing the Gospel and by living out the life of Christ and sharing the Gospel in love.

It is not enough to reflect Christ to one another in the church. We are also to take the message of Christ to the world outside of our community of faith. Paul desires to see the Colossians as active participants in the progress of the Gospel through responding to the issues and questions of the world.

1 Thessalonians
Introduction to 1 Thessalonians

First Thessalonians is a short letter written to a predominantly Gentile church of new converts. It provides all the basic requirements for holy living (a regular "walk" with God), as well as great insight into the importance and specifics of the anticipated return of Jesus. As such, it is a worthwhile study for believers of all ages.

Author
Early church authorities agree that Paul is the author of this epistle, and little serious opposition has been raised since. With the possible exception of Galatians (for which the date is debated), this is most likely Paul's first letter among those that are included in scripture.

Occasion/Purpose
The church at Thessalonica was facing persecution, yet it was continuing to grow and had developed a dynamic testimony of faith. Paul's letter was an effort to

comfort and motivate the believers there with the truth of the Lord's sure return.

Paul had taken the Gospel to Thessalonica, but had to leave abruptly when persecution broke out, for the good of other believers in the city (Acts 17:1–10). It would have been natural to wonder if, after his hasty departure, the new Gentile converts would soon drift back to their old ways. Paul had wanted to return on numerous occasions, and had been frustrated when unable to (2:18). So he was overjoyed when Timothy arrived from Thessalonica with a glowing report of their continued faithfulness (3:6–10). This letter was written in response to that report and in anticipation of a personal visit by Paul (3:11).

Themes
The primary doctrinal issue of 1 Thessalonians is the second coming of Christ. Jesus' return is mentioned at the end of every chapter of this letter, and it is the focus of the end of the epistle. In addition, Paul's emphasis on holy living is a call to unity, and he uses the term "brothers and sisters" (*adelphoi*) twenty-eight times in 1 and 2 Thessalonians.

Contribution to the Bible
As an early letter of Paul, this epistle shows that even then he was both emotionally vulnerable and theologically strong—a combination that would continue to make him an outstanding writer and church leader. Specifically, 1 Thessalonians contains perhaps the clearest picture of the rapture that is connected with Jesus' second coming (4:15–17).

Background & Context
Originally called Therma because of many hot springs in the surrounding area, the city of Thessalonica had been renamed in the 300s BC, in honor of the half-sister of Alexander the Great. It was conquered by Rome in 168 BC and became capital of the province of Macedonia. Today known as Thessaloniki (or Salonica), it is again the capital of Macedonia and one of the few cities from New Testament times that still exists, with a population of three hundred thousand.

The city's strategic location, with access to a major Roman military highway (the Egnatian Way) and a sheltered harbor, attracted many people. As a result, Thessalonica was a wealthy city, though it had also developed a reputation for evil and licentiousness.

A Faith That Inspires Others (1:1–10)
Having heard of the persecution and suffering within the church in Thessalonica, Paul wrote to encourage the believers. His opening in this section is filled with genuine praise. Not only were the Thessalonians enduring difficult times, they were also setting an example that other churches were noticing. Theirs was a faith that was helping others grow stronger.

Background & Context

The Gospel is spread through actions as well as words. Paul followed the example of Christ (1 Corinthians 11:1). The Thessalonians followed Paul's example (1:6). And as a result, people throughout all of Greece (Macedonia and Achaia) saw the example being set by the Thessalonians (1:7).

Macedonia and Achaia (1:7-8) were Roman provinces that comprised what is now Greece. Because of the faithful witness of the Thessalonians, the Gospel was heard through the entire land like the peal of a trumpet. The change in the lives of the Thessalonians was clearly evident. Many had been idolaters and some probably continued to battle the pull of their past. Yet they had welcomed God's message by faith and were putting their trust in Jesus.

The Gospel had revealed the foolishness of their faith in empty idols and pointed them to the truth of the living God. The Thessalonians did not put off their old life *in order* to be saved; it was their understanding of and belief in the message of the Gospel that led to salvation. Their salvation came only because of their willingness to acknowledge what God had already done for them.

Paul's Association with the Thessalonians (2:1–20)

After a warm and encouraging greeting (1:1), in this section Paul begins to recall his personal experiences in Thessalonica. He has fond memories, and will compare himself to both a loving mother and concerned father. He writes as an evangelist as well as an edifier of believers.

Concern and Encouragement (3:1–13)

Paul spent the previous section answering a number of accusations leveled against him by people who opposed the Gospel and his presentation of it. Now that he has set straight the false insinuations of his opponents, he continues to express personal concern for the Thessalonian believers. As their spiritual parent, he wants to see their faith continue to develop. Two key ideas he stresses in this section are spiritual stability and spiritual growth.

Holy Living (4:1–12)

In the previous section, Paul was rejoicing over the arrival of a message from Timothy that affirmed the ongoing faithfulness of the believers in Thessalonica. He had expressed thanksgiving for the church, reviewed his ministry with them, and shown his deep concern for their sufferings. At this point, Paul now begins a series of exhortations regarding appropriate Christian living.

Living in Expectation of Christ's Return (4:13–5:28)

Paul has already alluded to the return of Jesus several times throughout this letter

(1:10; 2:19; 3:13). Here he turns his full attention to what the Thessalonians could expect. They were a church under persecution, and the anticipated return of the One to whom they were being faithful was an ongoing comfort for them. Still, they had a number of questions that Paul answers in this section.

2 Thessalonians
Introduction to 2 Thessalonians

The second letter to the Thessalonian church is a timely follow-up to 1 Thessalonians, and as such, deals with the same concerns for the believers in Thessalonica. (See the introduction to 1 Thessalonians.) Yet some in the church were not responding to the first Epistle, so 2 Thessalonians has a more urgent tone.

Author
Paul's authorship of 2 Thessalonians has not been as widely accepted as that of 1 Thessalonians. The early church never doubted it, but as skeptics arose in the nineteenth century and began to dispute the divine inspiration of the Bible, 2 Thessalonians was one of the books that was challenged based on vocabulary (due to a few words not otherwise used by Paul) and the writer's approach to future events (for example, warning signs for the day of the Lord and references to the man of lawlessness that weren't found in 1 Thessalonians). Yet most scholars have been convinced that the similarities between the two letters far outweigh the differences, and support the authorship of Paul.

Occasion/Purpose
As persecution in Thessalonica continued to increase, one of Paul's primary purposes in this letter is to offer additional encouragement and comfort. He offers incentive to persevere while also attempting to correct any potential confusion resulting from a forged letter, using his name but twisting his teachings. And while Paul writes, he adds instructions to discipline those who use their spiritual beliefs as an excuse not to work.

Though believed to be written very soon after 1 Thessalonians, the persecution of the Thessalonian church seems to have intensified since the previous letter (1:4–5). So Paul writes this follow-up epistle from Corinth after Silas and Timothy inform him of the recent developments in Thessalonica.

Themes
The primary intent of 2 Thessalonians is to refute false rumors and clarify the truth about the expected return of Jesus. But in that context, a second emphasis of the letter is the problem of idleness among certain church members.

Contribution to the Bible
Second Thessalonians contains scripture's only reference to the "man of lawlessness," at least by that title (2:3). And the letter's exhortations to avoid idleness

provide valuable guidelines for those who continue to anticipate the coming of Christ.

Responding to Persecution (1:1–12)

Paul had written 1 Thessalonians largely to encourage the believers in Thessalonica to remain faithful as they encountered persecution from various sources. But not long after sending the first letter, he heard that the opposition was getting worse, not better. Much of what he says in this opening section is in acknowledgement of what they were facing.

Background & Context

The historical circumstances for 1 and 2 Thessalonians are so similar that most people believe this epistle was written within six months of the first one. (See the introduction to 1 Thessalonians.)

Holding to Reliable Teachings (2:1–17)

The suffering of the Thessalonian church has been mentioned several times so far in 1 and 2 Thessalonians. We know these believers were facing a lot of persecution from outsiders. But in this section, we discover some false teachings that had begun to circulate regarding the return of Christ, creating even more stress on those who were trying to remain faithful. Paul will set the record straight and then encourage the struggling believers to stand firm.

Remaining Faithful. . .and Active (3:1–18)

As Paul begins to bring this letter to a close, he emphasizes how his (and his associates') confidence lies not in human plans or promotions, but rather in God Himself. The ultimate success of any ministry depends on the faithfulness of the Lord and His Word, even though He chooses to use frail human instruments to accomplish it.

Background & Context

Perhaps it was more than simple laziness causing the Thessalonians' reluctance to work for a living. The Jewish people took pride in their work and taught all males a trade. The Greeks, however, considered manual labor to be fit only for slaves. Having come from such a culture, possibly pride was a prominent motive for the nonworking Thessalonians.

---

1 Timothy
Introduction to 1 Timothy

First Timothy is a letter from a faith mentor to one of his dearest disciples. It is a look into the first-century relationships that made up the early church, and the issues with which they grappled.

Author

The author of this letter introduces himself as the apostle Paul. Of all the letters of Paul, the Pastoral Epistles (1 Timothy, 2 Timothy, and Titus) are by far the most disputed in terms of authorship. Differences of language, style, and theology have caused many scholars to doubt that Paul was the original author. Some believe that a disciple of Paul wrote these after his death. Others think he may also have used one of his missionary companions to write out these letters (see Romans 16:22 for an example of this), and this scribe left his own stylistic mark. In any case, the differences are not as great as is sometimes supposed, and there are many features of the letter consistent with Paul's language and style. Evangelical scholars continue to assert that these letters came from the apostle's hand.

Occasion/Purpose

Paul wrote this letter from Macedonia sometime after being released from his first Roman imprisonment—around AD 63–64. Paul had left his protégé, Timothy, to minister at the church in Ephesus (1:3). At this particular time, the church was plagued by false teachers and dissension. Paul was going to be delayed in returning to Ephesus to be with Timothy and guide him in person, so he wrote this letter to offer guidance on how to choose and strengthen the leader of the church and train them to preserve godliness and reject false teaching.

Themes

1 Timothy is one of the three New Testament books identified as the Pastoral Epistles, along with 2 Timothy and Titus. Paul wrote this letter, as he did the other two, to assistants who were leading communities of faith. In the letter, he offers them instructions in their role as shepherds. In the first century, this included standing against heresy and teaching sound doctrine. Understandably then, the themes of 1 Timothy are along those lines—church leadership, sound doctrine, faith in practice, and church order.

Though this letter is addressed to Timothy, there are several indications that the full intention was for the letter to be shared with the congregation and even throughout the region.

Opening Words (1:1–20)

The opening of Paul's letter to Timothy reveals it to be both personal and official. It also reveals much of Timothy's task in Ephesus—facing teachers of false doctrine.

The Life of the Church (2:1–15)

There has been much conversation in the church since Paul wrote the words in this chapter regarding the behavior of the women in the Ephesian community of faith. When applying this teaching universally to the modern church, it's important to keep in mind that Paul was writing for a specific situation—to help Timothy know how to deal with the false teachers assailing the community. It may not be safe to assume that Paul would have given these exact same instructions had Timothy been facing a different situation.

In both chapters 2 and 3, Paul describes the kinds of people who should be leaders in the church. He is not listing the responsibilities of those leaders so much as describing the kind of people they should be.

Background & Context

While Paul's instructions regarding women in the church have given him a discriminatory reputation among some people, it is important to see the reason he is calling for order in the church and what that order is supposed to accomplish. This particular church was facing an attack on its doctrine. It was important for these believers to establish an order for their worship and their communication to preserve the truth and protect themselves from those who didn't speak the truth. If this body of believers allowed themselves to fall into chaos, they would only be prey for any new, louder doctrine that came along. Paul's call for order in the relationships and practices of the body are important to contemporary churches just as they were in the first century.

Church Leaders (3:1–16)

First Timothy is considered one of the Pastoral Epistles (along with 2 Timothy and Titus) because Paul was *pastoring* his protégé in the organization and character of the church and the principles of its leadership. It would make sense then, that Paul would discuss the kind of people that Timothy would choose to lead the church with him. The instructions here are not exhaustive lists, but they offer a glimpse into the kind of mature person that can effectively rise to leadership in the local church.

The Local Church (4:1–16)

Chapter 4 picks up right where the last chapter leaves off. Paul takes the logical next step from the responsibility and role of the church to the obstacles that prevent this fellowship from being all that God had called it to be. This section includes both warnings against false teachers and instructions for Timothy in his leadership role.

Instructions for Specific Groups (5:1–6:2)

The rest of Paul's first letter to Timothy includes very specific instructions for dealing with a variety of groups within the church. Using his gift of exhortation in varying contexts, Timothy was to exhort older men respectfully as fathers, younger men relationally as brothers, older women tenderly as mothers, and younger women with dignity as sisters. The majority of these instructions relate to widows and the church's care for them.

Exhortations (6:3–21)

This final section of Paul's first letter to Timothy functions much as the closing to many letters. Rather than being a section all on one theme, it is a smattering of information: additional information on false teachers, teachings about wealth, personal notes, and a closing doxology.

2 Timothy
Introduction to 2 Timothy

Paul wrote this letter to Timothy, someone who came to faith through Paul's ministry, then worked as a colleague, and finally took on a leadership role at the church in Ephesus. The instructions in this letter serve to give Timothy guidance in leading the church, which included battling with false teachers.

Author

Of all the letters of Paul, the Pastoral Epistles (1 Timothy, 2 Timothy, and Titus) are by far the most disputed in terms of authorship. Differences of language, style, and theology have caused many scholars to doubt that Paul was the original author. Some believe that a disciple of Paul wrote these after his death. Others think he may also have used one of his missionary companions to write out these letters (see Romans 16:22 for an example of this), and this scribe left his own stylistic mark. In any case, the differences are not as great as is sometimes supposed, and there are many features of the letter consistent with Paul's language and style. Evangelical scholars continue to assert that these letters came from the apostle's hand.

Occasion/Purpose

Paul wrote this letter to Timothy, someone who came to faith through Paul's ministry, then worked as a colleague, and finally took on a leadership role at the church in Ephesus. The instructions in this letter serve to give Timothy guidance in leading the church, which included battling with false teachers.

When Paul wrote this letter, he was in prison in Rome and had been deserted by most of his colleagues. He was also aware that his life was reaching its end and may have had some sense of passing the torch of leadership on.

Timothy was in Ephesus, troubled by corrupted doctrine that was affecting his congregation. Paul reached out to Timothy through this letter to offer guidance and to connect and communicate as old friends will do.

Themes

The themes of 2 Timothy center on the need for boldness in leadership and the need for faithfulness in the Christian walk. Additional themes are instruction in church leadership and how to identify false doctrine and do away with the needless controversy it creates.

Contribution to the Bible

Along with 1 Timothy and Titus, 2 Timothy offers a real-life look at the church, its conflicts, and its leadership in the first century. It offers some key insights regarding scripture itself (3:16–17).

Greetings and Salutations (1:1–18)

Paul opens this letter, as he does many of his other letters, with a salutation and personal greetings. This letter is a peek not only into first-century Christianity, but a personal window into the relationships that made up the church—both those that involved valued solidarity and those that involved obstacles and conflicts.

Background & Context

Paul and Barnabas visited Timothy's hometown of Lystra (in Galatia) on their first missionary journey. It is likely where Paul first met Timothy and his family. When Paul visited Lystra again on his second missionary journey, he was so impressed with Timothy's faith that he took him along as a missionary companion. Timothy was one of his closest and most trusted associates from that point onward.

Perseverance (2:1–26)

Rather than focus on the doctrines that have been tainted by false teachings, which is a topic that makes up much of the Pastoral Letters, chapter 2 opens with a warm exhortation from Paul to Timothy regarding Christian service.

The Last Days (3:1–17)

This next section of Paul's letter casts a shadow. There are difficult days ahead, and Paul predicts that the uphill battle against sin will only get steeper over time.

In Conclusion (4:1–22)

This final chapter begins with a solemn charge to young Timothy "in the presence of God and of Christ Jesus, who will judge the living and the dead" (4:1 NIV). The opening introduction adds urgency to all that follows. These final words come from a man who has spent time on both sides of Jesus—persecuting Him and proclaiming Him. Writing from prison, Paul shares his mission with Timothy.

Titus
Introduction to Titus

The book of Titus and 1 and 2 Timothy comprise Paul's Pastoral Epistles—not an entirely accurate name for the three letters. Titus and Timothy were not pastors, at least not by the modern definition. Still, both Timothy and Titus were Paul's associates who did a lot of legwork for him, and his letters to them about the expectations of church leaders is a valuable guideline for spiritual leadership.

Author

Of all the letters of Paul, the Pastoral Epistles are by far the most disputed in terms of authorship. Differences of language, style, and theology have caused many (more liberal) scholars to doubt that Paul was the original author. Some believe that a disciple of Paul wrote these after Paul's death. Yet the differences in style, vocabulary, and theology are not as great as is often supposed, and they can be satisfactorily accounted for by the different themes and by the fact that these letters were written later in Paul's life. Paul may also have used one of his missionary companions to write out these letters (see Romans 16:22 for an example of this), and this scribe left his own stylistic mark. Because of the many Pauline themes and personal touches, evangelical scholars continue to assert that these letters came from the apostle's hand.

Occasion/Purpose

Titus is not mentioned in Acts, as are many of Paul's other associates, but his name appears in various epistles. Paul's ministry had initiated Titus's conversion to Christianity, and the Gentile convert soon had taken on the responsibility of traveling and ministering with Paul, and at other times on his own. This was one of the latter cases, and Paul had left Titus in Crete while the apostle was elsewhere, perhaps in Corinth. Paul desired to stay in touch with his protégé and offers him some practical advice for overseeing a church.

Crete is an island in the Mediterranean, about 150 miles long and anywhere from seven to thirty miles wide. In Greek mythology, it is the birthplace of Zeus, and the Cretans claimed that his tomb was on their island as well. The citizens of Crete had a reputation that was less than stellar (1:12).

Titus, a young minister, had been entrusted to oversee the believers there. Paul was writing to both encourage him and give him some practical instructions regarding church leadership (qualifications of elders, basic teachings, dealing with problems, etc.). A proper understanding of the Gospel of Christ was especially needed in the hedonistic and idolatrous culture of Crete.

Themes

Six times in this short letter Paul makes a reference to "good works"—not as a requirement for God's forgiveness and redemption, but in response to God's free gift of salvation. And he regularly connects such proper behavior with sound doctrine.

Paul also directs the reader's attention to "our Savior," a phrase that appears six times in three distinct couplets. Each couplet has a distinct reference to both God and Jesus (1:3–4; 2:10; 3:4, 6).

Contribution to the Bible

Along with 1 Timothy, Titus is a primary source for clearly stated requirements for church overseers (1:5–9). In addition, Paul's concise description of salvation (2:11–14) is a doctrinal delight in its detail as well as its simplicity.

A Call for Authentic Beliefs and Leadership (1:1–16)

After Paul had introduced the Gospel to such a broad geographic area, it was necessary for him to delegate authority in following up with young and growing churches. To this end, he had placed Titus in Crete—a challenging mission field for anyone. Clearly, the church would need good and strong leadership. So Paul opens his letter to Titus with criteria for church elders and authorizes him to deal with some difficult problems already arising among the believers.

A Call for Authentic Behavior (2:1–15)

After giving Titus a list of requirements for church leaders (1:6–9), Paul now provides guidelines for different groups within the church. As he does, he also provides some personal encouragement for Titus in the challenging position he held.

Background & Context

Many people question why Paul (or scripture in general) seems to condone slavery. But the question itself exposes a misconception. The Bible never endorses slavery, yet since slavery was so widespread in the ancient world, scripture addresses the issue. Slaves were held to certain standards, but so were slave owners. And in most places where the truths of scripture were introduced and implemented, the acceptance of slavery began to decline. Furthermore, the Gospel does address the even worse problem of *spiritual* slavery, and how through Christ's sacrificial death all people are able to break the chains of sin and experience freedom and forgiveness. In this regard, there is no distinction between male and female, Jew and Gentile, slave and free person (Galatians 3:28).

A Call for Authentic Relationships (3:1–15)

Paul had written this letter to encourage Titus (chapter 1) and provide instructions for various groups within the church (chapter 2). In conclusion, he provides a few more guidelines for the entire church—reminders of how the believers should behave in response to their salvation. Afterward, he signs off as he usually does, with a few personal comments and greetings.

Philemon

Introduction to Philemon

Of the thirteen epistles traditionally attributed to Paul in scripture, his letter to Philemon is the most personal. Most were written to entire churches. The three Pastoral Epistles (1 and 2 Timothy and Titus) were to individuals but had church-wide applications. Philemon, too, contains public greetings and was intended to be read publicly. Philemon's situation was very specific, yet Paul's advice, as usual, contains wisdom appropriate for all believers.

Author

Paul identifies himself as the author (verses 1, 9, 19), and there is nothing in the letter theologically or grammatically to suggest otherwise.

Occasion/Purpose

Paul had come upon a runaway slave named Onesimus and had convinced him to return to his owner, Philemon. This letter is Paul's appeal to Philemon to forgive the slave and accept him back into the household.

It appears that Paul was in prison as he wrote (verses 1, 9), which would probably have been during his two-year house arrest in Rome (Acts 28:16, 30). As usual, Paul made the most of his time, ministering through the mail when he couldn't travel in person.

Themes

The theme of Philemon is forgiveness, not as a great theological concept but as a necessity of an effective Christian life. Whether or not Philemon wanted to forgive the offense of Onesimus as his slave, he was obligated to do so as a Christian brother.

Contribution to the Bible

The short letter to Philemon is important in its view on first-century slavery. Some ask why Paul (or other biblical writers) didn't come right out and condemn the practice. Yet if Philemon heeded Paul's appeal, both slave and master would find themselves equal as servants of Christ. The new relationship would certainly undermine the institution of slavery.

A Short Story of Forgiveness and Second Chances (1–25)

Paul uses a great deal of tact in this Epistle, so the facts of the matter are revealed slowly. But a slave named Onesimus has run away from his master, Philemon, apparently after stealing from him. In God's providence, Onesimus meets Paul, who facilitates his conversion to Christianity and sends him back to Philemon with this letter.

Background & Context
Paul's imprisonment and trial (AD 61-63) were during the rule of Nero

before he had become such a nemesis to the Christian movement. The letter to Philemon was likely delivered at the same time as the letter to the Colossians (Colossians 4:7–9) and near the time of Ephesians (Ephesians 6:21).

Hebrews
Introduction to Hebrews

The book of Hebrews is rightly identified as a letter (or "epistle") because it was written to a specific group of people to address problems and concerns of that community. Like a letter, it contains some personal comments and greetings (13:22–25). But in contrast to most other New Testament letters, Hebrews is fundamentally a sermon—a word of exhortation (13:22). It can be read aloud in less than an hour, and, like most sermons today, is structured around the citation, exposition, and application of scripture. It is not unlike a traditional contemporary sermon.

Author
No one can say with certainty who wrote Hebrews. Some attribute it to Paul, yet in every other Pauline letter, the apostle opens by identifying himself. In addition, the author's statement about hearing the Gospel from others (2:3) does not jibe with Paul's other statements that emphasize his receiving the Gospel directly from Christ (Galatians 1:11–12, for example). Furthermore, the language, style, and theological perspective are very different from Paul's elsewhere. Other educated guesses for authorship include Barnabas, Luke, and Apollos. Perhaps the best perspective comes from the insight of the early Christian theologian Origen. Concerning the author of Hebrews, he commented, "God alone knows."

Occasion/Purpose
The original recipients of this letter, as the title indicates, were Jewish Christians. They had suffered persecution for their new faith and had stood firm. . .at first. But as time passed, they had begun to waver and were tempted to return to the comfort of their old, familiar ways. Some had apparently already made the decision to leave the Christian faith and return to Judaism, which placed added pressure on the ones who were still in the church.

No one is certain where the letter was written (perhaps Italy [13:24], although it is equally possible that the *recipients* were in Italy). Still, the occasion of the letter remains clear. The author was well informed about his readers and knew that, while they had once been faithful to Christ and active in the church, some had left to return to the familiarity of Judaism and others were preparing to join them. The writer makes an impassioned plea for them to reconsider, and he lays out a series of strong arguments to verify that Christ is superior to any of their other options. Indeed, Jesus is the *only* option that provides lasting salvation. To reject Him is not only foolish, but spiritually dangerous.

Themes

Hebrews competes with Galatians for being the most single-minded book in the New Testament. The author makes numerous arguments around a single theme: the absolute necessity of persevering in the Christian faith. Any portion of the letter becomes more pertinent when the reader acknowledges this overriding theme.

Contribution to the Bible

Hebrews presents a masterful explanation of the preeminence of Christ—His superiority to Moses, priests, angels, and everything else. The book also shows not a contrast between the "old" ways of the ancient Israelites with those of the "new" Christian era, but rather the similarity between Old Testament and New Testament believers: Both received the Gospel, are saved by grace through faith, look forward to the promised rest of God, and so forth. Hebrews also provides some of the Bible's most direct warnings about the consequences of rejecting Christ and ignoring the work He has completed to provide salvation for humankind.

The Supremacy of Christ (1:1–14)

In response to hearing about a number of Jewish Christians beginning to leave the church in order to return to the familiarity of their traditional rites and rituals, the author sends this letter to show them exactly what they are abandoning. In the opening chapters, he describes the superiority of Jesus by making a number of contrasts. In this section he begins by comparing Jesus to angels.

Background & Context

It appears clear that Hebrews was written prior to the destruction of Jerusalem in AD 70. The author's comment in 2:3 indicates that he is addressing only the second generation of Christians, so a date in the 60s of the first century seems most likely.

Such a Great Salvation (2:1–18)

After an emphatic opening showing that Jesus is far superior to any other prophet and even the angels, the author now applies that knowledge to personal faith. Throughout the letter he will repeatedly return to the importance of persevering in the Christian faith.

Jesus Compared to Moses (3:1–19)

Knowing of his readers' high regard for angels, the writer of Hebrews has just concluded a section of how Jesus is far superior to the angelic beings. In this section he turns his attention to another hero of the Jewish people—Moses. While his readers had good reason to admire Moses for his faithfulness and great accomplishments, his deeds pale when contrasted to the life of Jesus Christ.

Rest for the Faithful (4:1–13)

The writer of Hebrews began a persuasive argument in 3:7 that continues in this section. He is reminding his hearers of the history of Israel in the wilderness and of the people's failure to enter the rest of God because of their unbelief. He is also warning them that if they turn away from God, they must expect the same consequences. In this section he continues his comparison of the first-century Hebrew Christians to the Israelites of the Exodus.

Jesus Compared to Aaron (4:14–5:10)

So far in his letter, the author of Hebrews has demonstrated how Christ is superior to the Old Testament prophets, to the angels, and to Moses. In this section he continues his series of contrasts by comparing Jesus to Aaron and other well-respected high priests.

Steady Growth and Stronger Hope (5:11–6:20)

In the author's alternations between exposition and application, this section brings us to another section of application. He is preparing to move on to another segment about the importance of Jesus Christ, but first he pauses to prepare his hearers. His preparation includes a scolding, yet what he has to say is a reminder, in no uncertain terms, of the basic theme of the letter.

Jesus Compared to Melchizedek (7:1–28)

Continuing his explanation of how Jesus Christ is superior to the Levitical priests in regard to providing salvation, in this section the author focuses on Melchizedek. He has already mentioned the Old Testament character a few times (5:6, 10; 6:20) but will now explain the significance of *when* he appears in scripture and *how* his ministry prefigured that of Jesus.

Background & Context

At the time when Hebrews was written, Jewish Christians were still participating (and rightly so) in sacrificial worship in the Jerusalem temple, yet most still had an incorrect or incomplete perception of the significance of such rites. Many Jews of the first century looked at the Mosaic arrangements as a complete way of salvation. They were comfortable with the system, so they felt no need for a redeemer who would die for their sins. Because they perceived their sacrifices as salvation itself, they didn't see that the sacrifices actually symbolized something (or someone) else.

The Work of a High Priest (8:1–13)

The author of Hebrews continues his ongoing discussion of comparisons and contrasts between the role of Jesus as High Priest and the priests who came before Him—Aaron and Melchizedek among them. In this section he shifts his perspective a bit, focusing not only on *what* Jesus does in His role of High Priest, but also *where*. And he makes some significant observations pertaining to the new covenant contrasted to the old covenant.

Sacrifice and Salvation (9:1–28)

In the previous section the author had begun a discussion of the superiority of Christ's priestly work to that of the Levitical priests, but had included a brief parenthetical section about the difference between the broken Mosaic covenant and the "better covenant" that had replaced it. In this section he will return to his original thought and describe how the sacrificial blood of Christ would at last provide genuine and lasting cleansing for sin.

The Only Meaningful Sacrifice (10:1–39)

The author has been elaborating on the significance of the person and work of Jesus Christ in the role of High Priest, especially in contrast to the work of the Levitical priests. In this section he continues and concludes that line of thought, reemphasizing some of what he has already said and adding new applications to the information he has been providing.

Noteworthy Faith (11:1–40)

After a lengthy and somewhat complicated plea for his readers to strengthen their faith and hold out for all the wonderful things God had promised them, the writer now turns to their history as a means of persuasion. He provides example after example of people who demonstrated faith that led to positive results. They were all people who chose to be faithful despite never receiving what they had been promised—something he is asking his readers to do.

The Loving Discipline of God (12:1–29)

This section of Hebrews continues the author's thought from the previous section. The reason he has just listed so many exemplary people of faith is so his readers would be inspired to imitate them. Here he provides practical insight for what to expect as his listeners begin to recommit themselves to Christ and return to the faith they were being lured away from. He begins with a positive petition but adds a severe warning for anyone who continues to resist God.

Background & Context

The same word translated "begged" in verse 19 is translated "refuse" in verse 25. Such an observation suggests that the Old Testament Israelites weren't so much awed by the presence of God as resistant to hearing His Word. Perhaps they didn't make the request (to hear no further Word spoken to them) out of reverence for God, but rather out of the craven fear that comes from unbelief. This view can be supported by their behavior with the golden calf less than a month later. In addition, the quotation by Moses (12:21) was not taken from the Exodus account on Sinai, but from Deuteronomy, where Moses was reflecting on the sin of the people with the golden calf. It seems he was not expressing fear about being in the presence of God, but about what would happen to Israel as a result of their unbelief and disobedience.

Practical Applications for Persevering Faith (13:1–25)

This section appears to take an abrupt turn. It seems strange that the writer pauses in the delivery of his long sermon on the absolute necessity of having a persevering faith in Christ to list some specific duties that may not seem to bear directly on what he had previously written. Yet it is characteristic of the Bible to specify particular ways in which a believer should practice and work out the faith to which he or she has been summoned in any given passage. Hebrews is no different in this respect.

Background & Context

Animal sacrifices were no longer necessary. Rather, believers were to offer God a sacrifice of praise (13:15-16)—a confession of His sufficiency and a commitment to do good works. The good deeds have nothing to do with acquiring salvation, but are in response to the forgiveness and righteousness God provides. The language of the Old Testament is brought into the New as yet another proof that the liturgical teaching of the Old Testament is still a valuable model for principles and practices of worship. Offering sacrifices to God is still completely appropriate, but the blood of animals is no longer necessary. Sacrifices of praise connect the worshipper's daily life with his or her worship of God. It is a response far greater than some cash or a check dropped into the offering plate each Sunday.

James
Introduction to James

James's instructions echo those found in the Old Testament, but they also repeat Jesus' own teachings. James is teaching new believers what it means to live out their faith in Christ as Lord. (The Greek word *pistis*, translated "faith," appears fifteen times in the letter.)

Author

James was the natural son of Joseph and Mary and the younger half brother of Jesus, since they shared a mother but not a father. James is always mentioned first in the lists of Jesus' siblings (Matthew 13:55; Mark 6:3), indicating that he was most likely the eldest of Jesus' half siblings. He is also mentioned in Acts 15:13;

21:18; 1 Corinthians 15:7; Galatians 1:19; 2:9, 12; James 1:1; and Jude 1.

Although he did not believe in Jesus as his Lord during Jesus' early earthly ministry (John 7:5), after the Resurrection James became the leader of the Jerusalem church from AD 44–62. He presided over the Jerusalem Council (Acts 15), and he was considered by Paul to be a pillar of the church, alongside Peter and John (Galatians 2:9). According to Josephus, a first-century Jewish historian, the Jewish Sanhedrin sentenced James to a martyr's death in AD 62.

Occasion/Purpose

The book of James is one of seven letters in the New Testament called the "general" or "catholic" epistles (*catholic* meaning "universal") because it is addressed to a general Christian audience, rather than a specific congregation. Its tone is one of pastoral exhortation. More than fifty of the 108 verses in the letter are imperatives, but James writes his commands in a way that is filled with care and concern for his brothers. Because of its teaching flavor, many scholars consider James more of a sermon in written form than a letter.

James was a Jewish Christian writing to a Jewish Christian audience. The letter is replete with Old Testament teachings and allusions, but it is clear that James wrote from a distinctly Christian perspective and from the experience of one who had spent time with Jesus. The audience was a group of Christians who were experiencing persecution for their faith. James wrote to them to encourage them in the face of trials and to help them know how to stand firm in the faith.

Themes

James's letter is a pragmatist's dream. He gives his wise instruction in a distinctive rubber-meets-the-road way that only a firsthand witness can. He shows that it is not good enough to have faith without works, but believers must do right acts for the right reasons. James's overall concern is consistency in practicing faith through obedient acts that produce results—truly hearing God equals obeying Him. Submitting to God means living out what one says he or she believes. Loving one's neighbors affects the tongue. Caring for the oppressed is a result of obedience to a just God. James calls for submission to Christ in genuine faith that works.

Facing Trials and Living Out Faith (1:1–27)

Early in the church, Christians were gaining their own identity apart from Jews, but this new identity came through much persecution. James urges the believers to persevere in the midst of trials in order to strengthen their faith so they may become righteous in their actions. The call in this chapter is to live with unconditional obedience to God.

Background & Context

Many scholars date James as early as AD 45-48, which would make it perhaps the earliest New Testament Epistle. There are several reasons for this conclusion:

- The Council of Jerusalem took place about AD 50, yet it is not mentioned in James. In fact, there is no reference to a conflict about requirements for Gentile Christians, the well-known debate of the Council, so it is assumed that James's letter predates it.
- Church leaders are called by Jewish terms, *teachers* and *elders*, rather than later church terms, *overseers* and *deacons*.
- The synagogue is mentioned as the meeting place of Christians (2:2).
- James addresses his letter only to Jewish Christians ("the twelve tribes scattered among the nations," James 1:1 TNIV), which suggests that the mission to the Gentiles had not yet begun. James may well be writing to the Jewish Christians who were dispersed from their homeland during the persecution described in Acts 8.

Love, Faith, and Action (2:1–26)

In the second chapter of his letter, James again calls for consistency in living out faith. The first half of this chapter deals with consistency in loving others regardless of their socioeconomic status; the second half calls for consistency in one's works and words.

This chapter in James has seemed troublesome to some. At issue is the relationship between faith and works. James agrees that one is saved by faith alone and not by works, but he emphasizes that genuine faith produces fruit. James concludes that workless faith—like faithless works—is unmeritorious before our heavenly Father.

Background & Context

The Jews had started a practice of seating those with privilege or position closer to the front where the Torah and other scripture were kept on scrolls, while other "less important" people were seated in the back. This practice continued in some Christian churches in the first century. Similar preferential treatment takes place in churches still today, but James says it should stop.

Wise Living (3:1–18)

This passage includes James's famous teachings on the power of speech. He refers to the combination of thought and speech, and the precariously instantaneous connection between the two by talking about the power of the tongue.

James says the tongue is challenging to tame. It is as unmanageable as a raging fire and as harmful as poison. What's more, it is disproportionately influential: It bears tremendous weight for its relatively small mass. Usually this influence is negative, but when managed properly it can wage a significantly positive force.

Put It in Perspective (4:1–17)
James is writing to believers who did not always find it easy to get along. There were pockets of disunity, arguments, disagreements, criticisms, and personal attacks taking place among these believers. His words go to the heart of the problem and address what is probably the most basic human sin: pride. He challenges believers to submit to God wholeheartedly.

Wealth, Waiting, and Prayer (5:1–20)
In the final chapter of his letter, James continues his focus on having an eternal perspective. He begins with a focus on material wealth and a warning to the rich who find their security in the here and now. Then he encourages believers to endure in the present by focusing on Christ. Finally, he points readers to trusting in God by praying earnestly.

1 Peter
Introduction to 1 Peter

First Peter is a great book to shatter any false expectations about who God is and what it means to serve God. It gives us realistic expectations about what this world has to offer and what perspective can help us through the tough times.

Author
This letter was written by Peter, one of Jesus' twelve disciples, who became a leader of the first-century Christian church. Because of the high quality of the Greek language used in this letter, some have doubted that Peter, the common fisherman, could have been the author. This argument is not strong, however. Greek was widely spoken in Galilee, and so Peter may well have been fluent in the language. Peter also notes at the end of the letter that he wrote "with the help of Silvanus" (or, Silas; 5:12). Like other New Testament writers (see Romans 16:22; Galatians 6:11), Peter may have dictated the letter to Silas, who improved the style and quality of the Greek.

Occasion/Purpose
Peter writes to believers living in Asia Minor to encourage them to faithfully endure persecution in light of the glorious salvation Christ has accomplished for them, and to see their suffering as a normal part of their service to God.

Peter addresses this letter to "God's elect, strangers in the world, scattered throughout Pontus, Galatia, Cappadocia, Asia, and Bithynia" (1:1)—the provinces of Asia Minor (present-day Turkey). The churches in this region were made up of both Jewish and Gentile Christians, though they were primarily Gentile. Several of Peter's statements suggest his audience is mostly Gentile (1:14; 2:10; 4:3–4).

Peter's purpose is stated in 1 Peter 5:12, where he tells the believers to stand firm in the true grace of God. The believers were experiencing a great deal of opposition and persecution because of their faith (1:6; 3:13–17; 4:12–19). Peter addresses them as "strangers" (NIV) or "exiles" (TNIV), living in a world that was growing increasingly hostile to Christians. By standing firm in the grace of God, they would be able to endure their "fiery ordeal" (4:12), knowing that there was a divine purpose behind their suffering and pain.

The letter was probably written in the early to mid AD 60s, shortly before or during the severe persecutions instigated by the Roman emperor Nero. Some have said that the context of the letter is the later empire-wide persecutions of Domitian (AD 81–96) or Trajan (AD 98–117). But in Peter, the persecutions seem to be local trials and hatred, not official state-sanctioned persecution. In later persecution, sacrifices to the emperors were a key issue. This does not appear to be the case in this letter. While Christianity had not yet been banned officially, there was a growing hatred for Christians, especially because (1) they lived differently, (2) they refused to worship pagan gods, and (3) they boldly preached the Gospel. Peter says, "Do not be surprised" at such persecution, because you are resident aliens in this world (2 Corinthians 5:20; Philippians 3:20; 1 Peter 4:12).

Peter claims to be writing from "Babylon" (5:13), which is probably a cryptic reference to Rome. The reasons for this are as follows:

- Literal Babylon on the Euphrates was almost deserted by New Testament times.
- "Babylon" appears to be used as a symbolic title for Rome in Revelation 17:3–6, 9, 18, and in other literature.
- Church tradition says nothing about Peter's travels to Babylon but tells us he went to Rome and was martyred there.
- John Mark is with Peter when he writes this letter (5:13). Mark is mentioned with Paul during his first imprisonment in Rome (Colossians 4:10) and probably came to him there during his second imprisonment (2 Timothy 4:11).

Themes
Major themes in 1 Peter include submission to authority, suffering because of faith in Christ, and shepherding the flock of believers. In these themes we are given the proper expectations that we are to have when we consider what it means to be a Christian.

God's Plan for Humanity (1:1–2:3)
This letter begins with the traditional greeting, identifying Peter as an apostle of Jesus and stating to whom he is writing. The author is the same Peter who was called by Jesus to be an apostle and the same Peter who struggled with learning how to follow God by faith and not in the power of his own emotional zeal.

God's Plan for the Church (2:4–25)
How do we live out this purification of our souls? How do we identify ourselves to the world around us? How do we relate to the governmental structure of our cultures? These are the kinds of questions Peter addresses in this passage.

Background & Context

Keep in mind which government Peter called these people to submit to—a government that did not respect Christianity, that supported practices that were offensive to God, and in months and years to come would begin a persecution of the church that would last for hundreds of years. Nevertheless, Peter wants them to see God's design for government and to submit for the Lord's sake. Of course there is a line in the sand—if the authority calls us to disobey God then we must reject their rule. But, short of that circumstance, we are not above the day-to-day ruling of the law.

God's Plan for the Christian (3:1–22)

What do the roles of husbands and wives reveal to the world about God? Peter reminds his readers not just of the acts of submission, but of the heart of submission—to God first, then within our relationships.

God's Plan for Suffering (4:1–19)

Peter's goal in both of his letters is to prepare the church to endure suffering. He does this by showing the reader the intrinsic value of suffering. When we suffer in this world, God uses it to mold us into the image of Christ. The reality of being molded into the image of Christ is a very important part of our formation. In this section, Peter wants us to see how suffering is used to achieve this goal.

Living Soberly (5:1–14)

Peter begins this final section of his letter talking about the role of the elders within the church. He also offers believers some final instructions concerning living in this world. By reminding the elders of their importance, mission, and future, Peter reveals the proper environment necessary for the flock to live soberly in a world that is drunk on its own pleasure and self-deception.

Background & Context

The position of a shepherd in the first century was not a position of honor. The fact that Peter uses this term to describe leaders brings an automatic idea of humility and service.

2 Peter
Introduction to 2 Peter

Late in the first century, the church was in an increasingly vulnerable position. In addition to the continuing threat of persecution, false teachers began to arise and distort the true message. At the same time, the apostles, who had established the church and provided its early leadership, were beginning to die off or suffer martyrdom. This letter deals with the problems that come when false teachers sneak into the Christian fold with the goal of turning people away from the message of Christ and enticing them with their own false message grounded in worldly wisdom and human achievement.

Author
The writer of this book identifies himself as Peter, one of Jesus' twelve disciples. Many have questioned Peter's authorship because of language differences with 1 Peter, among other things. However, conservative scholars still agree that while acknowledging the difficulties of the letter's authorship, Peter is a viable option.

Occasion/Purpose
Peter's goal in writing is to fortify the church against false teaching. He wants to give the standard of truth to the church so that once he and the rest of the apostles are gone, the church will be able to stand strong against heresy. In order for the standard of truth to be established, Peter must show the true knowledge of God, the nature of the false teachers, and how to stand firm in the midst of both.

Peter is near the end of his life. This letter was probably written from Rome, about three years after Peter's first letter, around AD 67.

Themes
Themes in 2 Peter include false teachers (2:1–22; 3:3–5) and Jesus' return (3:3–14).

Contribution to the Bible
The trials that Peter deals with in his first letter focus on conflict against the church coming from the outside in the form of persecution. 2 Peter is different in that it deals with the conflict and the trials that arise *within* the church because of false teaching.

The True Knowledge of God Explained (1:1–21)
In the first four verses, Peter declares that he is the true apostle, states the authentic message that is to be believed, and reveals what the authentic Christian life really is. He does this so the readers will not succumb to the perversion of the Gospel that was being preached in their midst. The truths outlined in these verses, as well as in all of chapter 1, represent the core doctrines that were being twisted by false teachers.

Background & Context
False teachers had sought to overrun the church and destroy the foundation of the doctrine under which the church was established. Peter writes about the importance of the Gospel so that the church would be strengthened and secure in the midst of false teaching. The letter has many words, phrases, and themes in common with the letter of Jude, and scholars debate which was written first and which author borrowed from the other.

The True Knowledge of God Attacked (2:1–22)
This section continues where chapter 1 leaves off, comparing the Old Testament prophets to the false teachers who had invaded the lives of Peter's readers.

The True Knowledge of God Protected (3:1–18)
Chapter 3 transitions from a description of the false teachers to encouragement for the readers. It is a chapter of reminders meant to help the church understand who God is, how to stay true to His message, and how to live in a world with false teaching.

Background & Context
In the Old Testament, the "Day of the Lord" was the future time when God would vindicate His holy name, bring judgment on those who refuse to believe, and gather His people into a new kingdom of righteousness and peace (Zephaniah 1:14-18; Malachi 4:1-3).

In the New Testament, beginning with Jesus, the day took on the connotation of Jesus' final return and judgment (Matthew 24:42-44; Acts 2:20; 1 Thessalonians 5:2-4).

1 John
Introduction to 1 John

The New Testament book we refer to as 1 John is a letter to a community of faith. Much of this letter is written to combat heresy regarding the identity of Jesus. The conflict over this heresy caused part of the congregation to split from the rest. John writes to ground the community in a true picture of not only Jesus' identity, but the identity of the children of God in light of who Jesus is.

Author
Determining the author of 1 John is somewhat different from determining the author of 2 and 3 John. In the case of 1 John, no author is identified in the work

itself. However, the author does identify himself as an eyewitness of Jesus' ministry. He also speaks with an apostolic kind of authority and writes in a similar style to the Gospel of John. There is good evidence, both historical and internal, that supports the traditional view of John the apostle as author.

Occasion/Purpose

The purpose statement for 1 John can be found in 5:13. We can deduce from this verse that the author is writing to believers and that his purpose is to assure them that they do indeed possess eternal life. Although this letter is written in response to a specific situation (the false teachers who had withdrawn from fellowship), it has a relevant message for the church at large.

John appears to be writing to a community to which he is well-known, and to which he may belong. Because this Christian community has undergone a serious split, and a substantial part of the community has withdrawn from fellowship over doctrinal issues, John writes to reassure them of their faith.

The group that has split off is continuing to propagate its own beliefs, seeking to persuade more community members to join them. John writes to warn members of the community to resist the proselytizing efforts of these false teachers by bolstering their understanding of the truth.

Themes

While this letter is written to combat theological opponents, the themes of walking in light and confessing Jesus as Christ are repeated throughout all of it.

In John's attempts to assure the believers of their eternal life (5:13), he also repeatedly emphasizes two basic components of that assurance: obedience to God and the love of fellow Christians.

God Is Light (1:1–10)

The use of a prologue to begin a work is characteristic of both the Gospel of John and 1 John. This section of John's first letter lays the foundation for the rest.

Obeying the Light (2:1–29)

This section contains three claims to intimate knowledge of God (2:4, 6, 9). As with the three "if we say" clauses in chapter 1 (1:6, 8, 10), these claims indirectly reflect the claims of the false teachers. The focus of the subject matter shifts from awareness and acknowledgment of sin to obedience of God's commandments. The concept of fellowship, introduced in the prologue (1:4), is replaced by an emphasis on knowing and loving God along with one's fellow believers.

Background & Context

In the New Testament, blindness is frequently a spiritual condition associated with deliberate disbelief. Particularly applicable to verses 9-11 is John 12:39-40, where deliberate refusal to believe, in spite of the miracles Jesus had performed, led to an inability to believe. Just as those who refuse to come to the light are left in darkness, so those who refuse to love fellow members of the Christian community are said to be in darkness.

God Is Love (3:1–24)
Within this section, the first 3 verses are a parenthesis in which John reflects on what it means to be fathered by God, a subject he has already mentioned at the end of 2:29. The flow of the argument against the false teachers is then resumed by verse 4.

Understanding God's Love (4:1–21)
Since the book of 1 John has a rather free structure, many interpreters divide it in a multitude of ways, breaking sections in a variety of places. With almost no exception, though, the opening six verses of chapter 4 are kept together as a section standing on its own. It opens this chapter, which focuses on understanding God's love.

God Is Life (5:1–21)
In this section, John will explain that the means by which believers conquer the world (including, of course, the false teachers, who are now part of the world according to 1 John 4:5) is their faith: faith in what Jesus has done during His earthly life and ministry, including His sacrificial death on the cross. For John, this is a faith the false teachers do not possess.

2 John
Introduction to 2 John

Second John is a personal letter written to warn a sister congregation some distance away. In its original Greek manuscript, it is shorter than any other New Testament book, except 3 John (with 219 words). The length of both 2 and 3 John is governed by the size of a single sheet of papyrus, which would have measured about 25 by 20 centimeters.

Author
As with the Gospel of John, the author does not explicitly identify himself as the apostle John. Instead, he uses the designation *the elder*. He obviously assumes the readers know him. However, the style of writing is unmistakably similar to that of 1 John. Also, as early as the second century, Christian historians and theologians recognized the author as the apostle John, one of the original twelve disciples.

Occasion/Purpose
The purpose of this letter is to warn its readers of the missionary efforts of false teachers and the dangers of welcoming them whenever they should arrive.

Both 1 and 2 John are written in response to the same kinds of false teachers. This letter offers specific instructions about how to deal with the traveling preachers who were being sent out to local congregations. There is no conclusive evidence for the actual date, but this book was probably written around the same time as 1 John (around AD 90), while John was in Ephesus.

Themes
Second John has the same themes that can be found in other writings by John: how to know the truth, how to live a life of love within that truth, and how to identify false teaching regarding the Christian faith.

Walking in Love (1–13)
Second John is written in a format characteristic of first-century letters. It begins with an introduction (verses 1–3), which mentions the sender and the addressee, and includes a greeting. Many letters of this period follow the greeting with an expression of thanksgiving or a wish for the health of the addressee. Although no explicit expression of thanksgiving is found in 2 John, John's expression of joy in verse 4 may be roughly equivalent.

3 John
Introduction to 3 John

Third John, like 2 John, is written in the standard correspondence format for the first century. It is slightly shorter than 2 John and is the shortest book of the New Testament. It is the only one of the three New Testament letters to be addressed to a named individual.

Author
As with the Gospel of John, the author does not explicitly identify himself as the apostle John, but instead uses the designation *the elder*. As early as the second century, though, Christian historians and theologians recognized the author as the apostle John, one of the original twelve disciples.

Occasion/Purpose
John wrote this letter to commend two church leaders, Gaius and Demetrius, and to send a warning about Diotrephes, a man who opposed John's leadership.

The problem with Diotrephes was not a problem with heresy (as in 1 and 2 John) as much as authority. He was evidently trying to diminish John's authority as well as censure those sent by John. It was this behavior that prompted John to write to Gaius.

Themes

John's third, short letter deals with the themes of hospitality toward the traveling teachers who spread the Gospel in the first century. It also speaks to pride and its effect on leadership within a community.

Walking in Truth (1–15)

Third John begins with an introductory formula (verses 1–2) that mentions the sender and the addressee. The greeting, a standard part of the introduction, is omitted, but unlike 2 John, the letter includes a health wish (verse 3).

Jude
Introduction to Jude

Truth and discernment are two key themes of this book. A believer's security in God's love opens and closes the letter, but the meat of the content pertains to the false teachers in the midst and the need for believers to stand firm in the truth.

Author

The author of this letter is Jude, the brother of James. Most likely these brothers are the same brothers listed in Matthew 13:55 and Mark 6:3 as Jesus' half brothers, born to Joseph and Mary after Jesus' birth. It was common in the history of the church to shorten the name of Judas to Jude, in the interest of changing one's name from that of the great betrayer, Judas Iscariot. While these two brothers did not have faith in Jesus as Lord during His lifetime (John 7:5), they became leaders in the first-century Christian church, and each wrote a New Testament letter.

Occasion/Purpose

This epistle is a passionate plea for the readers to contend for their faith. In light of a growing heresy in the church that understood grace as a license for immorality, Jude wrote to an unidentified group of Christ-followers to call them back to faith.

We don't know exactly when Jude was written, but many estimate around AD 65. The content of Jude and 2 Peter are closely related, and this has prompted discussion about which came first and which provided reference for the other.

While it had been Jude's intent to write to this particular group of believers on the topic of salvation (verse 3), what prompted this letter was news of false teaching.

Themes

Truth and discernment are two key themes of this book. A believer's security in God's love opens and closes the letter, but the meat of the content pertains to the false teachers in the midst and the need for believers to stand firm in the truth.

Contending for the Faith (1–4)

In this section, Jude gives his reasons for writing and a strongly worded identification of the enemies of the faith.

The Description of False Teachers (5–16)

Jude wants his readers to see the true nature of false teachers so that they will not try to please them or keep them close. False teachers are not people to be reasoned with; they are a danger to the congregation and, as Jude will point out, need be avoided.

Background & Context

Jude lists three more examples from the Old Testament that shed light on these false teachers (verse 11):

1. Like Cain, who offered up his sacrifice to the Lord on his own strength without faith, the false teachers try to please God on their terms and seek to do their work in the flesh (Genesis 4:1-16).
2. Like Balaam, the prophet who led the people of God astray for money, the false teachers follow their passion for wealth at the expense of the people (Numbers 22:1-34).
3. Like Korah's followers, who rebelled against Moses and were swallowed up in the earth, these teachers will be judged (Numbers 16:1-35).

In verses 12-13, Jude describes these troublesome teachers as sunken reefs (concealed danger), self-focused feasters, waterless clouds (empty promises), fruitless trees (twice dead because they came to faith, then fell away), waves carrying impurities to the beach (see Isaiah 57:20), and shooting stars that fall into the darkness.

The Defense against False Teachers (17–23)

Up to this point Jude has been making his case against the false teachers, but here he focuses on his main point. Discernment and mercy are requirements for this community—discernment so one does not get carried away by false teaching and mercy to reach out to those who have been influenced by heresy.

The Doxology (24–25)

As Jude brings his Epistle to a close, he focuses on the sustaining power of God.

Revelation
Introduction to Revelation

The word *revelation* means "unveiling," or "disclosure." This is a book that reveals how the person, righteousness, and judgment of Jesus are going to be revealed in all of the fullness and power of God.

Understanding a symbolic book like this requires putting together whole sections rather than reading select verses in isolation. The meaning of Revelation comes from unfolding the entire book chapter by chapter. The message is God's sovereignty over all.

Author

As with most New Testament books, through the centuries there has been discussion as to the author of this letter. While the writer identifies himself as John (1:1), some have wondered if it is safe to assume that this means the apostle John. Many of the arguments on this topic center around the language differences from the other New Testament books attributed to the apostle (the Gospel of John and 1 John). There has been no irrefutable evidence, though, to sway conservative scholars from accepting John's authorship.

Occasion/Purpose

The church in the first century was suffering. Many of the original apostles had been martyred for the faith, and John had been arrested and placed in exile on the island of Patmos. The fires of persecution were burning, and the immediate future seemed to hold only increasing difficulty. The first-century Christians needed spiritual, mental, emotional, and physical stability to stand firm in their trials. The overall purpose of this letter is to encourage those Christians. They needed to know that the kingdom of God would overcome the kingdoms of the world, and that all those who oppose God and oppress God's children would be brought to justice.

Since so many of the images in Revelation are often interpreted in relation to governments and political leaders, discussions about when the book was written focus on which emperor was ruling at the time. Many suggest that Nero must have been ruling, but most suggest that John wrote during the time of Domitian, which would have placed the writing of this vision letter around AD 90–95. One of the biggest supports for this date is the fact that emperor worship—which is repeatedly alluded to in John's visions—was a much greater issue during Domitian's rule than during Nero's.

Themes

First, John's book reveals significant aspects of the character and future work of Jesus Christ, the Lamb of God. Secondly, the eternality and sovereignty of God is a major theme. The idea that God is outside of time and sovereign over human history is encouraging, because we can know that He is above the things in the earth that drive us down. God is holding all things together, and therefore, no matter how much it looks like evil is winning, that is not the reality.

Contribution to the Bible

Revelation is the only book of prophecy in the New Testament and the only book that focuses so heavily on the end times. It offers us a symbolic, but rich, vision of the end of the age that is mentioned in places in the other New Testament writings.

Eternal Hope (1:1–20)

The book of Revelation, while a type of literature known as "apocalyptic" (a Greek word meaning "revelation"), is written in the form of a letter. It opens with a greeting typical for a New Testament Epistle.

John opens his letter with the truth of God's power and eternal nature. This would have been an encouragement to his readers who were facing increasing persecution for their faith. The first-century Christians needed spiritual, mental, emotional, and physical stability to stand firm in their trials. They would have been strengthened by the knowledge that God has a plan, and no matter how much it looks like evil is winning, that is not the reality.

Background & Context

Verse 4 begins a section of letters to seven churches in Asia. These seven churches are all located in the western part of what we know today as Turkey. They all face differing circumstances and struggle with a variety of issues. Though these letters address the specific situations of each church, all together they offer a wealth of application for the church at large today.

Letters to the Churches (2:1–3:22)

While some see these churches as only symbolic, it is more likely these were messages to specific congregations. What we do know about the cities addressed here meshes with the specific messages John writes. The situations of these churches vary, and thus John addresses many issues that churches still face today.

These letters do not represent a collection of letters that were once circulated separately, but were from the beginning part of the book of Revelation. The whole book was meant to circulate among the seven churches.

Background & Context

Little is known about the church of Philadelphia apart from this passage. Like most of the other churches, it was probably founded through Paul's ministry to Ephesus. One interesting note is that this church lasted for centuries. The people stood firm in the face of major persecution.

Oh, Worship the King (4:1–11)

From this point on, John's writing transitions from the letters to the church to the vision of heaven. He begins with a vision of God Himself.

The Lion and the Lamb (5:1–14)

In chapter 5, John's visions transition from God the Creator to Jesus the Redeemer. Here the nature of Jesus will come into view when we see the final judgment of the world taking place. Jesus will be the Judge; thus He is called the Lion. Yet Jesus is also the Savior of the world; thus He is called the Lamb. As the Lamb, He took the sin of humanity so that they might stand redeemed before God.

The Four Horsemen of the Apocalypse (6:1–17)
Beginning in chapter 6, and continuing into chapters 7 and 8, the scroll is unrolled and its seals are broken. Rather than reading the scroll, John experiences it in visions.

The unrolling of the scroll marks the judgment of God upon the earth—justice brought to the world. The first four seals on the scroll reveal the sin of humanity unleashed on the earth.

The Dramatic Pause (7:1–17)
Chapter 7 describes a pause between the sixth and seventh seal. This pause sets up the events just prior to the wrath of God being poured out on the earth. It is a moment God stops the clock to provide divine protection.

The Wrath of God (8:1–13)
Here is the beginning of the wrath of God. The judgment of Jesus is going to be carried out. This is the great moment of justice that suffering believers have been praying for.

The Day of the Lord (9:1–21)
Just as the last three seals pertain to things of heaven rather than earth, the last three trumpets deal with the realm of the supernatural—in this case, though, it's the demonic rather than angelic realm.

The Messenger, the Message, and a Meal (10:1–11)
Just as there was a pause between the sixth and the seventh seal, there is now a pause between the sixth and seventh trumpet. This pause is composed of two main sections: First an angel and a little book, then two witnesses come to declare the glory and wrath of God.

The section provides a specific warning. God has judged people in general. Now He will judge the leaders of the world system that sets its agenda against God.

Two Witnesses and One Last Trumpet (11:1–19)
In this chapter we will see a measuring of the temple and two witnesses emerging to give testimony. As with much of Revelation, these events can be interpreted either literally or symbolically. If taken symbolically, many interpret the measuring of the temple to reflect a description of the emerging Christian church based on the familiar temple of Jerusalem. By the same token, a symbolic interpretation often sees the two witnesses as a reflection of the martyrs of the church who give testimony with their lives, rather than two specific men. Whichever interpretive path, this section continues the theme of God's judgment as He begins to hold the world outside of the church accountable.

The Seven Signs (12:1–17)

Chapter 12 begins a series of seven visions that will extend into chapter 14. These visions do not have a repeating symbol, like the seven seals or seven trumpets. But they are similar in that they flesh out the conflict between God and His church and the forces of evil that would seek to destroy both.

The Antichrist and the False Prophet (13:1–18)

At this point in Revelation, we have seen the judgment of God on the earth in a general sense. This judgment has been carried out toward the earth and the people of the earth.

In chapter 10, God begins to deal directly with Satan and all those who have intentionally and directly supported his efforts to oppose Jesus. This final judgment on Satan is the reason worship breaks out at the end of chapter 11.

Chapter 12 describes the plight of Israel (the woman), Jesus (the child of the woman), Satan (the dragon), and the church (the other offspring of the woman). Satan, as revealed in this chapter, has one goal—to destroy the Messiah. Because he cannot destroy the Messiah, he seeks to do away with Israel. Because he cannot do away with Israel, he goes after the church.

In chapter 13, the story line continues with a final move of Satan in trying to oppose the Messiah through a false messiah—otherwise referred to by the contemporary church as the Antichrist. (Chapter 14 will show that this attempt will not be successful.) Also in chapter 13, we will see the description of the man whom the Antichrist will possess, referred to as the false prophet.

The Protection and Power of God (14:1–20)

In chapter 14, we see God's response to the attack of the two beasts described in chapter 13. The beast's goal has been to stop the Messiah, destroy the Jews, and persecute the church. Here God claims His own and begins the final harvest.

Background & Context

This is the first of several times in Revelation that Babylon is mentioned (16:19; 17:5; 18:1-24). The actual city of Babylon began after the Flood with the story of the tower of Babel (Genesis 10:10; 11:9).

Throughout the history of the Bible, Babylon represented pride, power, and wickedness. Some say that John was using Babylon here to represent Rome. Certainly his original readers would have seen Rome as the oppressive power they were experiencing. But there is a much broader interpretation as well. Babylon can represent the pride and wickedness of humanity that opposes God.

Prelude to Destruction (15:1–8)

Chapters 15–16 include another sevenfold image. In this instance, the image is of seven angels pouring out the contents of bowls. The contents contain God's wrath—His final judgment.

Background & Context

Understanding the temple is a key to understanding many of the terms John uses to describe his visions in Revelation. For instance, there were bowls in the temple that served a significant role in worship. In the sin offering (Leviticus 4), blood was put in a bowl and then sprinkled and poured out during the ceremony. The bowls are used similarly here in the vision of the seven angels with seven plagues. In this case, the angels do not receive bowls with blood; instead, they receive bowls with anger and judgment. The eternal God who cannot be in the presence of sin will fill these bowls with His wrath, and they will be poured out on the earth.

Verse 8 describes the temple as filled with smoke. In the scriptures, smoke has often accompanied majesty and power. It was one of the signs of the presence of God (Exodus 40:34-35) and one of the signs of the awesome wrath of God. In this closing verse of chapter 15, God's glory, all the attributes of His character, and His power fill the temple, and there is no room for anything else until the plagues are poured out by the angels. All must stop and watch the mighty power of God on display.

The Six Bowls (16:1–21)

In the judgments up to this point, there has been partial destruction. A portion of the stars, a portion of the earth, or a portion of the sea was destroyed, but not the whole of anything. In this case, total destruction will begin. All of the people who worship the beast are affected, all of nature is affected, and the end is destruction.

Seven bowls of judgment are described in the upcoming chapters, and they symbolize the final events of God's punishment of those who reject Him.

The Destruction of Babylon (17:1–18)

Thus far in Revelation, John's message has carried the theme of God's sovereignty. No matter what powers *seem* to exist, God is the One with the ultimate power and with the choice to decide when to display that power.

With chapter 17, the theme of the remainder of the book becomes the final judgment of God. He has chosen to display His power against evil, and the final throw-down is in sight.

Chapter 17 is built upon the vision of a woman, a prostitute, who seems to symbolize the same thing that Babylon symbolizes in 16:19—civilization convinced it doesn't need God.

The Funeral of Humanity (18:1–24)

Chapter 18 records the destruction of Babylon. There are similarities here with the Old Testament accounts of the destruction of Tyre (Ezekiel 26–28) and with the destruction of the actual city of Babylon (Jeremiah 50–51).

When Babylon is destroyed, the entire infrastructure of humanity will be destroyed. This will create an undoing of the world that will leave humans hopeless. For John's original readers, this prophecy would have held some significance regarding the Roman Empire, but it is also the picture of all human civilizations that focus on earthly accomplishments rather than the power of the Creator.

Worship and Wrath (19:1–21)

Chapter 19 includes the great marriage ceremony of the Lamb and the return of Jesus. It is a chapter of both worship and victory, including the final destruction of the beast and his prophet.

The Completion of the Promises of God (20:1–15)

To this point in Revelation, we have seen all those who stood on the side of the beast destroyed, except one. That is Satan himself. In this section, Satan receives his judgment.

There are many interpretations of the events John describes here, as well as a variety of timetables proposed for those events. The underlying truth remains, though, that John's visions reinforce God's ability and decision to deal with sin once and for all.

All Things Bright and Beautiful (21:1–27)

Having described the fate of evil in the previous chapters, the remaining two chapters of Revelation describe visions of a new world established and ruled by God. This is the fate of the faithful, a spiritual destiny described here in earthly terms.

Eden Restored (22:1–21)

Chapter 22 continues John's vision of the new heaven and earth begun in chapter 21. Then the chapter closes with an epilogue of observations about the collection of visions that make up the book of Revelation and the promise that Jesus is coming again.

Dictionary/ Concordance
of Key Bible Names, Places, Terms, and Topics

Like the first page of a computer search engine's results, this section of *The Complete Bible Companion* provides key verse references on a broad range of topics— some crucial to the Christian faith and others simply interesting.

Unlike a computer search engine, this resource is not exhaustive. Rather, it is a quick snapshot of each name, place, term, or topic, and will not require you to search through thousands of entries in order to find one crucial verse. Where a topic has limited references in the Bible, every one may be here. But where a subject is dealt with extensively in scripture, we have chosen those related to major events in the Bible or that have a clear practical application to the Christian walk. The focus of this dictionary/concordance is to include verses that help, encourage, and provide clear direction for a searching believer.

Since similar verses often appear in several Gospels (the books of Matthew, Mark, Luke, and John), we have chosen one, usually from the book of Matthew. Readers may want to use a study Bible to compare these to the other Gospels.

Where longer passages cover a topic, we have included a few key references. Often the first and last references in a chapter have been shown, in order to "bracket" the topic. Readers may want to study the verses in between for a more complete view of the subject.

Not every reference contains the topic word; where possible, we have tried to include helpful references that use a similar word. We hope this provides a more complete view of these subjects.

Additional information on many of the people and places in the following section can be found in the "Complete List of Individuals Named in Scripture" beginning on page 379 and in "Archaeological Evidences for the Bible" beginning on page 537. An extensive section of maps begins on page 591.

A

Aaron: Elder brother of Moses and Miriam (Num. 26:59); the spokesman of Moses (Exod. 4:14); mouthpiece and encourager of Moses before the Lord and the people of Israel, and in the court of the Pharaoh (Exod. 4:30); miracle worker of the Exodus (Exod. 7:19); consecrated to the priesthood by Moses (Exod. 29); death of (Num. 20:22–29).

Abba: An Aramaic word meaning "father," used by Jesus while praying in the garden of Gethsemane (Mark 14:32, 36). The apostle Paul also used it to describe the believer's sonship with God the Father (Rom. 8:15).

Abed-nego: Name given by the prince of Chaldean eunuchs to Azariah, one of the three friends and fellow captives of Daniel at Babylon (Dan. 1:7). He refused to bow to the golden image of Nebuchadnezzar and was condemned to the fiery furnace, from which he miraculously escaped (Dan. 3).

Abel: Second son of Adam and Eve. A keeper of sheep, murdered by his brother Cain (Gen. 4:2–8). See also Heb. 11:4; 1 John 3:12; Matt. 23:35.

Abide: To trust God and live in a way that glorifies Him.
a under the shadow of the
Almighty. . .Ps. 91:1
should not a in darkness. . .
John 12:46
If a man a not in me. . .John 15:6
a in me, and my words a in you
. . .John 15:7
ye shall a in my love. . .John 15:10
little children, a in him. . .1 John
2:28

Abigail: Wife of Nabal of Carmel, and afterward of David. Noted for her beauty and wisdom (1 Sam. 25:3, 14–44).

Ability: The skill to perform an action.
They gave after their a. . .Ezra 2:69
according to his several a. . .
Matt. 25:15
every man according to his a. . .
Acts 11:29

Abimelech: A line of Philistine kings, like the Pharaohs and Caesars. Kings of Gerar (Gen. 20; 21; 26:1).

Abomination: Something detestable to God (Gen. 46:34); referring to animals and acts (Lev. 11:13); to idolatry (2 Kings 23:13; Jer. 44:4); and to sins in general (Isa. 66:3).
an a unto the Lord. . .Deut. 27:15
wickedness is an a. . .Prov. 8:7
Lying lips are a. . .Prov. 12:22
thoughts of the wicked are an a. . .
Prov. 15:26
the scorner is an a to men. . .
Prov. 24:9
a in the sight of God. . .Luke 16:15
See *Obscenity.*

Abortion: Destruction of an unborn human life.
God created man in his own image
. . .Gen. 1:27
Thou shalt not kill. . .Exod. 20:13
did not one fashion us in the
womb?. . .Job 31:15
formed thee in the belly I knew
thee. . .Jer. 1:5
even from his mother's womb. . .
Luke 1:15

Abraham/Abram: Son of Terah, a dweller in Ur of the Chaldees (Gen. 11:25–32). Founder of the Jewish nation. Migrated from Chaldea to Haran. Moved then to Canaan, to Egypt, and back to Canaan, where he settled in Mamre. There confirmed in the thrice-repeated promise that his descendants would become a mighty nation, and his name was changed from Abram to Abraham. Died at the age of 175 (Gen. 7–26).

Absalom: A son of David (2 Sam. 3:3); killed his brother Amnon (2 Sam. 13); conspired to take over his father's throne (2 Sam. 14–17); defeated and killed (2 Sam. 18).

Abstain: To refrain from eating or drinking harmful substances or from participating in sinful actions.
> a from meats offered to idols. . .
> Acts 15:29
> a from fornication. . .1 Thess. 4:3
> A from all appearance of evil. . .
> 1 Thess. 5:22
> a from fleshly lusts. . .1 Pet. 2:11

Abundance/Abundant/Abundantly: To be blessed with more than enough; a plentiful supply.
> and a't in goodness. . .Exod. 34:6
> trusted in the a of his riches. . .
> Ps. 52:7
> did cast in of their a. . .Mark 12:44
> not in the a of the things. . .
> Luke 12:15
> to do exceeding a'ly. . .Eph. 3:20
> according to his a't mercy. . .
> 1 Pet. 1:3

Abundant Life: The rich, fulfilling life that God offers to believers.
> thee the desires of thine heart. . .
> Ps. 37:4
> things shall be added unto you. . .
> Matt. 6:33
> In him was life. . .John 1:4
> ask any thing in my name. . .
> John 14:14
> able to do exceeding abundantly
> . . .Eph. 3:20
> my God shall supply all your need
> . . .Phil. 4:19

Accept/Acceptable/Accepted: To receive divine approval.
> shalt thou not be a'ed? . . .Gen. 4:7
> The Lord thy God a thee. . .
> 2 Sam. 24:23
> a'able to the Lord than sacrifice
> . . . Prov. 21:3
> sacrifice, holy, a'able unto God. . .
> Rom. 12:1
> serveth Christ is a'able to God. . .
> Rom. 14:18
> the Gentiles might be a'able. . .
> Rom. 15:16
> good and a'able before God. . .
> 1 Tim. 5:4

Achan: The Judahite who was stoned to death for concealing the spoils of Jericho (Josh. 7:16–26).

Adam: 1. The first man, created by God on the sixth day and placed in the garden of Eden. Tempted to eat of the forbidden fruit, fell under God's disfavor, and driven out of the garden. Subject to the curse of sorrow and toil. Died at the age of 930 (Gen. 1–5). 2. A word used generically for man and woman (Gen. 1:26–27; Job 20:4; Ps. 68:18; 76:10). 3. A city of Reuben (Josh. 3:16).

Addiction: Compulsive need for a habit-forming substance.
> the drunkard and the glutton. . .
> Prov. 23:21
> as a drunken man staggereth. . .
> Isa. 19:14
> not in rioting and drunkenness. . .
> Rom. 13:13
> nor drunkards, nor revilers. . .
> 1 Cor. 6:10
> be not drunk with wine. . .Eph. 5:18

See *Alcohol; Drink/Drinking; Wine.*

Adolescence: See *Youth.*

Adonai: A word for *God.* The Israelites spoke this word where the word *Jehovah* occurred.

Adoption: Receiving a stranger into the family as one's own child (Exod. 2:10, Esther 2:7). Figuratively, reception into the family of God (Rom. 8:15–17; Gal. 4:5; Eph. 1:5).
  received the Spirit of a. . .Rom. 8:15
  waiting for the a. . .Rom. 8:23
  we might receive the a of sons. . .
    Gal. 4:5

Adoration: The act of paying homage to God; as in bending the knee, raising the hands, inclining the head, and prostrating the body. (Gen. 17:3; Ps. 95:6; Matt. 28:9).

Adultery: Under O.T. law, the crime of unchastity, wherein a man, married or single, had illicit intercourse with a woman who was not his wife. Punished by fire (Gen. 38:24), and by stoning (Deut. 22:22–24).
  Thou shalt not commit a. . .
    Exod. 20:14
  a with another man's wife. . .
    Lev. 20:10
  a with her already in his heart. . .
    Matt. 5:28
  a woman taken in a. . .John 8:3
  A, fornication, uncleanness. . .
    Gal. 5:19

Adversary/Adversaries: An opponent or an enemy; a word often used for Satan.
  render vengeance to his a'ies. . .
    Deut. 32:43
  how long shall the a reproach?
    . . .Ps. 74:10
  vengeance on his a'ies. . .Nah.1:2
  Agree with thine a quickly. . .
    Matt. 5:25
  your a the devil. . .1 Pet. 5:8
See *Enemy/Enemies.*

Adversity: Difficult or troublesome circumstances.
  God did vex them with all a. . .
    2 Chron.15:6
  brother is born for a.. . .Prov. 17:17
  give you the bread of a. . .
    Isa. 30:20

Advice: Recommendation from others regarding a course of action.
  Lord, who hath given me counsel
    . . .Ps. 16:7
  counsel of the most High. . .
    Ps. 107:11
  the counsels of the wicked. . .
    Prov. 12:5
  Hear counsel, and receive instruction
    . . .Prov. 19:20
See *Counsel/Counsels.*

Advocate: In N.T., a helper, intercessor, or comforter. A word for the Holy Spirit (John 14:16; 15:26; 16:7; Acts 24:1); Christ serves as our advocate (1 John 2:1).

Affection: A tender attachment to, or fondness for, a person or thing.
  kisses of an enemy are deceitful. . .
    Prov. 27:6
  not ceased to kiss my feet. . .
    Luke 7:45
  without natural a, implacable. . .
    Rom. 1:31
  Salute one another with an holy
    kiss. . .Rom. 16:16
  Set your a on things above. . .
    Col. 3:2
  Without natural a. . .2 Tim. 3:3

Affliction/Afflictions: Any condition that causes pain or suffering.
  the poor in his a. . .Job 36:15
  Look upon mine a. . .Ps. 25:18
  my comfort in my a. . .Ps. 119:50
  my refuge in the day of a. . .
    Jer. 16:19
  partaker of the a's of the gospel. . .
    2 Tim. 1:8
  endure a's. . .2 Tim. 4:5

Choosing rather to suffer a. . .
Heb. 11:25
See *Trouble.*

Affluence: See *Rich/Riches.*

Afraid: See *Fear.*

Agate: A species of precious quartz; second stone in the third row of the high priest's breastplate (Exod. 28:19; 39:12; Isa. 54:12; Ezek. 27:16).

Age: Attained years of one's earthly life.
mine a is as nothing before thee. . .
Ps. 39:5
Cast me not off in the time of old
a. . .Ps. 71:9
And even to your old a I am he. . .
Isa. 46:4
See *Elderly, the.*

Agree/Agreed: To be of one mind or opinion.
together, except they be a'd?. . .
Amos 3:3
A with thine adversary. . .Matt. 5:25
you shall a on earth. . .Matt. 18:19

Agriculture: Cultivation of the land to grow plants and livestock.
shall yield their fruit. . .Lev. 26:4
sendeth waters upon the fields. . .
Job 5:10
the cattle upon a thousand hills
. . .Ps. 50:10
thy barns be filled with plenty
. . .Prov. 3:10

Agrippa: See *Herod,* No. 6.

Ahab: Seventh king of Israel (1 Kings 16:29). He married Jezebel of Tyre, who introduced the worship of Baal and Astarte; killed by a chance arrow (1 Kings 18–22; 2 Chron. 18).

Ai: An ancient city of Canaan (Gen. 12:8, where it is spelled Hai); captured and destroyed by Joshua (Josh. 7:3–5; 9:3; 10:1; 12:9).

Alabaster: A mineral suitable for carving and fine polish, used for vases, ointment boxes, sculptures, etc. (Matt. 26:7; Mark 14:3; Luke 7:37).

Alcohol: Any beverage produced through a process of fermentation. Wine was the most common such drink in Bible times.
he drank of the wine. . .Gen. 9:21
Wine is a mocker. . .Prov. 20:1
not for kings to drink wine. . .
Prov. 31:4
as a drunken man staggereth. . .
Isa. 19:14
be not drunk with wine. . .Eph. 5:18
See *Addiction; Debauchery; Drink/ Drinking; Drunkenness.*

Alexandria: The Grecian, Roman, and Christian capital of Egypt, founded by Alexander the Great in 332 BC. Famous in early church history as a Christian center (Acts 18:24; 27:6; 28:11).

Alien: A stranger or foreigner from another country.
I have been an a in a strange land
. . .Exod. 18:3
an a in their sight. . .Job 19:15
an a unto my mother's children. . .
Ps. 69:8

Alive: Having life in one's body; the new life in Christ.
I kill, and I make a. . .Deut. 32:39
heard that he was a. . .Mark 16:11
he shewed himself a. . .Acts 1:3
but a unto God. . .Rom. 6:11
Christ shall all be made a. . .
1 Cor. 15:22
I am a for evermore. . .Rev. 1:18

Almighty: A divine title that emphasizes God's unlimited power.
> I am the A God. . .Gen. 17:1
> God A bless thee. . .Gen. 28:3
> the A, who shall bless thee. . .
>   Gen. 49:25
> the name of God A. . .Exod. 6:3
> the A hath given me life. . .
>   Job 33:4
> under the shadow of the A. . .
>   Ps. 91:1
> Holy, holy, holy, Lord God A. . .
>   Rev. 4:8

Alms: Charitable giving for the poor, required by Mosaic Law (Lev. 19:9; Ruth 2:2.
> do not your a before men. . .
>   Matt. 6:1
> thine a may be in secret. . .
>   Matt. 6:4
> Sell that ye have, and give a. . .
>   Luke 12:33

See *Give/Given/Giveth; Poor, the.*

Alpha: First letter of the Greek alphabet. Used with omega, the last letter, to express beginning and end (Isa. 41:4; 44:6; Rev. 1:8; 1:11; 21:6; 22:13).

Altar: The first altars were simple memorial stones (Gen. 8:20; 12:7); afterward they were sites where offerings were placed (Exod. 17:15–16; 27:1–8).
> build an a unto the Lord. . .
>   Deut. 27:5
> Solomon stood before the a. . .
>   1 Kings 8:22
> offer polluted bread upon mine a
>   . . .Mal. 1:7
> bring thy gift to the a. . .Matt. 5:23
> greater, the gift, or the a. . .
>   Matt. 23:19

Ambassador: A person who represented one government at the seat of another (Num. 20:14; Josh. 9:4; Judg. 11:17–19); ministers are called

ambassadors of Christ (2 Cor. 5:20).

Amen: A word used to fix the stamp of truth upon a statement or declaration (Num. 5:22; Deut. 27:15; Matt. 6:13; 1 Cor. 14:16).

Amethyst: A purplish quartz, ranking among the precious stones and forming the third stone in the third row of the high priest's breastplate (Exod. 28:19; 39:12).

Amos: One of the minor prophets of the O.T. Lived during reigns of Uzziah and Jeroboam II of Judah (Amos 1:1–7; 7:14–15). His book rebukes the sins of Israel and closes with God's promise.

Ananias: 1. An early believer in Jerusalem whose dishonesty led to a tragic ending (Acts 5:1–11). 2. A Jewish disciple at Damascus (Acts 9:10–27; 22:12). 3. A high priest, AD 48 (Acts 23:2–5; 24:1).

Andrew: An apostle of Christ (John 1:35–40; Matt. 4:18); brother of Simon Peter, native of Bethsaida, and fisherman. Original disciple of John the Baptist (Mark 13:3; John 6:6–13; 12:22).

Angel/Angels: A messenger (2 Sam. 2:5; Luke 7:24). In a spiritual sense, a messenger of God (Gen. 24:7; Heb. 1:14).
> *Angels as messengers*
> there came two a's to Sodom. . .
>   Gen. 19:1
> a's of God ascending. . .Gen. 28:12
> a said unto her, Fear not, Mary. . .
>   Luke 1:30
> *Angels as protection*
> he shall send his a before thee. . .
>   Gen. 24:7

a of God, which went before. . .
    Exod. 14:19
give his a's charge over thee. . .
    Ps. 91:11
Jesus and angels
a's came and ministered. . .
    Matt. 4:11
shall send forth his a's. . .Matt. 13:41
twelve legions of a's? . . .
    Matt. 26:53
a's of God ascending. . .John 1:51
the a's said he at any time. . .
    Heb. 1:5
People and angels
a's of God over one sinner. . .
    Luke 15:10
tongues of men and of a's. . .
    1 Cor. 13:1
entertained a's unawares. . .
    Heb. 13:2
a's of the seven churches. . .
    Rev. 1:20
Qualities of angels
wisdom of an a of God. . .
    2 Sam. 14:20
a little lower than the a's. . .Ps. 8:5
Who maketh his a's spirits. . .
    Ps. 104:4
See *Angel of the Lord.*

Angel of the Lord: An angel of high
rank who appeared at important times
in Israel's history. In the O.T., this angel sometimes appeared to be a preincarnate manifestation of Jesus.
And the a o t L found her. . .
    Gen. 16:7
the a o t L called. . .Gen. 22:11
a o t L appeared unto him. . .
    Exod. 3:2
a o t L stood in the way. . .
    Num 22:22
a o t L appeared unto him. . .
    Judg. 6:12
a o t L appeared unto the woman
    . . .Judg. 13:3
the a o t L went out. . .2 Kings 19:35
a o t L appeared unto him. . .
    Matt. 1:20
a o t L had bidden him. . .Matt. 1:24
a o t L appeareth in a dream. . .
    Matt. 2:19

appeared unto him an a o t L. . .
    Luke 1:11
a o t L came upon them. . .Luke 2:9

Anger of the Lord: God's wrath
against sin and corruption.
His anger against idolatry
lest the a of the LORD. . .Deut. 6:15
a of the LORD was hot. . .Judg. 2:14
His ager against sin
LORD's a was kindled against Israel
    . . .Num. 32:13
we are consumed by thine a. . .
    Ps. 90:7
shall be saved from wrath through
    him. . .Rom. 5:9
His anger as judgment
his a, wrath, and indignation. . .
    Ps. 78:49
both with wrath and fierce a. . .
    Isa. 13:9
Limitations of His anger
gracious and merciful, slow to a. . .
    Neh. 9:17
his a endureth but a moment. . .
    Ps. 30:5
turned he his a away. . .Ps. 78:38
See *Wrath of God.*

Anger/Angry, Righteous: Justified
anger against sin or injustice.
Moses' a waxed hot. . .Exod. 32:19
And his a was kindled. . .Judg. 14:19
about on them with a. . .Mark 3:5
Be ye a'ry, and sin not. . .Eph. 4:26

Anger/Angry, Sin of: Loss of one's
temper, and consequently self-control.
Avoiding anger
thine a be hot against me. . .
    Judg. 6:39
rebuke me not in thine a. . .Ps. 6:1
all these; a, wrath, malice. . .
    Col. 3:8
Examples of anger
Balaam's a was kindled. . .
    Num. 22:27
Saul's a was kindled. . .1 Sam. 20:30
he was very a'ry. . .Jon. 4:1

Foolishness of anger
wrath killeth the foolish man. . .
    Job 5:2
soon a'ry dealeth foolishly. . .
    Prov. 14:17
a resteth in the bosom. . .
    Eccles. 7:9
Provoking anger
grievous words stir up a. . .
    Prov. 15:1
wrath bringeth forth strife. . .
    Prov. 30:33
provoke not your children to a. . .
    Col. 3:21
Warnings against anger
Cease from a, and forsake wrath
    . . .Ps. 37:8
wise men turn away wrath. . .
    Prov. 29:8
a'ry with his brother. . .Matt. 5:22
See *Sin*.

Anguish: Emotional or mental stress.
    Moses for a of spirit. . .Exod. 6:9
    Trouble and a have taken hold. . .
        Ps. 119:143
    much affliction and a of heart. . .
        2 Cor. 2:4

Anise: A plant of the parsley family, producing aromatic seeds used in medicine and cooking, and with which tithes were paid (Matt. 23:23).

Anna: A prophetess at Jerusalem who recognized the infant Jesus as the Messiah (Luke 2:36).

Anoint: To pour oil or ointment on a person for a specific purpose, a common practice in Bible times (Gen. 28:18); a mark of respect (Luke 7:46); or of induction to a priestly office (Exod. 6:15); or to kingly office (1 Sam. 9:16); or as an act of healing (Mark 6:13).

Anointed/Anointing: To set a person apart for special service to God or others.
    spices for a'ing oil. . .Exod. 25:6

walk before mine a. . .1 Sam. 2:35
horn of oil, and a him. . .1 Sam. 16:13
washed, and a himself. . .
    2 Sam. 12:20
Saying, Touch not mine a. . .
    1 Chron. 16:22
a me to preach good tidings. . .
    Isa. 61:1
a with oil many. . .Mark 6:13
God a Jesus of Nazareth. . .
    Acts 10:38

Antichrist: The archenemy of Christ; a word applied to those who hold heretical opinions of the incarnation (1 John 2:18; 4:3; 2 John 7).

Antioch: 1. Capital of the Greek kings of Syria, on the Orontes River. The first Gentile church was founded here, and disciples were first called Christians here (Acts 11:19–21, 26). 2. A city of Pisidia (Acts 13:14). Starting point of the persecutions which followed Paul all through Asia Minor (Acts 14).

Anxiety: Emotional turmoil caused by worry.
    Take no thought for your life. . .
        Matt. 6:25
    be ye not troubled. . .Mark 13:7
    Why are ye troubled? . . .
        Luke 24:38
    Let not your heart be troubled. . .
        John 14:1
See *Worry*.

Apostasy: A renunciation of one's faith, a turning away from a previous loyalty.
    in time of temptation fall away. . .
        Luke 8:13
    come a falling away. . .2 Thess. 2:3
    If they shall fall away. . .Heb. 6:6

Apostle/Apostles: Official name of Jesus' twelve disciples (Matt. 10:1–42; John 16:13; Mark 26:20). In a broad sense, anyone commissioned to preach the Gospel (2 Cor. 8:23; Phil. 2:25).

The word is also applied to Christ (Heb. 3:1).

the names of the twelve a's. . .
  Matt. 10:2
a's were many signs and wonders
  . . .Acts 5:12
brought him to the a's. . .Acts 9:27
a's and elders came together. . .
  Acts 15:6
called to be an a. . .Rom. 1:1
the a of the Gentiles. . .Rom. 11:13
least of the a's. . .1 Cor. 15:9

Apparel: See *Garment/Garments*.

Appearance, Physical: A person's outward features.

man looketh on the outward a. . .
  1 Sam. 16:7
add one cubit unto his stature? . . .
  Matt. 6:27
increased in wisdom and stature
  . . .Luke 2:52
Judge not according to the a. . .
  John 7:24
look on things after the outward a?
  . . .2 Cor. 10:7

Approve/Approved: To be accepted, especially by the Lord.

a man a'd of God. . .Acts 2:22
and a'd of men. . .Rom. 14:18
shew thyself a'd unto God. . .
  2 Tim. 2:15

Aquila: A Jewish convert of Pontus and valuable assistant to the apostle Paul (Acts 18:2; 1 Cor. 16:19; Rom. 16:3).

Archangel: A chief angel, or one higher in rank than normal angels (1 Thess. 4:16; Jude 9).

Areopagus: A rocky hill near the center of Athens, where the court of justice sat and where Paul preached to the philosophers of the city (Acts 17:19–34).

Arguments: Quarrels or disputes.
  Arguments and the mouth
  and fill my mouth with a. . .
    Job 23:4
  the strife of tongues. . .Ps. 31:20
  Arguments and sin
  froward man soweth strife. . .
    Prov. 16:28
  loveth transgression that loveth
    strife. . .Prov. 17:19
  strife is, there is confusion. . .
    James 3:16
  Avoiding arguments
  house full of sacrifices with strife
    . . .Prov. 17:1
  strife and reproach shall cease. . .
    Prov. 22:10
  if any man have a quarrel against
    any. . .Col. 3:13
  Stirring up arguments
  Hatred stirreth up strifes. . .
    Prov. 10:12
  The beginning of strife. . .Prov. 17:14
  a proud heart stirreth up strife. . .
    Prov. 28:25

Ark: 1. The vessel in which Noah and his family were saved (Gen. 6–8). 2. A little boat of reeds in which the infant Moses was placed (Exod. 2:3).

Ark of the Covenant: Built at God's direction (Exod. 15). A chest of shittim wood for tabernacle use, lined and covered with gold, whose lid was the mercy seat, on either end of which were cherubs. Golden rings were on the sides, through which poles were inserted for carrying. Captured by the Philistines (1 Sam. 9:10–11); returned to Kirjath-Jearim and brought then by David to Jerusalem (2 Sam. 6:1; 1 Chron. 15:25, 28); placed in the temple by Solomon (2 Chron. 5:2–10).

the a o t c of the Lord. . .Num.
  10:33
put it in the side of the a o t c. . .
  Deut. 31:26
a o t c of the Lord came into. . .
  1 Sam. 4:5

stood before the a o t c. . .
1 Kings 3:15
priests brought in the a o t c. . .
2 Chron. 5:7

Armageddon: The place where evil is
to be overthrown in the end time.
by the waters of Megiddo. . .
Judg. 5:19
in the valley of Jezreel. . .
Judg. 6:33
upon the great river Euphrates. .
Rev. 16:12
called in the Hebrew tongue A. . .
Rev. 16:16

Arrogance/Arrogancy: A prideful or
superior attitude.
let not a'y come out of your mouth
. . .1 Sam. 2:3
hate evil: pride, and a'y. . .Prov. 8:13
a'y of the proud to cease. . .
Isa. 13:11

Ascension, the: Jesus' return to God
the Father after His resurrection.
Thou hast ascended on high. . .
Ps. 68:18
he was received up into heaven. . .
Mark 16:19
I ascend unto my Father. . .
John 20:17
he ascended up on high. . .Eph. 4:8

Asp: The hooded venomous serpent
known as the African cobra (Deut.
32:22; Job 20:14–16; Isa. 11:8; Rom.
3:13).

Ass: A patient beast of burden and rid-
ing animal even for kings (Gen. 22:3;
1 Chron. 27:30; Job 1:3; Zech. 9:9;
Matt. 11:1–9).

Assembly/Assemblies/Assembling:
A gathering of people, particularly followers of the Lord.
Assembly of saints
a of the congregation. . .Exod. 12:6

a of the children of Israel. . .
Num. 8:9
the a of the saints. . .Ps. 89:7
forsaking the a'ing of ourselves. . .
Heb. 10:25
Asembly of sinners
a'ies of violent men. . .Ps. 86:14
an a of treacherous men. . .Jer. 9:2
a of the mockers. . .Jer. 15:17

Assurance: Total confidence in God's
promises.
given a unto all men. . .Acts 17:31
full a of hope. . .Heb. 6:11
in full a of faith. . .Heb. 10:22

Assyria: That ancient empire on
the Tigris River whose capital was
Nineveh (Gen. 2:14; 10:11–22). Assyrian kings frequently invaded Israel
(2 Kings 15:19; 16:7–9; 2 Chron.
28:20). Assyria was overthrown by the
Medes and Babylonians in 625 BC, after an existence of 1,200 years.

Astrologers: Magicians who claimed
to be able to foretell the future by
studying the stars.
lift up thine eyes unto heaven. . .
Deut. 4:19
be not dismayed at the signs of
heaven. . .Jer. 10:2
better than all the magicians and a
. . .Dan. 1:20
we have seen his star in the east
. . .Matt. 2:2
See *Magic/Magicians*.

Athens: Capital of Attica and chief seat
of Grecian learning and civilization.
The apostle Paul preached on its Areopagus or Mars' Hill (Acts 17:19–22).

Athletics: Sports and games that require physical activity.
wrestled a man with him. . .
Gen. 32:24
they which run in a race run all. . .
1 Cor. 9:24

I have not run in vain. . .Phil. 2:16
run with patience the race. . .
    Heb. 12:1

Atonement: The expiation of sin and propitiation of God by the incarnation, life, suffering, and death of Christ. The day of atonement was an annual day of fasting and humiliation (Exod. 30:16; Lev. 16; 23:27–32).
    for a sin offering for a. . .
        Exod. 29:36
    an a for your sin. . .Exod. 32:30
    to make an a for Israel. . .
        1 Chron. 6:49
    we have now received the a. . .
        Rom. 5:11

Attributes of God: The qualities or characteristics of God that set Him apart as a divine being.
    Eternal
    Lord shall reign for ever. . .
        Exod. 15:18
    eternal God is thy refuge. . .
        Deut. 33:27
    his eternal power and Godhead. . .
        Rom. 1:20
    Holy
    for he is an holy God. . .Josh. 24:19
    none holy as the Lord. . .1 Sam. 2:2
    the holy Spirit of God. . .Eph. 4:30
    Infinite
    his understanding is infinite. . .
        Ps. 147:5
    Invisible
    invisible, the only wise God. . .
        1 Tim. 1:17
    Longsuffering
    The Lord is longsuffering. . .
        Num. 14:18
    the God of patience. . .Rom. 15:5
    the longsuffering of our Lord. . .
        2 Pet. 3:15
    Loving
    according to thy lovingkindness. . .
        Ps. 51:1
    God so loved the world. . .John 3:16
    separate us from the love of God
        . . .Rom. 8:39
    God is love. . .1 John 4:8

    Merciful
    shewing mercy unto thousands. . .
        Exod. 20:6
    the greatness of thy mercy. . .
        Neh. 13:22
    his mercy endureth for ever. . .
        Ps. 136:2
    Omnipotent
    the power, and the glory. . .
        1 Chron. 29:11
    ruleth by his power for ever. . .
        Ps. 66:7
    Lord God omnipotent reigneth. . .
        Rev. 19:6
    Omnipresent
    shall I flee from thy presence? . . .
        Ps. 139:7
    and move, and have our being. . .
        Acts 17:28
    never leave thee, nor forsake thee
        . . .Heb. 13:5
    Omniscient
    art acquainted with all my ways. . .
        Ps. 139:3
    his understanding is infinite. . .
        Ps. 147:5
    Powerful
    made the earth by his power. . .
        Jer. 10:12
    power on earth to forgive sins. . .
        Mark 2:10
    the glory of his power. . .
        2 Thess. 1:9
    Righteous
    God of Israel, thou art righteous. . .
        Ezra 9:15
    heavens shall declare his
        righteousness. . .Ps. 50:6
    Gracious is the Lord, and righteous
        . . .Ps. 116:5

Authority: Exercise of power, particularly that granted by the Lord.
    taught them as one having a. . .
        Matt. 7:29
    power and a over all devils. . .
        Luke 9:1
    a to execute judgment. . .John 5:27
    all a and power. . .1 Cor. 15:24

Avenge/Avenger: To retaliate against another for some harmful action.
    Thou shalt not a. . .Lev. 19:18

the Lord a me of thee. . .
   1 Sam. 24:12
a themselves on their enemies. . .
   Esther 8:13
God a his own elect. . .Luke 18:7
Dearly beloved, a not yourselves
   . . .Rom. 12:19
Lord is the a'r of all. . .1 Thess. 4:6

B

Baal: 1. Supreme male god of the Phoenicians and Canaanites, worshipped with self-torture and human offerings (Judg. 2:11; Isa. 46:1; Jer. 19:5). The Israelites were infected with Baal worship (Num. 22:41; Deut. 4:16). 2. Grandson of Saul (1 Chron. 8:30).

Balaam: Son of Beor, or Bosor (Deut. 23:4). A man of note and given to prophecy. Killed in battle with the Israelites (Num. 22–24, 31; Rev. 2:14).

Babble/Babbler/Babbling/Babblings: Nonsensical utterances.
   who hath b'ing? . . .Prov. 23:29
   What will this b'r say? . . .Acts 17:18
   shun profane and vain b'ings. . .
      2 Tim. 2:16

Babel, Tower of: The brick structure, built in the plain of Shinar, and intended to prevent the very confusion and dispersion it brought about (Gen. 11:4–9).

Babylon: Capital city of the Babylonian empire. Situated on both sides of the Euphrates River, 200 miles above its junction with the Tigris (Gen. 10:10; Jer. 51:58; Isa. 14:1–3). Once the capital of Assyria (2 Chron. 33:11). Reached height of its splendor and strength under Nebuchadnezzar (Isa. 13:19; Jer. 51:41). Chief home of the captive Jews. Captured by Cyrus the Persian, through his leader Darius in 539 BC, as prophesied (Jer. 51:31, 39).

Backbiting/Backbitings: Criticizing or condemning others when their backs are turned.
   he that uttereth a slander. . .
      Prov. 10:18
   A talebearer revealeth secrets. . .
      Prov. 11:13
   a talebearer revealeth secrets. . .
      Prov. 20:19
   strifes, b's, whisperings. . .
      2 Cor. 12:20
   without murmurings and disputings
      . . .Phil. 2:14
   tattlers also and busybodies. . .
      1 Tim. 5:13

Backslider/Backsliding/Backslidings: A believer who grows cold in his commitment to God.
   The b in heart. . .Prov. 14:14
   b'ings shall reprove thee. . .Jer. 2:19
   Turn, O b'ing children. . .Jer. 3:14
   I will heal their b'ing. . .Hosea 14:4

Balances: Used among the ancients for weighing gold and silver, and in commerce and trade (Lev. 19:36; Mic. 6:11; Hosea 12:7).

Balm: The balm of Gilead, or Mecca balsam, exuded an agreeable balsamic resin, highly prized as an unguent and cosmetic, as the crushed leaves were for their sweet smell (Gen. 37:25; 43:11; Jer. 8:22; 46:11; Ezek. 27:17).

Baptism/Baptized: The ordinance commanded by Christ (Matt. 28:19), in which water is used to initiate the recipient into the Christian church. John's baptism was with water, Christ's "with the Holy Ghost and with fire" (Matt. 3:1–12; Luke 3:16); Jesus was baptized by John (Matt. 3:13–17).

Baptism and the Holy Spirit
b'd with the Holy Ghost. . .Acts 1:5
that these should not be b'd. . .
   Acts 10:47
Spirit are we all b'd. . .1 Cor. 12:13
Baptism and Jesus
Jesus, when he was b'd. . .
   Matt. 3:16
Jesus made and b'd more disciples
   . . .John 4:1
b'd in the name of the Lord. . .
   Acts 8:16
b'd into Christ. . .Gal. 3:27
Examples of baptism
arose, and was b'd. . .Acts 9:18
when she was b'd. . .Acts 16:15
b'd, he and all his. . .Acts 16:33
believed, and were b'd. . .Acts 18:8
arise, and be b'd. . .Acts 22:16
Baptism of John
publicans to be b'd. . .Luke 3:12
Unto what then were ye b'd?. . .
   Acts 19:3
Salvation and baptism
the b of repentance. . .Mark 1:4
is b'd shall be saved. . .Mark 16:16

Barabbas: The prisoner at Jerusalem who was released when Christ was condemned (Matt. 27:16–18; Mark 15:7; Luke 23:18; John 18:40).

Barnabas: Joseph or Joses, a convert of Cyprus and companion of the apostle Paul (Acts 4:36; 9:27; 11:25–26; 15:22–39).

Barren: Unable to bear children.
But Sarai was b. . .Gen. 11:30
but Rachel was b. . .Gen. 29:31
was b, and bare not. . .Judg. 13:2
Elisabeth was b. . .Luke 1:7

Bartholomew: One of the twelve apostles (Matt. 10:3; Mark 3:18; Luke 6:14; Acts 1:13). Perhaps Nathanael in John 1:45.

Bartimaeus: A blind beggar of Jericho who was healed by Jesus (Mark 10:46–52).

Baruch: 1. Jeremiah's friend, helper, and fellow prisoner (Jer. 36:4–32; 32:12; 43:3–7). 2. Nehemiah's assistant (Neh. 3:20).

Bath: A Jewish liquid measure, varying from 4¾ to 6½ gallons.

Bathe: The process of washing oneself in order to become ritually pure.
b himself in water. . .Lev. 15:5
Wash thyself therefore. . .Ruth 3:3
saw a woman washing herself. . .
   2 Sam. 11:2
wash mine hands in innocency. . .
   Ps. 26:6

Bathsheba: Wife of David and mother of Solomon (2 Sam. 6; 1 Kings 1:15; 2:13–22). Also called Bathshua (1 Chron. 3:5).

Beauty/Beautiful: Physical features that are pleasant to the eye.
Human beauty
Rachel was b'iful. . .Gen. 29:17
as Absalom for his b. . .2 Sam. 14:25
and b is vain. . .Prov. 31:30
How b'iful are thy feet. . .
   Song of Sol. 7:1
b is a fading flower. . .Isa. 28:1
Beauty of the Gospel
How b'iful upon the mountains. . .
   Isa. 52:7
How b'iful are the feet of them. . .
   Rom. 10:15
Beauty of holiness
b of holiness. . .1 Chron. 16:29
b of the Lord. . .Ps. 27:4
b for ashes. . .Isa. 61:3
Beauty of things
precious stones for b. . .
   2 Chron. 3:6
every thing b'iful in his time. . .
   Eccles. 3:11

Beer-sheba: An ancient site in southern Palestine; so named by Abraham (Gen. 21:31–33) or Isaac (Gen. 26:32–33).

Beggar/Begging: A person who makes his living by taking handouts from others.

> lifteth up the b. . .1 Sam. 2:8
> nor his seed b'ing bread. . .
> Ps. 37:25
> b named Lazarus. . .Luke 16:20
> See *Poor, the.*

Believe/Believed/Believeth: To accept or trust fully.

> *Believe in God*
> he b'd in the Lord. . .Gen. 15:6
> people of Nineveh b'd God. . .
> Jon. 3:5
> as Abraham b'd God. . .Gal. 3:6
> must b that he is. . .Heb. 11:6
> *Believe in Jesus*
> b'ing, ye shall receive. . .Matt. 21:22
> possible to him that b'th. . .
> Mark 9:23
> I b; help thou mine unbelief
> . . .Mark 9:24
> all men through him might b. . .
> John 1:7
> b'th on me shall never thirst. . .
> John 6:35
> b that thou hast sent me. . .
> John 11:42
> b that I am he. . .John 13:19
> b in God, b also in me. . .John 14:1
> justifier of him which b'th. . .
> Rom. 3:26
> b that we shall also live. . .Rom. 6:8
> b that Jesus died and rose again
> . . .1 Thess. 4:14
> *Believe in truth*
> Beareth all things, b'th all things. . .
> 1 Cor. 13:7
> *Salvation and belief*
> b'th and is baptized. . .Mark 16:16
> b and be saved. . .Luke 8:12
> *Believe in the Scriptures*
> they b'd the scripture. . .John 2:22
> For had ye b'd Moses. . .John 5:46

See *Coming to Christ; Conversion; Repentance; Salvation; Unbelief.*

Beloved: To be accepted and loved by the Lord.

> he giveth his b sleep. . .Ps. 127:2

> O Daniel, a man greatly b. . .
> Dan. 10:11
> This is my b Son. . .Matt. 3:17
> whom I have chosen; my b. . .
> Matt. 12:18
> elect of God, holy and b. . .Col. 3:12

Belshazzar: Last king of Babylon; ruling at the time of the great feast and handwriting on the wall, 539 BC (Dan. 5).

Belteshazzar: Name given to Daniel by Nebuchadnezzar (Dan. 1:7).

Benevolence: Kindness and generosity shown to others.

> shew the kindness of God. . .
> 2 Sam. 9:3
> render unto the wife due b. . .
> 1 Cor. 7:3
> having compassion one of another
> . . .1 Pet. 3:8
> to brotherly kindness charity. . .
> 2 Pet. 1:7

Benjamin: Youngest of Jacob's children (Gen. 35:16–18). Beloved by Jacob (Gen. 42); visited Egypt (Gen. 43); tribe distinguished as Jacob prophesied (Gen. 49:27).

Bereaved: To grieve because of loss or a sense of failure.

> b'd of my children. . Gen. 42:36
> consumed because of grief. . .
> Ps. 6:7
> my life is spent with grief. . .
> Ps. 31:10

Beryl: The first stone in the fourth row of the high priest's breastplate (Exod. 28:20).

Bethany: A village on Mount Olivet near Bethpage and home of Lazarus, Martha, and Mary (Matt. 21:17; Mark 11; Luke 19:29; John 11:18).

Bethesda: A pool near the sheep gate in Jerusalem where Jesus healed a man (John 5:2).

Bethlehem: 1. A town of Palestine, six miles south of Jerusalem. Home of Ruth (Ruth 1:19); birthplace of David (1 Sam. 17:12); birthplace of Christ (Matt. 2:1–2; Luke 2:15–18). 2. A town in Zebulun (Josh. 19:15).

Betray/Betrayed: To deliver a person to an enemy through treachery.
> b me to mine enemies. . .
> 1 Chron. 12:17
> Judas Iscariot, who also b'ed him
> . . .Matt. 10:4
> Son of man shall be b'ed. . .Matt. 17:22
> b'ed to be crucified. . .Matt. 26:2
> one of you shall b me. . .Matt. 26:21

Betroth/Betrothed: To engage to marry. A betrothed woman was regarded as the lawful wife of her spouse, and he could not break off the relationship without a divorce, while she, if unfaithful, would be considered an adulteress (Deut. 28:30; Hosea 2:19–20).
> hath b'ed a wife. . .Deut. 20:7
> Mary was espoused to Joseph. . .
> Matt. 1:18
> Mary his espoused wife. . .Luke 2:5
> I have espoused you. . .2 Cor. 11:2

See *Courtship; Marriage/Marry.*

Beulah: A symbolic name for the land of Israel, referring to its future prosperity (Isa. 62:4).

Bildad: The Shuhite friend of Job (Job 2:11, 8, 18, 25).

Birth: Bringing forth young from the womb.
> day of one's b. . .Eccles. 7:1
> b of Jesus Christ. . .Matt. 1:18
> rejoice at his b. . .Luke 1:14

Birthright: The firstborn son enjoyed the right of consecration (Exod. 22:29), great dignity (Gen. 49:3), a double portion of the paternal estate (Deut. 21:17), and the right to royal succession (2 Chron. 21:3).

Bishop: Overseer; an officer of the early church, identical with presbyter, or elder (Acts 20:17–18; 1 Tim. 3:1–13, 17; Titus 1:5–8; 1 Pet. 5; 1 Thess. 5:12; James 5:14).

Blame/Blamed: To find a person at fault and responsible for some event or circumstance.
> the ministry be not b'd. . .2 Cor. 6:3
> no man should b us. . .2 Cor. 8:20
> he was to be b'd. . .Gal. 2:11

Blameless: Without fault.
> that ye may be b. . .1 Cor. 1:8
> shall have put on incorruption. . .
> 1 Cor. 15:54
> A bishop then must be b. . .
> 1 Tim. 3:2
> deacon, being found b. . .1 Tim. 3:10

Blaspheme/Blasphemed/Blasphemers/Blasphemy: Speaking evil of God (Lev. 24:11; Ps. 74:18; Matt. 12:32; Col. 3:8); and of royalty (1 Kings 21:10). Punishable by death (Lev. 24:11–14).
> enemies of the Lord to b. . .
> 2 Sam. 12:14
> name of God is b'd. . .Rom. 2:24
> word of God be not b'd. . .Titus 2:5
> b against the Holy Ghost. . .
> Matt. 12:31
> anger, wrath, malice, b'y. . .Col. 3:8
> boasters, proud, b'rs. . .2 Tim. 3:2

Blemish/Blemishes: A defect that made an animal unsuitable as a sacrifice, or a priest unfit to offer sacrifices.
> lamb shall be without b. . .
> Exod. 12:5

No man that hath a b. . .Lev. 21:21
there was no b in him. . .
 2 Sam. 14:25
without b and without spot. . .
 1 Pet. 1:19

Bless/Blessed: The act of bestowing a gift or favor on others, usually an act of God.

Blessed by the Lord
b'ed the sabbath day. . .Exod. 20:11
b his people with peace. . .Ps. 29:11
b'ed art thou among women. . .
 Luke 1:28
b'ed are they that hear. . .Luke 11:28
B'ed are they whose iniquities. . .
 Rom. 4:7
The obedient believer is blessed
B'ed is the man that walketh. . .
 Ps. 1:1
B'ed is he whose transgression. . .
 Ps. 32:1
B'ed are the undefiled. . .Ps. 119:1
B'ed are the poor in spirit. . .
 Matt. 5:3

Blessing/Blessings: God's gift or special favor.
b's shall come on thee. . .Deut. 28:2
B's are upon the head. . .Prov. 10:6
shall abound with b's. . .Prov. 28:20
pour you out a b. . .Mal. 3:10

Blind/Blinded: The inability to see, either physically or spiritually.
stumblingblock before the b. . .
 Lev. 19:14
eyes of the b shall be opened. . .
 Isa. 35:5
b receive their sight. . .Matt. 11:5
if the b lead the b. . .Matt. 15:14
Woe unto you, ye b guides. . .
 Matt. 23:16
darkness hath b'ed his eyes. . .
 1 John 2:11
See *Deaf, Disabilities, Diseases, Dumb.*

Blood: The life-sustaining fluid that circulates through the body.
Blood of animals
ye shall not eat the b. . .Deut. 12:16

idols, and from b. . .Acts 21:25
Blood of Jesus
my b of the new testament. . .
 Matt. 26:28
purchased with his own b. . .
 Acts 20:28
body and b of the Lord. . .
 1 Cor. 11:27
redemption through his b. . .
 Col. 1:14
by his own b he entered. . .
 Heb. 9:12
precious b of Christ. . .1 Pet. 1:19
the b of the Lamb. . .Rev. 7:14
Blood of man
Whoso sheddeth man's b. . .
 Gen. 9:6
flesh and b hath not revealed. . .
 Matt. 16:17
one b all nations of men. . .
 Acts 17:26
wrestle not against flesh and b. . .
 Eph. 6:12

Boast/Boasters: To speak of one's accomplishments with pride and arrogance.
trust in their wealth, and b. . .
 Ps. 49:6
despiteful, proud, b'ers. . .Rom.
 1:30
lest any man should b. . .Eph. 2:9
covetous, b'ers, proud. . .2 Tim. 3:2

Boaz: 1. The Bethlehemite who married Ruth (Ruth 4:9–10; Matt. 1:5). 2. A brazen pillar in the porch of Solomon's temple (1 Kings 7:21; 2 Chron. 3:17; Jer. 52:21).

Body, Human: The physical part of a person.
whole b should be cast into hell. . .
 Matt. 5:29
them which kill the b. . .Matt. 10:28
Take, eat; this is my b. . .Matt. 26:26
sinneth against his own b. . .
 1 Cor. 6:18
b, and bring it into subjection. . .
 1 Cor. 9:27

Bold/Boldness/Boldly: Courage and forthrightness; brave utterance of the truth.
> b'ness of Peter and John. . .
> > Acts 4:13
> word of God with b'ness. . .
> > Acts 4:31
> we were b in our God. . .
> > 1 Thess. 2:2
> b'ly unto the throne of grace. . .
> > Heb. 4:16

See *Courage.*

Bondage: The state of being held against one's will by an oppressor.
> lives bitter with hard b. . .Exod. 1:14
> God hath not forsaken us in our b
> > . . .Ezra 9:9
> not received the spirit of b. . .
> > Rom. 8:15
> delivered from the b of corruption
> > . . .Rom. 8:21
> desire again to be in b?. . .Gal. 4:9

Born Again: To receive a new nature through conversion.
> Except a man be b a. . .John 3:3
> b a, not of corruptible seed. . .
> > 1 Pet. 1:23

See *New Life; Regeneration; Salvation.*

Borrow/Borrower: To use something that belongs to another.
> b ought of his neighbour. . .
> > Exod. 22:14
> but thou shalt not b. . .Deut. 15:6
> B'er is servant to the lender
> > . . .Prov. 22:7

Bosom: To lean on a person's chest, or bosom, implied great intimacy (John 13:23). Figuratively, heaven (Luke 16:23; 23:43).

Bounty/Bountiful/Bountifully: A generous and plentiful supply.
> he hath dealt b'ifully with me. . .
> > Ps. 13:6
> a b'iful eye shall be blessed. . .
> > Prov. 22:9

> b, and not as of covetousness. . .
> > 2 Cor. 9:5
> He which soweth b'ifully shall reap
> > . . .2 Cor. 9:6

Branch, Jesus as the: A title of Jesus that emphasizes His succession through the lineage of David.
> stem of Jesse, and a B. . .Isa. 11:1
> unto David a righteous B. . .
> > Jer. 23:5
> man whose name is The B. . .
> > Zech. 6:12

Bread: Early use (Gen. 18:5–6; Exod. 12:34; Jer. 7:18). Made of wheat, barley, rye, fitches, and spelt, in loaves or rolls, leavened or unleavened; the kneading being in troughs, bowls, or on flat plates, and the baking in portable ovens of earthenware or upon heated stones.

Breastplate: Worn by the high priest (Exod. 28:15); embroidered, about ten inches square; its upper corners fastened with gold or lace to the ephod, its lower to the girdle (Exod. 28:28); adorned with twelve precious stones (Exod. 28:12–29).

Bribe/Bribes: Gifts or favors given to win the favor of others.
> after lucre, and took b's. . .
> > 1 Sam. 8:3
> right hand is full of b's. . .Ps. 26:10
> they take a b. . .Amos 5:12

Bride: A woman just married or about to be married.
> b adorneth herself. . .Isa. 61:10
> hath the b is the bridegroom. . .
> > John 3:29
> b, the Lamb's wife. . .Rev. 21:9
> Spirit and the b. . .Rev. 22:17

See *Bridegroom.*

Bridegroom: A man just married or about to be married.

as a b coming out. . .Ps. 19:5
the voice of the b. . .Jer. 33:11
to meet the b. . .Matt. 25:1

See *Bride*.

Broken/Brokenhearted: To be severed into pieces; to be overcome with despair.

I am like a b vessel. . .Ps. 31:12
them that are of a b heart. . .
Ps. 34:18
sent me to heal the b'hearted. . .
Luke 4:18
which is b for you. . .1 Cor. 11:24

Brother/Brother's/Brotherly/Brotherhood: A strong attachment to others, just as if they were part of one's family.

Caring for a brother
Am I my b's keeper? . . .Gen. 4:9
shall the weak b perish. . .1 Cor. 8:11
b or sister be naked. . .James 2:15
Hatred for a brother
b shall deliver up the b. . .
Matt. 10:21
hateth his b is in darkness. . .
1 John 2:11
Judging a brother
dost thou judge thy b? . . .
Rom. 14:10
occasion to fall in his b's way. . .
Rom. 14:13
Loving a brother
to another with b'ly love. . .
Rom. 12:10
Love the b'hood. . .1 Pet. 2:17
He that loveth his b. . .1 John 2:10
Offenses against a brother
b hath ought against thee. . .
Matt. 5:23
mote that is in thy b's eye. . .
Matt. 7:3
Sinning against a brother
if thy b shall trespass. . .Matt. 18:15
a b be a fornicator. . .1 Cor. 5:11
admonish him as a b. . .2 Thess.
3:15

Buckler: A small, round shield used to deflect blows in hand-to-hand combat (Ps. 18:2, 30; 91:4; Prov. 2:7).

Build/Builder/Builders/Buildest/Building/Builded: To erect a structure by following an orderly plan; believers as God's creation.

Building and God
stone which the b'ers rejected. . .
Matt. 21:42
b'er and maker is God. . .Heb. 11:10
Building the church
I will b my church. . .Matt. 16:18
Physical buildings
my barns, and b greater. . .
Luke 12:18
intending to b a tower. . .Luke 14:28
what house will ye b me? . . .
Acts 7:49
Spiritual building
lest I should b upon. . .Rom. 15:20
ye are God's b'ing. . .1 Cor. 3:9
b'ed together for an habitation
. . .Eph. 2:22
The temple
to b it in three days. . .Matt. 26:61
Seest thou these great b'ings?
. . .Mark 13:2

Bulrush: The papyrus plant from which paper was made (Exod. 2:3–5; Job 8:11).

Burden/Burdens: A difficult situation or problem.

Cast thy b upon the Lord. . .
Ps. 55:22
no greater b than these. . .
Acts 15:28
Bear ye one another's b's. . .
Gal. 6:2

Bury/Burial/Buried: Proper disposal of one's body after death.

first to go and b my father. . .
Matt. 8:21
she did it for my b'ial. . .Matt. 26:12
B'ied with him in baptism. . .
Col. 2:12

See *Death, Mortal/Mortality*

Burnt offering: An offering that was totally consumed by fire (Lev. 8; 9; 14; 29).

Business: Commerce or trade.
have a perfect and just weight. . .
Deut. 25:15
a man diligent in his b? . . .
Prov. 22:29
Not slothful in b. . .Rom. 12:11
Lydia, a seller of purple. . .
Acts 16:14
buy and sell, and get gain. . .
James 4:13
See *Honest/Honestly/Honesty; Partner/ Partners.*

Busybody/Busybodies: One who meddles in the affairs of others; a gossip.
words of a talebearer are as wounds. . .Prov. 18:8
a talebearer revealeth secrets. . .
Prov. 20:19
tattlers also and b's. . .1 Tim. 5:13
b in other men's matters. . .
1 Pet. 4:15

C

Caesar: With Julius Caesar and Augustus, Caesar was a surname, but with the latter it became an official title and remained so until the death of Nero. In Luke 2:1, Augustus Caesar is meant; in Luke 3:1, Tiberius Caesar; in Acts 11:28, Claudius Caesar; in Acts 25:8 and Phil. 4:22, Nero.

Caesarea: Political capital of Palestine, on the Mediterranean Sea, and official residence of Herodian kings and Roman procurators; home of Philip and Cornelius (Acts 8:40; 10; 11:1–18).

Caesarea Philippi: A city of Galilee marking the northern limit of Christ's pilgrimage, and probable scene of His transfiguration (Matt. 16:13–20; 17:1–10; Mark 8:27).

Caiaphas: The Jewish high priest who presided at the trial of Jesus and recommended that He be executed (Matt. 26:3–57; John 18:13–28).

Cain: 1. Eldest son of Adam (Gen. 4). 2. A city in the lowlands of Judah (Josh. 15:57).

Calamus: Identified with the lemongrass or sweet flag (Exod. 30:23; Song of Sol. 4:14; Ezek. 27:19). "Sweet cane" (Isa. 43:24; Jer. 6:20).

Caleb: 1. Son of Hezron (1 Chron. 2:18–19, 42, 50). Chelubai in 1 Chron. 2:9. 2. The spy of Judah (Num. 13:6; Josh. 14–15; 1 Sam. 30:14). 3. Son of Hur (1 Chron. 2:50). 4. Caleb's district (1 Sam. 30:14).

Calling: The call to service that is part of every believer's salvation experience.
the gifts and c of God. . .Rom. 11:29
abide in the same c. . .1 Cor. 7:20
prize of the high c of God. . .
Phil. 3:14

Calvary: Latin for Greek *kranion,* "skull" (referring to shape, and Hebrew *Golgotha*). Site of the crucifixion. Calvary, only in Luke 23:33.
come unto a place called Golgotha . . .Matt. 27:33
bring him unto the place Golgotha . . .Mark 15:22
the place, which is called C. . .
Luke 23:33
See *Cross.*

Cana: A town of Galilee, seven miles north of Nazareth, where Jesus performed His first miracle (John 2:1–11; 4:46; 21:2).

Canaan: 1. Fourth son of Ham (Gen. 10:6–19; 1 Chron. 1:8–13). 2. The country between the Mediterranean Sea and the Jordan River, given by God to the Israelites (Exod. 6:4; Lev. 25:38). "Holy Land" after the captivity (Zech. 2:13). Palestine, from Philistia.

Cankerworm: A variety of caterpillar. But in Joel 1:4; 2:25; Nah. 3:15–16, probably an underdeveloped locust.

Canon: A word first applied to the scriptures by Amphilochius about AD 380 (Gal. 6:16; Phil. 3:16). The O.T. canon was fixed by the Jews, and accepted by the time of Christ. The N.T. canon was ratified by the third council of Carthage in AD 397.

Capernaum: A city on the northwest shore of the Sea of Galilee. Chief residence of Christ and His apostles (Matt. 4:12–16; Mark 2:1; Luke 7:1–5; John 6:17).

Capital Punishment: The death penalty, rendered for serious crimes such as murder.
by man shall his blood be shed. . .
  Gen. 9:6
shall surely be put to death. . .
  Exod. 31:14
worthy of death be put to death. . .
  Deut. 17:6
life shall go for life. . .Deut. 19:21
delivered him to be crucified. . .
  Matt. 27:26
See *Death Penalty*.

Captain: 1. Title for a leader of a band of ten, fifty, hundred, or thousand (Deut. 1:15; Josh. 10:24; Judg. 11:6,

11. 2. Civic meaning (Isa. 1:10; 3:3). "Captain of the guard," commander of the Praetorian troops of Rome (Acts 28:16), "Captain of the temple," chief of the temple watchmen (Acts 4:1).

Captive/Captives: People imprisoned or held against their will.
lead thy captivity c. . .Judg. 5:12
c out of the land of Israel. . .
  2 Kings 5:2
carried them c to Assyria. . .
  2 Kings 15:29
preach deliverance to the c's. . .
  Luke 4:18
he led captivity c. . .Eph. 4:8
See *Prisoner/Prisoners*.

Captivity: Six partial captivities are mentioned in Judges. Israel had several (2 Kings 15:29; 1 Chron. 5:26), the final one being that by Shalmaneser, 721 BC (2 Kings 17:6). Judah was captive to Assyria, 713 BC, and finally to Nebuchadnezzar, 606–562 BC. Israel's last captivity was to Rome (AD 71).
into c'ity from Jerusalem to
  Babylon. . .2 Kings 24:15
which were come out of the c'ity
  . . .Ezra 8:35
my people are gone into c'ity. . .
  Isa. 5:13
c'ity to the law of sin. . .Rom. 7:23
bringing into c'ity every thought. . .
  2 Cor. 10:5
See *Captive/Captives; Prisoner/Prisoners*.

Carbuncle: A gem of deep red color (Isa. 54:12). A stone in the high priest's breastplate (Exod. 28:17; 39:10).

Care/Careful/Cares: The troubles and concerns of everyday life.
the c of this world. . .Matt. 13:22
choked with c's and riches. . .
  Luke 8:14
Be c'ful for nothing. . .Phil. 4:6
Casting all your c upon him. . .
  1 Pet. 5:7

Carmel: 1. A prominent mountain in northern Israel where the prophet Elijah demonstrated the power of God in a dramatic encounter with the priests of the pagan god Baal (1 Kings 18:17–39). 2. A city of Judah (1 Sam. 15:12; 25:2–44; 2 Chron. 26:10).

Carnal/Carnally: Worldliness; to give in to the desires of the flesh.
thou shalt not lie c'ly. . .Lev. 18:20
to be c'ly minded is death. . .
Rom. 8:6
ye are yet c. . .1 Cor. 3:3
weapons of our warfare are not c
. . .2 Cor. 10:4

Cedar: A cone-bearing tree whose reddish fragrant wood was much prized (1 Kings 7:2; Ps. 92:12; Song of Sol. 5:15; Isa. 2:13; Ezek. 31:6).

Censer: A small, portable vessel of copper (Num. 16:39; Lev. 16:12) or gold (1 Kings 7:50; Heb. 9:4), used to carry the coals on which incense was burned at the altar.

Census: Twelve different censuses are noted in the O.T. (Exod. 38:26; Num. 1:2; 26; 2 Sam. 24:9; 1 Kings 12:21; 2 Chron. 2:17–18; 2 Chron. 13:3; 14; 25:5–6; 26:13; Ezek. 2:64; 8:1–14). The census in Luke 2:1–3 was for taxation.

Centurion: A Roman officer who had command of a hundred soldiers (Matt. 8:5; Mark 15:39; Luke 7:1–10; Acts 10:1).

Cephas: Another name for Simon Peter, a disciple of Jesus (John 1:42).

Chaff: Debris carried away by the wind when the wheat harvest was

thrown into the air (Ps. 1:4; Isa. 17:13; Hosea 13:3; Zeph. 2:2).

Chance: Something that happens unpredictably.
a c that happened to us. . .
1 Sam. 6:9
c happeneth to them all. . .
Eccles. 9:11
by c there came down. . .Luke 10:31

Change/Changed/Changeth: To replace one circumstance or object with another.
and they shall be c'd. . .Ps. 102:26
with them that are given to c. . .
Prov. 24:21
he c'th the times and the seasons
. . .Dan. 2:21
I am the Lord, I c not. . .Mal. 3:6
but we shall all be c'd. . .1 Cor. 15:51
c'd into the same image. . .
2 Cor. 3:18

Characteristics of God: See *Attributes of God.*

Charity: A word for love in the King James Version of the Bible.
now abideth faith, hope, c. . .
1 Cor. 13:13
Follow after c. . .1 Cor. 14:1
put on c. . .Col. 3:14
above all things have fervent c. . .
1 Pet. 4:8

Chaste/Chastity: Personal purity and integrity, particularly in sexual behavior.
whatsoever things are pure. . .
Phil. 4:8
keep thyself pure. . .1 Tim. 5:22
the bed undefiled. . .Heb. 13:4
behold your c conversation. . .
1 Pet. 3:2
See *Modest/Modesty.*

Chastisement: God's discipline that corrects and guides people.
c of our peace. . .Isa. 53:5
if ye be without c. . .Heb. 12:8

Cheat/Cheating: To practice fraud or trickery.
> Divers weights are an abomination . . .Prov. 20:23
> deceive not with thy lips. . . Prov. 24:28
> cursed be the deceiver. . .Mal. 1:14

See *Deceit/Deceitful/Deceitfully/Deceitfulness.*

Cheerful/Cheerfulness: An upbeat, joyful, or positive attitude.
> maketh a c countenance. . . Prov. 15:13
> mercy, with c'ness. . .Rom. 12:8
> God loveth a c giver. . .2 Cor. 9:7

Cherith: The place where the prophet Elijah was fed by ravens (1 Kings 17:3–5).

Cherub/Cherubim: Guards of Eden (Gen. 3:24) and the mercy seat (Exod. 25:18). Wrought in wood or gold (Exod. 36:5; 37:7–9). Of immense size in Solomon's temple (1 Kings 6:27); four-winged and four-faced (Ezek. 1:6; 10:14; Rev. 4:8).

Chief Priest: See *High Priest.*

Child/Children: One's formative years during which values are taught.
> c'ren are an heritage. . .Ps. 127:3
> c'ren arise up, and call her blessed . . .Prov. 31:28
> unto us a c is born. . .Isa. 9:6
> a little c shall lead them. . .Isa. 11:6
> kingdom of God as a little c. . . Mark 10:15
> C'ren, obey your parents. . . Eph. 6:1

See *Daughter/Daughters; Family; Son/Sons; Youth.*

Child Rearing: The process of bringing up children and teaching them how to live.

> Train up a child in the way. . .Prov. 22:6
> a child left to himself. . .Prov. 29:15
> Study to shew thyself approved. . . 2 Tim. 2:15
> from a child thou hast known. . . 2 Tim. 3:15

Choices: Exercising sound judgment and making good decisions.
> choose you this day. . .Josh. 24:15
> choose the fear of the Lord. . . Prov. 1:29
> name is rather to be chosen. . . Prov. 22:1

Chosen People: A name for the Israelites as well as the Christian church.
> c thee to be a peculiar p. . . Deut. 14:2
> ye are a chosen generation. . . 1 Pet. 2:9

Christ: The Messiah (Matt. 16:16; Mark 8:29; John 4:25; Rom. 10:4; Phil 2:11). A title of Jesus, the Savior: at first with the article, "The Christ;" later, as part of a proper name, "Jesus Christ."

Christian/Christians: Followers of Christ. First called by this name at Antioch, Syria, AD 43 (Acts 11:26; 26:28). Believers were first called "followers of the Way."
> found any of this way. . .Acts 9:2
> called C's first in Antioch. . .Acts 11:26
> no small stir about that way. . . Acts 19:23
> I persecuted this way. . .Acts 22:4
> knowledge of that way. . .Acts 24:22
> persuadest me to be a C. . . Acts 26:28
> any man suffer as a C. . .1 Pet. 4:16

See *Christianity; Church/Churches; Congregation.*

Christianity: The body of beliefs accepted by followers of Jesus.

by faith in Christ Jesus. . .Gal. 3:26
your faith in Christ. . .Col. 2:5
See *Christian/Christians; Church/Churches; Congregation.*

Chronicles: Thirteenth and fourteenth books of the O.T. They focus on the history of Israel, covering a period of about 3,500 years.

Church/Churches: A congregation of religious worshippers (Acts 7:38; Mat. 16:18). Visible (Acts 2; Col. 1:24). Invisible (Heb. 12:23).
 c which was at Jerusalem. . .
  Acts 8:1
 ordained them elders in every c. . .
  Acts 14:23
 c of God which is at Corinth. . .
  1 Cor. 1:2
 care of the c of God? . . .1 Tim. 3:5
 John to the seven c'es. . .Rev. 1:4
See *Christian/Christians; Christianity; Church Leaders; Church, Universal; Congregation.*

Church Leaders: Those who serve the church in leadership positions. The word *minister* refers to all believers.
 Bishop
 bishop, he desireth a good work. . .
  1 Tim. 3:1
 bishop must be blameless. . .
  Titus 1:7
 Deacon/Deacons
 must the deacons be grave. . .
  1 Tim. 3:8
 deacons be the husbands of one
  wife. . .1 Tim. 3:12
 Evangelist/Evangelists
 Philip the evangelist. . .Acts 21:8
 do the work of an evangelist. . .
  2 Tim. 4:5
 Minister/Ministers
 let him be your minister. . .
  Matt. 20:26
 minister of Jesus Christ. . .Rom.
  15:16
 ministers by whom ye believed. . .
  1 Cor. 3:5

ministers of the new testament. . .
  2 Cor. 3:6
 I was made a minister. . .Eph. 3:7
 Paul am made a minister. . .Col.
  1:23
See *Pastor.*

Circumcision: A rite, symbolizing God's covenant, performed on Israelite males on the eighth day after birth (Gen. 17; Exod. 7:44; Lev. 12:3; John 7:22).
 covenant of c. . .Acts 7:8
 profit is there of c? . . .Rom. 3:1
 minister of the c. . .Rom. 15:8
 C is nothing. . .1 Cor. 7:19

Cleopas: One of the two disciples to whom Christ appeared on the road to Emmaus (Luke 24:18).

Clean/Cleanse/Cleansed/Cleanseth/ Cleansing: To make a person ceremonially pure and suitable for entering God's presence. Jesus' sacrifice did away with the need for ceremonial cleansing.
 Physical cleansing
 thou canst make me c. . .Matt. 8:2
 offer for thy c'sing. . .Mark 1:44
 all things are c unto you. . .
  Luke 11:41
 Spiritual cleansing
 ye are c. . .John 13:10
 What God hath c'sed. . .Acts 10:15
 he might sanctify and c'se. . .
  Eph. 5:26
 those that were c. . .2 Pet. 2:18
 c'se us from all unrighteousness. . .
  1 John 1:9

Cock: An adult male domestic fowl (Matt. 26:34, 74).

Colosse: A city in Phrygia. Paul wrote to the church in this city (Col. 1:2; 4:13).

Comfort, Physical: Enjoying contentment and security.
> My bed shall c me. . .Job 7:13
> c me with apples. . .Song of Sol. 2:5

See *Comfort/Comforted/Comforts; Spiritual.*

Comfort/Comforted/Comforts, Spiritual: The sense of well-being that God gives to all believers.
> thy staff they c me. . .Ps. 23:4
> soul refused to be c'ed. . .Ps. 77:2
> thy c's delight my soul. . .Ps. 94:19
> c all that mourn. . .Isa. 61:2
> c of the Holy Ghost. . .Acts 9:31
> God of all c. . .2 Cor. 1:3
> ourselves are c'ed of God. . .
> 2 Cor. 1:4

See *Comfort, Physical; Consolation/ Consolations; Encouragement.*

Comforter: Defender and helper. A title for the Holy Spirit and Christ (John 14:16, 26; 15:26; 16:7).
> he shall give you another C. . .
> John 14:16
> C, which is the Holy Ghost. . .
> John 14:26
> when the C is come. . .John 15:26

See *Holy Ghost.*

Coming to Christ: Accepting Jesus Christ as Lord and Savior.
> believeth on him that sent me. . .
> John 5:24
> Believe on the Lord Jesus Christ
> . . .Acts 16:31
> shalt believe in thine heart. . .
> Rom. 10:9

See *Believe/Believed/Believeth/Believest; Conversion; Repentance; Salvation.*

Communication: A person-to-person exchange of information.
> your c be, Yea, yea. . .Matt. 5:37
> great plainness of speech. . .
> 2 Cor. 3:12
> no corrupt c proceed. . .Eph. 4:29
> speech be alway with grace. . .
> Col. 4:6

Communion: Mutual love, confidence, and fellowship (1 Cor. 10:16; 2 Cor. 13:14; 1 John 1:3). The Lord's Supper is called the "Holy Communion."
> Jesus took bread, and blessed it. . .
> Matt. 26:26
> he took the cup. . .Luke 22:17
> c of the blood of Christ? . . .
> 1 Cor. 10:16

Companion: A friend or associate.
> c of all them that fear thee. . .
> Ps. 119:63
> thy c, and the wife. . .Mal. 2:14

Compassion: Love and acceptance of others.
> art a God full of c. . .Ps. 86:15
> moved with c on them. . .Matt. 9:36
> having c one of another. . .1 Pet. 3:8

See *Concern for Others.*

Complain/Complained/Complainers/Complaint: To express discontent or disagreement.
> c'ed, it displeased the Lord. . .
> Num. 11:1
> I c'ed, and my spirit. . .Ps. 77:3
> poured out my c't before him. . .
> Ps. 142:2
> Wherefore doth a living man c. . .
> Lam. 3:39
> These are murmurers, c'ers. . .
> Jude 1:16

See *Discontentment/Discontented; Murmur/Murmured/Murmurers/ Murmurings.*

Comprehend/Comprehended: To understand.
> which we cannot c. . .Job 37:5
> darkness c'ed it not. . .John 1:5
> c with all saints. . .Eph. 3:18

See *Understanding.*

Conceit/Conceits: A prideful, haughty attitude.
> high wall in his own c. . .Prov. 18:11
> wise in his own c. . .Prov. 26:5

Be not wise in your own c's. . .
   Rom. 12:16

Concern for Others: A spirit of compassion.
   no man cared for my soul. . .
      Ps. 142:4
   hath pity upon the poor. . .
      Prov. 19:17
   have the same care. . .1 Cor. 12:25
   pray one for another. . .James 5:16
See *Compassion.*

Concubine: A secondary wife, betrothed according to custom (Gen. 21:14; 25:6; Exod. 21:7). Concubinage is repudiated in the N.T. (Matt. 19:4–9; 1 Cor. 7:2–4).

Condemnation: The declaration of a person as guilty and deserving of punishment.
   art in the same c? . . .Luke 23:40
   shall not come into c. . .John 5:24
   therefore now no c. . .Rom. 8:1
   lest ye fall into c. . .James 5:12
See *Consequences of Sin.*

Conduct: Daily deeds and behavior.
   The just shall live by faith. . .Rom.
      1:17
   live peaceably with all men. . .
      Rom. 12:18
   also walk in the Spirit. . .Gal. 5:25
   live soberly, righteously. . .Titus 2:12
See *Conversation.*

Confident/Confidence: Having assurance.
   than to put c'ce in man. . .Ps. 118:8
   fear of the Lord is strong c'ce. . .
      Prov. 14:26
   Being c of this very thing. . .Phil. 1:6
   I can do all things through Christ
      . . .Phil. 4:13
   Cast not away therefore your c'ce
      . . .Heb. 10:35

Conflict: A disagreement or quarrel.

them that fight against me. . .
   Ps. 35:1
fighting daily oppresseth me. . .
   Ps. 56:1
Fight the good fight of faith. . .
   1 Tim. 6:12
fightings among you? . . .James 4:1
See *Contention/Contentions/Contentious.*

Confusion: Puzzlement or perplexity; lack of clarity about an issue.
   let me never be put to c. . .Ps. 71:1
   not the author of c. . .1 Cor. 14:33
   perplexed, but not in despair. . .
      2 Cor. 4:8
   strife is, there is c. . .James 3:16

Congregation: A gathering of believers for worship.
   the c of the righteous. . .Ps. 1:5
   thanks in the great c. . .Ps. 35:18
   c of saints. . .Ps. 149:1

Consecrate: To dedicate or devote something to God. The tribe of Levi was consecrated to the priesthood (Exod. 32:28–29). Other things in the Bible consecrated to God were vessels (Josh. 6:19), profits (Mic. 4:13), fields (Lev. 27:28), cattle (2 Chron. 29:33), persons (Num. 6:9–13), and nations (Exod. 19:6).

Conservation: Caring for God's world, the physical creation.
   created the heaven and the earth
      . . .Gen. 1:1
   replenish the earth. . .Gen. 1:28
   for all the earth is mine. . .
      Exod. 19:5
   Lord made heaven and earth. . .
      Exod. 20:11
See *Earth; Ecology.*

Consolation/Consolations: The state of being comfortable and at ease.
   Are the c's of God small. . .Job 15:11
   God of patience and c. . .Rom. 15:5
   hath given us everlasting c. . .
      2 Thess. 2:16

See *Comfort/Comforted/Comforts, Spiritual; Encouragement.*

Content/Contentment: Satisfaction with one's life and circumstances.
be c with your wages. . .Luke 3:14
godliness with c'ment is great gain
. . .1 Tim. 6:6
let us be therewith c. . .1 Tim. 6:8

Contention/Contentions/Contentious: A quarrel or argument.
therefore leave off c. . .Prov. 17:14
A fool's lips enter into c. . .
Prov. 18:6
c'us man to kindle strife. . .
Prov. 26:21
there are c's among you. . .1 Cor. 1:11
See *Complain/Complained/Complainers/Complaint; Conflict; Discontentment/Discontented; Murmur/Murmured/Murmurers/Murmurings; Quarrel.*

Conversation: A consistent lifestyle of faith and righteous conduct.
our c in the world. . .2 Cor. 1:12
in c, in charity. . .1 Tim. 4:12
c be without covetousness. . .
Heb. 13:5
holy in all manner of c. . .1 Pet. 1:15
See *Conduct.*

Conversion: Regeneration by the power of God through faith in Jesus Christ.
whosoever believeth in him
. . .John 3:16
Except ye be converted. . .
Matt. 18:3
be converted, that your sins. . .
Acts 3:19
Believe on the Lord Jesus Christ
. . .Acts 16:31
See *Believe/Believed/Believeth/Believest; Coming to Christ; Knowing God; New Life; Repentance; Salvation.*

Convocation: A holy assembly of God's people, usually called to receive

some special message from Him (Exod. 12:16; Lev. 23:2; Num. 28:18).

Corinth: Capital of Achaia in Greece. Destroyed by Rome in 146 BC. Rebuilt by Julius Caesar in 46 BC, as a Roman colony. Paul founded a church here (Acts 18:1; 20:2–3).

Cornelius: A Roman centurion and the first Gentile convert (Acts 10:1–33).

Corporal Punishment: Physical discipline such as spanking.
Forty stripes he may give him. . .
Deut. 25:3
spareth his rod hateth his son. . .
Prov. 13:24
the rod of correction. . .Prov. 22:15
rod and reproof give wisdom. . .
Prov. 29:15

Correction: Discipline designed to bring about appropriate behavior.
neither be weary of his c. . .
Prov. 3:11
Withhold not c from the child. . .
Prov. 23:13
for reproof, for. . .2 Tim. 3:16

Corruption: The world's tendency toward decay and confusion.
and not see c. . .Ps. 49:9
from the pit of c. . .Isa. 38:17
brought up my life from c. . .
Jon. 2:6
It is sown in c. . .1 Cor. 15:42

Council: In N.T., 1. The Sanhedrin, the Jewish supreme court (Matt. 26:59). 2. Lesser courts (Matt. 10:17; Mark 13:9).

Counsel/Counsels: Guidance and advice.
he hath c and understanding. . .
Job 12:13
guide me with thy c. . .Ps. 73:24

walked in their own c's. . .Ps. 81:12
no c is, the people fall. . .Prov. 11:14
hearkeneth unto c is wise. . .
Prov. 12:15
See *Advice; Decision Making.*

Countenance. The face or a facial expression.
Lord lift up his c. . .Num. 6:26
through the pride of his c. . .
Ps. 10:4
in the light of thy c. . .Ps. 89:15
maketh a cheerful c. . .Prov. 15:13

Courage: The strength to withstand danger or fear.
Be strong and of a good c. . .
Deut. 31:6
be of good c. . .Ps. 27:14
thanked God, and took c. . .
Acts 28:15
See *Bold/Boldness/Boldly.*

Courtship: The process of getting to know each other that precedes marriage. In Bible times, marriages were arranged by the parents of the bride and groom.
take a wife unto my son. . .
Gen. 24:38
serve thee seven years for Rachel
. . .Gen. 29:18
Mary was espoused to Joseph. . .
Matt. 1:18
and the bed undefiled. . .Heb. 13:4
See *Betroth/Betrothed; Marriage/Marry.*

Covenant: An agreement between two parties. God's covenant with Israel was first established with Abraham, then renewed with succeeding generations (Gen. 9:15; 11:30–31). The covenant of the law was established through Moses (Exod. 20:24), of the Gospel through Christ (Gal. 3; Heb. 8).
I will establish my c. . .Gen. 9:11
made a c with Abram. . .Gen. 15:18
make a c with our God. . .Ezra 10:3
My c will I not break. . .Ps. 89:34

mediator of a better c. . .Heb. 8:6
blood of the everlasting c. . .
Heb. 13:20

Covet/Covetousness: Strong desire. Rightful desire is good (1 Cor. 12:31), but wrongful desire is sinful (Exod. 20:24; Prov. 28:16; Luke 12:15–34; 1 Tim. 6:9–10).
not c thy neighbour's house. . .
Exod. 20:17
beware of c'ousness. . .Luke 12:15
c earnestly the best gifts. . .
1 Cor. 12:31
and c'ousness, which is idolatry. . .
Col. 3:5

Cracknels: Hard, brittle cakes (1 Kings 14:3).

Create/Created: To bring something into existence.
God c'd the heaven. . .Gen. 1:1
God c'd man in his own image. . .
Gen. 1:27
Male and female c'd he them. . .
Gen. 5:2
hath not one God c'd us?. . .
Mal. 2:10
c'd all things by Jesus Christ. . .
Eph. 3:9
See *Creation.*

Creation: The physical universe created by the Lord.
from the beginning of the c. . .
Mark 10:6
invisible things of him from the c
. . .Rom. 1:20
the whole c groaneth. . .Rom. 8:22
See *Create/Created.*

Creator: A title of God that emphasizes His formation of the physical universe.
Remember now thy C in. . .
Eccles. 12:1
C of the ends of the earth. . .
Isa. 40:28
creature more than the C. . .
Rom. 1:25

Credit: To take possession of something with the promise to pay for it in the future.

> If thou lend money. . .Exod. 22:25
> not lend upon usury. . .Deut. 23:19
> thou dost lend thy brother. . .
>   Deut. 24:10
> borrower is servant to the lender
>   . . .Prov. 22:7

See *Gambling; Money.*

Crete: One of the largest islands in the Mediterranean Sea. Paul founded a church here and placed it in charge of Titus (Acts 2:11; 27:1–12; Titus 1:5–13).

Crib: A stall for cattle, and the manger or rack for hay or straw (Job 39:9; Prov. 14:4; Isa. 1:3).

Crime: An illegal act.
Extortion
> thy neighbours by extortion. . .
>   Ezek. 22:12
> full of extortion and excess. . .
>   Matt. 23:25

Theft
> shall be sold for his theft. . .
>   Exod. 22:3
> Thefts, covetousness. . .Mark 7:22

See *Adultery; Blaspheme/Blasphemy/ Blasphemed/Blasphemers/Blasphemy; Murder/Murders; Rape.*

Criminals: See *Crime.*

Cross: The wooden stake on which Jesus was executed (John 19:17–18). Now a sacred emblem.

> his c, and follow me. . .Matt. 16:24
> bearing his c went forth. . .
>   John 19:17
> offence of the c. . .Gal. 5:11
> c of our Lord Jesus. . .Gal. 6:14
> even the death of the c. . .Phil. 2:8
> through the blood of his c. . .
>   Col. 1:20
> endured the c. . .Heb. 12:2

See *Calvary.*

Crucified: A method of capital punishment by nailing a person to a cross (Gal. 11:19; Esther 7:10). The limbs sometimes were broken to hasten death (John 19:31). Burial was denied (Deut. 21:22–23), but an exception was allowed in Christ's case (Matt. 27:58).

> delivered him to be c. . .Matt. 27:26
> And they c him. . .Matt. 27:35
> two thieves c with him. . .Matt.
>   27:38
> Jesus, whom ye have c. . .Acts 2:36
> our old man is c. . .Rom. 6:6
> we preach Christ c. . .1 Cor. 1:23
> I am c with Christ. . .Gal. 2:20

Cruse: A bottle, flask, or jug for holding liquids (1 Sam. 26:11; 1 Kings 17:12; 19:6).

Crying: Shedding tears, or weeping.
> tears have been my meat. . .Ps.
>   42:3
> a time to weep. . .Eccles. 3:4
> Blessed are ye that weep now. . .
>   Luke 6:21
> wash his feet with tears. . .Luke
>   7:38

Cubit: The distance from an adult's elbow to the end of the middle finger, or about 22 inches (Gen. 6:15; 1 Sam. 17:4).

Currency: Any item used as legal tender. In the Bible, the shekel and talent were weights, not coins, but eventually they became standardized as currency.

> worth four hundred shekels. . .
>   Gen. 23:15
> thirty shekels of silver. . .Exod.
>   21:32
> sparrows sold for a farthing? . . .
>   Matt. 10:29
> they brought unto him a penny. . .
>   Matt. 22:19

one he gave five talents. . .Matt.
25:15
he took out two pence. . .Luke
10:35
See *Money.*

Curse/Cursing: To call for evil or misfortune to fall upon another person.
profane my holy name. . .Lev. 22:32
clothed himself with c'ing. . .
Ps. 109:18
full of c'ing and bitterness. . .
Rom. 3:14
same mouth proceedeth blessing
and c'ing. . .James 3:10
See *Profane/Profanity.*

Cyprus: A large island in the Mediterranean Sea. Christianity was introduced here quite early (Acts 11:19); birthplace of Barnabas (Acts 4:36); Paul visited this island (Acts 13:4–13).

D

Dagon: National male idol of the Philistines (1 Chron. 10:10). Noted temples at Ashdod (1 Sam. 5:1–7); Gaza (Judg. 16:23); Beth-dagon (Josh. 15:41); and Asher (Josh. 19:27). Represented with human heads and face and a fish's body.

Damascus: A city of Asia, 133 miles northeast of Jerusalem (Gen. 14:15; 15:2). Adjacent region called "Syria of Damascus" (2 Sam. 8:5). Taken by David (2 Sam. 8:6); and by Jeroboam (2 Kings 14:28). Scene of Paul's conversion (Acts 9:1–27; 22:1–16).

Damnation: Consignment to everlasting punishment (Matt. 23:33; Mark 3:29; John 5:29; 2 Peter 2:3).
wicked shall be turned into hell. . .
Ps. 9:17

shall be in danger of hell fire. . .
Matt. 5:22
judgment seat of Christ. . .2 Cor.
5:10
but after this the judgment. . .
Heb. 9:27
See *Hell; Unsaved.*

Dan: Fifth son of Jacob (Gen. 30:6; 49:16). Land allotment (Josh. 19:40–46). A portion of the tribe moved north (Josh. 19:47–48; Judg. 18).

Daniel: 1. Fourth of the major prophets. Carried captive to Babylon in 604 BC. Named Belteshazzar (Daniel 1–2); made a governor under Darius (Dan. 6:2). Last vision on the Tigris River in the third year of Cyrus, 534 BC (Dan. 10:10–4). 2. Second son of David (1 Chron. 3:1).

Darius: 1. Darius the Mede (Dan. 5:31; 6; 9:1; 11:1). Captured Babylon from Belshazzar in 538 BC. 2. Darius Hystaspes, king of Persia, 521–486 BC. He restored the captive Jews (Ezek. 4:5, 24; 6:14–15; Hag. 1:1, 15; Zech. 1:1, 7). 3. Darius the Persian (Neh. 12:22).

Darkness: The absence of light; a metaphor for life without God.
the Lord will lighten my d. . .
2 Sam. 22:29
brought them out of d. . .Ps. 107:14
cast out into outer d. . .Matt. 8:12
to them that sit in d. . .Luke 1:79
light shineth in d. . .John 1:5
not walk in d. . .John 8:12
in him is no d at all. . .1 John 1:5

Daughter/Daughters: A female offspring.
if a man sell his d. . .Exod. 21:7
Many d's have done virtuously. . .
Prov. 31:29
he that loveth son or d. . .Matt.
10:37

your d's shall prophesy. . .Acts 2:17
See *Woman; Youth.*

David: Youngest son of Jesse (1 Sam. 16:8–12); born at Bethlehem. Anointed king by Samuel (1 Sam. 16:13). Re-anointed at Hebron (2 Sam. 2:4). United his kingdom and raised it to great strength and splendor. Died at the age of 70 in 1015 BC, after a reign of seven and a half years over Judah and thirty-three years over the entire kingdom of Israel. History told in 1 Sam. 16–1 Kings 2.

David, City of: See *Jerusalem.*

Deacon: A subordinate minister or officer in the early Christian church (Acts 6:1–6). Qualifications of (1 Tim. 3:8–12).

Deaconess: A female officer in the early church (Rom. 16:1; 1 Tim. 5:10).

Dead Sea: Not so called until the second century. In the O.T., called the Salt Sea and the Sea of the Plain.

Deaf: Unable to hear.
maketh the dumb, or d. . .Exod. 4:11
d shall be unstopped. . .Isa. 35:5
the d hear. . .Matt. 11:5
See *Blind/Blinded; Disabilities; Diseases; Dumb.*

Death: The end of physical existence.
d of the righteous. . .Num. 23:10
valley of the shadow of d. . .Ps. 23:4
shall not see d? . . .Ps. 89:48
passed from d unto life. . .John 5:24
wages of sin is d. . .Rom. 6:23
See *Bury/Burial/Buried; Mortal/ Mortality.*

Death Penalty: Execution; punishment for extreme crimes such as murder.
surely be put to death. . .Exod. 21:16
that man shall die. . .Deut. 17:12
lay with her shall die. . .Deut. 22:25
See *Capital Punishment; Death.*

Debauchery: Moral corruption.
chambering and wantonness. . . Rom. 13:13
uncleanness, lasciviousness. . . Gal. 5:19
lasciviousness, lusts. . .1 Pet. 4:3
See *Adultery; Alcohol; Drink/Drinking; Lasciviousness.*

Deborah: 1. Nurse of Rebekah (Gen. 35:8; 24:59). 2. Prophetess and judge (Judg. 4:5–14; 5).

Debt: See *Credit; Money.*

Deceit/Deceitful/Deceitfulness: Dishonesty or deception.
bloody and d'ful men. . .Ps. 55:23
counsels of the wicked are d. . . Prov. 12:5
kisses of an enemy are d'ful. . . Prov. 27:6
The heart is d'ful. . .Jer. 17:9
d'fulness of riches. . .Matt. 13:22
See *Cheat/Cheating.*

Decision Making: To weigh the merits of several choices and decide on one.
choose you this day. . .Josh. 24:15
choose the fear of the Lord. . . Prov. 1:29
choose none of his ways. . . Prov. 3:31
See *Counsel/Counsels.*

Defiled: Contamination; to make something impure through sin and rebellion.
lay with her, and d'd her. . . Gen. 34:2

d'd with their own works. . .
Ps. 106:39
d'd my holy name. . .Ezek. 43:8
See *Impurity.*

Defraud/Defrauded: To deprive a person of something through deception.
Shalt not d thy neighbour. . .
Lev. 19:13
suffer yourselves to be d'ed? . . .
1 Cor. 6:7
D ye not one the other. . .1 Cor. 7:5

Deity of Christ: Jesus in His divine nature as the Son of God.
Son of the living God. . .Matt. 16:16
making himself equal with God. . .
John 5:18
seen me hath seen the Father. . .
John 14:9
being in the form of God. . .Phil. 2:6
image of the invisible God. . .Col. 1:15
by him were all things created. . .
Col. 1:16
fulness of the Godhead bodily. . .
Col. 2:9

Delilah: A woman of Sorek who discovered the secret of Samson's strength and betrayed him to the Philistines (Judg. 16:4–20).

Deliverer: A person who rescues others from an enemy or unfavorable circumstances; a divine title.
the Lord raised up a d. . .Judg. 3:9
my fortress, and my d. . .Ps. 18:2
my high tower, and my d. . .Ps. 144:2

Delusion: The state of being misled or deceived.
imaginations of the thoughts. . .
1 Chron. 28:9
deviseth wicked imaginations. . .
Prov. 6:18
became vain in their imaginations
. . .Rom. 1:21

Demetrius: 1. A silversmith at Ephesus (Acts 19:24–30). 2. A disciple (3 John 12).

Demon Possession: To be possessed and controlled by demons or evil spirits.
two possessed with devils. . .Matt. 8:28
vexed with a devil. . .Matt. 15:22
Jesus rebuked the devil. . .Matt. 17:18
which hath a dumb spirit. . .Mark 9:17
See *Devil/Devils.*

Denarius: A Roman silver coin. The "penny" of the N.T. (Matt. 20:2).

Deny: To refuse to admit or acknowledge.
lest ye d your God. . .Josh. 24:27
shall d me before men. . .Matt. 10:33
let him d himself. . .Matt. 16:24
thou shalt d me thrice. . .Matt. 26:34
in works they d him. . .Titus 1:16

Depression: A state of extreme sadness or remorse.
cast down, O my soul? . . .Ps. 43:5
eat the bread of sorrows. . .Ps. 127:2
See *Empty/Emptiness; Sorrow/Sorrows.*

Derbe: A city of Lycaonia in Asia Minor (Acts 14:20; 20:4).

Desire/Desires: Extreme longing for something.
boasteth of his heart's d. . .Ps. 10:3
d's of thine heart. . .Ps. 37:4
d of the righteous. . .Prov. 10:24
d spiritual gifts. . .1 Cor. 14:1
d the office of a bishop. . .1 Tim. 3:1

Desire/Desires, Sexual: Strong sexual impulses.
d shall be to thy husband. . .Gen. 3:16

d thy neighbour's wife. . .Deut. 5:21

Despise/Despised/Despisest: Hatred or malice toward others.
> they d'd my judgments. . .Lev. 26:43
> fools d wisdom. . .Prov. 1:7
> d'd and rejected. . .Isa. 53:3
> d'st thou the riches. . .Rom. 2:4
> no man d thy youth. . .1 Tim. 4:12

See *Hate/Hated/Hateth*.

Destruction: Ruin, wreckage, or havoc.
> down into the pit of d. . .Ps. 55:23
> foolish is near d. . .Prov. 10:14
> Pride goeth before d. . .Prov. 16:18
> punished with everlasting d. . . 2 Thess. 1:9

Devil: A word for Satan, meaning "adversary" (Matt. 16:23; Mark 8:33; Luke 22:3; 1 Pet. 5:8; Rev. 20:2).
> to be tempted of the d. . .Matt. 4:1
> stand against the wiles of the d. . . Eph. 6:11
> Resist the d. . .James 4:7
> your adversary the d. . .1 Pet. 5:8

See *Demon Possession*.

Devotion: Faithfulness and loyalty to the Lord.
> walked before thee in truth. . . 2 Kings 20:3
> serve him with a perfect heart. . . 1 Chron. 28:9
> the Lord without distraction. . . 1 Cor. 7:35

See *Good Work/Good Works*.

Devotions: Regular meditation on the Lord and His blessings.
> Be still, and know that I am God. . . Ps. 46:10
> daily shall he be praised. . .Ps. 72:15
> Praying always with all prayer. . . Eph. 6:18
> desire the sincere milk of the word . .1 Pet. 2:2

See *Prayer; Word of God*.

Diamond: Pure crystallized carbon. Third stone in the second row of the high priest's breastplate (Exod. 28:18; Ezek. 28:13).

Diana: A Roman goddess. The Artemis of the Greeks. Her temple at Ephesus was regarded as one of the seven wonders of the world (Acts 19:24–28).

Didymus: Surname of Thomas, one of Jesus' disciples (John 11:16; 20:24; 21:2).

Diet: The food a person eats for nourishment.
> shalt eat the herb of the field. . . Gen. 3:18
> not good to eat much honey. . . Prov. 25:27
> life is more than meat. . .Luke 12:23
> body is the temple of the Holy Ghost. . .1 Cor. 6:19

See *Fast/Fasting*.

Diligent/Diligently/Diligence: Earnest and energetic effort.
> keep thy soul d'ly. . .Deut. 4:9
> substance of a d man. . .Prov. 12:27
> them that d'ly seek him. . .Heb. 11:6
> give d'ce to make your calling. . . 2 Pet. 1:10

See *Industry*.

Disabilities: Physical limitations.
> he fell, and became lame. . .2 Sam. 4:4
> Then shall the lame man leap. . . Isa. 35:6
> the maimed, the lame, the blind. . . Luke 14:13
> a certain man lame. . .Acts 3:2

See *Blind/Blinded; Deaf; Diseases; Dumb*.

Disappoint/Disappointed: A reaction to crushed expectations.
> and were not confounded. . .Ps. 22:5
> Without counsel purposes are d'ed. . .Prov. 15:22

hope maketh not ashamed. . .
Rom. 5:5

Discern/Discerneth/Discerning: To weigh all the facts and make a wise decision.
wise man's heart d'eth. . .
Eccles. 8:5
ye do not d this time? . . .
Luke 12:56
another d'ing of spirits. . .
1 Cor. 12:10

Disciple/Disciples: A follower of Christ (Matt. 10:24); of John the Baptist (Matt. 9:14). Applied especially to the twelve (Matt. 10:1; 11:1; 20:17).
d is not above his master. . .Matt. 10:24
commanding his twelve d's. . .
Matt. 11:1
When his d's heard it. . .Matt. 19:25
D's, and findeth them asleep. . .
Matt. 26:40
he cannot be my d. . .Luke 14:26
d, whom Jesus loved. . .John 20:2
d's were called Christians. . .
Acts 11:26
d's were filled with joy. . .Acts 13:52
strengthening all the d's. . .
Acts 18:23

Discipline: To control one's impulses; to train or teach.
if ye will obey my voice. . .Exod. 19:5
that ye should obey it. . .Rom. 6:12
See *Obedience.*

Discontentment/Discontented: Dissatisfaction with one's circumstances.
every one that was d'ed. . .1 Sam. 22:2
neither will he rest content. . .
Prov. 6:35
See *Complain/Complained/Complainers/Complaint; Contention/Contentions/Contentious.*

Discord: Lack of harmony or agreement.
soweth d among brethren. . .
Prov. 6:19
arose a great dissension. . .
Acts 23:10
not in strife and envying. . .
Rom. 13:13

Discretion: To decide carefully; to exercise good judgment.
guide his affairs with d. . .Ps. 112:5
D shall preserve thee. . .Prov. 2:11
keep sound wisdom and d. . .
Prov. 3:21

Discrimination: Showing favoritism toward some individuals or groups while rejecting others.
Love your enemies. . .Matt. 5:44
love thy neighbour as thyself. . .
Matt. 19:19
that ye love one another. . .
John 15:17
not call any man common or unclean. . .Acts 10:28
ye are all one in Christ Jesus. . .
Gal. 3:28
neither Greek nor Jew. . .Col. 3:11
See *Equality; Favoritism.*

Diseases: Illnesses that attack the human body.
one plague more upon Pharaoh . . .Exod. 11:1
none of these d. . .Exod. 15:26
those that died in the plague . . .Num. 25:9
immediately his leprosy was cleansed. . .Matt. 8:3
as many as had plagues. . .Mark 3:10
See *Blind/Blinded; Deaf; Disabilities; Dumb.*

Disgrace: Humiliation or shame.
mine enemies be ashamed. . .
Ps. 6:10
Turn away my reproach. . .Ps. 119:39
worthy to suffer shame. . .Acts 5:41

Dishonesty: Lack of forthrightness in dealing with others.
> all that do unrighteously. . .
> Deut. 25:16
> false balance is abomination
> . . .Prov. 11:1
> hidden things of d. . .2 Cor. 4:2

Dishonour: To treat someone or oneself in a degrading manner.
> my shame, and my d. . .Ps. 69:19
> to d their own bodies. . .Rom. 1:24
> It is sown in d. . .1 Cor. 15:43

Disobedient/Disobedience: Refusing to obey.
> Nevertheless they were d. . .
> Neh. 9:26
> d to parents. . .Rom. 1:30
> children of d'ce. . .Eph. 2:2

Disrespect: Lack of respect toward others.
> My friends scorn me. . .Job 16:20
> sitteth in the seat of the scornful
> . . .Ps. 1:1
> laughed him to scorn. . .Matt. 9:24

Distress/Distressed: Extreme trouble or discouragement.
> In my d I called upon. . .Ps. 18:6
> shall tribulation, or d. . .Rom. 8:35
> on every side, yet not d'ed. . .
> 2 Cor. 4:8

Diversity. See *Discrimination*.

Dives: A traditional name for the rich man in Luke 16:19–31.

Divination: The use of superstition to discover the divine will; by rods (Hosea 4:12), arrows (Ezek. 21:21), cups (Gen. 44:5), the liver (Ezek. 21:21), dreams (Deut. 13:3; Zech. 10:2), and consulting oracles (Isa. 41:21–24; 44:7). The practice of divination was forbidden (Lev. 19:26).

Divinity: See *Deity of Christ*.

Divorce/Divorced/Divorcement: Breaking of the marriage covenant.
> he may not put her away. . .
> Deut. 22:19
> write her a bill of d'ment. . .
> Deut. 24:1
> d'd committeth adultery. . .
> Matt. 5:32
> let not man put asunder. . .
> Matt. 19:6

See *Adultery; Fornication/Fornications; Lawsuits.*

Doctrine: A system of religious beliefs.
> astonished at his d. . .Matt. 7:28
> the apostles' d. . .Acts 2:42
> every wind of d. . .Eph. 4:14
> is profitable for d. . .2 Tim. 3:16

Dominion: Man's rule over God's creation.
> replenish the earth, and subdue it
> . . .Gen. 1:28
> Thou madest him to have d. . .Ps. 8:6

Dorcas: A believer from Joppa whom Peter raised from the dead (Acts 9:36–42). Also known as Tabitha.

Doubt/Doubted/Doubts: To be hesitant and uncertain.
> dissolving of d's. . .Dan. 5:12
> have faith, and d not. . .Matt. 21:21
> but some d'ed. . .Matt. 28:17
> shall not d in his heart. . .Mark 11:23

See *Feelings.*

Dowry: The consideration paid the father of the bride by the bridegroom (Gen. 29:18; 34:12; 1 Sam. 18:25; Hosea 3:2).

Drachma/Drachm: A silver coin of Greece, corresponding to the Roman denarius. A piece of silver (Luke 15:8–9).

Dream/Dreamed/Dreams: Thoughts or images that come to a person while asleep.
> Joseph d'ed a d...Gen. 37:5
> that Pharaoh d'ed...Gen. 41:1
> or a dreamer of d's...Deut. 13:1
> interpreting of d's...Dan. 5:12
> old men shall d d's...Joel 2:28
> being warned of God in a d...
> Matt. 2:12

Drink/Drinking: The consumtion of alcoholic beverages.
> Do not drink wine nor strong d...
> Lev. 10:9
> he is a glutton, and a drunkard...
> Deut. 21:20
> a drunken man staggereth in his vomit...Isa. 19:14
> not in rioting and drunkenness...
> Rom. 13:13
> be not drunk with wine, wherein is excess...Eph. 5:18

See *Addiction; Alcohol; Debauchery; Drunkenness; Wine.*

Drugs: Chemicals or substances that produce a feeling of exhilaration.
> Let not sin therefore reign...
> Rom. 6:12
> ye are the temple of God...
> 1 Cor. 3:16
> glorify God in your body...
> 1 Cor. 6:20
> body, and bring it into subjection
> ...1 Cor. 9:27

Drunkenness: Intoxication caused by drinking too much wine or strong drink.
> **Avoiding drink and drunkards**
> not in rioting and d...Rom. 13:13
> a drunkard, or an extortioner...
> 1 Cor. 5:11
> be not drunk with wine, wherein is excess...Eph. 5:18
> **Examples of drunkenness**
> for he was very drunken...
> 1 Sam. 25:36
> and he made him drunk...
> 2 Sam. 11:13

> **God's kingdom and drunkenness**
> nor drunkards, nor revilers...
> 1 Cor. 6:10
> d, revellings...Gal. 5:21

See *Alcohol; Drink/Drinking.*

Dulcimer: The bagpipe (Dan. 3:5–15).

Dumb: Unable to speak; a disability usually associated with deafness in the Bible.
> who maketh the d...Exod. 4:11
> d man possessed...Matt. 9:32
> lame, blind, d...Matt. 15:30

See *Blind/Blinded; Deaf; Disabilities; Diseases.*

Duty: Obligatory tasks, especially service that the Lord deserves from all believers.
> whole d of man...Eccles. 12:13
> that which was our d to do...
> Luke 17:10

Dwelling: A place where people live.
> heaven thy d place...1 Kings 8:43
> thou hast been our d place...Ps. 90:1
> d in the light...1 Tim. 6:16

E

Earnest: Pledge (Gen. 38:17); surety (Prov. 17:18); hostage (2 Kings 14:14); deposit or advance (2 Cor. 1:22; Eph. 1:14).
> the e of the Spirit...2 Cor. 5:5
> the e of our inheritance...Eph. 1:14

Earth: The planet on which humans live; created by the Lord.
> created the heaven and the e...
> Gen. 1:1
> replenish the e...Gen. 1:28
> flood of waters upon the e...
> Gen. 6:17
> the e is the Lord's...1 Cor. 10:26

See *Conservation; Ecology.*

Eat: To take food into the body for nourishment.
> thou mayest freely e. . .Gen. 2:16
> shall e and be satisfied. . .Ps. 22:26
> what ye shall e. . .Matt. 6:25
> take thine ease, e, drink. . .Luke 12:19
> e of the tree of life. . .Rev. 2:7

See *Food; Health.*

Ebenezer: A memorial stone (1 Sam. 4:1–5; 7:12).

Ebony: A hard, heavy, dark wood, used for ornamental work and musical instruments (Ezek. 27:15).

Ecology: The natural laws and systems by which the earth functions.
> created the heaven and the earth . . .Gen. 1:1
> replenish the earth. . .Gen. 1:28
> for all the earth is mine. . .Exod. 19:5
> precious fruit of the earth. . .James 5:7

See *Conservation; Earth.*

Eden: First residence of man (Gen. 2:15). Paradise. Site not known.

Edify/Edifieth/Edifying: To build up or encourage another person.
> one may e another. . .Rom. 14:19
> but charity e'eth. . .1 Cor. 8:1
> Let all things be done unto e'ing. . . 1 Cor. 14:26
> e'ing of itself in love. . .Eph. 4:16

See *Learn/Learned/Learning.*

Edom: Name given to Esau, his country and people (Gen. 32:3–19; 33:1–16). Also called Idumea and Mount Seir. It lay south of Palestine and Moab.

Education: The process of training by formal instruction.

> know wisdom and instruction. . . Prov. 1:2
> Whoso loveth instruction. . . Prov. 12:1
> Moses was learned. . .Acts 7:22
> doctrine which ye have learned. . . Rom. 16:17

See *Learn/Learned/Learning.*

Egypt: Northeastern country of Africa; the Hebrew "Mizraim" (Gen. 10:6) and the "Land of Ham" (Ps. 105:23, 27). Bondage place of the Israelites (Exod. 1–14). Noted for the Nile River, rich soil, and gigantic ruins. Ancient religion was monotheistic, with the sun as the central object and attributes of nature in form of trinities. Vast temples and numerous priests. Kings called Pharaohs, who perpetuated their reigns in obelisks, temples, sculptures, sphinxes, pyramids, etc. Conquered Judea (1 Kings 14:25–26).

Elder: Highest in tribal authority (Gen. 24:2; Exod. 3:16; 4:29; Num. 22:7). One of the seventy leaders (Num. 11:25) or Sanhedrin (Judg. 2:7; 2 Sam. 17:4; Jer. 29:1). An official in the early Christian church, like a presbyter or bishop (Acts 20:17, 28).

Elderly, the: People in the senior years of life.
> aged understand judgment. . . Job 32:9
> when I am old and greyheaded. . . Ps. 71:18
> bring forth fruit in old age. . . Ps. 92:14
> are the crown of old men. . . Prov. 17:6
> old men shall dream dreams. . . Acts 2:17

See *Age.*

Elect: One called to everlasting life; the saved collectively (Matt. 24:22;

Mark 13:27; Luke 18:7; Rom. 8:33; Titus 1:1).

Israel mine e. . .Isa. 45:4
e shall long enjoy the work. . .
Isa. 65:22
to the charge of God's e? . . .
Rom. 8:33
e of God, holy and beloved. . .
Col. 3:12
E according to the foreknowledge
. . .1 Pet. 1:2
See *Election.*

Election: God's plan to bring salvation to the world.

according to the e of grace. . .
Rom. 11:5
as touching the e. . .Rom. 11:28
your calling and e sure. . .2 Pet. 1:10
See *Elect; Foreknowledge of God; Predestinate/Predestinated.*

Eli: A descendent of Aaron (Lev. 10:12). First of a line of high priests (1 Sam 1:9–17; 2:22–36; 3:1–14); and judge of Israel for forty years (1 Sam. 4:14–18). Line extinguished (1 Kings 2:26–27).

Elijah: A prophet of Gilead; appeared suddenly; was fed by ravens; restored the widow's son (1 Kings 17:1–24); invoked fire on the prophets of Baal (1 Kings 18:17–40); anointed Hazael, Jehu, and Elisha (1 Kings 19); denounced Ahab and Jezebel (1 Kings 21:17–24); was taken to heaven in a chariot of fire (2 Kings 2); reappeared on the Mount of Transfiguration (Luke 9:28–35). Called Elias in N.T. (Matt. 17:3).

Elisabeth: Wife of Zacharias and mother of John the Baptist (Luke 1:36–80).

Elisha: A prophet anointed by Elijah (1 Kings 19:16–21). Prophesied during a period of about sixty years.

Life and work described in 2 Kings 2–9; 13:14–21.

Emerald: A bright green variety of beryl. The emerald of Exod. 28:18; 39:11; Ezek. 27:16; 28:13; Rev. 4:3 is supposedly the carbuncle, a fiery garnet.

Emmanuel: A name for the Messiah, meaning "God with us" (Matt. 1:23). See *Immanuel.*

Emmaus: A village of Palestine about seven miles from Jerusalem (Luke 24:13).

Employment: Engagement in meaningful and profitable labor.

Six days shalt thou labour. . .
Exod. 20:9
goeth forth unto his work. . .
Ps. 104:23
sleep of a labouring man. . .Eccles. 5:12
labourer is worthy of his hire. . .
Luke 10:7
See *Work.*

Empty/Emptiness: A metaphor for physical and spiritual poverty.

brought me home again e. . .Ruth 1:21
his soul is e. . .Isa. 29:8
he was sad at that saying. . .
Mark 10:22
hath sent e'ness away. . .Luke 1:53
See *Depression.*

Encouragement: Inspiration and hope; the courage to go on.

in the comfort of the Holy Ghost . . .Acts 9:31
God of patience and consolation . . .Rom. 15:5
given us everlasting consolation. . .
2 Thess. 2:16
exhort one another daily. . .Heb. 3:13

See *Comfort/Comforted/Comforteth/ Comforts; Consolation/Consolations.*

Endure/Endureth: To persevere and continue to be faithful to the Lord, in spite of difficult circumstances.
e'th to the end. . .Matt. 10:22
therefore e hardness. . .2 Tim. 2:3
e afflictions. . .2 Tim. 4:5
man that e'th temptation. . .James 1:12
See *Perseverance.*

Enemy/Enemies: An adversary or foe.
saved from mine e'ies. . .Ps. 18:3
Love your e'ies. . .Matt. 5:44
The last e that. . .1 Cor. 15:26
See *Adversary/Adversaries.*

Engagement: See *Betroth/Betrothed; Courtship; Marriage/Marry.*

Enjoyment: See *Pleasure/Pleasures.*

Enoch: 1. A son of Cain (Gen. 4:17). 2. Father of Methuselah (Gen. 5:18–24; Heb. 11:5–13; Jude 14).

Ensign: A simple device, elevated on a pole, bearing an emblem to distinguish the tribes and army divisions (Num. 1:52; Song of Sol. 2:4; Isa. 13:2; 18:3).

Enter/Entered: To go or come in.
E into his gates. . .Ps. 100:4
e into the kingdom. . .Matt. 19:24
e not into temptation. . .Matt. 26:41
his own blood he e'ed. . .Heb. 9:12

Entertainment: Amusements or diversions provided for one's enjoyment.
that he may make us sport. . . Judg. 16:25
entertained angels unawares. . . Heb. 13:2
excess of wine, revellings. . .1 Pet. 4:3

Entice/Enticed/Enticeth: Drawing another person into sin.
if a man e a maid. . .Exod. 22:16
if sinners e thee. . .Prov. 1:10
A violent man e'th. . .Prov. 16:29
his own lust, and e'd. . .James 1:14

Envy/Envying: Jealousy or resentment toward other people or their possessions.
e slayeth the silly. . .Job 5:2
full of e, murder. . .Rom. 1:29
not in strife and e'ing. . .Rom. 13:13
where e'ing and strife. . .James 3:16

Ephah: 1. First son of Midian (Gen. 25:4; 1 Chron. 1:33; Isa. 60:6). 2. Caleb's concubine (1 Chron. 2:46). 3. A Hebrew dry measure, estimated at two and one-third to three and one-fourth pecks (Ruth 2:17; Num. 5:15). 4. A Hebrew liquid measure equal to seven and a half gallons.

Ephesus: Capital of Ionia, on the Aegean Sea. Noted for its commerce, learning, and architecture. Paul visited it (Acts 18:1–20) and founded a church there, to which he addressed one of his epistles (Acts 19:1–10; 20:17–38).

Ephod: 1. A sleeveless linen garment for priests, covering the breast and back (Exod. 28:4–35; 1 Sam. 22:18). Worn later by other than priests (1 Chron. 15:27). 2. A Manassite (Num. 34:23).

Ephraim: 1. Second son of Joseph (Gen. 41:52). Obtained Jacob's blessing (Gen. 48:8–20). 2. Site of Absalom's sheep farm (2 Sam. 13:23). 3. Place to which Christ withdrew (John 11:54). 4. A gate of Jerusalem (2 Kings 14:13; Neh. 8:16). 5. "Mount of," in

Ephraim (1 Sam. 1:1). 6. "The wood of," east of Jordan (2 Sam. 18:6).

Epicureans: A sect of pleasure-loving philosophers at Athens (Acts 17:18).

Epistle: In O.T., a letter (2 Sam. 11:14; 2 Kings 5:5–6; 2 Chron. 11:12; Exod. 4:6–11. In N.T., a formal tract containing Christian doctrine and salutary advice.

Equality: God's treatment of all people the same, regardless of nationality and ethnicity.
not call any man common or unclean. . .Acts 10:28
for there is no difference. . .Rom. 3:22
ye are all one in Christ Jesus. . . Gal. 3:28
neither Greek nor Jew. . .Col. 3:11

Error/Errors: A mistake or misguided action.
Who can understand his e's? . . . Ps. 19:12
utter e against the Lord. . .Isa. 32:6
from the e of his way. . .James 5:20
them who live in e. . .2 Pet. 2:18
e of the wicked. . .2 Pet. 3:17
See *Fail/Faileth.*

Esaias: N.T. name of the prophet Isaiah (Matt. 3:3).

Esau: Eldest son of Isaac and twin brother of Jacob (Gen. 25:25). Called also Edom. Sold his birthright to Jacob (Gen. 25:26–34; 36:1–10). Gave his name, Edom, to a country and to his descendants (Gen. 26, 36).

Espouse: See *Betroth/Betrothed.*

Esther: Persian name of Hadassah, Mordecai's cousin, who married King Ahasuerus and saved the lives of her countrymen. Her book, the seventeenth of the O.T., tells her story.

Eternal Life: Abundant life both here and hereafter—a promise of Jesus to His followers.
I may have e l? . . .Matt. 19:16
but have e l. . .John 3:15
give unto them e l. . .John 10:28
gift of God is e l. . .Rom. 6:23
promised us, even e l. . .1 John 2:25
See *Eternity; Heaven/Heavens; Immortal/Immortality; Reward, Eternal; Salvation.*

Eternity
One that inhabiteth e. . .Isa. 57:15
be with me in paradise. . .Luke 23:43
hath ascended up to heaven. . . John 3:13
laid up for you in heaven. . .Col. 1:5
See *Eternal Life; Heaven/Heavens; Reward, Eternal.*

Ethiopia: The country south of Egypt (Ezek. 29:10); settled by Hamites (Gen. 10:6); merchants (Isa. 45:14; Jer. 13:23; Job 28:19); wealthy (Acts 8:27–37); strong military (2 Chron. 12:3; 14:9–12; 2 Kings 17:4).

Eucharist. Communion, or the Lord's Supper.
Jesus took bread, and blessed it. . . Matt. 26:26
He took the cup. . .Luke 22:17
communion of the body of Christ? . . .1 Cor. 10:16
See *Lord's Supper.*

Eunice: Mother of Timothy (Acts 16:1; 2 Tim. 1:5).

Eunuch: A castrated male. Eunuchs became court officials (2 Kings 9:32; Esther 2:3; Acts 8:27); could not enter the congregation (Deut. 23:1). A celibate (Matt. 19:12).

Euphrates: A great river of western Asia, rising in Armenia and emptying into the Persian Gulf. Boundary of Eden (Gen. 2:14); "great river" (Gen. 15:18; Deut. 1:7); eastern boundary of the Promised Land (Deut. 11:24; Josh. 1:4); and of David's conquests (2 Sam. 8:3; 1 Chron. 18:3).

Eve: The first woman; made from man and for him (Gen. 2:18–25; 3–4).

Everlasting Life: See *Eternal Life.*

Evil: A force that opposes God and righteousness.
    knowledge of good and e. . .Gen. 2:9
    I will fear no e. . .Ps. 23:4
    Seek good, and not e. . .Amos 5:14
    e hateth the light. . .John 3:20
    Abhor that which is e. . .Rom. 12:9
See *Wickedness.*

Exalt/Exalted/Exalteth: To elevate by praise, particularly praise of the Lord in worship.
    let us e his name. . .Ps. 34:3
    Be thou e'ed, O God. . .Ps. 108:5
    Righteousness e'eth a nation. . .
        Prov. 14:34
    e himself shall be abased. . .
        Matt. 23:12
    God also hath highly e'ed him. . .
        Phil. 2:9

Example/Examples: A pattern worthy of imitation.
    I have given you an e. . .John 13:15
    be thou an e. . .1 Tim. 4:12
    e of unbelief. . .Heb. 4:11
    being e's to the flock. . .1 Pet. 5:3

Excellent: Eminently good; first class.
    how e is thy name. . .Ps. 8:1

    he hath done e things. . .Isa. 12:5
    a more e way. . .1 Cor. 12:31

Excuse: A reason given to justify one's actions.
    no cloak for their sin. . .John 15:22
    they are without e. . .Rom. 1:20

Execution: See *Capital Punishment.*

Exercise: Physical activity for building up the body.
    there wrestled a man. . .Gen. 32:24
    run, and not be weary. . .Isa. 40:31
    body is the temple. . .1 Cor. 6:19
    run with patience. . .Heb. 12:1
See *Health.*

Exodus: Second book of the Bible and the Pentateuch. Written by Moses. Historic from chapters 1–18; legislative from 19 to end. Its history covers the period (about 142 years) of Jewish preparation to leave Egypt, the departure, the desert wanderings, and the arrival at Sinai. Its legislation comprises the giving of the law at Sinai, directions for the priesthood, and the establishment of the tabernacle and its services.

Exploitation: Mistreatment of others, particularly the poor and helpless.
    not oppress an hired servant. . .
        Deut. 24:14
    Rob not the poor. . .Prov. 22:22
    oppress not the widow. . .Zech. 7:10

Eye/Eyes, Physical: The body's organ of sight.
    E for e. . .Exod. 21:24
    I will lift up mine e's. . .Ps. 121:1
    their e's received sight. . .Matt. 20:34
    E hath not seen. . .1 Cor. 2:9
    tears from their e's. . .Rev. 21:4

Eye/Eyes, Spiritual: Sensitivity to the will and commands of the Lord.

e's shall be opened. . .Gen. 3:5
Open thou mine e's. . .Ps. 119:18
right e offend thee. . .Matt. 5:29
mote that is in thy brother's e. . .
   Matt. 7:3
e's of your understanding. . .
   Eph. 1:18

Ezekiel: One of the four major prophets; carried captive to Babylon in 598 BC; entered the prophetic calling in the fifth year of his captivity (Ezek. 1:1–3). Chapters 1–24 contain predictions before the fall of Jerusalem, and 25–48 predictions after that event. Chapters 40–48 contain visions of the temple.

Ezra: A scribe and priest who returned from Babylon to Jerusalem with his countrymen in 458 BC. He collected and revised the previous O.T. writing and largely settled the O.T. canon. His book tells the story of the return and the establishment of a new order of things at Jerusalem and in Judea.

F

Fail/Faileth: To be unsuccessful.
he will not f thee. . .Deut. 31:6
thy foot shall not stumble. . .
   Prov. 3:23
thy faith f not. . .Luke 22:32
Charity never f'eth. . .1 Cor. 13:8

Fairness: Impartial treatment of all people; justice.
thou dost establish equity. . .
   Ps. 99:4
judgment, and equity. . .Prov. 1:3
reprove with equity. . .Isa. 11:4
See *Justice.*

Faith: Confidence in the promises of God; an essential element of salvation.
Doubt and faith
f as a grain of mustard. . .Matt. 17:20

f, and doubt not. . .Matt. 21:21
Established in faith
propitiation through f. . .Rom. 3:25
f cometh by hearing. . .Rom. 10:17
saved through f. . .Eph. 2:8
Great faith
not found so great f. . .Matt. 8:10
f hath made thee whole. . .Matt. 9:22
Stephen, a man full of f. . .Acts 6:5
Living in faith
just shall live by his f. . .Hab. 2:4
f, hope, charity. . .1 Cor. 13:13
f is the substance. . .Heb. 11:1

Faithful: Steadfast and loyal.
Lord preserveth the f. . .Ps. 31:23
thou good and f servant. . .
   Matt. 25:21
God is f. . .1 Cor. 1:9

Faithfulness, Marital: Staying true to one's marriage partner.
rejoice with the wife of thy youth
   . . .Prov. 5:18
the wife of thy covenant. . .
   Mal. 2:14
Marriage is honourable in all. . .
   Heb. 13:4

Fall, the: The sin of disobedience committee by Adam and Eve that has infected all humankind.
she took of the fruit thereof. . .
   Gen. 3:6
The serpent beguiled me. . .
   Gen. 3:13
by one man sin entered. . .
   Rom. 5:12
since by man came death. . .
   1 Cor. 15:21

Falling into Sin: Giving in to temptation and committing sin.
For all have sinned. . .Rom. 3:23
if we sin willfully. . .Heb. 10:26
If we confess our sins. . .1 John 1:9

False Gods: Idols that people worship instead of the one true God.
through the fire to Molech. . .

Lev. 18:21
Baal and Ashtaroth. . .Judg. 2:13
high place for Chemosh. . .1 Kings 11:7
walk after other gods. . .Jer. 7:9
See *Idol/Idols; Idolatry/Idolaters.*

Falsehood: Misrepresenting the truth;
lies.
their deceit is f. . .Ps. 119:118
right hand of f. . .Ps. 144:8
trusted in f. . .Jer. 13:25

False Teaching: Heretical doctrines
spread by false teachers.
prophet that teacheth lies. . .
Isa. 9:15
For such are false apostles. . .
2 Cor. 11:13
false prophet that wrought
miracles. . .Rev. 19:20
beast and the false prophet. . .
Rev. 20:10

Fame: Popular acclaim.
f of David went out. . .1 Chron. 14:17
his f went throughout. . .Matt. 4:24
f of Jesus. . .Matt. 14:1

Family: A group of people united by
ties of blood or adoption.
thy father and thy mother. . .
Exod. 20:12
keep thy father's commandment
. . .Prov. 6:20
Children, obey your parents. . .
Eph. 6:1
provoke not your children. . .
Col. 3:21
See *Child/Children; Father/Fathers;
Husband/Husbands; Mother/Mothers;
Parents; Wife/Wives.*

Fasting: Going without food as a spiritual discipline.
humbled my soul with f. . .Ps. 35:13
f, and with weeping. . .Joel 2:12
yourselves to f and prayer. . .1 Cor.
7:5
See *Diet.*

Father/Fathers: Male parent in a family relationship.
man leave his f. . .Gen. 2:24
Honour thy f. . .Exod. 20:12
iniquity of the f's. . .Jer. 32:18
He that loveth f. . .Matt. 10:37
See *Family; Parents.*

Father, God the. A title of God that
compares Him to an earthly, loving
father.
The everlasting F. . .Isa. 9:6
Have we not all one f? . . .Mal. 2:10
knoweth the Son, but the F
. . .Matt. 11:27
F loveth the Son. . .John 3:35
man hath seen the F. . .John 6:46
I and my F are one. . .John 10:30

Faultless: Without fault; morally
pure.
Blessed are the undefiled. . .Ps.
119:1
holy, harmless, undefiled. . .Heb.
7:26
present you f. . .Jude 1:24

Favoritism: Showing special favor or
partiality toward some people.
God is no respecter of persons. . .
Acts 10:34
neither is there respect of persons
. . .Eph. 6:9
without partiality. . .James 3:17
See *Discrimination.*

Favour: Friendly regard shown toward
others.
found f in my sight. . .1 Sam. 16:22
she obtained grace and f. . .
Esther 2:17
obtaineth f of the Lord. . .Prov.
18:22
f with God and man. . .Luke 2:52

Fear: Emotional response to a threat
to one's safety.
Esau: for I f him. . .Gen. 32:11
I will f no evil. . .Ps. 23:4
f not them which kill. . .Matt. 10:28

not given us the spirit of f. . .2 Tim. 1:7

Fear of God: An attitude of reverence and respect for the Lord.
f the Lord your God for ever. . .
Josh. 4:24
Let all the earth f the Lord. . .Ps.
33:8
f of the Lord prolongeth days. . .
Prov. 10:27

Feasts: Celebrations for joyous events (Gen. 21:8; 29:22; Mark 6:21–22). Numerous religious feasts were observed by the Israelites (Exod. 12:16; Lev. 23:21–24; Jude 12).

Feelings: Human emotions such as love and hate.
Isaac, whom thou lovest. . .Gen.
22:2
whom shall I fear? . . .Ps. 27:1
and a time to hate. . .Eccles. 3:8
love is strong as death. . .Song of
Sol. 8:6
no fear in love. . .1 John 4:18
See *Doubt/Doubted/Doubts; Fear; Hate/Hated/Hateth; Love, Brotherly.*

Felix: A procurator of Judea (Acts 23:26).

Fellowship: A friendly association with others, particularly other believers.
apostles' doctrine and f. . .Acts
2:42
right hands of f. . .Gal. 2:9
no f with the unfruitful works. . .
Eph. 5:11
f in the gospel. . .Phil. 1:5
f of his sufferings. . .Phil. 3:10

Festus: A Roman procurator before whom Paul appeared (Acts 24:27).

Fetters: Instruments of brass or iron for fastening the feet of prisoners (Ps. 105:18; 149:8).

Fight/Fightings: A hostile disagreement or quarrel.
The Lord shall f for you. . .Exod.
14:14
f against them that fight. . .Ps. 35:1
even to f against God. . .Acts 5:39
without were f'ings. . .2 Cor. 7:5
I have fought a good f. . .2 Tim. 4:7

Filled with the Spirit: To receive the Holy Spirit after conversion.
f w t s of wisdom. . .Exod. 28:3
Peter, filled with the Holy Ghost. . .
Acts 4:8
be f w t S. . .Eph. 5:18

Filthy/Filthiness: Moral corruption.
righteousnesses are as f rags. . .Isa.
64:6
cleanse ourselves from all f'iness
. . .2 Cor. 7:1
not greedy of f lucre. . .1 Tim. 3:3
vexed with the f conversation. . .
2 Pet. 2:7

Financial Gain: See *Money; Rich/Riches.*

Finished Work of Christ: The death of Christ on the cross that purchased our salvation.
Son therefore shall make you free. . .
John 8:36
he said, It is finished. . .John 19:30
as in Adam all die, even so in
Christ. . .1 Cor. 15:22
he is the propitiation for our sins
. . .1 John 2:2
See *Propitiation; Reconcile/Reconciled/Reconciling; Redemption.*

Firstborn: The first child to be born into a family; the first offspring of livestock.
will smite all the f. . .Exod. 12:12
Sanctify unto me all the f. . .
Exod. 13:2
all the f are mine. . .Num. 3:13
brought forth her f son. . .Matt. 1:25
f from the dead. . .Col. 1:1?

Firstfruits: The first of the crops presented to the Lord as a special offering. The word is also used to describe the first of anything, for example, Jesus as the firstfruits of the glorious resurrection that all believers will experience.

f of thy labours. . .Exod. 23:16
f of the Spirit. . .Rom. 8:23
f of them that slept. . .1 Cor. 15:20
Christ the f. . .1 Cor. 15:23
f of his creatures. . .James 1:18

Flagon: A small vessel for liquids (Isa. 22:24; 2 Sam. 6:19; 1 Chron. 16:3; Song of Sol. 2:5).

Flatter/Flattereth/Flattery: To praise a person excessively, particularly out of self-interest.

speaketh f'y to his friends. . .Job 17:5
For he f'eth himself. . .Ps. 36:2
stranger which f'eth. . .Prov. 2:16
f'y of the tongue. . .Prov. 6:24

Flesh: A word for the human body, in contrast to the spiritual nature.

they shall be one f. . .Gen. 2:24
my spirit upon all f. . .Joel 2:28
f and blood hath not. . .Matt. 16:17
Word was made f. . .John 1:14
Christ is come in the f. . .1 John 4:2

Flood: The deluge that God sent on the earth in Noah's time (Gen. 6–8; Matt. 24:37; 2 Pet. 2:5; 3:6).

f of waters was upon. . .Gen. 7:6
f was forty days. . .Gen. 7:17
shall no more become a f. . .
Gen. 9:15
Noah lived after the f. . .Gen. 9:28
other side of the f. . .Josh. 24:14
f upon the world. . .2 Pet. 2:5

Flower/Flowers: A colorful blooming plant.

He cometh forth like a f. . .Job 14:2
The f's appear on the earth. . .Song of Sol. 2:12

withereth, the f fadeth. . .Isa. 40:7
Consider the lilies of the field. . .
Matt. 6:28

Folly: Lack of good sense and sound judgment.

fool layeth open his f. . .Prov. 13:16
The simple inherit f. . .Prov. 14:18
fool according to his f. . .Prov. 26:4
foolishness with God. . .1 Cor. 3:19
ignorance of foolish men. . .1 Pet. 2:15
See *Fool/Fools*.

Food: Plants and animals eaten for nourishment.

green herb for meat. . .Gen. 1:30
fish, which we did eat. . .Num. 11:5
A land of wheat, and barley. . .
Deut. 8:8
giving him f and raiment. . .
Deut. 10:18
Give us this day our daily bread. . .
Matt. 6:11
five loaves, and two fishes. . .
Matt. 14:17
See *Eat/Eateth*.

Fool/Fools: A person without wisdom who is noted for his shallow reasoning ability.

f hath said in his heart. . .Ps. 14:1
folly of f's is deceit. . .Prov. 14:8
trusteth in his own heart is a f. . .
Prov. 28:26
Ye f's and blind. . .Matt. 23:17
f's for Christ's sake. . .1 Cor. 4:10
See *Folly*.

Footstool: A low piece of furniture for resting the feet, used by kings (2 Chron. 9:18). The earth is God's footstool (1 Chron. 28:2; Ps. 99:5).

Forbearance: See *Longsuffering*.

Foreigner: See *Alien*.

Foreknowledge of God: God's knowledge of everything, even events before they happen.

his understanding is infinite. .
Ps. 147:5
his people which he foreknew. . .
Rom. 11:2
Elect according to the f of G. . .
1 Pet. 1:2

See *Election; Predestinate/Predestinated; Sovereignty of God.*

Forgive/Forgiveness/Forgiving: To pardon the wrongful acts of others. Believers are blessed by God's forgiveness of our sins.

f us our debts. . .Matt. 6:12
power on earth to f sins. . .Matt. 9:6
I f him? till seven times? . . .Matt. 18:21
f us our sins. . .Luke 11:4
if he repent, f him. . .Luke 17:3
the f'ness of sins. . .Eph. 1:7
f'ing one another. . .Eph. 4:32

Fornication/Fornications: Sexual relations between two people who are not married to each other.

saving for the cause of f. . .Matt. 5:32
the body is not for f. . .1 Cor. 6:13
Adultery, f, uncleanness. . .Gal. 5:19
abstain from f. . .1 Thess. 4:3

See *Adultery; Divorce/Divorced/Divorcement; Impurity; Living Together.*

Forsake/Forsaken: To renounce or turn away from.

he will not f thee. . .Deut. 4:31
if thou f him. . .1 Chron. 28:9
why hast thou f'n me? . . .Ps. 22:1
never leave thee, nor f thee. . .
Heb. 13:5

Foundation/Foundations, Firm: The solid base on which a building is erected; often used metaphorically of our grounding in Christ.

laid the f on a rock. . .Luke 6:48

I have laid the f. . .1 Cor. 3:10
For other f can no man. . .1 Cor. 3:11
f of the apostles and prophets. . .
Eph. 2:20
city which hath f's. . .Heb. 11:10

Fountain/Fountains: A source of fresh, flowing water; a metaphor for eternal life.

living f's of waters. . .Rev. 7:17
f of the water of life. . .Rev. 21:6

Frankincense: The yellowish gum used in sacrifices (Exod. 30:7–9; Lev. 16:12–13; Rev. 8:3). A mixture of gums and spices (Exodus 30:34–38).

Fraud: See *Defraud/Defrauded.*

Freedom: Having civil and spiritual liberty.

proclaim liberty to the captives. . .
Isa. 61:1
set at liberty them that are bruised. . .Luke 4:18
Spirit of the Lord is, there is liberty
. . .2 Cor. 3:17
As free, and not using your liberty
. . .1 Pet. 2:16

Free Will: Humankind's God-given ability to follow or refuse the Lord's purpose for their lives.

therefore choose life. . .Deut. 30:19
and ye would not!. . .Matt. 23:37
all men to be saved. . .1 Tim. 2:4
not willing that any should perish
. . .2 Pet. 3:9

Friend/Friends/Friendship: A close acquaintance who is loved and esteemed.

Faithful friend
A f loveth at all times. . .Prov. 17:17
Faithful are the wounds of a f. . .
Prov. 27:6
a man lay down his life for his f's. . .
John 15:13
God as friend
as a man speaketh unto his f. . .
Exod. 33:11

Abraham thy f. . .2 Chron. 20:7
he was called the F of God. . .
  James 2:23
Making friends
A man that hath f's. . .Prov. 18:24
no f'ship with an angry man. . .
  Prov. 22:24
Mistakes concerning friends
if thou be surety for thy f. . .Prov.
  6:1
blesseth his f with a loud voice. . .
  Prov. 27:14
Unfaithful friends
familiar f's have forgotten me. . .
  Job 19:14
my f's stand aloof. . .Ps. 38:11
f'ship of the world is enmity. . .
  James 4:4

Frontlets: Parchment strips inscribed with scriptural texts (Exod. 13:2–17; Deut. 6:4–22); worn on forehead or the arm (Matt. 23:5; Mark 7:3–4; Luke 5:33).

Fruit/Fruits, Spiritual: Good works performed by believers.
  f's meet for repentance. . .Matt. 3:8
  Ye shall know them by their f's. . .
    Matt. 7:16
  f's of your righteousness. . .2 Cor.
    9:10
  But the f of the Spirit. . .Gal. 5:22
  full of mercy and good f's. . .
    James 3:17

Frustration: A negative feeling caused by failure or unresolved problems.
  cursing, vexation, and rebuke. . .
    Deut. 28:20
  vanity and vexation of spirit. . .
    Eccles. 1:14
  vexation of his heart. . .Eccles. 2:22

G

Gabbatha: The pavement on which Christ was sentenced (John 19:13).

Gabriel: An angel who announced significant Bible events (Dan. 8:16; 9:21; Luke 1:11, 19, 26, 38).

Gain: To realize an increase.
  g thereof than fine gold. . .Prov.
    3:14
  He that is greedy of g. . .Prov. 15:27
  if he shall g the whole world. . .
    Matt. 16:26
  and to die is g. . .Phil. 1:21
  what things were g to me. . .Phil.
    3:7

Galatia: A central province of Asia Minor, and part of the apostle Paul's missionary field (Acts 16:6; 18:23; 2 Tim. 4:10).

Galilee: Originally the circuit containing the twenty towns given by Solomon to Hiram (Josh. 20:7; 1 Kings 9:11; 2 Kings 15:29). In the time of Christ, one of the largest provinces of Palestine, in which He spent the greater part of His life and ministry (Luke 13:1; 23:6; John 1:43–47; Acts 1:11).

Galilee, Sea of: See *Gennesaret.*

Gall: The fluid secreted by the liver. Bitter (Job 16:13); poison (Job 20:14, 25; Deut. 32:33); hemlock (Hosea 10:4); probably myrrh in Matt. 27:34 as in Mark 15:23; great troubles (Jer. 8:14; Acts 8:23).

Gambling: To engage in a game of chance to try to increase one's possessions.
  Better is little with the fear. . .
    Prov. 15:16
  Lay not up for yourselves
    treasures. . .Matt. 6:19
  where your treasure is. . .Matt. 6:21
  love of money is the root of all evil
    . . .1 Tim. 6:10

Garden: A plot where vegetables or fruit trees are grown.
    g eastward in Eden. . .Gen. 2:8
    Eden the g of God. . .Ezek. 28:13
    crucified there was a g. . .John 19:41

Garment/Garments: A word for *clothes.*
    wax old as a g. . .Isa. 50:9
    new cloth unto an old g. . .Matt. 9:16
    hem of his g. . .Matt. 9:20
    not having a wedding g? . . . Matt. 22:12
    parted his g's. . .Matt. 27:35
    cast their g's on him. . .Mark 11:7

Gate/Gates: An entrance, door, or opening into a house or walled city.
    Lot sat in the g of Sodom. . .Gen. 19:1
    king arose, and sat in the g. . . 2 Sam. 19:8
    ye g's; and be ye lift up. . .Ps. 24:7
    g's of hell shall not prevail. . . Matt. 16:18

Gath: A city in Philistia (Josh. 13:3; 1 Sam. 6:17); home of Goliath (1 Sam. 17:4); refuge of David (1 Sam. 21:10).

Gaza: A city of Philistia (Gen. 10:19); assigned to Judah (Josh. 10:41; 15:47; Judg. 1:18); scene of Samson's exploits (Judg. 16; 1 Kings 4:24; Acts 8:26).

Generosity: Willingness to share one's possessions with others.
    offer so willingly. . .1 Chron. 29:14
    brought they in abundantly. . . 2 Chron. 31:5
    gave much alms. . .Acts 10:2
    soweth bountifully shall reap. . . 2 Cor. 9:6
See *Give/Given/Giveth.*

Genesis: First book of the Bible and the Pentateuch. Chapters 1–11 give history of Creation, Adam, the flood, Noah, first inhabitants, and Babel. Balance devoted to history of the patriarchs Abraham, Isaac, Jacob, and Joseph. Covers a period of nearly 2,500 years. Authorship attributed to Moses.

Gennesaret: 1. The small region northwest of the Sea of Galilee (Matt. 14:34; Mark 6:53). 2. "Sea of Chinnereth" in O.T. (Num. 34:11; Josh. 12:3); and "Sea of Galilee" in N.T.; enlargement of the Jordan River; thirteen miles long, six miles wide, seven hundred feet below the bed of the ocean. "Lake of Gennesaret" (Luke 5:1); "Sea of Tiberias" (John 6:1); "the sea" (Matt. 4:15).

Gentiles: In O.T. sense, all peoples not Jewish (Gen. 10:5; 14:1; Neh. 5:8). In N.T., Greeks and Romans seem to represent the Gentiles (Luke 2:32; Acts 26:17–20; Rom. 1:14– 16; 9:24).
    Gentiles come to faith
    G shall come to thy light. . .Isa. 60:3
    his name shall the G trust. . . Matt. 12:21
    salvation is come unto the G. . . Rom. 11:11
    Praise the Lord, all ye G. . .Rom. 15:11
    Judgment of Gentiles
    judgment to the G. . .Isa. 42:1
    shew judgment to the G. . .Matt. 12:18
    Light to Gentiles
    for a light of the G. . .Isa. 42:6
    light to lighten the G. . .Luke 2:32
    Power of Gentiles
    shall deliver him to the G. . . Matt. 20:19
    into the hands of the G. . .Acts 21:11
    Times of the Gentiles
    times of the G be fulfilled. . . Luke 21:24
    Witness to Gentiles

bear my name before the G. . .
   Acts 9:15
we turn to the G. . .Acts 13:46
apostle of the G. . .Rom. 11:13
See *Heathen.*

Gentle/Gentleness: A mild, easy-going spirit; similar to meekness.
   g'ness of Christ. . .2 Cor. 10:1
   we were g among you. . .1 Thess.
     2:7
   g, shewing all meekness. . .Titus 3:2

Gideon: The powerful warrior of Manasseh, and judge of Israel for forty years (Judg. 6–9).

Gift/Gifts, Spiritual: Talents or abilities bestowed on believers by the Holy Spirit for the benefit of the church.
   g's and calling of God. . .Rom. 11:29
   concerning spiritual g's. . .1 Cor. 12:1
   diversities of g's. . .1 Cor. 12:4
   then g's of healings. . .1 Cor. 12:28
   covet earnestly the best g's. . .
     1 Cor. 12:31
   desire spiritual g's. . .1 Cor. 14:1
   g's of the Holy Ghost. . .Heb. 2:4

Gilead: 1. Mount and land of Gilead, east of the Jordan River (Gen. 31:21–25; Num. 32:1; Josh. 17:6). 2. A mountain near Jezreel (Judg. 7:3). 3. Grandson of Manasseh (Num. 26:29–30). 4. Father of Jephthah (Judg. 11:1–2).

Gilgal: First encampment of the Israelites west of the Jordan River (Josh. 4:19–20; 5:9–10). Became a city and headquarters (Josh. 9:6; 15:7). Saul crowned there (1 Sam. 7:16; 10:8; 11:14–15).

Give/Given/Giveth: To grant something to another with no expectation of repayment.
   shall g as he is able. . .Deut. 16:17

He that g'th unto the poor. . .
   Prov. 28:27
G, and it shall be g'n. . .Luke 6:38
whomsoever much is g'n. . .
   Luke 12:48
half of my goods I g to the poor. . .
   Luke 19:8
See *Alms; Generosity; Poor, the.*

Glad/Gladness: A joyful or happy attitude.
   with g'ness of heart. . .Deut. 28:47
   I will be g and rejoice. . .Ps. 9:2
   girded me with g'ness. . .Ps. 30:11
   Serve the Lord with g'ness. . .
     Ps. 100:2
   g when they said. . .Ps. 122:1

Gleaning: Collecting leftover grain in fields. Field gleanings were reserved for the poor (Lev. 19:9– 10; Ruth 2:2).

Glory: A visible manifestation of the Lord's presence.
   his g and his greatness. . .Deut.
     5:24
   heavens declare the g. . .Ps. 19:1
   riches in g by Christ. . .Phil. 4:19
   appear with him in g. . .Col. 3:4
   his g shall be revealed. . .1 Pet. 4:13
   receive a crown of g. . .1 Pet. 5:4
See *Shining/Glory of God.*

Glutton/Gluttonous: Eating or drinking to excess.
   a g, and a drunkard. . .Deut. 21:20
   the drunkard and the g. . .Prov.
     23:21

Goals: The ends toward which efforts are directed.
   teach us to number our days. . .Ps.
     90:12
   Commit thy works unto the Lord. . .
     Prov. 16:3
   seek that ye may excel. . .1 Cor.
     14:12
   I press toward the mark. . .Phil. 3:14

God: See *Attributes of God.*

Godhead: God the supreme being in all His nature and attributes (Acts 17:29; Rom. 1:20; Col. 2:9).

Godly/Godliness: Holy living and righteous behavior.
g sorrow worketh repentance. . .
2 Cor. 7:10
great is the mystery of g'iness. . .
1 Tim. 3:16
g'iness is profitable. . .1 Tim. 4:8
Having a form of g'iness. . .2 Tim. 3:5
And to g'iness brotherly kindness . . .2 Pet. 1:7

God's Condescension: The Lord's conscious effort to bless humankind and bring people into His holy presence.
shewing mercy unto thousands. . .
Exod. 20:6
the greatness of thy mercy. . .Neh. 13:22
gracious and full of compassion . . .Ps. 111:4
God, who is rich in mercy. . .Eph. 2:4

God's Will: The Lord's plan and desire for all people.
have no other gods before me . . .Exod. 20:3
serve him with all your hear t. . .Deut. 11:13
Thy word is a lamp. . .Ps. 119:105
love thy neighbour as thyself . . .Matt. 19:19
good, and acceptable, and perfect, will. . .Rom. 12:2
do all to the glory of God. . .
1 Cor. 10:31
If any of you lack wisdom. . .
James 1:5

Golgotha: Hebrew name of the spot where Christ was crucified (Matt. 27:33; Mark 15:22; John 19:17).

Goliath: 1. The Philistine giant who defied the army of Israel (1 Sam. 17:4–54). 2. Another Goliath in 2 Sam. 21:19–22.

Gomer: 1. Eldest son of Japheth (Gen. 10:2–3; 1 Chron. 1:5–6). 2. Wife of Hosea (Hosea 1:3).

Gomorrah: A city of the plain destroyed by fire (Gen. 14:1–11; 18:20; 19:24–28; Deut. 29:23; 32:32; Matt. 10:15; Mark 6:11).

Good: What is right, appropriate, and commendable.
Good behavior
thou g and faithful servant. . .Matt. 25:21
overcome evil with g. . .Rom. 12:21
g and acceptable before God. . .
1 Tim. 5:4
Doing good
none that doeth g. . .Ps. 14:1
Depart from evil, and do g. . .
Ps. 34:14
Trust in the Lord, and do g. . .
Ps. 37:3
God is good
G and upright is the Lord. . .
Ps. 25:8
none g but one, that is, God . . .Mark 10:18
I am the g shepherd. . .John 10:11
A good man
steps of a g man. . .Ps. 37:23
A g man sheweth favour. . .Ps. 112:5
a g man shall be satisfied. . .
Prov. 14:14

Goodness: Purity and righteousness; a fruit of the Spirit in the lives of believers.
abundant in g and truth. . .Exod. 34:6
g and mercy shall follow. . .Ps. 23:6
praise the Lord for his g. . .
Ps. 107:15
riches of his g. . .Rom. 2:4

Good Work/Good Works: Good deeds and acts of kindness performed by believers.

> they may see your g w's. . .Matt. 5:16
> abound to every g w. . .2 Cor. 9:8
> begun a g w in you. . .Phil. 1:6
> fruitful in every g w. . .Col. 1:10
> rich in g w's. . .1 Tim. 6:18

See *Devotion.*

Gospel, the: The good news about Jesus and His atoning death for humankind.

> bringeth good tidings of good. . .Isa. 52:7
> preach good tidings. . .Isa. 61:1
> good tidings of great joy. . .Luke 2:10

Gossip: Fruitless tales, rumors, or idle talk.

> words of a talebearer are as . . .Prov. 18:8
> a talebearer revealeth secrets . . .Prov. 20:19
> strifes, backbitings, whisperings . . .2 Cor. 12:20
> busybody in other men's matters . . .1 Pet. 4:15

Government: A system of authority and power for maintaining order in society.

> Joseph was the governor. . . Gen. 42:6
> g shall be upon his shoulder. . . Isa. 9:6
> out of thee shall come a Governor . . .Matt. 2:6
> Pontius Pilate being governor . . .Luke 3:1

See *King, Earthly; Prince/Princes.*

Grace: God's unmerited favor and love that make salvation possible.
> *Believers and grace*
> g did much more abound. . .Rom. 5:20
> not under the law, but under g . . .Rom. 6:14

> by g are ye saved. . .Eph. 2:8
> But grow in g. . .2 Pet. 3:18
> *Finding of grace*
> But Noah found g. .Gen. 6:8
> found g in my sight. . .Exod. 33:17
> *God and grace*
> g of God was upon him. . . Luke 2:40
> full of g and truth. . .John 1:14
> justified freely by his g. . .Rom. 3:24
> according to the riches of his g . . .Eph. 1:7
> being justified by his g. . .Titus 3:7

Gratitude: A spirit of thanksgiving, particularly for God's blessings.

> Offer unto God thanksgiving. . . Ps. 50:14
> magnify him with thanksgiving . . .Ps. 69:30
> Enter into his gates with thanksgiving. . .Ps. 100:4

Great Commission: Jesus' orders to His followers to spread the Gospel.

> Go ye therefore, and teach . . .Matt. 28:19
> they ceased not to teach. . . Acts 5:42
> arose, and was baptized. . . Acts 9:18
> teaching and preaching. . . Acts 15:35
> believed, and were baptized . . .Acts 18:8

See *Baptism/Baptized; Teach/Teaching.*

Greaves: Armor to protect the shins in hand-to-hand combat (1 Sam. 17:6).

Greece/Greeks/Grecians: The well-known country and its people in southeast Europe; country also called Hellas. "Javan" in O.T. (Gen. 10:2–5; Isa. 66:19; Ezek. 27:13, 19); but direct in Dan. 8:21; 10:20; Joel 3:6; Acts 20:2. Greek was the original N.T. language.

Greed/Greedily/Greediness/Greedy: Obsessive desire for material things.

He that is g'y of gain. . .Prov. 15:27
He coveteth g'ily all the day
. . .Prov. 21:26
work all uncleanness with g'iness
. . .Eph. 4:19
not g'y of filthy lucre. . .1 Tim. 3:8
See *Materialism.*

Grief/Griefs: Sorrow over a loss or the troubles of life.
consumed because of g. . .Ps. 6:7
my life is spent with g. . .Ps. 31:10
acquainted with g. . .Isa. 53:3
he hath borne our g's. . .Isa. 53:4
See *Mourn/Mourning.*

Groan/Groaneth/Groaning/Groanings: A deep, guttural moan; symbolic of humankind's condition apart from God.
God heard their g'ing. . .Exod. 2:24
weary with my g'ing. . .Ps. 6:6
the whole creation g'eth. . .
Rom. 8:22
g'ings which cannot be uttered
. . .Rom. 8:26
we g, earnestly desiring to. . .
2 Cor. 5:2

Grow/Groweth: To increase and expand.
g up into him. . .Eph. 4:15
faith g'eth exceedingly. . .2 Thess.
1:3
But g in grace. . .2 Pet. 3:18

Grudge: A feeling of resentment or ill will toward others.
Esau hated Jacob because. . .
Gen. 27:41
nor bear any g. . .Lev. 19:18
G not one against another. . .
James 5:9

Guests: See *Hospitality.*

Guide/Guides: To direct or instruct another person.
lead me, and g me. . .Ps. 31:3
g even unto death. . .Ps. 48:14

g me with thy counsel. . .Ps. 73:24
ye blind g's. . .Matt. 23:16
g you into all truth. . .John 16:13

Guilty/Guiltless: Remorse for sin and wrongdoing.
will not hold him g'less. . .Exod.
20:7
which is g of death. . .Num. 35:31
condemned the g'less. . .Matt. 12:7
world may become g. . .Rom. 3:19
he is g of all. . .James 2:10

H

Habakkuk: A minor prophet during the reigns of Jehoiakim and Josiah. His book denounces Babylonia and concludes with a striking poem and prayer.

Hadassah: Hebrew name of Esther (Esther 2:7).

Hades: Place of departed spirits. Greek equivalent of Hebrew "sheol," unseen world. Hell in KJV; Hades in some translations (Matt. 11:23; 16:18; Acts 2:31; Rev. 1:18).

Hagar: 1. Abraham's concubine (Gen. 16:3); mother of Ishmael (21:9–21). 2. Type of law and bondage (Gal. 4:24–25).

Haggai: A minor prophet. His book exhorts the Jews to support the work of Zerubbabel.

Hall: Court of a high priest's house (Luke 22:55; Matt. 27:27).

Ham: Third son of Noah (Gen. 5:32; 9:22). Father of the Hamitic races (Gen. 10:6).

Haman: Prime minister under King Ahasuerus of Persia. His schemes against the Jews are described in the book of Esther.

Hand of the Lord: A metaphor for God's power.
> h o t L was against the city. . .
>> 1 Sam. 5:9
> fall now into the h o t L. . .
>> 2 Sam. 24:14
> h o t L was on Elijah. . .1 Kings 18:46
> h o t L was upon me. . .Ezek. 37:1

Hannah: Mother of Samuel (1 Sam. 1–2).

Happy: A joyful, carefree spirit.
> h is the man whom God. . .Job 5:17
> on the poor, h is he. . .Prov. 14:21
> keepeth the law, h is he. . .Prov. 29:18
> Christ, h are ye. . .1 Pet. 4:14

Hardening of the Heart: A metaphorical expression for a stubborn and unyielding attitude.
> harden the hearts of the Egyptians. . .Exod. 14:17
> hardened his heart from turning . . .2 Chron. 36:13
> Harden not your heart. . .Ps. 95:8
> their heart was hardened. . .Mark 6:52
> unbelief and hardness of heart . . .Mark 16:14
> his voice, harden not your hearts . . .Heb. 4:7

Harlot/Harlots: A prostitute(Gen. 38:15). Harlotry forbidden (Lev. 19:29). Type of idolatry (Isa. 1:21; Ezek. 16).
> he thought her to be an h. . . Gen. 38:15
> came into an h's house, named Rahab. . .Josh. 2:1
> keepeth company with h's. . . Prov. 29:3
> thou hast played the h. . .Jer. 3:1

publicans and the h's go. . .
> Matt. 21:31

Harmony: Cooperation; working together.
> how pleasant it is for brethren . . .Ps. 133:1
> unity of the Spirit. . .Eph. 4:3
> be ye all of one mind. . .1 Pet. 3:8
See *Peace.*

Harvest: The gathering of crops at the end of the growing season.
> h truly is plenteous. . .Matt. 9:37
> grow together until the h. . . Matt. 13:30
> white already to h. . .John 4:35
See *Lost/Unsaved; Unsaved; Witness/ Witnessing.*

Hate/Hated/Hateth: Extreme animosity or contempt toward another person.
> *Hatred of brother*
> Thou shalt not h thy brother. . . Lev. 19:17
> h'th his brother. . .1 John 2:9
> *Hatred of enemies*
> h thine enemy. . .Matt. 5:43
> do good to them which h you . . .Luke 6:27
> *God and hatred*
> which the Lord thy God h'th . . .Deut. 16:22
> love, and a time to h. . .Eccles. 3:8
> h not his father. . .Luke 14:26
> *Sin and hatred*
> they that h the righteous. . . Ps. 34:21
> Ye that love the Lord, h evil. . . Ps. 97:10
> fear of the Lord is to h evil. . . Prov. 8:13
> what I h, that do I. . .Rom. 7:15
See *Despise/Despised/Despisest; Feelings.*

Haughty/Haughtiness: An arrogant and prideful spirit.
> h spirit before a fall. . .Prov. 16:18
> Proud and h scorner. . .Prov. 21:24

h'iness of men. . .Isa. 2:17
h shall be humbled. . .Isa. 10:33

Haves and Have Nots: See *Oppression; Poor, the.*

Heal: To restore to health and wholeness.
I wound, and I h. . .Deut. 32:39
will h their land. . .2 Chron. 7:14
a time to h. . .Eccles. 3:3
h all manner of sickness. . .
Matt. 10:1
Is it lawful to h. . .Matt. 12:10
See *Physician/Physicians; Recover/ Recovering.*

Health: Sound of body and mind.
thy saving h among all nations. . .
Ps. 67:2
tongue of the wise is h. . .Prov. 12:18
h to the bones. . .Prov. 16:24
See *Exercise.*

Hear/Heareth: In the biblical sense, to hear is to obey.
H me when I call. . .Ps. 4:1
h the words of the wise. . .
Prov. 22:17
He that h'eth, let him h. . .
Ezek. 3:27
any man h my words. . .John 12:47
how shall they h. . .Rom. 10:14
See *Listen.*

Heart: The center of one's existence, including emotions and attitudes.
My h rejoiceth in the Lord. . .
1 Sam. 2:1
with my whole h. . .Ps. 111:1
as he thinketh in his h. . .Prov. 23:7
new h also will I give. . .Ezek. 36:26
there will your h be. . .Matt. 6:21
Let not your h be troubled. . .
John 14:1

Heathen: A word for non-Jews, unbelievers, and worshippers of false gods.
Why do the h rage. . .Ps. 2:1
exalted among the h. . .Ps. 46:10

Declare his glory among the h
. . .Ps. 96:3
repetitions, as the h do. . .Matt. 6:7
preach him among the h. . .Gal. 1:16
See *Gentiles.*

Heaven: Eternal life; the place reserved for those who have placed their faith in Jesus Christ as Lord and Savior.
Our Father which art in h. . .
Matt. 6:9
in earth, as it is in h. . .Matt. 6:10
treasures in h. . .Matt. 6:20
names are written in h. . .
Luke 10:20
shall descend from h. . .
1 Thess. 4:16
See *Eternity; Eternal Life; Reward, Eternal.*

Hebrew/Hebrews: The nation that descended from Abraham. Also referred to as Israelites, descendants of Jacob, or Israel (Gen. 32:28).
Abram the H. . .Gen. 14:13
H midwives. . .Exod. 1:15
Egyptian smiting an H. . .Exod. 2:11
H of the H's. . .Phil. 3:5
See *Israel/Israelites; Jew/Jews.*

Hebron: Ancient city of Judah, twenty miles south of Jerusalem (Gen. 13:18; Num. 13:22); Arba in Josh. 21:11; Judg. 1:10).

Heir/Heirs: The eldest son in a family became head of the clan and inherited the largest share of the paternal estate. The word also describes believers in Jesus Christ.
joint-h's with Christ. . .Rom. 8:17
h's according to the promise. . .
Gal. 3:29
we should be made h's. . .Titus 3:7
appointed h of all things. . .Heb. 1:2
h's together of the grace. . .
1 Pet. 3:7

Hell: Hebrew "sheol," translated "grave" (1 Sam. 2:6); "pit" (Num. 16:30); "hell" (Job 11:8) in O.T. In N.T., Hades and Gehenna are translated "hell" (Acts 2:27; Matt. 5:29). Gehenna, or Valley of Hinnom, alone implies a place of burning or torture.

h compassed me about. . .
    2 Sam. 22:6
wilt not leave my soul in h. . .
    Ps. 16:10
if I make my bed in h. . .Ps. 139:8
h shall not prevail. . .Matt. 16:18
cast them down to h. . .2 Pet. 2:4

See *Damnation; Perdition; Unsaved.*

Help/Helper: To give assistance or support to another. God is the ultimate help for His people.

h'er of the fatherless. . .Ps. 10:14
Lord, be thou my h'er. . .Ps. 30:10
very present h in trouble. . .Ps. 46:1
h thou mine unbelief. . .Mark 9:24

Heresy: False tachings and beliefs.

Let us go after other gods. . .Deut.
    13:2
there shall arise false Christs
    . . .Matt. 24:24
For such are false apostles. . .
    2 Cor. 11:13
certain men crept in unawares
    . . .Jude 1:4

Heritage: Our legacy or inheritance from the past.

give it you for an h. . .Exod. 6:8
I have a goodly h. . .Ps. 16:6
children are an h. . .Ps. 127:3

Herod: 1. Herod the Great, tetrarch of Judea, 41 BC; King of Judah 41–4 BC; liberal, yet tyrannical and cruel. Issued murderous edict against children of Bethlehem (Matt. 2:16). 2. Herod Antipas, son of former; tetrarch of Galilee and Perea, 4 BC–AD 39; murderer of John the Baptist (Matt. 14:1; Luke 3:19; 23:7–15; Acts 13:1). 3. Herod Philip, son of Herod the Great. Married Herodias (Matt. 14:3; Mark 6:17; Luke 3:19). Lived and died in private life. 4. Herod Philip II, son of Herod the Great and tetrarch of Batanea, Ituraea, etc., 4 BC–AD 34 (Luke 3:1). 5. Herod Agrippa I, grandson of Herod the Great; tetrarch of Galilee; king of his grandfather's realm, AD 37–44 (Acts 12:1–19). 6. Herod Agrippa II, son of former and king of consolidated tetrarchies, AD 50–100 (Acts 25:13–27; 26:1–28).

Herodias: Granddaughter of Herod the Great. Wife of her uncle Herod Philip and her step-uncle. She requested the head of John the Baptist (Matt. 14:3–6; Mark 6:17; Luke 3:19).

Hezekiah: Twelfth king of Judah, 726–698 BC. Noted for abolition of idolatry and powerful resistance to neighboring nations (2 Kings 18–20; 2 Chron. 29–32).

Hidden Things: See *Mystery/Mysteries.*

High Places: Altars, temples, and dedicated places originally on high ground (Gen. 12:8; Judg. 6:25; Isa. 65:7; Jer. 3:6). When the groves and mounts of idolatry overshadowed true worship, "high places" became a reproach.

High Priest: Chief priest, Aaron being the first. Originally a life office, limited to a line or family (Exod. 28:1; Lev. 21:10; Num. 3:32; 20:8; Deut. 10:6).

Hiring: See *Employment.*

Holy/Holiness: Moral purity; to be set apart for service to God.

glorious in h'ness. . .Exod. 15:11

sabbath day, to keep it h. . .
   Exod. 20:8
therefore, and be ye h. . .Lev. 20:7
none h as the Lord. . .1 Sam. 2:2
H, h, h, is the Lord. . .Isa. 6:3
to present you h. . .Col. 1:22
partakers of his h'ness. . .Heb. 12:10

Holy Ghost. KJV term for the Holy Spirit.
   baptize you with the H G. . .
     Matt. 3:11
   blasphemy against the H G. . .
     Matt. 12:31
   H G shall teach you. . .Luke 12:12
   power of the H G. . .Rom. 15:13
   temple of the H G. . .1 Cor. 6:19
   H G which dwelleth in us. . .
     2 Tim. 1:14
   partakers of the H G. . .Heb. 6:4
See *Comforter.*

Home: One's place of residence.
   giveth meat to her household. . .
     Prov. 31:15
   the ways of her household. . .
     Prov. 31:27
   chaste, keepers at h. . .Titus 2:5

Homosexuality: A sexual relationship between members of the same sex.
   Thou shalt not lie with mankind. . .
     Lev. 18:22
   God gave them up unto vile
     affections. . .Rom. 1:26
   nor adulterers, nor effeminate. . .
     1 Cor. 6:9
   defile themselves with mankind
     . . .1 Tim. 1:10
   going after strange flesh. . .Jude 1:7

Honest/Honestly/Honesty: Speaking the truth and acting without deceit toward others.
   Let us walk h'ly. . .Rom. 13:13
   whatsoever things are h. . .Phil. 4:8
   all godliness and h'y. . .1 Tim. 2:2
See *Business; Truth.*

Honour/Honoureth: Respect toward God and other people.

H thy father and thy mother
   . . .Exod. 20:12
crowned him with glory and h
   . . .Ps. 8:5
H the Lord with thy. . .Prov. 3:9
prophet is not without h. . .Matt. 13:57
h'eth me with their lips. . .Matt. 15:8

Hope: A steadfast faith in God's promises.
   h thou in God. . .Ps. 42:11
   I h in thy word. . .Ps. 119:81
   whose h the Lord is. . .Jer. 17:7
   h of the promise. . .Acts 26:6
   we are saved by h. . .Rom. 8:24
   faith, h, charity. . .1 Cor. 13:13

Hophni: Dishonest son of Eli (1 Sam. 1:3; 2:12–17; 3:11–14; 4:11).

Hosanna: "Save, we pray" (Ps. 118:25–26). The cry of the crowd when Christ entered Jerusalem (Matt. 21:9–15; Mark 11:9–10).

Hosea: First of the minor prophets. Prophetic career, 784–725 BC, in Israel. Denounced the idolatries of Israel and Samaria.

Hospitality: Kindness and graciousness toward others, especially fellow believers.
   given to h. . .Rom. 12:13
   Use h one to another. . .1 Pet. 4:9

Hosts, Lord of: See *Lord of Hosts.*

Humble/Humbled: A meek and kind spirit; the opposite of pride and arrogance.
   h themselves, and pray. . .
     2 Chron. 7:14
   thou didst h thyself. . .
     2 Chron. 34:27
   h himself shall be exalted. . .
     Matt. 23:12
   he h'd himself. . .Phil. 2:8
See *Humility.*

Humiliation: A state of shame or extreme remorse.
>till they were ashamed. . .Judg. 3:25
>against me my reproach. . .Job 19:5
>wait on thee be ashamed. . . Ps. 25:3
>hope maketh not ashamed. . . Rom. 5:5

See *Reproach/Reproached.*

Humility: A compassionate, gentle attitude.
>before honour is h. . .Prov. 15:33
>By h and the fear. . .Prov. 22:4
>be clothed with h. . .1 Pet. 5:5

See *Humble/Humbled.*

Humor: Something comical or amusing.
>A merry heart maketh. . .Prov. 15:13
>Then I commended mirth. . .Eccles. 8:15
>eat, drink, and be merry. . . Luke 12:19
>Is any merry? . . .James 5:13

See *Laugh/Laughter.*

Hunger/Hungered, Physical: Intense desire of the body for food.
>If thine enemy be hungry. . . Prov. 25:21
>when saw we thee an h'red. . . Matt. 25:37
>if thine enemy h. . .Rom. 12:20
>if any man h. . .1 Cor. 11:34

Hunger, Spiritual: Desire of one's spiritual nature for fellowship with God.
>My soul thirsteth for God. . . Ps. 42:2
>fainteth for thy salvation. . . Ps. 119:81
>h and thirst after righteousness . . .Matt. 5:6
>cometh to me shall never h. . . John 6:35
>If any man thirst. . .John 7:37

Husband/Husbands: The male partner in a marriage.
>desire shall be to thy h. . .Gen. 3:16
>h also, and he praiseth. . . Prov. 31:28
>H's, love your wives. . .Eph. 5:25
>h of one wife. . .1 Tim. 3:2

See *Family; Marriage/Marry; Spouse/ Spouses.*

Hypocrite/Hypocrites/Hypocrisy: A person who plays a role, or pretends to be something he is not.
>h's hope shall perish. . .Job 8:13
>h's do in the synagogues. . . Matt. 6:2
>h, of a sad countenance. . . Matt. 6:16
>h, first cast out. . .Matt. 7:5
>partiality, and without h'sy. . . James 3:17

Hyssop: A bushy herb of the mint family (Exod. 12:22; Lev. 14:4, 6, 51; 1 Kings 4:33; John 19:29).

I

"I Am" Statements of Jesus. Jesus' description of Himself and His unique nature. All these statements appear in the writings of the apostle John.
>I that speak unto thee a. . .John 4:26
>I a the bread of life. . .John 6:35
>I a the light of the world. . . John 8:12
>I a from above. . .John 8:23
>Before Abraham was, I a. . . John 8:58
>I a the door. . .John 10:9
>I a the good shepherd. . .John 10:11
>I a the Son of God? . . .John 10:36
>I a the resurrection. . .John 11:25
>may believe that I a he. . .John 13:19
>I a the way. . .John 14:6
>I a the true vine. . .John 15:1
>saith unto them, I a he. . .John 18:5

I a Alpha and Omega. . .Rev. 1:8
See *Name of Jesus.*

Idle/Idleness: Inactivity; laziness.
Go to the ant, thou sluggard. . .
Prov. 6:6
eateth not the bread of i'ness. . .
Prov. 31:27
through i'ness of the hands. . .
Eccles. 10:18
every i word that men. . .
Matt. 12:36

Idols: Objects of worship, other than
God (Gen. 31:19); idolatry forbidden
(Exod. 20:3–4; Deut. 4:16–19); yet
it existed, especially under the judges
and later kings (Judg. 2:10–23; Isa.
57:5–8).
Turn ye not unto i. . .Lev. 19:4
gods of the people are i. . .
1 Chron. 16:26
abstain from pollutions of i. . .
Acts 15:20
from meats offered to i. . .
Acts 15:29
things offered unto i. . .1 Cor. 8:1
See *False Gods, Idolatry/Idolaters; Superstition/Superstitious.*

Idolatry/Idolaters
i he shall utterly abolish. . .Isa. 2:18
or covetous, or an i'ater. . .
1 Cor. 5:11
nor i'aters, nor adulterers. . .
1 Cor. 6:9
flee from i. . .1 Cor. 10:14
See *False Gods; Idol/Idols; Superstition/Superstitious.*

Imagination/Imaginations: KJV
term for *thoughts,* particularly evil
impulses.
i of man's heart. . .Gen. 8:21
imagine mischiefs in their heart. . .
Ps. 140:2
deviseth wicked i's. . .Prov. 6:18
vain in their i's. . .Rom. 1:21

Immanuel: Name of the Messiah,
meaning "God with us" (Matt. 1:23).

Immortal/Immortality: Something
that never dies; eternal life.
mortal must put on i'ity. . .1 Cor.
15:53
King eternal, i, invisible. . .1 Tim. 1:17
Who only hath i'ity. . .1 Tim. 6:16
See *Eternal Life.*

Impatience: Restlessness; lack of
perseverance.
maketh haste to be rich. . .
Prov. 28:20
hasty to utter any thing. . .
Eccles. 5:2
Be not hasty in thy spirit. . .
Eccles. 7:9

Impossible: Incapable of accomplishment.
nothing shall be i unto you. . .
Matt. 17:20
with God nothing shall be i. . .
Luke 1:37
i for God to lie. . .Heb. 6:18

Imprisonment: See *Prisoner/Prisoners.*

Impurity: Uncleanness; characterized
by sin.
purge away thy dross. . .Isa. 1:25
any man common or unclean
. . .Act 10:28
gave them up to uncleanness
. . .Rom. 1:24
not called us unto uncleanness. . .
1 Thess. 4:7
See *Adultery; Defile/Defiled; Fornication/Fornications.*

Impute/Imputed/Imputeth/Imputing: To transfer something to another
person.
God i'eth righteousness. . .Rom. 4:6
Lord will not i sin. . .Rom. 4:8
righteousness might be i'ed. . .
Rom. 4:11

not i'ing their trespasses. . .
2 Cor. 5:19

Incense: A mixture of gums, spices, etc. (Exod. 30:34–38), made up the official incense burned morning and evening on the altar of incense (Exod. 30:1–10). Used also in idolatrous worship (2 Chron. 34:25; Jer. 11:12–17) and by angels (Rev. 8:3).

Incest. Sexual relations with members of one's own family.
nakedness of thy father's wife . . .Lev. 18:8
nakedness of thy sister. . .Lev. 18:9
nakedness of thy son's daughter . . .Lev. 18:10
nakedness of thy father's sister . . .Lev. 18:12
nakedness of thy mother's sister . . .Lev. 18:13
nakedness of thy daughter in law . . .Lev. 18:15
nakedness of thy brother's wife . . .Lev. 18:16

Indignation: Anger or wrath.
Pour out thine i. . .Ps. 69:24
hast filled me with i. . .Jer. 15:17
cup of his i. . .Rev. 14:10

Industry: Working busily; the opposite of idleness.
industrious, he made him ruler. . . 1 Kings 11:28
substance of a diligent man. . . Prov. 12:27
diligent in his business? . . . Prov. 22:29
See *Diligent/Diligently/Diligence.*

Infertility: See *Barren.*

Influence: Power exerted over the minds or behavior of others.
light so shine before men. . . Matt. 5:16
confess me before men. . . Matt. 10:32
not as pleasing men. . .1 Thess. 2:4

Inheritance: A gift that can't be earned, as in God's salvation for believers.
their land for an i. . .Deut. 4:38
portion of mine i. . .Ps. 16:5
we have obtained an i. . .Eph. 1:11
partakers of the i. . .Col. 1:12
See *Heir.*

Iniquity: A word for sin or wickedness.
O Lord, pardon mine i. . .Ps. 25:11
I was shapen in i. . .Ps. 51:5
workers of i do flourish. . .Ps. 92:7
i of us all. . .Isa. 53:6
See *Sin.*

Inn: In the O.T., a stopping place for caravans (Gen. 42:27; Exod. 4:24); in the N.T., an inn afforded food and shelter for man and beast (Luke 10:34–35).

Innocent: Not guilty; free of wrongdoing.
i blood be not shed. . .Deut. 19:10
wilt not hold me i. . .Job 9:28
betrayed the i blood. . .Matt. 27:4

Instruction: Advice or teaching passed on to others.
despise wisdom and i. . .Prov. 1:7
Take fast hold of i. . .Prov. 4:13
Give i to a wise man. . .Prov. 9:9
Whoso loveth i. . .Prov. 12:1

Integrity: Incorruptibility; firm adherence to righteousness.
walked, in i of heart. . .1 Kings 9:4
still he holdeth fast his i. . .Job 2:3
God may know mine i. . .Job 31:6
upholdest me in mine i. . .Ps. 41:12

Intercession/Intercessions: Prayer offered on behalf of others.
i for the transgressors. . .Isa. 53:12
Praying always with all. . .Eph. 6:18
supplications, prayers, i's. . . 1 Tim. 2:1
pray one for another. . .James 5:16

Iron: 1. City of Naphtali (Josh. 19:38). 2. Iron, the metal, and copper early known (Gen. 4:22). Prepared in furnaces (1 Kings 8:51); used for tools (Deut. 27:5); weapons (1 Sam. 17:7); implements (2 Sam. 12:31); war chariots (Josh. 17:16).

Isaac: Son of Abraham (Gen. 17:17–22). Second of the patriarchs and father of Jacob and Esau (Gen. 21–35); Poetically, a word for Israel (Amos 7:9, 16).

Isaiah: Son of Amos (Isa. 1:1) and first of the major prophets. His book, the twenty-third of the O.T., covers sixty years of prophecy (1:1) at Jerusalem. It condemns the sins of the Jews and other nations and foreshadows the coming of Christ. Called "prince of prophets."

Israel/Israelites: Name given to Jacob (Gen. 32:28; 35:10); became the name of God's people (Exod. 3:16); narrowed to northern kingdom after the revolt of the ten tribes from Judah (1 Sam. 11:8; 2 Sam. 20:1; 1 Kings 12:16) with Shechem as capital (1 Kings 12:25) and Tirzah as royal residence (14:17); afterward, capital at Samaria (16:24). Kingdom lasted 254 years, with 19 kings, 975–721 BC, when it fell prey to the Assyrians. The returned of Israel blended with those of Judah.
> all the I'ites passed over. . .
>   Josh. 3:17
> I for an inheritance. . .Josh. 13:6
> I, the priests, Levites. . .1 Chron. 9:2
> Are they I'ites? . . .2 Cor. 11:22

See *Hebrew/Hebrews.*

Issachar: Fifth son of Jacob by Leah (Gen. 30:17–18). Tribe characteristics foretold (Gen. 49:14–15). Land allotment was north of Manasseh, from Carmel to the Jordan River (Josh. 19:17–23).

Ivory: A substance from the tusks of elephants (1 Kings 10:22; 2 Chron. 9:17–21; Ezek. 27:15).

J

Jabez: An Israelite known for his prayer for success (1 Chron. 4:9–10).

Jacinth: Zircon, a varicolored gem (Rev. 9:17; 21:20).

Jacob: Son of Isaac and second-born twin with Esau (Gen. 25:24–34). Bought Esau's birthright, fled to Padan-aram, married Rachel and Leah, wandered to Hebron, name changed to Israel, drifted to Egypt, where he died at the age of 147 years (Gen. 25–50).

Jah: In poetry, a shortened form of the divine name *Jehovah* (Ps. 68:4).

James: 1. "The Greater" or "Elder," son of Zebedee and brother of John (Matt. 4:21–22). A fisherman of Galilee, called by Jesus about AD 28, and styled Boanerges (Matt. 10:2–3; Mark 3:14–18; Luke 6:12–16; Acts 1:13). Labored at Jerusalem. Beheaded by Herod AD 44. 2. "The Less," another apostle, son of Alphaeus (Matt. 10:3; Mark 3:18; Luke 6:15). 3. Christ's brother, or more likely cousin, and identical with James the Less (Gal. 1:19). Compare Matt. 13:55; Mark 6:3; Acts 12:17. Resident at Jerusalem and author of the epistle of James, written before AD 62 to the scattered Jews, urging good works as the groundwork and evidence of faith.

Japheth: Son of Noah (Gen. 5:32; 6:10; 9:27; 10:21). His generations peopled the "Isles of the Gentiles," and type the Indo-European and Caucasian races (Gen. 10:1–5).

Jasper: A colored quartz. Last stone in the high priest's breastplate and first in New Jerusalem foundation (Exod. 28:20; Rev. 21:19).

Jealous/Jealousy: Resentful toward others for their good fortune. God's "jealousy" is a metaphor for His desire for worship and honor that belong exclusively to Him.

> God am a j God. . .Exod. 20:5
> provoked him to j'y. . .Deut. 32:16
> j for my holy name. . .Ezek. 39:25
> provoke the Lord to j'y? . . .
>   1 Cor. 10:22

Jehoshaphat: 1. Father of Jehu (2 Kings 9:2–14). 2. Son and successor of Asa on the throne of Judah, 914–890 BC. A God-fearing king in close alliance with Israel (1 Kings 15:24; 2 Kings 8:16; 2 Chron. 17–21:1).

Jehovah: "He that is." "I am" (Exod. 3:14). The self-existent and eternal one. Hebrew word for *God*, generally rendered as "Lord."

Jehovah-jireh: "God will provide." Abraham's name for spot where Isaac was offered (Gen. 22:14).

Jehovah-nissi: "God my banner." The altar built in honor of Joshua's victory (Exod. 17:15).

Jehovah-shalom: "God is peace." Gideon's altar in Ophrah (Judg. 6:24).

Jeremiah: 1. Second of the major prophets. His prophecies cover reigns of Josiah, Jehoiakim, and Zedekiah, 628–586 BC, and constitute the twenty-fourth O.T. book. His prophecies are noted for boldness and beauty, and chiefly denunciative of Judah and her policy. Withdrew to Egypt, probably where he died. 2. Seven others in O.T. (2 Kings 23:31; 1 Chron. 12:4–13; 5:24; Neh. 10:2; 12:1, 12, 34; Jer. 35:3). Greek forms of his name were *Jeremias* and *Jeremy* (Matt. 2:17; 16:14; 27:9).

Jericho: Ancient city of Canaan, five miles west of the Jordan River and eighteen miles from Jerusalem. Strongly fortified, and conquered by Joshua; fell to Benjamin (Deut. 34:3; Num. 22:1; Josh. 6; 1 Kings 16:34; Matt. 20:29; Mark 10:46).

Jeroboam: 1. First king of Israel after the division, 975–954 BC. Plotter for Solomon's throne (1 Kings 11:26–40); fled to Egypt; returned on death of Solomon; set up kingdom of ten tribes; established idolatry; warred with Judah; defeated by Abijah; soon after died (1 Kings 12–14; 2 Chron. 10–13). 2. Jeroboam II, thirteenth king of Israel; successor to Joash. Reigned in 825–784 BC. Idolatrous, but mighty and illustrious. Raised Israel to greatest splendor (2 Kings 14:23–29; 15:8–9; Amos 1; 2:6–16).

Jerusalem: Capital of the Israelite monarchy and of the kingdom of Judah, twenty-four miles west of the Jordan River and thirty-seven miles east

of the Mediterranean Sea. "Salem"
(Ps. 76:2); "Jebus" (Judg. 19:10–11).
"Jebus-salem," Jerusalem (Josh. 10:1).
"City of David," Zion (1 Kings 8:1; 2
Kings 14:20). "City of Judah" (2 Chron.
25:28). "City of God" (Ps. 46:4). "City
of the Great King" (Ps. 48:2); "The
holy city" (Neh. 11:1). Captured and
rebuilt by David, and made his capital
(2 Sam. 5:6–13; 1 Chron. 11:4–9).
Destroyed by Nebuchadnezzar, 588
BC. Rebuilt by returned captives.
Captured by Alexander the Great, 332
BC; by Antiochus, 203 BC; by Rome,
63 BC.

Jerusalem, New: Metaphorically, the
spiritual church (Rev. 3:12; 21). Compare Gal. 4:26; Heb. 12:22.

Jesse: Father of David (1 Sam. 16:1–
18).

Jesus Christ: Jesus the Savior; Christ,
or Messiah, the Anointed One. Jesus
the Christ. Name given to the long
promised Prophet and King (Matt.
11:3; Acts 19:4). Only-begotten of
God. Born of Mary at Bethlehem, 5
BC; reared at Nazareth, baptized at
age thirty (Luke 3:23). Ministerial
career, extending over Galilee, Judea,
and Perea, began AD 27 and ended
with the crucifixion, AD 30. Matthew,
Mark, and Luke record His Galilean
ministry; John His Judean ministry.
The four Gospels embrace Christ's
biography.
 Jesus Christ as God
 J C is the Son of God. . .Acts 8:37
 J C is Lord. . .Phil. 2:11
 Belief in Jesus Christ
 Believe on the Lord J C. . .Acts
 16:31
 by faith of J C. . .Rom. 3:22
 The Christian life and Jesus Christ

through J C our Lord. . .Rom. 6:11
the day of J C. . .Phil. 1:6
Spirit of J C. . .Phil. 1:19
 Eternal life through Jesus Christ
 true God, and J C. . .John 17:3
 eternal life through J C. . .Rom.
 6:23
 Grace of Jesus Christ
 truth came by J C. . .John 1:17
 grace of our Lord J C. . .2 Cor. 8:9
 Redemption of Jesus Christ
 J C, and him crucified. . .1 Cor. 2:2
 cross of our Lord J C. . .Gal. 6:14
 blood of J C. . .1 John 1:7
 J C the righteous. . .1 John 2:1
See *Deity of Christ; Messiah.*

Jew/Jews: Contraction of *Judah.* Man
of Judea (2 Kings 16:6; 25:25). After
captivity, Hebrews in general (Exod.
4:12; Dan. 3:8–12). Antithesis of
Christian in N.T. (Rom. 1:16).
 was a certain J. . .Esther 2:5
 Mordecai the J. . .Esther 5:13
 knew that he was a J. . .Acts 19:34
 to the J first. . .Rom. 1:16
 neither J nor Greek. . .Gal. 3:28
See *Hebrew/Hebrews.*

Jewel/Jewels: Precious stones worn as
ornaments.
 j's of silver. . .Gen. 24:53
 j of gold in a swine's. . .Prov. 11:22
 make up my j's. . .Mal. 3:17

Jewelry: See *Jewel/Jewels.*

Jezebel: Idolatrous wife of Ahab (1
Kings 16:29–33; 17–21; 2 Kings
9:30–37).

Jezreel: 1. A city in the plain of Jezreel.
Ahab's royal residence (Josh. 19:18; 1
Kings 21:1; 2 Kings 9:30). 2. Valley
of, stretches from Jezreel to Jordan.
Greek form, *Esdraelon.* 3. Town of Judah (Josh. 15:56; 1 Sam. 27:3). 4. Son
of Hosea (Hosea 1:4).

Joash: 1. Son of Ahaziah and his successor on the throne of Judah, 878–839 BC. Cruel and idolatrous. Murdered by his servants (2 Kings 11–12; 2 Chron. 24). 2. Son and successor of Jehoahaz on the throne of Israel, 840–825 BC. Successful warrior (2 Kings 8:9–25; 14:1–16; 2 Chron. 25:17–25). 3. Father of Gideon (Judg. 6:11–31). 4. One of David's heroes (1 Chron. 12:3).

Job: 1. The pious and wealthy patriarch of Uz, whose poem makes up the eighteenth O.T. book, and first of the poetical books. It is a dramatic narrative of his life of trouble, demonstrating whether goodness can exist without reward. Poetry noted for its sublimity, pathos, and beauty. 2. Son of Issachar (Gen. 46:13). Jashub (1 Chron. 7:1).

Jobs: See *Employment; Labour.*

Joel: 1. Son of Pethuel and second of the minor prophets. Probably of Judah and contemporary with Uzziah, 810–758 BC. His book, twenty-ninth of the O.T., depicts calamities, rises into exhortation, and foreshadows the Messiah. 2. Son of Samuel (1 Sam. 8:2).

John: 1. Kinsman of the high priest (Acts 4:6). 2. Hebrew name of Mark (Acts 12:25; 13:5; 15:37). 3. John the Baptist, son of Zacharias. Birth foretold (Luke 1). Born about six months before Christ. Retired to wilderness. Emerged to preach and baptize. Baptized Jesus (Matt. 3). Imprisoned by Herod (Luke 3:1–22). Beheaded (Matt. 14:1– 12). 4. John, apostle and evangelist; son of Zebedee (Matt. 4:21). A fisherman of Galilee (Luke 5:1–10). A favorite apostle, noted for zeal and firmness (John 13:23; 19:26; 20:2; 21:7). He remained at Jerusalem until about AD 65, when he went to Ephesus. Banished to Patmos; released AD 96. His writings, completed at Ephesus, include the fourth Gospel, giving Christ's ministry in Judea; his three epistles; and Revelation.

Joking: See *Humor; Laugh/Laughter.*

Jonah: Son of Amittai. Commissioned to denounce Nineveh. His book, the thirty-second of the O.T. and fifth of the minor prophets, narrates his refusal, escape from drowning, final acceptance, and successful ministry. Its lesson is God's providence over all nations.

Jonathan: Eldest son of Saul and friend of David (1 Sam. 13:2–3; 18:1–4; 19:1–7; 20). Fell in battle of Gilboa. David lamented his death (2 Sam. 1:17–27).

Joppa: Mediterranean seaport of Jerusalem (1 Kings 5:9; 2 Chron. 2:16; Ezek. 3:7); now Jaffa.

Jordan: Chief river of Palestine, rising in the Anti-Lebanon mountain range, flowing southward, enlarging into the Sea of Galilee, emptying into the Dead Sea. A swift, narrow, yet fordable stream, with an entire course of about two hundred miles (Gen. 13:10; Josh. 2:7; Judg. 3:28; 2 Sam. 10:17; Matt. 3:13).

Joseph: 1. Son of Jacob and Rachel (Gen. 37:3); sold into Egypt; promoted to high office by the Pharaoh; rescued his family from famine; settled them in Goshen; died at advanced age; bones carried back to Shechem (Josh. 24:32). 2. Three of Christ's ancestors (Luke 3:24, 26, 30). 3. Husband of Mary, earthly father of Jesus, and a carpenter at Nazareth (Matt. 1:19; Luke 3:23; John 1:45). 4. Of Arimathea, a member of the Sanhedrim, who acknowledged Christ (Matt. 27:57–59; Mark 15:43; Luke 23:51). 5. The apostle Barsabas, substituted for Judas (Acts 1:23).

Joshua: 1. Jehoshuah (1 Chron. 7:27). Oshea (Num. 13:8). Jesus (Acts 7:45; Heb. 4:8). Son of Nun, of the tribe of Ephraim. The great warrior of the Israelites during the desert wanderings and conquest and apportionment of Canaan (Exod. 17:9–14; 1 Chron. 7:27; Num. 13:8, 16; 27:18–23). His book, sixth of the O.T., contains the history of his conquests and governorship, 1451–1426 BC. 2. A governor of Jerusalem (2 Kings 23:8) 3. A high priest (Hag. 1:1, 14).

Josiah: 1. Son and successor of Amon on the throne of Judah, 641–610 BC. He abolished idolatry, propagated the newly discovered law, aided Assyria against Egypt, and fell in the battle of Esdraelon (2 Kings 22:1–23:30; 2 Chron. 34–35). 2. Son of Zephaniah (Zech 6:10).

Jot: The Greek *I, iota.* A little thing (Matt. 5:18).

Journey: A day's journey, indefinite. Sabbath day's journey, 2,000 paces, or three-quarters of a mile from the walls of a city (Deut. 1:2; Acts 1:12).

Joy/Joyful: Great delight or positive feelings, particularly toward the Lord for His blessings.

j, of the Lord is your strength. . . Neh. 8:10
j cometh in the morning. . .Ps. 30:5
my soul shall be j'ful. . .Ps. 35:9
j of thy salvation. . .Ps. 51:12
good tidings of great j. . .Luke 2:10
your j might be full. . .John 15:11
count it all j. . .James 1:2

Jubal: Son of Lamech and inventor of the harp and organ (Gen. 4:19–21).

Jubilee: Year of, celebrated every fiftieth year; ushered in by blowing of trumpets; land rested; alienated lands reverted; slaves freed; outer circle of seventh or sabbatical system, year, month, and day (Lev. 25:8–55).

j shall that fiftieth year be. . .Lev. 25:11
until the year of j. . .Lev. 25:28
from the year of j. . .Lev. 27:17
j of the children of Israel. . .Num. 36:4

Judaea/Judea: A district in southern Palestine in N.T. times; a Roman province annexed to Syria when Jesus was born (Matt. 2:1).

Judah: 1. Fourth son of Jacob (Gen. 29:35; 37:26–28; 43:3–10). His tribe was the largest (Num. 1:26–27). Allotted the southern section of Canaan (Josh. 15:1–63). 2. Kingdom of, formed on disruption of Solomon's empire, out of Judah, Benjamin, Simeon, and part of Dan, with Jerusalem as capital, 975 BC. Had nineteen kings and lasted for 389 years, until overrun by Nebuchadnezzar, 586 BC. Outlived its rival, Israel, some 135 years. 3. City of Jerusalem (2 Chron. 25:28). 4. A town in Naphtali (Josh. 19:34).

Judas: Greek form of *Judah*. 1. Judah (Matt. 1:2–3). 2. Iscariot, or of Kerioth. Betrayer of Christ (Matt. 10:4; Mark 3:19; Luke 6:16; John 6:17; 12:6; 13:29). 3. Man of Damascus (Acts 9:11). 4. Surname of Barsabas, a prophet (Acts 15:22, 32). 5. A Galilean apostate (Acts 5:37).

Jude: Judas, brother of James the Less (Luke 6:16; John 14:22; Acts 1:13; Jude 1:1). Thaddaeus, Lebbaeus (Matt. 10:3; Mark 3:18). An apostle and author of the epistle which bears his name, the twenty-sixth N.T. book. Written about AD 65. Place unknown.

Judge/Judgest: To investigate the facts carefully and make a wise decision.
   j thy neighbour. . .Lev. 19:15
   J not, that ye be. . .Matt. 7:1
   thou j'st another. . .Rom. 2:1
   j not mine own self. . .1 Cor. 4:3

Judge, God as: A title of God that emphasizes His role as the ultimate standard of justice and fairness.
   Shall not the J. . .Gen. 18:25
   j the fatherless. . .Ps. 10:18
   j among the nations. . .Isa. 2:4
   not to j the world. . .John 12:47
See *Judgment/Judgments, God's.*

Judgment, Day of: The final judgment in the end time.
   Gomorrha in the d o j. . .Matt. 10:15
   account thereof in the d o j
      . . .Matt. 12:36
   day of wrath and revelation
      . . .Rom. 2:5
   boldness in the d o j. . .1 John 4:17
See *Judgment/Judgments, God's.*

Judgment, God's: The Lord's actions in His role as judge.
   all his ways are j. . .Deut. 32:4
   every work into j. . .Eccles. 12:14
   j run down as waters. . .Amos 5:24

   For j I am come. . .John 9:39
   j seat of Christ. . .Rom. 14:10
   after this the j. . .Heb. 9:27
See *Judge, God as; Judgment, Day of.*

Judgment, Human: The God-given ability to investigate a problem or situation and make a wise decision.
   j of thy poor. . .Exod. 23:6
   Teach me good j. . .Ps. 119:66
   To do justice and j. . .Prov. 21:3
   j, mercy, and faith. . .Matt. 23:23

Judges: Governors of Israel between Joshua and the kings. Qualification were martial or moral prowess. Rule arbitrary. Fifteen are recorded. Period, 1400–1091 BC. Book of Judges, seventh of the O.T., was probably compiled by Samuel. Its history is that of a tumultuous period, completing Joshua's conquests and leading to legitimate kingly rule.

Judgment Hall: Pilate's residence in Jerusalem (John 18:28, 33; 19:9). Praetorium or court (Acts 23:35).

Justice: Fair and impartial treatment of all people.
   do j to the afflicted. . .Ps. 82:3
   done judgment and j. . .Ps. 119:121
   To do j and judgment. . .Prov. 21:3
   execute judgment and j. . .Jer. 23:5
See *Fairness.*

Justification: God's pardon and acceptance of the just through faith (Rom. 3:20–31; 4:25).

Justify/Justified: God's declaration that makes a believer just or right in His sight—a result of His grace.
   I will not j the wicked. . .Exod. 23:7
   j'ied from all things. . .Acts 13:39
   j'ied freely by his grace. . .
      Rom. 3:24
   not j'ied by the works. . .Gal. 2:16
   might be j'ied by faith. . .Gal. 3:24

K

Kadesh: A Stopping place of the Is-raelites near borders of Canaan, and scene of Miriam's death (Num. 13:26; 20:1). Kadesh-barnea (Deut. 2:14; Josh. 15:3). Enmishpat (Gen. 14:7).

Kidron: The brook or ravine between Jerusalem and Mount Olivet (2 Sam. 15:23; 2 Kings 23:6). Cedron (John 18:1).

Kill/Killed: To take a human life. The word usually refers to the crime of murder.
Thou shalt not k. . .Exod. 20:13
A time to k. . .Eccles. 3:3
them which k the body. . .
Matt. 10:28
go ye about to k me? . . .John 7:19
k'ed the Prince of life. . .Acts 3:15
See *Murder/Murders.*

Kind/Kindly/Kindness: Cordiality toward others.
his merciful k'ness is great. . .Ps. 117:2
the law of k'ness. . .Prov. 31:26
Be k'ly affectioned. . .Rom. 12:10
suffereth long, and is k. .1 Cor. 13:4
k one to another. . .Eph. 4:32

King, Earthly: A civil official who ruled over a nation or kingdom.
Melchizedek k of Salem. . .Gen. 14:18
Pharaoh k of Egypt. . .Gen. 41:46
k Solomon exceeded. . .1 Kings 10:23
k of Assyria departed. . .Isa. 37:37
Nebuchadnezzar the k. . .Jer. 27:8
See *Government; Leader/Leaders; Ruler/Rulers.*

King, God as: A title of God that emphasizes His dominion over all the earth.

The Lord is K. . .Ps. 10:16
K of glory shall come in. . .Ps. 24:7
K over all the earth. . .Ps. 47:2
Holy One of Israel is our k. . .Ps. 89:18
great K above all gods. . .Ps. 95:3
the K, the Lord of hosts. . .Isa. 6:5
righteous Branch, and a K. . .Jer. 23:5
K of k, and Lord of lords. . .Tim. 6:15

Kingdom of God: God's rule in hu-man hearts; a kingdom established by Jesus.
seek ye first the k o G. . .Matt. 6:33
k o G is at hand. . .Mark 1:15
of such is the k o G. . .Mark 10:14
seek ye the k o G. . .Luke 12:31
shall not inherit the k o G? . . .1 Cor. 6:9
See *Kingdom of Heaven.*

Kingdom of Heaven: A phrase that means the same thing as "kingdom of God."
k o h is at hand. . .Matt. 3:2
enter into the k o h. . .Matt. 5:20
mysteries of the k o h. . .Matt. 13:11
keys of the k o h. . .Matt. 16:19
of such is the k o h. . .Matt. 19:14
See *Kingdom of God.*

Kiss: Form of salutation (Gen. 29:13); token of allegiance (1 Sam. 10:1); pledge of Christian brotherhood (Rom. 16:16; 1 Pet. 5:14).

Knowing God: The ability of human-kind to understand and have fellow-ship with God.
know that my redeemer liveth . . .Job 19:25
know that I am God. . .Ps. 46:10
delight to know my ways. . .Isa. 58:2
for all shall know me. . .Heb. 8:11
dwelleth in him, and he in him. . .1 John 3:24
See *Conversion; New Life; Salvation.*

Knowledge: Information acquired through study or personal experience.
Lord is a God of k. . .1 Sam. 2:3
Such k is too wonderful. . .Ps. 139:6
To give k of salvation. . .Luke 1:77
to another the word of k. . .1 Cor. 12:8
whether there be k. . .1 Cor. 13:8
See *Learn/Learned/Learning.*

L

Laban: 1. Father-in-law of Jacob (Gen. 24–30). 2. A landmark (Deut. 1:1).

Labour: Human effort; work.
Six days shalt thou l. . .Exod. 20:9
L not to be rich. . .Prov. 23:4
good reward for their l. . .
Eccles. 4:9
l for that which satisfieth not?
. . .Isa. 55:2

Lamb of God: A title of Christ that emphasizes His redemptive suffering.
as a lamb to the slaughter. . .Isa. 53:7
Behold the L o G! . . .John 1:36
a lamb without blemish. . .1 Pet. 1:19
fell down before the Lamb. . .
Rev. 5:8
Worthy is the Lamb. . .Rev. 5:12
marriage supper of the Lamb
. . .Rev. 19:9

Lame: Unable to walk.
was l of his feet. . .2 Sam. 4:4
the l walk. . .Matt. 11:5
a certain man l. . .Acts 3:2
l, were healed. . .Acts 8:7

Lamech: 1. Father of Noah (Gen. 5:28–32). 2. Father of Jubal, inventor of the harp and organ (Gen. 4:18–26).

Laodicea: A city of Phrygia and seat of an early Christian church (Col. 2:1; 4:15; Rev. 1:11; 3:14–22).

Lasciviousness: Unbridled lust; a sin characteristic of unbelievers.
fornication and l. . .2 Cor. 12:21
fornication, uncleanness, l. . .
Gal. 5:19
themselves over unto l. . .Eph. 4:19
See *Adultery; Debauchery.*

Last Day: The final judgment in the end time.
raise him up at the l d. . .John 6:40
resurrection at the l d. . .John 11:24
judge him in the l d. . .John 12:48
See *Second Coming of Christ.*

Laugh/Laughter: Mirth, joy, or merriment.
God hath made me to l. . .Gen. 21:6
our mouth filled with l'ter. . .
Ps. 126:2
a time to l. . .Eccles. 3:4
l'ter be turned to mourning
. . .James 4:9
See *Humor.*

Law/Laws: The civil, moral, and ceremonial law among God's people(Matt. 5:17; John 1:17; Acts 25:8).
my statutes, and my l's. . .Gen. 26:5
this book of the l. . .Deut. 30:10
the l of the Lord. . .Ps. 1:2
come to destroy the l. . .Matt. 5:17
The l and the prophets. . .
Luke 16:16

Lawsuits: Cases brought before a court of law.
Agree with thine adversary. . .
Matt. 5:25
any man will sue thee. . .Matt. 5:40
brother shall trespass against thee. . .Matt. 18:15
goeth to law with brother. . .
1 Cor. 6:6
See *Divorce/Divorced/Divorcement.*

Lazarus: 1. Brother of Mary and Martha (John 11:1; 12:1–22). 2. A type of poverty and distress in Jesus' parable (Luke 16:19–31).

Laziness: See *Idle, Idleness.*

Leader/Leaders: People responsible for teaching and guiding others.
> l's of this people. . .Isa. 9:16
> l and commander to the people
> . . .Isa. 55:4
> blind l's of the blind. . .Matt. 15:14

See *Government; King, Earthly; Ruler/ Rulers.*

Leah: Jacob's wife through the deceit of her father, Laban (Gen. 29–30; 49:31).

Learn/Learned/Learning: To acquire knowledge through study or personal experience.
> l to fear the Lord. . .Deut. 31:13
> will increase l'ing. . .Prov. 1:5
> l'ed, in whatsoever state I am. . .
> Phil. 4:11
> l to maintain good works. . .
> Titus 3:14

See *Edify/Edifieth/Edifying; Education; Knowledge; Literacy.*

Leaven: 1. A fermentation agent used in bread (Matt. 13:33). Passover bread was unleavened (Exod. 7:15–17). 2. Corrupt doctrines (Matt. 16:6); evil passions (1 Cor. 5:7–8).
> put away l. . .Exod. 12:15
> kingdom of heaven is like unto l
> . . .Matt. 13:33
> Purge out therefore the old l. . .
> 1 Cor. 5:7

Lebanon: Two mountain ranges running northeast, between which was Coelo-Syria. The west is Libanus, or Lebanon proper. The eastern

is Anti-Libanus, and skirted Palestine on the north (Deut. 1:7; Josh. 1:4). Many scripture allusions (Isa. 10:34; Jer. 22:23).

Leek: A vegetable closely related to the onion (Num. 11:5).

Legalism: Faith gone wrong, because it puts more emphasis on following the letter of the law than on following the Spirit.
> bind heavy burdens. . .Matt. 23:4
> unto another gospel. . .Gal. 1:6
> yoke of bondage. . .Gal. 5:1
> an Hebrew of the Hebrews. . .
> Phil. 3:5
> which is in the law, blameless
> . . .Phil. 3:6

See *Pharisee/Pharisees.*

Legion: A division of the Roman army consisting of several thousand men (Matt. 26:53; Mark 5:9).

Lend/Lendeth: To place property under the care of others, with the stipulation that it be returned or repaid in the future.
> l him sufficient. . .Deut. 15:8
> sheweth favour, and l'eth. . .
> Ps. 112:5
> l'eth unto the Lord. . .Prov. 19:17
> l, hoping for nothing. . .Luke 6:35

See *Usury.*

Lentil: A vegetable similar to the pea or bean (Gen. 25:34; 2 Sam. 17:28).

Levi: 1. Third son of Jacob (Gen. 29:34); avenged Dinah's wrong (34:25–31); cursed (49:5–7); went to Egypt (Exod. 6:16); blessed (Exod. 32:25–28). 2. Two of Christ's ancestors (Luke 3:24, 29). 3. Original name of Matthew (Mark 2:14; Luke 5:27, 29; compare Matt. 9:9).

Libya: The African nation west of Egypt and contiguous with the Mediterranean (Ezek. 30:5; Acts 2:10).

Lies: Falsehoods; untruths.
not bear false witness. . .
Exod. 20:16
speaketh l shall perish. . .Prov. 19:9
Speaking l in hypocrisy. . .1 Tim. 4:2

Life, Breath of: Life-giving oxygen; a gift of God.
the b o l. . .Gen. 2:7
wherein is the b o l. . .Gen. 6:17
breath of the Almighty. . .Job 33:4
giveth to all life, and breath. . .
Acts 17:25

Life, Brevity of: The few short years granted to humans in this life.
l should prolong my l? . . .Job 6:11
My days are swifter. . .Job 7:6
teach us to number our days. . .
Ps. 90:12
l? It is even a vapour. . .James 4:14

Life Eternal. See *Eternal Life.*

Lifestyle: The typical way of life of a person or group.
Live joyfully with the wife. . .
Eccles. 9:9
Take no thought for your life. . .
Matt. 6:25
The just shall live by faith. . .
Rom. 1:17
live peaceably with all men. . .
Rom. 12:18
live unto righteousness. . .
1 Pet. 2:24

Light: Illumination. Light is often used as a metaphor for God's gift of salvation.
Let there be l. . .Gen. 1:3
The Lord is my l. . .Ps. 27:1
l unto my path. . .Ps. 119:105
Gentiles shall come to thy l. . .
Isa. 60:3

Ye are the l of the world. . .
Matt. 5:14
A l to lighten the Gentiles. . .
Luke 2:32
That was the true L. . .John 1:9
l of the glorious gospel. . .
2 Cor. 4:4

Ligure: Possibly amber. First stone in the third row of the high priest's breastplate (Exod. 28:19; 39:12).

Lips: See *Speech.*

Listen: In the biblical sense, to listen is to hear and obey.
hearken unto me. . .Ps. 34:11
Hear, O my son, and receive. . .
Prov. 4:10
heareth his father's instruction. . .
Prov. 13:1
My sheep hear my voice. . .
John 10:27
be swift to hear. . .James 1:19
and not hearers only. . .James 1:22
See *Hear/Heareth.*

Literacy: The ability to read and write.
thou shalt read this law. . .
Deut. 31:11
read in the book. . .Neh. 8:8
read that which was spoken. . .
Matt. 22:31
epistle is read among you. . .
Col. 4:16
See *Learn/Learned/Learning.*

Living Together: An unmarried couple sharing the same household.
men of her city shall stone her
. . .Deut. 22:21
ravished with a strange woman
. . .Prov. 5:20
Marriage is honourable. . .Heb. 13:4
See *Fornication/Fornication; Marriage/ Marry.*

Lois: Timothy's grandmother (2 Tim. 1:5).

Loneliness: Living a solitary life; cut off from others.
man should be alone. . .Gen. 2:18
I am desolate and afflicted. . .
Ps. 25:16
my heart within me is desolate
. . .Ps. 143:4
never leave thee, nor forsake thee.
. .Heb. 13:5

Longeth/Longing: Intense desire.
panteth my soul after thee. . .
Ps. 42:1
My soul I, yea. . .Ps. 84:2
satisfieth the l'ing soul. . .Ps. 107:9

Longsuffering: Patience or perseverance.
The Lord is l. . .Num. 14:18
I, forbearing one another. . .
Eph. 4:2
patience and l. . .Col. 1:11
l of our Lord is salvation. . .
2 Pet. 3:15

Lord: A word for God that refers to His supreme rule (Gen. 15:4; Ps. 7; 100).

Lord of Hosts: A title of God that emphasizes His rule over the hosts of heaven, or the heavenly bodies.
L o h was with him. . .1 Chron. 11:9
L o h is his name. . .Isa. 47:4
Thus speaketh the L o h. . .
Zech. 7:9
messenger of the L o h. . .Mal. 2:7

Lord's Day: First day of the week; resurrection day of Christ (Rev. 1:10). Sunday, after AD 321.

Lordship of Christ: Jesus' universal authority and rule in the world.
he is Lord of all. . .Acts 10:36
on the Lord Jesus Christ. . .
Rom. 13:14
he is Lord of lords. . .Rev. 17:14

Lord's Supper: Instituted by Christ the night before the crucifixion as a reminder of His covenant with humankind (Matt. 26:19; Mark 14:16; Luke 22:13). "Breaking of bread" (Acts 2:42); "Communion" (1 Cor. 10:16); "Lord's Supper" (1 Cor. 11:20).
Take, eat; this is my body. . .Matt. 26:26
which is shed for many. . .Matt. 26:28
he was betrayed took bread. . .
1 Cor. 11:23
this cup is the new testament. . .
1 Cor. 11:25
See *Eucharist.*

Lose/Loss/Lost: To suffer deprivation of one's possessions or of life itself.
salt have l't his savour. . .Matt. 5:13
findeth his life shall l it. . .Matt. 10:39
l his own soul? . . .Matt. 16:26
he shall suffer l's. . .1 Cor. 3:15
l count all things but l's. . .Phil. 3:8

Lost/Unsaved: The state of those who have not accepted Jesus Christ as Lord and Savior.
save that which was l. . .Matt. 18:11
ye shall all likewise perish. . .
Luke 13:3
was l, and is found. . .Luke 15:24
none of them is l. . .John 17:12
gavest me have I l none. . .
John 18:9
See *Harvest; Unsaved.*

Lot: Abraham's nephew (Gen. 11:27–31). Settled in Jordan valley (Gen. 13:1–13); escaped to mountains (Gen. 19). Ancestor of the Moabites and Ammonites.

Lots, Casting of: Small objects used to determine God's will and to make choices.
c l upon the two goats. . .Lev. 16:8

land shall be divided by lot. . .
    Num. 26:55
c l upon my vesture. . .Ps. 22:18
Come, and let us c l. . .Jon. 1:7
parted his garments, c l. . .Matt.
    27:35

Lots, Feast of: See *Purim.*

Love, Brotherly: Love for others, particularly fellow believers.
    be of one mind, live in peace. . .
        2 Cor. 13:11
    being knit together in love. . .
        Col. 2:2
    ought also to love one another. . .
        1 John 4:11
    loveth God love his brother also
        . . .1 John 4:21
See *Feelings.*

Love, God's: God's concern and compassion for His people.
    Lord loved Israel for ever. . .1 Kings
        10:9
    For God so loved the world
        . . .John 3:16
    God commendeth his l. . .Rom. 5:8
    God, who loved me, and gave. . .
        Gal. 2:20
    great l wherewith he loved us. . .
        Eph. 2:4
    l of Christ, which passeth. . .
        Eph. 3:19
    for God is l. . .1 John 4:8

Loving God: Love of believers for the Lord whom they serve.
    love the Lord thy God. . .Deut. 6:5
    mercy with them that love him. . .
        Deut. 7:9
    to them that love God. . .Rom. 8:28
    But if any man love God. . .
        1 Cor. 8:3

Lovingkindness: God's gentle and steadfast love and mercy for His people.
    How excellent is thy l. . .Ps. 36:7
    thy l is better than life. . .Ps. 63:3
    To shew forth thy l. . .Ps. 92:2
    crowneth thee with l. . .Ps. 103:4

l unto thousands. . .Jer. 32:18

Lucifer: A reference to the king of Babylon (Isa. 14:12).

Luke: Evangelist and physician (Col. 4:14; 2 Tim. 4:11). Author of third Gospel and the book of Acts.

Lust/Lusts: Intense and inappropriate sexual desire.
    L not after her beauty. . .Prov. 6:25
    looketh on a woman to l. . .
        Matt. 5:28
    not fulfil the l of the flesh. . .
        Gal. 5:16
    Flee also youthful l's. . .2 Tim. 2:22
    abstain from fleshly l's. . .1 Pet. 2:11
    through the l's of the flesh. . .
        2 Pet. 2:18
See *Entice/Enticed/Enticeth.*

Lydia: 1. A province of Asia Minor, on the Mediterranean Sea. 2. Female convert of Thyatira (Acts 16:14).

Lying: Telling falsehoods and untruths.
    l lips be put to silence. . .Ps. 31:18
    A proud look, a l tongue. . .
        Prov. 6:17
    L lips are abomination. . .
        Prov. 12:22
    A righteous man hateth l. . .
        Prov. 13:5
    Wherefore putting away l. . .
        Eph. 4:25

Lystra: City of Lycaonia, where Paul was honored (Acts 14:6–18), and then rejected and stoned (Acts 14:19–21).

M

Macedonia: The ancient empire north of Greece whose greatest kings were Philip and Alexander the Great. Often visited by the apostle Paul, who made here his first European converts (Acts 16:9–12; 17:1–15; 20:1–6).

Mad/Madness: Insanity or bizarre behavior.
Lord shall smite thee with m'ness
. . .Deut. 28:28
feigned himself m in their hands
. . .1 Sam. 21:13
they were filled with m'ness
. . .Luke 6:11
much learning doth make thee m
. . .Acts 26:24

Magi: Oriental priests and learned men. A Median and Persian caste of royal advisers (Jer. 39:3; Matt. 2:1–11).

Magicians: People who practiced illusion or sleight of hand to entertain others or work miracles.
called for all the m of Egypt
. . .Gen. 41:8
ten times better than all the m
. . .Dan. 1:20
astrologers, the m, the
soothsayers. . .Dan. 2:27
shalt have no more soothsayers
. . .Mic. 5:12
See *Astrologers; Occult, the; Sorcery/Sorcerer/Sorcerers; Witch/Witchcraft.*

Majesty: A word for God's power and glory.
with God is terrible m. . .Job 37:22
the Lord is full of m. . .Ps. 29:4
he is clothed with m. . .Ps. 93:1
hand of the M on high. . .Heb. 1:3

Malachi: Last of the minor prophets. His book foretells the coming of Christ and John the Baptist.

Malchus: The servant whose ear Peter cut off (Matt. 26:51; Luke 22:50).

Malefactor/Malefactors: A lawbreaker or one who commits wrong against others.
thieves break through and steal. . .
Matt. 6:19
crucified him, and the m's. . .
Luke 23:33
because he was a thief. . .John 12:6
If he were not a m. .John 18:30
Nor thieves, nor covetous. . .
1 Cor. 6:10
hateth his brother is a murderer
. . .1 John 3:15

Malice: Contempt or hatred.
Whose hatred is covered by
deceit. . .Prov. 26:26
leaven of m and wickedness. . .
1 Cor. 5:8
away from you, with all m. . .
Eph. 4:31
living in m and envy. . .Titus 3:3
laying aside all m. . .1 Pet. 2:1

Mammon: A word for money, wealth, or riches (Matt. 6:24; Luke 16:9).

Mamre: The Amorite chief who gave his name to the plain where Abraham lived for a time (Gen. 14:13–24). Hebron (Gen. 23:19).

Man/Mankind: A word often used for all people or humanity in general.
m became a living soul. . .Gen. 2:7
image of God made he m. . .Gen. 9:6
breath of all m'kind. . .Job 12:10
What is m, that thou art mindful
. . .Ps. 8:4
what can m do unto me? . . .
Ps. 118:6
since by m came death. . .
1 Cor. 15:21
our outward m perish. . .2 Cor. 4:16
found in fashion as a m. . .Phil. 2:8

Manasseh: 1. First son of Joseph (Gen. 41:51). The tribe divided and occupied both sides of the Jordan River

(Josh. 16–17). 2. Son and successor of Hezekiah on the throne of Judah, 698–643 BC. Idolatrous (2 Kings 21:1–18). Captive in Babylon; repented; restored (2 Chron. 33:1–20).

Mandrake: A narcotic plant resembling rhubarb, bearing a yellow, aromatic fruit (Gen. 30:14–16; Song of Sol. 7:13).

Manger: A feeding crib or trough for cattle. The stall, and even the cattle yard (Luke 2:7–16; 8:15).

Manna: A bread substitute provided by the Lord for the wandering Israelites (Exod. 16:14–36; Num. 11:7–9; Deut. 8:3; Josh. 5:12).
  eat m forty years. . .Exod. 16:35
  m ceased on the morrow. . .
    Josh. 5:12
  Our fathers did eat m. . .John 6:31
  golden pot that had m. . .Heb. 9:4

Mantle: Blanket (Judg. 4:18); garment (1 Sam. 15:27); sleeved wrapper (Isa. 3:22); chief outer garment (1 Kings 19:13–19).

Mara: Naomi called herself by this name (Ruth 1:20), meaning "bitter."

Mark: John Mark (Acts 12:12, 25; 15:37). John (Acts 8:5, 13). Mark (Acts 15:39). Convert of Peter (1 Pet. 5:13). Companion of Paul (Col. 4:10). Author of the second Gospel, which was probably written in Rome.

Marriage/Marry: The union of a man and a woman in commitment to each other as husband and wife.
  m'y her that is divorced. . .
    Matt. 5:32
  and shall m'y another. . .Matt. 19:9

  m in Cana of Galilee. . .John 2:1
  better to m'y than to burn. . .
    1 Cor. 7:9
  M is honourable in all. . .Heb. 13:4
  m of the Lamb. . .Rev. 19:7
See *Betroth/Betrothed; Courtship; Husband/Husbands; Living Together; Wife.*

Mars' Hill: A landmark in the city of Athens (Acts 17:22). See *Areopagus.*

Martha: Sister of Mary and Lazarus (Luke 10:38–42; John 11:5–28).

Martyr/Martyrs: Believers who give their lives rather than renounce their faith.
  blood of thy m Stephen. . .
    Acts 22:20
  m's of Jesus. . .Rev. 17:6

Mary: 1. The betrothed of Joseph and mother of Christ (Matt. 1:18–25; Mark 6:3; Luke 8:19; John 2:1–5). 2. Wife of Cleophas (Matt. 27:56, 61; Luke 24:1–10). 3. Mother of John Mark (Acts 12:12; Col. 4:10). 4. Sister of Martha and Lazarus (Luke 10:41–42; John 11–12). 5. Mary Magdalene, i.e., of Magdala (Matt. 28:1–10; John 20:1–18). 6. A Roman convert (Rom. 16:6).

Master/Masters. A title of Christ and a word for a person who ruled over a household, or a slave.
  your m, the Lord's anointed. . .
    1 Sam. 26:16
  No man can serve two m's. . .
    Matt. 6:24
  disciple is not above his m. . .
    Matt. 10:24
  Good M, what good thing. . .
    Matt. 19:16
  be subject to your m's. . .1 Pet. 2:18

Materialism: An intense desire for money and material things.

Wherefore do ye spend money...
Isa. 55:2
kept back part of the price...
Acts 5:2
God may be purchased with
money...Acts 8:20
love of money is the root...
1 Tim. 6:10
See *Greed/Greedily/Greediness/Greedy;
Usury.*

Matthew: The apostle and evangelist. "Levi" (Luke 5:27–29); Son of Alphaeus (Mark 2:14); tax collector at Capernaum when called (Matt. 9:9). His Gospel is the first book of the N.T., AD 60–66.

Matthias: Apostle chosen to fill the place of Judas (Acts 1:26).

Mediator, Christ as: A title of Christ that emphasizes His work of reconciliation between God and humankind.
one God, and one m...1 Tim. 2:5
m of the new testament...Heb. 9:15
Jesus the m...Heb. 12:24

Medicine/Medicines: A substance for healing sickness.
doeth good like a m...Prov. 17:22
thou hast no healing m's...Jer. 30:13
wine mingled with myrrh...Mark 15:23
wine for thy stomach's sake...1 Tim. 5:23

Meditate/Meditation: Contemplation of spiritual truth.
doth he m day and night...Ps. 1:2
m'ion of my heart...Ps. 19:14
m'ion of him shall be sweet...
Ps. 104:34
m in thy statutes...Ps. 119:23

Meek/Meekness: Humility and a gentle spirit.

Moses was very m...Num. 12:3
m shall inherit the earth...Ps. 37:11
Lord lifteth up the m...Ps. 147:6
Blessed are the m...Matt. 5:5
m and lowly in heart...Matt. 11:29
love, patience, m'ness...1 Tim. 6:11

Melchizedek: King of Salem, and priest (Gen. 14:18– 20). Prototype of Christ (Ps. 110:4; Heb. 5–7). Melchisedec in N.T.

Melita: The island of Malta in the Mediterranean Sea south of Sicily (Acts (27–28).

Membership, Church: Belonging to a local church, a body of baptized believers.
every one members one of
another...Rom. 12:5
Bear ye one another's burdens
...Gal. 6:2
Submitting yourselves one to
another...Eph. 5:21
edify one another...1 Thess. 5:11
Not forsaking the assembling
...Heb. 10:25

Memorial: A physical reminder of an important event from the past.
these stones shall be for a m
...Josh. 4:7
keep my name in remembrance
...2 Sam. 18:18
told for a m of her...Matt. 26:13
in remembrance of his mercy...
Luke 1:54
or a m before God...Acts 10:4
do in remembrance of me...
1 Cor. 11:24

Mene: First word of Belshazzar's warning. Entire, *Mene*, "he is numbered"; *Tekel*, "he is weighed"; *Upharsin*, "they are divided" (Dan. 5:25–28).

Mental Illness: See *Mad/Madness.*

Mercy/Mercies: God's compassion for us and our compassion for others.

for his m'ies are great. . .
2 Sam. 24:14
Have m upon me, O God. . .Ps. 51:1
I desired m, and not sacrifice
. . .Hosea 6:6
they shall obtain m. . .Matt. 5:7

Mercy Seat: Lid of the ark of the covenant (Exod. 25:17–22); therefore, a covering, or atonement for sin (Heb. 9:5).

Meshach: Babylonian name of Mishael, Daniel's companion (Dan. 1:6–7; 3).

Mesopotamia: The country between the Tigris and Euphrates rivers (Gen. 24:10; Deut. 23:4; Judg. 3:8–10; Acts 2:9; 7:2).

Message/Messenger: A communication sent to another.

the Lord hath not spoken. . .
Deut. 18:22
m by the hand of a fool. . .
Prov. 26:6
m'enger of the covenant. . .Mal. 3:1
send my m'enger before thy face
. . .Matt. 11:10

Messiah: A title of Christ, meaning "Anointed One" (Lev. 4:3, 5, 16; 1 Sam. 2:10, 3512:3–5). The Messiah was foretold throughout the Old Testament in many prophecies.

in thy seed shall all the nations
. . .Gen. 22:18
I know that my redeemer liveth
. . .Job 19:25
Thou art my Son. . .Ps. 2:7
Thy seed will I establish for ever
. . .Ps. 89:4
he shall judge among the nations
. . .Isa. 2:4
a virgin shall conceive. . .Isa. 7:14

government shall be upon. . .
Isa. 9:6
Gentiles shall come to thy light
. . .Isa. 60:3
shall M be cut off. . .Dan. 9:26
See *Jesus Christ.*

Methuselah: Grandfather of Noah; oldest of those who lived before the flood; lived 969 years (Gen. 5:21–27).

Micah: Sixth of the minor prophets. Prophesied 750– 698 BC. He foretold the destruction of Samaria and Jerusalem and prefigured the Messiah.

Michael: Prince of angels (Dan. 10:13; 12:1; Rev. 12:7).

Midian: Son of Abraham, and founder of the Midianites (Gen. 25:2; Exod. 3:1; Num. 22:4; Judg. 7:13).

Might/Mighty: A word for power, particularly the power and authority of God.

and thy m'y hand. . .Deut. 3:24
his m'y power to be known. . .
Ps. 106:8
Not by m, nor by power. . .
Zech. 4:6
in the power of his m. . .Eph. 6:10

Mind: The reasoning faculty of human beings.

imaginations of the thoughts. . .
1 Chron. 28:9
whose m is stayed on thee. . .
Isa. 26:3
and with all thy m. . .Matt. 22:37
over to a reprobate m. . .Rom. 1:28
by the renewing of your m. . .
Rom. 12:2
have the m of Christ. . .1 Cor. 2:16

Minister/Ministry: A person who performs service in the name of the Lord.

let him be your m. . .Matt. 20:26
they had fulfilled their m'ry. . .
Acts 12:25
m of Jesus Christ. . .Rom. 15:16
m'ry of reconciliation. . .2 Cor. 5:18
for the work of the m'ry. . .Eph. 4:12

Miracle/Miracles: A supernatural event (Num. 22:28; 1 Kings 17:6; Matt. 9:18–33; 14:25).
man which shall do a m. . .
Mark 9:39
This beginning of m's. . .John 2:11
no man can do these m's. . .
John 3:2
m's and wonders and signs. . .
Acts 2:22
m's by the hands of Paul. . .
Acts 19:11

Miriam: Sister of Moses and Aaron. Musician and prophetess (Exod. 2:4–10; 15:20–21; Num. 12:1–15; 20:1; 1 Chron. 6:3).

Mischief/Mischiefs: KJV word for wrongdoing or evil acts.
practised m against him. . .1 Sam. 23:9
away the m of Haman. . .Esther 8:3
The tongue deviseth m's. . .Ps. 52:2
swift in running to m. . .Prov. 6:18

Misery: Extreme unhappiness and emotional distress.
thou shalt forget thy m. . .Job 11:16
cast down, O my soul?. . .Ps. 42:5
remember his m no more. . .
Prov. 31:7
Destruction and m are. . .Rom. 3:16

Mite: Half a farthing, or one-fifth of a cent (Mark 12:41– 44; Luke 21:1–4).

Mitre: The priestly headdress of linen that bore the inscription, "Holiness to the Lord" (Exod. 28:4, 36–39; 29:6; 39:28–30; Lev. 8:9; 16:4).

Mizpah/Mizpeh: 1. Jacob's covenant stones (Gen. 31:47–49). 2. Hivite section in northern Palestine (Josh. 11:3–8). 3. A city in Judah (Josh. 15:38). 4. A city of Benjamin (Josh. 18:26; 1 Sam. 10:17–21; 1 Kings 15:22).

Moab: Son of Lot by his daughter, and ancestor of the Moabites. The country lay east of the Dead Sea and south of the Arnon River (Num. 21:13–15; 22; Judg. 11:18). Though idolatrous, worshipping Chemosh, they were a strong, progressive people holding Israel subject (Judg. 3:12–14); but finally subdued (Judg. 3:15–30; 2 Sam. 8:2; Isa. 15–16; Ruth 1–2).

Mock/Mocked/Mocker: To ridicule and insult another person.
Fools make a m at sin. . .Prov. 14:9
Wine is a m'er. . .Prov. 20:1
m'ed him, saying, Hail, King. . .
Matt. 27:29
some m'ed: and others said. . .
Acts 17:32
God is not m'ed. . .Gal. 6:7

Modest/Modesty: Correct and appropriate behavior.
she took a vail, and covered. . .
Gen. 24:65
To be discreet, chaste. . .Titus 2:5
See *Chaste/Chastity.*

Money: Gold and silver passed by weight among the Israelites (Gen. 17:13; 23:16). The N.T. coins (Matt. 17:27; 22:19; Mark 12:42) were Roman or Grecian.
cannot serve God and mammon. . .
Matt. 6:24
Shew me the tribute m. . .
Matt. 22:19
the unrighteous mammon. . .
Luke 16:11
love of m is the root. . .1 Tim. 6:10
not for filthy lucre. . .1 Pet. 5:2
See *Currency; Gambling.*

Money Changers: Those who made a business of supplying the annual half-shekel offering at a premium (Exod. 30:13–15; Matt. 21:12; Mark 11:15).

Mordecai: A Benjamite captive at the court of Ahasuerus, and deliverer of the Jews from the plot of Haman. He appears in the book of Esther.

Morning: The early part of the day.
m were the first day. . .Gen. 1:5
joy cometh in the m. . .Ps. 30:5
m, and at noon, will I pray. . .
Ps. 55:17
lovingkindness in the m. . .Ps. 92:2
They are new every m. . .Lam. 3:23
bright and m star. . .Rev. 22:16

Mortal/Mortality: The human condition which leads eventually to physical death.
reign in your m body. . .Rom. 6:12
m must put on immortality. . .
1 Cor. 15:53
manifest in our m flesh. . .
2 Cor. 4:11
m'ity might be swallowed. . .
2 Cor. 5:4
See *Bury/Burial/Buried; Death.*

Moses: The great leader and lawgiver of the Israelites. Son of Amram, a Levite. Born in Egypt, about 1571 BC. Adopted by Pharaoh's daughter, liberally educated, fled to Midian (Exod. 2). Called to lead the exodus from Egypt (Exod. 3–19). Promulgated the law (Exod. 10–11; Lev.; Num.; Deut.). Died on Nebo at 120 years of age. Reputed author of the Pentateuch.

Mother: The female parent in a family relationship.
leave his father and his m. . .
Gen. 2:24
m of all living. . .Gen. 3:20

Honour thy father and thy m. . .
Exod. 20:12
his m Mary was espoused. . .
Matt. 1:18
loveth father or m more. . .
Matt. 10:37
See *Family; Parents.*

Mourn/Mourning: To express grief or sorrow.
m'ing into dancing. . .Ps. 30:11
m'ing all the day long. . .Ps. 38:6
a time to m. . .Eccles. 3:4
to comfort all that m. . .Isa. 61:2
Blessed are they that m. . .
Matt. 5:4
See *Grief/Griefs.*

Mouth/Mouths: An organ of human communication. The mouth is also used as a metaphor for speech.
Who hath made man's m? . . .
Exod. 4:11
The m of the righteous. . .Ps. 37:30
m shall shew forth thy praise. . .
Ps. 51:15
He that keepeth his m. . .Prov. 13:3
open my m in parables. . .Matt.
13:35

Murder/Murders: The unlawful killing of another person.
m's, adulteries, fornications. . .
Matt. 15:19
Thou shalt do no m. . .Matt. 19:18
full of envy, m, debate. . .Rom. 1:29
Envyings, m's, drunkenness. . .Gal.
5:21
See *Crime; Kill/Killed/Killeth; Murderer/Murderers.*

Murderer/Murderers
The m rising with the light. . .Job
24:14
He was a m. . .John 8:44
betrayers and m's. . .Acts 7:52
suffer as a m. . .1 Pet. 4:15
hateth his brother is a m. . .1 John
3:15
See *Murder/Murders.*

**Murmur/Murmured/Murmurers/
Murmurings:** KJV word for criticizing and complaining.
> m'ed against Moses and Aaron. . .
> Exod. 16:2
> take away their m'ings. . .
> Num. 17:10
> m'ed against his disciples. . .
> Luke 5:30
> Pharisees and scribes m'ed. . .
> Luke 15:2
> without m'ings and disputings. . .
> Phil. 2:14
> These are m'ers, complainers. . .
> Jude 1:16

See *Complain/Complained/Complainers/Complaint; Contention/Contentions/Contentious; Quarrel.*

Musick: Vocal and instrumental praise performed in worship.
> I will sing unto the Lord. . .
> Exod. 15:1
> with singing, and with harps. . .
> 1 Chron. 13:8
> he heard m and dancing. . .
> Luke 15:25
> singing and making melody. . .
> Eph. 5:19

Myrrh: A gum resin much prized and variously used (Exod. 30:23; Est. 2:12; Ps. 45:8; Prov. 7:17; Mark 15:23; John 19:39).

Mystery/Mysteries: Something unknown except through divine revelation.
> revelation of the m. . .Rom. 16:25
> Behold, I shew you a m. . .1 Cor.
> 15:51
> the m of the gospel. . .Eph. 6:19
> to speak the m of Christ. . .Col. 4:3
> Holding the m of the faith. . .
> 1 Tim. 3:9

See *Secret/Secrets.*

N

Naaman: The leprous Syrian army commander who was cured by Elisha's orders (2 Kings 5).

Nabal: The Carmelite shepherd who refused to give food to David and his men (1 Sam. 15).

Nahum: Seventh of minor prophets. Probably an exile in Assyria. Approximate time of prophecy, 726–698 BC. It relates to the fall of Nineveh. Noted for vigor and beauty.

Naked/Nakedness: Lack of physical clothing. In a spiritual sense, spiritual inadequacy before God.
> knew that they were n. . .Gen. 3:7
> N came I out of my mother's
> . . .Job 1:21
> they have seen her n'ness. . .
> Lam. 1:8
> N, and ye clothed me. . .
> Matt. 25:36
> or n'ness, or peril. . .Rom. 8:35

Name of God: The expression "name of God" often represents the person of God Himself.
> called upon the n. . .Gen. 12:8
> n o G Almighty. . .Exod. 6:3
> whose n is Jealous. . .Exod. 34:14
> call on the n of the Lord. . .
> 1 Kings 18:24
> Hallowed be thy n. . .Matt. 6:9
> n of the Father. . .Matt. 28:19
> Father, glorify thy n. . .John 12:28

Name of Jesus: The expression "name of Jesus" often represents the person of Jesus Himself.
> call his n Jesus. . .Matt. 1:21
> shall call his n Emmanuel. . .
> Matt. 1:23
> in his n shall the Gentiles trust
> . . .Matt. 12:21

have life through his n. . .
John 20:31
none other n under heaven. . .
Acts 4:12
n which is above every n. . .Phil. 2:9
See *"I Am" Statements of Jesus.*

Naomi: Mother-in-law of Ruth (Ruth 1:22).

Naphtali: Fifth son of Jacob (Gen. 30:8). Large tribe at Sinai and Jordan (Num. 1:43; 26:50). Settled in northern Canaan (Josh. 19:32–39). Tribe carried captive in reign of Pekah (2 Kings 15:29).

Nathan: 1. Distinguished prophet, royal adviser, and biographer of David and Solomon (2 Sam. 7:2–17; 7:1–22; 1 Kings 1:8–45). 2. A son of David (1 Chron. 3:5; Luke 3:31).

Nathanael: A disciple of Christ and native of Cana in Galilee (John 1:47–51; 21:2.

Nation/Nations: A people bound together by customs, traditions, and civil rule.
make of thee a great n. . .Gen. 12:2
priests, and an holy n. . .Exod. 19:6
Righteousness exalteth a n. . .
Prov. 14:34
I will make them one n. . .
Ezek. 37:22
teach all n's. . .Matt. 28:19
holy n, a peculiar people. . .
1 Pet. 2:9

Nativity, the: The coming of Christ into the world in the form of a baby.
Thy seed will I establish for ever. . .
Ps. 89:4
Behold, a virgin shall conceive
. . .Isa. 7:14
he that is born King of the Jews?
. . .Matt. 2:2

young child with Mary his mother
. . .Matt. 2:11
Hail, thou that art highly favoured
. . .Luke 1:28
she brought forth her firstborn
son. . .Luke 2:7
unto you is born this day. . .
Luke 2:11
See *Virgin Birth.*

Natural Man: A person who has not been redeemed by Christ.
our old man is crucified. . .Rom. 6:6
n m receiveth not. . .1 Cor. 2:14
by nature the children of wrath. . .
Eph. 2:3

Nazareth: A town of Galilee, now En-nazirah. Hometown of Jesus (Matt. 4:13; Mark 1:9; Luke 1:26; 4:16, 29; John 1:45–46).

Nazarite: One bound by a temporary or permanent vow (Num. 6:1–21; Amos 2:11–12; Acts 21:20–26).
this is the law of the N. . .Num. 6:13
N may drink wine. . .Num. 6:20
child shall be a N. . .Judg. 13:5
for I have been a N. . .Judg. 16:17
See *Vow/Vowed/Vows.*

Nebo: 1. A mountain of Moab, from which Moses viewed the Promised Land (Deut. 32:49; 34:1). 2. A Reubenite city (Num. 32:3, 38; 33:47). 3. A Babylonian god, presiding over learning. Counterpart of the Greek Hermes (Isa. 46:1; Jer. 48:1).

Nebuchadnezzar: King of the Babylonian Empire, 605–561 BC. Brought empire to greatest height of prosperity. Defeated Pharaoh-necho at Carchemish (Jer. 46:2–26). Captured Jerusalem (2 Kings 24–25; Dan. 1–4).

Neglect/Neglected: To disregard or pay no attention to.
> not forsake the house of our God
> . . .Neh. 10:39
> n to hear them. . .Matt. 18:17
> n'ed in the daily ministration
> . . .Acts 6:1
> n so great salvation. . .Heb. 2:3

Nehemiah: 1. The Israelite captive who returned, as leader of his people, to rebuild Jerusalem and administer its affairs. His book, the sixteenth of the O.T., 445– 433 BC, tells of his work. 2. An assistant wall builder (Neh. 3:16).

New Life: The life that replaces a person's old, sinful nature through the process of regeneration.
> Except a man be born again
> . . .John 3:3
> born of water and of the Spirit
> . . .John 3:5
> Ye must be born again. . .John 3:7
> but have eternal life. . .John 3:15
> walk in newness of life. . .Rom. 6:4
> in Christ, he is a new creature. . .
> 2 Cor. 5:17

See *Born Again; Conversion; Knowing God; Regeneration; Salvation.*

Nicodemus: The Pharisee ruler and timid convert who assisted at Christ's burial (John 3:1–10; 7:50; 19:39).

Night: The dark part of the day; a metaphor for sin and lostness.
> the darkness he called N. . .
> Gen. 1:5
> giveth songs in the n. . .Job 35:10
> came to Jesus by n. . .John 3:2
> if a man walk in the n. . .John 11:10
> cometh as a thief in the n. . .
> 1 Thess. 5:2
> there shall be no n. . .Rev. 21:25

Nile: The great river of Egypt, worshipped as a god, famous for its annual and fertilizing overflows. Name not mentioned in scripture, but alluded to as "the river" (Gen. 12:1; Exod. 2:3); "the river of Egypt" (Gen. 15:18); "flood of Egypt" (Amos 8:8); Sihor, "black" (Josh. 8:3); Shihor, "dark blue" (1 Chron. 13:5).

Nineveh: Capital of Assyria, on the Tigris River. Founded by Asshur (Gen. 10:11). At the height of its wealth and splendor during time of Jonah to Nahum, and focus of their prophecies. Taken by the Medes about 750 BC, and destroyed by combined Medes and Babylonians, 606 BC (Jon.; Nah. 1–3).

Noah: 1. Ninth in descent from Adam (Gen. 5:28–32). Saved from the flood with his three sons (Gen. 7–8). Repeopled the earth (Gen. 9–10). Died at the age of 950 years. 2. A daughter of Zelophehad (Num. 26:33).

Nod: The land to which Cain fled after he murdered his brother (Gen. 4:16).

Nourishment: See *Eat/Eateth; Food.*

Numbers: Many numbers in the Bible have special meaning, for example, seven, indicating perfection.
> seventh day God ended. . .Gen. 2:2
> forty days and forty nights. . .
> Gen. 7:12
> not destroy it for ten's sake. . .
> Gen. 18:32
> Jacob served seven years. . .
> Gen. 29:20
> seventh year shall be a sabbath
> . . .Lev. 25:4
> called unto him his twelve
> disciples. . .Matt. 10:1
> Until seventy times seven. . .
> Matt. 18:22

an hundred and forty and four
thousand. . .Rev. 7:4

O

Oath/Oaths: Appeals to God to attest the truth of a statement or promise (Gen. 21:23; 26:3; Heb. 6:16).
Joseph took an o. . .Gen. 50:25
an o of the Lord. . .Exod. 22:11
perform unto the Lord thine o's. . .
Matt. 5:33
neither by any other o. . .
James 5:12
See *Vow/Vowed/Vows*.

Obadiah: 1. A court officer under Ahab (1 Kings 18:3– 16). 2. A teacher of the law (2 Chron. 17:7). 3. Fourth of the minor prophets. Prophesied after capture of Jerusalem. His book, thirty-first of the O.T., is a denunciation of Edom.

Obedience: To follow God's commands.
so by the o of one. . .Rom. 5:19
for the o of faith. . .Rom. 16:26
when your o is fulfilled. . .
2 Cor. 10:6
yet learned he o. . .Heb. 5:8

Obesity: See *Glutton/Gluttonous*.

Obey/Obeyed: To submit to authority, particularly the Lord's.
Abraham o'ed my voice. . .
Gen. 26:5
if ye o the commandments. . .
Deut. 11:27
to o is better than sacrifice. . .
1 Sam. 15:22
unclean spirits, and they do o him
. . .Mark 1:27
Children, o your parents. . .Eph. 6:1

Obscenity: Something repulsive and abominable to God.
abominable and filthy is man
. . .Job 15:16
ashamed of thy lewd way. . .
Ezek. 16:27
In thy filthiness is lewdness
. . .Ezek. 24:13
Neither filthiness, nor foolish. . .
Eph. 5:4
See *Abomination*.

Occult, the: Black magic, witchcraft, and superstition; prohibited by the Lord.
not suffer a witch to live. . .
Exod. 22:18
neither shall ye use enchantment
. . .Lev. 19:26
such as have familiar spirits. . .
Lev. 20:6
or a wizard, or a necromancer
. . .Deut. 18:11
familiar spirits, and the wizards
. . .1 Sam. 28:3
soothsayers like the Philistines
. . .Isa. 2:6
shalt have no more soothsayers
. . .Mic. 5:12
bewitched them with sorceries
. . .Acts 8:11
See *Magicians; Sorcery/Sorcerer/Sorcerers; Witch/Witchcraft*.

Offence/Offences: KJV word for sin or wrongdoing.
for a rock of o. . .Isa. 8:14
Who was delivered for our o's
. . .Rom. 4:25
by one man's o death. . .Rom. 5:17
stumblingstone and rock of o
. . .Rom. 9:33

Offering/Offerings: Either bloody, as of animals; or bloodless, as of vegetables. They embraced the burnt, sin, trespass, peace, and meat offerings (Lev. 1–9).
lamb for a burnt o. . .Gen. 22:8
delightest not in burnt o. . .Ps. 51:16

freewill o's of my mouth. . .
Ps. 119:108
more than all whole burnt o's
. . .Mark 12:33
given himself for us an o. . .Eph. 5:2
See *Sacrifice/Sacrifices; Tithe/Tithes.*

Olives/Olivet: The Mount of Olives, or
Olivet, is the ridge east of Jerusalem, beyond the Kidron Brook. So named because of its olive trees. On its slopes were
Gethsemane, Bethphage, and Bethany
(2 Sam. 15:30; Zech. 14:4; Matt. 21:1;
Mark 11:1; John 8:1; Acts 1:12).

Omega: The last letter of the Greek
alphabet (Rev. 1:8, 11; 21:6; 22:13).

Onesimus: Slave of Philemon, at
Colosse, on whose behalf Paul wrote
the epistle to Philemon (Col. 4:9;
Phile. 10, 15).

Onyx: A crystalline quartz (Exod.
28:9–12; 1 Chron. 29:2).

Oppose/Opposition: See *Persecution.*

Oppression: Domination and mis-
treatment of others.
I have also seen the o. . .Exod. 3:9
For the o of the poor. . .Ps. 12:5
Deliver me from the o. . .Ps. 119:134
See *Persecute/Persecuted/Persecutest;
Persecution.*

Oracle: In O.T. sense, the holy place
where God declared His will (1 Kings
6:5; 8:6). Divine revelation (Acts 7:38;
Rom. 3:2).

Ordain/Ordained: To set a person
or thing apart for a special purpose or
function.
chosen you, and o'ed you. . .
John 15:16

he which was o'ed of God. . .
Acts 10:42
o'ed to eternal life. . .Acts 13:48
powers that be are o'ed of God
. . .Rom. 13:1

Orphans: Children without earthly
parents.
thou art the helper of the
fatherless. . .Ps. 10:14
Defend the poor and fatherless. . .
Ps. 82:3
widow, and the fatherless. . .
Mal. 3:5
To visit the fatherless. . .James 1:27

Outcast/Outcasts: Dispossessed people; those without a home.
I will cast out the nations. . .Exod.
34:24
together the o's of Israel. . .Ps. 147:2
o's in the land of Egypt. . .Isa. 27:13

Outward Appearance: See *Appearance, Physical.*

Overcome/Overcometh: To emerge
victorious from troubling circumstances.
I have o the world. . .John 16:33
o evil with good. . .Rom. 12:21
ye have o the wicked one. . .
1 John 2:13
Him that o'th will I make. . .Rev. 3:12
See *Triumph/Triumphed/Triumphing.*

P

Pagan: See *Heathen; Gentiles.*
Pain: Physical suffering or discomfort.
wicked man travaileth with p
. . .Job 15:20
I found trouble and sorrow. . .
Ps. 116:3
p, as of a woman. . .Jer. 6:24
See *Sorrow/Sorrows.*

Palestina/Palestine: Philistia, land of the Philistines (Ps. 60:8); Palestina (Exod. 15:14); Palestine (Joel 3:4); Canaan (Gen. 12:5); Holy Land (Zech. 2:12) The indefinitely bounded region promised to Abraham, lying between the Mediterranean Sea. the Jordan River, and the Dead Sea. It also embraced the Israelite settlements beyond the Jordan (Gen. 15:18; 17:8; Num. 24:2–12).

Palsy: Partial or total death of muscle and nerve (1 Kings 13:4–6; Matt. 4:24; Luke 6:6).

Pamphylia: A seacoast province of Asia Minor. Its chief town was Perga, where Paul preached (Acts 13:13; 14:24; 27:5).

Paphos: A town on island of Cyprus visited by Paul (Acts 13:6–13).

Papyrus: The writing paper of the Egyptians, Greeks, and Romans, made from the papyrus plant (Job 40:21).

Parable: Allegorical representation of something real in nature or human affairs, with a moral lesson. A favorite method of Oriental teaching (2 Sam. 12:1–4; Isa. 5:1–7). Christ spoke many parables (Matt. 13:3–8; 24–32).
> mote that is in thy brother's eye . . .Matt. 7:3
> wise man, which built his house . . .Matt. 7:24
> unclean spirit is gone out of a man . . .Matt. 12:43
> sower went forth to sow. . . Matt. 13:3
> a grain of mustard seed. . . Matt. 13:31
> one pearl of great price. . . Matt. 13:46

> sheep, and one of them be gone astray. . .Matt. 18:12
> labourers into his vineyard. . . Matt. 20:1
> A certain man had two sons . . .Matt. 21:28
> householder, which planted a vineyard. . .Matt. 21:33
> king, which made a marriage for his son. . .Matt. 22:2
> ten virgins, which took their lamps . . .Matt. 25:1
> one he gave five talents. . . Matt. 25:15
> creditor which had two debtors . . .Luke 7:41
> I am the true vine. . .John 15:1

Paradise: "Garden of Eden;" and, figuratively, the dwelling place of happy souls—heaven (Luke 23:43; 2 Cor. 12:4; Rev. 2:7).

Paradoxes of the Gospel: Seemingly contradictory statements Jesus used to teach truths of God's kingdom.
> Blessed are the poor in spirit . . .Matt. 5:3
> Blessed are ye, when men shall revile. . .Matt. 5:11
> He that findeth his life shall lose it . . .Matt. 10:39
> So the last shall be first. . . Matt. 20:16
> exalteth himself shall be abased . . .Luke 14:11
> the good that I would I do not . . .Rom. 7:19
> weep, as though they wept not. . . 1 Cor. 7:30
> as dying, and, behold, we live. . . 2 Cor. 6:9
> as poor, yet making many rich. . . 2 Cor. 6:10
> I am weak, then am I strong. . . 2 Cor. 12:10
> to live is Christ, and to die is gain . . .Phil. 1:21
> the poor of this world rich . . .James 2:5

Parchment: Skin of sheep or goats prepared as a writing material (2 Tim. 4:13).

Parents: Adults responsible for the rearing of children.

rise up against their p. . .Matt. 10:21

p brought in the child Jesus
. . .Luke 2:27

who did sin, this man, or his p
. . .John 9:2

Children, obey your p. . .Eph. 6:1

See *Family; Father/Fathers; Mother/ Mothers.*

Partner/Partners: A companion, colleague, or fellow worker.

Whoso is p with a thief. . .
Prov. 29:24

which were p's with Simon. . .
Luke 5:10

not unequally yoked together. . .
2 Cor. 6:14

count me therefore a p. . .
Philem. 1:17

Passion of Christ: The suffering of Christ on the cross.

I am poured out like water. . .
Ps. 22:14

He is despised and rejected of men. . .Isa. 53:3

he was wounded for our transgressions. . .Isa. 53:5

whom they have pierced. . .
Zech. 12:10

suffer many things of the elders
. . .Matt. 16:21

to give his life a ransom for many
. . .Matt. 20:28

that he must suffer many things
. . .Mark 9:12

shewed himself alive after his p
. . .Acts 1:3

Christ must needs have suffered
. . .Acts 17:3

That Christ should suffer. . .
Acts 26:23

Passover: First of three great Jewish feasts, instituted in honor of the "passing over" of the Israelite households by the destroying angel (Exod. 12; 13:3–10; Lev. 23:4–14); called the "feast of unleavened bread." The Christian Passover is "The Lord's Supper" (Matt. 27:62; Luke 22:1–20; John 19:42).

it is the Lord's p. . .Exod. 12:11

I have desired to eat this p. . .
Luke 22:15

that they might eat the p. . .
John 18:28

Christ our p is sacrificed. . .
1 Cor. 5:7

Through faith he kept the p. . .
Heb. 11:28

Pastor: Figuratively, one who keeps Christ's flocks (Eph. 4:11).

Path/Paths of Life: A metaphor for behavior and the choices one makes in life.

shew me the p o l. . .Ps. 16:11

p's of righteousness. . .Ps. 23:3

a light unto my p. . .Ps. 119:105

he shall direct thy p's. . .Prov. 3:6

ponder the p o l. . .Prov. 5:6

ask for the old p's. . .Jer. 6:16

make straight p's. . .Heb. 12:13

Patience/Patient/Patiently: Endurance and perseverance.

the Lord, and wait p'tly. . .Ps. 37:7

tribulation worketh p. . .Rom. 5:3

God of p and consolation. . .
Rom. 15:5

p't waiting for Christ. . .2 Thess. 3:5

run with p the race. . .Heb. 12:1

See *Longsuffering; Perseverance; Wait/ Waiteth/Waiting.*

Patmos: The rocky island in the Aegean Sea to which the apostle John was banished (Rev. 1:9).

Paul: In Hebrew, Saul. Born at Tarsus in Cilicia, of Benjamite parents, about the beginning of the first century; a Pharisee in faith; a tentmaker by trade

(Phil. 3:5; Acts 18:3). Studied law with Gamaliel at Jerusalem; persecuted early Christians; converted near Damascus (Acts 5:34; 7:58). Commissioned an apostle to the Gentiles (Acts 36:13–20). Carried the Gospel to Asia Minor, Greece, and Rome. Author of fourteen epistles, amplifying the Christian faith.

Pay/Payeth: To buy or make a purchase.
p double unto his neighbour
. . .Exod. 22:9
sell the oil, and p. . .2 Kings 4:7
wicked borroweth, and p'eth not
. . .Ps. 37:21
your master p tribute? . . .
Matt. 17:24
till he should p all. . .Matt. 18:34

Pavilion: Movable tent or dwelling. Applied to tabernacle, booth, den, etc. (1 Kings 20:12; Ps. 18:11; Jer. 43:10).

Peace: Harmony and accord; a gift of God to His people.
bless his people with p. . .Ps. 29:11
keep him in perfect p. . .Isa. 26:3
P, p; when there is no p. . .Jer. 6:14
p, good will toward men. . .
Luke 2:14
P I leave with you. . .John 14:27
we have p with God. . .Rom. 5:1
p of God, which passeth. . .Phil. 4:7
See *Harmony; Peacemakers.*

Peacemakers: Believers who cultivate peace and harmony in all their relationships.
Blessed are the p. . .Matt. 5:9
have peace one with another
. . .Mark 9:50
live peaceably with all men. . .
Rom. 12:18
preparation of the gospel of
peace. . .Eph. 6:15
See *Peace.*

Peer Pressure: The temptation to "follow the crowd."
Depart from evil, and do good
. . .Ps. 34:14
companion of all them that fear
thee. . .Ps. 119:63
a companion of fools. . .Prov. 13:20
Whoso is partner with a thief
. . .Prov. 29:24
ye ought to walk and to please
God. . .1 Thess. 4:1
See *Pleasing God.*

Peniel: Place beyond the Jordan River where Jacob wrestled with an angel (Gen. 32:30). Penuel (Judg. 8:17; 1 Kings 12:25).

Penny: The Roman silver denarius. The Greek silver drachma was a corresponding coin (Matt. 20:2; 22:19–21; Mark 6:37; Luke 20:24).

Pentateuch: Greek name for the first five O.T. books, or books of Moses. Called Torah, "the law," by Hebrews.

Pentecost: The Hebrew harvest festival, celebrated on the fiftieth day after the Passover, or on the date of the giving of the law at Sinai (Exod. 23:16; 34:22; Lev. 23:12–22; Num. 28). In the Christian church, Pentecost is celebrated seven weeks after Easter, to commemorate the day in Acts 2:1–14.

People of God: People who belong to God and follow His commands.
this day to be his peculiar people
. . .Deut. 26:18
a rest to the p o G. . .Heb. 4:9
an holy nation, a peculiar people
. . .1 Pet. 2:9
are now the p o G. . .1 Pet. 2:10

Perceive: To have insight and understanding.

that ye may p and see. . .1 Sam.
12:17
ye shall see, and shall not p. . .
Matt. 13:14
I p that virtue is gone out. . .Luke
8:46
I p that God is no respecter. . .Acts
10:34
Hereby p we the love of God. . .
1 John 3:16

Perdition: The state of the damned, or those who have rejected Christ.
lost, but the son of p. . .John 17:12
day of judgment and p. . .2 Pet. 3:7
and goeth into p. . .Rev. 17:11
See *Hell.*

Perfect/Perfection: A state of completion or fulfillment.
Noah was a just man and p. . .
Gen. 6:9
The law of the Lord is p. . .Ps. 19:7
Be ye therefore p. . .Matt. 5:48
acceptable, and p, will of God. . .
Rom. 12:2
when that which is p is come. . .
1 Cor. 13:10
made p in weakness. . .2 Cor. 12:9
p in Christ Jesus. . .Col. 1:28
let us go on unto p'ion. . .Heb. 6:1
p love casteth out fear. . .1 John
4:18

Perga: A city of Pamphylia (Acts 13:13).

Pergamos: A city of Mysia, in Asia Minor, celebrated for its library which was transferred to Alexandria. Seat of one of the "seven churches" of Asia Minor (Rev. 1:11; 2:12–17).

Perish: KJV word for *die.*
the ungodly shall p. . .Ps. 1:6
is no vision, the people p. . .
Prov. 29:18
shall p with the sword. . .
Matt. 26:52

not p, but have eternal life. . .
John 3:15
though our outward man p. . .
2 Cor. 4:16
not willing that any should p. . .
2 Pet. 3:9

Persecute/Persecuted/Persecution: Oppression and mistreatment of believers because of their faith in Christ.
wicked in his pride doth p. . .
Ps. 10:2
p'd for righteousness' sake. . .
Matt. 5:10
use you, and p you. . .Matt. 5:44
If they have p'd me. . .John 15:20
I am Jesus whom thou p'st. . .
Acts 9:5
distress, or p'ion, or famine. . .
Rom. 8:35
P'd, but not forsaken. . .2 Cor. 4:9
p'ion for the cross of Christ. . .Gal.
6:12
See *Oppression; Persecute/Persecuted/ Persecution.*

Perseverance: Persistence or endurance in spite of difficult circumstances.
with all p and supplication. . .Eph.
6:18
let us run with patience. . .Heb. 12:1
Blessed is the man that endureth
. . .James 1:12
we count them happy which
endure. . .James 5:11
See *Endure/Endureth; Patience/Patient/ Patiently.*

Persia: Originally the country around the head of the Persian Gulf; afterward, the great empire, including all western Asia and parts of Europe and Africa. Reached its height under Cyrus, 486–485 BC. Conquered by Alexander the Great, 330 BC (Ezek. 38:5; 2 Chron. 36:20–23; Ezek. 1:8).

Perversion: Confusion or moral corruption.

they have wrought confusion
...Lev. 20:12
them over to a reprobate mind
...Rom. 1:28
defile themselves with mankind
...1 Tim. 1:10
going after strange flesh...Jude 1:7

Pestilence: Calamities and plagues (Exod. 9:14; 11:1; 1 Kings 8:37).

Peter: Simon, or Simeon; son of Jonas (Matt. 16:17; Acts 15:14). A fisherman, resident of Capernaum (Matt. 8:14); called by Jesus (Matt. 4:18–20); name changed to Peter (John 1:42); Founder of Christian church among the Jews (Acts 2); spokesman of the apostles (Acts 10); author of two epistles; probably a martyr at Rome.

Pharaoh: General name of Egyptian kings. Only a few are definitely named in the Bible. Several are alluded to (Gen. 12:15; Exod. 1:81; 1 Chron. 4:18; 1 Kings 11:18–22; 2 Kings 18:21; Jer. 37:5–8).

Pharisee/Pharisees: A Jewish sect, strictly orthodox in religion, and politically opposed to foreign supremacy (Matt. 23:23–33; Luke 18:9–14).
the P's were offended...Matt. 15:12
beware of the leaven of the P's
...Matt. 16:6
P's, named Nicodemus...John 3:1
P, named Gamaliel...Acts 5:34
P, the son of a P...Acts 23:6
See *Legalism*.

Philadelphia: A city of Lydia in Asia Minor and seat of one of the "seven churches" of Asia (Rev. 1:11; 3:7–13).

Philemon: A Christian convert at Colosse in Phrygia, to whom Paul wrote an epistle during his captivity at Rome, in favor of Onesimus, Philemon's servant.

Philip: 1. One of the twelve apostles of Jesus (Matt. 10:3; Mark 3:18; Luke 6:14). 2. The evangelist and deacon, resident at Caesarea, and preacher throughout Samaria (Acts 6:5). 3. The tetrarch. 4. Husband of Herodias (Matt. 14:3).

Philippi: City in Macedonia, founded by Philip II, twelve miles from the port of Neapolis. Paul founded a vigorous church there (Acts 16; 20:1–6).

Philistia: The plain and coastal country in southwestern Palestine that gave its name to Palestine (Ps. 60:8; 87:4; 108:9).

Phinehas: 1. Chief of the Korhite Levites, and high priest (Exod. 6:25; Num. 25:6–15). 2. Wicked son of Eli (1 Sam. 1:3; 2:34; 14:3).

Phoenicia: The small coastal country north of Palestine, noted for its commercial enterprise, learning, and skill in arts. Included in the Land of Promise but never conquered (Josh. 13:4–6). David and Solomon employed its sailors and artisans (2 Sam. 5:11; 1 Kings 5). Phenicia (Acts 21:2). Phenice (Acts 11:19). In O.T., referred to as Tyre and Sidon, or coasts of Tyre and Sidon.

Phrygia: An undefined section of Asia Minor, from which several Roman provinces were formed (Acts 2:10; 16:6; 18:23).

Physician/Physicians: A specialist in medicine and healing.
ye are all p's of no value...Job 13:4

is there no p there? . . .Jer. 8:22
whole need not a p. . .Luke 5:31
Luke, the beloved p. . .Col. 4:14
See *Heal.*

Piety: See *Godliness.*

Pilate: Pontius Pilate (Matt. 27:2). Sixth Roman procurator of Judea, AD 26–36. Official residence at Caesarea, with judicial visits to other places. Christ was brought before him at Jerusalem for judgment. He found no guilt in Jesus, but lost his moral courage in the presence of the mob. Eventually banished to Gaul (Luke 23:1–7; John 18:27–40; 19).

Pisgah: The high place in Moab where Moses viewed the Promised Land (Num. 21:20; Deut. 3:27; 4:49; 34:1).

Pisidia: A province of Asia Minor, with Antioch as its capital. Twice visited by the apostle Paul (Acts 13:14; 14:21–24).

Pitch: Asphalt or bitumen, found in the Dead Sea region. Used for mortar, cement, caulk, etc., (Gen. 6:14; 11:3; Exod. 2:3; Isa. 34:9).

Pity: See *Compassion.*

Plague: A widespread disease (Lev. 13:2–8; 26:25). Any calamitous visitation (Mark 5:29; Luke 7:21). The judgments of God on Egypt are called plagues (Exod. 7–12).

Pleasing God: Engaging in behavior that honors God.
This also shall please the Lord
. . .Ps. 69:31
in the flesh cannot please God
. . .Rom. 8:8

well pleasing unto the Lord. . .
Col. 3:20
ought to walk and to please God
. . .1 Thess. 4:1

Pleasure/Pleasures: Sensual gratification.
at thy right hand there are p's
. . .Ps. 16:11
thou that art given to p's. . .Isa. 47:8
and p's of this life. . .Luke 8:14
lovers of p's. . .2 Tim. 3:4

Plenty: A state of abundance; having more than enough.
seven years of great p. . .Gen. 41:29
in p of justice. . .Job 37:23
thy barns be filled with p. . .
Prov. 3:10
shall have p of bread. . .Prov. 28:19

Pollution: See *Ecology.*

Poor, the: People who have few material possessions and may even lack the basic essentials of life.
p of thy people may eat. . .
Exod. 23:11
p shall never cease. . .Deut. 15:11
Defend the p and fatherless. . .
Ps. 82:3
He that oppresseth the p. . .
Prov. 14:31
a strength to the p. . .Isa. 25:4
have the p always with you. . .
Matt. 26:11
See *Beggar/Begging; Give/Given/Giveth.*

Popularity: The state of being held in high esteem by others.
despise me shall be lightly
esteemed. . .1 Sam. 2:30
regardeth the rich. . .Job 34:19
we did esteem him stricken. . .
Isa. 53:4

Pornography: Materials that depict erotic behavior and stimulate sexual impulses.

rejoice with the wife of thy youth
. . .Prov. 5:18
lusts of their own hearts. . .
Rom. 1:24
Let not sin therefore reign. . .
Rom. 6:12
not fulfil the lust of the flesh. . .
Gal. 5:16

Possession by Demons: See *Demon Possession.*

Possession/Possessions/Possessing:
Ownership of material objects.
for an everlasting p. . .Gen. 48:4
for he had great p's. . .Matt. 19:22
sold their p's. . .Acts 2:45
and yet p'ing all things. . .
2 Cor. 6:10

Potiphar: Captain of Pharaoh's guard (Gen. 37:36; 39).

Potsherd: A piece of broken pottery (Prov. 26:23).

Potter, God as: A title of God that demonstrates His ability to shape us as He desires.
esteemed as the p's clay. . .
Isa. 29:16
the clay, and thou our p. . .Isa. 64:8
cannot I do with you as this p?
. . .Jer. 18:6
p power over the clay. . .Rom. 9:21

Potter's Field: The burial ground for strangers bought with the money that Judas accepted to betray Jesus (Matt. 27:7).

Pound: A weight; the maneh (1 Kings 10:17; Ezek. 2:69; Neh. 7:71). One-sixtieth of a Grecian talent (Luke 19:13–27).

Poverty: See *Poor, the.*

Power, God's: The Lord's unlimited strength.
The Father's power
God is my strength and p. . .
2 Sam. 22:33
p and a stretched out arm. . .
2 Kings 17:36
redeemed by thy great p. . .
Neh. 1:10
his p who can understand? . . .
Job 26:14
God exalteth by his p. .Job 36:22
made the earth by his p. . .Jer. 10:12
slow to anger, and great in p. . .
Nah. 1:3
Christ's power
All p is given unto me. . .Matt. 28:18
his word was with p. . .Luke 4:32
p over all flesh. . .John 17:2
p of our Lord Jesus Christ. . .
1 Cor. 5:4
The Holy Spirit's power
in the p of the Spirit. . .Luke 4:14
p of the Spirit of God. . .Rom. 15:19

Power, Human: Physical strength and influence.
ye shall have no p to stand. . .
Lev. 26:37
p to become the sons . . .John 1:12
ye shall receive p. . .Acts 1:8
p which the Lord hath given . . .
2 Cor. 13:10

Praetorium: The court, hearing hall, and judgment hall of a Roman governor (Matt. 27:27; Mark 15:16; John 18:28; Acts 23:35).

Praise/Praises/Praised: To exalt the Lord and count Him worthy of our obedience.
who is worthy to be p'd. . .
2 Sam. 22:4
sing p's unto thy name. . .Ps. 18:49
heaven and earth p him. . .
Ps. 69:34
p thy great and terrible name
. . .Ps. 99:3
Lord's name is to be p'd. . .Ps. 113:3

Pray/Prayer: To offer reverent petitions to God.

ceasing to p for you. . .1 Sam. 12:23
hear thou in heaven their p'er. . .
1 Kings 8:45
morning will I direct my p'er. . .
Ps. 5:3
p'er of the upright is his delight
. . .Prov. 15:8
house of p'er for all people. . .
Isa. 56:7
p for them which despitefully
. . .Matt. 5:44
manner therefore p ye. . .Matt. 6:9
every thing by p'er and
supplication. . .Phil. 4:6
P without ceasing. . .1 Thess. 5:17
p'er of faith shall save the sick
. . .James 5:15
See *Devotions; Word of God.*

Preach/Preached/Preaching : To proclaim the truths of the Gospel.

p good tidings unto the meek
. . .Isa. 61:1
p'ing the gospel of the kingdom
. . .Matt. 4:23
foolishness of p'ing. . .1 Cor. 1:21
But we p Christ crucified. . .
1 Cor. 1:23
For we p not ourselves. . .
2 Cor. 4:5
p'ed unto the spirits in prison. . .
1 Pet. 3:19
See *Witness/Witnessing.*

Predestinate/Predestinated: God's plan of salvation of those who choose to obey Him.

p, them he also called. . .Rom. 8:30
Having p'd us unto. . .Eph. 1:5
p'd according to the purpose. . .
Eph. 1:11
See *Election; Foreknowledge of God; Sovereignty of God.*

Premarital Sex: See *Adultery; Fornication/Fornications; Living Together; Marriage/Marry.*

Presence of God: The Lord's nearness to His people.

at the presence of the Lord. . .
1 Chron. 16:33
went forth from the presence of
the Lord. . .Job 1:12
perish at the p o G. . .Ps. 68:2
stand in the p o G. . .Luke 1:19

Pride: Arrogance, vanity, or conceit.

break the p of your power. . .
Lev. 26:19
wicked in his p doth persecute
. . .Ps. 10:2
P goeth before destruction. . .
Prov. 16:18
those that walk in p. . .Dan. 4:37
and the p of life. . .1 John 2:16

Priesthood of Believers: The doctrine that each believer has direct access to God through Jesus Christ and, consequently, a ministry to perform on His behalf.

kingdom of priests, and an holy
nation. . .Exod. 19:6
veil of the temple was rent. . .
Matt. 27:51
the Spirit is given to every man. . .
1 Cor. 12:7
And he gave some, apostles
. . .Eph. 4:11
one mediator between God and
men. . .1 Tim. 2:5
we have a great high priest. . .
Heb. 4:14
royal priesthood, an holy nation
. . .1 Pet. 2:9
they shall be priests of God. . .
Rev. 20:6

Prince/Princes: A civil ruler; a title applied to Christ.

The P of Peace. . .Isa. 9:6
p's also shall worship. . .Isa. 49:7
unto the Messiah the P. . .Dan. 9:25
killed the P of life . . .Acts 3:15
p of the kings of the earth. . .
Rev. 1:5
See *Government; Ruler/Rulers.*

Prisoner/Prisoners: A place of confinement for lawbreakers.
>The Lord looseth the p's. . .
>>Ps. 146:7
>notable p, called Barabbas. . .
>>Matt. 27:16
>the p's heard them. . .Acts 16:25
>p of Jesus Christ. . .Eph. 3:1

See *Captive/Captives; Captivity.*

Proconsul: A Roman official, beneath a consul, who exercised authority in a province. Appointed by the Roman senate (Acts 13:7; 19:38).

Procrastination: See *Idle/Idleness.*

Profane/Profanity: To treat what is holy as common.
>p the name of thy God. . .Lev. 19:12
>His mouth is full of cursing. . .
>>Ps. 10:7
>mouth is full of cursing. . .Rom. 3:14
>shun p and vain babblings. . .
>>2 Tim. 2:16

See *Curse/Cursing.*

Profit/Profitable/Profited/Profiteth: Gain or increase in value.
>What p hath a man. . .Eccles. 1:3
>For what is a man p'ed. . .
>>Matt. 16:26
>charity, it p'eth me nothing. . .
>>1 Cor. 13:3
>bodily exercise p'eth little. . .
>>1 Tim. 4:8
>p'able for doctrine. . .2 Tim. 3:16

Prognosticator: A conjurer and fortune-teller who claimed to receive direction from the heavenly bodies (Isa. 47:13).

Promise/Promised/Promises: A pledge or guarantee, particularly of some blessing from the Lord.
>*Divine promises*
>God of thy fathers hath p'd. . .
>>Deut. 6:3

doth his p fail for evermore? . . .
>>Ps. 77:8
>p of the Holy Ghost. . .Acts 2:33
>Having therefore these p's. . .
>>2 Cor. 7:1
>not slack concerning his p. . .
>>2 Pet. 3:9
>p'd us, even eternal life. . .
>>1 John 2:25
>*Human promises*
>which thou hast p'd. . .Deut. 23:23
>he p'd with an oath. . .Matt. 14:7

See *Promised Land.*

Promised Land: The territory that God promised to Abraham and his descendants.
>unto a land that I will shew thee
>>. . .Gen. 12:1
>I will make of thee a great nation
>>. . .Gen. 12:2
>seed will I give this land. . .Gen. 12:7
>bring thee again into this land
>>. . .Gen. 28:15
>the land which I gave Abraham
>>. . .Gen. 35:12
>sojourned in the land of promise
>>. . .Heb. 11:9

See *Promise/Promised/Promises.*

Proof/Proofs: Evidence that compels acceptance.
>by many infallible p's. . .Acts 1:3
>the p of your love. . .2 Cor. 8:24
>make full p of thy ministry. . .
>>2 Tim. 4:5

Prophecy/Prophecies: The prediction of future events.
>whether p, let us prophesy. . .
>>Rom. 12:6
>though I have the gift of p. . .
>>1 Cor. 13:2
>p'ies, they shall fail. . .1 Cor. 13:8
>words of the book of this p. . .
>>Rev. 22:19

Prophet/Prophets: One who tells the future under God's inspiration (Matt. 23:34). The prophetic order included political as well as spiritual advisers. The books of seventeen prophets appear in the O.T. Christ is the preeminent and eternal prophet (Luke 24:27, 44).

Lord's people were p's. . .
Num. 11:29
A p is not without honour. . .
Matt. 13:57
false p's shall rise. . .Matt. 24:11
p of the Highest. . .Luke 1:76
apostles; and some, p's. . .Eph. 4:11

Propitiation: The process by which sins are nullified or covered.

God hath set forth to be a p. . .
Rom. 3:25
he is the p for our sins. . .1 John 2:2
his Son to be the p. . .1 John 4:10
See *Finished Work of Christ.*

Proselyte: A convert to the Jewish faith. "Stranger" in O.T. (Deut. 10:18–19; Matt. 23:15; Acts 13:43).

Prosperity: Economic well-being; thriving materially.

spend their days in p. . .Job 36:11
saw the p of the wicked. . .Ps. 73:3
In the day of p be joyful. . .
Eccles. 7:14

Prostitution: See *Harlot/Harlots.*

Protection: Being shielded from danger.
my rock, and my fortress. . .
2 Sam. 22:2
made an hedge about him. . .
Job 1:10
The Lord is good, a strong hold
. . .Nah. 1:7

Proverb: A wise utterance or saying (Num. 21:27). The proverbs, collected and poetically arranged by Solomon, or by his authority, make up the twentieth O.T. book.

Prudent: To have discernment, wisdom, or understanding.

p't are crowned with knowledge
. . .Prov. 14:18
he that regardeth reproof is p't
. . .Prov. 15:5
heart of the p't getteth knowledge
. . .Prov. 18:15
things from the wise and p't
. . .Matt. 11:25

Publican: Gatherer of public revenue; tax collector, abhorred by the Jews (Matt. 18:17; Luke 3:12–13; 19:2).

Punish/Punished/Punishment: To penalize for a crime or wrongful act.

p'ment is greater. . .Gen. 4:13
God hast p'ed us less. . .Ezra 9:13
wrath shall suffer p'ment. . .
Prov. 19:19
p you according to the fruit. . .
Jer. 21:14
go away into everlasting p'ment
. . .Matt. 25:46

Purification: A ritualistic form and sanitary precaution among the Israelites (Lev. 14:4–32; Mark 7:3–4; John 11:55).

Purim: The Jewish festival commemorating the preservation of the Jews in Persia. Celebrated yearly on the fourteenth and fifteenth day of the month Adar (Esther 3:7; 9:20–32).

Purpose/Purposed: God's determination to work His will.

time to every p under the heaven. . .
Eccles. 3:1
Lord of hosts hath p'd. . .Isa. 14:27
called according to his p. . .
Rom. 8:28
predestinated according to the p
. . .Eph. 1:11
according to his own p and grace
. . .2 Tim. 1:9

Q

Quarrel: A ground of dispute or verbal argument.

> he seeketh a q against me. . .
> 2 Kings 5:7
> man have a q against any. . .
> Col. 3:13

See *Contention/Contentions/Contentious; Murmur/Murmured/Murmurers/ Murmurings.*

Quaternion: A Roman guard of four soldiers, two of whom watched prisoners within the door, and two who watched the door outside (Acts 12:4–10).

Queen: A female ruler or the wife or mother of a king.

> when the q of Sheba heard. . .
> 1 Kings 10:1
> Vashti the q made a feast. . .
> Esther 1:9
> the king saw Esther the q. . .
> Esther 5:2
> Candace q of the Ethiopians
> . . .Acts 8:27

Queen of Heaven: The moon, worshipped as Astoreth or Astarte by disobedient Israelites Hebrews (Jer. 7:18; 44:17–25).

Quench: To extinguish or snuff out.

> that thou q not the light of Israel
> . . .2 Sam. 21:17
> Many waters cannot q love. . .
> Song of Sol. 8:7
> smoking flax shall he not q. . .
> Isa. 42:3
> Q not the Spirit. . .1 Thess. 5:19

Quiver: A case or cover for arrows (Gen. 27:3; Job 39:23).

R

Rabbi: A title of respect applied to Hebrew doctors and teachers. Applied also to priests and to Christ (Matt. 23:7; Mark 9:5; John 1:38). "Rabboni" (John 20:16).

Raca: A term of contempt and reproach (Matt. 5:22).

Rachel: Daughter of Laban, wife of Jacob, and mother of Joseph and Benjamin (Gen. 29–35).

Rahab: 1. The harlot of Jericho who hid the Israelite spies (Josh. 2:1–21; 6:17–25; Ruth 4:21; Matt. 1:5). 2. Symbolic term for Egypt, implying insolence and violence (Ps. 89:10; Isa. 51:9).

Rainbow: A sign of the covenant that the earth would not again be destroyed by water (Gen. 9:12–17).

Ram: 1. A male sheep (Gen. 22:13). 2. The battering ram for breaking down gates and walls (Ezek. 4:2; 21:22).

Ransom: To redeem or buy.

> give every man a r for his soul
> . . .Exod. 30:12
> to give his life a r for many. . .
> Matt. 20:28
> Who gave himself a r for all. . .
> 1 Tim. 2:6

Rape: The crime of forced sexual relations.

> lay with her, and defiled her. . .
> Gen. 34:2
> knew her, and abused her. . .
> Judg. 19:25
> forced her, and lay with her. . .
> 2 Sam. 13:14

Reaping/Sowing: The biblical concept of repayment in kind.
> sow in tears shall reap in joy. . .
> Ps. 126:5
> soweth iniquity shall reap vanity
> . . .Prov. 22:8
> shall reap the whirlwind. . .
> Hosea 8:7
> sow not, neither do they reap
> . . .Matt. 6:26
> soweth sparingly shall reap. . .
> 2 Cor. 9:6

Rebekah: Wife of Isaac and mother of Jacob and Esau (Gen. 22:23; 24–28; 49:31).

Rebel/Rebelled/Rebellion/Rebellious: To disobey one in authority, particularly the authority of the Lord.
> then ye r'led against the
> commandment. . .Deut. 9:23
> a stubborn and r'lious son. . .
> Deut. 21:18
> disobedient, and r'led against
> thee. . .Neh. 9:26
> those that r against the light. . .
> Job 24:13
> An evil man seeketh only r'lion
> . . .Prov. 17:11
> Woe to the r'lious children. . .
> Isa. 30:1

Rebuke: To criticize sharply.
> O Lord, r me not in thine anger
> . . .Ps. 6:1
> Open r is better. . .Prov. 27:5
> hear the r of the wise. . .Eccles. 7:5
> As many as I love, I r. . .Rev. 3:19

Recompense: To pay back in kind.
> The Lord r thy work. . .Ruth 2:12
> the labourer is worthy of his hire
> . . .Luke 10:7
> R to no man evil for evil. . .Rom.
> 12:17

Reconcile/Reconciled/Reconciling: To bring opposing parties or people

together.
> be r'd to thy brother. . .Matt. 5:24
> we were r'd to God. . .Rom. 5:10
> be the r'ing of the world. . .
> Rom. 11:15
> hath r'd us to himself by Jesus
> Christ. . .2 Cor. 5:18
> r all things unto himself. . .Col. 1:20

See *Finished Work of Christ.*

Recover/Recovering: To regain or take back to a normal position.
> he would r him of his leprosy. . .
> 2 Kings 5:3
> so wilt thou r me. . .Isa. 38:16
> r'ing of sight to the blind. . .
> Luke 4:18

See *Heal.*

Redeem/Redeemed: In O.T., buying back a forfeited estate. Metaphorically, freeing from bondage (Exod. 6:6; Isa. 43:1). In N.T., rescuing or ransoming from sin and its consequences (Matt. 20:28; Gal. 3:13; 1 Pet. 1:18).
> the Lord thy God r'ed thee. . .
> Deut. 15:15
> r us for thy mercies' sake. . .
> Ps. 44:26
> Let the r'ed of the Lord. . .Ps. 107:2
> r'ed us to God by thy blood. . .
> Rev. 5:9

Redeemer: A title of God and Jesus that emphasizes their work of redemption.
> I know that my r liveth. . .Job 19:25
> Lord, my strength, and my r. . .
> Ps. 19:14
> his r the Lord of hosts. . .Isa. 44:6
> saith the Lord thy R. . .Isa. 54:8
> art our father, our r. . .Isa. 63:16

Redemption: God's provision of salvation for sinners.
> He sent r unto his people. . .
> Ps. 111:9
> for your r draweth nigh. . .
> Luke 21:28
> r that is in Christ Jesus. . .
> Rom. 3:24

we have r through his blood. . .
    Col. 1:14
having obtained eternal r for us
    . . .Heb. 9:12
See *Finished Work of Christ.*

Red Sea: The arm of the Gulf of Aden which separates Egypt from Arabia. "The sea" (Exod. 14:2, 9, 16, 21, 28). "Egyptian sea" (Isa. 11:15). "Sea of *Suph*," "weedy or reedy sea," translated, "Red Sea" (Exod. 10:19; Num. 21:4).

Refreshed/Refresheth/Refreshing, Spiritual: To restore one's strength.
    he rested, and was r. . .Exod. 31:17
    he r'eth the soul. . .Prov. 25:13
    times of r'ing shall come. . .
        Acts 3:19

Refuge, Cities of: The six Levitical cities set apart for the temporary escape of involuntary manslayers (Num. 35:6, 11–32; Deut. 19:7–9; Josh. 20:2–8).

Refuge, Spiritual: Safety and security under the Lord's protection.
    The eternal God is thy r. . .
        Deut. 33:27
    He is my r and my fortress. . .
        Ps. 91:2
    the rock of my r. . .Ps. 94:22
    r in the day of affliction. . .Jer. 16:19

Regeneration: The renovation of the world at and after the second coming of Christ (Matt. 19:28). The new birth from the Holy Spirit (Titus 3:5).
    Except a man be born again
        . . .John 3:3
    alive unto God through Jesus
        . . .Rom. 6:11
    by the washing of r. . .Titus 3:5
See *Born Again; New Life; Salvation.*

Rehoboam: Son of Solomon (1 Kings 11:43; 14:21) and successor to his father's throne, 975–958 BC. During his reign, the ten tribes, under Jeroboam, revolted and set up the kingdom of Israel. Shishak of Egypt captured Jerusalem from him (1 Kings 14:21–31).

Reject/Rejected: To refuse to accept.
    they have r'ed me. . .1 Sam. 8:7
    I have r'ed him from reigning. . .
        1 Sam. 16:1
    despised and r'ed of men. . .
        Isa. 53:3
    ye r the commandment of God
        . . .Mark 7:9
    The stone which the builders r'ed
        . . .Luke 20:17

Rejoice/Rejoiced: To be glad and joyful about one's circumstances or the Lord's blessings.
    glad and r in thy mercy. . .Ps. 31:7
    r and be glad in it. . .Ps. 118:24
    saw the star, they r'd. . .Matt. 2:10
    many shall r at his birth. . .Luke 1:14
    R in the Lord always. . .Phil. 4:4

Remember: To recall some event or feeling from the past.
    R the sabbath day. . .Exod. 20:8
    R his marvellous works. . .
        1 Chron. 16:12
    R now thy Creator. . .Eccles. 12:1
    I will r their sin no more. . .
        Jer. 31:34

Remission: A release from guilt or penalty. The word also carries the idea of making payment for a demand.
    repentance for the r of sins
        . . .Mark 1:4
    r of sins should be preached
        . . .Luke 24:47
    Jesus Christ for the r of sins
        . . .Acts 2:38
    shedding of blood is no r. . .
        Heb. 9:22

Remnant: A small group of God's people who remain faithful to Him.
    The r shall return. . .Isa. 10:21
    gather the r of my flock. . .Jer. 23:3
    Yet will I leave a r. . .Ezek. 6:8
    a r shall be saved. . .Rom. 9:27

Renew/Renewed/Renewing: To restore or revive.
    r a right spirit within me. . .Ps. 51:10
    r our days as of old. . .Lam. 5:21
    be r'ed in the spirit. . .Eph. 4:23
    r'ing of the Holy Ghost. . .Titus 3:5
See *Revive.*

Repentance: Turning from sin to acceptance of God's will.
    fruits meet for r. . .Matt. 3:8
    r and remission of sins. . .
        Luke 24:47
    to the Gentiles granted r. . .
        Acts 11:18
    godly sorrow worketh r. . .
        2 Cor. 7:10
See *Believe/Believed/Believeth/Believest; Coming to Christ; Conversion; Salvation.*

Reproach/Reproached: To rebuke or disapprove.
    the r of the foolish. . .Ps. 39:8
    Remove from me r and contempt
        . . .Ps. 119:22
    lest he fall into r. . .1 Tim. 3:7
    bearing his r. . .Heb. 13:13
    r'ed for the name of Christ. . .
        1 Pet. 4:14
See *Humiliation.*

Reproof/Reproofs: Criticism for a fault.
    in whose mouth are no r's. . .
        Ps. 38:14
    they despised all my r. . .Prov. 1:30
    he that hateth r is brutish. . .
        Prov. 12:1

Reputation: Held in high esteem by others.
    good name is better than precious
        . . .Eccles. 7:1
    in r for wisdom and honour
        . . .Eccles. 10:1
    But made himself of no r. . .Phil. 2:7

Rest: To cease from work.
    seventh day thou shalt r. . .
        Exod. 23:12
    seventh year shall be a sabbath of
        r. . .Lev. 25:4
    find r for your souls. . .Jer. 6:16
    I will give you r. . .Matt. 11:28
    shall not enter into my r. . .Heb. 3:11

Restitution: To repay a person for a property loss or a wrongful action committed against him.
    he should make full r. . .Exod. 22:3
    r unto the owner thereof. . .
        Exod. 22:12
    according to his substance shall
        the r. . .Job 20:18

Restore/Restoreth: To give back or return to a previous state.
    He r'th my soul. . .Ps. 23:3
    R unto me the joy. . .Ps. 51:12
    For I will r health unto thee. . .
        Jer. 30:17
    I r him fourfold. . .Luke 19:8

Resurrection: The rising again from the dead (Ps. 16:10–11; Matt. 16:21; 20:19; Acts 2:31).
    that there is no r. . .Matt. 22:23
    the r of the just. . .Luke 14:14
    r at the last day. . .John 11:24
    say that there is no r. . .Acts 23:8
    they might obtain a better r. . .
        Heb. 11:35
See *Resurrection of Christ.*

Resurrection of Christ: Jesus' restoration to life after His death on the cross.
    I am the r, and the life. . .John 11:25
    spake of the r of Christ. . .Acts 2:31
    witness of the r of the Lord Jesus. . .
        Acts 4:33
    in the likeness of his r. . .Rom. 6:5
    the power of his r. . .Phil. 3:10

r of Jesus Christ from the dead
. . .1 Pet. 1:3
See *Resurrection*.

Retirement: The final years of life after one's working career has ended.
in the time of old age. . .Ps. 71:9
when I am old and grayheaded
. . .Ps. 71:18
the crown of old men. . .Prov. 17:6
she was of a great age. . .Luke 2:36
never leave thee, nor forsake thee
. . .Heb. 13:5

Reuben: Eldest son of Jacob and Leah (Gen. 29:32). Lost his birthright through crime (Gen. 35:22; 49:3–4). Tribe numerous and pastoral, settled east of the Jordan River (Num. 1:20–21; Josh. 13:15–23).

Revelation/Revelations: Revealing truth through divine agency or by supernatural means (2 Cor. 12:1–7).
speak to you either by r. . .
1 Cor. 14:6
visions and r's of the Lord. . .
2 Cor. 12:1
the r of Jesus Christ. . .Gal. 1:12
spirit of wisdom and r. . .Eph. 1:17

Revelation, Book of: Last of N.T. books; written by the apostle John about AD 95–97, probably at Ephesus. It is a record of his inspired visions while a prisoner on the island of Patmos. It presents a prophetic panorama of church history to the end of time.

Revenge: See *Avenge/Avenger; Vengeance*.

Revile/Reviled/Revilers: To condemn or abuse verbally.
when men shall r you. . .Matt. 5:11
crucified with him r'd him. . .
Mark 15:32
nor drunkards, nor r'rs. . .1 Cor. 6:10

Revive: To renew, particularly in a spiritual sense.
Wilt thou not r us again. . .Ps. 85:6
to r the heart of the contrite ones
. . .Isa. 57:15
O Lord, r thy work. . .Hab. 3:2
See *Renew/Renewed/Renewing*.

Reward, Eternal: Eternal life in heaven promised to believers.
your r in heaven. . .Matt. 5:12
away into everlasting punishment
. . .Matt. 25:46
the r of the inheritance. . .Col. 3:24
the author of eternal salvation
. . .Heb. 5:9
See *Eternity; Eternal Life; Heaven/Heavens*.

Rich/Riches: Material goods and earthly treasures.
Lord maketh poor, and maketh r
. . .1 Sam. 2:7
trusteth in his r'es shall fall. . .
Prov. 11:28
Labour not to be r. . .Prov. 23:4
r man glory in his r'es. . .Jer. 9:23
r man shall hardly enter. . .
Matt. 19:23
woe unto you that are r! . . .
Luke 6:24
is not r toward God. . .Luke 12:21

Right: Morally correct.
that which is r in his sight. . .
Exod. 15:26
just and r is he. . .Deut. 32:4
statutes of the Lord are r. . .Ps. 19:8
ways of the Lord are r. . .
Hosea 14:9

Righteousness: Moral excellence.
counted it to him for r. . .Gen. 15:6
The Lord executeth r. . .Ps. 103:6
R exalteth a nation. . .Prov. 14:34
hunger and thirst after r. . .
Matt. 5:6
persecuted for r sake. . .Matt. 5:10
follow after r. . .1 Tim. 6:11

Riot/Rioting: To engage in revelry.
> not in r'ing and drunkenness
> . . .Rom. 13:13
> not accused of r or unruly. . .
> Titus 1:6
> to the same excess of r. . .1 Pet. 4:4

Rob/Robber/Robbery: To steal from others.
> R not the poor. . .Prov. 22:22
> Will a man r God? . . .Mal. 3:8
> Now Barabbas was a r'ber. . .
> John 18:40
> thought it not r'bery. . .Phil. 2:6

Rock, God as: A title of God that emphasizes the security He provides for believers.
> the R of his salvation. . .Deut. 32:15
> The Lord is my r. . .2 Sam. 22:2
> my r; in him will I. . .2 Sam. 22:3
> my r, and my fortress. . .Ps. 18:2
> God is the r of my refuge. . .
> Ps. 94:22
> stumblingstone and r of offence
> . . .Rom. 9:33

Roll: The book of ancient times, consisting of long strips of linen, papyrus, or parchment written upon and wrapped on a stick (Isa. 8:1; Ezek. 2:9–10).

Rome/Romans: Located on the Tiber River, fifteen miles from the sea. Founded 752 BC; governed by kings until 509 BC; then by consuls until Augustus Caesar became emperor, in 30 BC. In the Christian era, Rome was the virtual mistress of the civilized world. The empire declined rapidly after removal of the capital to Constantinople by Constantine in AD 328. The Gospel was introduced early among the Romans, but Christians were persecuted until the time of Constantine. Palestine was ruled from Rome by kings, procurators, governors, or proconsuls. Paul wrote his celebrated epistle to the Romans from

Corinth, about AD 58, to show that Jew and Gentile were both subject to sin and in equal need of justification and sanctification.

Ruby: A valuable gem; but the original word is thought to mean "coral" or "pearl" (Job 28:18; Prov. 3:15).

Ruin: Destruction.
> brought his strong holds to r. . .
> Ps. 89:40
> flattering mouth worketh r. . .
> Prov. 26:28
> the r of that house was great
> . . .Luke 6:49

Ruler/Rulers: An official with authority over others.
> r's take counsel together. . .Ps. 2:2
> If a r hearken to lies. . .Prov. 29:12
> brought before r's and kings
> . . .Mark 13:9
> Nicodemus, a r of the Jews. . .
> John 3:1
> against the r's of the darkness
> . . .Eph. 6:12

See *King, Earthly; Prince/Princes.*

Rumour/Rumours: Idle and destructive talk.
> heard a r from the Lord. . .
> Jer. 49:14
> hear of wars and r's of wars
> . . .Matt. 24:6
> r of him went forth. . .Luke 7:17

Ruth: The Moabite wife of Mahlon, then Boaz, and an ancestor of David. Her story appears in the book of Ruth.

S

Sabaoth: A word used usually with Jehovah, "Lord of Hosts"—hosts signifying the powers of earth and heaven (Isa. 1:9; Rom. 9:29; James 4:4).

Sabbath: Rest day, or seventh day of the week (Gen. 2:2–3). Became a Mosaic institution for rest and festal occasions (Exod. 16:23–30; Deut. 5:12–15). Day for consulting prophets (2 Kings 4:23). A day of teaching and joy (Neh. 8:1–12). Among Christians, the day after the Hebrew Sabbath, or seventh day, gradually became the Sabbath, or first day, in commemoration of the resurrection of Christ; thus, "The Lord's Day" (John 20:26; Acts 20:6–11).

> Remember the s day. . .Exod. 20:8
> the seventh day is the s. . .
>   Exod. 20:10
> Lord even of the s day. . .Matt. 12:8
> do well on the s days. . .Matt. 12:12

Sabbath Day's Journey: Travel on the Sabbath was limited (Exod. 16:29). Custom seemed to sanction 2,000 paces from the walls of a city as sufficient for all needs on the day of rest (Acts 1:12).

Sabbatical Year: By the Mosaic code, each seventh year was sacred. The land rested, the poor were entitled to what grew, and debtors were released (Exod. 23:10–11; Lev. 25:2–7; Deut. 15:1–18).

Sackbut: A wind instrument; trombone. But in Dan. 3:5–15, a stringed instrument of triangular shape with from four to twenty strings.

Sackcloth: A coarse, goat-hair cloth used for making sacks and rough garments. The latter were worn next to the skin by mourners and repentants (Gen. 37:34; 43:25; 2 Sam. 3:31; 1 Kings 21:27; 2 Kings 6:30).

Sacrifice/Sacrifices: An atoning offering to God. Sacrificial offerings were numerous, consisting of burnt offering (Lev. 1:1–17); trespass offering (Lev. 7:1–10), and peace-offering (Lev. 7:11–34); the latter also a "freewill" offering. Among Christians, all sacrificial offerings merged in the universal offering of Christ's body (Heb. 9–10).

> to obey is better than s. . .
>   1 Sam. 15:22
> s's of God are a broken. . .Ps. 51:17
> will have mercy, and not s. . .
>   Matt. 9:13
> present your bodies a living s
>   . . .Rom. 12:1
> no more s for sins. . .Heb. 10:26
> offer up spiritual s's. . .1 Pet. 2:5

See *Offering/Offerings.*

Sadducees: A Jewish sect whose chief beliefs were rejection of the divinity of the Mosaic oral law and traditions, rejection of the later O.T. books, but acceptance of the Mosaic teachings, denial of angel and spiritual existence, and immortality of the soul, and belief in the absolute moral freedom of man. Their hatred of Christianity was as bitter as that of the Pharisees (Matt. 3:7; Mark 12:18; Luke 20:27).

Sadness: See *Sorrow/Sorrowed/Sorrows.*

Safe/Safely/Safety: Free from harm or danger.

> dwell in the land in s'ty. . .Lev. 25:18
> only makest me dwell in s'ty. . .
>   Ps. 4:8
> And he led them on s'ly. . .
>   Ps. 78:53
> hearkeneth unto me shall dwell
>   s'ly. . .Prov. 1:33
> multitude of counsellors there is
>   s'ty. . .Prov. 11:14
> runneth into it, and is s. . .
>   Prov. 18:10

Saints: In the O.T., followers of the Lord; in the N.T., everyone who has accepted Jesus as Savior.

fear the Lord, ye his s...Ps. 34:9
is the death of his s...Ps. 116:15
Let the s be joyful...Ps. 149:5
maketh intercession for the s
...Rom. 8:27
For the perfecting of the s...
Eph. 4:12

Salt: A mineral used to season and preserve food.

she became a pillar of s...
Gen. 19:26
by a covenant of s?...
2 Chron. 13:5
unsavoury be eaten without s?
...Job 6:6
the s of the earth...Matt. 5:13
s have lost his saltness...
Mark 9:50
with grace, seasoned with s...
Col. 4:6

Salt Sea: The Dead Sea. "Sea of the plain" (Deut. 4:49); "Salt sea" (Deut. 3:17); "East sea" (Ezek. 47:18); "The sea" (Ezek. 47:8); "Vale of Siddim" (Gen. 14:3). Situated sixteen miles east of Jerusalem; forty-six miles long by ten miles wide; 1,300 feet below the level of the Mediterranean Sea; waters intensely salty; receives waters of the Jordan River from the north; no outlet.

Salvation: A word for both temporal deliverance (Exod. 14:13) and spiritual deliverance (2 Cor. 7:10; Eph. 1:13; Heb. 2:3).

see the s of the Lord...Exod. 14:13
my light and my s...Ps. 27:1
power of God unto s...Rom. 1:16
confession is made unto s...Rom. 10:10
take the helmet of s...Eph. 6:17
work out your own s...Phil. 2:12
if we neglect so great s...Heb. 2:3

See *Born Again; Coming to Christ; Conversion; Eternal Life; Immortal/ Immortality; Knowing God; New Life; Regeneration; Repentance.*

Samaria: 1. Synonymous with the kingdom of Israel, lay to the north of Judah. It varied in size at different times, but in general embraced the territory of the ten revolting tribes on either side of the Jordan River (1 Kings 13:32). Named from its capital, Samaria. In N.T. times, Samaria was one of the three subdivisions of Palestine, lying between Judea on the south and Galilee on the north. 2. Capital of the kingdom of Samaria or Israel, and located thirty miles north of Jerusalem. Founded by Omri, king of Israel, about 925 BC, and called Samaria, after Shemer, from whom he bought the ground (1 Kings 16:23–24). It became a beautiful and strong city and remained the capital until Shalmaneser, the Assyrian, destroyed it and the empire, 721 BC (2 Kings 18:9–12). Herod rebuilt it and restored much of its ancient splendor, naming it Sebaste, in honor of Augustus, who gave it to him. Philip preached the Gospel there (Acts 9:5–9).

Samson: Son of Manoah and judge of Israel for twenty years (Judg. 13:3–25). Noted for his great strength, marvelous exploits, and moral weakness. He married a Philistine woman (Exod. 34:16; Deut. 7:3), whom he deserted (Judg. 16), and then wished to return to (Judg. 15:1–8). The secret of his strength was finally detected by Delilah and he was imprisoned and made blind. He killed himself and numerous enemies by pulling down the pillars of the building in which they were feasting (Judg. 16).

Samuel: Son of Elkanah and Hannah, celebrated Hebrew and last of the judges (1 Sam. 1:19–28). Educated under Eli (1 Sam. 3:4–14) and became his successor in the prophetic office. The people then demanded a king; Samuel anointed Saul as king (1 Sam. 12) and also anointed David, Saul's successor (1 Sam. 16:13). He died at Ramah (1 Sam. 25:1).

Sanballat: A Persian officer in Samaria who opposed Ezra and Nehemiah (Neh. 2:10; 4:1–9; 13:28).

Sanctify/Sanctified/ Sanctification: To prepare or set apart persons or things for holy use (Exod. 13:2). To establish union with Christ by faith (John 17:17); to exercise the graces of knowledge, such as faith, love, repentance, humility, etc., toward God and man (2 Thess. 2:13; 1 Pet. 1:2).

> S yourselves therefore. . .Lev. 20:7
> sabbath day to s it. . .Deut. 5:12
> being s'ied by the Holy Ghost
>   . . .Rom. 15:16
> he might s and cleanse it. . .
>   Eph. 5:26
> will of God, even your s'ication. . .
>   1 Thess. 4:3
> s'ied the people with his own
>   blood. . .Heb. 13:12
> s the Lord God in your hearts. . .
>   1 Pet. 3:15

Sanctuary: A holy or sanctified place (Ps. 20:2). The inner part of the temple in which the ark of the covenant was kept, and which none but the high priest might enter, and he only once a year, on the day of atonement (Lev. 4:6). Any place of public worship of God (Ps. 63:17); heaven (Ps. 102:19); place of refuge (Isa. 8:14).

Sanhedrin: The supreme council of the Jewish nation (Num. 11:16–17). The "great Sanhedrin" was composed of seventy-one priests, scribes, and elders, and presided over by the high priest. The "lesser Sanhedrins" were provincial courts in the towns, and composed of twenty-three members appointed by the great Sanhedrin. Usually "council" in N.T. (Matt. 5:22; Mark 14:55; John 11:47).

Sapphire: A light blue gem, next to the diamond in hardness (Exod. 24:10). Second stone in second row of the high priest's breastplate (Exod. 28:18). A foundation stone of the holy Jerusalem (Rev. 21:19).

Sarah: Wife of Abraham; mother of Isaac (Gen. 11:29; 21:2–3). Name changed from Sarai to Sarah (Gen. 17:15–16). Commended for her faith (Heb. 11:11); and obedience (1 Peter 3:6). Died at the age of 127 (Gen. 23).

Sardis: Capital of Lydia in Asia Minor; once noted for its beauty and wealth, but no longer (Rev. 3:1–6). Seat of one of the seven churches of Asia Minor (Rev. 3:1).

Satan: In O.T., a common noun, meaning "enemy" or "adversary" (1 Sam. 29:4), except in Job 1:6, 12; 2:1; Zech. 3:1, where the word becomes a proper noun, and the spiritual representative of evil. In N.T., chief of the evil spirits; great adversary of man; the devil (Matt. 4:10; 25:41); "the prince of this world;" "the wicked one;" and "the tempter."

> S, Hast thou considered my
>   servant Job. . .Job 2:3
> Get thee behind me, S. . .
>   Matt. 16:23

forty days, tempted of S. . .
Mark 1:13
Then entered S into Judas. . .
Luke 22:3
S hath desired to have you. . .
Luke 22:31
deliver such an one unto S. . .
1 Cor. 5:5
S shall be loosed. . .Rev. 20:7

Saul: 1. A Benjamite, son of Kish, and the first king of Israel. Anointed by Samuel; killed with his sons at Gilboa. His versatile career is described in 1 Samuel 9–31. 2. Hebrew name of the apostle Paul (Acts 13:9).

Save/Saved: To be delivered from sin.
whosoever will s his life. . .Matt.
16:25
world through him might be s'd
. . .John 3:17
name of the Lord shall be s'd
. . .Acts 2:21
For by grace are ye s'd. . .Eph. 2:8
will have all men to be s'd. . .
1 Tim. 2:4
according to his mercy he s'd us
. . .Titus 3:5
can faith s him? . . .James 2:14

Saviour/Saviours: A divine title that emphasizes the work of salvation for sinners.
and my refuge, my s. . .2 Sam. 22:3
beside me there is no s. . .Isa. 43:11
thy S and thy Redeemer. . .
Isa. 49:26
rejoiced in God my S. . .Luke 1:47
Christ, the S of the world. . .
John 4:42
he is the s of the body. . .Eph. 5:23
who is the S of all men. . .
1 Tim. 4:10

Scarlet: A color much prized by an-cients (Exod. 25:4; Prov. 31:21).

Scorn/Scorner/Scornful: Contempt and ridicule.

in the seat of the s'ful. . .Ps. 1:1
a s'er heareth not rebuke. . .
Prov. 13:1
And they laughed him to s. . .
Mark 5:40

Scribe: Hebrew writer who appears to have been at first a court or military official (Exod. 5:6; Judg. 5:14); then secretary or recorder for kings, priests, and prophets (2 Sam. 8:17); and finally a secretary of state, doctor, or teacher (Ezek. 7:6).

Scripture/Scriptures: The sacred writing contained in the Old and New Testaments.
not knowing the s's. . .Matt. 22:29
s was fulfilled, which saith. . .Mark
15:28
that they might understand the s's
. . .Luke 24:45
Search the s's. . .John 5:39
All s is given by inspiration. . .
2 Tim. 3:16
See *Word of God.*

Searching for God: See *Seeking God.*

Seasons of Life: See *Age; Elderly, the; Youth.*

Second Coming of Christ: Christ's return to earth in the end time.
hour your Lord doth come. . .
Matt. 24:42
shall so come in like manner
. . .Acts 1:11
the Lord's death till he come. . .
1 Cor. 11:26
coming of our Lord Jesus Christ
. . .1 Thess. 3:13
the brightness of his coming. . .
2 Thess. 2:8
power and coming of our Lord. . .
2 Pet. 1:16
day of the Lord will come as a
thief. . .2 Pet. 3:10
See *Last Day.*

Secret/Secrets
  s things belong unto the Lord
      . . .Deut. 29:29
  s place of the most High. . .Ps. 91:1
  revealeth the deep and s things
      . . .Dan. 2:22
  God in heaven that revealeth s's
      . . .Dan. 2:28
  thy Father which is in s. . .Matt. 6:6
See *Mystery/Mysteries.*

Security: See *Safe/Safely/Safety.*
  he will not forsake thee. . .Deut.
      4:31
  God is a refuge for us. . .Ps. 62:8
  runneth into it, and is safe. . .
      Prov. 18:10
  I will in no wise cast out. . .
      John 6:37
  never leave thee, nor forsake thee
      . . .Heb. 13:5

Seeking God: Desiring to have fellow-ship with the Lord.
  and pray, and seek my face. . .
      2 Chron. 7:14
  early will I seek thee. . .Ps. 63:1
  seek me early shall find me. . .
      Prov. 8:17
  Seek ye the Lord while he may
      . . .Isa. 55:6
  seek ye first the kingdom. . .
      Matt. 6:33

Selah: A word of frequent occurrence in the Psalms, perhaps meaning an interlude in vocal music (Ps. 9:16; Hab. 3:3, 9, 13).

Self-Control: Disciplined control of one's actions and emotions.
  I have refrained my feet. . .
      Ps. 119:101
  he that refraineth his lips. . .
      Prov. 10:19
  righteousness, temperance, and
      judgment. . .Acts 24:25
  and to temperance patience. . .
      2 Pet. 1:6
See *Self-Denial.*

Self-Denial: Voluntary denial of one's desires.
  let him deny himself, and take. . .
      Matt. 16:24
  denying ungodliness and worldly
      lusts. . .Titus 2:12
See *Self-Control.*

Self-Esteem: A confidence and satisfaction with oneself.
  God created man in his own
      image. . .Gen. 1:27
  Christ died for us. . .Rom. 5:8
  not to think of himself more highly
      . . .Rom. 12:3
  Ye are bought with a price. . .
      1 Cor. 7:23
  loved me, and gave himself for me
      . . .Gal. 2:20
  esteem other better than
      themselves. . .Phil. 2:3

Separate/Separated: To be set apart for service to God.
  s themselves unto the Lord
      . . .Num. 6:2
  S me Barnabas and Saul. . .
      Acts 13:2
  shall be able to s us. . .Rom. 8:39
  be ye s, saith the Lord. . .2 Cor. 6:17

Sepulchre: A tomb (2 Kings 23:16; Isa. 22:16; Matt. 27:60; Mark 16:2).

Seraphim: An order of celestial beings, pictured in Isaiah's vision as surrounding the throne of God (Isa. 6:2–7).

Servant/Servants: One who serves the wants and needs of others.
  nor the s above his lord. . .Matt.
      10:24
  Behold my s. . .Matt. 12:18
  let him be your s. . .Matt. 20:27
  last of all, and s of all. . .Mark 9:35
  No s can serve two masters
      . . .Luke 16:13
  no more a s, but a son. . .Gal. 4:7
See *Bondage; Serve.*

Serve: To give oneself for the benefit of others, particularly the interests of the Lord.

> Lord thy God, and s him. . .Deut. 6:13
> all nations shall s him. . .Ps. 72:11
> s the Lord with gladness. . . Ps. 100:2
> No man can s two masters. . . Matt. 6:24
> by love s one another. . .Gal. 5:13

See *Servant/Servants.*

Shadrach: Babylonian name given to Hananiah (Dan. 1:7–21; 2–3).

Shame: Disgrace or loss of self-respect.

> will ye turn my glory into s? . . . Ps. 4:2
> pride cometh, then cometh s . . .Prov. 11:2
> suffer s for his name. . .Acts 5:41
> glory is in their s. . .Phil. 3:19
> cross, despising the s. . .Heb. 12:2

Sharon: 1. The plain skirting the Mediterranean Sea coast from Judah to Caesarea. It is an extension of the lowlands of Judah and was renowned for its fertility (Acts 9:35). 2. A town or district east of the Jordan River, and perhaps in Gilead (1 Chron. 5:16).

Shekel: A weight for weighing uncoined money, of Assyrian and Babylonian origin. There seem to have been two standards, that of the sanctuary and of the king (Exod. 30:13; 2 Sam. 14:26). Both were about half an ounce. Later, a Jewish silver coin, with bronze half- and quarter-shekels.

Shem: Oldest son of Noah, preserved with his father in the ark (Gen. 5:32). Blessed by Noah for his conduct (Gen. 9:18–27). His descendents are the Hebrews, Arameans, Persians, Assyrians, and Arabians, whose languages are called Semitic.

Shepherd: A highly honorable occupation among the Israelites (Gen. 29:6; 30:29–35; Exod. 2:16–22). Jehovah as (Ps. 80:1); kings as (Ezek. 34:10); Christ as (John 10:11). Also applied to teachers, pastors, and ministers of the Gospel.

Shewbread: Unleavened bread baked in twelve loaves corresponding to the twelve tribes and placed fresh every Sabbath on the golden table of the sanctuary; eaten only by the priests (Exod 25:30; Lev. 24:8). Called "shewbread," "bread of the face," or "bread of the setting before," because it stood continually before the Lord.

Shiloh: 1. A disputed rendering; referred to a town and to the Messiah (Gen. 49:10; Isa. 9:6). 2. A city in Ephraim, midway between Bethel and Shechem. The ark of the covenant remained there for three hundred years, until captured by the Philistines (Josh. 18:1, 8–10; Judg. 21:19–23).

Shining/Glory of God: The bright, physical sign of God's presence.

> glory of the Lord filled. . . Exod. 40:34
> fire came down from heaven. . . 2 Chron. 7:1
> his raiment became s. . .Mark 9:3
> glory of the Lord shone round . . .Luke 2:9

See *Glory.*

Sight: The ability to see, either physically or spiritually.

> pleasant to the s. . .Gen. 2:9
> The blind receive their s. . . Matt. 11:5

received him out of their s. . .
  Acts 1:9
walk by faith, not by s. . .2 Cor. 5:7

Signs: Miracles or events that foretell future events.
  multiply my s and my wonders. . .
    Exod. 7:3
  How great are his s! . . .Dan. 4:3
  Except ye see s and wonders
    . . .John 4:48
  many other s truly did Jesus
    . . .John 20:30
See *Miracle/Miracles.*

Silas: An eminent member of the early Christian church. Called Silvanus in Paul's epistles. Resided at Jerusalem as teacher, and fellow-prisoner with Paul at Philippi (Acts 15:22, 32–34, 40; 17:14; 18:5; 2 Cor. 1:19).

Siloam: 1. A pool at Jerusalem, on the south side, near the opening of the Tyrophean valley into the Kidron valley. Originally a part of the water supply of the city (Neh. 3:15; Isa. 8:6). 2. A tower whose fall killed eighteen men (Luke 13:4).

Simeon: 1. Son of Jacob and Leah (Gen. 29:33). For the crime in Gen. 34:25–30, his father denounced him (Gen. 49:5–7). 2. Son of Judah in genealogy of Christ (Luke 3:30). 3. Simon Peter (Acts 15:14). 4. A man who blessed the child Jesus in the temple (Luke 2:25–35). 5. Simeon Niger (Acts 13:1).

Simon: 1. A native of Samaria and famous sorcerer, who professed Christ for mercenary purposes (Acts 8:9–24). 2. Simon Peter (Matt. 4:18). 3. Simon the Canaanite, or Simon Zelotes, a member of the party of Zealots who

advocated the Jewish ritual, and an apostle (Matt. 10:4). 4. Simon, the brother of Jesus (Matt. 13:55). 5. Simon the Pharisee, in whose house a woman anointed the feet of Jesus (Luke 7:36–50). 6. Simon, the leper of Bethany (Matt. 26:6). 7. Simon the Cyrene, who was compelled to bear Christ's cross (Matt. 27:32). 8. The tanner of Joppa with whom Peter lodged (Acts 9:43). 9. Simon, the father of Judas Iscariot (John 6:71).

Sin: Rebellion against God.
Dangers of sin
s lieth at the door. . .Gen. 4:7
wages of s is death. . .Rom. 6:23
sting of death is s. . .1 Cor. 15:56
Humanity and sin
is without s among you. . .John 8:7
by one man s entered. . .Rom. 5:12
say that we have no s. . .1 John 1:8
Redemption and sin
whose s is covered. . .Ps. 32:1
he bare the s of many. . .Isa. 53:12
remember their s no more. . .
  Jer. 31:34
made him to be s for us. . .
  2 Cor. 5:21
See *Iniquity; Transgression/Transgressions; Trespass.*

Sinai: The peninsula of Sinai lies between the two great arms of the Red Sea: the Gulf of Akaba on the east, and the Gulf of Suez on the west. This region contains the mountain system of Horeb or Sinai. God, Moses, and the burning bush at Sinai (Exod. 3:1–5); Israelites encamped at Sinai (Exod. 19:1–2); law delivered to Moses at Sinai (Exod. 19:3–25).

Sincere/Sincerity: Freedom from pretense or hypocrisy.
  whose spirit there is no guile. . .
    Ps. 32:2
  in whom is no guile! . . .John 1:47

in simplicity and godly s'ity. . .
    2 Cor. 1:12
to prove the s'ity of your love. . .
    2 Cor. 8:8

Single: Not married.
    eunuchs, which have made
        themselves. . .Matt. 19:12
    neither marry, nor are given. . .
        Luke 20:35
    let her remain unmarried. . .
        1 Cor. 7:11
    The unmarried woman careth. . .
        1 Cor. 7:34

Sinner/Sinners: Those who commit sin; all people.
    standeth in the way of s's. . .Ps. 1:1
    wickedness overthroweth the s
        . . .Prov. 13:6
    over one s that repenteth. . .
        Luke 15:7
    be merciful to me a s. . .Luke 18:13
    we were yet s's, Christ died
        . . .Rom. 5:8
See *Sin*.

Sisera: Captain of King Jabin's forces when defeated by Barak. Slain by Jael (Judg. 4–5).

Slander/Slanderers/Slandereth: Malicious and destructive statements against another person.
    I have heard the s of many. . .
        Ps. 31:13
    Whoso privily s'eth his neighbour
        . . .Ps. 101:5
    grave, not s'ers, sober. . .1 Tim. 3:11

Slavery: See *Bondage; Servant/Servants*.

Sleep: Restoration of the body through deep rest.
    deep s to fall upon Adam. . .
        Gen. 2:21
    shall neither slumber nor s. . .
        Ps. 121:4

wilt thou s, O sluggard? . . .
    Prov. 6:9
The s of a labouring man. . .
    Eccles. 5:12
being fallen into a deep s. . .
    Acts 20:9

Slothful: See *Idle/Idleness*.

Snobbery: A prideful, superior attitude.
    respect of persons is not good
        . . .Prov. 28:21
    Mind not high things. . .Rom. 12:16
    no one of you be puffed up. . .
        1 Cor. 4:6
    if ye have respect to persons
        . . .James 2:9

Sodom: Most prominent of the cities in the plain of Siddim. Destroyed by fire from heaven (Gen. 10:19; 13:10–13). Often referred to in scripture as a symbol of wickedness and warning to sinners (Deut. 29:23; Isa. 1:9–10; Matt. 10:15; Rev. 11:8).

Solomon: Last of David's sons by Bathsheba. Placed in Nathan's care; secured the throne according to David's pledge (1 Kings 1:13–53). Built the palace and temple, grew famous for wisdom, encouraged literature, died leaving his kingdom divided and on the edge of decay (1 Kings 2–11; 2 Chron. 1–9).

Son/Sons: A male descendant.
    a foolish s is the heaviness. . .
        Prov. 10:1
    s's of the living God. . .Hosea 1:10
    Is not this the carpenter's s?
        . . .Matt. 13:55
    become the s's of God. . .John 1:12
    receive the adoption of s's. . .
        Gal. 4:5
See *Child/Children; Youth*.

Son/Son of God: A term applied to the angels (Job 38:7); to Adam (Luke 3:38); to believers (Rom. 8:14); but preeminently to Christ, signifying His divine origin and nature (Dan. 3:25; Matt. 11:27; John 1:18; 5:19–26).

This is my beloved S. . .Matt. 3:17
thou art the S o G. . .Matt. 14:33
S of the living God. . .Matt. 16:16
the only begotten S. . .John 1:18
this is the S o G. . .John 1:34
spared not his own S. . .Rom. 8:32

Son of Man: In a limited sense, "man" (Num. 23:19; Job 25:6). In a broader, higher sense, "the Messiah." In the N.T. sense, where the term is used some eighty times, it means Christ in His incarnate form (Dan. 7:13; Matt. 9:6; 12:8; Mark 2:10; John 1:51).

Soothsayer: One who claimed to be able to foretell future events (Dan. 2:27).

Sorcery/Sorcerer/Sorcerers: Magic and divination.

astrologers, and the s'ers. . .Dan. 2:2
in the same city used s. . .Acts 8:9
But Elymas the s'er. . .Acts 13:8
For without are dogs, and s'ers . . .Rev. 22:15

See *Magicians; Occult, the; Witch/ Witchcraft.*

Sorrow/Sorrows: Grief or extreme sadness.

s is turned into joy. . .Job 41:22
my s is continually before me. . . Ps. 38:17
and carried our s's. . .Isa. 53:4
godly s worketh repentance. . . 2 Cor. 7:10

See *Depression; Pain.*

Soul: KJV word for life or spirit.

man became a living s. . .Gen. 2:7

cast down, O my s? . . .Ps. 42:5
lose his own s? . . .Matt. 16:26
heart, and with all thy s. . .Matt. 22:37

Sound Mind/Thinking: Right or appropriate reasoning.

whose mind is stayed on thee . . .Isa. 26:3
renewing of your mind. . .Rom. 12:2
same mind one toward another . . .Rom. 12:16
renewed in the spirit of your mind . . .Eph. 4:23
Let this mind be in you. . .Phil. 2:5
and of a s m. . .2 Tim. 1:7

Sovereignty of God: The Lord's unlimited power and supreme rule in the world.

Whatsoever the Lord pleased. . . Ps. 135:6
I have made the earth. . .Isa. 45:12
an everlasting dominion. . . Dan. 4:34
power over all flesh. . .John 17:2
who hath resisted his will? . . . Rom. 9:19
by him were all things created. . . Col. 1:16

See *Foreknowledge of God; Predestinate/ Predestinated.*

Spanking: See *Corporal Punishment.*

Special to God: See *Beloved.*

Speech: Spoken communication.

I am slow of s. . .Exod. 4:10
continued his s until midnight . . .Acts 20:7
not with excellency of s. . .1 Cor. 2:1
Great is my boldness of s. . . 2 Cor. 7:4
s be always with grace. . .Col. 4:6

See *Tongue.*

Spikenard: A fragrant and costly ointment made from the spikenard plant of India (Song of Sol. 1:12; 4:13–14; Mark 14:3; John 12:3).

Spirit: The breath (2 Thess. 2:8); the vital principle (Eccl. 8:8); elsewhere, the soul. Holy Spirit, or Ghost, is the third person in the Trinity (2 Cor. 13:14; Acts 15:28).

Spirit, Holy: See *Holy Ghost.*

Spite/Spitefully: See *Malice.*

Sports: See *Athletics.*

Spouse/Spouses: A husband or wife.
my s; thou hast ravished my heart
. . .Song of Sol. 4:9
your s's shall commit adultery
. . .Hosea 4:13
See *Husband/Husbands; Wife.*

Star/Stars: A luminous body visible in the night sky.
he made the s's also. . .Gen. 1:16
When the morning s's sang
together. . .Job 38:7
we have seen his s. . .Matt. 2:2
in his right hand seven s's. . .
Rev. 1:16
the bright and morning s. . .
Rev. 22:16

Stargazers: See *Astrologers.*

Stature: One's physical height; a metaphor for spiritual growth.
man of great s. . .2 Sam. 21:20
add one cubit unto his s? . . .
Matt. 6:27
Jesus increased in wisdom and s
. . .Luke 2:52
s of the fulness of Christ. . .
Eph. 4:13

Statutes: Laws or decrees created by either God or a civil ruler. Ye shall therefore keep my s. . .Lev. 18:5
not put away his s. . .Ps. 18:22
s of the Lord are right. . .Ps. 19:8
See *Law/Laws.*

Steadfastness: Persistence and perseverance.
renew a right spirit within me
. . .Ps. 51:10
his heart is fixed, trusting. . .
Ps. 112:7
whose mind is stayed on thee
. . .Isa. 26:3

Steal: To take possessions that belong to others.
Thou shalt not s. . .Exod. 20:15
thieves break through and s
. . .Matt. 6:19
him that stole s no more. . .
Eph. 4:28

Stephen: First Christian martyr. A Greek convert of strong faith and great eloquence. Arrested and tried; stoned to death; Saul's conversion followed Stephen's death (Acts 6:5–15; 7; 8:1–3).

Steward/Stewards: A manager or administrator.
s's of the mysteries of God. . .
1 Cor. 4:1
as good s's of the manifold grace
. . .1 Pet. 4:10

Stoics: Members of a Grecian philosophical school, or sect, founded by Zeno, who taught in the *stoa*, or porch, of the Agora at Athens (Acts 17:18).

Stranger: See *Alien.*

Strength/Strengtheneth: Energy, both physical and spiritual.
The Lord is my s and song. . .
Exod. 15:2
joy of the Lord is your s. . .
Neh. 8:10
s in the time of trouble. . .Ps. 37:39
God is our refuge and s. . .Ps. 46:1
confidence shall be your s. . .
Isa. 30:15
shall renew their s. . .Isa. 40:31

Christ which s'eneth me. . .
Phil. 4:13
my s is made perfect. . .2 Cor. 12:9

Stress: See *Overwhelm/Overwhelmed; Strife; Struggles; Trouble.*

Strife/Strifes: Bitter conflict.
Hatred stirreth up s's. . .Prov. 10:12
man to cease from s. . .Prov. 20:3
nothing be done through s. . .
Phil. 2:3
For where envying and s is. . .
James 3:16

Strive/Striving: To put forth great effort.
shall not always s with man. . .
Gen. 6:3
He shall not s, nor cry. . .Matt. 12:19
S to enter in. . .Luke 13:24
s'ing together for the faith. . .
Phil. 1:27
must not s; but be gentle. . .
2 Tim. 2:24

Stubborn/Stubbornness: An unyielding, obstinate spirit.
it is a stiffnecked people. . .
Exod. 32:9
a s and rebellious generation. . .
Ps. 78:8
Ye stiffnecked and uncircumcised
in heart. . .Acts 7:51

Study: See *Learn/Learned/Learning.*

Stumblingblock: A hindrance to belief or understanding.
no man put a s. . .Rom. 14:13
s to them that are weak. . .
1 Cor. 8:9

Subjection: Under the Lord's authority and direction.
brought them into s. . .Jer. 34:16
s unto the gospel of Christ. . .
2 Cor. 9:13
all things in s under his feet. . .
Heb. 2:8

Submit/Submitted/Submitting: To yield to authority.
s'ted themselves unto Solomon. . .
1 Chron. 29:24
every one s himself. . .Ps. 68:30
s'ted themselves unto him. . .
Ps. 81:15
have not s'ted themselves. . .
Rom. 10:3
S'ting yourselves one to another
. . .Eph. 5:21
Wives, s yourselves. . .Col. 3:18

Substance Abuse: See *Addiction; Alcohol; Drink/Drinking; Drugs.*

Success: A favorable outcome for one's efforts.
then thou shalt have good s
. . .Josh. 1:8
whatsoever he doeth shall
prosper. . .Ps. 1:3
riches, and honour, and life. . .
Prov. 22:4
Give, and it shall be given. . .
Luke 6:38
least is faithful also in much
. . .Luke 16:10

Suffering: See *Pain.*

Suicide: The act of taking one's own life.
therefore choose life. . .Deut. 30:19
Saul took a sword, and fell upon it
. . .1 Sam. 31:4
went and hanged himself. . .
Matt. 27:5
those days shall men seek death
. . .Rev. 9:6

Superstition/Superstitious: Ideas based on ignorance or fear.
Turn ye not unto idols. . .Lev. 19:4
against him of their own s. . .
Acts 25:19
all things ye are too s'us. . .
Acts 17:22
See *Idol/Idols; Idolatry/Idolaters.*

Supplication/Supplications: An earnest prayer or request to God.
> heard my voice and my s's. . .
> Ps. 116:1
> Daniel praying and making s
> . . .Dan. 6:11
> one accord in prayer and s. . .
> Acts 1:14
> s with thanksgiving. . .Phil. 4:6

Surety: Responsibility for debt, regulated by the Mosaic law (Gen. 44:32; Exod. 22:25–26). A pledge or guarantee that a debt would be paid.
> I will be s for him. . .Gen. 43:9
> if thou be s for thy friend. . .
> Prov. 6:1
> Jesus made a s. . .Heb. 7:22

Sustain/Sustained: To give support or relief to.
> s them in the wilderness. . .Neh. 9:21
> for the Lord s'd me. . .Ps. 3:5
> his righteousness, it s'd him. . .Isa. 59:16

Swear: See *Oath/Oaths.*

Sycamore: A tree of the fig species growing in Egypt and Palestine and valued for its fruit and durable wood (1 Kings 10:27; 1 Chron. 27:28; Luke 19:4).

Synagogue/Synagogues: The Jewish assembly for social and religious purposes seems to have had its origin during the captivity, or to have been an outgrowth of it (Ezek. 8:15; Neh. 8:2). Often elaborate and costly, presided over by a chief, or rabbi, assisted by a council of elders (Mark 5:22, 35; Luke 4:20; Acts 18:8).
> teaching in their s's. . .Matt. 4:23
> put you out of the s's. . .John 16:2
> preached Christ in the s's. . .Acts 9:20
> And he went into the s. . .Acts 19:8
> but are the s of Satan. . .Rev. 2:9

Syria: The country north of Canaan, extending from the Tigris River to the Mediterranean Sea, and northward to the Taurus mountain ranges. Damascus was its capital. Persistent enemy of the Israelites (1 Kings 15:18–20; 2 Kings 6:8–33).

T

Tabernacle/Tabernacles: Tent of Jehovah, or movable sanctuary, which Moses was directed to build in the wilderness (Exod. 25:8). Its plan, materials, and furnishings are described in Exod. 25:9–40; 26–27). The word is also used to describe the homes of the righteous.
> thou shalt make the t. . .Exod. 26:1
> who shall abide in thy t? . . .Ps. 15:1
> make here three t's. . .Matt. 17:4
> earthly house of this t. . .2 Cor. 5:1
> greater and more perfect t. . .
> Heb. 9:11

Tabernacles, Feast of: Third of the three great Hebrew feasts. Commemorated the long tent life of the Israelites. Called also "feast of ingathering" (Exod. 23:16).

Tabitha: See *Dorcas.*

Tabret: A small drum or tambourine (1 Sam. 18:6).

Talebearer: See *Gossip.*

Talent: A Hebrew weight and denomination for money, equal to 3,000 shekels, or 93¾ pounds of silver (Exod. 38:25; Matt. 18:24).

Tarshish/Tharshish: 1. The city with which the Phoenicians traded. Associated with Tartessus in Spain (Jer. 10:9). 2. Another Tarshish is inferable from the statement that Solomon's ships at Ezion-geber on the Red Sea traded with Tarshish or Tharshish (1 Kings 9:26).

Tarsus: Chief city of Cilicia, Asia Minor, on the Cydnus River, six miles from the Mediterranean Sea. Birthplace of Paul and rival of Athens and Alexandria in literature and fine arts (Acts 9:11, 30; 11:25; 21:39; 22:3).

Tartan: An army official, similar to a general or commander-in-chief (2 Kings 18:17; Isa. 20:1).

Tax/Taxes: First Hebrew taxes were tithes, firstfruits, redemption money, for use of the priests. These were increased under the kings and became burdensome (1 Kings 10:28–29; 12:4). Tithe tax became a poll tax (Neh. 10:32–33). The enrollment, or census (Luke 2:2; Acts 5:37), was for the purpose of Roman taxation.
> all the world should be t. . .Luke 2:1
> And all went to be t. . .Luke 2:3
> in the days of the t'ing. . .Acts 5:37

Teach/Teaching: To communicate knowledge or religious truth to others.
> t them diligently unto thy children . . .Deut. 6:7
> Train up a child. . .Prov. 22:6
> T'ing them to observe all things . . .Matt. 28:20
> t'ing and admonishing one another . . .Col. 3:16

Temper: See *Anger/Angry, Sin of.*

Temperance/Temperate: Moderation or self-discipline.
> mastery is t'te in all things. . . 1 Cor. 9:25
> Meekness, t: against such. . . Gal. 5:23
> sober, just, holy, t'te. . .Titus 1:8

Temple: 1. Solomon's temple erected at Jerusalem on Mount Moriah. David's proposal for permanent temple, but forbidden by the prophet Nathan (1 Chron. 17; 2 Sam. 7:7–29). Solomon completed the work (1 Chron. 11–12; 28–29). 2. The temple of Zerubbabel. Completion; destruction; restoration (Ezek. 3–6). 3. Herod the Great removed the decayed temple of Zerubbabel and began the erection of a new one. Destroyed by the Romans, thus fulfilling Mark 13:2.
> laid the foundation of the t. . . Ezra 3:10
> The Lord is in his holy t. . .Ps. 11:4
> his train filled the t. . .Isa. 6:1
> one greater than the t. . .Matt. 12:6
> veil of the t was rent. . .Matt. 27:51
> ye are the t of God. . .1 Cor. 3:16

Temptation/Temptations: Testing or enticement to sin.
> t in the wilderness. . .Ps. 95:8
> lead us not into t. . .Matt. 6:13
> in time of t fall away. . .Luke 8:13
> ye fall into divers t's. . .James 1:2
> man that endureth t. . .James 1:12

Tempter: See *Satan.*

Tender/Tenderhearted: Compassion for others.
> thy t mercies and thy lovingkindnesses. . .Ps. 25:6
> t mercies are over all his works . . .Ps. 145:9
> the t mercy of our God. . .Luke 1:78
> t'hearted, forgiving one another . . .Eph. 4:32

Teraphim: Little images kept in Eastern households for private consultation and worship. This type of idolatry or superstition was denounced by the Lord (Gen. 31:19, 34–35; Judg. 18:17; 1 Sam. 15:23; 2 Kings 23:24; Hosea 3:4).

Terrorism: See *Murder/Murders; Murderer/Murderers; Violence.*

Tertius: Paul's scribe in writing his epistle to the Romans (Rom. 16:22).

Tertullus: A Roman lawyer or orator hired by the high priest and Sanhedrim to prosecute the apostle Paul before the procurator Felix (Acts 24:1–9).

Testify: To make a statement based on personal experience or belief.
I t among you this day. . .
  Deut. 32:46
though our iniquities t against us
  . . .Jer. 14:7
t that we have seen. . .John 3:11
to t that it is he. . .Acts 10:42

Tetrarch: Originally an official who governed a part of a country divided into four parts, or tetrarchies; but under Roman rule, it came to mean any ruler or petty prince of the republic and empire, especially in Syria (Matt. 14:1; Luke 3:1; 9:7; Acts 13:1). Sometimes the tetrarch was called the king (Matt. 14:9; Mark 6:14, 22).

Thaddeus: Surname of the apostle Jude, and another form of Lebbaeus (Matt. 10:3; Mark 3:18).

Thankful/Thanksgiving: To express one's gratitude, particularly for God's blessings.
Offer unto God t'sgiving. . .
  Ps. 50:14
before his presence with t'sgiving
  . . .Ps. 95:2
be t unto him, and bless. . .
  Ps. 100:4
supplication with t'sgiving. . .
  Phil. 4:6
one body; and be ye t. . .Col. 3:15

Thanks: See *Thankful/Thanksgiving.*

Theophilus: The person, probably an official, to whom Luke addressed his Gospel and his history of the Acts of the Apostles (Luke 1:3; Acts 1:1).

Thessalonica: An important city of Macedonia, at the head of the Gulf of Thessalonica. Paul visited it during his second tour and founded a strong church there, to whose members he wrote two epistles (Acts 17:1–9).

Thirst/Thirsteth/Thirsty: The body's intense desire for water. Thirst is also a biblical picture of a person's desire for God.
My soul t'eth for God. . .Ps. 42:2
hunger and t after righteousness. . .
  Matt. 5:6
t'y, and ye gave me drink. . .
  Matt. 25:35
believeth on me shall never t
  . . .John 6:35
If any man t. . .John 7:37

Thomas: The apostle whose name in Greek was Didymus, "twin" (Matt. 10:3; Mark 3:18; Luke 6:15; John 11:16; 14:5–6; 20:24–29; Acts 1:13).

Thought/Thoughts: Ideas and impressions produced by the human mind.
every imagination of the t's. . .
  Gen. 6:5
I hate vain t's. . .Ps. 119:113
try me, and know my t's. . .
  Ps. 139:23
my t's are not your t's. . .Isa. 55:8
Take no t for your life. . .Matt. 6:25
bringing into captivity every t. . .
  2 Cor. 10:5

Thummin: See *Urim and Thummim.*

Tigris River: Great eastern tributary of the Euphrates River, rising in the Armenian mountains and flowing southeastwardly 1,146 miles. "Hiddekel," one of the rivers of Eden (Gen. 2:14).

Timbrel: A musical instrument similar to the tambourine (Exod. 15:20; Judg. 11:34; Ps. 68:25).

Time/Times
My t's are in thy hand. . .Ps. 31:15
Remember how short my t is. . .
 Ps. 89:47
a t to every purpose. . .Eccles. 3:1
My t is not yet come. . .John 7:6
Redeeming the t. . .Eph. 5:16

Timothy: A young man converted under Paul who became a close friend and valuable assistant of the apostle (Rom. 16:21; Heb. 13:23). Recipient of two of Paul's epistles.

Tithe/Tithes: One-tenth of all produce of lands and livestock was set apart, under the Levitical law, for the support of the Levites, and a tenth of their tenth went to the priests. There were tithe regulations among other nations (Gen. 14:20; 28:22; Lev. 27:30–33; Deut. 12:17–18). The Pharisees tithed their mint, anise, cumin, and rue (Matt. 23:23).
And he gave him t's of all. . .
 Gen. 14:20
all the t of the land. . .Lev. 27:30
all the t's into the storehouse
 . . .Mal. 3:10
pay t of mint and anise. . .
 Matt. 23:23
See *Offering/Offerings.*

Tittle: Jot; iota; any minute quantity (Matt. 5:18; Luke 16:17).

Titus: A distinguished Greek who became a Christian convert and a companion of Paul in his trials and on his missionary tours (Titus 1:4; Gal. 2:3–5; 2 Cor. 8:6, 16, 23). Paul wrote an epistle to Titus to instruct him in his ministerial duties on the island of Crete.

Tolerance. Acceptance of other people, in spite of their differences.
That ye love one another. . .John
 13:34
in honour preferring one another
 . . .Rom. 12:10
Husbands, love your wives. . .
 Eph. 5:25
Forbearing one another. . .Col. 3:13
ought also to love one another. . .
 1 John 4:11

Tongue: The part of the body that utters speech.
Keep thy t from evil. . .Ps. 34:13
I sin not with my t. . .Ps. 39:1
A wholesome t is a tree. . .
 Prov. 15:4
keepeth his mouth and his t. . .
 Prov. 21:23
every t should confess. . .Phil. 2:11
t can no man tame. . .James 3:8
See *Speech.*

Tongues, Speaking in: Ecstatic utterances.
they shall speak with new t. . .
 Mark 16:17
every man in our own tongue. . .
 Acts 2:8
spake with t, and prophesied. . .
 Acts 19:6
t of men and of angels. . .1 Cor. 13:1

Topaz: A precious stone corresponding to the modern chrysolite, which the Israelites obtained from Ethiopia (Job 28:19). Topaz was the second stone in the first row of the high priest's breastplate (Exod. 28:17), and a foundation stone of the New Jerusalem (Rev. 21:20).

Tophet/Topheth: Part of the valley of Hinnom near Jerusalem. Perhaps once a pleasure garden, but afterward polluted by the abomination caused by the worship of Baal and Molech (2 Kings 23:10; Jer. 7:31; 19:13). A place of judgment (Jer. 19:6–14).

Tradition. Additions to the original Mosaic Law that eventually became as important as the original law itself.
> the t of the elders?. . .Matt. 15:2
> none effect by your t. . .Matt. 15:6
> ye hold the t of men. . .Mark 7:8
> received by t from your fathers
> . . .1 Pet. 1:18

Traitor/Traitors: One who betrays another.
> Judas Iscariot, which also was the t. . .Luke 6:16
> T's, heady, highminded. . .2 Tim. 3:4

Transfiguration: The supernatural change in the appearance of Christ. It proved His messiahship and symbolized His glory (Matt. 17:1–13; Mark 9:2–13; Luke 9:28–36).

Transformed/Transforming
> be ye t by the renewing. . . Rom. 12:2
> deceitful workers, t'ing themselves. . .2 Cor. 11:13
> t as the ministers of righteousness . . .2 Cor. 11:15

Transgression/Transgressions: A word for sin that emphasizes the breaking of God's law.
> forgiving iniquity and t. . .Num. 14:18
> he whose t is forgiven. . .Ps. 32:1
> blot out my t's. . .Ps. 51:1
> he was wounded for our t's. . . Isa. 53:5
See *Sin; Trespass.*

Treasure/Treasures, Spiritual: Good deeds done in the Lord's name.
> t's upon earth, where moth. . .Matt. 6:19
> t's in heaven, where. . .Matt. 6:20
> For where your t is. . .Matt. 6:21
> shalt have t in heaven. . .Matt. 19:21

Treasury: The place in the temple where gifts were received (1 Chron. 9:26; Mark 12:41; Luke 21:1; John 8:20).

Trespass/Trespasses: To violate the personal or property rights of another (Lev. 5:6). To violate a law of God (Matt. 6:15).
> if ye forgive men their t'es. . . Matt. 6:14
> If thy brother t against thee. . . Luke 17:3
> t against thee seven times. . . Luke 17:4
> not imputing their t'es unto them. . . 2 Cor. 5:19
> who were dead in t'es. . .Eph. 2:1
See *Sin; Transgression/Transgressions.*

Trial: Trouble or suffering.
> a great t of affliction. . .2 Cor. 8:2
> concerning the fiery t. . .1 Pet. 4:12

Tribe: The division of the people that sprang from the twelve sons of Jacob, and was carried on through their descendents (Gen. 48:5; Num. 26:5–51). Each tribe was headed by a prince, and each possessed considerable independence. They waged war separately and among themselves (Judg. 1:2–4; 1 Chron. 5:18–22; 2 Sam. 2:4–9). Finally ten tribes revolted and set up the separate kingdom of Israel (19:41–43; 1 Kings 12).

Tribulation: Extreme suffering or distress.
> deliver me out of all t. . .1 Sam. 26:24

then shall be great t. . .Matt. 24:21
shall t, or distress. . .Rom. 8:35
came out of great t. . .Rev. 7:14

Tribute: A payment made as a token of submission, or for the sake of peace, or in pursuance of a treaty (Gen. 49:15).

Triumph/Triumphed/Triumphing:
To overcome against great odds.
he hath t'ed gloriously. . .Exod. 15:1
t'ing of the wicked is short. . .
Job 20:5
I will t in the works. . .Ps. 92:4
causeth us to t in Christ. . .2 Cor. 2:14
See *Overcome/Overcometh; Victory.*

Troas: An important city in Mysia, Asia Minor. Founded by Alexander the Great; key of commerce between Europe and Asia. Paul visited Troas more than once (Acts 16:8–11; 20:5–10; 2 Tim. 4:13).

Trouble: Difficult circumstances.
man is born unto t. . .Job 5:7
a refuge in times of t. . .Ps. 9:9
deliver him in time of t. . .Ps. 41:1
present help in t. . .Ps. 46:1
See *Affliction/Afflictions.*

Trumpets, Feast of: The feast of the new moon (Num. 29:1–6; Lev. 23:24–25). It was the New Year's Day of the Jewish civil year and was ushered in by the blowing of trumpets and observed by offerings.

Trust: To put one's confidence in a person or thing.
in him will I t. . .2 Sam. 22:3
afraid, I will t in thee. . .Ps. 56:3
Put not your t in princes. . .
Ps. 146:3
name shall the Gentiles t. . .
Matt. 12:21

we should not t in ourselves. . .
2 Cor. 1:9

Truth: What is reliable and consistent with God's revelation.
abundant in goodness and t. . .
Exod. 34:6
his t endureth to all generations. . .
Ps. 100:5
grace and t came by Jesus. . .
John 1:17
And ye shall know the t. . .
John 8:32
the Spirit of t. . .John 16:13
speaking the t in love. . .Eph. 4:15

Tychicus: A disciple of Paul (Acts 20:4) and his messenger and spokesman (Eph. 6:21–22; Col. 4:7–8).

Tyre: A commercial city of Phoenicia on the Mediterranean Sea coast. It fell to the lot of Asher, but was never conquered (Josh. 19:29). Denounced by the prophets (Isa. 23:1–17; Jer. 27:3). Visited by Paul (Acts 21:3–4).

U

Unbelief: Refusal to believe in God.
ye did not believe the Lord. . .
Deut. 1:32
seen me, and believe not. . .
John 6:36
I will not believe. . .John 20:25
ignorantly in u. . .1 Tim. 1:13
See *Believe/Believed/Believeth.*

Uncertainty: See *Doubt/Doubted/Doubts.*

Uncleanness: See *Impurity.*

Understanding: Spiritual insight, a gift of God.
Through thy precepts I get u. . .
Ps. 119:104

his u is infinite. . .Ps. 147:5
which passeth all u. . .Phil. 4:7
hath given us an u. . .1 John 5:20
See *Comprehend/Comprehended.*

Unity: Harmony and cooperation.
dwell together in u! . . .Ps. 133:1
keep the u of the Spirit. . .Eph. 4:3
are one bread, and one body. . .
1 Cor. 10:17

Unjust/Unjustly: Dishonesty;
unfairness.
u man is an abomination. . .
Prov. 29:27
uprightness will he deal u'ly. . .
Isa. 26:10
rain on the just and on the u
. . .Matt. 5:45
both of the just and u. . .Acts 24:15

Unleavened Bread: Bread baked
without yeast and eaten during the
observance of Passover.
observe the feast of u b. . .Exod.
12:17
eat u b seven days. . .Exod. 23:15
And a basket of u b. . .Num. 6:15
u b shall be eaten. . .Ezek. 45:21

Unmerciful: To show harsh judgment
of others.
remembered not to shew mercy
. . .Ps. 109:16
shew them no mercy. . .Isa. 47:6
no more have mercy. . .Hosea 1:6
without natural affection,
implacable, u. . .Rom. 1:31

Unrighteous/Unrighteousness: Immoral behavior.
u man his thoughts. . .Isa. 55:7
faithful in the u mammon. . .
Luke 16:11
members as instruments of u'ness
. . .Rom. 6:13
u shall not inherit the kingdom. . .
1 Cor. 6:9
hath righteousness with u'ness?
. . .2 Cor. 6:14
cleanse us from all u'ness. . .
1 John 1:9

Unsaved: The condition of those who
refuse to believe or follow God.
believeth not shall be damned. . .
Mark 16:16
be damned who believed not. . .
2 Thess. 2:12
See *Damnation; Harvest; Hell; Lost/
Unsaved.*

Upright: See *Righteousness.*

Ur: Place where Abraham lived with
his father, Terah, and his wife, Sarah,
before they started for the land of Canaan (Gen. 11:28, 31; 15:7; Acts 7:2).

Uriah: 1. A Hittite (2 Sam. 11:3), and
commander of one of the thirty divisions
of David's army (2 Sam. 23:39; 1 Chron.
11:41). He was husband of the beautiful
Bathsheba, with whom David committed adultery (2 Sam. 11:4–5). He had
Uriah killed to cover up his crime (2
Sam. 11:15–17). 2. A high priest in the
reign of Ahaz (Isa. 8:20), and probably
the same as Urijah in 2 Kings 16:10–16.
3. A priest of the family of Hakkoz, in
the time of Ezra (Exod. 8:33).

Urim and Thummim: Two objects
in the breastplate of the high priest
(Exod. 28:30), perhaps colored stones
cast as lots to help determine God's
will (Num. 27:21).

Usury: Exorbitant or unlawful interest
for money loaned; but in a Bible sense,
the taking of any interest at all. The
Law of Moses prohibited the Israelites
from exacting interest of one another
on loans, though not of foreigners
(Lev. 25:36–37; Deut. 23:19–20).
Take thou no u of him. . .Lev. 25:36
let us leave off this u. . .Neh. 5:10
u and unjust gain increaseth
. . .Prov. 28:8
See *Lend/Lendeth; Materialism.*

Uz: 1. Job's country (Job 1:1). Located east or southeast of Palestine (Job 1:3); adjacent to the Sabeans or Chaldeans (Job 1:15), and to the Edomites, who once occupied it as conquerors (Lam. 4:21); grouped with Egypt, Philistia, and Moab (Jer. 25:19–21). 2. The first son of Aram, son of Shem (Gen. 10:23). 3. Son of Nahor by Milcah (Gen. 22:21).

Uzziah: Son and successor of Amaziah on the throne of Judah, 810–758 BC (2 Chron. 26:1–3). Called Azariah (2 Kings 14:21); godly king, excellent general, and renowned city builder. Entered the temple and burned incense in violation of the law (Num. 16:40; 18:7); stricken with leprosy and forced to live in a separate house until he died (2 Kings 15:1–7; 2 Chron. 26).

V

Vanity: Anything that is useless, empty, or futile.
> they followed v, and became vain
> . . .2 Kings 17:15
> They speak v every one. . .Ps. 12:2
> soweth iniquity shall reap v. . .
> Prov. 22:8
> all is v and vexation of spirit
> . . .Eccles. 1:14

Vashti: Wife of King Ahasuerus and queen of Persia (Esther 1:9–22).

Vengeance: Retaliation against another person, or "getting even."
> To me belongeth v. . .Deut. 32:35
> day of v of our God. . .Isa. 61:2
> these be the days of v. . .Luke 21:22
> V is mine; I will repay. . .Rom. 12:19

Victory: Success in a struggle against difficulties.
> Lord wrought a great v. . .
> 2 Sam. 23:10
> swallow up death in v. . .Isa. 25:8
> O grave, where is thy v? . . .
> 1 Cor. 15:55
> v that overcometh the world. . .
> 1 John 5:4

See *Triumph/Triumphed/Triumphing.*

Vine: A favorite Oriental plant of many varieties (Gen. 9:20). Subject of frequent metaphor (Deut. 32:32); symbol of contentment (1 Kings 4:25); rebellious Israel compared to "wild grapes" (Isa. 5:2); "empty vine" (Hosea 10:1); symbol of spiritual union (John 15:1–5).

Violence: Acts of physical force.
> earth was filled with v. . .Gen. 6:11
> v covereth them as a garment
> . . .Ps. 73:6
> v covereth the mouth. . .Prov. 10:6
> who store up v and robbery
> . . .Amos 3:10

Virgin Birth: The miraculous conception of Jesus by the Holy Spirit.
> Behold, a virgin shall conceive. . .
> Isa. 7:14
> that which is conceived in her. . .
> Matt. 1:20
> a virgin shall be with child. . .
> Matt. 1:23
> shalt conceive in thy womb. . .
> Luke 1:31
> seeing I know not a man? . . .
> Luke 1:34

See *Nativity, the.*

Virtue/Virtuous: Moral excellence.
> Who can find a v'ous woman? . . .
> Prov. 31:10
> if there be any v. . .Phil. 4:8
> add to your faith v. . .2 Pet. 1:5

Vision: An inspired dream, fantasy, or apparition (Num. 24:4; Isa. 6; Ezek. 1:8–10; Dan. 7–8; Acts 26:13–19).

Vow/Vowed/Vows: A solemn promise made to God (Num. 6:1–2; Deut. 23:21–23).
> Nazarite who hath v'ed. . .
> Num. 6:21
> When thou shalt v a v. . .
> Deut. 23:21
> Jephthah v'ed a v. . .Judg. 11:30
> God, hast heard my v's. . .Ps. 61:5
> for he had a v. . .Acts 18:18

See *Nazarite; Oath/Oaths.*

W

Wait/Waiteth/Waiting: To bide one's time.
> Our soul w'eth for the Lord. . .
> Ps. 33:20
> those that w upon the Lord. . .
> Ps. 37:9
> w'ing for the adoption. . .Rom. 8:23
> patient w'ing for Christ. . .
> 2 Thess. 3:5

See *Patience/Patient/Patiently.*

Wages: Payment for work rendered.
> thou shalt give him his hire. . .
> Deut. 24:15
> earneth w to put it. . .Hag. 1:6
> labourer is worthy of his hire. . .
> Luke 10:7
> the w of sin is death. . .Rom. 6:23

Walk, Christian: To walk in Christ is to follow His will.
> w in newness of life. . .Rom. 6:4
> w by faith. . .2 Cor. 5:7
> also w in the Spirit. . .Gal. 5:25
> w worthy of the vocation. . .
> Eph. 4:1
> if we w in the light. . .1 John 1:7

Wander/Wandereth/Wanderers: To move about aimlessly.
> w in the wilderness forty years
> . . .Num. 14:33
> causeth them to w. . .Ps. 107:40
> w'eth out of the way. . .Prov. 21:16

> w'ers among the nations. . .
> Hosea 9:17

Warfare, Spiritual: Struggle against Satan and His temptations.
> we do not war after the flesh. . .
> 2 Cor. 10:3
> ye fight and war, yet ye. . .
> James 4:2
> which war against the soul. . .
> 1 Pet. 2:11

Washing: The custom of washing hands before meals or of feet after a journey or on entering a stranger's house was not only a polite ceremony but a religious observance (Matt. 15:2; Mark 7:3; Luke 11:38). The first act of hospitality toward a guest was to offer a basin of water for washing the feet (Gen. 18:4; Exod. 3:19; Luke 7:37–38, 44; John 13:5–14).

Water/Waters, Living: A metaphor for salvation and eternal life.
> the fountain of l w's. . .Jer. 2:13
> that l w's shall go out. . .Zech. 14:8
> would have given thee l w. . .
> John 4:10

Way, the: A name for the Christian movement in the book of Acts.
> found any of this w. . .Acts 9:2
> w of God more perfectly. . .
> Acts 18:26
> no small stir about that w. . .
> Acts 19:23
> I persecuted this w. . .Acts 22:4

Weak/Weaker/Weakness: Diminished physical strength.
> O Lord; for I am w. . .Ps. 6:2
> bear the infirmities of the w. . .
> Rom. 15:1
> w'ness of God is stronger. . .
> 1 Cor. 1:25
> to them that are w. . .1 Cor. 8:9
> as unto the w'er vessel. . .1 Pet. 3:7

Wealth: See *Money; Rich/Riches.*

Welfare: See *Alms; Poor, the.*

Wickedness: Evil and wrongdoing; another word for sin.
　　land become full of w. . .Lev. 19:29
　　Ye have plowed w. . .Hosea 10:13
　　unrighteousness, fornication,
　　　w. . .Rom. 1:29
　　spiritual w in high places. . .
　　　Eph. 6:12
See *Evil.*

Widow/Widows: A woman whose husband has died.
　　Ye shall not afflict any w. . .
　　　Exod. 22:22
　　take a w's raiment to pledge
　　　. . .Deut. 24:17
　　And oppress not the w. . .
　　　Zech. 7:10
　　came a certain poor w. . .
　　　Mark 12:42
　　Honour w's that are w's. . .1 Tim. 5:3

Wife: A married woman.
　　shall cleave to his w. . .Matt. 19:5
　　husband render unto the w. . .
　　　1 Cor. 7:3
　　husband is sanctified by the w. . .
　　　1 Cor. 7:14
　　the head of the w. . .Eph. 5:23
　　be joined unto his w. . .Eph. 5:31
See *Family; Marriage/Marry; Spouse/ Spouses; Woman.*

Wilderness: An area of wasteland, with stretches of pasturage (Josh. 15:61; Isa. 42:11). The wilderness in which the Israelites spent forty years (Deut. 1:1; Josh. 5:6) was the great peninsula of Sinai, lying between Seir, Edom, and the Gulf of Akaba on the east, and the Gulf of Suez and Egypt on the west.

Will of God: See *God's Will.*

Wine: A common fermented beverage of Bible times. It was also used as a temple offering and medication.
　　not drink w nor strong drink. . .
　　　Lev. 10:9
　　W is a mocker. . .Prov. 20:1
　　new w into old bottles. . .Matt. 9:17
　　water that was made w. . .John 2:9
　　w for thy stomach's sake. . .
　　　1 Tim. 5:23
See *Alcohol; Drink/Drinking.*

Wisdom: Knowledge guided by insight and understanding.
　　price of w is above rubies. . .
　　　Job 28:18
　　by w made the heavens. . .Ps. 136:5
　　W is better than weapons of war
　　　. . .Eccles. 9:18
　　wise man glory in his w. . .Jer. 9:23
　　foolish the w of this world? . . .
　　　1 Cor. 1:20
　　If any of you lack w. . .James 1:5

Wise Men: See *Magi.*

Witness/Witnessing: To give testimony, particularly about God's actions.
　　for a w unto all nations. . .Matt.
　　　24:14
　　Go ye therefore, and teach
　　　. . .Matt. 28:19
　　w'ing both to small and great
　　　. . .Acts 26:22
See *Harvest; Preach/Preached/Preaching.*

Woman: A female of the human species.
　　she shall be called W. . .Gen. 2:23
　　virtuous w is a crown. . .Prov. 12:4
　　find a virtuous w? . . .Prov. 31:10
　　looketh on a w to lust. . .Matt. 5:28
　　man created for the w. . .1 Cor. 11:9
See *Daughter/Daughters; Wife.*

Wonders: See *Miracle/Miracles; Signs.*

Word of God: Truths spoken by God; the Bible.

word of the Lord is tried. . .
   Ps. 18:30
Every w o G is pure. . .Prov. 30:5
In the beginning was the Word
   . . .John 1:1
the w o G increased. . .Acts 6:7
w o G abideth in you. . .1 John 2:14
See *Devotions; Prayer; Scripture/
Scriptures.*

Work: See *Labour.*

Work/Works of God: The wondrous
deeds of the Lord.
   God ended his w. . .Gen. 2:2
   his w is perfect. . .Deut. 32:4
   Remember his marvellous w's. . .
      1 Chron. 16:12
   the w of thy fingers. . .Ps. 8:3
   I must w the w's. . .John 9:4
   I have finished the w. . .John 17:4

Work/Works, Good: Gracious deeds
performed by believers.
   they may see your g w's. . .
      Matt. 5:16
   fruitful in every g w. . .Col. 1:10
   your work of faith. . .1 Thess. 1:3
   furnished unto all g w's. . .2 Tim.
      3:17
   careful to maintain g w's. . .Titus 3:8

Works of the Flesh: Sinful acts.
   ye live after the flesh. . .Rom. 8:13
   fulfil the lust of the flesh. . .
      Gal. 5:16
   w o t f are manifest. . .Gal. 5:19
   fulfilling the desires of the flesh
      . . .Eph. 2:3

World, the: The earth. The word is
often used metaphorically for human
ambition.
   he shall judge the w. . .Ps. 96:13
   the light of the w. . .Matt. 5:14
   he shall gain the whole w. . .
      Matt. 16:26
   taketh away the sin of the
      w. . .John 1:29
   God so loved the w. . .John 3:16

I have overcome the w. . .
   John 16:33
be not conformed to this w. . .
   Rom. 12:2
wisdom of this w is foolishness. . .
   1 Cor. 3:19
reconciling the w unto himself. . .
   2 Cor. 5:19

Worry: Anxiety over worldly matters.
   Take no thought for your life
      . . .Matt. 6:25
   Let not your heart be troubled
      . . .John 14:27
See *Anxiety.*

Worship: Praise and adoration of
God.
   thou shalt w no other god. . .
      Exod. 34:14
   All the earth shall w thee. . .
      Ps. 66:4
   are come to w him. . .Matt. 2:2
   angels of God w him. . .Heb. 1:6
   w him that liveth for ever. . .
      Rev. 4:10

Worthy: Something of value or merit.
   who is w to be praised. . .2 Sam.
      22:4
   is not w of me. . .Matt. 10:37
   fruits w of repentance. . .Luke 3:8
   walk w of the vocation. . .Eph. 4:1
   w of the kingdom of God. . .
      2 Thess. 1:5

Wrath of God: A metaphor for God's
judgment.
   when his wrath is kindled. . .Ps. 2:12
      sware in my wrath. . .Ps. 95:11 w o
      G is revealed. . .Rom. 1:18 day of
      his wrath is come. . .Rev. 6:17
See *Anger of the Lord.*

Wrongdoing: See *Sin.*

Y

Year of Jubilee: See *Jubilee.*

Yoke: An implement placed on the necks of oxen to equip them for pulling a plow. The word is also used metaphorically for subjection (1 Kings 12:4, 9–11; Isa. 9:4). Breaking of the yoke meant repudiation of authority (Nah. 1:13).

Youth: The adolescent years of life.
> fear the Lord from my y. . .1 Kings 18:12
> taught me from my y. . .Ps. 71:17
> The glory of young men. . . Prov. 20:29
> childhood and y are vanity . . .Eccles. 11:10
> Let no man despise thy y. . . 1 Tim. 4:12
> Flee also youthful lusts. . . 2 Tim. 2:22

See *Child/Children; Daughter/Daughters; Son/Sons.*

Z

Zacchaeus: The rich chief tax collector at Jericho who climbed a tree to see Jesus pass by, was invited down, became the host of Jesus, and was converted (Luke 19:1–10).

Zacharias: 1. Father of John the Baptist (Luke 1:5–25, 57–80). 2. Son of Barachias, who was killed between the temple and the altar (Matt. 23:35; Luke 6:51).

Zaphnath-paaneah: A name given by the Pharaoh to Joseph upon his promotion to a high place in the royal service (Gen. 41:45).

Zealots: A fanatical Jewish party that sought to overthrow Roman authority.

Zebedee: A fisherman of Galilee and father of the apostles James and John (Matt. 4:21; 27:56; Mark 1:19–20).

Zechariah: 1. Son of Berechiah (Zech. 1:1); of Iddo, (Ezek. 5:1). Eleventh of the minor prophets and contemporary of Haggai, born in Babylon during the captivity; returned with Zerubbabel (Ezek. 6:14). Time of prophecies is thought to be between 520–518 BC, during the period of building the second temple. His book is the thirty-eighth of the O.T. 2. A priest who blew the trumpet before the ark of the covenant on its return (1 Chron. 15:24). 3. One of the temple rulers in the reign of Josiah (2 Chron. 35:8). 4. A witness for Isaiah (Isa. 8:2).

Zelotes: A name added to that of the apostle Simon to distinguish him from Simon Peter, and to emphasize his membership in the party of Zealots (Luke 6:15).

Zephaniah: Ninth in order of the twelve minor prophets. Son of Cushi and descendent of Hezekiah. Prophecy denounced Judah, Nineveh, and surrounding nations, and recorded many promises of Gospel blessing.

Zerubbabel: Leader of the first colony of captives back to Jerusalem (Exod. 2:2); laid the foundation of the new temple (Zech. 4:6–10); began the work or reconstruction and finally succeeded in completing the structure, restored the order of priests according to the institution of David (Ezek. 6:14–22; Hag. 1:12, 15; 2:2–4). Zorobabel in N.T. (Matt. 1:12).

Zion/Sion: One of the hills on which Jerusalem was built. David captured the city from the Jebusites and strengthened its fortifications, calling it "The City of David" (2 Sam. 5:6–9; 1 Chron. 6:5–8). The O.T. poets and prophets exalted the word *Zion,* so that it came to be known as a sacred capital (Ps. 2:6); holy place, (Ps. 87:2); God's chosen people (Ps. 51:18); the Christian church (Heb. 12:22); the heavenly city (Rev. 14:1).

Zodiac: See *Astrologers; Star/Stars.*

Complete List of
Individuals
Named
in Scripture

The Bible is the story of God's dealing with people. From the very beginning, when He created Adam and Eve, the Lord desired a relationship with humans, who were made "in the image of God" (Genesis 1:27). Some bore God's image well, many did not. . .and the Bible is very honest about both the good and bad.

This section of *The Complete Bible Companion* provides details on every individual named in scripture. For every personal name in the King James Version—2,026 names covering nearly 3,400 individuals—you'll find relevant information including

- the number of men and/or women by that name
- the number of times that name is mentioned
- a brief biography for many individuals
- related scripture references (one for every person by that name)
- name meanings, if from the Hebrew or Greek

For more prominent Bible characters, you will find additional information and scripture references in the "Dictionary/Concordance of Key Bible Names, Places, Terms, and Topics" beginning on page 257.

A

Aaron
(Meaning uncertain)
1 man/350 references
Older brother of Moses and
first priest of Israel.
Exodus 4:14

Abagtha
1 man/1 reference
Esther 1:10

Abda
(Work)
2 men/2 references
1 Kings 4:6; Nehemiah 11:17

Abdeel
(Serving God)
1 man/1 reference
Jeremiah 36:26

Abdi
(Serviceable)
2 men/3 references
1 Chronicles 6:44; Ezra 10:26

Abdiel
(Servant of God)
1 man/1 reference
1 Chronicles 5:15

Abdon
(Servitude)
4 men/6 references
Most notably, twelfth judge of Israel.
Judges 12:13; 1 Chronicles 8:23; 1
Chronicles 8:30; 2 Chronicles 34:20

Abed-nego
1 man/15 references
Babylonian name for Azariah, one of
Daniel's companions in exile.
Daniel 1:7

Abel
(Emptiness or *vanity)*
1 man/12 references
Second son of Adam and Eve,
murdered by his jealous brother,
Cain.
Genesis 4:2

Abi
(Fatherly)
1 woman/1 reference
Mother of Judah's good king
Hezekiah.
2 Kings 18:2

Abia
(Worshipper of God)
2 men/4 references
Notably, a grandson of Solomon and
king of Judah. Also called Abijah.
1 Chronicles 3:10; Luke 1:5

Abiah
(Worshipper of God)
2 men/1 woman/4 references
Notably, second son of the prophet
Samuel.
1 Samuel 8:2; 1 Chronicles 2:24;
1 Chronicles 7:8

Abi-albon
(Father of strength)
1 man/1 reference
A "mighty man" of King David.
2 Samuel 23:31

Abiasaph
(Gatherer)
1 man/1 reference
Exodus 6:24

Abiathar
(Father of abundance)
1 man/31 references
Priest and trusted counselor of King
David.
1 Samuel 22:20

Abida
(Knowing)
1 man/1 reference
1 Chronicles 1:33

Abidah
(Knowing)
1 man/1 reference
Genesis 25:4

Abidan
(Judge)
1 man/5 references
Numbers 1:11

Abiel
(Possessor of God)
2 men/3 references
1 Samuel 9:1; 1 Chronicles 11:32

Abiezer
(Helpful)
2 men/7 references
Joshua 17:2; 2 Samuel 23:27

Abigail
(Source of joy)
2 women/17 references
Notably, widow of Nabal and wife of
King David.
1 Samuel 25:3; 2 Samuel 17:25

Abihail
(Possessor of might)
3 men/2 women/6 references
Numbers 3:35; 1 Chronicles 2:29; 1
Chronicles 5:14; 2 Chronicles 11:18;
Esther 2:15

Abihu
(Worshipper of God)
1 man/12 references
Exodus 6:23

Abihud
(Possessor of renown)
1 man/1 reference
1 Chronicles 8:3

Abijah
(Worshipper of God)
5 men/1 woman/20 references
Most notably, a son of King
Rehoboam of Judah and successor to
the throne. Also known as Abia.
1 Kings 14:1; 1 Chronicles 24:10;
2 Chronicles 11:20; 2 Chronicles 29:1;
Nehemiah 10:7; Nehemiah 12:4

Abijam
(Seaman)
1 man/5 references
An evil king of Judah.
1 Kings 14:31

Abimael
(Father of Mael)
1 man/2 references
Genesis 10:28

Abimelech
(Father of the king)
3 men/66 references
Philistine king who took Abraham's
wife, Sarah, as concubine after
Abraham called her his sister. Also a
son of Gideon who killed all but one
of his brothers and was made king.
Genesis 20:2; Judges 8:31;
1 Chronicles 18:16

Abinadab
(Liberal or generous)
4 men/13 references
A son (also known as Ishui) of Israel's
king Saul, who died with Saul in
battle on Mount Gilboa. Also a
brother of King David.
1 Samuel 7:1; 1 Samuel 16:8; 1 Samuel 31:2;
1 Kings 4:11

Abinoam
(Gracious)
1 man/4 references
Judges 4:6

Abiram
(Lofty)
2 men/11 references
Notably, a man who conspired
against Moses and was swallowed by
the earth.
Numbers 16:1; 1 Kings 16:34

Abishag
(Blundering)
1 woman/5 references
Beautiful young woman called to
serve the dying King David by lying
with him to keep him warm.
1 Kings 1:3

Abishai
(Generous)
1 man/25 references
Brother of David's commander, Joab.
Became a military leader himself.
1 Samuel 26:6

Abishalom
(Friendly)
1 man/2 references
1 Kings 15:2

Abishua
(Prosperous)
2 men/5 references
1 Chronicles 6:4; 1 Chronicles 8:4

Abishur
(Mason)
1 man/2 references
1 Chronicles 2:28

Abital
(Fresh)
1 woman/2 references
A wife of King David.
2 Samuel 3:4

Abitub
(Good)
1 man/1 reference
1 Chronicles 8:11

Abiud
(My father is majesty)
1 man/2 references
Matthew 1:13

Abner
(Enlightening)
1 man/63 references
Uncle of King Saul of Israel and
captain of his army. Later supported
David's kingship.
1 Samuel 14:50

Abraham
(Father of a multitude)
1 man/250 references
New name for Abram, whom God
called out of Ur of the Chaldees and
into the Promised Land. The name
was a symbol of the covenant between
God and Abraham, to build a nation
through Abraham and his wife, Sarai
(renamed Sarah).
Genesis 17:5

Abram
(High father)
1 man/58 references
A man from Ur of the Chaldees,
married to Sarai *(renamed Sarah)*. God
called him to the Promised Land and
promised to bless him. When Abram
was ninety years old, God made a
covenant with him and changed his
name to Abraham.
Genesis 11:26

Absalom
(Friendly)
1 man/102 references
King David's son by his wife Maacah.
2 Samuel 3:3

Achaicus
1 man/1 reference
Corinthian Christian who visited the apostle Paul in Ephesus.
1 Corinthians 16:17

Achan
(Troublesome)
1 man/6 references
Israelite who ignored Joshua's command that nothing in Jericho should live or be taken from the city.
Joshua 7:1

Achar
(Troublesome)
1 man/1 reference
Variant spelling of Achan, "the troubler of Israel."
1 Chronicles 2:7

Achaz
1 man/2 references
Same as Ahaz.
Matthew 1:9

Achbor
3 men/7 references
Genesis 36:38; 2 Kings 22:12;
Jeremiah 26:22

Achim
1 man/2 references
Matthew 1:14

Achish
2 men/21 references
Notably, Philistine king of Gath.
1 Samuel 21:10; 1 Kings 2:39

Achsa
(Anklet)
1 woman/1 reference
Same as Achsah.
1 Chronicles 2:49

Achsah
(Anklet)
1 woman/4 references
Caleb's daughter, whom he promised in marriage to the man who could capture the city of Kirjathsepher. Same as Achsa.
Joshua 15:16

Adah
(Ornament)
2 women/8 references
Wife of Lamech, the first man in scripture to have two wives. Also, a wife of Esau. Same as Bashemath.
Genesis 4:19; Genesis 36:2

Adaiah
(God has adorned)
9 men/9 references
2 Kings 22:1; 1 Chronicles 6:41; 1 Chronicles 8:21; 1 Chronicles 9:12; 2 Chronicles 23:1; Ezra 10:29; Ezra 10:39; Nehemiah 11:5; Nehemiah 11:12

Adalia
1 man/1 reference
Esther 9:8

Adam
(Ruddy)
1 man/30 references
The first man, created by God to have dominion over the earth. His first act was to name the animals; then God created Adam's wife, Eve.
Genesis 2:19

Adbeel
(Disciplined of God)
1 man/2 references
Genesis 25:13

Addar
(Ample)
1 man/1 reference
1 Chronicles 8:3

Addi
1 man/1 reference
Luke 3:28

Ader
(An arrangement)
1 man/1 reference
1 Chronicles 8:15

Adiel
(Ornament of God)
3 men/3 references
1 Chronicles 4:36; 1 Chronicles 9:12;
1 Chronicles 27:25

Adin
(Voluptuous)
3 men/4 references
Ezra 2:15; Nehemiah 10:16; Ezra 8:6

Adina
(Effeminacy)
1 man/1 reference
One of King David's valiant warriors.
1 Chronicles 11:42

Adino
(Slender)
1 man/1 reference
A "mighty man" of King David.
2 Samuel 23:8

Adlai
1 man/1 reference
1 Chronicles 27:29

Admatha
1 man/1 reference
One of seven Persian princes serving
under King Ahasuerus.
Esther 1:14

Adna
(Pleasure)
2 men/2 references
Ezra 10:30; Nehemiah 12:15

Adnah
(Pleasure)
2 men/2 references
Notably, captain in David's army.
1 Chronicles 12:20; 2 Chronicles 17:14

Adoni-bezek
(Lord of Bezek)
1 man/3 references
Ruler of a Canaanite city who ran
from the army of Judah during its
cleansing of the Promised Land.
Judges 1:5

Adonijah
(Worshipper of God)
3 men/26 references
Most notably, son of King David who
attempted to take the throne, though
David had promised it to Solomon.
2 Samuel 3:4; 2 Chronicles 17:8;
Nehemiah 10:16

Adonikam
(High)
1 man/3 references
Ezra 2:13

Adoniram
(Lord of height)
1 man/2 references
King Solomon's official over forced
labor for building the temple.
1 Kings 4:6

Adoni-zedec
(Lord of justice)
1 man/2 references
Pagan king of Jerusalem during
Joshua's conquest of the Promised
Land.
Joshua 10:1

Adoram
(Lord of height)
2 men/2 references

Notably, King David's official over forced labor.
2 Samuel 20:24; 1 Kings 12:18

Adrammelech
(Splendor of the king)
1 man/2 references
Son of the Assyrian king Sennacherib, who, with his brother Sharezer, killed his father with a sword.
2 Kings 19:37

Adriel
(Flock of God)
Man who married Saul's daughter Merab, who had been promised to David.
2 Samuel 18:19

Aeneas
1 man/2 references
Lame man of Lydda healed by the apostle Peter.
Acts 9:33

Agabus
(Locust)
1 man/2 references
Early Christian prophet from Jerusalem.
Acts 11:28

Agag
(Flame)
2 men/8 references
Notably, king mentioned by Balaam in his prophecy concerning God's blessing on Israel. Also, king of the Amalekites whom King Saul of Israel spared in defiance of God's command.
Numbers 24:7; 1 Samuel 15:8

Agar
1 woman/2 references
Greek form of the name *Hagar*, used in the New Testament.
Galatians 4:24

Agee
1 man/1 reference
2 Samuel 23:11

Agrippa
(Wild horse tamer)
1 man/12 references
Herod Agrippa II, great-grandson of Herod the Great. Same as Herod.
Acts 25:13

Agur
(Gathered)
1 man/1 reference
Little-known biblical writer who penned the thirtieth chapter of Proverbs.
Proverbs 30:1

Ahab
(Friend of his father)
2 men/94 references
Notably, an evil king of Israel who humbled himself before God.
1 Kings 16:28; Jeremiah 29:21

Aharah
(After his brother)
1 man/1 reference
1 Chronicles 8:1

Aharhel
(Safe)
1 man/1 reference
1 Chronicles 4:8

Ahasai
(Seizer)
1 man/1 reference
Nehemiah 11:13

Ahasbai
1 man/1 reference
2 Samuel 23:34

Ahasuerus

3 men/31 references

Most notably, Persian king who reigned over an empire that ran from India to Ethiopia and replaced his queen Vashti with Esther, whom he was unaware was a Jew. Also, king of Media and the father of Darius the Mede.

Ezra 4:6; Daniel 9:1; Esther 1:1

Ahaz

(Possessor)

2 men/42 references

Notably, king of Judah who became deeply involved in paganism.

2 Kings 15:38; 1 Chronicles 8:35

Ahaziah

(God has seized)

2 men/37 references

Notably, king of Israel and the son of Ahab, who walked in the pagan ways of his parents. Also, king of Judah.

1 Kings 22:40; 2 Kings 8:24

Ahban

(Possessor of understanding)

1 man/1 reference

1 Chronicles 2:29

Aher

(Hinder)

1 man/1 reference

1 Chronicles 7:12

Ahi

(Brotherly)

2 men/2 references

1 Chronicles 5:15; 1 Chronicles 7:34

Ahiah

(Worshipper of God)

3 men/4 references

Most notably, priest who was with King Saul at Gibeah when Jonathan

and his armor bearer conquered the Philistines.

1 Samuel 14:3; 1 Kings 4:3; 1 Chronicles 8:7

Ahiam

(Uncle)

1 man/2 references

One of King David's valiant warriors.

2 Samuel 23:33

Ahian

(Brotherly)

1 man/1 reference

1 Chronicles 7:19

Ahiezer

(Brother of help)

2 men/6 references

Notably, man of the tribe of Dan who helped Aaron number the Israelites, serving as captain of his tribe. Also, "mighty man" of David.

Numbers 1:12; 1 Chronicles 12:3

Ahihud

(Possessor of renown, mysterious)

2 men/2 references

Notably, prince of the tribe of Asher when the Israelites entered the Promised Land.

Numbers 34:27; 1 Chronicles 8:7

Ahijah

(Worshipper of God)

6 men/20 references

Most notably, prophet who prophesied the division of Israel into the countries of Israel and Judah.

1 Kings 11:29; 1 Kings 15:27; 1 Chronicles 2:25; 1 Chronicles 11:36; 1 Chronicles 26:20; Nehemiah 10:26

Ahikam

(High)

1 man/20 references

Man sent to consult Huldah the prophetess after King Josiah

rediscovered the book of the law and
supported Jeremiah, protecting him
from death.
2 Kings 22:12

Ahilud
(Brother of one born)
1 man/5 references
2 Samuel 8:16

Ahimaaz
(Brother of anger)
3 men/15 references
1 Samuel 14:50; 2 Samuel 15:27; 1 Kings 4:15

Ahiman
(Gift)
2 men/4 references
Notably, one of the gigantic children
of Anak who was killed after Joshua's
death, as Judah battled against the
Canaanites.
Numbers 13:22; 1 Chronicles 9:17

Ahimelech
(Brother of the king)
2 men/16 references
Notably, priest of Nob who gave
David the hallowed bread to feed his
men when David was fleeing from
Saul.
1 Samuel 21:1; 1 Samuel 26:6

Ahimoth
(Brother of death)
1 man/1 reference
1 Chronicles 6:25

Ahinadab
(Brother of liberality)
1 man/1 reference
One of King Solomon's twelve
officials over provisions.
1 Kings 4:14

Ahinoam
(Brother of pleasantness)
2 women/7 references
Notably, wife of Saul, Israel's first
king.
1 Samuel 14:50; 1 Samuel 25:43

Ahio
(Brotherly)
3 men/6 references
Most notably, son of Abinadab who
went before the ark of the covenant
then transported it into Jerusalem.
2 Samuel 6:3; 1 Chronicles 8:14;
1 Chronicles 8:31

Ahira
(Brother of wrong)
1 man/5 references
Prince of the tribe of Napthali, after
the Exodus.
Numbers 1:15

Ahiram
(High)
1 man/1 reference
Numbers 26:38

Ahisamach
(Brother of support)
1 man/3 references
Exodus 31:6

Ahishahar
(Brother of the dawn)
1 man/1 reference
1 Chronicles 7:10

Ahishar
(Brother of the singer)
1 man/1 reference
King Solomon's official over his
household.
1 Kings 4:6

Ahithophel
(Brother of folly)
1 man/20 references
King David's counselor who conspired with David's son Absalom to overthrow the throne.
2 Samuel 15:12

Ahitub
(Brother of goodness)
4 men/15 references
1 Samuel 14:3; 2 Samuel 8:17; 1 Chronicles 6:11; 1 Chronicles 9:11

Ahlai
(Wishful)
1 man/1 woman/2 references
1 Chronicles 2:31; 1 Chronicles 11:41

Ahoah
(Brotherly)
1 man/1 reference
1 Chronicles 8:4

Aholiab
(Tent of his father)
1 man/5 references
Engraver and embroiderer given special ability by God to work on the tabernacle, "a cunning workman."
Exodus 31:6

Aholibamah
(Tent of the height)
1 man/1 woman/8 references
Genesis 36:2; Genesis 36:41

Ahumai
(Neighbor of water)
1 man/1 reference
1 Chronicles 4:2

Ahuzam
(Seizure)
1 man/1 reference
1 Chronicles 4:6

Ahuzzath
(Possession)
1 man/1 reference
Genesis 26:26

Aiah
(Hawk)
2 men/5 references
1 Chronicles 1:40; 2 Samuel 3:7

Ajah
(Hawk)
1 man/1 reference
Genesis 36:24

Akan
(Tortuous)
1 man/1 reference
Same as Jaakan and Jakan.
Genesis 36:27

Akkub
(Insidious)
5 men/8 references
1 Chronicles 3:24; 1 Chronicles 9:17; Ezra 2:42; Ezra 2:45; Nehemiah 8:7

Alameth
(A covering)
1 man/1 reference
1 Chronicles 7:8

Alemeth
(A covering)
1 man/2 references
1 Chronicles 8:36

Alexander
(Man-defender)
4 men/6 references
Mark 15:21; Acts 4:6; Acts 19:33; 1 Timothy 1:20

Aliah
(Perverseness)
1 man/1 reference
Same as Alvah.
1 Chronicles 1:51

Alian
(Lofty)
1 man/1 reference
Same as Alvan.
1 Chronicles 1:40

Allon
(Oak)
1 man/1 reference
1 Chronicles 4:37

Almodad
1 man/2 references
Genesis 10:26

Alphaeus
2 men/5 references
Notably, father of one of two apostles
named James.
Matthew 10:3; Mark 2:14

Alvah
(Perverseness)
1 man/1 reference
"Duke of Edom." Same as Aliah.
Genesis 36:40

Alvan
(Lofty)
1 man/1 reference
Genesis 36:23

Amal
(Worry)
1 man/1 reference
1 Chronicles 7:35

Amalek
1 man/3 references
Genesis 36:12

Amariah
(God has promised)
9 men/16 references
1 Chronicles 6:7; 1 Chronicles 6:11;
1 Chronicles 23:19; 2 Chronicles 19:11;
2 Chronicles 31:15; Ezra 10:42; Nehemiah
10:3; Nehemiah 11:4; Zephaniah 1:1

Amasa
(Burden)
2 men/16 references
Notably, King David's nephew who
became Absalom's commander during
Absalom's rebellion against his father.
2 Samuel 17:25; 2 Chronicles 28:12

Amasai
(Burdensome)
3 men/5 references
Most notably, chief captain in
David's army. Also, Levite who
blew a trumpet before the ark of the
covenant when David brought it to
Jerusalem.
1 Chronicles 6:25; 1 Chronicles 12:18;
1 Chronicles 15:24

Amashai
(Burdensome)
1 man/1 reference
Jewish exile from the tribe of Levi
who resettled Jerusalem.
Nehemiah 11:13

Amasiah
(God has loaded)
1 man/1 reference
Warrior who raised 200,000 brave
men for King Jehoshaphat.
2 Chronicles 17:16

Amaziah
(Strength of God)
4 men/40 references
Most notably, son and successor of
King Joash of Judah.
2 Kings 12:21; 1 Chronicles 4:34;
1 Chronicles 6:45; Amos 7:10

Ami
(Skilled)
1 man/1 reference
Ezra 2:57

Aminadab
(People of liberality)
1 man/3 references
Matthew 1:4

Amittai
(Truthful)
1 man/2 references
Father of the prophet Jonah, who
preached in Nineveh.
2 Kings 14:25

Ammiel
(People of God)
4 men/6 references
Most notably, one of twelve spies
sent by Moses to Canaan. Also, man
who housed Saul's crippled son,
Mephibosheth, after the king's death.
Numbers 13:12; 2 Samuel 9:4; 1 Chronicles
3:5; 1 Chronicles 26:5

Ammihud
(People of splendor)
5 men/10 references
Numbers 1:10; Numbers 34:20; Numbers
34:28; 2 Samuel 13:37; 1 Chronicles 9:4

Amminadab
(People of liberality)
4 men/13 references
Exodus 6:23; Numbers 1:7; 1 Chronicles
6:22; 1 Chronicles 15:10

Ammishaddai
(People of the Almighty)
1 man/5 references
Numbers 1:12

Ammizabad
(People of endowment)
1 man/1 reference
Army officer of King David.
1 Chronicles 27:6

Amnon
(Faithful)
2 men/28 references
Notably, David's firstborn son. He
fell in love with his half sister Tamar
and raped her. Tamar's full brother,
Absalom, eventually had him killed.
2 Samuel 3:2; 1 Chronicles 4:20

Amok
(Deep)
1 man/2 references
Exiled priest who returned to Judah
under Zerubbabel.
Nehemiah 12:7

Amon
(Skilled)
3 men/19 references
1 Kings 22:26; 2 Kings 21:18; Nehemiah 7:59

Amos
(Burdensome)
2 men/8 references
Notably, Judean prophet during the
reigns of King Uzziah of Judah and
King Jeroboam of Israel.
Amos 1:1; Luke 3:25

Amoz
(Strong)
1 man/13 references
Father of the prophet Isaiah.
2 Kings 19:2

Amplias
(Enlarged)
1 man/1 reference
Romans 16:8

Amram
(High people)
3 men/14 references
Most notably, father of Moses, Aaron,
and Miriam.
Exodus 6:18; Ezra 10:34; 1 Chronicles 1:41

Amraphel
1 man/2 references
King of Shinar in the days of Abram.
Genesis 14:1

Amzi
(Strong)
2 men/2 references
1 Chronicles 6:46; Nehemiah 11:12

Anah
(Answer)
2 men/1 woman /12 references
Genesis 36:2; Genesis 36:20;
Genesis 36:24

Anaiah
(God has answered)
2 men/2 references
Notably, priest who assisted Ezra in
reading the book of the law to the
people of Jerusalem.
Nehemiah 8:4; Nehemiah 10:22

Anak
(Strangling)
1 man/9 references
Founder of a tribe in Hebron. His
gigantic sons lived there when
Joshua's spies searched the land.
Numbers 13:22

Anan
(Cloud)
1 man/1 reference
Jewish leader who renewed the
covenant under Nehemiah.
Nehemiah 10:26

Anani
(Cloudy)
1 man/1 reference
1 Chronicles 3:24

Ananiah
(God has covered)
1 man/1 reference
Nehemiah 3:23

Ananias
(God has favored)
3 men/11 references
Most notably, Christian who lied to
the apostle Peter, saying that he and
his wife, Sapphira, had donated the
full price of a land sale to the church.
He died for his sin.
Acts 5:1; Acts 9:10; Acts 23:2

Anath
(Answer)
1 man/2 references
Judges 3:31

Anathoth
(Answers)
2 men/2 references
1 Chronicles 7:8; Nehemiah 10:19

Andrew
(Manly)
1 man/13 references
Brother of Peter and one of Jesus'
disciples and apostles.
Matthew 4:18

Andronicus
(Man of victory)
1 man/1 reference
Roman Christian who spent time in
jail with the apostle Paul and who
may have been related to Paul.
Romans 16:7

Aner
(Boy)
1 man/2 references
Genesis 14:13

Aniam
(Groaning of the people)
1 man/1 reference
1 Chronicles 7:19

Anna
(Favored)
1 woman/1 reference
Widowed prophetess who lived in the temple and recognized Jesus as the Messiah when He was first brought to the temple.
Luke 2:36

Annas
(God has favored)
1 man/4 references
High priest during Jesus' ministry.
Luke 3:2

Antipas
(Instead of father)
1 man/1 reference
Christian martyr commended by Jesus.
Revelation 2:13

Antothijah
(Answers of God)
1 man/1 reference
1 Chronicles 8:24

Anub
(Borne)
1 man/1 reference
1 Chronicles 4:8

Apelles
1 man/1 reference
Romans 16:10

Aphiah
(Breeze)
1 man/1 reference
1 Samuel 9:1

Aphses
(Sever)
One of twenty-four priests in David's time who was chosen by lot to serve in the tabernacle.
1 Chronicles 24:15

Apollos
(The sun)
1 man/10 references
Jewish preacher from Alexandria.
Acts 18:24

Appaim
(Two nostrils)
1 man/2 references
1 Chronicles 2:30

Apphia
1 woman/1 reference
Christian woman of Colosse.
Philemon 1:2

Aquila
(Eagle)
1 man/6 references
Tentmaker, married to Priscilla. Together this couple helped Paul's ministry.
Acts 18:2

Ara
(Lion)
1 man/1 reference
1 Chronicles 7:38

Arad
(Fugitive)
2 men/3 references
Notably, Canaanite king who fought the Israelites as they entered the Promised Land.
Numbers 21:1; 1 Chronicles 8:15

Arah
(Wayfaring)
3 men/4 references
1 Chronicles 7:39; Ezra 2:5; Nehemiah 6:18

Aram
(The highland)
3 men/8 references
Genesis 10:22; Genesis 22:21;
1 Chronicles 7:34

Aran
(Shrill)
1 man/2 reference
Genesis 36:28

Araunah
(Strong)
1 man/9 references
Jebusite who sold his threshing floor
to King David so the king could
build an altar and make a sacrifice
there. Same as Ornan.
2 Samuel 24:16

Arba
(Four)
1 man/3 references
Joshua 15:13

Archelaus
(People-ruling)
1 man/1 reference
Matthew 2:22

Archippus
(Horse-ruler)
1 man/2 references
Colossians 4:17

Ard
(Fugitive)
2 men/3 references
Genesis 46:21; Numbers 26:40

Ardon
(Roaming)
1 Chronicles 2:18

Areli
(Heroic)
1 man/2 references
Genesis 46:16

Aretas
1 man/1 reference
Arabian king who ruled over Syria.
2 Corinthians 11:32

Argob
(Stony)
1 man/1 reference
Israelite official assassinated along
with King Pekahiah.
2 Kings 15:25

Aridai
1 man/1 reference
Esther 9:9

Aridatha
1 man/1 reference
Esther 9:8

Arieh
(Lion)
1 man/1 reference
Israelite official assassinated along
with King Pekahiah.
2 Kings 15:25

Ariel
(Lion of God)
1 man/1 reference
Jewish exile charged with finding
Levites and temple servants to travel
to Jerusalem with Ezra.
Ezra 8:16

Arioch
2 men/7 references
Notably, king of Ellasar in the days
of Abram. Also, captain of King
Nebuchadnezzar's guard, who took
Daniel to the king when the wise
men could not interpret his dream.
Genesis 14:1; Daniel 2:14

Arisai
1 man/1 reference
Esther 9:9

Aristarchus
(Best ruling)
1 man/5 references
One of Paul's companions who
accompanied him on various travels,
including his trip to Rome.
Acts 19:29

Aristobulus
(Best counseling)
1 man/1 reference
Romans 16:10

Armoni
(Palatial)
1 man/1 reference
Son of King Saul.
2 Samuel 21:8

Arnan
(Noisy)
1 man/1 reference
1 Chronicles 3:21

Arod
(Fugitive)
1 man/1 reference
Numbers 26:17

Arphaxad
1 man/10 references
Genesis 10:22

Artaxerxes
3 men/15 references
Most notably, Persian king who
received letters objecting to the
rebuilding of Jerusalem from those
who opposed the Jews. Also called
Longimanus.
Ezra 4:7; Ezra 6:14; Ezra 7:1

Artemas
(Gift of Artemis)
1 man/1 reference
Titus 3:12

Arza
(Earthiness)
1 man/1 reference
Palace steward of Israel's king Elah.
1 Kings 16:9

Asa
2 men/60 references
Notably, king of Judah who reigned
forty-one years and removed many
idols from Judah.
1 Kings 15:8; 1 Chronicles 9:16

Asahel
(God has made)
4 men/18 references
Most notably, brother of Joab, who
was David's army commander. Also,
Levite sent by King Jehoshaphat to
teach the law of the Lord throughout
the nation of Judah.
2 Samuel 2:18; 2 Chronicles 17:8;
2 Chronicles 31:13; Ezra 10:15

Asahiah
(God has made)
1 man/2 references
Servant of King Josiah who was part
of a delegation sent to the prophetess
Huldah after the "book of the law"
was discovered in the temple. Same as
Asaiah.
2 Kings 22:12

Asaiah

(God has made)
5 men/6 references
Same as Asahiah.
1 Chronicles 4:36; 1 Chronicles 6:30;
1 Chronicles 9:5; 1 Chronicles 15:6;
2 Chronicles 34:20

Asaph

(Collector)
5 men/45 references
2 Kings 18:18; 1 Chronicles 6:39;
1 Chronicles 9:15; 1 Chronicles 26:1;
Nehemiah 2:8

Asareel

(Right of God)
1 man/1 reference
1 Chronicles 4:16

Asarelah

(Right toward God)
1 man/1 reference
1 Chronicles 25:2

Asenath

1 woman/3 references
Daughter of an Egyptian priest, she
was given as a wife to Joseph by the
pharaoh.
Genesis 41:45

Aser

(Happy)
1 man/2 references
Greek form of the Hebrew name
Asher; one of twelve tribes of Israel.
Luke 2:36

Ashbea

(Adjurer)
1 man/1 reference
1 Chronicles 4:21

Ashbel

(Flowing)
1 man/3 references
Genesis 46:21

Ashchenaz

1 man/1 reference
Same as Ashkenaz.
1 Chronicles 1:6

Asher

(Happy)
1 man/9 references
Genesis 30:13

Ashkenaz

1 man/1 reference
Genesis 10:3

Ashpenaz

1 man/1 reference
Chief eunuch of the Babylonian king
Nebuchadnezzar.
Daniel 1:3

Ashriel

(Right of God)
1 man/1 reference
1 Chronicles 7:14

Ashur

(Successful)
1 man/2 references
1 Chronicles 2:24

Ashvath

(Bright)
1 man/1 reference
1 Chronicles 7:33

Asiel

(Made of God)
1 man/1 reference
1 Chronicles 4:35

Asnah

1 man/1 reference
Ezra 2:50

Asnapper
1 man/1 reference
An Assyrian king who resettled
Samaria with other people, after the
Israelites were captured.
Ezra 4:10

Aspatha
1 man/1 reference
Esther 9:7

Asriel
(Right of God)
1 man/2 references
Numbers 26:31

Asshur
(Successful)
2 men/3 references
Genesis 10:11; Genesis 10:22

Assir
(Prisoner)
3 men/5 references
Exodus 6:24; 1 Chronicles 6:23;
1 Chronicles 3:17

Asyncritus
(Incomparable)
1 man/1 reference
Romans 16:14

Atarah
(Crown)
1 woman/1 reference
1 Chronicles 2:26

Ater
(Maimed)
3 men/5 references
Ezra 2:16; Ezra 2:42; Nehemiah 10:17

Athaiah
(God has helped)
1 man/1 reference
Nehemiah 11:4

Athaliah
(God has constrained)
2 men/1 woman/17 references
Notably, wife of Jehoram and mother
of Ahaziah, two kings of Judah.
2 Kings 8:26; 1 Chronicles 8:26; Ezra 8:7

Athlai
(Constricted)
1 man/1 reference
Ezra 10:28

Attai
(Timely)
3 men/4 references
1 Chronicles 2:35; 1 Chronicles 12:11;
2 Chronicles 11:20

Augustus
(August)
1 man/4 references
Roman emperor who called for the
census that brought Mary and Joseph
to Bethlehem and still ruled when
Paul appealed to Caesar during his
imprisonment in Jerusalem. Also
called Caesar Augustus.
Luke 2:1

Azaliah
(God has reserved)
1 man/2 references
2 Kings 22:3

Azaniah
(Heard by God)
1 man/1 reference
Levite who renewed the covenant
under Nehemiah.
Nehemiah 10:9

Azarael
(God has helped)
1 man/1 reference
Priest who helped to dedicate the
rebuilt walls of Jerusalem by playing a
musical instrument.
Nehemiah 12:36

Azareel
(God has helped)
5 men/5 references
Most notably, a "mighty man" who supported the future king David during his conflict with Saul. Also, leader of the tribe of Dan in the days of King David.
1 Chronicles 12:6; 1 Chronicles 25:18; 1 Chronicles 27:22; Ezra 10:41; Nehemiah 11:13

Azariah
(God has helped)
28 men/49 references
Most notably, officer in Solomon's army. Also, king of Judah who was obedient to God but did not remove the idolatrous altars from the high places. Same as Uzziah. Also, prophet who encouraged King Asa of Judah to follow the Lord. Also, chief priest during the reign of King Hezekiah of Judah. Also, man who repaired Jerusalem's walls under Nehemiah. Also, Hebrew name for Abed-nego, one of Daniel's companions in exile.
1 Kings 4:2; 1 Kings 4:5; 2 Kings 14:21; 1 Chronicles 2:8; 1 Chronicles 2:38; 1 Chronicles 6:9; 1 Chronicles 6:10; 1 Chronicles 6:13; 1 Chronicles 6:36; 2 Chronicles 15:1; 2 Chronicles 21:2; 2 Chronicles 22:6; 2 Chronicles 23:1; 2 Chronicles 26:17; 2 Chronicles 28:12; 2 Chronicles 29:12; 2 Chronicles 31:10; Ezra 7:3; Nehemiah 3:23; Nehemiah 7:7; Nehemiah 8:7; Nehemiah 10:2; Nehemiah 12:33; Jeremiah 43:2; Daniel 1:6

Azaz
(Strong)
1 man/1 reference
1 Chronicles 5:8

Azaziah
(God has strengthened)
3 men/3 references
Most notably, Levite musician who performed in celebration when King David brought the ark of the covenant to Jerusalem.
1 Chronicles 15:21; 1 Chronicles 27:20; 2 Chronicles 31:13

Azbuk
(Stern depopulator)
1 man/1 reference
Nehemiah 3:16

Azel
(Noble)
1 man/6 references
1 Chronicles 8:37

Azgad
(Stern troop)
3 men/4 references
Ezra 2:12; Ezra 8:12; Nehemiah 10:15

Aziel
(Strengthened of God)
1 man/1 reference
Levite musician who performed in celebration when King David brought the ark of the covenant to Jerusalem. Same as Jaaziel.
1 Chronicles 15:20

Aziza
(Strengthfulness)
1 man/1 reference
Ezra 10:27

Azmaveth
(Strong one of death)
4 men/6 references
Most notably, one of King David's valiant warriors.
2 Samuel 23:31; 1 Chronicles 8:36; 1 Chronicles 12:3; 1 Chronicles 27:25

Azor
(Helpful)
1 man/2 references
Matthew 1:13

Azriel
(Help of God)
3 men/3 references
Most notably, one of the "mighty men of valour, famous men" who led the half tribe of Manasseh.
1 Chronicles 5:24; 1 Chronicles 27:19; Jeremiah 36:26

Azrikam
(Help of an enemy)
4 men/6 references
1 Chronicles 3:23; 1 Chronicles 8:38; 1 Chronicles 9:14; 2 Chronicles 28:7

Azubah
(Desertion)
2 women/4 references
1 Kings 22:42; 1 Chronicles 2:18

Azur
(Helpful)
2 men/2 references
Jeremiah 28:1; Ezekiel 11:1

Azzan
(Strong one)
1 man/1 reference
Numbers 34:26

Azzur
(Helpful)
1 man/1 reference
Jewish leader who renewed the covenant under Nehemiah.
Nehemiah 10:17

B

Baal
(Master)
2 men/3 references
1 Chronicles 5:5; 1 Chronicles 8:30

Baal-hanan
(Possessor of grace)
2 men/5 references
Notably, king of Edom. Also, Gederite who had charge of King David's olive and sycamore trees.
Genesis 36:38; 1 Chronicles 27:28

Baalis
(In exultation)
1 man/1 reference
Ammonite king who sent an assassin against Gedaliah, the Babylonianappointed governor of Judah.
Jeremiah 40:14

Baana
(In affliction)
2 men/2 references
One of King Solomon's twelve officials over provisions.
1 Kings 4:12; Nehemiah 3:4

Baanah
(In affliction)
4 men/10 references
Most notably, leader of one of the raiding bands of Saul's son. Also, one of King Solomon's twelve officials over provisions.
2 Samuel 4:22; 2 Samuel 22:39; 1 Kings 4:16; Ezra 2:2

Baara
(Brutish)
1 woman/1 reference
1 Chronicles 8:8

Baaseiah
(In the work of God)
1 man/1 reference
1 Chronicles 6:40

Baasha
(Offensiveness)
1 man/28 references
Idolatrous king of Israel.
1 Kings 15:16

Bakbakkar
(Searcher)
1 man/1 reference
1 Chronicles 9:15

Bakbuk
(Bottle)
1 man/2 references
Ezra 2:51

Bakbukiah
1 man/3 references
(Emptying of God)
Nehemiah 11:17

Balaam
(Foreigner)
1 man/63 references
Mesopotamian prophet, sent for by
Balak, king of Moab, to curse the
Israelites. His donkey spoke to him
when the angel of the Lord barred the
donkey's way.
Numbers 22:5

Balac
(Waster)
1 man/1 reference
Greek form of the name *Balak*; a king
of Moab.
Revelation 2:14

Baladan
(Bel is his lord)
1 man/2 references
2 Kings 20:12

Balak
(Waster)
1 man/43 references
King of Moab who sent for the
Mesopotamian prophet Balaam to
curse the Israelites.
Numbers 22:2

Bani
(Built)
10 men/15 references
Most notably, a "mighty man" of
King David.
2 Samuel 23:36; 1 Chronicles 6:46;
1 Chronicles 9:4; Ezra 2:10; Ezra 10:34;
Ezra 10:38; Nehemiah 3:17; Nehemiah 9:4;
Nehemiah 10:14; Nehemiah 11:22

Barabbas
(Son of Abba)
1 man/11 references
Prison inmate when Jesus came to
trial. When given the choice by
Pilate of which of the two should be
released, the people chose Barabbas.
Matthew 27:16

Barachel
(God has blessed)
1 man/2 references
Job 32:2

Barachias
(Blessing of God)
1 man/1 reference
Matthew 23:35

Barak
(Lightning)
1 man/14 references
Judge Deborah's battle captain who
refused to enter battle without her
support.
Judges 4:6

Bariah
(Fugitive)
1 man/1 reference
1 Chronicles 3:22

Bar-jesus
(Son of Jesus)
1 man/1 reference
Jewish sorcerer, also called Elymas.
Acts 13:6

Barjona
(Son of Jonas)
1 man/1 reference
Another name for the apostle Peter, used by Jesus Christ.
Matthew 16:17

Barkos
1 man/2 references
Ezra 2:53

Barnabas
(Son of prophecy)
1 man/29 references
Introduced Saul to the apostles and spoke up for him. Also traveled on missionary journeys with Paul and Mark. Same as Joses.
Acts 4:36

Barsabas
(Son of Sabas)
2 men/2 references
Notably, also called Joseph Justus, potential apostolic replacement for Judas Iscariot who lost by lot to the other candidate, Matthias. Same as Joseph and Justus.
Acts 1:23; Acts 15:22

Bartholomew
(Son of Tolmai)
1 man/4 references
One of Jesus' disciples. Probably the same as Nathanael.
Matthew 10:3

Bartimaeus
(Son of Timaeus)
1 man/1 reference
Blind beggar of Jericho who shouted for Jesus' attention and Jesus healed him.
Mark 10:46

Baruch
(Blessed)
3 men/26 references
Most notably, rebuilder of the walls of Jerusalem and a priest who renewed the covenant under Nehemiah. Also, scribe who wrote down all the words the prophet Jeremiah received from God.
Nehemiah 3:20; Nehemiah 11:5; Jeremiah 32:12

Barzillai
(Iron-hearted)
2 men/12 references
Notably, elderly man who brought food and supplies to King David and his soldiers.
2 Samuel 17:27; 2 Samuel 21:8

Bashemath
(Fragrance)
2 women/6 references
Notably, Hittite wife of Esau. Same as Adah. Also possibly the same as Bashemath.
Genesis 26:34; Genesis 36:3

Basmath
(Fragrance)
1 woman/1 reference
1 Kings 4:15

Bath-sheba
(Daughter of an oath)
1 woman/11 references
Wife of the warrior Uriah the Hittite. King David committed adultery with her, and she became pregnant then married him when Uriah died.
2 Samuel 11:3

Bath-shua
(Daughter of wealth)
1 woman/1 reference
Form of the name *Bath-sheba*; a wife
of King David.
1 Chronicles 3:5

Bavai
1 man/1 reference
Man who repaired Jerusalem's walls
under Nehemiah.
Nehemiah 3:18

Bazlith
(Peeling)
1 man/1 reference
Nehemiah 7:54

Bazluth
(Peeling)
1 man/1 reference
Same as Bazlith.
Ezra 2:52

Bealiah
(God is master)
1 man/1 reference
"Mighty man" who supported the
future king David during his conflict
with Saul.
1 Chronicles 12:5

Bebai
3 men/6 references
Ezra 2:11; Ezra 8:11; Nehemiah 10:15

Becher
(Young camel)
2 men/5 references
Genesis 46:21; Numbers 26:35

Bechorath
(Firstborn)
1 man/1 reference
1 Samuel 9:1

Bedad
(Solitary)
1 man/2 references
Genesis 36:35

Bedan
(Servile)
2 men/2 references
Notably, judge of Israel who delivered
the nation from its enemies.
1 Samuel 12:11; 1 Chronicles 7:17

Bedeiah
(Servant of Jehovah)
1 man/1 reference
Ezra 10:35

Beeliada
(Baal has known)
Son of King David, born in
Jerusalem.
1 Chronicles 14:7

Beera
(A well)
1 man/1 reference
1 Chronicles 7:37

Beerah
(A well)
1 man/1 reference
1 Chronicles 5:6

Beeri
(Fountained)
1 men/2 references
Genesis 26:34; Hosea 1:1

Bela
(A gulp)
3 men/11 references
Most notably, king of Edom.
Genesis 36:32; Numbers 26:38;
1 Chronicles 5:8

Belah
(A gulp)
1 man/1 reference
Form of the name *Bela*; a son of
Benjamin.
Genesis 46:21

Belshazzar
1 man/8 references
Babylonian king who saw
handwriting on the wall and sought
to have it interpreted. When his
own soothsayers could not do so, the
prophet Daniel read it to him.
Daniel 5:1

Belteshazzar
1 man/10 references
Babylonian name given to the exiled
Israelite Daniel upon entering King
Nebuchadnezzar's service.
Daniel 1:7

Ben
(Son)
1 man/1 reference
Levite musician who performed in
celebration when King David brought
the ark of the covenant to Jerusalem.
1 Chronicles 15:18

Benaiah
(God has built)
12 men/42 references
Most notably, one of David's three
mighty men and a commander in
King David's army.
2 Samuel 8:18; 2 Samuel 23:30;
1 Chronicles 4:36; 1 Chronicles 15:18;
1 Chronicles 27:34; 2 Chronicles 20:14;
2 Chronicles 31:13; Ezra 10:25; Ezra 10:30;
Ezra 10:35; Ezra 10:43; Ezekiel 11:1

Benammi
(Son of my people)
1 man/1 reference
Genesis 19:38

Ben-hadad
(Son of Hadad)
3 men/26 references
Most notably, king of Syria who
supported Asa, king of Judah, against
Israel.
1 Kings 15:18; 1 Kings 20:1; 2 Kings 13:3

Ben-hail
(Son of might)
1 man/1 reference
Prince of Judah sent by King
Jehoshaphat to teach the law of the
Lord throughout the nation.
2 Chronicles 17:7

Ben-hanan
(Son of Chanan)
1 man/1 reference
1 Chronicles 4:20

Beninu
(Our son)
1 man/1 reference
Nehemiah 10:13

Benjamin
(Son of the right hand)
5 men/20 references
Most notably, Jacob's youngest son
and the only full brother of Joseph.
Genesis 35:18; 1 Chronicles 7:10; Ezra
10:32; Nehemiah 3:23; Nehemiah 12:34

Beno
(Son)
1 man/2 references
1 Chronicles 24:26

Ben-oni
(Son of my sorrow)
1 man/1 reference
Name given by Rachel to her second
son as she was dying in childbirth.
The boy's father, Jacob, called him
Benjamin.
Genesis 35:18

Ben-zoheth
(Son of Zocheth)
1 man/1 reference
1 Chronicles 4:20

Beor
(A lamp)
2 men/10 references
Same as Bosor.
Genesis 36:32; Numbers 22:5

Bera
1 man/1 reference
King of Sodom in the days of Abram.
Genesis 14:2

Berachah
(Benediction)
1 man/1 reference
"Mighty man" who supported the
future king David during his conflict
with Saul.
1 Chronicles 12:3

Berachiah
(Blessing of God)
1 man/1 reference
Same as Berechiah.
1 Chronicles 6:39

Beraiah
(God has created)
1 man/1 reference
1 Chronicles 8:21

Berechiah
(Blessing of God)
7 men/10 references
1 Chronicles 3:20; 1 Chronicles 9:16;
1 Chronicles 15:17; 1 Chronicles 15:23;
2 Chronicles 28:12; Nehemiah 3:4;
Zechariah 1:1

Bered
(Hail)
1 man/1 reference
1 Chronicles 7:20

Beri
(Fountained)
1 man/1 reference
1 Chronicles 7:36

Beriah
(In trouble)
4 men/11 references
Genesis 46:17; 1 Chronicles 7:23; 1
Chronicles 8:13; 1 Chronicles 23:10

Bernice
(Victorious)
1 woman/3 references
Daughter of Herod Agrippa and sister
of Agrippa II.
Acts 25:13

Berodach-baladan
1 man/1 reference
Babylonian king who sent wishes for
recovery to Judah's ill king Hezekiah.
2 Kings 20:12

Besai
(Domineering)
1 man/2 references
Ezra 2:49

Besodeiah
(In the counsel of Jehovah)
1 man/1 reference
Nehemiah 3:6

Bethlehem

(Native of Bethlehem)
1 man/3 references
1 Chronicles 2:51

Beth-rapha

(House of the giant)
1 man/1 reference
1 Chronicles 4:12

Bethuel

(Destroyed of God)
1 man/9 references
Genesis 22:22

Beth-zur

(House of the rock)
1 man/1 reference
1 Chronicles 2:45

Bezai

(Domineering)
2 men/3 references
Ezra 2:17; Nehemiah 10:18

Bezaleel

(In the shadow of God)
2 men, 9 references
Notably, craftsman given special ability by God to work on the tabernacle.
Exodus 31:2; Ezra 10:30

Bezer

(Inaccessible)
1 man/1 reference
1 Chronicles 7:37

Bichri

(Youthful)
1 man/8 references
2 Samuel 20:1

Bidkar

(Assassin)
1 man/1 reference
Army captain serving Israel's king Jehu.
2 Kings 9:25

Bigtha

1 man/1 reference
Eunuch serving the Persian king Ahasuerus in Esther's time.
Esther 1:10

Bigthan

1 man/1 reference
One of two palace doorkeepers who conspired to kill their king, Ahasuerus of Persia. The plot was uncovered by Mordecai, and both doorkeepers were hanged. Same as Bigthana.
Esther 2:21

Bigthana

1 man/1 reference
Same as Bigthan.
Esther 6:2

Bigvai

4 men/6 references
Ezra 2:2; Ezra 2:14; Ezra 8:14;
Nehemiah 10:16

Bildad

1 man/5 references
One of three friends of Job who mourned Job's losses for a week then accused him of wrongdoing.
Job 2:11

Bilgah

(Stopping)
2 men/3 references
Notably, one of twenty-four priests in David's time who was chosen by lot to serve in the tabernacle.
1 Chronicles 24:14; Nehemiah 12:5

Bilgai
(Stoppable)
1 man/1 reference
Priest who renewed the covenant
under Nehemiah.
Nehemiah 10:8

Bilhah
(Timid)
1 woman/10 references
Rachel's handmaid, whom she gave to
Jacob to bear children for her. Bilhah
had two sons, Dan and Naphtali.
Genesis 29:29

Bilhan
(Timid)
2 men/4 references
Genesis 36:27; 1 Chronicles 7:10

Bilshan
1 man/2 references
Ezra 2:2

Bimhal
(With pruning)
1 man/1 reference
1 Chronicles 7:33

Binea
1 man/2 references
1 Chronicles 8:37

Binnui
(Built up)
6 men/7 references
Ezra 8:33; Ezra 10:30; Ezra 10:38;
Nehemiah 3:24; Nehemiah 7:15;
Nehemiah 12:8

Birsha
(With wickedness)
1 man/1 reference
King of Sodom in the days of Abram.
Genesis 14:2

Birzavith
(Holes)
1 man/1 reference
1 Chronicles 7:31

Bishlam
1 man/1 reference
Man who tried to stop the rebuilding
of Jerusalem's walls.
Ezra 4:7

Bithiah
(Daughter of God)
1 woman/1 reference
1 Chronicles 4:18

Biztha
1 man/1 reference
Eunuch serving the Persian king
Ahasuerus in Esther's time.
Esther 1:10

Blastus
(To germinate)
1 man/1 reference
Eunuch serving Herod Agrippa I.
Acts 12:20

Boanerges
(Sons of commotion)
2 men/1 reference
Nickname given to the disciples
James and John, the sons of Zebedee,
by Jesus.
Mark 3:17

Boaz
1 man/22 references
Relative of Naomi who acted as
kinsman-redeemer for her and her
daughter-in-law Ruth, marrying Ruth
and having a son with her. Same as
Booz.
Ruth 2:1

Bocheru
(Firstborn)
1 man/2 references
1 Chronicles 8:38

Booz
1 man/3 references
Greek form of the name *Boaz*; hero of
the story of Ruth.
Matthew 1:5

Bosor
(A lamp)
1 man/1 reference
Same as Beor.
2 Peter 2:15

Bukki
(Wasteful)
2 men/5 references
1 Chronicles 6:5; Numbers 34:22

Bukkiah
(Wasting of God)
1 man/2 references
1 Chronicles 25:4

Bunah
(Discretion)
1 man/1 reference
1 Chronicles 2:25

Bunni
(Built)
3 men/3 references
Most notably, one of a group of
Levites who led a revival among the
Israelites in the time of Nehemiah.
Nehemiah 9:4; Nehemiah 10:15;
Nehemiah 11:15

Buz
(Disrespect)
2 men/2 references
Genesis 22:21; 1 Chronicles 5:14

Buzi
(Disrespect)
1 man/1 reference
Ezekiel 1:3

C

Caiaphas
(The dell)
1 man/9 references
Jewish high priest who judged Jesus at
His trial.
Matthew 26:3

Cain
(Lance)
1 man/19 references
Adam and Eve's first son who became
jealous of his brother Abel and
killed him when God refused Cain's
unrighteous offering but accepted
Abel's offering.
Genesis 4:1

Cainan
(Fixed)
1 man/7 references
Genesis 5:9

Calcol
(Sustenance)
1 man/1 reference
1 Chronicles 2:6

Caleb
(Forcible)
3 men/36 references
Most notably, sent by Moses to spy
out Canaan before the Israelites
entered the Promised Land. Of the
twelve, only he and Joshua entered
the Promised Land.
Numbers 13:6; 1 Chronicles 2:18;
1 Chronicles 2:50

Canaan
(Humiliated)
1 man/9 references
Genesis 9:18

Candace
1 woman/1 reference
Queen of Ethiopia whose treasurer
was converted to Christianity by
Philip the evangelist.
Acts 8:27

Carcas
1 man/1 reference
Eunuch serving the Persian king
Ahasuerus in Esther's time.
Esther 1:10

Careah
(Bald)
1 man/1 reference
2 Kings 25:23

Carmi
(Gardener)
2 men/8 references
Joshua 7:1; Genesis 46:9

Carpus
(Fruit)
1 man/1 reference
2 Timothy 4:13

Carshena
1 man/1 reference
One of seven Persian princes serving
under King Ahasuerus.
Esther 1:14

Cephas
(The rock)
1 man/6 references
Name Jesus gave the apostle Peter. It
is used most often in the book of 1
Corinthians.
John 1:42

Chalcol
(Sustenance)
1 man/1 reference
Wise man mentioned in comparison
to Solomon's wisdom.
1 Kings 4:31

Chedorlaomer
1 man/5 references
King of Elam in the days of Abram.
Genesis 14:1

Chelal
(Complete)
1 man/1 reference
Ezra 10:30

Chelluh
(Completed)
1 man/1 reference
Ezra 10:35

Chelub
(Basket)
2 men/2 references
1 Chronicles 4:11; 1 Chronicles 27:26

Chelubai
(Forcible)
1 man/1 reference
Same as Caleb.
1 Chronicles 2:9

Chenaanah
(Humiliated)
2 men/5 references
Notably, false prophet who told King
Ahab to fight against Ramothgilead.
1 Kings 22:11; 1 Chronicles 7:10

Chenani
(Planted)
1 man/1 reference
One of a group of Levites who led
a revival among the Israelites in the
time of Nehemiah.
Nehemiah 9:4

Chenaniah
(God has planted)
2 men/3 references
Notably, Levite musician, "the master
of the song," who led singers in
celebration when King David brought
the ark of the covenant to Jerusalem.
1 Chronicles 15:22; 1 Chronicles 26:29

Cheran
1 man/2 references
Genesis 36:26

Cherub
1 man/2 references
Ezra 2:59

Chesed
1 man/1 reference
Genesis 22:22

Chileab
(Restraint of his father)
1 man/1 reference
2 Samuel 3:3

Chilion
(Pining)
1 man/3 references
Ruth 1:2

Chimham
(Pining)
1 man/4 references
2 Samuel 19:37

Chislon
(Hopeful)
1 man/1 reference
Numbers 34:21

Chloe
(Green)
1 woman/1 reference
Corinthian Christian and
acquaintance of Paul.
1 Corinthians 1:11

Chushan-rishathaim
(Cushan of double wickedness)
1 man/4 references
Mesopotamian king into whose hands
God gave the disobedient Israelites.
Judges 3:8

Chuza
1 man/1 reference
King Herod's household manager
whose wife, Joanna, financially
supported the ministry of Jesus.
Luke 8:3

Cis
(A bow)
1 man/1 reference
Same as Kish.
Acts 13:21

Claudia
1 woman/1 reference
2 Timothy 4:21

Claudius
2 men/3 references
Most notably, Roman emperor who
ruled when a famine affected the
empire.
Acts 11:28; Acts 23:26

Clement
(Merciful)
1 man/1 reference
Philippians 4:3

Cleopas
(Renowned father)
1 man/1 reference
Christian who met Jesus on the road
to Emmaus.
Luke 24:18

Cleophas
1 man/1 reference
John 19:25

Col-hozeh
(Every seer)
1 man/2 references
Nehemiah 3:15

Conaniah
(God has sustained)
1 man/1 reference
Levite (worship leader) who
distributed sacrificial animals for
the Passover celebration under King
Josiah.
2 Chronicles 35:9

Coniah
(God will establish)
1 man/3 references
An alternative name for Judah's king
Jehoiachin. Same as Jeconiah.
Jeremiah 22:24

Cononiah
(God has sustained)
1 man/2 references
Levite (worship leader) in charge
of tithes and offerings during King
Hezekiah's reign.
2 Chronicles 31:12

Core
(Ice)
1 man/1 reference
Greek form of the name *Korah;* a man
who led a rebellion against Moses.
Jude 1:11

Cornelius
1 man/10 references
God-fearing centurion of the Italian
band.
Acts 10:1

Cosam
(Divination)
1 man/1 reference
Luke 3:28

Coz
(Thorn)
1 man/1 reference
1 Chronicles 4:8

Cozbi
(False)
1 woman/2 references
Numbers 25:15

Crescens
(Growing)
1 man/1 reference
Coworker of Paul who left the apostle
in Rome before preaching in Galatia.
2 Timothy 4:10

Crispus
(Crisp)
1 man/2 references
Head of the Corinthian synagogue
who, along with his household,
believed in Jesus and was baptized by
Paul.
Acts 18:8

Cush
2 men/7 references
Genesis 10:6; Psalm 7 (title)

Cushan
1 man/1 reference
Mesopotamian king into whose hands
God gave the disobedient Israelites.
Same as Chushan-rishathaim.
Habakkuk 3:7

Cushi
(A Cushite)
3 men/10 references
Most notably, messenger who
brought David the news that his son
Absalom was dead.
2 Samuel 18:21; Jeremiah 36:14;
Zephaniah 1:1

Cyrenius
1 man/1 reference
Roman governor of Syria at the time
when Jesus was born.
Luke 2:2

Cyrus
1 man/23 references
King of Persia who commanded that
the temple in Jerusalem be rebuilt.
2 Chronicles 36:22

D

Dalaiah
(God has delivered)
1 man/1 reference
1 Chronicles 3:24

Dalphon
(Dripping)
1 man/1 reference
Esther 9:7

Damaris
(Gentle)
1 woman/1 reference
Acts 17:34

Dan
(Judge)
1 man/10 references
Genesis 30:6

Daniel
(Judge of God)
3 men/83 references
Most notably, Old Testament
major prophet who, as a child, was
taken into exile in Babylon. Was
condemned to the lions' den for
praying to God, but God kept him
safe. Also, son of David, born to his
wife Abigail.
1 Chronicles 3:1; Ezra 8:2; Ezekiel 14:14

Dara
(Pearl of knowledge)
1 man/1 reference
1 Chronicles 2:6

Darda
(Pearl of knowledge)
1 man/1 reference
Wise man whose wisdom is compared
to Solomon's.
1 Kings 4:31

Darius
3 men/25 references
Most notably, king of Persia. Also,
Darius the Mede, king of Persia,
during Daniel's lifetime.
Ezra 4:5; Nehemiah 12:22; Daniel 5:31

Darkon
1 man/2 references
Ezra 2:56

Dathan
1 man/10 references
Conspirer against Moses. Because of
his disobedience, the ground broke
open at Dathan's feet and swallowed
him, his family, and his possessions.
Numbers 16:1

David
(Loving)
1 man/1139 references
Popular king of Israel. As a young
shepherd and musician, he was
anointed king by the prophet
Samuel. He defeated the Philistine
giant Goliath, then defeated the
Philistines and brought the ark of the
covenant to Jerusalem. He fell into
sin with Bathsheba and killed her
husband, Uriah. He repented, and
scripture refers to David as a man
after God's own heart.
Ruth 4:17

Debir
(Shrine)
1 man/1 reference
Pagan king of Eglon during Joshua's
conquest of the Promised Land.
Joshua 10:3

Deborah
(Bee)
2 women/10 references
Notably, nurse who accompanied
Rebekah when she married Isaac.
Also, Israel's only female judge and
prophetess, who held court under a
palm tree.
Genesis 35:8; Judges 4:4

Dedan
2 men/5 references
Genesis 10:7; Genesis 25:3

Dekar
(Stab)
1 man/1 reference
1 Kings 4:9

Delaiah
(God has delivered)
4 men/6 references
Most notably, one of twenty-
four priests in David's time who
was chosen by lot to serve in the
tabernacle.
1 Chronicles 24:18; Ezra 2:60; Nehemiah
6:10; Jeremiah 36:12

Delilah
(Languishing)
1 woman/6 references
Woman Samson fell in love with
who was bribed by the Philistines to
discover the source of his strength.
When she shared his secret, his hair
was shaved, and the Philistines could
then overpower him.
Judges 16:4

Demas
1 man/3 references
Christian worker who was with Paul
at Corinth, leaving when he was
attracted by worldly things.
Colossians 4:14

Demetrius
2 men/3 references
Notably, silversmith of Ephesus
who opposed Paul and his teachings
because they tended to destroy his
business of making pagan shrines.
Acts 19:24; 3 John 1:12

Deuel
(Known of God)
1 man/4 references
Numbers 1:14

Diblaim
(Two cakes)
1 man/1 reference
Hosea 1:3

Dibri
(Wordy)
1 man/1 reference
Leviticus 24:11

Didymus
(Twin)
1 man/3 references
Alternate name for Thomas, one of
the twelve disciples of Jesus.
John 11:16

Diklah
1 man/2 references
Genesis 10:27

Dinah
(Justice)
1 man/8 references
Genesis 30:21

Dionysius
(Reveler)
1 man/1 reference
Man of Athens converted under the
ministry of the apostle Paul.
Acts 17:34

Diotrephes
(Jove-nourished)
1 man/1 reference
Arrogant church member condemned
by the apostle John.
3 John 1:9

Dishan
(Antelope)
1 man/5 references
Genesis 36:21

Dishon
(Antelope)
2 men/7 references
Genesis 36:21; Genesis 36:25

Dodai
(Sick)
1 man/1 reference
Commander in King David's army.
1 Chronicles 27:4

Dodavah
(Love of God)
1 man/1 reference
2 Chronicles 20:37

Dodo
(Loving)
3 men/5 references
Judges 10:1; 2 Samuel 23:9; 2 Samuel 23:24

Doeg
(Anxious)
1 man/6 references
King Saul's chief herdsman.
1 Samuel 21:7

Dorcas
(Gazelle)
1 woman/2 references
Christian of Joppa who did many
good works. When she died, her
friends called Peter, who raised her
back to life. Same as Tabitha.
Acts 9:36

Drusilla
1 woman/1 reference
Wife of Felix, the Roman governor of
Judea in Paul's time.
Acts 24:24

Dumah
(Silence)
1 man/2 references
Genesis 25:14

E

Ebal
(Bare)
2 men/3 references
Genesis 36:23; 1 Chronicles 1:22

Ebed
(Servant)
2 men/6 references
Judges 9:26; Ezra 8:6

Ebed-melech
(Servant of a king)
1 man/6 references
Ethiopian eunuch who rescued
Jeremiah from a dungeon by
reporting his situation to King
Zedekiah.
Jeremiah 38:7

Ebiasaph
(Gatherer)
1 man/3 references
1 Chronicles 6:23

Eden
(Pleasure)
2 men/2 references
Notably, Levite who cleansed the
Jerusalem temple during the revival
of King Hezekiah's day. Also, priest
in the time of King Hezekiah who
helped to distribute the people's
freewill offerings to his fellow priests.
2 Chronicles 29:12; 2 Chronicles 31:15

Eder
(Arrangement)
1 man/2 references
1 Chronicles 23:23

Edom
(Red)
1 man/3 references
Name given to Esau when he sold his
birthright to his brother, Jacob, for a
meal.
Genesis 25:30

Eglah
(Calf)
1 woman/2 references
2 Samuel 3:5

Eglon
(Calflike)
1 man/5 references
King of Moab who attacked Israel.
Judges 3:12

Ehi
(Brotherly)
1 man/1 reference
Genesis 46:21

Ehud
(United)
2 men/10 references
Second judge of Israel who subdued
the oppressing Moabites. Noted as
being a left-handed man.
Judges 3:15; 1 Chronicles 7:10

Eker
(A transplanted person)
1 man/1 reference
1 Chronicles 2:27

Eladah
(God has decked)
1 man/1 reference
1 Chronicles 7:20

Elah
(Oak)
6 men/14 references
Genesis 36:41; 1 Kings 4:18; 1 Kings 16:6;
2 Kings 15:30; 1 Chronicles 4:15;
1 Chronicles 9:8

Elam
(Distant)
9 men/13 references
Genesis 10:22; 1 Chronicles 8:24;
1 Chronicles 26:3; Ezra 2:7; Ezra 2:31;
Ezra 8:7; Ezra 10:2; Nehemiah 10:14;
Nehemiah 12:42

Elasah
(God has made)
2 men/2 references
Ezra 10:22; Jeremiah 29:3

Eldaah
(God of knowledge)
1 man/2 references
Genesis 25:4

Eldad
(God has loved)
1 man/2 references
Numbers 11:26

Elead
(God has testified)
1 man/1 reference
1 Chronicles 7:21

Eleasah
(God has made)
2 men/4 references
1 Chronicles 2:39; 1 Chronicles 8:37

Eleazar
(God is helper)
8 men/74 references
Most notably, chief over the Levites, overseeing temple worship. Became high priest after Aaron's death.
Exodus 6:23; 1 Samuel 7:1; 2 Samuel 23:9; 1 Chronicles 23:21; Ezra 8:33; Ezra 10:25; Nehemiah 12:42; Matthew 1:15

Elhanan
(God is gracious)
2 men/4 references
Killed Goliath's brother.
2 Samuel 21:19; 2 Samuel 23:24

Eli
(Lofty)
1 man/33 references
High priest in Shiloh who rebuked Hannah for being drunk as she prayed for God to give her a child. Samuel was born, and she brought him to Eli, dedicating him to God. Eli acted as Samuel's foster father and trained him in the priesthood.
1 Samuel 1:3

Eliab
(God of his father)
6 men/21 references
Most notably, prince of Zebulun, assisting Moses in taking the census of his tribe.
Numbers 1:9; Numbers 16:1; 1 Samuel 16:6; 1 Chronicles 6:27; 1 Chronicles 12:9; 1 Chronicles 15:18

Eliada
(God is knowing)
2 men/3 references
2 Samuel 5:16; 2 Chronicles 17:17

Eliadah
(God is knowing)
1 man/1 reference
1 Kings 11:23

Eliah
(God of Jehovah)
1 man/2 references
1 Chronicles 8:27

Eliahba
(God will hide)
1 man/2 references
2 Samuel 23:32

Eliakim
(God of raising)
4 men/15 references
Most notably, palace administrator for King Hezekiah of Judah.
2 Kings 18:18; 2 Kings 23:34; Nehemiah 12:41; Matthew 1:13

Eliam
(God of the people)
2 men/2 references
2 Samuel 11:3; 2 Samuel 23:34

Elias
(God of Jehovah)
1 man/30 references
Greek form of the name *Elijah*.
Matthew 11:14

Eliasaph
(God is gatherer)
2 men/6 references
Notably, prince of Gad who helped Moses take a census of his tribe.
Numbers 1:14; Numbers 3:24

Eliashib
(God will restore)
7 men/17 references
1 Chronicles 3:24; 1 Chronicles 24:12; Ezra 10:6; Ezra 10:24; Ezra 10:27; Ezra 10:36; Nehemiah 3:1

Eliathah
(God of his consent)
1 man/2 references
1 Chronicles 25:4

Elidad
(God of his love)
1 man/1 reference
Prince of the tribe of Benjamin when the Israelites entered the Promised Land.
Numbers 34:21

Eliel
(God of his God)
10 men/10 references
Most notably, one of the "mighty men of valour, famous men" leading the half tribe of Manasseh.
1 Chronicles 5:24; 1 Chronicles 6:34; 1 Chronicles 8:20; 1 Chronicles 8:22; 1 Chronicles 11:46; 1 Chronicles 11:47; 1 Chronicles 12:11; 1 Chronicles 15:9; 1 Chronicles 15:11; 2 Chronicles 31:13

Elienai
(Toward Jehovah are my eyes)
1 man/1 reference
1 Chronicles 8:20

Eliezer
(God of help)
10 men/15 references
Most notably, steward of Abraham's house and Abraham's presumed heir before the miraculous birth of Isaac.
Genesis 15:2; Exodus 18:4; 1 Chronicles 15:24; 1 Chronicles 27:16; 2 Chronicles 20:37; Ezra 8:16; Ezra 10:18; Ezra 10:23; Ezra 10:31; Luke 3:29

Elihoenai
(Toward Jehovah are my eyes)
1 man/1 reference
Ezra 8:4

Elihoreph
(God of autumn)
1 man/1 reference
Scribe serving Israel's king Solomon.
1 Kings 4:3

Elihu
(God of him)
5 men/11 references
Most notably, young man who became a mediator in the discussion between Job and his comforters. Also, a warrior who defected to David at Ziklag and became an army commander.
1 Samuel 1:1; 1 Chronicles 12:20; 1 Chronicles 26:7; 1 Chronicles 27:18; Job 32:2

Elijah
(God of Jehovah)
2 men/69 references
Most notably, a major prophet. His prophecy that no rain would fall in Israel except at his command angered wicked King Ahab. At Mount Carmel, he had a showdown with the priests of Baal that proved the Lord was God. Later Elijah went up into heaven in a whirlwind. Same as Elias.
1 Kings 17:1; Ezra 10:21

Elika
(God of rejection)
1 man/1 reference
2 Samuel 23:25

Elimelech
(God of the king)
1 man/6 references
Naomi's husband.
Ruth 1:2

Elioenai
(Toward Jehovah are my eyes)
7 men/8 references
1 Chronicles 3:23; 1 Chronicles 4:36;
1 Chronicles 7:8; 1 Chronicles 26:3; Ezra
10:22; Ezra 10:27; Nehemiah 12:41

Eliphal
(God of judgment)
1 man/1 reference
One of King David's valiant warriors.
1 Chronicles 11:35

Eliphalet
(God of deliverance)
1 man/2 references
2 Samuel 5:16

Eliphaz
(God of gold)
2 men/15 references
Most notably, one of three friends
of Job who mourned his losses
for a week then accused him of
wrongdoing.
Genesis 36:4; Job 2:11

Elipheleh
(God of his distinction)
1 man/2 references
Levite musician who performed in
celebration when King David brought
the ark of the covenant to Jerusalem.
1 Chronicles 15:18

Eliphelet
(God of deliverance)
6 men/6 references
Most notably, one of King David's
"mighty men."
2 Samuel 23:34; 1 Chronicles 3:6;
1 Chronicles 3:8; 1 Chronicles 8:39; Ezra
8:13; Ezra 10:33

Elisabeth
(God of the oath)
1 woman/9 references

Wife of Zacharias, cousin of Jesus'
mother, Mary, and mother of John
the Baptist.
Luke 1:5

Eliseus
(God of supplication)
1 man/1 reference
Greek form of the Old Testament
name *Elisha.*
Luke 4:27

Elisha
(God of supplication)
1 man/58 references
Elijah's successor and disciple, Elisha
saw Elijah carried up to heaven in
a whirlwind of fire and received a
double portion of his spirit. Elisha
then took the role of prophet.
1 Kings 19:16

Elishah
1 man/3 references
Genesis 10:4

Elishama
(God of hearing)
7 men/17 references
Numbers 1:10; 2 Samuel 5:16; Jeremiah
41:1; 1 Chronicles 2:41; 2 Chronicles 17:8;
2 Kings 25:25; Jeremiah 36:12

Elishaphat
(God of judgment)
1 man/1 reference
Commander who entered into a
covenant with the priest Jehoiada,
young King Joash's protector.
2 Chronicles 23:1

Elisheba
(God of the oath)
1 woman/1 reference
Exodus 6:23

Elishua
(God of supplication)
1 man/2 references
Same as Elishama.
2 Samuel 5:15

Eliud
(God of majesty)
1 man/2 references
Matthew 1:14

Elizaphan
(God of treasure)
2 men/3 references
Notably, prince of the tribe of
Zebulun when the Israelites entered
the Promised Land. Same as
Elzaphan.
Numbers 3:30; Numbers 34:25

Elizur
(God of the rock)
1 man/5 references
Prince of Reuben who helped Moses
take a census of his tribe and led the
tribe out of Sinai.
Numbers 1:5

Elkanah
(God has obtained)
8 men/20 references
Most notably, father of the prophet
Samuel. Also, "mighty man" of King
David.
Exodus 6:24; 1 Samuel 1:1; 1 Chronicles
6:25; 1 Chronicles 6:26; 1 Chronicles 9:16;
1 Chronicles 12:6; 1 Chronicles 15:23;
2 Chronicles 28:7

Elmodam
1 man/1 reference
Luke 3:28

Elnaam
(God is his delight)
1 man/1 reference
1 Chronicles 11:46

Elnathan
(God is the giver)
4 men/7 references
2 Kings 24:8; Ezra 8:16; Ezra 8:16; Ezra 8:16

Elon
(Oak grove)
3 men/6 references
Most notably, eleventh judge of Israel
who led the nation for ten years.
Genesis 26:34; Genesis 46:14; Judges 12:11

Elpaal
(God act)
1 man/3 references
1 Chronicles 8:11

Elpalet
(Meaning)
1 man/1 reference
1 Chronicles 14:5

Eluzai
(God is defensive)
1 man/1 reference
"Mighty man" who supported the
future king David during his conflict
with Saul.
1 Chronicles 12:5

Elymas
1 man/1 reference
Jewish sorcerer miraculously blinded
for opposing the apostle Paul's
preaching of the Gospel. Same as Bar-
jesus.
Acts 13:8

Elzabad
(God has bestowed)
2 men/2 references
Notably, one of several warriors from
the tribe of Gad who left Saul to join
David during his conflict with the
king.
1 Chronicles 12:12; 1 Chronicles 26:7

Elzaphan
(God of treasure)
1 man/2 references
Same as Elizaphan.
Exodus 6:22

Emmanuel
(God with us)
1 man/1 reference
Prophetic name for Jesus, given by
the angel of the Lord to Joseph,
husband of Mary.
Matthew 1:23

Emmor
(Ass)
1 man/1 reference
Prince of Shechem whose sons sold
Abraham a tomb.
Acts 7:16

Enan
(Having eyes)
1 man/5 references
Numbers 1:15

Enoch
(Initiated)
2 men/11 references
Notably, Cain's eldest son, after
whom he named a city. Also,
descendant of Seth, son of Adam.
He was immediately translated into
eternity. Same as Henoch.
Genesis 4:17; Genesis 5:18

Enos
(Mortal)
1 man/7 references
Same as Enosh.
Genesis 4:26

Enosh
(Mortal)
1 man/1 reference
Another form of the name *Enos*; son
of Seth.
1 Chronicles 1:1

Epaenetus
(Praised)
1 man/1 reference
Christian acquaintance of the apostle
Paul in Rome and the first Christian
convert from Achaia.
Romans 16:5

Epaphras
(Devoted)
1 man/3 references
Native of Colossae and fellow servant,
with Paul, to the Colossian church.
Colossians 1:7

Epaphroditus
(Devoted)
1 man/2 references
Fellow laborer with Paul whom the
apostle sent to the church at Philippi.
Philippians 2:25

Ephah
(Obscurity)
2 men/1 woman/5 references
Genesis 25:4; 1 Chronicles 2:46;
1 Chronicles 2:47

Ephai
(Birdlike)
1 man/1 reference
Jeremiah 40:8

Epher
(Gazelle)
3 men/4 references
Most notably, one of the "mighty
men of valour, famous men" leading
the half tribe of Manasseh.
Genesis 25:4; 1 Chronicles 4:17;
1 Chronicles 5:24

Ephlal
(Judge)
1 man/2 references
1 Chronicles 2:37

Ephod
(Girdle)
1 man/1 reference
Numbers 34:23

Ephraim
(Double fruit)
1 man/11 references
Joseph and his wife Asenath's second son, adopted and blessed by Jacob.
Genesis 41:52

Ephratah
(Fruitfulness)
1 woman/2 references
Same as Ephrath.
1 Chronicles 2:50

Ephrath
(Fruitfulness)
1 woman/1 reference
Alternative form of the name *Ephratah*.
1 Chronicles 2:19

Ephron
(Fawnlike)
1 man/12 references
Hittite from whom Abraham bought the cave of Machpelah, where he buried Sarah.
Genesis 23:8

Er
(Watchful)
3 men/11 references
Most notably, Judah's firstborn son, who was wicked.
Genesis 38:3; 1 Chronicles 4:21; Luke 3:28

Eran
(Watchful)
1 man/1 reference
Numbers 26:36

Erastus
(Beloved)
2 men/3 references
Notably, companion of Timothy on a mission to Macedonia.
Acts 19:22; Romans 16:23

Eri
(Watchful)
1 man/2 references
Genesis 46:16

Esaias
(God has saved)
1 man/21 references
Greek form of the name *Isaiah*, used in the New Testament.
Matthew 3:3

Esar-haddon
1 man/3 references
Son of Sennacherib who inherited the throne of Assyria.
2 Kings 19:37

Esau
(Rough)
1 man/82 references
Son of Isaac and Rebekah and twin brother of Jacob, a good hunter and the favorite of his father, but he sold his birthright to Jacob for some lentil stew.
Genesis 25:25

Esh-baal
(Man of Baal)
1 man/2 references
1 Chronicles 8:33

Eshban
(Vigorous)
1 man/2 references
Genesis 36:26

Eshcol
(Bunch of grapes)
1 man/2 references
Genesis 14:13

Eshek
(Oppression)
1 man/1 reference
1 Chronicles 8:39

Eshtemoa
(Obedience)
1 man/2 references
1 Chronicles 4:17

Eshton
(Restful)
1 man/2 references
1 Chronicles 4:11

Esli
(Toward Jehovah are my eyes)
1 man/1 reference
Luke 3:25

Esrom
(Courtyard)
1 man/3 references
Matthew 1:3

Esther
1 woman/56 references
Jewish wife of Persian King
Ahasuerus, whose counselor, Haman,
plotted to kill the Jewish people.
Esther's cousin Mordecai, who had
raised her, convinced the new queen
to confront her husband. She told the
king of Haman's plan and her people
were saved. Same as Hadassah.
Esther 2:7

Etam
(Hawk-ground)
1 man/1 reference
1 Chronicles 4:3

Ethan
(Permanent)
4 men/8 references
Notably, wise man who wrote Psalm
89.
1 Kings 4:31; 1 Chronicles 2:6; 1 Chronicles
6:42; 1 Chronicles 6:44

Ethbaal
(With Baal)
1 man/1 reference
1 Kings 16:31

Ethnan
(Gift)
1 man/1 reference
1 Chronicles 4:7

Ethni
(Munificence)
1 man/1 reference
1 Chronicles 6:41

Eubulus
(Good-willer)
1 man/1 reference
2 Timothy 4:21

Eunice
(Victorious)
1 woman/1 reference
The Jewish mother of the apostle
Paul's protégé Timothy.
2 Timothy 1:5

Euodias
(Fine traveling)
1 woman/1 reference
Christian woman of Philippi who had
conflict with another church member,
Syntyche.
Philippians 4:2

Eutychus
(Fortunate)
1 man/1 reference
Young man of Troas who drifted off
to sleep during a late-night sermon
of the apostle Paul. He fell from his
window seat three floors to his death.
Paul brought him back to life.
Acts 20:9

Eve
(Life-giver)
1 woman/4 references
Adam's wife, "the mother of all living."
Tempted by the serpent, Eve ate the
fruit of the tree of the knowledge of
good and evil and offered it to her
husband, who also ate. For her part
in the sin, Eve would suffer greatly
during childbirth, desire her husband,
and be ruled over by him.
Genesis 3:20

Evi
(Desirous)
1 man/2 references
Midianite king killed by the Israelites
at God's command.
Numbers 31:8

Evil-merodach
(Soldier of Merodak)
1 man/2 references
Successor to Babylonian king
Nebuchadnezzar.
2 Kings 25:27

Ezar
(Treasure)
1 man/1 reference
1 Chronicles 1:38

Ezbai
(Hyssoplike)
1 man/1 reference
1 Chronicles 11:37

Ezbon
2 men/2 references
Genesis 46:16; 1 Chronicles 7:7

Ezekias
(Strengthened of God)
1 man/2 references
Greek form of the name *Hezekiah*,
used in the New Testament.
Matthew 1:9

Ezekiel
(God will strengthen)
1 man/2 references
Priest taken into exile when
Nebuchadnezzar, king of Babylon,
carried off most of Jerusalem.
Probably best known for his
prophetic vision of the dry bones that
came to life.
Ezekiel 1:3

Ezer
(Treasure, help)
6 men/9 references
Genesis 36:21; 1 Chronicles 4:4;
1 Chronicles 7:21; 1 Chronicles 12:9;
Nehemiah 3:19; Nehemiah 12:42

Ezra
(Aid)
3 men/26 references
Most notably, Israelite scribe and
teacher of the law who returned from
the Babylonian Exile along with some
priests, Levites, temple servants, and
other Israelites.
1 Chronicles 4:17; Ezra 7:1; Nehemiah 12:1

Ezri
(Helpful)
1 man/1 reference
Superintendent of agriculture who
served under King David.
1 Chronicles 27:26

F

Felix
(Happy)
1 man/9 references
Governor of Judea before whom
Paul appeared after the Roman guard
rescued him from his appearance at
the Jewish council.
Acts 23:24

Festus
(Festal)
1 man/13 references
Governor of Judea who replaced
Felix. Also called Porcius Festus.
Acts 24:27

Fortunatus
(Fortunate)
1 man/1 reference
Corinthian Christian who visited the
apostle Paul in Ephesus.
1 Corinthians 16:17

G

Gaal
(Loathing)
1 man/9 references
Judges 9:26

Gabbai
(Collective)
1 man/1 reference
Nehemiah 11:8

Gad
(Attack)
2 men/19 references
Notably, son of Jacob and Leah's
handmaid Zilpah.
Genesis 30:11; 1 Samuel 22:5

Gaddi
(Fortunate)
1 man/1 reference
Numbers 13:11

Gaddiel
(Fortune of God)
1 man/1 reference
Numbers 13:10

Gadi
(Fortunate)
1 man/2 references
2 Kings 15:14

Gaham
(Flame)
1 man/1 reference
Genesis 22:24

Gahar
(Lurker)
1 man/2 references
Ezra 2:47

Gaius
4 men/5 references
Most notably, Corinthian Christian
who hosted the apostle Paul when he
wrote the letter to the Romans. Also,
the "wellbeloved" of John, addressee
of John's third letter.
Acts 19:29; Acts 20:4; Romans 16:23;
3 John 1

Galal
(Great)
2 men/3 references
1 Chronicles 9:15; 1 Chronicles 9:16

Gallio
1 man/3 references
Deputy (proconsul) of Achaia who
refused to hear the case when the Jews
accused Paul of breaking the law.
Acts 18:12

Gamaliel
(Reward of God)
2 men/7 references
Notably, leader of the tribe of Manasseh under Moses during the Exodus.
Numbers 1:10; Acts 5:34

Gamul
(Rewarded)
1 man/1 reference
1 Chronicles 24:17

Gareb
(Scabby)
1 man/2 references
One of King David's valiant warriors.
2 Samuel 23:38

Gashmu
(A shower)
1 man/1 reference
Nehemiah 6:6

Gatam
1 man/3 references
Genesis 36:11

Gazez
(Shearer)
2 men/2 references
1 Chronicles 2:46; 1 Chronicles 2:46

Gazzam
(Devourer)
1 man/2 references
Ezra 2:48

Geber
(Warrior)
2 men/2 references
1 Kings 4:13; 1 Kings 4:19

Gedaliah
(God has become great)
5 men/32 references
Most notably, ruler appointed by Nebuchadnezzar over the remnant of Jews left behind in Judah at the time of the Babylonian Exile.
2 Kings 25:22; 1 Chronicles 25:3; Ezra 10:18; Zephaniah 1:1; Jeremiah 38:1

Gedeon
(Warrior)
1 man/1 reference
Greek form of the name *Gideon*, used in the New Testament.
Hebrews 11:32

Gedor
(Enclosure)
2 men/4 references
More notably, leader of the tribe of Benjamin who lived in Jerusalem.
1 Chronicles 8:31; 1 Chronicles 4:4

Gehazi
(Valley of a visionary)
1 man/12 references
Prophet Elisha's servant.
2 Kings 4:12

Gemalli
(Camel driver)
1 man/1 reference
Numbers 13:12

Gemariah
(God has perfected)
2 men/5 references
Notably, scribe and prince of Judah in whose room Baruch read the prophecies of Jeremiah.
Jeremiah 36:10; Jeremiah 29:3

Genubath
(Theft)
1 man/2 references
1 Kings 11:20

Gera
(Grain)
4 men/9 references
Genesis 46:21; Judges 3:15; 2 Samuel 16:5;
1 Chronicles 8:3

Gershom
(Refugee)
4 men/14 references
Exodus 2:22; Judges 18:30; 1 Chronicles
6:16; Ezra 8:2

Gershon
(Refugee)
1 man/18 references
Same as Gershom.
Genesis 46:11

Gesham
(Lumpish)
1 man/1 reference
1 Chronicles 2:47

Geshem
(A shower)
1 man/3 references
Arabian who opposed Nehemiah's
rebuilding of the walls of Jerusalem.
Nehemiah 2:19

Gether
1 man/2 references
Genesis 10:23

Geuel
(Majesty of God)
1 man/1 reference
Numbers 13:15

Gibbar
(Warrior)
1 man/1 reference
Ezra 2:20

Gibea
(A hill)
1 man/1 reference
1 Chronicles 2:49

Giddalti
(I have made great)
1 man/2 references
1 Chronicles 25:4

Giddel
(Stout)
2 men/4 references
Ezra 2:47; Ezra 2:56

Gideon
(Warrior)
1 man/39 references
Fifth judge of Israel who sought proof
of God's will by placing a fleece on
the ground and asking God to make
either the fleece or the ground wet;
God answered his request. Same as
Gedeon, Jerubbaal, and Jerubbesheth.
Judges 6:11

Gideoni
(Warlike)
1 man/5 references
Numbers 1:11

Gilalai
(Dungy)
1 man/1 reference
Priest who helped to dedicate the
rebuilt walls of Jerusalem by playing a
musical instrument.
Nehemiah 12:36

Gilead
(Heap of testimony)
3 men/13 references
Numbers 26:29; Judges 11:1;
1 Chronicles 5:14

Ginath
1 man/2 references
1 Kings 16:21

Ginnetho
(Gardener)
1 man/1 reference
Nehemiah 12:4

Ginnethon
(Gardener)
1 man/2 references
Nehemiah 10:6

Gispa
1 man/1 reference
Nehemiah 11:21

Gog
2 men/11 references
Notably, prince of Magog, a place
perhaps in Scythia, against whom
Ezekiel prophesied.
1 Chronicles 5:4; Ezekiel 38:2

Goliath
(Exile)
1 man/6 references
Nine-foot-nine-inch-tall Philistine
champion who challenged any
Israelite to a fight; the losing nation
would become the winner's servants.
David fought Goliath with a slingshot
and killed him and then cut off his
head.
1 Samuel 17:4

Gomer
(Completion)
1 man/1 woman/5 references
Notably, the unfaithful wife of the
prophet Hosea who represented the
unfaithfulness of God's people.
Genesis 10:2; Hosea 1:3

Guni
(Protected)
2 men/4 references
Genesis 46:24; 1 Chronicles 5:15

H

Haahashtari
(Courier)
1 man/1 reference
1 Chronicles 4:6

Habaiah
(God has hidden)
1 man/2 references
Ezra 2:6

Habakkuk
(Embrace)
1 man/2 references
Old Testament minor prophet who
served during the reign of King Josiah
of Judah.
Habakkuk 1:1

Habaziniah
1 man/1 reference
Jeremiah 35:3

Hachaliah
(Darkness of God)
1 man/2 references
Nehemiah 1:1

Hachmoni
(Skillful)
1 man/1 reference
1 Chronicles 27:32

Hadad
4 men/14 references
Most notably, king of Edom.
Genesis 36:35; 1 Kings 11:14; 1 Chronicles
1:30; 1 Chronicles 1:51

Hadadezer
(Hadad is his help)
1 man/9 references
Syrian king of Zobah whose troops
David defeated along with the
Syrians of Damascus who supported

Hadadezer. Same as Hadarezer.
2 Samuel 8:3

Hadar
(Magnificence)
2 men/2 references
Genesis 25:15; Genesis 36:39

Hadarezer
(Hadad is his help)
1 man/12 references
Same as Hadadezer.
2 Samuel 10:16

Hadassah
(Myrtle)
1 woman/1 reference
Alternative name for Esther, the
Jewish woman who became queen
of Persia and saved her people from
destruction.
Esther 2:7

Hadlai
(Idle)
1 man/1 reference
2 Chronicles 28:12

Hadoram
3 men/4 references
Genesis 10:27; 1 Chronicles 18:10;
2 Chronicles 10:18

Hagab
(Locust)
1 man/1 reference
Same as Hagaba and Hagabah.
Ezra 2:46

Hagaba
(Locust)
1 man/1 reference
Same as Hagab and Hagabah.
Nehemiah 7:48

Hagabah
(Locust)
1 man/1 reference
Same as Hagab and Hagaba.
Ezra 2:45

Hagar
1 woman/12 references
Sarai's Egyptian maid who became
a surrogate wife to Abram so he and
Sarai could have a child.
Genesis 16:1

Haggai
(Festive)
1 man/11 references
Prophet of Judah who wrote the book
that bears his name.
Ezra 5:1

Haggeri
1 man/1 reference
1 Chronicles 11:38

Haggi
(Festive)
1 man/2 references
Genesis 46:16

Haggiah
(Festival of God)
1 man/1 reference
1 Chronicles 6:30

Haggith
(Festive)
1 woman/5 references
One of several wives of King David
and mother of David's son Adonijah.
2 Samuel 3:4

Hakkatan
(Small)
1 man/1 reference
Ezra 8:12

Hakkoz
(Thorn)
1 man/1 reference
One of twenty-four priests in David's
time who was chosen by lot to serve
in the tabernacle.
1 Chronicles 24:10

Hakupha
(Crooked)
1 man/2 references
Ezra 2:51

Hallohesh
(Enchanter)
1 man/1 reference
Same as Halohesh.
Nehemiah 10:24

Halohesh
(Enchanter)
1 man/1 reference
Same as Hallohesh.
Nehemiah 3:12

Ham
(Hot)
1 man/12 references
Youngest of Noah's three sons.
Genesis 5:32

Haman
1 man/53 references
King Ahasuerus's wicked counselor
who plotted to eradicate the
Jews from the Persian kingdom.
Ahasuerus, angry at the deceit of his
counselor, had him hanged on the
gallows that Haman had erected to
destroy Mordecai.
Esther 3:1

Hammedatha
1 man/5 references
Esther 3:1

Hammelech
(King)
1 man/2 references
Jeremiah 36:26

Hammoleketh
(Queen)
1 woman/1 reference
1 Chronicles 7:18

Hamor
(Ass)
1 man/13 references
Genesis 33:19

Hamuel
(Anger of God)
1 man/1 reference
1 Chronicles 4:26

Hamul
(Pitied)
1 man/3 references
Genesis 46:12

Hamutal
(Father-in-law of dew)
1 woman/3 references
2 Kings 23:31

Hanameel
(God has favored)
1 man/4 references
Jeremiah 32:7

Hanan
(Favor)
9 men/12 references
1 Chronicles 8:23; 1 Chronicles 8:38;
1 Chronicles 11:43; Ezra 2:46; Nehemiah
8:7; Nehemiah 10:10; Nehemiah 10:22;
Nehemiah 10:26; Jeremiah 35:4

Hanani
(Gracious)
6 men/11 references
1 Chronicles 25:4; 2 Chronicles 16:7;

1 Kings 16:1; Ezra 10:20; Nehemiah 1:2; Nehemiah 12:36

Hananiah

(God has favored)
14 men/29 references
Most notably, Hebrew name of Daniel's friend, better known as Shadrach.
1 Chronicles 3:19; 1 Chronicles 8:24; 1 Chronicles 25:4; 1 Chronicles 26:11; Ezra 10:28; Nehemiah 3:8; Nehemiah 3:30; Nehemiah 7:2; Nehemiah 10:23; Nehemiah 12:41; Jeremiah 28:1; Jeremiah 36:12; Jeremiah 37:13; Daniel 1:6

Haniel

(Favor of God)
1 man/1 reference
1 Chronicles 7:39

Hannah

(Favored)
1 woman/13 references
Wife of Elkanah who could not bear a child and went to the temple to pray, promising God that if He gave her a child, she would give the boy to Him for his whole life. She conceived, bore Samuel, and fulfilled her pledge.
1 Samuel 1:2

Hanniel

(Favor of God)
1 man/1 reference
Prince of the tribe of Manasseh when the Israelites entered the Promised Land.
Numbers 34:23

Hanoch

(Initiated, favor of God)
2 men/5 references
Same as Henoch.
Genesis 25:4; Genesis 46:9

Hanun

(Favored)
3 men/11 references
Most notably, Ammonite king.
2 Samuel 10:1; Nehemiah 3:30; Nehemiah 3:13

Haran

(Rest, mountaineer, parched)
3 men/9 references
Most notably, brother of Abram and father of Lot. Also, head Levite who was part of King David's religious leadership reorganization.
Genesis 11:26; 1 Chronicles 2:46; 1 Chronicles 23:9

Harbona

1 man/1 reference
Eunuch serving the Persian king Ahasuerus in Esther's time. Same as Harbonah.
Esther 1:10

Harbonah

1 man/1 reference
Same as Harbona.
Esther 7:9

Hareph

(Reproachful)
1 man/1 reference
1 Chronicles 2:51

Harhaiah

(Fearing God)
1 man/1 reference
Nehemiah 3:8

Harhas

(Shining)
1 man/1 reference
Same as Hasrah.
2 Kings 22:14

Harhur
(Inflammation)
1 man/2 references
Ezra 2:51

Harim
(Snub-nosed)
5 men/11 references
Most notably, one of twenty-four priests in David's time who was chosen by lot to serve in the tabernacle.
1 Chronicles 24:8; Ezra 2:32; Ezra 10:31; Nehemiah 10:5; Nehemiah 10:27

Hariph
(Autumnal)
2 men/2 references
Nehemiah 7:24; Nehemiah 10:19

Harnepher
1 man/1 reference
1 Chronicles 7:36

Haroeh
(Prophet)
1 man/1 reference
1 Chronicles 2:52

Harsha
(Magician)
1 man/2 references
Ezra 2:52

Harum
(High)
1 man/1 reference
1 Chronicles 4:8

Harumaph
(Snub-nosed)
1 man/1 reference
Nehemiah 3:10

Haruz
(Earnest)
1 man/1 reference
2 Kings 21:19

Hasadiah
(God has favored)
1 man/1 reference
1 Chronicles 3:20

Hasenuah
(Pointed)
1 man/1 reference
1 Chronicles 9:7

Hashabiah
(God has regarded)
14 men/15 references
Most notably, leader of the tribe of Levi in the days of King David. Also, priest trusted by Ezra to carry money and temple vessels to Israel.
1 Chronicles 6:45; 1 Chronicles 9:14; 1 Chronicles 25:3; 1 Chronicles 26:30; 1 Chronicles 27:17; 2 Chronicles 35:9; Ezra 8:19; Ezra 8:24; Nehemiah 3:17; Nehemiah 10:11; Nehemiah 11:15; Nehemiah 11:22; Nehemiah 12:21; Nehemiah 12:24

Hashabnah
(Inventiveness)
1 man/1 reference
Nehemiah 10:25

Hashabniah
(Thought of God)
2 man/2 references
Nehemiah 3:10; Nehemiah 9:5

Hashbadana
(Considerate judge)
1 man/1 reference
Priest who assisted Ezra in reading the book of the law to the people of Jerusalem.
Nehemiah 8:4

Hashem
(Wealthy)
1 man/1 reference
1 Chronicles 11:34

Hashub
(Intelligent)
4 men/4 references
Nehemiah 3:11; Nehemiah 3:23; Nehemiah 10:23; Nehemiah 11:15

Hashubah
(Estimation)
1 man/1 reference
1 Chronicles 3:20

Hashum
(Enriched)
3 men/5 references
Priest who assisted Ezra in reading the book of the law to the people of Jerusalem.
Ezra 2:19; Nehemiah 8:4; Nehemiah 10:18

Hashupha
(Nakedness)
1 man/1 reference
Nehemiah 7:46

Hasrah
(Want)
1 man/1 reference
Grandfather of Shallum, husband of the prophetess Huldah in the days of King Josiah. Same as Harhas.
2 Chronicles 34:22

Hassenaah
(Thorny)
1 man/1 reference
Nehemiah 3:3

Hasshub
(Intelligent)
1 man/1 reference
1 Chronicles 9:14

Hasupha
(Nakedness)
1 man/1 reference
Ezra 2:43

Hatach
1 man/4 references
One of King Ahasuerus's eunuchs who attended Queen Esther. He acted as a messenger between her and Mordecai when Mordecai discovered Haman's plot.
Esther 4:5

Hathath
(Dismay)
1 man/1 reference
1 Chronicles 4:13

Hatipha
(Robber)
1 man/2 references
Ezra 2:54

Hatita
(Explorer)
1 man/2 references
Ezra 2:42

Hattil
(Fluctuating)
1 man/2 references
Ezra 2:57

Hattush
5 men/5 references
1 Chronicles 3:22; Ezra 8:2; Nehemiah 3:10; Nehemiah 10:4; Nehemiah 12:12

Havilah
(Circular)
2 men/4 references
Genesis 10:7; Genesis 10:29

Hazael
(God has seen)
1 man/23 references
King of Syria anointed to his position
by Elijah.
1 Kings 19:15

Hazaiah
(God has seen)
1 man/1 reference
Nehemiah 11:5

Hazarmaveth
(Village of death)
1 man/2 references
Genesis 10:26

Hazelelponi
(Shade-facing)
1 man/1 reference
1 Chronicles 4:3

Haziel
(Seen of God)
1 man/1 reference
Chief Levite who was part of
King David's religious-leadership
reorganization.
1 Chronicles 23:9

Hazo
(Seer)
1 man/1 reference
Abraham's brother.
Genesis 22:22

Heber
(Community, across)
6 men/14 references
Heber the Kenite, husband of Jael,
the woman who killed the Canaanite
commander Sisera.
Genesis 46:17; Judges 4:11; 1 Chronicles
4:18; 1 Chronicles 5:13; 1 Chronicles 8:17; 1
Chronicles 8:22

Hebron
(Association)
2 men/10 references
Exodus 6:18; 1 Chronicles 2:42

Hegai
1 man/3 references
Keeper of the harem for King
Ahasuerus of Persia. He treated Esther
preferentially, and she took his advice
on what to take when she went to the
king. Same as Hege.
Esther 2:8

Hege
1 man/1 reference
Alternative name for Hegai, servant
of the Persian king Ahasuerus.
Esther 2:3

Helah
(Rust)
1 woman/2 references
Wife of Ashur, descendant of
Abraham through Jacob's son Judah.
1 Chronicles 4:5

Heldai
(Worldliness)
2 men/2 references
Notably, commander in King
David's army overseeing twenty-four
thousand men in the twelfth month
of each year. Also, same as Helem.
1 Chronicles 27:15; Zechariah 6:10

Heleb
(Fatness)
1 man/1 reference
One of King David's valiant warriors.
Same as Heled.
2 Samuel 23:29

Heled
(To glide)
1 man/1 reference
One of King David's valiant warriors.
Same as Heleb.
1 Chronicles 11:30

Helek
(Portion)
1 man/2 references
Numbers 26:30

Helem
(Dream)
2 men/2 references
Same as Heldai.
1 Chronicles 7:35; Zechariah 6:14

Helez
(Strength)
2 men/5 references
Commander in King David's army
overseeing twenty-four thousand men
in the seventh month of each year.
2 Samuel 23:26; 1 Chronicles 2:39

Heli
(Lofty)
1 man/1 reference
Father of Jesus' earthly father, Joseph.
Luke 3:23

Helkai
(Apportioned)
1 man/1 reference
Nehemiah 12:15

Helon
(Strong)
1 man/5 references
Helped Moses take a census of his
tribe.
Numbers 1:9

Hemam
(Raging)
1 man/1 reference
Genesis 36:22

Heman
(Faithful)
2 men/16 references
Notably, wise man mentioned in
comparison to Solomon's wisdom.
Also, one of the key musicians serving
in the Jerusalem temple.
1 Kings 4:31; 1 Chronicles 6:33

Hemath
(Walled)
1 man/1 reference
1 Chronicles 2:55

Hemdan
(Pleasant)
1 man/1 reference
Genesis 36:26

Hen
(Grace)
1 man/1 reference
Son of Zephaniah who received a
memorial crown in the temple.
Zechariah 6:14

Henadad
(Favor of Hadad)
1 man/4 references
Ezra 3:9

Henoch
(Initiated)
2 men/2 references
Notably, same as Enoch. Also, same
as Hanoch.
1 Chronicles 1:3; 1 Chronicles 1:33

Hepher
(Shame)
3 men/7 references
Most notably, one of King David's
valiant warriors.
Numbers 26:32; 1 Chronicles 4:6;
1 Chronicles 11:36

Hephzibah
(My delight is in her)
1 woman/1 reference
Wife of Judah's good king Hezekiah
and mother of the evil king
Manasseh.
2 Kings 21:1

Heresh
(Magical craft)
1 man/1 reference
1 Chronicles 9:15

Hermas
(To utter)
1 man/1 reference
Christian acquaintance of the apostle
Paul, greeted in Paul's letter to the
Romans.
Romans 16:14

Hermes
(To utter)
1 man/1 reference
Christian acquaintance of the apostle
Paul, greeted in Paul's letter to the
Romans.
Romans 16:14

Hermogenes
(Born of Hermes)
1 man/1 reference
Asian Christian who turned away
from Paul.
2 Timothy 1:15

Herod
(Heroic)
4 men/44 references
Most notably, known as Herod the
Great, evil king of Judea. When the
wise men from the East appeared,
looking for the king of the Jews,
Herod feared for his throne and killed
all the male toddlers and infants in
Bethlehem. But Joseph and his family
escaped into Egypt and returned
upon Herod's death. Also, Herod
Antipas, son of Herod the Great,
tetrarch of Galilee and Perea. He
promised to grant any request to his
stepdaughter and sorrowfully fulfilled
her request—John the Baptist's head
on a plate. Hearing of Jesus' miracles,
he believed John had returned from
the dead. When Pilate learned that
Jesus was from Galilee, he passed
him on to Herod to judge. Herod
mocked Him and dressed Him in fine
clothing. Also, grandson of Herod the
Great who ruled over the tetrarchy of
Philip and Lysanias, Herod Agrippa
I had the apostle James killed and
arrested and also imprisoned Peter.
Also, son of Herod Agrippa I, Herod
Agrippa II. Heard Paul's case with
his sister, Bernice, with whom he had
an incestuous relationship. Same as
Agrippa.
Matthew 2:1; Matthew 14:1; Acts 12:1;
Acts 25:13

Herodias
(Heroic)
1 woman/6 references
Granddaughter of Herod the
Great whose second marriage was
opposed by John the Baptist. When
Herodias's daughter asked what she
should request from Herod Antipas,
she pushed her to ask for John the
Baptist's head on a plate.
Matthew 14:3

Herodion
(Heroic)
1 man/1 reference
Relative of the apostle Paul.
Romans 16:11

Hesed
(Favor)
1 man/1 reference
1 Kings 4:10

Heth
(Terror)
1 man/14 references
Genesis 10:15

Hezeki
(Strong)
1 man/1 reference
1 Chronicles 8:17

Hezekiah
(Strengthened of God)
3 men/128 references
Most notably, king of Judah, son of Ahaz, who did right in God's eyes, removing pagan worship from the kingdom and keeping God's commandments. Same as Ezekias.
2 Kings 16:20; 1 Chronicles 3:23; Ezra 2:16

Hezion
(Vision)
1 man/1 reference
1 Kings 15:18

Hezir
(Protected)
2 men/2 references
Notably, one of twenty-four priests in David's time who was chosen by lot to serve in the tabernacle.
1 Chronicles 24:15; Nehemiah 10:20

Hezrai
(Enclosure)
1 man/1 reference
One of King David's valiant warriors. Same as Hezro.
2 Samuel 23:35

Hezro
(Enclosure)
1 man/1 reference
Same as Hezrai.
1 Chronicles 11:37

Hezron
(Courtyard)
2 men/16 references
Genesis 46:9; Genesis 46:12

Hiddai
1 man/1 reference
One of King David's warriors known as the "mighty men."
2 Samuel 23:30

Hiel
(Living of God)
1 man/1 reference
Rebuilder of Jericho.
1 Kings 16:34

Hilkiah
(Portion of God)
6 men/34 references
Most notably, high priest during the reign of King Josiah of Judah. Also, father of the prophet Jeremiah. Also, priest and father of Eliakim. Also, priest who assisted Ezra in reading the book of the law to the people of Jerusalem.
2 Kings 18:18; 2 Kings 22:4; 1 Chronicles 6:45; 1 Chronicles 26:11; Nehemiah 8:4; Jeremiah 1:1

Hillel
(Praising)
1 man/2 references
Father of Israel's twelfth judge, Abdon.
Judges 12:13

Hirah
(Splendor)
1 man/2 references
Genesis 38:1

Hiram
(Milk)
2 men/23 references
Notably, king of Tyre who provided cedar trees and workmen for building the temple in Israel.
2 Samuel 5:11; 1 Kings 7:13

Hizkiah
(Strengthened of God)
1 man/1 reference
Zephaniah 1:1

Hizkijah
(Strengthened of God)
1 man/1 reference
Nehemiah 10:17

Hobab
(Cherished)
1 man/2 references
Father-in-law of Moses. Same as Jethro.
Numbers 10:29

Hod
(How?)
1 man/1 reference
1 Chronicles 7:37

Hodaiah
(Majesty of God)
1 man/1 reference
1 Chronicles 3:24

Hodaviah
(Majesty of God)
3 men/3 references
Most notably, leader of the half tribe of Manasseh.
1 Chronicles 5:24; 1 Chronicles 9:7; Ezra 2:40

Hodesh
(A month)
1 woman/1 reference
1 Chronicles 8:9

Hodevah
(Majesty of God)
1 man/1 reference
Nehemiah 7:43

Hodiah
(Celebrated)
1 woman/1 reference
1 Chronicles 4:19

Hodijah
(Celebrated)
2 men/5 references
Notably, Levite who helped Ezra explain the law to exiles returned to Jerusalem.
Nehemiah 8:7; Nehemiah 10:18

Hoglah
(Partridge)
1 woman/4 references
Numbers 26:33

Hoham
1 man/1 reference
Pagan king of Hebron during Joshua's conquest of the Promised Land, allied with four other rulers to attack Gibeon, which had deceptively made a peace treaty with the Israelites.
Joshua 10:3

Homam
(Raging)
1 man/1 reference
1 Chronicles 1:39

Hophni
(Pugilist)
1 man/5 references
Son of the high priest Eli. Hophni did not know the Lord, misused his

priestly office, and disobeyed the law.
1 Samuel 1:3

Horam

(High)
1 man/1 reference
King of Gezer who was killed, along
with all of his people, by Joshua's
army during the conquest of the
Promised Land.
Joshua 10:33

Hori

(Cave dweller)
2 men/4 references
Genesis 36:22; Numbers 13:5

Hosah

(Hopeful)
1 man/4 references
Levite who was chosen by lot to
guard the west side of the house of
the Lord.
1 Chronicles 16:38

Hosea

(Deliverer)
1 man/3 references
Minor prophet told by God to marry
a prostitute named Gomer. In the
Old Testament book that bears his
name, Hosea called God's people
away from idolatry and back into an
intimate relationship with Him.
Hosea 1:1

Hoshaiah

(God has saved)
2 men/3 references
Notably, prince of Judah who
participated in the dedication of
Jerusalem's rebuilt walls. Also, captain
of the Israelite forces and father
of Azariah, who refused to believe
Jeremiah's warning not to escape into
Egypt.
Nehemiah 12:32; Jeremiah 42:1

Hoshama

(Jehovah has heard)
1 man/1 reference
1 Chronicles 3:18

Hoshea

(Deliverer)
4 men/11 references
Most notably, another name of
Joshua, successor to Moses as leader
of Israel. Also, leader of the tribe of
Ephraim in the days of King David.
Deuteronomy 32:44; 2 Kings 15:30;
1 Chronicles 27:20; 2 Nehemiah 10:23

Hotham

(Seal)
1 man/1 reference
1 Chronicles 7:32

Hothan

(Seal)
1 man/1 reference
1 Chronicles 11:44

Hothir

(He has caused to remain)
1 man/2 references
1 Chronicles 25:4

Hul

(Circle)
1 man/2 references
Genesis 10:23

Huldah

(Weasel)
1 woman/2 references
Prophetess who spoke to King Josiah's
messengers about a coming judgment
of God on Judah.
2 Kings 22:14

Hupham

(Protection)
1 man/1 reference
Numbers 26:39

Huppah
(Canopy)
1 man/1 reference
One of twenty-four priests in David's
time who was chosen by lot to serve
in the tabernacle.
1 Chronicles 24:13

Huppim
(Canopies)
1 man/3 references
Genesis 46:21

Hur
(White)
7 men/16 references
Most notably, Israelite who held up
Moses' hand as the battle against the
Amalekites raged so Israel could win.
Also, Midianite king killed by the
Israelites. Also, father of Caleb, who
spied out the land of Canaan.
Exodus 17:10; Exodus 31:2; Numbers 31:8;
1 Kings 4:8; 1 Chronicles 2:50; 1 Chronicles
4:1; Nehemiah 3:9

Hurai
(Linen worker)
1 man/1 reference
One of King David's valiant warriors.
1 Chronicles 11:32

Huram
(Whiteness)
3 men/12 references
Variation of the name Hiram.
1 Chronicles 8:5; 2 Chronicles 2:3;
2 Chronicles 4:11

Huri
(Linen worker)
1 man/1 reference
1 Chronicles 5:14

Hushah
(Haste)
1 man/1 reference
1 Chronicles 4:4

Hushai
(Hasty)
1 man/14 references
David's friend who remained in
Jerusalem when Absalom ousted the
king from the city.
2 Samuel 15:32

Husham
(Hastily)
1 man/4 references
King of Edom.
Genesis 36:34

Hushim
(Hasters)
2 men/1 woman/4 references
One of two wives of a Benjamite
named Shaharaim. He divorced her
in favor of other wives in Moab.
Genesis 46:23; 1 Chronicles 7:12;
1 Chronicles 8:8

Huz
(Consultation)
1 man/1 reference
Firstborn son of Nahor, Abraham's
brother.
Genesis 22:21

Hymenaeus
(Nuptial)
1 man/2 references
Man whom Paul accused of
blasphemy.
1 Timothy 1:20

I

Ibhar
(Choice)
1 man/3 references
Son of King David, born in
Jerusalem.
2 Samuel 5:15

Ibneiah
(Built of God)
1 man/1 reference
1 Chronicles 9:8

Ibnijah
(Building of God)
1 man/1 reference
1 Chronicles 9:8

Ibri
(Eberite [Hebrew])
1 man/1 reference
Levite worship leader during David's
reign. Lots were cast to determine his
duties.
1 Chronicles 24:27

Ibzan
(Splendid)
1 man/2 references
Tenth judge of Israel, who led the
nation for seven years.
Judges 12:8

I-chabod
(There is no glory)
1 man/2 references
1 Samuel 4:21

Idbash
(Honeyed)
1 man/1 reference
1 Chronicles 4:3

Iddo
(Timely, appointed)
7 men/14 references
Most notably, leader of the half
tribe of Manasseh in the days of
King David. Also, prophet who
recorded the acts of kings Solomon,
Rehoboam, and Abijah.
1 Kings 4:14; 1 Chronicles 6:21; 1 Chronicles
27:21; 2 Chronicles 9:29; Ezra 5:1; Ezra 8:17;
Nehemiah 12:4

Igal
(Avenger)
2 men/2 references
Notably, one of twelve spies sent by
Moses to spy out the land of Canaan.
Also, one of King David's warriors
known as the "mighty men."
Numbers 13:7; 2 Samuel 23:36

Igdaliah
(Magnified of God)
1 man/1 reference
Jeremiah 35:4

Igeal
(Avenger)
1 man/1 reference
1 Chronicles 3:22

Ikkesh
(Perverse)
1 man/3 references
2 Samuel 23:36

Ilai
(Elevated)
1 man/1 reference
1 Chronicles 11:29

Imla
(Full)
1 man/2 references
Father of Micaiah, prophet in the time
of Israel's king Ahab. Same as Imlah.
2 Chronicles 18:7

Imlah
(Full)
1 man/2 references
Father of Micaiah, a prophet in the
time of Israel's king Ahab. Same as
Imla.
1 Kings 22:8

Immanuel
(With us is God)
1 man/2 references
Prophetic name for a child promised
to King Ahaz of Judah. Various Old
Testament–era children have been
identified as the fulfillment, but this
most clearly prophesies the coming
of Jesus.
Isaiah 7:14

Immer
(Talkative)
5 men/10 references
Most notably, one of twenty-
four priests in David's time who
was chosen by lot to serve in the
tabernacle.
1 Chronicles 9:12; 1 Chronicles 24:14; Ezra
2:59; Nehemiah 3:29; Jeremiah 20:1

Imna
(He will restrain)
1 man/1 reference
1 Chronicles 7:35

Imnah
(Prosperity)
2 men/2 references
1 Chronicles 7:30; 2 Chronicles 31:14

Imrah
(Interchange)
1 man/1 reference
1 Chronicles 7:36

Imri
(Force)
2 men/2 references
1 Chronicles 9:4; Nehemiah 3:2

Iphedeiah
(God will liberate)
1 man/1 reference
1 Chronicles 8:25

Ir
(City)
1 man/1 reference
1 Chronicles 7:12

Ira
(Wakefulness)
3 men/6 references
Most notably, royal official serving
under Israel's king David. Also,
commander in King David's army
overseeing twenty-four thousand men
in the sixth month of each year.
2 Samuel 20:26; 2 Samuel 23:26;
2 Samuel 23:28

Irad
(Fugitive)
1 man/2 references
Genesis 4:18

Iram
1 man/2 references
(City-wise)
"Duke of Edom," leader in the family
line of Esau.
Genesis 36:43

Iri
(Urbane)
1 man/1 reference
1 Chronicles 7:7

Irijah

(Fearful of God)
1 man/2 references
Sentry who seized the prophet
Jeremiah, accusing him of deserting
to the Chaldeans.
Jeremiah 37:13

Irnahash

(City of a serpent)
1 man/1 reference
1 Chronicles 4:12

Iru

(City-wise)
1 man/1 reference
1 Chronicles 4:15

Isaac

(Laughter)
1 man/132 references
Son of Abraham and Sarah whom
God promised to the long-barren
couple. Almost sacrificed by his father
but saved by God when it was evident
Abraham would fully obey His
command. Husband of Rebekah, and
father of two sons, Esau and Jacob.
Genesis 17:19

Isaiah

(God has saved)
1 man/32 references
Aristocratic prophet of Jerusalem
who warned against making treaties
with foreign nations. Isaiah married
a prophetess and had at least two
children. Same as Esaias.
2 Kings 19:2

Iscah

(Observant)
1 woman/1 reference
Genesis 11:29

Iscariot

(Inhabitant of Kerioth)
1 man/11 references
Name identifying Judas, the disciple
who betrayed Jesus. Same as Judas.
Matthew 10:4

Ishbah

(He will praise)
1 man/1 reference
1 Chronicles 4:17

Ishbak

(He will leave)
1 man/2 references
A son of Abraham by his second wife,
Keturah.
Genesis 25:2

Ishbi-benob

(His dwelling is in Nob)
1 man/1 reference
Philistine giant who planned to kill
King David in battle but was felled by
David's soldier Abishai.
2 Samuel 21:16

Ish-bosheth

(Man of shame)
1 man/12 references
King Saul's son who was made king
over Israel by Abner, captain of Saul's
army.
2 Samuel 2:8

Ishi

(Saving)
4 men/5 references
1 Chronicles 2:31; 1 Chronicles 4:20;
1 Chronicles 4:42; 1 Chronicles 5:24

Ishiah

(God will lend)
1 man/1 reference
1 Chronicles 7:3

Ishijah
(God will lend)
1 man/1 reference
Ezra 10:31

Ishma
(Desolate)
1 man/1 reference
1 Chronicles 4:3

Ishmael
(God will hear)
6 men/48 references
Most notably, son of Hagar, Sarai's
maid, and Abram, born after Sarai
encouraged her husband to have a
child with her maid. God rejected
Ishmael, who was not the son of
His covenant promise, but He
promised to bless Ishmael and make
him fruitful so he would found a
great nation. Also, official who ruled
over the household of Judah's King
Jehoshaphat.
Genesis 16:11; 2 Kings 25:23; 1 Chronicles
8:38; 2 Chronicles 19:11; 2 Chronicles 23:1;
Ezra 10:22

Ishmaiah
(God will hear)
1 man/1 reference
Leader of the tribe of Zebulun in the
days of King David.
1 Chronicles 27:19

Ishmerai
(Preservative)
1 man/1 reference
1 Chronicles 8:18

Ishod
(Man of renown)
1 man/1 reference
1 Chronicles 7:18

Ishpan
(He will hide)
1 man/1 reference
1 Chronicles 8:22

Ishuah
(He will level)
1 man/1 reference
Genesis 46:17

Ishuai
(Level)
1 man/1 reference
1 Chronicles 7:30

Ishui
(Level)
1 man/1 reference
One of three sons of Israel's king Saul.
Ishui and his brothers died with Saul
in a battle against the Philistines on
Mount Gilboa. Same as Abinadab.
1 Samuel 14:49

Ismachiah
(God will sustain)
1 man/1 reference
Temple overseer of offerings during
the reign of King Hezekiah of Judah.
2 Chronicles 31:13

Ismaiah
(God will hear)
1 man/1 reference
One of King David's warriors known
as the "mighty men." Part of an elite
group called "the thirty."
1 Chronicles 12:4

Ispah
(He will scratch)
1 man/1 reference
1 Chronicles 8:16

Israel
(He will rule as God)
1 man/55 references
Name given to Jacob by God when
he wrestled with Him at Peniel.
Later God again appeared to Jacob,
confirmed His covenant promises,
and blessed him. Of his twelve
sons, Israel loved Joseph more
than the others, gave him a coat of
many colors to show his preferred
status, and put him in a position of
authority. Israel blessed Joseph's sons,
Ephraim and Manasseh, taking them
as his own sons. Same as Jacob.
Genesis 32:28

Issachar
(He will bring a reward)
2 men/8 references
Notably, Leah and Jacob's fifth son
and Jacob's ninth son. His mother
saw him as God's payment to her
because she gave her servant Zilpah
to Jacob.
Genesis 30:18; 1 Chronicles 26:5

Isshiah
(God will lend)
2 men/3 references
Notably, Levite worship leader during
David's reign.
1 Chronicles 24:21; 1 Chronicles 24:25

Isuah
(Level)
1 man/1 reference
1 Chronicles 7:30

Isui
(Level)
1 man/1 reference
Genesis 46:17

Ithai
(Near)
1 man/1 reference
1 Chronicles 11:31

Ithamar
(Coast of the palm tree)
1 man/21 references
Son of Aaron and his wife, Elisheba,
who served as a priest. Moses
became angry at Ithamar because he
would not eat the sin offering in the
tabernacle.
Exodus 6:23

Ithiel
(God has arrived)
2 men/3 references
Notably, man to whom Agur spoke
the words of Proverbs 30.
Nehemiah 11:7; Proverbs 30:1

Ithmah
(Orphanage)
1 man/1 reference
One of King David's valiant warriors.
1 Chronicles 11:46

Ithra
(Excellence)
1 man/1 reference
2 Samuel 17:25

Ithran
(Excellent)
2 men/3 references
Genesis 36:26; 1 Chronicles 7:37

Ithream
(Excellence of people)
1 man/2 references
Sixth son of David, born to his wife
Eglah in Hebron.
2 Samuel 3:5

Ittai
(Near)
2 men/8 references
Notably, Gittite who remained
faithful to David when Absalom tried
to overthrow the king. David set
Ittai over a third of the people who
followed him out of Jerusalem. Also,
one of King David's warriors known
as the "mighty men."
2 Samuel 15:19; 2 Samuel 23:29

Izehar
(Anointing)
1 man/1 reference
Numbers 3:19

Izhar
(Anointing)
1 man/8 references
Exodus 6:18

Izrahiah
(God will shine)
1 man/2 references
1 Chronicles 7:3

Izri
(Trough)
1 man/1 reference
One of twenty-four Levite musicians
who was chosen by lot to serve in the
house of the Lord.
1 Chronicles 25:11

J

Jaakan
(To twist)
1 man/1 reference
Deuteronomy 10:6

Jaakobah
(Heel catcher)
1 man/1 reference
1 Chronicles 4:36

Jaala
(Roe)
1 man/1 reference
Same as Jaalah.
Nehemiah 7:58

Jaalah
(Roe)
1 man/1 reference
Same as Jaala.
Ezra 2:56

Jaalam
(Occult)
1 man/4 references
Son of Esau.
Genesis 36:5

Jaanai
(Responsive)
1 man/1 reference
1 Chronicles 5:12

Jaare-oregim
(Woods of weavers)
1 man/1 reference
Father of Elhanan. Same as Jair.
2 Samuel 21:19

Jaasau
(They will do)
1 man/1 reference
Ezra 10:37

Jaasiel
(Made of God)
1 man/1 reference
Leader of the tribe of Benjamin in the
days of King David.
1 Chronicles 27:21

Jaazaniah
(Heard of God)
4 men/4 references
Most notably, captain of the army
of Judah under Nebuchadnezzar's

governor, Gedaliah. Also called Jezaniah. Also, prince of Judah whom God described as devising mischief and giving wicked counsel.
2 Kings 25:23; Jeremiah 35:3; Ezekiel 8:11; Ezekiel 11:1

Jaaziah
(Emboldened of God)
1 men/2 references
Levite worship leader during David's reign. Lots were cast to determine his duties.
1 Chronicles 24:26

Jaaziel
(Emboldened of God)
1 man/1 reference
Levite musician who performed in celebration when King David brought the ark of the covenant to Jerusalem. Same as Aziel.
1 Chronicles 15:18

Jabal
(Stream)
1 man/1 reference
Genesis 4:20

Jabesh
(Dry)
1 man/3 references
2 Kings 15:10

Jabez
(To grieve)
1 man/3 references
Pious man of the line of Judah who prayed for God's blessing, that He would enlarge his border, and that God's hand would be with him and keep him from harm.
1 Chronicles 4:9

Jabin
(Intelligent)
2 men/8 references
Notably, king of Hazor who raised armies against Joshua and his invading troops. Also, king of Canaan who had Sisera as the captain of his army.
Joshua 11:1; Judges 4:2

Jachan
(Troublesome)
1 man/1 reference
1 Chronicles 5:13

Jachin
(He will establish)
3 men/6 references
Most notably, one of twenty-four priests in David's time who was chosen by lot to serve in the tabernacle.
Genesis 46:10; 1 Chronicles 9:10; 1 Chronicles 24:17

Jacob
(Supplanter)
2 men/280 references
Notably, Isaac and Rebekah's son and twin brother of Esau who exchanged a bowl of stew for his brother's birthright. He also gained Isaac's blessing by deception. God promised him many descendants and blessed the earth through them. Jacob married Laban's daughters, Leah and Rachel. From them and their handmaids, Jacob had twelve sons, the founders of Israel's twelve tribes. He met God, wrestled with Him, and was renamed Israel. Same as Israel.
Genesis 25:26; Matthew 1:15

Jada
(Knowing)
1 man/2 references
1 Chronicles 2:28

Jadau
(Praised)
1 man/1 reference
Ezra 10:43

Jaddua
(Knowing)
2 men/3 references
Nehemiah 10:21; Nehemiah 12:11

Jadon
(Thankful)
1 man/1 reference
Nehemiah 3:7

Jael
(Ibex)
1 woman/6 references
Wife of Heber the Kenite who killed the Canaanite commander Sisera when he fled to her tent following his defeat by the Israelites.
Judges 4:17

Jahath
(Unity)
5 men/8 references
Most notably, Levite worship leader during David's reign. Also, Levite worship leader who oversaw the repair of the temple under King Josiah.
1 Chronicles 4:2; 1 Chronicles 6:20;
1 Chronicles 23:10; 1 Chronicles 24:22;
2 Chronicles 34:12

Jahaziah
(God will behold)
1 man/1 reference
Man who oversaw the Israelites who needed to put away "strange" (foreign) wives under Ezra.
Ezra 10:15

Jahaziel
(Beheld of God)
5 men/6 references
Most notably, a "mighty man" of King David. Also, priest who blew a trumpet when David brought the ark of the Lord to Jerusalem. Also, Levite worship leader who prophesied before King Jehoshaphat of Judah when Edom attacked.
1 Chronicles 12:4; 1 Chronicles 16:6;
1 Chronicles 23:19; 2 Chronicles 20:14;
Ezra 8:5

Jahdai
(Jehovah fired)
1 man/1 reference
1 Chronicles 2:47

Jahdiel
(Unity of God)
1 man/1 reference
One of the men leading the half tribe of Manasseh.
1 Chronicles 5:24

Jahdo
(His unity, together)
1 man/1 reference
1 Chronicles 5:14

Jahleel
(Wait for God)
1 man/2 references
Genesis 46:14

Jahmai
(Hot)
1 man/1 reference
1 Chronicles 7:2

Jahzeel
(God will allot)
1 man/2 references
Same as Jahziel.
Genesis 46:24

Jahzerah
(Protection)
1 man/1 reference
1 Chronicles 9:12

Jahziel
(Allotted of God)
1 man/1 reference
Same as Jahzeel.
1 Chronicles 7:13

Jair
(Enlightener)
4 men/9 references
Most notably, descendant of
Manasseh who captured twenty-three
cities of Bashan and named them
Havvothjair. Also, the eighth judge of
Israel, who led the nation for twenty-
two years and is known for having
thirty sons who rode thirty donkeys.
Numbers 32:41; Judges 10:3; 1 Chronicles
20:5; Esther 2:5

Jairus
(Enlightener)
1 man/2 references
Synagogue ruler who asked Jesus to
come and heal his daughter. She died
before they could reach her, but Jesus
brought her back to life.
Mark 5:22

Jakan
(Tortuous)
1 man/1 reference
Same as Akan or Jaakan.
1 Chronicles 1:42

Jakeh
(Obedient)
1 man/1 reference
Proverbs 30:1

Jakim
(He will raise)
2 men/2 references
Most notably, one of twenty-
four priests in David's time who
was chosen by lot to serve in the
tabernacle.
1 Chronicles 8:19; 1 Chronicles 24:12

Jalon
(Lodging)
1 man/1 reference
1 Chronicles 4:17

Jambres
1 man/1 reference
Opponent of Moses mentioned by
the apostle Paul as an example of
apostasy.
2 Timothy 3:8

James
3 men/42 references
Most notably, Jesus' brother, called
James the less (younger) who became
a leader in the Jerusalem church, and
believed by many to be the writer
of the book of James in the New
Testament. Also, Zebedee's son and
John's brother, a fisherman called by
Jesus to become a fisher of men as
one of His disciples, and years later,
executed by Herod Agrippa I. Also,
son of Alphaeus and disciple of Jesus.
Matthew 4:21; Matthew 10:3;
Matthew 13:55

Jamin
(Right hand)
3 men/6 references
Most notably, Levite who helped
Ezra to explain the law to exiles who
returned to Jerusalem.
Genesis 46:10; 1 Chronicles 2:27;
Nehemiah 8:7

Jamlech
(He will make king)
1 man/1 reference
1 Chronicles 4:34

Janna
(Oppressor)
1 man/1 reference
Forebear of Jesus' earthly father,
Joseph.
Luke 3:24

Jannes
(To cure)
1 man/1 reference
Opponent of Moses mentioned by
the apostle Paul as an example of
apostasy.
2 Timothy 3:8

Japheth
(Expansion)
1 man/11 references
Noah's third son, who joined his
family in the ark.
Genesis 5:32

Japhia
(Bright)
2 men/4 references
Notably, king of Lachish during
Joshua's conquest of the Promised
Land who allied with four other
rulers to attack Gibeon, which had
deceptively made a peace treaty
with the Israelites. Also, son of King
David, born in Jerusalem.
Joshua 10:3; 2 Samuel 5:15

Japhlet
(He will deliver)
1 man/3 references
1 Chronicles 7:32

Jarah
(Honey in the comb)
1 man/2 references
Same as Jehoadah.
1 Chronicles 9:42

Jareb
(He will contend)
1 man/2 references
Assyrian king mentioned in the
prophecies of Hosea.
Hosea 5:13

Jared
(A descent)
1 man/6 references
Second-longest-lived individual in the
Bible at 962 years. Same as Jered.
Genesis 5:15

Jaresiah
(Uncertain)
1 man/1 references
1 Chronicles 8:27

Jarha
1 man/2 references
Egyptian servant of Sheshan,
descendant of Abraham through
Jacob's son Judah.
1 Chronicles 2:34

Jarib
(He will contend)
3 men/3 references
1 Chronicles 4:24; Ezra 8:16; Ezra 10:18

Jaroah
(Born at the new moon)
1 man/1 reference
1 Chronicles 5:14

Jashen
(Sleepy)
1 man/1 reference
2 Samuel 23:32

Jashobeam
(People will return)
2 men/3 references
Notably, commander in King
David's army, overseeing twenty-four
thousand men in the first month of
each year. One of David's "mighty
men," who once single-handedly
killed three hundred enemy soldiers.
1 Chronicles 11:11; 1 Chronicles 12:6

Jashub
(He will return)
2 men/3 references
Notably, descendant of Abraham
through Jacob's son Issachar. Same
as Job.
Numbers 26:24; Ezra 10:29

Jashubi-lehem
(Returner of bread)
1 man/1 reference
1 Chronicles 4:22

Jasiel
(Made of God)
1 man/1 reference
One of King David's valiant warriors.
1 Chronicles 11:47

Jason
(About to cure)
2 men/5 references
Notably, Christian from Thessalonica
who was taken along with other
Christians by jealous Jews to the city
officials. Also, relative of Paul, living
in Rome, who was greeted in the
apostle's letter to the Romans.
Acts 17:5; Romans 16:21

Jathniel
(Continued of God)
1 man/1 reference
1 Chronicles 26:2

Javan
(Effervescing)
1 man/4 references
Grandson of Noah through his son
Japheth.
Genesis 10:2

Jaziz
(He will make prominent)
1 man/1 reference
Called Jaziz the Hagarite, in charge of
King David's flocks.
1 Chronicles 27:31

Jeaterai
(Stepping)
1 man/1 reference
1 Chronicles 6:21

Jeberechiah
(Blessed of God)
1 man/1 reference
Isaiah 8:2

Jecamiah
(God will rise)
1 man/1 reference
Descendant of Abraham through
Jacob's son Judah, in the line of the
nation of Judah's second-to-last king,
Jeconiah (also known as Jehoiachin).
Same as Jekamiah.
1 Chronicles 3:18

Jecholiah
(Jehovah will enable)
1 woman/1 reference
Mother of Judah's good king Azariah,
also known as Uzziah. Same as Jecoliah.
2 Kings 15:2

Jechonias
(Jehovah will establish)
1 man/2 references
Greek form of the name *Jeconiah*,
used in the New Testament.
Matthew 1:11

Jecoliah
(God will enable)
1 woman/1 reference
Mother of Judah's good king Uzziah, also known as Azariah. Same as Jecholiah.
2 Chronicles 26:3

Jeconiah
(God will establish)
1 man/7 references
King of Judah and son of King Jehoiakim, carried to Babylon along with his nobles by King Nebuchadnezzar. Same as Coniah, Jechonias, and Jehoiachin.
1 Chronicles 3:16

Jedaiah
(Praised of God)
5 men/13 references
Most notably, rebuilder of the walls of Jerusalem under Nehemiah. Also, one of twenty-four priests in David's time who was chosen by lot to serve in the tabernacle.
1 Chronicles 4:37; 1 Chronicles 9:10; Nehemiah 3:10; Nehemiah 11:10; Nehemiah 12:7

Jediael
(Knowing God)
4 men/6 references
Most notably, one of King David's valiant warriors. Also, captain of thousands for the tribe of Manasseh, which supported David against Saul.
1 Chronicles 7:6; 1 Chronicles 11:45; 1 Chronicles 12:20; 1 Chronicles 26:2

Jedidah
(Beloved)
1 woman/1 reference
Mother of Judah's good king Josiah.
2 Kings 22:1

Jedidiah
(Beloved of God)
1 man/1 reference
God's special name for Solomon, as delivered by the prophet Nathan.
2 Samuel 12:25

Jeduthun
(Laudatory)
1 man/17 references
Descendant of Abraham through Jacob's son Levi. One of the key musicians serving in the Jerusalem temple.
1 Chronicles 9:16

Jeezer
(Helpless)
1 man/1 reference
Descendant of Joseph's son Manasseh and son of Gilead.
Numbers 26:30

Jehaleleel
(Praising God)
1 man/1 reference
1 Chronicles 4:16

Jehalelel
(Praising God)
1 man/1 reference
2 Chronicles 29:12

Jehdeiah
(Unity of God)
2 men/2 references
Notably, official responsible for King David's herds of donkeys.
1 Chronicles 24:20; 1 Chronicles 27:30

Jehezekel
(God will strengthen)
1 man/1 reference
One of twenty-four priests in David's time, chosen by lot to serve in the tabernacle.
1 Chronicles 24:16

Jehiah
(God will live)
1 man/1 reference
A doorkeeper of the ark of the covenant under King David.
1 Chronicles 15:24

Jehiel
(God will live)
13 men/16 references
Most notably, Levite musician who performed in celebration when King David brought the ark of the covenant to Jerusalem. Also, leader of the Gershonites who cared for the precious stones donated for Solomon's temple. Also, tutor to King David's sons. Also, one of King David's valiant warriors.
1 Chronicles 9:35 1 Chronicles 11:44; 1 Chronicles 15:18; 1 Chronicles 23:8; 1 Chronicles 27:32; 2 Chronicles 21:2; 2 Chronicles 29:14; 2 Chronicles 31:13; 2 Chronicles 35:8; Ezra 8:9; Ezra 10:2; Ezra 10:21; Ezra 10:26

Jehieli
(God will live)
1 man/2 references
Levite whose sons were in charge of the temple treasury.
1 Chronicles 26:21

Jehizkiah
(Strengthened of God)
1 man/1 reference
Man of the tribe of Ephraim who counseled his nation of Israel against enslaving fellow Jews from Judah who were captured in a civil war. Helped feed and clothe the prisoners before sending them home.
2 Chronicles 28:12

Jehoadah
(Jehovah adorned)
1 man/2 references
Descendant of Abraham through Jacob's son Benjamin, through the line of King Saul and his son Jonathan. Same as Jarah.
1 Chronicles 8:36

Jehoaddan
(Jehovah pleased)
1 woman/2 references
Mother of Amaziah, king of Judah.
2 Kings 14:2

Jehoahaz
(Jehovah seized)
3 men/23 references
Most notably, king of Israel and son of King Jehu, doing evil in God's sight. Also, king of Judah, son of King Josiah. Evil king who reigned only three months. Same as Shallum.
2 Kings 10:35; 2 Kings 23:30; 2 Chronicles 21:17

Jehoash
(Jehovah fired)
2 men/17 references
Another name for Joash. Also, evil king of Israel, son of King Jehoahaz. Fought King Amaziah of Judah, broke down Jerusalem's wall, and took gold and silver from the temple and the king.
2 Kings 11:21; 2 Kings 13:10

Jehohanan
(Jehovah favored)
6 men/6 references
Most notably, military captain of Judah who stood next to Adnah, the commander. Also, priest who helped to dedicate the rebuilt wall of Jerusalem by giving thanks.
1 Chronicles 26:3; 2 Chronicles 17:15; 2 Chronicles 23:1; Ezra 10:28; Nehemiah 12:13; Nehemiah 12:42

Jehoiachin
(Jehovah will establish)
1 man/10 references
King of Judah and son of King Jehoiakim, this evil king reigned only three months before King Nebuchadnezzar of Babylon carried him and the best of his people to Babylon. In the thirty-seventh year of Jehoiachin's captivity, King Evil-merodach brought him out of prison and gave him preferential treatment. Same as Coniah, Jeconiah, and Jeconias.
2 Kings 24:6

Jehoiada
(Jehovah known)
6 men/52 references
Most notably, father of Benaiah, commander in King David's army, who also served Solomon. Also, high priest who made a covenant with the army's leaders to protect young King Joash.
2 Samuel 8:18; 2 Kings 11:4; 1 Chronicles 12:27; 1 Chronicles 27:34; Nehemiah 3:6; Jeremiah 29:26

Jehoiakim
(Jehovah will raise)
1 man/37 references
Originally named Eliakim, Egyptian pharaoh Necho made him king of Judah and changed his name to Jehoiakim. Jehoiakim rebelled, and when Jeremiah's prophetic warning words were read to this wicked king, he burned the scroll they were written on. Same as Eliakim.
2 Kings 23:34

Jehoiarib
(Jehovah will contend)
2 men/2 references
Notably, priest who returned to Jerusalem after the Babylonian captivity. Also, one of twenty-four priests of David's time who was chosen by lot to serve in the tabernacle.
1 Chronicles 9:10; 1 Chronicles 24:7

Jehonadab
(Jehovah largessed)
1 man/3 references
A Rechabite known for spiritual austerity. Saw destruction of the temple of Baal, with all the worshippers in it.
2 Kings 10:15

Jehonathan
(Jehovah given)
3 men/3 references
Most notably, official in charge of King David's storehouses. Also, Levite sent by King Jehoshaphat to teach the law of the Lord throughout the nation of Judah.
1 Chronicles 27:25; 2 Chronicles 17:8; Nehemiah 12:18

Jehoram
(Jehovah raised)
3 men/23 references
Most notably, firstborn son of King Jehoshaphat of Judah. He led his nation into idolatry. Same as Joram. Also, king of Israel who did not stop his nation from worshipping idols. Also, priest who taught the law of the Lord throughout Judah.
1 Kings 22:50; 2 Kings 1:17; 2 Chronicles 17:8

Jehoshabeath
(Jehovah sworn)
1 woman/2 references
Daughter of Judah's king Jehoram and sister of Judah's king Ahaziah. After Ahaziah was killed, Jehoshabeath saved her infant nephew, Joash,

from a family massacre engineered by Ahaziah's mother, Athaliah, who wanted to make herself queen. Same as Jehosheba.
2 Chronicles 22:11

Jehoshaphat
(Jehovah judged)
5 men/83 references
Most notably, official in King David's court who was his recorder. Also, king of Judah who inherited the throne from his father, Asa. Also, one of King Solomon's twelve officials over provisions. Also, father of Jehu, king of Israel.
2 Samuel 8:16; 1 Kings 4:17; 1 Kings 15:24; 2 Kings 9:2; 1 Chronicles 15:24

Jehosheba
(Jehovah sworn)
1 woman/2 references
King Joash's aunt, who protected him from his wicked grandmother Athaliah. Same as Jehoshabeath.
2 Kings 11:2

Jehoshua
(Jehovah saved)
1 man/1 reference
Variant name for Joshua, son of Nun, successor to Moses.
Numbers 13:16

Jehoshuah
(Jehovah saved)
1 man/1 reference
Variant name for Joshua, son of Nun, successor to Moses.
1 Chronicles 7:27

Jehozabad
(Jehovah endowed)
3 men/4 references
Most notably, one of two royal officials who conspired to kill Judah's

king Joash. Also, commander in the army of King Jehoshaphat of Israel.
2 Kings 12:21; 1 Chronicles 26:4; 2 Chronicles 17:18

Jehozadak
(Jehovah righted)
1 man/2 references
1 Chronicles 6:14

Jehu
(Jehovah [is] He)
5 men/59 references
Most notably, prophet who prophesied the destruction of Baasha, king of Israel, and Baasha's heirs. Also, king of Israel anointed to destroy King Ahab and his dynasty. Also, "mighty man" of King David.
1 Kings 16:1; 1 Kings 19:16; 1 Chronicles 2:38; 1 Chronicles 4:35; 1 Chronicles 12:3

Jehubbah
(Hidden)
1 man/1 reference
1 Chronicles 7:34

Jehucal
(Potent)
1 man/1 reference
Jeremiah 37:3

Jehudi
(Descendant of Jehudah)
1 man/4 references
Jeremiah 36:14

Jehudijah
(Female descendant of Jehudah)
1 woman/1 reference
Wife of Ezra.
1 Chronicles 4:18

Jehush
(Hasty)
1 man/1 reference
1 Chronicles 8:39

Jeiel

(Carried away of God)
8 men/11 references
Most notably, Levite worship leader
who played a harp as the ark of the
covenant was brought into Jerusalem.
1 Chronicles 5:7; 1 Chronicles 15:18;
2 Chronicles 20:14; 2 Chronicles 26:11;
2 Chronicles 29:13; 2 Chronicles 35:9;
Ezra 8:13; Ezra 10:43

Jekameam

(The people will rise)
1 man/2 references
1 Chronicles 23:19

Jekamiah

(God will rise)
1 man/2 references
Same as Jecamiah.
1 Chronicles 2:41

Jekuthiel

(Obedience of God)
1 man/1 reference
1 Chronicles 4:18

Jemima

(Dove)
1 woman/1 reference
Oldest daughter of Job, born after
God restored his fortunes.
Job 42:14

Jemuel

(Day of God)
1 man/2 references
Same as Nemuel.
Genesis 46:10

Jephthae

(He will open)
1 man/1 reference
Greek form of the name *Jephthah*,
used in the New Testament.
Hebrews 11:32

Jephthah

(He will open)
1 man/29 references
Eighth judge of Israel who
promised God that he would give
Him whatever greeted him when
he returned home, should he be
victorious in battle. After winning,
his daughter came to greet him.
Following a two-month reprieve,
Jephthah kept his vow. Same as
Jephthae.
Judges 11:1

Jephunneh

(He will be prepared)
2 men/16 references
Numbers 13:6; 1 Chronicles 7:38

Jerah

(Month)
1 man/2 references
Genesis 10:26

Jerahmeel

(God will be compassionate)
3 men/8 references
1 Chronicles 2:9; 1 Chronicles 24:29;
Jeremiah 36:26

Jered

(A descent)
2 men/2 references
Second-longest-lived individual in the
Bible at 962 years. Same as Jared.
1 Chronicles 1:2; 1 Chronicles 4:18

Jeremai

(Elevated)
1 man/1 reference
Ezra 10:33

Jeremiah

(God will rise)
7 men/146 references
Most notably, prophet of Judah who

had gloomy prophecies, condemning Judah for idolatry and calling the nation to repentance. Same as Jeremias and Jeremy. Also, leader of the half tribe of Manasseh. Also, one of King David's mightiest warriors known as "the thirty."
2 Kings 23:31; 1 Chronicles 5:24; 1 Chronicles 12:4; 1 Chronicles 12:10; 1 Chronicles 12:13; 2 Chronicles 35:25; Nehemiah 10:2

Jeremias
(God will rise)
1 man/1 reference
Greek form of the name *Jeremiah*, used in the New Testament. Same as Jeremiah.
Matthew 16:14

Jeremoth
(Elevations)
5 men/5 references
Most notably, one of twenty-four Levite musicians who was chosen by lot to serve in the house of the Lord. Same as Jerimoth.
1 Chronicles 8:14; 1 Chronicles 23:23; 1 Chronicles 25:22; Ezra 10:26; Ezra 10:27

Jeremy
(God will rise)
1 man/2 references
Latin form of the name *Jeremiah*, used in the New Testament. Same as Jeremiah.
Matthew 2:17

Jeriah
(God will throw)
1 man/2 references
1 Chronicles 23:19

Jeribai
(Contentious)
1 man/1 reference
One of King David's valiant warriors.
1 Chronicles 11:46

Jeriel
(Thrown of God)
1 man/1 reference
1 Chronicles 7:2

Jerijah
1 man/1 reference
Chief of Hebronites whom King David gave authority over the Reubenites, Gadites, and half tribe of Manasseh.
1 Chronicles 26:31

Jerimoth
(Elevations)
8 men/8 references
Most notably, "mighty man" who supported the future king David during his conflict with Saul. Also, leader of the tribe of Naphtali in the days of King David. Same as Jeremoth.
1 Chronicles 7:7; 1 Chronicles 7:8; 1 Chronicles 12:5; 1 Chronicles 24:30; 1 Chronicles 25:4; 1 Chronicles 27:19; 2 Chronicles; 11:18; 2 Chronicles 31:13

Jerioth
(Curtains)
1 woman/1 reference
1 Chronicles 2:18

Jeroboam
(The people will contend)
2 men/104 references
Most notably, servant of King Solomon who had authority over forced labor for the tribes of Ephraim and Manasseh and established idolatrous worship in Israel. Because of his disobedience, God cut off all the men of Jeroboam's household. Also, king of Israel, son of King Joash, who continued idolatrous worship.
1 Kings 11:26; 2 Kings 13:13

Jeroham
(Compassionate)
7 men/10 references
Most notably, prince of the tribe of
Dan, assigned to rule by King David.
1 Samuel 1:1; 1 Chronicles 8:27; 1 Chronicles
9:8; 1 Chronicles 9:12; 1 Chronicles 12:7;
1 Chronicles 27:22; 2 Chronicles 23:1

Jerubbaal
(Baal will contend)
1 man/14 references
Name given to Gideon by his father
after he destroyed the altars to Baal.
Judges 6:32

Jerubbesheth
(Shame will contend)
1 man/1 reference
Alternative name for the judge
Gideon.
2 Samuel 11:21

Jerusha
(Possessed [married])
1 woman/1 reference
Mother of Jotham, king of Judah.
2 Kings 15:33

Jerushah
(Possessed [married])
1 woman/1 reference
Variant spelling of *Jerusha*; mother of
King Jotham of Judah.
2 Chronicles 27:1

Jesaiah
(God has saved)
2 men/2 references
1 Chronicles 3:21; Nehemiah 11:7

Jeshaiah
(God has saved)
4 men/5 references
Most notably, Levite worship leader
under King David.
1 Chronicles 25:3; 1 Chronicles 26:25; Ezra
8:7; Ezra 8:19

Jesharelah
(Right toward God)
1 man/1 reference
One of twenty-four Levite musicians
in David's time, chosen by lot to serve
in the house of the Lord.
1 Chronicles 25:14

Jeshebeab
(People will return)
1 man/1 reference
One of twenty-four priests in David's
time, chosen by lot to serve in the
tabernacle.
1 Chronicles 24:13

Jesher
(The right)
1 man/1 reference
1 Chronicles 2:18

Jeshishai
(Aged)
1 man/1 reference
1 Chronicles 5:14

Jeshohaiah
(God will empty)
1 man/1 reference
1 Chronicles 4:36

Jeshua
(He will save)
9 men/29 references
Most notably, high priest who
returned from exile with Zerubbabel
and built the temple altar with him.
Also, another form of the name *Joshua*.

1 Chronicles 24:11; Ezra 2:2; Ezra 2:6; Ezra 2:36; Ezra 8:33; Nehemiah 3:19; Nehemiah 8:7; Nehemiah 8:17; Nehemiah 10:9

Jesiah
(God will lend)
2 men/2 references
Notably, "mighty man" who supported the future king David during his conflict with Saul.
1 Chronicles 12:6; 1 Chronicles 23:20

Jesimiel
(God will place)
1 man/1 reference
1 Chronicles 4:36

Jesse
(Extant)
1 man/47 references
Father of David, who had seven sons pass before the prophet Samuel before David was brought before Samuel and anointed king. Jesus' earthly lineage stems from Jesse, through David.
Ruth 4:17

Jesui
(Level)
1 man/1 reference
Numbers 26:44

Jesus
(Jehovah saved)
3 men/983 references
Most notably, God's Son and humanity's Savior, incarnated within the womb of Mary and born in Bethlehem. At about age thirty, He began His ministry, calling twelve disciples to follow Him. With them, He traveled through Israel, preaching about God and healing many people. Later, Judas betrayed Him, and Jesus, who had done no wrong, died for humanity's sin on the cross. Some time later, after His resurrection, He ascended to heaven and will someday return for those who believe in Him. He will establish a New Jerusalem, where He will live with them forever. Also, another form of the name *Joshua.*
Matthew 1:1; Hebrews 4:8; Colossians 4:11

Jether
(Superiority)
5 men/8 references
Most notably, Gideon's son who fearfully disobeyed when his father told him to kill Zebah and Zalmunna.
Judges 8:20; 1 Kings 2:5; 1 Chronicles 2:32; 1 Chronicles 4:17; 1 Chronicles 7:38

Jetheth
1 man/2 references
A "duke of Edom," a leader in the family line of Esau.
Genesis 36:40

Jethro
(His excellence)
1 man/10 references
Moses' father-in-law, for whom Moses kept flocks until God called him to Egypt. For a time, Moses' wife, Zipporah, and her two sons lived with Jethro. He advised Moses to appoint those who could help him rule over the people. Same as Hobab.
Exodus 3:1

Jetur
(Encircled, enclosed)
1 man/2 references
Genesis 25:15

Jeuel
(Carried away of God)
1 man/1 reference
Jewish exile from the tribe of Judah

who resettled Jerusalem.
1 Chronicles 9:6

Jeush
(Hasty)
4 men/8 references
Most notably, son of Esau. Also, son
of Judah's king Rehoboam and a
grandson of Solomon.
Genesis 36:5; 1 Chronicles 7:10;
1 Chronicles 23:10; 2 Chronicles 11:19

Jeuz
(Counselor)
1 man/1 reference
1 Chronicles 8:10

Jezaniah
(Heard of God)
1 man/2 references
Captain of Israel's forces under
Nebuchadnezzar's governor Gedaliah.
Same as Jaazaniah.
Jeremiah 40:8

Jezebel
(Chaste)
1 woman/22 references
Sidonian princess who married King
Ahab of Israel, Jezebel persecuted
Israel's prophets, including Elijah,
after he killed the priests of her god
Baal. God ordered Jehu to strike
Jezebel down. Jehu commanded her
slaves to throw her from a window,
and she died.
1 Kings 16:31

Jezer
(Form)
1 man/3 references
Genesis 46:24

Jeziah
(Sprinkled of God)
1 man/1 reference
Ezra 10:25

Jeziel
(Sprinkled of God)
1 man/1 reference
"Mighty man" who supported the
future king David during his conflict
with Saul.
1 Chronicles 12:3

Jezliah
(He will draw out)
1 man/1 reference
1 Chronicles 8:18

Jezoar
(He will shine)
1 man/1 reference
1 Chronicles 4:7

Jezrahiah
(God will shine)
1 man/1 reference
Priest who helped to dedicate the
rebuilt wall of Jerusalem by leading
the singing.
Nehemiah 12:42

Jezreel
(God will sow)
2 men/4 references
Notably, firstborn son of the prophet
Hosea whose name signified the
judgment God planned for the
rebellious people of Judah.
1 Chronicles 4:3; Hosea 1:4

Jibsam
(Fragrant)
1 man/1 reference
1 Chronicles 7:2

Jidlaph
(Tearful)
1 man/1 reference
Son of Nahor, Abraham's brother.
Genesis 22:22

Jimna
(Prosperity)
1 man/1 reference
Same as Jimnah.
Numbers 26:44

Jimnah
(Prosperity)
1 man/1 reference
Variant spelling of *Jimna.*
Genesis 46:17

Joab
(Jehovah fathered)
5 men/146 references
Most notably, commander of David's
army. He obeyed David's command
to put Uriah the Hittite on the front
lines so he would be killed.
1 Samuel 26:6; 1 Chronicles 2:54;
1 Chronicles 4:14; Ezra 2:6; Ezra 8:9

Joah
(Jehovah brothered)
4 men/11 references
Most notably, officer of King
Hezekiah of Judah. Also, official
under King Josiah of Judah, whom
the king sent to repair the temple.
2 Kings 18:18; 1 Chronicles 6:21;
1 Chronicles 26:4; 2 Chronicles 34:8

Joahaz
(Jehovah seized)
1 man/1 reference
2 Chronicles 34:8

Joanna
1 man/1 woman/3 references
Notably, wife of one of King Herod's
officials, she followed Jesus and
provided for His financial needs.
Luke 3:27; Luke 8:3

Joash
(Jehovah hastened)
8 men/49 references
Most notably, king of Judah, son
of King Ahaziah, hidden from his
wicked grandmother Athaliah then
protected by the priest Jehoiada. He
followed the Lord but did not remove
idolatry from the nation. Same as
Jehoash. Also, a king of Israel. Also,
official over stores of oil under King
David. Also, "mighty man" who
supported the future king David
during his conflict with Saul.
Judges 6:11; 1 Kings 22:26; 2 Kings 11:2;
2 Kings 13:9; 1 Chronicles 4:22;
1 Chronicles 7:8; 1 Chronicles 27:28;
1 Chronicles 12:3

Joatham
1 man/2 references
Matthew 1:9

Job
(Hated, persecuted)
2 men/60 references
Notably, righteous man from Uz
whom God tested to prove to Satan
that Job was not faithful to Him
because of His blessings. Job lost
his cattle and servants; then all his
children were killed. Yet he continued
to worship God. When he suffered an
affliction, three friends came to share
his misery. At first they were silent but
then accused Job of doing something
wrong. God rebuked his three friends
and restored all of Job's original
blessings. Also, same as Jashub.
Genesis 46:13; Job 1:1

Jobab
(Howler)
5 men/9 references
Most notably, king of Madon who
joined an alliance to attack the

Israelites under Joshua. Also, king of Edom.
Genesis 10:29; Genesis 36:33; Joshua 11:1; 1 Chronicles 8:9; 1 Chronicles 8:18

Jochebed
(Jehovah gloried)
1 woman/2 references
Wife of Amram and mother of Moses, Aaron, and Miriam.
Exodus 6:20

Joed
(Appointer)
1 man/1 reference
Nehemiah 11:7

Joel
(Jehovah is his God)
14 men/20 references
Most notably, Old Testament minor prophet who spoke of the coming day of the Lord and prophesied that God would pour out His Spirit on all flesh in the last days. Also, firstborn son of the prophet Samuel, serving as a judge in Beersheba. Same as Vashni. Also, one of King David's valiant warriors. Also, among a group of Levites appointed by King David to bring the ark of the covenant from the house of Obed-edom to Jerusalem.
1 Samuel 8:2; 1 Chronicles 4:35; 1 Chronicles 5:4; 1 Chronicles 5:12; 1 Chronicles 6:36; 1 Chronicles 7:3; 1 Chronicles 11:38; 1 Chronicles 15:7; 1 Chronicles 26:22; 1 Chronicles 27:20; 2 Chronicles 29:12; Ezra 10:43; Nehemiah 11:9; Joel 1:1

Joelah
(To ascend)
1 man/1 reference
A "mighty man" who supported the future king David during his conflict with Saul.
1 Chronicles 12:7

Joezer
(Jehovah is his help)
1 man/1 reference
"Mighty man" who supported the future king David during his conflict with Saul.
1 Chronicles 12:6

Jogli
(Exiled)
1 man/1 reference
Prince of the tribe of Dan when the Israelites entered the Promised Land.
Numbers 34:22

Joha
(Jehovah revived)
2 men/2 references
Notably, one of King David's valiant warriors.
1 Chronicles 8:16; 1 Chronicles 11:45

Johanan
(Jehovah favored)
11 men/27 references
Most notably, rebellious Jewish leader. Also, "mighty man" who supported the future king David during his conflict with Saul. Same as Jonathan.
2 Kings 25:23; 1 Chronicles 3:15; 1 Chronicles 3:24; 1 Chronicles 6:9; 1 Chronicles 12:4; 1 Chronicles 12:12; 2 Chronicles 28:12; Ezra 8:12; Ezra 10:6; Nehemiah 6:18; Nehemiah 12:22

John
4 men/133 references
Most notably, called "the Baptist." Jesus' cousin who preached repentance in the desert and baptized those who confessed their sins in the Jordan River. He also baptized Jesus and was later imprisoned. Herod promised his stepdaughter whatever she wanted, and her mother, Herodias, pressed her to ask for John

the Baptist's head, which Herod reluctantly granted. Also, son of Zebedee and brother of James and became Jesus' disciple when called to leave their fishing boat and follow Him. Known as the disciple whom Jesus loved. Writer of the Gospel, the letters that bear his name, and the book of Revelation. Also, one called Mark. Joined Barnabas and Paul on Paul's first missionary journey but left them at Perga, causing Paul to lose confidence in him for a time.
Matthew 3:1; Matthew 4:21; Acts 4:6; Acts 12:12

Joiada
(Jehovah knows)
1 man/4 references
Nehemiah 12:10

Joiakim
(Jehovah will raise)
1 man/4 references
Nehemiah 12:10

Joiarib
(Jehovah will contend)
3 men/5 references
Most notably, Jewish exile charged with finding Levites and temple servants to travel to Jerusalem with Ezra.
Ezra 8:16; Nehemiah 11:5; Nehemiah 11:10

Jokim
(Jehovah will establish)
1 man/1 reference
1 Chronicles 4:22

Jokshan
(Insidious)
1 man/4 references
Son of Abraham by his second wife, Keturah.
Genesis 25:2

Joktan
(He will be made little)
1 man/6 references
Genesis 10:25

Jona
(A dove)
1 man/1 reference
Greek form of the name *Jonah*, used in the New Testament.
John 1:42

Jonadab
(Jehovah largessed)
2 men/12 references
Notably, friend and cousin of David's son Amnon who advised him to pretend to be ill so his half sister Tamar would come to him.
2 Samuel 13:3; Jeremiah 35:6

Jonah
(A dove)
1 man/19 references
Old Testament minor prophet whom God commanded to preach in Nineveh. He fled on a ship headed for Tarshish and was thrown overboard when a tempest struck the ship. He was swallowed by a fish, which later vomited him onto land. He then went to Nineveh and the people repented. Same as Jona and Jonas.
2 Kings 14:25

Jonan
1 man/1 reference
Luke 3:30

Jonas
2 men/12 references
Notably, Greek form of the name *Jonah*, used in the New Testament. Also, father of Simon Peter.
Matthew 12:39; John 21:15

Jonathan
(Jehovah given)
14 men/121 references
Most notably, eldest son of King Saul
and close friend of David, making
a covenant with him to protect him
from his father. Also, scribe in whose
home Jeremiah was imprisoned. Also,
same as Johanan.
Judges 18:30; 1 Samuel 13:2; 2 Samuel
15:27; 2 Samuel 21:21; 2 Samuel 23:32;
1 Chronicles 2:32; 1 Chronicles 27:32; Ezra
8:6; Ezra 10:15; Nehemiah 12:11; Nehemiah
12:14; Nehemiah 12:35; Jeremiah 37:15;
Jeremiah 40:8

Jorah
(Rainy)
1 man/1 reference
Ezra 2:18

Jorai
(Rainy)
1 man/1 reference
1 Chronicles 5:13

Joram
(Jehovah raised)
4 men/29 references
Most notably, king of Judah and son
of King Jehoshaphat. Also, son of
King Ahab and king of Israel. Same as
Jehoram.
2 Samuel 8:10; 2 Kings 8:21; 2 Kings 8:16;
1 Chronicles 26:25

Jorim
1 man/1 reference
Luke 3:29

Jorkoam
(People will be poured forth)
1 man/1 reference
1 Chronicles 2:44

Josabad
(Jehovah endowed)
1 man/1 reference
"Mighty man" who supported King
David during his conflict with Saul.
1 Chronicles 12:4

Josaphat
1 man/2 references
Matthew 1:8

Jose
1 man/1 reference
Luke 3:29

Josedech
(Jehovah righted)
1 man/6 references
Haggai 1:1

Joseph
(Let him add)
11 men/250 references
Most notably, husband of Mary
and earthly father of Jesus. He
was betrothed to Mary when she
conceived Jesus and traveled with
her to Bethlehem, where the child
was born. Also, son of Jacob and
Rachel. Due to his father's favoritism,
his jealous brothers plotted to kill
him but then chose to sell him as a
slave. In Egypt, he was employed by
the captain of Pharaoh's guard and
was falsely accused of impropriety.
After interpreting Pharaoh's dream,
he became second-in-command,
carrying his country through famine
and eventually reconciling with
his brothers. Also, wealthy man
of Arimathea and member of the
Sanhedrin who became Jesus' disciple,
providing the tomb for Jesus after His
crucifixion.
Genesis 30:24; Numbers 13:7; 1 Chronicles
25:2; Ezra 10:42; Nehemiah 12:14; Matthew

1:16; Matthew 27:57; Luke 3:24; Luke 3:26;
Luke 3:30; Acts 1:23

Joses
3 men/6 references
Most notably, one of four brothers of
Jesus, as recorded in the Gospels of
Matthew and Mark. Also, son of one
of the Marys who witnessed Jesus'
crucifixion. Also, another name for
Barnabas.
Matthew 13:55; Matthew 27:56; Acts 4:36

Joshah
(Jehovah set)
1 man/1 reference
1 Chronicles 4:34

Joshaphat
(Jehovah judged)
1 man/1 reference
One of King David's valiant warriors.
1 Chronicles 11:43

Joshaviah
(Jehovah set)
1 man//1 reference
One of King David's valiant warriors.
1 Chronicles 11:46

Joshbekashah
(Hard seat)
1 man/2 references
1 Chronicles 25:4

Joshua
(Jehovah saved)
4 men/216 references
Most notably, son of Nun and Moses'
right-hand man. Spied out Canaan
and came back with a positive report.
For his faith, he was one of only two
men of his generation who entered
the Promised Land. Became Moses'
successor as Israel's leader. Led the
Israelites in defeating Jericho with

trumpets, the ark of the covenant,
and their voices. The walls fell flat
from God's power. Same as Hoshea
and Jesus.
Exodus 17:9; 1 Samuel 6:14; 2 Kings 23:8;
Haggai 1:1

Josiah
(Founded of God)
2 men/53 references
Notably, son of King Amon of Judah.
He became king when he was eight
years old and followed the Lord
closely through his life.
1 Kings 13:2; Zechariah 6:10

Josias
(Founded of God)
1 man/2 references
Matthew 1:10

Josibiah
(Jehovah will cause to dwell)
1 man/1 reference
1 Chronicles 4:35

Josiphiah
(God is adding)
1 man/1 reference
Ezra 8:10

Jotham
(Jehovah is perfect)
3 men/24 references
Most notably, son of Azariah, king of
Judah, who governed for his father,
who had become a leper.
Judges 9:5; 2 Kings 15:5; 1 Chronicles 2:47

Jozabad
(Jehovah has conferred)
8 men/9 references
Most notably, mighty man of valor
who joined David at Ziklag.
1 Chronicles 12:20; 2 Chronicles 31:13;
2 Chronicles 35:9; Ezra 8:33; Ezra 10:22;
Ezra 10:23; Nehemiah 8:7; Nehemiah 11:16

Jozachar
(Jehovah remembered)
1 man/1 reference
Servant of King Joash of Judah
who conspired against him and
murdered him.
2 Kings 12:21

Jozadak
(Jehovah righted)
1 man/5 references
Ezra 3:2

Jubal
(Stream)
1 man/1 reference
Genesis 4:21

Jucal
(Potent)
1 man/1 reference
Prince of Judah who urged King
Zedekiah to kill Jeremiah because of
his negative prophecy.
Jeremiah 38:1

Juda
(Judah)
4 men/4 references
Most notably, one of four brothers of
Jesus, as recorded in Mark's Gospel.
Same as Judas.
Mark 6:3; Luke 3:26; Luke 3:30; Luke 3:33

Judah
(Celebrated)
7 men/49 references
Most notably, son of Jacob and Leah,
who convinced his brothers not to
kill Joseph but to sell him instead. In
Egypt, Judah spoke up for Benjamin
when he was accused of stealing
Joseph's cup and offered himself in
Benjamin's place. His father's final
blessing described Judah as one whom
his brothers would praise.

Genesis 29:35; Ezra 3:9; Ezra 10:23;
Nehemiah 11:9; Nehemiah 12:8; Nehemiah
12:34; Nehemiah 12:36

Judas
(Celebrated)
7 men/33 references
Most notably, disciple who betrayed
Jesus, usually identified as Judas
Iscariot. Also, one of four brothers
of Jesus, as recorded by Matthew's
Gospel. Same as Juda. Also, "the
brother of James," another of
Jesus' disciples, not to be confused
with Judas Iscariot. Same as Jude,
Lebbaeus, and Thaddaeus. Also, man
of Damascus with whom Saul stayed
while he was blinded. Also, Greek
form of the name *Judah*.
Matthew 10:4; Matthew 13:55; Luke 6:16;
Acts 5:37; Acts 9:11; Acts 15:22; Matthew 1:2

Jude
1 man/1 reference
Disciple of Jesus, author of the
epistle of Jude, and the brother of
James. Same as Judas, Lebbaeus, and
Thaddaeus.
Jude 1:1

Judith
(Jew, descendant of Judah)
1 woman/1 reference
Genesis 26:34

Julia
1 woman/1 reference
Christian acquaintance of the apostle
Paul, greeted in his letter to the
Romans.
Romans 16:15

Julius
1 man/2 references
Acts 27:1

Junia
1 woman/1 reference
Roman Christian who spent time in
jail with the apostle Paul and who
also may have been related to Paul.
Romans 16:7

Jushabhesed
(Jehovah is perfect)
1 man/1 reference
1 Chronicles 3:20

Justus
(Just)
3 men/3 references
Most notably, surname of Joseph,
potential apostolic replacement for
Judas Iscariot who lost by lot to the
other candidate, Matthias. Same as
Barsabas. Also, Corinthian Christian
in whose home Paul stayed. Also,
Christian Jew and fellow worker with
the apostle Paul in Rome.
Acts 1:23; Acts 18:7; Colossians 4:11

K

Kadmiel
(Presence of God)
3 men/8 references
Ezra 2:40; Ezra 3:9; Nehemiah 9:4

Kallai
(Frivolous)
1 man/1 reference
Nehemiah 12:20

Kareah
(Bald)
1 man/13 references
Jeremiah 40:8

Kedar
(Dusky)
1 man/2 references
Genesis 25:13

Kedemah
(Precedence)
1 man/2 references
Genesis 25:15

Keilah
(Enclosing, citadel)
1 man/1 reference
1 Chronicles 4:19

Kelaiah
(Insignificance)
1 man/1 reference
Same as Kelita.
Ezra 10:23

Kelita
(Maiming)
2 men/3 references
Same as Kelaiah.
Ezra 10:23; Nehemiah 8:7

Kemuel
(Raised of God)
3 men/3 references
Most notably, prince of the tribe of
Ephraim when the Israelites entered
the Promised Land.
Genesis 22:21; Numbers 34:24;
1 Chronicles 27:17

Kenan
(A nest)
1 man/1 reference
Sixth-longest-lived person in the
Bible, at 910 years.
1 Chronicles 1:2

Kenaz
(Hunter)
4 men/11 references
Genesis 36:11; Genesis 36:42; Joshua
15:17; 1 Chronicles 4:15

Keren-happuch
(Horn of cosmetic)
1 woman/1 reference
Youngest of three daughters born to
Job when God restored his fortunes.
Job 42:14

Keros
(Ankled)
1 man/2 references
Ezra 2:44

Keturah
(Perfumed)
1 woman/4 references
Abraham's concubine and wife, whom
he may have married following Sarah's
death, but her children were not part
of God's promised line.
Genesis 25:1

Kezia
(Cassia)
1 woman/1 reference
Second of three daughters born to Job
when God restored his fortunes.
Job 42:14

Kirjath-jearim
(City of forests)
1 man/3 references
1 Chronicles 2:50

Kish
(A bow)
5 men/21 references
Father of King Saul. Same as Cis.
1 Samuel 9:1; 1 Chronicles 8:30;
1 Chronicles 23:21; 2 Chronicles 29:12;
Esther 2:5

Kishi
(War, battle)
1 man/1 reference
1 Chronicles 6:44

Kittim
(Islander)
1 man/2 references
Genesis 10:4

Kohath
(Allied)
1 man/32 references
Genesis 46:11

Kolaiah
(Voice of God)
2 men/2 references
Notably, father of Ahab, a false
prophet at the time of the Babylonian
Exile.
Nehemiah 11:7; Jeremiah 29:21

Korah
(To make bald)
5 men/37 references
Most notably, descendant of Levi and
Kohath who opposed Moses when
the prophet said all the Israelites were
not holy. Also, descendant of Abraham through Jacob's son Levi. Korah's
sons are named in the titles of eleven
psalms: 42, 44–49, 84–85, and 87–88.
Genesis 36:5; Genesis 36:16; Exodus 6:21; 1
Chronicles 2:43; 1 Chronicles 6:22

Kore
2 men/4 references
1 Chronicles 9:19; 2 Chronicles 31:14

Koz
2 men/4 references
Ezra 2:61; Nehemiah 3:4

Kushaiah
(Entrapped of God)
1 man/1 reference
1 Chronicles 15:17

L

Laadah
1 man/1 reference
1 Chronicles 4:21

Laadan
2 men/7 references
1 Chronicles 7:26; 1 Chronicles 23:7

Laban
(To be white or to make bricks)
1 man/55 references
Called Laban the Syrian, brother of Rebekah who approved of her marriage to Isaac. Uncle of Jacob who employed him for seven years in exchange for marriage to his daughter Rachel. Laban tricked Jacob into marrying his first daughter, Leah, then offered Rachel to Jacob for another seven years of service.
Genesis 24:29

Lael
(Belonging to God)
1 man/1 reference
Chief of the Gershonites when Moses led Israel.
Numbers 3:24

Lahad
(To glow, to be earnest)
1 man/1 reference
1 Chronicles 4:2

Lahmi
(Foodful)
1 man/1 reference
Brother of Philistine giant Goliath.
1 Chronicles 20:5

Laish
(Crushing)
1 man/2 references
1 Samuel 25:44

Lamech
1 man/12 references
Descendant of Cain through Cain's son Enoch. Lamech's father was Methuselah, and Lamech was the father of Noah. Lamech is the first man whom the Bible records as having more than one wife.
Genesis 4:18

Lapidoth
(To shine, or a lamp or flame)
1 man/1 reference
Husband of Israel's only female judge, Deborah.
Judges 4:4

Lazarus
1 man/11 references
Brother of Mary and Martha, and loved by Jesus. His sisters sent for Jesus when he became ill, but he died. After weeping at Lazarus's tomb, Jesus had the stone removed. He called Lazarus forth, and Lazarus walked out. Not to be confused with the beggar named Lazarus in Jesus' parable in Luke 16.
John 11:1

Leah
(Weary)
1 woman/34 references
Laban's older daughter who was less beautiful than her sister, Rachel. Jacob loved Rachel and arranged to marry her, but Laban insisted that Jacob marry Leah first, tricking Jacob into marriage with Leah. Leah had four children, then later had two more sons and a daughter.
Genesis 29:16

Lebana
(The white, the moon)
1 man/1 reference
Same as Lebanah.
Nehemiah 7:48

Lebanah
(*The white, the moon*)
1 man/1 reference
Same as Lebana.
Ezra 2:45

Lebbaeus
(*Uncertain*)
1 man/1 reference
Also called Thaddaeus, he was one
of Jesus' twelve disciples, as listed by
Matthew. Same as Judas and Jude.
Matthew 10:3

Lecah
(*A journey*)
1 man/1 reference
1 Chronicles 4:21

Lehabim
(*Flames*)
1 man/2 references
Genesis 10:13

Lemuel
(*Belonging to God*)
1 man/2 references
Otherwise unknown king credited
with writing Proverbs 31.
Proverbs 31:1

Letushim
(*Oppressed*)
1 man/1 reference
Genesis 25:3

Leummim
(*Night specter*)
1 man/1 reference
Genesis 25:3

Levi
(*Attached*)
4 men/21 references
Most notably, Leah and Jacob's third
child and founder of Israel's priestly
line. Also, son of Alphaeus, tax
collector who became Jesus' disciple.
Same as Matthew.
Genesis 29:34; Mark 2:14; Luke 3:24;
Luke 3:29

Libni
(*White*)
2 men/5 references
Exodus 6:17; 1 Chronicles 6:29

Likhi
(*Learned*)
1 man/1 reference
1 Chronicles 7:19

Linus
1 man/1 reference
Christian whose greetings Paul passed
on to Timothy when Paul wrote his
second letter to the young pastor.
2 Timothy 4:21

Lo-ammi
(*Not my people*)
1 man/1 reference
Third child of the prophet Hosea's
adulterous wife, Gomer.
Hosea 1:9

Lois
1 woman/1 reference
Grandmother of the apostle Paul's
protégé Timothy.
2 Timothy 1:5

Lo-ruhamah
(*Not pitied*)
1 woman/2 references
Second child of the prophet Hosea's
adulterous wife, Gomer.
Hosea 1:6

Lot
1 man/37 references
Abram's nephew, who traveled with

him to the Promised Land. Although warned not to look back at Sodom, his wife did and was turned into a pillar of salt.
Genesis 11:27

Lotan
(Covering)
1 man/7 references
Genesis 36:20

Lucas
1 man/2 references
A variation on the name *Luke*; biblical writer and traveling companion of the apostle Paul.
Philemon 1:24

Lucius
(Illuminative)
2 men/2 references
Notably, Lucius of Cyrene, prophet or teacher who ministered in Antioch when Paul and Barnabas were chosen for missionary work. Also, relative of Paul who lived in Rome and was greeted in the apostle's letter to the Romans.
Acts 13:1; Romans 16:21

Lud
1 man/2 references
Genesis 10:22

Ludim
(A Ludite)
1 man/2 references
Genesis 10:13

Luke
1 man/2 references
The "beloved physician," probably a Gentile believer who became a companion of Paul. Writer of a Gospel and the book of Acts, he was also an excellent historian, as is

shown by the exactness with which he describes the details of the Gospel events and the places where they happened. Same as Lucas.
Colossians 4:14

Lydia
1 woman/2 references
Woman of Thyatira who sold goods dyed with an expensive purple color. After hearing Paul's preaching, she became a Christian believer.
Acts 16:14

Lysanias
(Grief dispelling)
1 man/1 reference
Tetrarch of Abilene when John the Baptist began preaching.
Luke 3:1

Lysias
1 man/3 references
Roman soldier who heard information from Paul's nephew about a plot to kill Paul. Also called Claudius Lysias.
Acts 23:26

M

Maacah
(Depression)
1 man/1 woman/2 references
Notably, one of David's wives, daughter of Talmai, king of Geshur, and mother of Absalom. Same as Maachah. Also, king who provided soldiers to the Ammonites when they attacked King David.
2 Samuel 3:3; 2 Samuel 10:6

Maachah
(Depression)
4 men/6 women/18 references
Most notably, mother of King Asa
of Judah. Also, one of David's wives
who was daughter of Talmai, the king
of Geshur, and mother of Absalom.
Same as Maacah.
Genesis 22:24; 1 Kings 2:39; 1 Kings 15:2;
1 Kings 15:13; 1 Chronicles 2:48;
1 Chronicles 3:2; 1 Chronicles 7:15;
1 Chronicles 8:29; 1 Chronicles 11:43;
1 Chronicles 27:16

Maadai
(Ornamental)
1 man/1 reference
Ezra 10:34

Maadiah
(Ornament of God)
1 man/1 reference
Chief priest who went up to
Jerusalem with Zerubbabel.
Nehemiah 12:5

Maai
(Sympathetic)
1 man/1 reference
Priest who helped to dedicate the
rebuilt wall of Jerusalem by playing a
musical instrument.
Nehemiah 12:36

Maaseiah
(Work of God)
21 men/25 references
Most notably, Jerusalem's governor
who repaired the temple at King
Josiah's command. Also, a rebuilder
of the walls of Jerusalem under
Nehemiah. Also, priest who assisted
Ezra in reading the book of the law to
the people of Jerusalem. Also, priest
who helped to dedicate the rebuilt wall
of Jerusalem by giving thanks. Also,
priest who gave thanks with a trumpet

at the dedication of Jerusalem's rebuilt
walls. Also, false prophet against
whom Jeremiah prophesied.
1 Chronicles 15:18; 2 Chronicles 23:1;
2 Chronicles 26:11; 2 Chronicles 28:7;
2 Chronicles 34:8; Ezra 10:18; Ezra 10:21;
Ezra 10:22; Ezra 10:30; Nehemiah 3:23;
Nehemiah 8:4; Nehemiah 8:7; Nehemiah
10:25; Nehemiah 11:5; Nehemiah 11:7;
Nehemiah 12:41; Nehemiah 12:42;
Jeremiah 21:1; Jeremiah 29:21; Jeremiah
35:4; Jeremiah 32:12

Maasiai
(Operative)
1 man/1 reference
1 Chronicles 9:12

Maath
1 man/1 reference
Luke 3:26

Maaz
(Closure)
1 man/1 reference
1 Chronicles 2:27

Maaziah
(Rescue of God)
2 men/2 references
Notably, one of twenty-four priests in
David's time, chosen by lot to serve in
the tabernacle.
1 Chronicles 24:18; Nehemiah 10:8

Machbanai
(Native of Macbena)
1 man/1 reference
Warriors from the tribe of Gad who
left Saul to join David during his
conflict with the king.
1 Chronicles 12:13

Machbenah
(Knoll)
1 man/1 reference
1 Chronicles 2:49

Machi
(Pining)
1 man/1 reference
Numbers 13:15

Machir
(Salesman)
2 men/22 references
Notably, man who brought food and supplies to King David and his soldiers as they fled from the army of David's son Absalom.
Genesis 50:23; 2 Samuel 9:4

Machnadebai
(What is like a liberal man?)
1 man/1 reference
Ezra 10:40

Madai
(Mede)
1 man/2 references
Genesis 10:2

Madmannah
1 man/1 reference
1 Chronicles 2:49

Magbish
(Stiffening)
1 man/1 reference
Ezra 2:30

Magdalene
(Woman of Magdala)
1 woman/12 references
Surname of Mary.
Matthew 27:56

Magdiel
(Preciousness of God)
1 man/2 references
Genesis 36:43

Magog
1 man/2 references
Genesis 10:2

Magor-missabib
(Afright from around)
1 man/1 reference
Jeremiah 20:3

Magpiash
(Exterminator of the moth)
1 man/1 reference
Jewish leader who renewed the covenant under Nehemiah.
Nehemiah 2:10

Mahalah
(Sickness)
1 man/1 reference
1 Chronicles 7:18

Mahalaleel
(Praise of God)
2 men/7 references
Genesis 5:12; Nehemiah 11:4

Mahalath
(Sickness)
2 women/2 references
Genesis 28:9; 2 Chronicles 11:18

Mahali
(Sick)
1 man/1 reference
Exodus 6:19

Maharai
(Hasty)
1 man/3 references
Commander in King David's army overseeing twenty-four thousand men in the tenth month of each year.
2 Samuel 23:28

Mahath
(Erasure)
2 men/3 references
1 Chronicles 6:35; 2 Chronicles 31:13

Mahazioth
(Visions)
1 man/2 references
1 Chronicles 25:4

Maher-shalal-hash-baz
(Hasting is he to the booty)
1 man/2 references
Son of the prophet Isaiah, named
at God's command to describe the
Assyrian attack on Damascus and
Samaria.
Isaiah 8:1

Mahlah
(Sickness)
1 woman/4 references
One of Zelophehad's five daughters
who received his inheritance because
he had no sons.
Numbers 26:33

Mahli
(Sick)
2 men/11 references
Numbers 3:20; 1 Chronicles 6:47

Mahlon
(Sick)
1 man/4 references
Son of Naomi and her husband,
Elimelech. Died in Moab, forcing
Naomi and his wife, Ruth, to return
to Bethlehem.
Ruth 1:2

Mahol
(Dancing)
1 man/1 reference
1 Kings 4:31

Malachi
(Ministrative)
1 man/1 reference
Writer of the last book of the Old
Testament, who lived in the time of
Nehemiah and Ezra.
Malachi 1:1

Malcham
1 man/1 reference
1 Chronicles 8:9

Malchiah
(King of [appointed by] God)
7 men/9 references
Most notably, man who repaired
Jerusalem's walls under Nehemiah.
Also, priest who assisted Ezra in
reading the book of the law to the
people of Jerusalem.
1 Chronicles 6:40; Ezra 10:25; Ezra 10:31;
Nehemiah 3:14; Nehemiah 3:31; Nehemiah
8:4; Jeremiah 38:1

Malchiel
(King of [appointed by] God)
1 man/3 references
Genesis 46:17

Malchijah
(King of [appointed by] God)
5 men/6 references
Most notably, one of twenty-
four priests in David's time who
was chosen by lot to serve in the
tabernacle. Also, priest who helped to
dedicate the rebuilt walls of Jerusalem
by giving thanks.
1 Chronicles 9:12; 1 Chronicles 24:9; Ezra
10:25; Nehemiah 3:11; Nehemiah 10:3

Malchiram
(King of a high one [or exaltation])
1 man/1 reference
1 Chronicles 3:18

Malchi-shua
1 man/3 references
Son of King Saul. Same as
Melchishua.
1 Chronicles 8:33

Malchus
1 man/1 reference
High priest's servant whose ear Simon
Peter cut off when Jesus was arrested.
John 18:10

Maleleel
1 man/1 reference
Luke 3:37

Mallothi
(I have talked, loquacious)
1 man/2 references
1 Chronicles 25:4

Malluch
(Regnant)
5 men/6 references
Most notably, priest who renewed the
covenant under Nehemiah.
1 Chronicles 6:44; Ezra 10:29; Ezra 10:32;
Nehemiah 10:4; Nehemiah 10:27

Mamre
(Lusty [meaning "vigorous"])
1 man/2 references
Amorite ally of Abram who went with
him to recover Abram's nephew Lot
from the king of Sodom.
Genesis 14:13

Manaen
(Uncertain)
1 man/1 reference
Prophet or teacher at Antioch
when Barnabas and Saul were
commissioned as missionaries.
Acts 13:1

Manahath
(Rest)
1 man/2 references
Genesis 36:23

Manasseh
(Causing to forget)
5 men/55 references
Most notably, elder child of Joseph
and Asenath who was adopted, with
his brother, Ephraim, by Joseph's
father, Jacob. Also, priest of the tribe
of Dan, who worshipped idols, in the
period of the judges. Also, king of
Judah and son of King Hezekiah, he
was an evil ruler who led his nation
into idolatry, burning his sons as
offerings to the idols. He repented and
commanded his nation to follow God.
Genesis 41:51; Judges 18:30; 2 Kings 20:21;
Ezra 10:30; Ezra 10:33

Manasses
(Causing to forget)
1 man/2 references
Greek form of *Manasseh.*
Matthew 1:10

Manoah
(Rest)
1 man/18 references
Father of Samson, who received
instructions from an angel as to what
to do when his child was born.
Judges 13:2

Maoch
(Oppressed)
1 man/1 reference
1 Samuel 27:2

Maon
(A residence)
1 man/2 references
1 Chronicles 2:45

Mara

(Bitter)
1 woman/1 reference
Name Naomi gave herself after the
men of her family died and she felt
that God had dealt bitterly with her.
Ruth 1:20

Marcus

1 man/3 references
Latin form of *Mark*.
Colossians 4:10

Mareshah

(Summit)
2 men/2 references
1 Chronicles 2:42; 1 Chronicles 4:21

Mark

1 man/5 references
Nephew of Barnabas and fellow
missionary with Barnabas and Saul.
Writer of the Gospel that bears his
name. Same as Marcus.
Acts 12:12

Marsena

1 man/1 reference
One of seven Persian princes serving
under King Ahasuerus.
Esther 1:14

Martha

(Mistress)
1 woman/13 references
Sister of Lazarus and Mary who asked
Jesus to tell Mary to help her serve.
He told her that Mary had chosen
better in listening to His teaching.
Luke 10:38

Mary

7 women/54 references
Most notably, a virgin who received
news from an angel that she would
bear the Messiah and traveled to
Bethlehem with Joseph, where Jesus
was born. Mary stood by the cross
and saw her son crucified. Also, Mary
Magdalene, who had seven devils cast
out of her by Jesus and was present
throughout the crucifixion of Jesus,
and one of the group of women who
went to the tomb to anoint His body.
She saw the angels who reported that
Jesus had risen from the dead and
went to tell the disciples. As she wept
at the tomb, Jesus appeared to her
and spoke her name. Also, Mary, the
mother of James and Joses, with Mary
Magdalene and other women at the
crucifixion of Jesus and at the tomb
following His resurrection. Also, sister
of Lazarus and Martha who listened
at Jesus' feet while her sister became
sidetracked with household matters.
Matthew 1:16; Matthew 27:56; Matthew
27:56; John 19:25; Luke 10:39; Acts 12:12;
Romans 16:6

Mash

1 man/1 reference
Genesis 10:23

Massa

(Burden)
1 man/2 references
Son of Ishmael.
Genesis 25:14

Mathusala

1 man/1 reference
Luke 3:37

Matred

(Propulsive)
1 woman/2 references
Genesis 36:39

Matri

1 man/1 reference
1 Samuel 10:21

Mattan
2 men/3 references
Priest of Baal killed by the people of
Judah after Jehoiada made a covenant
between them, King Joash, and God.
2 Kings 11:18; Jeremiah 38:1

Mattaniah
(Gift of God)
9 men/16 references
Most notably, king who began to rule
in his uncle Jehoiachin's place when
Nebuchadnezzar, king of Babylon,
conquered Judah. Renamed Zedekiah.
2 Kings 24:17; 1 Chronicles 9:15;
1 Chronicles 25:4; 2 Chronicles 29:13;
Ezra 10:26; Ezra 10:27; Ezra 10:30;
Ezra 10:37; Nehemiah 13:13

Mattatha
(Gift of God)
1 man/1 reference
Luke 3:31

Mattathah
(Gift of God)
1 man/1 reference
Ezra 10:33

Mattathias
(Gift of God)
2 men/2 references
Luke 3:25; Luke 3:26

Mattenai
(Liberal)
3 men/2 references
Ezra 10:33; Ezra 10:37; Nehemiah 12:19

Matthan
1 man/2 references
Matthew 1:15

Matthat
(Gift of God)
2 men/2 references
Luke 3:24; Luke 3:29

Matthew
1 man/5 references
Tax collector (or publican), also called
Levi, who left his tax booth to follow
Jesus. Although Matthew does not
list himself as the writer of the Gospel
named after him, the early church
ascribed it to him. Same as Levi.
Matthew 9:9

Matthias
1 man/2 references
Apostolic replacement for Judas
Iscariot.
Acts 1:23

Mattithiah
(Gift of God)
5 men/8 references
Most notably, Levite musician who
performed in celebration when
King David brought the ark of the
covenant to Jerusalem. Also, priest
who assisted Ezra in reading the book
of the law to the people of Jerusalem.
Also, Levite official in charge of goods
baked in the temple sanctuary.
1 Chronicles 9:31; 1 Chronicles 15:18;
1 Chronicles 25:3; Ezra 10:43; Nehemiah 8:4

Mebunnai
(Built up)
1 man/1 reference
One of King David's warriors known
as the "mighty men."
2 Samuel 23:27

Medad
(Loving, affectionate)
1 man/2 references
Man who prophesied after God
sent the Israelites quail to eat in the
wilderness.
Numbers 11:26

Medan
(Discord, strife)
1 man/2 references
Son of Abraham by his second wife,
Keturah.
Genesis 25:2

Mehetabeel
(Bettered of God)
1 man/1 reference
Nehemiah 6:10

Mehetabel
(Bettered of God)
1 woman/2 references
Genesis 36:39

Mehida
(Junction)
1 man/2 references
Ezra 2:52

Mehir
(Price)
1 man/1 reference
1 Chronicles 4:11

Mehujael
(Smitten of God)
1 man/2 references
Genesis 4:18

Mehuman
1 man/1 reference
Eunuch serving the Persian king
Ahasuerus in Esther's time.
Esther 1:10

Mehunim
(A Muenite or inhabitant of Maon)
1 man/1 reference
Ezra 2:50

Melatiah
(God has delivered)
1 man/1 reference
Repaired Jerusalem's walls under
Nehemiah.
Nehemiah 3:7

Melchi
(My king)
2 men/2 references
Luke 3:24; Luke 3:28

Melchiah
(King of [appointed by] God)
1 man/1 reference
Jeremiah 21:1

Melchisedec
(King of right)
1 man/9 references
King and high priest of Salem
who blessed Abram. The writer of
Hebrews refers to Jesus as high priest
"after the order of Melchisedec," since
He was not a priest from the line of
Levi. Same as Melchizedek.
Hebrews 5:6

Melchi-shua
(King of wealth)
1 man/2 references
Son of King Saul, killed by the
Philistines along with his father and
two brothers. Same as Malchi-shua.
1 Samuel 14:49

Melchizedek
(King of right)
1 man/2 references
Hebrew form of the name
Melchisedec.
Genesis 14:18

Melea
1 man/1 reference
Luke 3:31

Melech
(King)
1 man/2 references
1 Chronicles 8:35

Melicu
(Regnant)
1 man/1 reference
Nehemiah 12:14

Melzar
1 man/2 references
Babylonian official in charge of
Daniel and his three friends.
Daniel 1:11

Memucan
1 man/3 references
One of seven Persian princes serving
under King Ahasuerus.
Esther 1:14

Menahem
(Comforter)
1 man/8 references
King of Israel who usurped the
throne from King Shallum. During
his tenyear reign, the idolatrous
Menahem did evil.
2 Kings 15:14

Menan
1 man/1 reference
Luke 3:31

Meonothai
(Habitative)
1 man/1 reference
1 Chronicles 4:14

Mephibosheth
(Dispeller of shame)
2 men/15 references
Notably, grandson of King Saul and
son of Jonathan. When David took
the throne of Israel, he treated the

lame Mephibosheth kindly because of
his friendship with Jonathan. Same as
Merib-baal. Also, one of King Saul's
sons whom David handed over to the
Gibeonites, who sought vengeance on
Saul's house.
2 Samuel 4:4; 2 Samuel 21:8

Merab
(Increase)
1 woman/3 references
King Saul's firstborn daughter who
was promised to David but married
another man.
1 Samuel 14:49

Meraiah
(Rebellion)
1 man/1 reference
Priest in the days of the high priest
Joiakim.
Nehemiah 12:12

Meraioth
(Rebellious)
3 men/7 references
1 Chronicles 6:6; 1 Chronicles 9:11;
Nehemiah 12:15

Merari
(Bitter)
1 man/39 references
Levi's third son, in charge of the
boards, bars, pillars, sockets, and
vessels of the tabernacle.
Genesis 46:11

Mered
(Rebellion)
1 man/2 references
1 Chronicles 4:17

Meremoth
(Heights)
3 men/6 references
Most notably, priest's son who

weighed the valuable utensils that King Artaxerxes of Persia and his officials had given Ezra to take back to Jerusalem's temple. Also, priest who renewed the covenant under Nehemiah.
Ezra 8:33; Ezra 10:36; Nehemiah 10:5

Meres
1 man/1 reference
One of seven Persian princes serving under King Ahasuerus.
Esther 1:14

Merib-baal
(Quarreler of Baal)
1 man/4 references
Same as Mephibosheth.
1 Chronicles 8:34

Merodach-baladan
1 man/1 reference
King of Babylon during the reign of King Hezekiah of Judah.
Isaiah 39:1

Mesha
(Safety)
3 men/3 references
King of Moab at the time of King Jehoram of Israel.
2 Kings 3:4; 1 Chronicles 2:42; 1 Chronicles 8:9

Meshach
1 man/15 references
Babylonian name for Mishael, one of Daniel's companions in exile. Survived the fiery furnace when cast there for not bowing down to an idol. Same as Mishael.
Daniel 1:7

Meshech
2 men/3 references
Genesis 10:2; 1 Chronicles 1:17

Meshelemiah
(Ally of God)
1 man/4 references
1 Chronicles 9:21

Meshezabeel
(Delivered of God)
2 men/3 references
Notably, Levite who renewed the covenant under Nehemiah.
Nehemiah 3:4; Nehemiah 10:21

Meshillemith
(Reconciliation)
1 man/1 reference
1 Chronicles 9:12

Meshillemoth
(Reconciliations)
2 men/2 references
2 Chronicles 28:12; Nehemiah 11:13

Meshobab
(Returned)
1 man/1 reference
1 Chronicles 4:34

Meshullam
(Allied)
21 men/25 references
Most notably, descendant of Benjamin and a chief of that tribe who lived in Jerusalem. Also, man who repaired Jerusalem's walls under Nehemiah. Also, priest who assisted Ezra in reading the book of the law to the people of Jerusalem. Also, priest who helped to dedicate Jerusalem's rebuilt walls.
2 Kings 22:3; 1 Chronicles 3:19; 1 Chronicles 5:13; 1 Chronicles 8:17; 1 Chronicles 9:7; 1 Chronicles 9:8; 1 Chronicles 9:11; 1 Chronicles 9:12; 2 Chronicles 34:12; Ezra 8:16; Ezra 10:15; Ezra 10:29; Nehemiah 3:4; Nehemiah 3:6; Nehemiah 8:4; Nehemiah 10:7; Nehemiah 10:20; Nehemiah 11:7; Nehemiah 12:13; Nehemiah 12:16; Nehemiah 12:25

Meshullemeth
(A mission or a favorable release)
1 woman/1 reference
Mother of King Amon of Judah.
2 Kings 21:19

Methusael
(Man who is of God)
1 man/2 references
Genesis 4:18

Methuselah
(Man of a dart)
1 man/6 references
Descendant of Seth who lived for 969 years, the longest-recorded life span in the Bible.
Genesis 5:21

Meunim
(A Meunite)
1 man/1 reference
Nehemiah 7:52

Mezahab
(Water of gold)
1 woman/2 references
Genesis 36:39

Miamin
(From the right hand)
2 men/2 references
Notably, chief priest who went up to Jerusalem with Zerubbabel.
Ezra 10:25; Nehemiah 12:5

Mibhar
(Select, the best)
1 man/1 reference
One of King David's warriors known as the "mighty men."
1 Chronicles 11:38

Mibsam
(Fragrant)
2 men/3 references
Notably, fourth son of Ishmael.
Genesis 25:13; 1 Chronicles 4:25

Mibzar
(Fortification, castle, or fortified city)
1 man/2 references
Genesis 36:42

Micah
(Who is like God?)
7 men/31 references
Most notably, Micah the Morasthite, the Old Testament minor prophet who ministered during the reign of Hezekiah, king of Judah.
Judges 17:1; 1 Chronicles 5:5; 1 Chronicles 8:34; 1 Chronicles 9:15; 1 Chronicles 23:20; 2 Chronicles 34:20; Jeremiah 26:18

Micaiah
1 man/18 references
Prophet whom King Ahab of Israel hated because he never prophesied anything good to him. When King Jehoshaphat asked Ahab for a prophet who would tell the truth, Ahab called for Micaiah.
1 Kings 22:8

Micha
3 men/4 references
Most notably, son of Mephibosheth and grandson of King Saul's son Jonathan.
2 Samuel 9:12; Nehemiah 10:11; Nehemiah 11:17

Michael
(Who is like God?)
10 men/10 references
Most notably, mighty man of valor who defected to David at Ziklag. Also, son of Judah's king Jehoshaphat.
Numbers 13:13; 1 Chronicles 5:13; 1 Chronicles 5:14; 1 Chronicles 6:40; 1 Chronicles 7:3; 1 Chronicles 8:16; 1 Chronicles 12:20; 1 Chronicles 27:18; 2 Chronicles 21:2; Ezra 8:8

Michah
(Who is like God?)
1 man/3 references
Levite worship leader during David's reign. Lots were cast to determine his duties.
1 Chronicles 24:24

Michaiah
(Who is like God?)
4 men/1 woman/7 references
Most notably, prince of Judah sent by King Jehoshaphat to teach the law of the Lord throughout the nation. Also, mother of King Abijah of Judah. Also, father of Achbor. Same as Micah. Also, priest who helped to dedicate the rebuilt walls of Jerusalem by giving thanks.
2 Kings 22:12; 2 Chronicles 13:12; 2 Chronicles 17:7; Nehemiah 12:35; Jeremiah 36:11

Michal
(Rivulet)
1 woman/18 references
Daughter of King Saul and wife of David. To win her, David killed two hundred of the enemy, fulfilling the king's request twice over. She warned her husband and let him out a window when Saul sought to kill David.
1 Samuel 14:49

Michri
(Salesman)
1 man/1 reference
1 Chronicles 9:8

Midian
(Brawling, contentious)
1 man/4 references
Son of Abraham by his second wife, Keturah.
Genesis 25:2

Mijamin
2 men/2 references
Notably, one of twenty-four priests in David's time who was chosen by lot to serve in the tabernacle. Also, priest who renewed the covenant under Nehemiah.
1 Chronicles 24:9; Nehemiah 10:7

Mikloth
(Rods)
2 men/4 references
Notably, one of David's officers who served him during the second month.
1 Chronicles 8:32; 1 Chronicles 27:4

Mikneiah
(Possession of God)
1 man/2 references
Levite musician who performed in celebration when King David brought the ark of the covenant to Jerusalem.
1 Chronicles 15:18

Milalai
(Talkative)
1 man/1 reference
Priest who helped to dedicate the rebuilt walls of Jerusalem by playing a musical instrument.
Nehemiah 12:36

Milcah
(Queen)
2 women/11 references
Notably, wife of Nahor, Abraham's brother. Also, one of Zelophehad's five daughters who received his inheritance because he had no sons. Each had to marry within their tribe, Manasseh.
Genesis 11:29; Numbers 26:33

Miniamin

(From the right hand)
2 men/3 references
Notably, priest in the time of King
Hezekiah. Also, priest who helped
dedicate the rebuilt wall of Jerusalem
by giving thanks.
2 Chronicles 31:15; Nehemiah 12:17

Miriam

(Rebelliously)
2 women/15 references
Notably, sister of Moses and Aaron
and a prophetess of Israel.
Exodus 15:20; 1 Chronicles 4:17

Mirma

(Deceiving, fraud)
1 man/1 reference
1 Chronicles 8:10

Mishael

(Who is what God is?)
3 men/8 references
Most notably, friend of the prophet
Daniel who would not defile himself
by eating the king's meat. Along with
two others, he would not worship
an idol and was cast into the fiery
furnace by King Nebuchadnezzar.
Also called Meshach. Also, priest who
assisted Ezra in reading the book of
the law to the people of Jerusalem.
Exodus 6:22; Daniel 1:6; Nehemiah 8:4

Misham

(Inspection)
1 man/1 reference
1 Chronicles 8:12

Mishma

(A report, hearing)
1 man/4 references
Genesis 25:14

Mishmannah

(Fatness)
1 man/1 reference
One of several warriors from the tribe
of Gad who left Saul to join David
during his conflict with the king.
1 Chronicles 12:10

Mispereth

(Enumeration)
1 man/1 reference
Nehemiah 7:7

Mithredath

1 man/2 references
Treasurer for Cyrus, king of Persia.
Joined in writing a letter of complaint
to King Artaxerxes about the
rebuilding of Jerusalem.
Ezra 1:8

Mizpar

(Number)
1 man/1 reference
Ezra 2:2

Mizraim

(Upper and Lower Egypt)
1 man/4 references
Genesis 10:6

Mizzah

(To faint with fear)
1 man/3 references
Genesis 36:13

Mnason

1 man/1 reference
Elderly Christian from Cyprus who
accompanied Paul to Jerusalem.
Acts 21:16

Moab

(From her [the mother's] father)
1 man/1 reference
Forefather of the Moabites.
Genesis 19:37

Moadiah
(Assembly of God)
1 man/1 reference
Priest under the leadership of Joiakim
following the return from exile.
Nehemiah 12:17

Molid
(Genitor)
1 man/1 reference
1 Chronicles 2:29

Mordecai
2 men/60 references
Most notably, an exiled Jew and
cousin of Queen Esther, wife of
the Persian king Ahasuerus. He
discovered a plot against the Jews, set
up by the king's scheming counselor,
Haman, and warned Esther,
encouraging her to confront the king.
Mordecai received all of Haman's
household as a reward.
Ezra 2:2; Esther 2:5

Moses
(Drawing out [of the water], rescued)
1 man/848 references
Old Testament prophet through
whom God gave Israel the law. When
Pharaoh commanded that all male
newborn Israelites should be killed,
Moses' mother placed him in a basket
in the Nile River, where he was
found by an Egyptian princess, who
raised him. Later, as God's prophet
in Egypt, Moses confronted Pharaoh.
Following the Exodus, God gave
Moses the Ten Commandments and
other laws. Moses and his people
wandered in the desert for forty years.
He died on Mount Nebo just before
Israel entered the Promised Land.
Exodus 2:10

Moza
2 men/5 references
1 Chronicles 2:46; 1 Chronicles 8:36

Muppim
(Wavings)
1 man/1 reference
Genesis 46:21

Mushi
(Sensitive)
1 man/8 references
Exodus 6:19

N

Naam
(Pleasure)
1 man/1 reference
Son of Caleb.
1 Chronicles 4:15

Naamah
(Pleasantness)
2 women/4 references
Notably, mother of King Rehoboam.
Genesis 4:22; 1 Kings 14:21

Naaman
(Pleasantness)
4 men/17 references
Most notably, leprous captain of
the Syrian army who came to the
prophet Elisha for healing. Angered
that Elisha told him to wash seven
times in the Jordan River, he had to
be persuaded to obey. When he did,
he was healed. Also, son of Benjamin
and a descendant of Abraham.
Genesis 46:21; Numbers 26:40;
1 Chronicles 8:7; 2 Kings 5:1

Naarah
(Girl)
1 woman/3 references
1 Chronicles 4:5

Naarai
(Youthful)
1 man/1 reference
One of King David's valiant warriors.
1 Chronicles 11:37

Naashon
(Enchanter)
1 man/1 reference
Exodus 6:23

Naasson
1 man/3 references
Matthew 1:4

Nabal
(Dolt)
1 man/22 references
First husband of Abigail, Nebal refused to give David and his men anything in return for their protection of his lands during David's battles with Saul. Abigail generously provided them with food; ten days later Nabal died.
1 Samuel 25:3

Naboth
(Fruits)
1 man/22 references
Owner of a vineyard that was coveted by King Ahab of Israel. After Naboth refused to trade it, Queen Jezebel had him stoned, and Ahab took possession of his land.
1 Kings 21:1

Nachon
(Prepared)
1 man/1 reference
2 Samuel 6:6

Nachor
(Snorer)
2 men/2 references
Notably, brother of Abraham. Same as Nahor.
Joshua 24:2; Luke 3:34

Nadab
(Liberal)
4 men/20 references
Most notably, son of Jeroboam, king of Israel, who inherited Jeroboam's throne and did evil and made his country sin. Also, son of Aaron who, along with his brother Abihu, offered strange fire before the Lord. God sent fire from His presence to consume them, and they died.
Exodus 6:23; 1 Kings 14:20; 1 Chronicles 2:28; 1 Chronicles 8:30

Nagge
1 man/1 reference
Luke 3:25

Naham
1 man/1 reference
1 Chronicles 4:19

Nahamani
(Consolatory)
1 man/1 reference
Nehemiah 7:7

Naharai
(Snorer)
1 man/1 reference
One of King David's valiant warriors. Same as Nahari.
1 Chronicles 11:39

Nahari
(Snorer)
1 man/1 reference
One of King David's valiant warriors. Same as Naharai.
2 Samuel 23:37

Nahash
3 men/9 references
Most notably, king of the
Ammonites.
1 Samuel 11:1; 2 Samuel 10:2; 2 Samuel 17:25

Nahath
(Quiet)
3 men/5 references
Most notably, temple overseer during
the reign of King Hezekiah of Judah.
Genesis 36:13; 1 Chronicles 6:26;
2 Chronicles 31:13

Nahbi
(Occult)
1 man/1 reference
One of the twelve spies sent by Moses
to spy out Canaan.
Numbers 13:14

Nahor
(Snorer)
2 men/17 references
Notably, grandfather of Abraham.
Also, brother of Abraham and son of
Terah, and married Milcah. Same as
Nachor.
Genesis 11:22; Genesis 11:26

Nahshon
(Enchanter)
1 man/9 references
Captain and prince of the tribe of
Judah, appointed by God through
Moses.
Numbers 1:7

Nahum
(Comfortable)
1 man/1 reference
Old Testament minor prophet who
preached to Judah after Assyria had
captured Israel.
Nahum 1:1

Naomi
(Pleasant)
1 woman/21 references
Elimelech's wife and mother-in-law to
Ruth. Naomi and her family moved
to Moab during a famine. Following
the deaths of her husband and two
sons, Naomi and Ruth returned to
Bethlehem, impoverished.
Ruth 1:2

Naphish
(Refreshed)
1 man/2 references
Son of Ishmael.
Genesis 25:15

Naphtali
(My wrestling)
1 man/8 references
Son of Jacob and founder of one of
Israel's twelve tribes.
Genesis 30:8

Narcissus
(Narcissus [flower])
1 man/1 reference
Head of a household of believers and
greeted by Paul in his letter to the
Romans.
Romans 16:11

Nathan
(Given)
10 men/43 references
Most notably, prophet who
confronted King David about his sin
with Bath-sheba. Also, son of King
David. Also, Jewish exile charged
with finding Levites and temple
servants to travel to Jerusalem with
Ezra. Also, one who will mourn at the
piercing of the Messiah when God
defends Jerusalem.
2 Samuel 5:14; 2 Samuel 7:2; 2 Samuel
23:36; 1 Kings 4:5; 1 Kings 4:5; 1 Chronicles

2:36; 1 Chronicles 11:38; Ezra 8:16; Ezra 10:39; Zechariah 12:12

Nathanael

1 man/6 references
Jesus' disciple from Cana, described by Him as an Israelite in whom there was no guile. Nathanael recognized Jesus as the Son of God and followed Him. Probably the same as Bartholomew.
John 1:45

Nathan-melech

(Given of the king)
1 man/1 reference
Court official under King Josiah of Judah.
2 Kings 23:11

Naum

1 man/1 reference
Luke 3:25

Neariah

(Servant of God)
2 men/3 references
Notably, captain over the sons of Simeon during the reign of King Hezekiah of Judah.
1 Chronicles 3:22; 1 Chronicles 4:42

Nebai

(Fruitful)
1 man/1 reference
Israelite who signed an agreement declaring that exiles from Babylon would repent and obey God.
Nehemiah 10:19

Nebaioth

(Fruitfulness)
1 man/1 reference
A variant spelling of *Nebajoth*.
1 Chronicles 1:29

Nebajoth

(Fruitfulness)
1 man/3 references
Ishmael's firstborn son. Same as Nebaioth.
Genesis 25:13

Nebat

(Regard)
1 man/25 references
Father of King Jeroboam.
1 Kings 11:26

Nebo

1 man/1 reference
Ezra 10:43

Nebuchadnezzar

1 man/60 references
King of Babylon who besieged Jerusalem, took its king, and brought Judah's people into exile, including the prophet Daniel, who interpreted the king's dream. Daniel and his friends Shadrach, Meshach, and Abednego refused to worship an idol, so Nebuchadnezzar had them thrown into a fiery furnace, but they were not consumed. Amazed, the king declared that no one should speak against their God. Same as Nebuchadrezzar.
2 Kings 24:1

Nebuchadrezzar

1 man/31 references
King of Babylon. A variant spelling of *Nebuchadnezzar*.
Jeremiah 21:2

Nebushasban

1 man/1 reference
Babylonian official who, at King Nebuchadnezzar's command, showed kindness to the prophet Jeremiah.
Jeremiah 39:13

Nebuzar-adan
1 man/15 references
Captain of the guard for King
Nebuchadnezzar of Babylon and
carried Israelite captives to Babylon.
2 Kings 25:8

Necho
1 man/3 references
King of Egypt who attacked
Carchemish.
2 Chronicles 35:20

Nedabiah
(Largesse of God)
1 man/1 reference
1 Chronicles 3:18

Nehemiah
(Consolation of God)
3 men/8 references
Notably, cupbearer sent at his own
request by Persian King Artaxerxes to
rebuild Jerusalem, where he ruled as
governor and rebuilt the walls. Also,
man who repaired Jerusalem's walls
under Nehemiah.
Ezra 2:2; Nehemiah 1:1; Nehemiah 3:16

Nehum
(Comforted)
1 man/1 reference
Nehemiah 7:7

Nehushta
(Copper)
1 woman/1 reference
Mother of King Jehoiachin of Judah.
2 Kings 24:8

Nekoda
(Distinction, marked)
2 men/4 references
Ezra 2:48; Ezra 2:60

Nemuel
(Day of God)
2 men/3 references
Notably, Reubenite counted in the
census taken by Moses and Aaron.
Same as Jemuel.
Numbers 26:9; Numbers 26:12

Nepheg
(To spring forth, a sprout)
2 men/4 references
Notably, son of King David.
Exodus 6:21; 2 Samuel 5:15

Nephishesim
(To scatter, expansions)
1 man/1 reference
Nehemiah 7:52

Nephusim
(To scatter, expansions)
1 man/1 reference
Ezra 2:50

Ner
(Lamp)
1 man/16 references
Grandfather of King Saul and father
of Abner.
1 Samuel 14:50

Nereus
(Wet)
1 man/1 reference
Christian whom Paul greeted in his
letter to the church at Rome.
Romans 16:15

Nergal-sharezer
2 men/3 references
Notably, prince of Babylon who
besieged Jerusalem during the reign
of King Zedekiah of Judah. Also,
another Babylonian prince who took
part in the destruction of Jerusalem
under King Nebuchadnezzar.
Jeremiah 39:3; Jeremiah 39:3

Neri
1 man/1 reference
Luke 3:27

Neriah
(Light of God)
1 man/10 references
Jeremiah 32:12

Nethaneel
(Given of God)
10 men/14 references
Most notably, head of the tribe of
Issachar during Israel's wandering.
Also, priest who blew a trumpet
before the ark of the covenant when
David brought it to Jerusalem. Also,
prince of Judah who taught the law
of the Lord throughout the nation.
Also, chief Levite who provided for
the first Passover celebration under
King Josiah of Judah. Also, priest who
helped to dedicate the rebuilt walls
of Jerusalem by playing a musical
instrument.
Numbers 1:8; 1 Chronicles 2:14;
1 Chronicles 15:24; 1 Chronicles 24:6;
1 Chronicles 26:4; 2 Chronicles 17:7;
2 Chronicles 35:9; Ezra 10:22;
Nehemiah 12:21; Nehemiah 12:36

Nethaniah
(Given of God)
4 men/20 references
Most notably, Levite sent by King
Jehoshaphat to teach the law of the
Lord throughout the nation of Judah.
2 Kings 25:23; 1 Chronicles 25:2;
2 Chronicles 17:8; Jeremiah 36:14

Neziah
(Conspicuous)
1 man/2 references
Ezra 2:54

Nicanor
(Victorious)
1 man/1 reference
One of seven men selected to serve
needy Christians in Jerusalem.
Acts 6:5

Nicodemus
(Victorious among his people)
1 man/5 references
Member of the Jewish Sanhedrin who
came to Jesus by night to question
Him about His miracles and was
told he must be born again. When
the Pharisees wanted to arrest Jesus,
Nicodemus stood up for Him. He
provided the spices with which Jesus'
body was wrapped after His death.
John 3:1

Nicolas
(Victorious over the people)
1 man/1 reference
One of seven men selected to serve
needy Christians in Jerusalem.
Acts 6:5

Niger
(Black)
1 man/1 reference
Prophet and teacher in the church
at Antioch in the time of the apostle
Paul. Also called Simeon.
Acts 13:1

Nimrod
1 man/4 references
Built the city of Nineveh.
Genesis 10:8

Nimshi
(Extricated)
1 man/5 references
1 Kings 19:16

Noadiah
(Convened of God)
1 man/1 woman/2 references
Notably, Levite who weighed the
temple vessels after the Babylonian
exile. Also, prophetess who opposed
Nehemiah as he rebuilt Jerusalem's
walls.
Ezra 8:33; Nehemiah 6:14

Noah
(Rest)
1 man/1 woman/53 references
Notably, the man God chose to build
an ark that would save both animals
and people. Same as Noe. Also, one
of Zelophehad's five daughters who
received his inheritance because he
had no sons.
Genesis 5:29; Numbers 26:33

Nobah
(A bark)
1 man/2 references
Man who took Kenath and its villages
for his inheritance when Moses divided
the Promised Land between the tribes.
Numbers 32:42

Noe
(Noah)
1 man/5 references
Greek spelling of *Noah*, used in the
New Testament.
Matthew 24:37

Nogah
(Brilliancy)
1 man/2 references
Son of King David.
1 Chronicles 3:7

Nohah
(Quietude)
1 man/1 reference
Benjamin's fourth son.
1 Chronicles 8:2

Non
(Perpetuity)
1 man/1 reference
Variant spelling of *Nun*; father of the
Israelite leader Joshua.
1 Chronicles 7:27

Nun
(Perpetuity)
1 man/29 references
Father of the Israelite leader Joshua.
Same as Non.
Exodus 33:11

Nymphas
(Nymph given)
1 woman/1 reference
Colossian Christian who had a house
church in her home.
Colossians 4:15

O

Obadiah
(Serving God)
13 men/20 references
Most notably, Old Testament minor
prophet who spoke God's words
against Edom. Also, "governor" of the
household of King Ahab of Israel and
a man who feared God. Also, ruler
of the tribe of Zebulun in the days
of King David. Also, prince of Judah
sent by King Jehoshaphat to teach
the law of the Lord throughout the
nation.
1 Kings 18:3; 1 Chronicles 3:21; 1 Chronicles
7:3; 1 Chronicles 8:38; 1 Chronicles 9:16;
1 Chronicles 12:9; 1 Chronicles 27:19;
2 Chronicles 17:7; 2 Chronicles 34:12;
Ezra 8:9; Nehemiah 10:5; Nehemiah 12:25;
Obadiah 1:1

Obal

1 man/1 reference
Genesis 10:28

Obed

(Serving)
5 men/13 references
Most notably, one of King David's
warriors known as the "mighty men."
Ruth 4:17; 1 Chronicles 2:37; 1 Chronicles
11:47; 1 Chronicles 26:7; 2 Chronicles 23:1

Obed-edom

(Worker of Edom)
3 men/20 references
Most notably, owner of a house where
the ark of the covenant was kept for
three months before David brought
it to Jerusalem. Also, Levite musician
who performed in celebration when
King David brought the ark of the
covenant to Jerusalem.
2 Samuel 6:10; 1 Chronicles 15:18;
2 Chronicles 25:24

Obil

(Mournful)
1 man/1 reference
Servant of King David who was in
charge of the royal camels.
1 Chronicles 27:30

Ocran

(Muddler)
1 man/5 references
Numbers 1:13

Oded

(Reiteration)
2 men/3 references
Notably, prophet who warned the
Israelites not to enslave their fellow
Jewish citizens.
2 Chronicles 15:1; 2 Chronicles 28:9

Og

(Round)
1 man/22 references
Amorite king of Bashan, whom
Moses defeated after Israel failed to
enter the Promised Land.
Numbers 21:33

Ohad

(Unity)
1 man/2 references
Genesis 46:10

Ohel

(A tent)
1 man/1 reference
1 Chronicles 3:20

Olympas

*(Olympian bestowed or heaven
descended)*
1 man/1 reference
Christian whom Paul greeted in his
letter to the church at Rome.
Romans 16:15

Omar

(Talkative)
1 man/3 references
Genesis 36:11

Omri

(Heaping)
4 men/18 references
Most notably, commander of Israel's
army under King Elah, he later
became king and did evil, causing
Israel to sin. Also, ruler of the tribe of
Issachar under David.
1 Kings 16:16; 1 Chronicles 7:8; 1 Chronicles
9:4; 1 Chronicles 27:18

On

(Ability, power, wealth)
1 man/1 reference
Numbers 16:1

Onam
(Strong)
2 men/4 references
Genesis 36:23; 1 Chronicles 2:26

Onan
(Strong)
1 man/8 references
Genesis 38:4

Onesimus
(Profitable)
1 man/2 references
Slave of Philemon. He fled his master
and met Paul, who led him to Christ.
Colossians 4:9

Onesiphorus
(Profit bearer)
1 man/2 references Ephesian
Christian whose household refreshed
Paul.
2 Timothy 1:16

Ophir
1 man/2 references
Genesis 10:29

Ophrah
(Female fawn)
1 man/1 reference
1 Chronicles 4:14

Oreb
(Mosquito)
1 man/5 references
Prince of Midian who was killed by
the tribe of Ephraim when Gideon
called the tribe to fight that nation.
Judges 7:25

Oren
1 man/1 reference
1 Chronicles 2:25

Ornan
(Strong)
1 man/12 references
Same as Araunah.
1 Chronicles 21:15

Orpah
(Mane)
1 woman/2 references
Naomi's daughter-in-law who did not
follow her to Bethlehem.
Ruth 1:4

Osee
1 man/1 reference
Greek form of the name *Hoshea*.
Romans 9:25

Oshea
(Deliverer)
1 man/2 references
Variant spelling of the name *Joshua*.
Numbers 13:8

Othni
(To force, forcible)
1 man/1 reference
1 Chronicles 26:7

Othniel
(Force of God)
1 man/6 references
Caleb's brother who delivered Israel
from the king of Mesopotamia and
judged Israel for forty years.
Joshua 15:17

Ozem
(To be strong, strength)
2 men/2 references
Notably, sixth son of Jesse and
brother of King David.
1 Chronicles 2:15; 1 Chronicles 2:25

Ozias
1 man/2 references
Matthew 1:8

Ozni
(Having quick ears)
1 man/1 reference
Numbers 26:16

P

Paarai
(Yawning)
1 man/1 reference
One of King David's warriors known as the "mighty men."
2 Samuel 23:35

Padon
(Ransom)
1 man/2 references
Ezra 2:44

Pagiel
(Accident of God)
1 man/5 references
Chief of the tribe of Asher who helped Moses take a census of Israel.
Numbers 1:13

Pahath-moab
(Pit of Moab)
3 men/6 references
Most notably, Jewish leader who renewed the covenant under Nehemiah.
Ezra 2:6; Ezra 8:4; Nehemiah 10:14

Palal
(Judge)
1 man/1 reference
Man who repaired Jerusalem's walls under Nehemiah.
Nehemiah 3:25

Pallu
(Distinguished)
1 man/4 references
Exodus 6:14

Palti
(Delivered)
1 man/1 reference
Spy from the tribe of Benjamin who reported that Israel could not take the Promised Land.
Numbers 13:9

Paltiel
(Deliverance of God)
1 man/1 reference
Prince of the tribe of Issachar when the Israelites entered the Promised Land.
Numbers 34:26

Parmashta
1 man/1 reference
Esther 9:9

Parmenas
(Constant)
1 man/1 reference
One of seven men selected to serve needy Christians in Jerusalem.
Acts 6:5

Parnach
1 man/1 reference
Numbers 34:25

Parosh
(A flea)
4 men/5 references
Ezra 2:3; Ezra 10:25; Nehemiah 3:25; Nehemiah 10:14

Parshandatha
1 man/1 reference
Esther 9:7

Pa ruah
(Blossomed)
1 man/1 reference
1 Kings 4:17

Pasach
(Divider)
1 man/1 reference
1 Chronicles 7:33

Paseah
(Limping)
3 men/3 references
Most notably, prince of Judah who
sought to have King Zedekiah kill
Jeremiah because of his negative
prophecy.
1 Chronicles 4:12; Ezra 2:49; Nehemiah 3:6

Pashur
(Liberation)
4 men/14 references
Most notably, priest and "chief
governor" of the temple who
responded to Jeremiah's prophecies by
hitting him and putting him in the
stocks near the temple. Also, priest
who renewed the covenant under
Nehemiah.
1 Chronicles 9:12; Nehemiah 10:3;
Jeremiah 20:1; Jeremiah 21:1

Patrobas
(Father's life)
1 man/1 reference
Christian whom Paul greeted in his
letter to the church at Rome.
Romans 16:14

Paul
(Little)
1 man/157 references
Latin form of the name Saul; God's
chosen apostle to the Gentiles who
zealously persecuted Christians until
he became one himself as he traveled

to Damascus and was confronted by
Jesus. He communicated with the
churches through his epistles to the
Romans, Corinthians, Galatians,
Colossians, and Thessalonians and
a letter to Titus. During his time of
imprisonment, he wrote additional
epistles that became scripture:
Ephesians, Philippians, the letters to
Timothy, and Philemon. Same as Saul.
Acts 13:9

Paulus
(Little)
1 man/1 reference
Sergius Paulus was a proconsul of
Cyprus who called on Barnabas and
Saul to share their faith with him.
Acts 13:7

Pedahel
(God has ransomed)
1 man/1 reference
Prince of the tribe of Naphtali when
the Israelites entered the Promised
Land.
Numbers 34:28

Pedahzur
(A rock [God] has ransomed)
1 man/5 references
Numbers 1:10

Pedaiah
(God has ransomed)
6 men/8 references
Most notably, priest who assisted Ezra
in reading the book of the law to the
people of Jerusalem. Nehemiah also
appointed him one of the temple
treasurers. Also, man who repaired
Jerusalem's walls under Nehemiah.
2 Kings 23:36; 1 Chronicles 3:18;
1 Chronicles 27:20; Nehemiah 3:25;
Nehemiah 8:4; Nehemiah 11:7

Pekah
(Watch)
1 man/11 references
Captain of King Pekahiah of Israel, he conspired against his king, killed him, and usurped his throne.
2 Kings 15:25

Pekahiah
(God has answered)
1 man/3 references
Evil ruler of Israel who succeeded his father, Menahem, as king.
2 Kings 15:22

Pelaiah
(God has distinguished)
3 men/3 references
Most notably, Levite who helped Israel to understand the law after Ezra read it to them.
1 Chronicles 3:24; Nehemiah 8:7; Nehemiah 10:10

Pelaliah
(God has judged)
1 man/1 reference
Nehemiah 11:12

Pelatiah
(God has delivered)
4 men/5 references
Most notably, Jewish leader who renewed the covenant under Nehemiah. Also, prince of Judah and a wicked counselor who died while Ezekiel prophesied against Jerusalem.
1 Chronicles 3:21; 1 Chronicles 4:42; Nehemiah 10:22; Ezekiel 11:1

Peleg
(Earthquake)
1 man/7 references
Same as Phalec.
Genesis 10:25

Pelet
(Escape)
2 men/2 references
Notably, "mighty man" who supported the future king David during his conflict with Saul.
1 Chronicles 2:47; 1 Chronicles 12:3

Peleth
(To flee, swiftness)
1 man/2 references
Numbers 16:1

Peninnah
(A pearl, round)
1 woman/3 references
Elkanah's wife who had children and provoked his other wife, Hannah, who was barren.
1 Samuel 1:2

Penuel
(Face of God)
2 men/2 references
1 Chronicles 4:4; 1 Chronicles 8:25

Peresh
1 man/1 reference
1 Chronicles 7:16

Perez
(A break)
2 men/3 references
Same as Pharez and Phares.
1 Chronicles 27:3; Nehemiah 11:4

Perida
(Dispersion)
1 man/1 reference
Same as Peruda.
Nehemiah 7:57

Persis
1 woman/1 reference
Christian whom Paul greeted and commended in his letter to the church at Rome.
Romans 16:12

Peruda
(Dispersions)
1 man/1 reference
Same as Perida.
Ezra 2:55

Peter
(A piece of rock)
1 man/162 references
Jesus' disciple, also called Simon Peter
and Simon Bar-Jonah, who was called
from his fishing to become a fisher
of men. He walked on water and was
the first to call Jesus "the Christ."
Peter cut off the ear of the high
priest's servant at Jesus' arrest then
denied Jesus three times. He wrote
the books of 1 and 2 Peter. Same as
Cephas.
Matthew 4:18

Pethahiah
(God has opened)
4 men/4 references
Most notably, one of twenty-
four priests in David's time who
was chosen by lot to serve in the
tabernacle. Also, Levite who led a
revival among the Israelites in the
time of Nehemiah.
1 Chronicles 24:16; Ezra 10:23; Nehemiah
9:5; Nehemiah 11:24

Pethuel
(Enlarged of God)
1 man/1 reference
Father of the Old Testament minor
prophet Joel.
Joel 1:1

Peulthai
(Laborious)
1 man/1 reference
1 Chronicles 26:5

Phalec
1 man/1 reference
Same as Peleg.
Luke 3:35

Phallu
(Distinguished)
1 man/1 reference
Genesis 46:9

Phalti
(Delivered)
1 man/1 reference
Michal's second husband, to whom
Saul married her after David fled.
Same as Phaltiel.
1 Samuel 25:44

Phaltiel
(Deliverance of God)
1 man/1 reference
Michal's second husband, from whom
King David claimed her. Same as
Phalti.
2 Samuel 3:15

Phanuel
1 man/1 reference
Father of the prophetess Anna, who
saw the baby Jesus in the temple.
Luke 2:36

Pharaoh-hophra
1 man/1 reference
King of Egypt who Jeremiah
prophesied would be given into the
hands of his enemies.
Jeremiah 44:30

Pharaoh-necho
1 man/1 reference
King of Egypt against whom
Jeremiah prophesied God would take
vengeance. Same as Pharaoh-nechoh.
Jeremiah 46:2

Pharaoh-nechoh
1 man/4 references
King of Egypt who fought Assyria
and King Josiah of Judah. Same as
Pharaoh-necho.
2 Kings 23:29

Phares
1 man/3 references
Same as Pharez and Perez.
Matthew 1:3

Pharez
1 man/12 references
Same as Phares and Perez.
Genesis 38:29

Pharosh
(A flea)
1 man/1 reference
Ezra 8:3

Phaseah
(Limping)
1 man/1 reference
Nehemiah 7:51

Phebe
(Bright)
1 woman/1 reference
Believer whom Paul recommended
that the Roman church assist.
Romans 16:1

Phichol
(Mouth of all)
1 man/3 references
Commander of the Philistine king
Abimelech's army in the time of
Abraham and Isaac.
Genesis 21:22

Philemon
(Friendly)
1 man/1 reference
Christian owner of the escaped slave
Onesimus.
Philemon 1:1

Philetus
(Amiable)
1 man/1 reference
False teacher who opposed Paul,
teaching that Christians would not be
physically resurrected.
2 Timothy 2:17

Philip
(Fond of horses)
3 men/36 references
Most notably, one of seven men selected
to serve needy Christians in Jerusalem.
He preached to the Ethiopian eunuch
and baptized him. Also called Philip
the evangelist. Also, disciple of Jesus
who introduced the soon-to-be disciple
Nathanael to Him. Also, one called
Herod Philip I, the tetrarch of Iturea,
and Trachonitis was a son of Herod the
Great. His wife, Herodias, left him and
married his half brother, Herod.
Matthew 10:3; Matthew 14:3; Acts 6:5

Philologus
(Fond of words)
1 man/1 reference
Christian whom Paul greeted in his
letter to the church at Rome.
Romans 16:15

Phinehas
(Mouth of a serpent)
3 men/25 references
Most notably, son of the high priest
Eli who did not know the Lord.
He misused his priestly office and
disobeyed the law.
Exodus 6:25; 1 Samuel 1:3; Ezra 8:33

Phlegon
(Blazing)
1 man/1 reference
Christian whom Paul greeted in his
letter to the church at Rome.
Romans 16:14

Phurah
(Foliage)
1 man/2 references
Servant of Gideon.
Judges 7:10

Phut
1 man/2 references
A grandson of Noah through his
son Ham.
Genesis 10:6

Phuvah
(A blast)
1 man/1 reference
Genesis 46:13

Phygellus
(Fugitive)
1 man/1 reference
Asian Christian who turned away
from Paul.
2 Timothy 1:15

Pilate
(Close pressed)
1 man/56 references
Procurator (governor) of Judea before
whom Jesus appeared after His trial
before the Jewish religious authorities.
Pilate understood He was innocent
but, out of fear, allowed the Jewish
leaders to condemn Jesus. Same as
Pontius Pilate.
Matthew 27:2

Pildash
1 man/1 reference
Genesis 22:22

Pileha
(Slicing)
1 man/1 reference
Jewish leader who renewed the
covenant under Nehemiah.
Nehemiah 10:24

Piltai
(A Paltite or descendant of Palti)
1 man/1 reference
Chief priest under Joiakim in the days
of Zerubbabel.
Nehemiah 12:17

Pinon
(Perplexity)
1 man/2 references
Genesis 36:41

Piram
(Wildly)
1 man/1 reference
Joshua 10:3

Pispah
(Dispersion)
1 man/1 reference
1 Chronicles 7:38

Pithon
(Expansive)
1 man/2 references
1 Chronicles 8:35

Pochereth
(To entrap)
1 man/2 references
Ezra 2:57

Pontius Pilate
*(Pontius, "bridged"; Pilate, "close
pressed")*
1 man/4 references
Pilate's family name and first name.
Same as Pilate.
Matthew 27:2

Poratha
1 man/1 reference
Esther 9:8

Porcius Festus
(Porcius, "swinish"; Festus, "festal")
1 man/1 reference
Governor of Judea who heard Paul's
case and sent him to Caesar. Also
called Festus.
Acts 24:27

Potiphar
1 man/2 references
Officer of Pharaoh and captain of
Pharaoh's guard, Potiphar became
master to the enslaved Joseph.
Genesis 37:36

Potipherah
1 man/3 references
Egyptian priest of On and father-in-
law of Joseph.
Genesis 41:45

Prisca
1 woman/1 reference
With her husband, Aquila, she was a
coworker of Paul. Same as Priscilla.
2 Timothy 4:19

Priscilla
1 woman/5 references
Wife of Aquila. This tent-making
couple worked with the apostle Paul
in their craft and in spreading the
Gospel and founded a house church
in their home. Same as Prisca.
Acts 18:2

Prochorus
(Before the dance)
1 man/1 reference
One of seven men selected to serve
needy Christians in Jerusalem.
Acts 6:5

Pua
(A blast)
1 man/1 reference
Same as Puah.
Numbers 26:23

Puah
(A blast)
2 men/1 woman/3 references
Same as Pua. Also, Hebrew midwife
who did not obey the command of
the king of Egypt to kill all male
Israelite babies.
1 Chronicles 7:1; Judges 10:1; Exodus 1:15

Publius
(Popular)
1 man/2 references
Chief official of Melita who housed
Paul and his companions after they
were shipwrecked on their way to
Rome.
Acts 28:7

Pudens
(Modest)
1 man/1 reference
Christian to whom Paul sent
greetings when he wrote Timothy.
2 Timothy 4:21

Pul
1 man/3 references
King of Assyria who exacted tribute
from Israel then brought the nation
into exile. Possibly the same as
Tiglath-pileser.
2 Kings 15:19

Put
1 man/1 reference
1 Chronicles 1:8

Putiel
(Contempt of God)
1 man/1 reference
Exodus 6:25

Q

Quartus
(Fourth)
1 man/1 reference
Christian in Corinth who sent his
greetings to fellow believers in Paul's
letter to Rome.
Romans 16:23

R

Raamah
(Mane)
1 man/4 references
Genesis 10:7

Raamiah
(God has shaken)
1 man/1 reference
Nehemiah 7:7

Rabmag
(Chief magician)
1 man/2 references
Babylonian prince who took part in
the destruction of Jerusalem under
King Nebuchadnezzar but showed
kindness to the prophet Jeremiah.
Jeremiah 39:3

Rabsaris
(Chief eunuch)
2 men/3 references
Notably, Babylonian prince who took
part in the destruction of Jerusalem
under King Nebuchadnezzar but
showed kindness to the prophet
Jeremiah. Also, Assyrian military
commander who participated in
King Sennacherib's failed attempt to
take Jerusalem in the days of King
Hezekiah and the prophet Isaiah.
Jeremiah 39:3; 2 Kings 18:17

Rab-shakeh
(Chief butler)
1 man/16 references
Assyrian field commander sent by
King Sennacherib to attack King
Hezekiah at Jerusalem. Same as
Rabshakeh.
2 Kings 18:17

Rabshakeh
(Chief butler)
1 man/16 references
Variant spelling of the name of the
Assyrian military commander
Rab-shakeh.
Isaiah 36:2

Rachab
(Proud)
1 woman/1 reference
Greek form of the name *Rahab*, used
in the New Testament.
Matthew 1:5

Rachel
(Ewe)
1 woman/47 references
Daughter of Laban and wife of Jacob,
promised to Jacob for seven years'
work. But Laban deceived Jacob,
giving her sister, Leah, to him in
marriage and requiring Jacob to work
another seven years to receive Rachel
as his bride. Leah had children, but
Rachel remained barren. Finally God
enabled Rachel to conceive, and she
bore Joseph and Benjamin. Same as
Rahel.
Genesis 29:6

Raddai
(Domineering)
1 man/1 reference
Fifth son of Jesse and older brother of
King David.
1 Chronicles 2:14

Ragau
(Friend)
1 man/1 reference
Greek form of the name *Reu*, used in
the New Testament.
Luke 3:35

Raguel
(Friend of God)
1 man/1 reference
Father-in-law of Moses. Same as
Reuel and Jethro.
Numbers 10:29

Rahab
(Proud)
1 woman/7 references
Prostitute of Jericho who hid the
two spies whom Joshua sent to look
over the city before Israel attacked it.
When Jericho fell to Joshua's troops,
he kept the spies' promise to spare her
and her family. Same as Rachab.
Joshua 2:1

Raham
(Pity)
1 man/1 reference
1 Chronicles 2:44

Rahel
(Ewe)
1 woman/1 reference
Variant spelling of the name of Jacob's
wife Rachel.
Jeremiah 31:15

Rakem
(Parti-colored)
1 man/1 reference
1 Chronicles 7:16

Ram
(High)
3 men/7 references
Ruth 4:19; 1 Chronicles 2:25; Job 32:2

Ramiah
(God has raised)
1 man/1 reference
Ezra 10:25

Ramoth
(Elevations)
1 man/1 reference
Ezra 10:29

Rapha
(Giant)
2 men/2 references
1 Chronicles 8:2; 1 Chronicles 8:37

Raphu
(Cured)
1 man/1 reference
Numbers 13:9

Reaia
(God has seen)
1 man/1 reference
1 Chronicles 5:5

Reaiah
(God has seen)
2 men/3 references
1 Chronicles 4:2; Ezra 2:47

Reba
(A fourth)
1 man/2 references
Midianite king killed by the Israelites
at God's command.
Numbers 31:8

Rebecca
(Fettering by beauty)
1 woman/1 reference
Greek form of the name *Rebekah*,
used in the New Testament.
Romans 9:10

Rebekah
(Fettering by beauty)
1 woman/30 references
Wife for Abraham's son, Isaac, discovered by Abraham's servant as she watered his camels. She agreed to marry Isaac and traveled to her new home. She was at first barren, but then conceived twins Esau and Jacob. Same as Rebecca.
Genesis 22:23

Rechab
(Rider)
3 men/13 references
Most notably, leader of one of the raiding bands of Saul's son Ishbosheth. Also, father of Jonadab, who commanded his descendants not to drink wine.
2 Samuel 4:2; 2 Kings 10:15; Nehemiah 3:14

Reelaiah
(Fearful of God)
1 man/1 reference
Ezra 2:2

Regem
(Stone heap)
1 man/1 reference
1 Chronicles 2:47

Regem-melech
(King's heap)
1 man/1 reference
Messenger sent to the prophet Zechariah to ask if the Jews should fast over their exile in Babylon.
Zechariah 7:2

Rehabiah
(God has enlarged)
1 man/5 references
1 Chronicles 23:17

Rehob
(Width)
2 men/3 references
Notably, father of Hadadezer, king of Zobah, whom King David conquered. Also, Jewish leader who renewed the covenant under Nehemiah.
2 Samuel 8:3; Nehemiah 10:11

Rehoboam
(A people has enlarged)
1 man/50 references
Son of King Solomon who inherited the kingdom of Israel. Same as Roboam.
1 Kings 11:43

Rehum
(Compassionate)
4 men/8 references
Most notably, officer of the Persian king Artaxerxes who joined in opposition to Zerubbabel's rebuilding of the temple in Jerusalem. Also, Levite who repaired the walls of Jerusalem under Nehemiah. Also, Jewish leader who renewed the covenant under Nehemiah.
Ezra 2:2; Ezra 4:8; Nehemiah 3:17; Nehemiah 10:25

Rei
(Social)
1 man/1 reference
Friend of King David who did not join in the attempted coup of David's son Adonijah.
1 Kings 1:8

Rekem
(Parti-colored)
2 men/4 references
Notably, Midianite king killed by the Israelites at God's command to Moses.
Numbers 31:8; 1 Chronicles 2:43

Remaliah
(God has bedecked)
1 man/13 references
Father of King Pekah of Israel.
2 Kings 15:25

Rephael
(God has cured)
1 man/1 reference
1 Chronicles 26:7

Rephah
(To sustain)
1 man/1 reference
1 Chronicles 7:25

Rephaiah
(God has cured)
5 men/5 references
Most notably, city official of
Jerusalem and rebuilder of the walls
under Nehemiah.
1 Chronicles 3:21; 1 Chronicles 4:42;
1 Chronicles 7:2; 1 Chronicles 9:43;
Nehemiah 3:9

Resheph
(Lightning)
1 man/1 reference
1 Chronicles 7:25

Reu
(Friend)
1 man/5 references
Same as Ragau.
Genesis 11:18

Reuben
(See ye a son)
1 man/26 references
Jacob and Leah's first son. Brother of
Joseph who was sorrowful when he
learned his brothers had sold Joseph
as a slave; Reuben had hoped to
return him to their father.
Genesis 29:32

Reuel
(Friend of God)
4 men/10 references
Most notably, father-in-law of Moses.
Same as Raguel and Jethro. Also, son
of Esau.
Genesis 36:4; Exodus 2:18; Numbers 2:14;
1 Chronicles 9:8

Reumah
(Raised)
1 woman/1 reference
Genesis 22:24

Rezia
(Delight)
1 man/1 reference
1 Chronicles 7:39

Rezin
(Delight)
2 men/10 references
Notably, king of Syria who attacked
Judah during the reigns of kings
Jotham and Ahaz.
2 Kings 15:37; Ezra 2:48

Rezon
(Prince)
1 man/1 reference
Rebel leader in Damascus who
became King Solomon's adversary.
1 Kings 11:23

Rhesa
(God has cured)
1 man/1 reference
Luke 3:27

Rhoda
(Rose)
1 woman/1 reference
Young woman serving in the
Jerusalem home of Mary, mother
of John Mark, who responded to
a knock at the gate. She heard the

voice of Peter, and in her excitement, she forgot to let Peter in, returning instead to those who were praying for his release.
Acts 12:13

Ribai
(Contentious)
1 man/2 references
2 Samuel 23:29

Rimmon
(Pomegranate)
1 man/3 references
2 Samuel 4:2

Rinnah
(Creaking)
1 man/1 reference
1 Chronicles 4:20

Riphath
1 man/2 references
Genesis 10:3

Rizpah
(Hot stone)
1 woman/4 references
Concubine of Saul.
2 Samuel 3:7

Roboam
(A people has enlarged)
1 man/2 references
Greek form of the name *Rehoboam*, used in the New Testament. Son of Solomon and first king of Judah, the southern portion of divided Israel.
Matthew 1:7

Rohgah
(Outcry)
1 man/1 reference
1 Chronicles 7:34

Romamti-ezer
(I have raised up a help)
1 man/2 references
1 Chronicles 25:4

Rosh
(To shake the head)
1 man/1 reference
Genesis 46:21

Rufus
(Red)
2 men/2 references
Notably, son of Simon, man from Cyrene forced by Roman soldiers to carry Jesus' cross to Golgotha, the crucifixion site. Also, acquaintance whom the apostle Paul greeted in his letter to the Romans.
Mark 15:21; Romans 16:13

Ruth
(Friend)
1 woman/13 references
Moabite daughter-in-law of Naomi, married to Naomi's son Mahlon. After Mahlon's death, she returned to Bethlehem with Naomi. There she gleaned barley in Boaz's field and she married him, her kinsman-redeemer.
Ruth 1:4

S

Sabta
1 man/1 reference
Same as Sabtah.
1 Chronicles 1:9

Sabtah
1 man/1 reference
Same as Sabta.
Genesis 10:7

Sabtecha
1 man/1 reference
Same as Sabtechah.
1 Chronicles 1:9

Sabtechah
1 man/1 reference
Same as Sabtecha.
Genesis 10:7

Sacar
(Recompense)
2 men/2 references
1 Chronicles 11:35; 1 Chronicles 26:4

Sadoc
(Just)
1 man/2 references
Matthew 1:14

Sala
(Spear)
1 man/1 reference
Greek form of the name *Salah*, used
in the New Testament.
Luke 3:35

Salah
(Spear)
1 man/1 reference
Same as Sala.
Genesis 10:24

Salathiel
(I have asked God)
1 man/4 references
1 Chronicles 3:17

Sallai
(Weighed)
2 men/2 references
Notably, man chosen by lot to resettle
Jerusalem after the Babylonian
Exile. Also, priest who returned to
Jerusalem with Zerubbabel.
Nehemiah 11:8; Nehemiah 12:20

Sallu
(Weighed)
2 men/3 references
Notably, man chosen by lot to resettle
Jerusalem after the Babylonian Exile.
Also, exiled priest who returned to
Judah under Zerubbabel.
1 Chronicles 9:7; Nehemiah 12:7

Salma
(Clothing)
1 man/4 references
Father of Boaz and a descendant of
Abraham through Jacob's son Judah.
Same as Salmon.
1 Chronicles 2:11

Salmon
(Clothing)
1 man/5 references
Father of Boaz and a forefather of
Jesus. Same as Salma.
Ruth 4:20

Salome
(Welfare)
1 woman/2 references
Follower of Jesus who witnessed His
death on the cross and later brought
spices to anoint His body—only to
find it gone due to His resurrection.
Mark 15:40

Salu
(Weighed)
1 man/1 reference
Numbers 25:14

Samgar-nebo
1 man/1 reference
Babylonian prince who took part in
the destruction of Jerusalem under
King Nebuchadnezzar.
Jeremiah 39:3

Samlah
(Dress)
1 man/4 references
King of Edom.
Genesis 36:36

Samson
(Sunlight)
1 man/39 references
Twelfth judge of Israel who was to
follow a Nazarite vow, which included
not cutting his hair, the source of his
strength. His wife, Delilah, betrayed
him after he revealed his secret to her.
His hair was shaved, but as his hair
grew, his strength returned. While
bound by the Philistines, he leaned on
the pillars of the temple and brought
it down, killing the worshippers and
himself.
Judges 13:24

Samuel
(Heard of God)
1 man/142 references
Prophet and judge of Israel. After
Samuel's birth, his mother gave him
to Eli to raise in the temple. God
spoke to him; Samuel mistakenly
thought Eli called, but Eli told him
that it was God's voice. Anointed Saul
king and later anointed David king in
Saul's place. Same as Shemuel.
1 Samuel 1:20

Sanballat
1 man/10 references
One of Nehemiah's opponents who
plotted to fight against Jerusalem as
he rebuilt the walls.
Nehemiah 2:10

Saph
(Containing)
1 man/1 reference
2 Samuel 21:18

Sapphira
(Sapphire)
1 woman/1 reference
Wife of Ananias who lied to the
apostle Peter and was struck dead.
Acts 5:1

Sara
(Female noble)
1 woman/2 references
Greek form of the name *Sarah*, used
in the New Testament.
Hebrews 11:1

Sarah
(Female noble)
2 women/41 references
Notably, the name God gave Sarai,
wife of Abram (Abraham), after He
promised she would bear a child.
When she was over ninety years old,
she bore Isaac.
Genesis 17:15; Numbers 26:46

Sarai
(Controlling)
1 woman/17 references
Barren wife of Abram who traveled
with her husband to Canaan at God's
calling. Sarai had no children, so she
gave her maid, Hagar, to Abram to bear
children for her; but Hagar despised
Sarai and fled. God changed her name
to Sarah, and she gave birth to a son
who would be the father of a multitude.
Genesis 11:29

Saraph
(Burning)
1 man/1 reference
1 Chronicles 4:22

Sargon
1 man/1 reference
King of Assyria in the days of the
prophet Isaiah.
Isaiah 20:1

Sarsechim
1 man/1 reference
Babylonian prince who took part in the destruction of Jerusalem under King Nebuchadnezzar.
Jeremiah 39:3

Saruch
(Tendril)
1 man/1 reference
Luke 3:35

Saul
(Asked)
3 men/422 references
Most notably, anointed king of Israel by the prophet Samuel, he fought the Philistines throughout his reign. He wrongly made a burnt offering, and the consequence was that his kingdom would not be established forever. Because of his sin, God rejected him as Israel's king. Samuel anointed David king, and Saul became increasingly jealous of and attempted to kill him. In fear, he consulted a witch, then soon died in battle. Also, zealous Jew who witnessed the martyrdom of Stephen and persecuted Christians. He was temporarily blinded and turned to Christ, preaching His message and traveling on missionary journeys, at which time scripture begins to call him Paul.
Genesis 36:37; 1 Samuel 9:2; Acts 7:58

Sceva
(Left-handed)
1 man/1 reference
Jewish chief priest in Ephesus whose seven sons were beaten by a demonpossessed man during an attempted exorcism.
Acts 19:14

Seba
1 man/2 references
Genesis 10:7

Secundus
(Second)
1 man/1 reference
Man from Thessalonica who was a traveling companion of the apostle Paul.
Acts 20:4

Segub
(Aloft)
2 men/3 references
1 Kings 16:34; 1 Chronicles 2:21

Seir
(Rough)
1 man/2 references
Genesis 36:20

Seled
(Exultation)
1 man/2 references
1 Chronicles 2:30

Sem
1 man/1 reference
Greek form of the name *Shem*, used in the New Testament.
Luke 3:36

Semachiah
(Supported of God)
1 man/1 reference
1 Chronicles 26:7

Semei
(Famous)
1 man/1 reference
Luke 3:26

Sennacherib
1 man/13 references
King of Assyria who attacked and

captured Judah's fortified cities during King Hezekiah's reign.
2 Kings 18:13

Senuah
(Pointed)
1 man/1 reference
Father of man chosen by lot to resettle Jerusalem after the Babylonian Exile.
Nehemiah 11:9

Seorim
(Barley)
1 man/1 reference
One of twenty-four priests in David's time who was chosen by lot to serve in the tabernacle.
1 Chronicles 24:8

Serah
(Superfluity)
1 woman/2 references
Genesis 46:17

Seraiah
(God has prevailed)
9 men/20 references
Most notably, scribe in King David's court. Also, high priest during King Zedekiah's reign. Also, priest who renewed the covenant under Nehemiah. Also, priest who resettled Jerusalem following the Babylonian Exile.
2 Samuel 8:17; 2 Kings 25:18; 2 Kings 25:23; 1 Chronicles 4:13; 1 Chronicles 4:35; Ezra 2:2; Nehemiah 11:11; Jeremiah 36:26; Jeremiah 51:59

Sered
(Trembling)
1 man/2 references
Genesis 46:14

Sergius
1 man/1 reference
Roman ruler of Cyprus during the apostle Paul's first missionary journey. Asked Paul and Barnabas to share the word of God with him. A false prophet interfered, but after Paul pronounced blindness on him, Sergius came to faith.
Acts 13:7

Serug
(Tendril)
1 man/5 references
Genesis 11:20

Seth
(Substituted)
1 man/8 references
Adam and Eve's third son, whom Eve bore after Abel was killed by his brother Cain. Same as Sheth.
Genesis 4:25

Sethur
(Hidden)
1 man/1 reference
One of twelve spies sent by Moses to spy out the land of Canaan.
Numbers 13:13

Shaaph
(Fluctuation)
1 Chronicles 2:47

Shaashgaz
1 man/1 reference
Eunuch serving Persian king Ahasuerus, overseeing the king's harem, including the future queen Esther.
Esther 2:14

Shabbcthai
(Restful)
3 men/3 references
Most notably, Levite who helped Ezra
to explain the law to exiles returned
to Jerusalem. Also, Levite who
oversaw the outside of the Jerusalem
temple in the time of Nehemiah.
Ezra 10:15; Nehemiah 8:7; Nehemiah 11:16

Shachia
(Captivation)
1 man/1 reference
1 Chronicles 8:10

Shadrach
1 man/15 references
Babylonian name for Hananiah,
one of Daniel's companions in exile.
Survived being cast into a fiery
furnace when he refused to bow to
an idol.
Daniel 1:7

Shage
1 man/1 reference
1 Chronicles 11:34

Shaharaim
(Double dawn)
1 man/1 reference
1 Chronicles 8:8

Shallum
(Retribution)
14 men/27 references
Most notably, fifth-to-last king of
the northern kingdom of Israel,
obtained the throne by assassinating
King Zachariah. Also, husband of
the prophetess Huldah during the
reign of King Josiah. Also, fourth son
of Judah's king Josiah who inherited
the throne from his father. Same as
Jehoahaz. Also, city official who, with
the aid of his daughters, helped to

rebuild the walls of Jerusalem under
Nehemiah.
2 Kings 15:10; 2 Kings 22:14; 1 Chronicles
2:40; 1 Chronicles 3:15; 1 Chronicles 4:25;
1 Chronicles 6:12; 1 Chronicles 7:13;
1 Chronicles 9:17; 2 Chronicles 28:12; Ezra
10:24; Ezra 10:42; Nehemiah 3:12; Jeremiah
32:7; Jeremiah 35:4

Shallun
(Retribution)
1 man/1 reference
Rebuilder of the walls of Jerusalem,
repaired the Fountain Gate.
Nehemiah 3:15

Shalmai
(Clothed)
1 man/2 references
Ezra 2:46

Shalman
1 man/1 reference
Variant spelling of the name
Shalmaneser; king of Assyria.
Hosea 10:14

Shalmaneser
1 man/2 references
King of Assyria who imprisoned King
Hoshea of Israel and besieged and
captured Samaria and brought Israel
into exile. Same as Shalman.
2 Kings 17:3

Shama
(Obedient)
1 man/1 reference
One of King David's valiant warriors.
1 Chronicles 11:44

Shamariah
1 man/1 reference
Son of Judah's king Rehoboam and a
grandson of Solomon.
2 Chronicles 11:19

Shamed
(Preserved)
1 man/1 reference
1 Chronicles 8:12

Shamer
(Preserved)
2 men/2 references
1 Chronicles 6:46; 1 Chronicles 7:34

Shamgar
1 man/2 references
Third judge of Israel who killed six
hundred Philistines with an ox goad.
Judges 3:31

Shamhuth
(Desolation)
1 man/1 reference
Commander in King David's army
overseeing twenty-four thousand men
in the fifth month of each year.
1 Chronicles 27:8

Shamir
(Observed)
1 man/1 reference
1 Chronicles 24:24

Shamma
(Desolation)
1 man/1 reference
1 Chronicles 7:37

Shammah
(Consternation)
4 men/8 references
Most notably, third son of Jesse and
an older brother of King David who
served as a soldier in King Saul's
army. Same as Shimea and Shimeah.
Also, one of King David's warriors
known as the "mighty men." Also,
one of King David's valiant warriors.
Genesis 36:13; 1 Samuel 16:9; 2 Samuel
23:11; 2 Samuel 23:25

Shammai
(Destructive)
3 men/6 references
1 Chronicles 2:28; 1 Chronicles 2:44;
1 Chronicles 4:17

Shammoth
(Ruins)
1 man/1 reference
One of King David's valiant warriors.
1 Chronicles 11:27

Shammua
(Renowned)
4 men/4 references
Most notably, son of King David.
Same as Shammuah. Also, one of
twelve spies sent by Moses to spy out
the land of Canaan.
Numbers 13:4; 1 Chronicles 14:4;
Nehemiah 11:17; Nehemiah 12:18

Shammuah
(Renowned)
1 man/1 reference
Son of King David. Same as
Shammua.
2 Samuel 5:14

Shamsherai
(Sunlike)
1 man/1 reference
1 Chronicles 8:26

Shapham
(Baldly)
1 man/1 reference
1 Chronicles 5:12

Shaphan
(Rock-rabbit)
4 men/30 references
Most notably, scribe for King Josiah
of Judah.
2 Kings 22:3; 2 Kings 22:12; Jeremiah 29:3;
Ezekiel 8:11

Shaphat
(Judge)
5 men/8 references
Most notably, one of twelve spies sent by Moses to spy out the land of Canaan. Also, father of the prophet Elisha. Also, King David's chief shepherd over herds in the valleys.
Numbers 13:5; 1 Kings 19:16; 1 Chronicles 3:22; 1 Chronicles 5:12; 1 Chronicles 27:29

Sharai
(Hostile)
1 man/1 reference
Ezra 10:40

Sharar
(Hostile)
1 man/1 reference
2 Samuel 23:33

Sharezer
1 man/2 references
Son of the Assyrian king Sennacherib who, with his brother Adrammelech, killed his father.
2 Kings 19:37

Shashai
(Whitish)
1 man/1 reference
Ezra 10:40

Shashak
(Pedestrian)
1 man/2 references
1 Chronicles 8:14

Shaul
(Asked)
3 men/7 references
Most notably, king of Edom in the days before Israel had a king.
Genesis 46:10; 1 Chronicles 1:48; 1 Chronicles 6:24

Shavsha
(Joyful)
1 man/1 reference
Scribe serving in the government of King David.
1 Chronicles 18:16

Sheal
(Request)
1 man/1 reference
Ezra 10:29

Shealtiel
(I have asked God)
1 man/9 references
Father of Zerubbabel, governor of Judah after the Babylonian Exile.
Ezra 3:2

Sheariah
(God has stormed)
1 man/2 references
1 Chronicles 8:38

Shear-jashub
(A remnant will return)
1 man/1 reference
Son of Isaiah who joined the prophet in delivering a message to Judah's king Ahaz.
Isaiah 7:3

Sheba
5 men/15 references
Most notably, Israelite who rebelled against King David.
Genesis 10:7; Genesis 10:28; Genesis 25:3; 2 Samuel 20:1; 1 Chronicles 5:13

Shebaniah
(God has grown)
4 men/7 references
Most notably, priest who blew a trumpet before the ark of the covenant when David brought it to Jerusalem. Also, one of a group of

Levites who led a revival among the Israelites in the time of Nehemiah. Also, priest who renewed the covenant under Nehemiah. Also, Levite who renewed the covenant under Nehemiah.
1 Chronicles 15:24; Nehemiah 9:4; Nehemiah 10:4; Nehemiah 10:12

Sheber
(Fracture)
1 man/1 reference
1 Chronicles 2:48

Shebna
(Growth)
2 men/9 references
Most notably, scribe for King Hezekiah of Judah who spoke to King Sennacherib's representative and also later took a message to the prophet Isaiah. Also, treasurer (steward) Isaiah prophesied against for building himself a kingly tomb.
2 Kings 18:18; Isaiah 22:15

Shebuel
(Captive of God)
2 men/3 references
1 Chronicles 23:16; 1 Chronicles 25:4

Shecaniah
(God has dwelt)
2 men/2 references
Notably, one of twenty-four priests in David's time who was chosen by lot to serve in the tabernacle. Also, priest in the time of King Hezekiah who helped to distribute freewill offerings to his fellow priests.
1 Chronicles 24:11; 2 Chronicles 31:15

Shechaniah
(God has dwelt)
7 men/8 references
Most notably, priest who returned to Jerusalem under Zerubbabel.

1 Chronicles 3:21; Ezra 8:3; Ezra 8:5; Ezra 10:2; Nehemiah 3:29; Nehemiah 6:18; Nehemiah 12:3

Shechem
(Neck)
3 men/19 references
Most notably, prince of the city of Shechem who raped Jacob's daughter, Dinah, then wanted to marry her. Simeon and Levi attacked the city; killed Shechem, his father, and all the males of the city; and brought Dinah home.
Genesis 34:2; Numbers 26:31; 1 Chronicles 7:19

Shedeur
(Spreader of light)
1 man/5 references
Numbers 1:5

Shehariah
(God has sought)
1 man/1 reference
1 Chronicles 8:26

Shelah
(Request)
2 men/11 references
Notably, son of Jacob's son Judah.
Genesis 38:5; 1 Chronicles 1:18

Shelemiah
(Thank-offering of God)
9 men/10 references
Most notably, Levite who was chosen by lot to guard the east side of the house of the Lord. Also, priest whom Nehemiah made treasurer to distribute the portions of the Levites. Also, man whom King Jehoiakim ordered to imprison the prophet Jeremiah and his scribe.
1 Chronicles 26:14; Ezra 10:39; Ezra 10:41; Nehemiah 3:30; Nehemiah 13:13; Jeremiah 36:14; Jeremiah 36:26; Jeremiah 37:3; Jeremiah 37:13

Sheleph
(Extract)
1 man/2 references
Genesis 10:26

Shelesh
(Triplet)
1 man/1 reference
1 Chronicles 7:35

Shelomi
(Peaceable)
1 man/1 reference
Numbers 34:27

Shelomith
(Peaceableness, pacification)
5 men/2 women/9 references
Most notably, Levite chief appointed under King David. Same as Shelomoth. Also, Levite in charge of the treasures that were dedicated to the temple. Also, son of Judah's king Rehoboam and grandson of Solomon.
Leviticus 24:11; 1 Chronicles 3:19; 1 Chronicles 23:9; 1 Chronicles 23:18; 1 Chronicles 26:25; 2 Chronicles 11:20; Ezra 8:10

Shelomoth
(Pacification)
1 man/1 reference
Same as Shelomith.
1 Chronicles 24:22

Shelumiel
(Peace of God)
1 man/5 references
Man of the tribe of Simeon who helped Aaron take a census.
Numbers 1:6

Shem
(Name)
1 man/17 references
Eldest son of Noah, he joined Noah in the ark. Same as Sem.
Genesis 5:32

Shema
(Heard)
4 men/5 references
Most notably, priest who assisted Ezra in reading the book of the law to the people of Jerusalem.
1 Chronicles 2:43; 1 Chronicles 5:8; 1 Chronicles 8:13; Nehemiah 8:4

Shemaah
(Annunciation)
1 man/1 reference
1 Chronicles 12:3

Shemaiah
(God has heard)
25 men/41 references
Most notably, prophet who told King Rehoboam not to fight Israel when it revolted against him. Also, one of a group of Levites appointed by King David to bring the ark of the covenant from the house of Obededom to Jerusalem. Also, one of a group of Levites who cleansed the Jerusalem temple during the revival in King Hezekiah's reign. Also, one of a group who distributed sacrificial animals to fellow Levites preparing to celebrate the Passover under King Josiah. Also, man who repaired Jerusalem's walls under Nehemiah. Also, priest who renewed the covenant under Nehemiah.
1 Kings 12:22; 1 Chronicles 3:22; 1 Chronicles 4:37; 1 Chronicles 5:4; 1 Chronicles 9:14; 1 Chronicles 9:16; 1 Chronicles 15:8; 1 Chronicles 24:6; 1 Chronicles 26:4; 2 Chronicles 17:8; 2 Chronicles 29:14; 2 Chronicles 31:15; 2 Chronicles 35:9; Ezra 8:13; Ezra 8:16; Ezra 10:21; Ezra 10:31; Nehemiah 3:29; Nehemiah 6:10; Nehemiah 10:8; Nehemiah 12:36; Nehemiah 12:42; Jeremiah 26:20; Jeremiah 29:24; Jeremiah 36:12

Shemariah
(God has guarded)
3 men/3 references
Most notably, "mighty man" who
supported the future king David
during his conflict with Saul.
1 Chronicles 12:5; Ezra 10:32; Ezra 10:41

Shemeber
(Illustrious)
1 man/1 reference
King of Zeboiim in the days of
Abram.
Genesis 14:2

Shemer
(Preserved)
1 man/1 reference
Owner of the hill of Samaria, which
he sold to King Omri of Israel.
1 Kings 16:24

Shemida
(Name of knowing)
1 man/2 references
Same as Shemidah.
Numbers 26:32

Shemidah
(Name of knowing)
1 man/1 reference
Same as Shemida.
1 Chronicles 7:19

Shemiramoth
(Name of heights)
2 men/4 references
Notably, Levite musician who
performed in celebration when
King David brought the ark of the
covenant to Jerusalem. Also, Levite
sent by King Jehoshaphat to teach
the law of the Lord throughout the
nation of Judah.
1 Chronicles 15:18; 2 Chronicles 17:8

Shemuel
(Heard of God)
3 men/3 references
Most notably, prince of the tribe of
Simeon when the Israelites entered
the Promised Land. Also, alternative
name for the prophet Samuel.
Numbers 34:20; 1 Chronicles 6:33;
1 Chronicles 7:2

Shenazar
1 man/1 reference
1 Chronicles 3:18

Shephathiah
(God has judged)
1 man/1 reference
1 Chronicles 9:8

Shephatiah
(God has judged)
9 men/12 references
Notably, fifth son of David, born to
his wife Abital. Also, "mighty man"
who supported the future king David
during his conflict with Saul. Also,
leader of the tribe of Simeon in the
days of King David. Also, son of
Judah's king Jehoshaphat.
2 Samuel 3:4; 1 Chronicles 12:5;
1 Chronicles 27:16; 2 Chronicles 21:2; Ezra
2:4; Ezra 2:57; Ezra 8:8; Nehemiah 11:4;
Jeremiah 38:1

Shephi
(Baldness)
1 man/1 reference
Same as Shepho.
1 Chronicles 1:40

Shepho
(Baldness)
1 man/1 reference
Same as Shephi.
Genesis 36:23

Shephuphan
(Serpentlike)
1 man/1 reference
1 Chronicles 8:5

Sherah
(Kindred)
1 woman/1 reference
1 Chronicles 7:24

Sherebiah
(God has brought heat)
2 men/8 references
Most notably, Levite whom Ezra
called to serve in the temple upon
his return to Jerusalem. Also, Levite
who renewed the covenant under
Nehemiah.
Ezra 8:18; Nehemiah 10:12

Sheresh
(Root)
1 man/1 reference
1 Chronicles 7:16

Sherezer
1 man/1 reference
Man sent by the people of Bethel to
the prophet Zechariah to seek God's
favor.
Zechariah 7:2

Sheshai
(Whitish)
1 man/3 references
One of the children of Anak, killed
after Joshua's death when Judah
battled the Canaanites.
Numbers 13:22

Sheshan
(Lily)
1 man/4 references
1 Chronicles 2:31

Sheshbazzar
1 man/4 references
Another name for Zerubbabel, the
leader of exiles who returned from
Babylon to Judah.
Ezra 1:8

Sheth
(Substituted)
2 men/2 references
Notably, leader of Moab mentioned
in one of Balaam's prophecies. Also,
variant spelling of the name *Seth*;
Adam's third son.
Numbers 24:17; 1 Chronicles 1:1

Shethar
1 man/1 reference
One of seven Persian princes serving
under King Ahasuerus.
Esther 1:14

Shethar-boznai
1 man/4 references
Persian official who objected to the
rebuilding of the Jewish temple.
Ezra 5:3

Sheva
(False)
2 men/2 references
Notably, scribe serving in the
government of King David.
2 Samuel 20:25; 1 Chronicles 2:49

Shilhi
(Armed)
1 man/2 references
Grandfather of Judah's king
Jehoshaphat.
1 Kings 22:42

Shillem
(Requital)
1 man/2 references
Genesis 46:24

Shiloni
(Inhabitant of Shiloh)
1 man/1 reference
Jewish exile from the tribe of Judah
who resettled Jerusalem.
Nehemiah 11:5

Shilshah
(Triplication)
1 man/1 reference
1 Chronicles 7:37

Shimea
(Annunciation)
4 men/4 references
Most notably, brother of King David.
Same as Shimeah, Shammah, and
Shimma. Also, son of King David,
born in Jerusalem to Bath-sheba (also
known as Bath-shua).
1 Chronicles 3:5; 1 Chronicles 6:30;
1 Chronicles 6:39; 1 Chronicles 20:7

Shimeah
(Annunciation)
2 men/4 references
Notably, brother of King David.
Same as Shimea, Shammah, and
Shimma.
2 Samuel 13:3; 1 Chronicles 8:32

Shimeam
(Annunciation)
1 man/1 reference
Cousin of King Saul.
1 Chronicles 9:38

Shimeath
(Annunciation)
1 woman/2 references
Mother of Zabad, royal official who
conspired to kill Judah's king Joash.
2 Kings 12:21

Shimei
(Famous)
18 men/42 references
Most notably, relative of King Saul
who cursed King David when he fled
Jerusalem. Later Shimei apologized to
David, who pardoned him. Same as
Shimi. Also, one of King Solomon's
twelve officials over provisions. Also,
King David's official who was in
charge of the vineyards. Also, Levite
appointed by King Hezekiah to care
for the temple contributions. Also,
head of a household whom Zechariah
prophesied would be set apart before
the day of the Lord.
Numbers 3:18; 2 Samuel 16:5; 1 Kings 1:8;
1 Kings 4:18; 1 Chronicles 3:19; 1 Chronicles
4:26; 1 Chronicles 5:4; 1 Chronicles 6:29;
1 Chronicles 23:9; 1 Chronicles 25:17;
1 Chronicles 27:27; 2 Chronicles; 29:14;
2 Chronicles 31:12; Ezra 10:23; Ezra 10:33;
Ezra 10:38; Esther 2:5; Zechariah 12:13

Shimeon
(Hearing)
1 man/1 reference
Ezra 10:31

Shimhi
(Famous)
1 man/1 reference
1 Chronicles 8:21

Shimi
(Famous)
1 man/1 reference
Same as Shimei.
Exodus 6:17

Shimma
(Annunciation)
1 man/1 reference
Third son of Jesse and an older
brother of David. Same as Shammah,
Shimea, and Shimeah.
1 Chronicles 2:13

Shimon
(Desert)
1 man/1 reference
1 Chronicles 4:20

Shimrath
(Guardship)
1 man/1 reference
1 Chronicles 8:21

Shimri
(Watchful)
3 men/3 references
Most notably, among the Levites who cleansed the Jerusalem temple during the revival in King Hezekiah's reign.
1 Chronicles 4:37; 1 Chronicles 11:45; 2 Chronicles 29:13

Shimrith
(Female guard)
1 woman/1 reference
Mother of Jehozabad, a royal official who conspired to kill Judah's king Joash. Same as Shomer.
2 Chronicles 24:26

Shimrom
(Guardianship)
1 man/1 reference
Same as Shimron.
1 Chronicles 7:1

Shimron
(Guardianship)
1 man/4 references
Same as Shimrom.
Genesis 46:13

Shimshai
(Sunny)
1 man/4 references
Scribe who wrote King Artaxerxes a letter objecting to the rebuilding of Jerusalem.
Ezra 4:8

Shinab
(Father has turned)
1 man/1 reference
King of Admah in the days of Abraham.
Genesis 14:2

Shiphi
(Copious)
1 man/1 reference
1 Chronicles 4:37

Shiphrah
(Brightness)
1 woman/1 reference
Hebrew midwife who did not obey the command of the king of Egypt to kill all male Israelite babies.
Exodus 1:15

Shiphtan
(Judgelike)
1 man/1 reference
Numbers 34:24

Shisha
(Whiteness)
1 man/1 reference
1 Kings 4:3

Shishak
1 man/7 references
King of Egypt to whom Jeroboam fled when Solomon discovered he had been anointed king over the ten northern tribes.
1 Kings 11:40

Shitrai
(Magisterial)
1 man/1 reference
King David's chief shepherd over herds in Sharon.
1 Chronicles 27:29

Shiza
1 man/1 reference
1 Chronicles 11:42

Shobab
(Rebellious)
2 men/4 references
Notably, son of King David.
2 Samuel 5:14; 1 Chronicles 2:18

Shobach
(Thicket)
1 man/2 references
Captain in the Syrian army of King
Hadarezer. Same as Shophach.
2 Samuel 10:16

Shobai
(Captor)
1 man/2 references
Ezra 2:42

Shobal
(Overflowing)
3 men/9 references
Genesis 36:20; 1 Chronicles 2:50;
1 Chronicles 4:1

Shobek
(Forsaking)
1 man/1 reference
Jewish leader who renewed the
covenant under Nehemiah.
Nehemiah 10:24

Shobi
(Captor)
1 man/1 reference
Man who brought food and supplies
to King David and his soldiers as they
fled from the army of David's son
Absalom, who was staging a coup.
2 Samuel 17:27

Shoham
(To blanch)
1 man/1 reference
1 Chronicles 24:27

Shomer
(Keeper)
1 man/1 woman/2 references
Same as Shimrith.
2 Kings 12:21; 1 Chronicles 7:32

Shophach
(Poured)
1 man/2 references
Captain in the Syrian army of King
Hadarezer. Same as Shobach.
1 Chronicles 19:16

Shua
(A cry)
2 women/2 references
Same as Shuah.
1 Chronicles 2:3; 1 Chronicles 7:32

Shuah
(Dell)
2 men/1 woman/5 references
Notably, son of Abraham by his
second wife, Keturah. Also, same as
Shua.
Genesis 25:2; Genesis 38:2;
1 Chronicles 4:11

Shual
(Jackal)
1 man/1 reference
1 Chronicles 7:36

Shubael
(God has favored)
2 men/3 references
Notably, one of twenty-four Levite
musicians who was chosen by lot to
serve in the house of the Lord.
1 Chronicles 24:20; 1 Chronicles 25:20

Shuham
(Humbly)
1 man/1 reference
Numbers 26:42

Shuni
(Rest)
1 man/2 references
Genesis 46:16

Shupham
(Serpentlike)
1 man/1 reference
Numbers 26:39

Shuppim
(Serpents)
2 men/3 references
Notably, Levite who was chosen by lot to guard the west side of the house of the Lord.
1 Chronicles 7:12; 1 Chronicles 26:16

Shuthelah
(Crash of breakage)
2 men/4 references
Numbers 26:35; 1 Chronicles 7:21

Sia
(Converse)
1 man/1 reference
Same as Siaha.
Nehemiah 7:47

Siaha
(Converse)
1 man/1 reference
Same as Sia.
Ezra 2:44

Sibbecai
(Corpselike)
1 man/2 references
Commander in King David's army overseeing twenty-four thousand men in the eighth month of each year.

Same as Sibbechai.
1 Chronicles 11:29

Sibbechai
1 man/2 references
One of King David's valiant warriors. Same as Sibbecai.
2 Samuel 21:18

Sidon
(Fishery)
1 man/1 reference
Genesis 10:15

Sihon
(Tempestuous)
1 man/37 references
Amorite king whom the Israelites defeated when he would not let them pass through his land as they turned back before the Promised Land.
Numbers 21:21

Silas
(Sylvan)
1 man/13 references
Prophet chosen by the Jerusalem Council to accompany Paul and Barnabas to the Gentiles. Same as Silvanus.
Acts 15:22

Silvanus
(Sylvan)
2 men/4 references
Notably, Latin name for Silas, who accompanied Paul on his missionary journeys. Also, a "faithful brother" by whom Peter wrote the epistle of 1 Peter.
2 Corinthians 1:19; 1 Peter 5:12

Simeon
(Hearing)
5 men/18 references
Most notably, devout man at the

Jerusalem temple who held the eight-day-old Jesus when His parents brought Him to the temple to present Him to the Lord. Also, second son of Jacob and Leah. Also, prophet and teacher in the church at Antioch during the apostle Paul's ministry. Also called Niger. Also, variant name for the apostle Simon Peter.
Genesis 29:33; Luke 2:25; Luke 3:30; Acts 13:1; Acts 15:14

Simon
(Hearing)
9 men/76 references
Most notably, disciple whom Jesus surnamed Peter, also called Simon Bar-jona. Also, one of Jesus' twelve disciples, called "the Canaanite" and "Zelotes" (the Zealot). Also, one of four brothers of Jesus, as recorded by Matthew's and Mark's Gospels. Also, man from Cyrene whom the Romans forced to carry Jesus' cross to the crucifixion site. Also, Pharisee who invited Jesus to eat in his home and thought Jesus should have known that the woman who anointed him with oil was a sinner. Also, sorcerer who became a Christian. Also, tanner of Joppa who lived by the sea and lodged Peter.
Matthew 4:18; Matthew 10:4; Matthew 13:55; Matthew 26:6; Matthew 27:32; Luke 7:40; John 6:71; Acts 8:9; Acts 9:43

Simri
(Watchful)
1 man/1 reference
1 Chronicles 26:10

Sippai
(Basinlike)
1 man/1 reference
Philistine warrior killed by one of King David's soldiers.
1 Chronicles 20:4

Sisamai
1 man/2 references
1 Chronicles 2:40

Sisera
2 men/21 references
Notably, captain under Jabin, king of Canaan, who fled to the tent of Jael, the wife of Heber the Kenite. She encouraged him to come in then killed him by nailing a tent peg into his temple.
Judges 4:2; Ezra 2:53

So
1 man/1 reference
King of Egypt approached by Israel's last king, Hoshea, for aid against the Assyrian Empire.
2 Kings 17:4

Socho
(Entwine)
1 man/1 reference
1 Chronicles 4:18

Sodi
(Confidant)
1 man/1 reference
Numbers 13:10

Solomon
(Peaceful)
1 man/306 references
Son of King David and Bath-sheba who became king over Israel and was blessed with wisdom, understanding, wealth, and honor. He dedicated the temple with a prayer and benediction. Had seven hundred wives and three hundred concubines; when he was old, his wives turned his heart away from God and he did evil, building pagan altars and worshipping there.
2 Samuel 5:14

Sopater
(Of a safe father)
1 man/1 reference
Man from Berea and traveling
companion of the apostle Paul.
Acts 20:4

Sophereth
(Scribe)
1 man/2 references
Ezra 2:55

Sosipater
(Of a safe father)
1 man/1 reference
Relative of Paul who lived in Rome,
greeted in the apostle's letter to the
Romans.
Romans 16:21

Sosthenes
(Of safe strength)
2 men/2 references
Notably, chief ruler of the synagogue
at Corinth. Also, coworker of Paul,
named in the greeting of the apostle's
first letter to the Corinthians.
Acts 18:17; 1 Corinthians 1:1

Sotai
(Roving)
1 man/2 references
Ezra 2:55

Stachys
(Head of grain)
1 man/1 reference
Christian acquaintance of the apostle
Paul in Rome.
Romans 16:9

Stephanas
1 man/3 refernces
Corinthian Christian whose
household, the first converts in
Achaia, was baptized by Paul.
1 Corinthians 1:16

Stephen
(Wreathe)
1 man/7 references
Man of the Jewish church ordained
to care for the physical needs of
church members. He was accused of
blasphemy and, after witnessing to
the Jewish council, was stoned by an
angry mob that included Saul.
Acts 6:5

Suah
(Wipe away)
1 man/1 reference
1 Chronicles 7:36

Susanna
(Lily)
1 woman/1 reference
Woman who followed Jesus and
provided for His financial needs.
Luke 8:3

Susi
(Horselike)
1 man/1 reference
Numbers 13:11

Syntyche
(Accident)
1 woman/1 reference
Christian woman of Philippi who had
conflict with another church member,
Euodias.
Philippians 4:2

T

Tabbaoth
(Rings)
1 man/2 references
Ezra 2:43

Tabeal
(Pleasing to God)
1 man/1 reference
Father of a man whom Syria and
Israel wanted to make king over
Judah in Ahaz's place.
Isaiah 7:6

Tabeel
(Pleasing to God)
1 man/1 reference
Man who tried to stop the rebuilding
of Jerusalem's wall.
Ezra 4:7

Tabitha
(The gazelle)
1 woman/2 references
Christian of Joppa who did many
good works. When she died, her
friends called Peter, who raised her
back to life. Same as Dorcas.
Acts 9:36

Tabrimon
(Pleasing to Rimmon)
1 man/1 reference
1 Kings 15:18

Tahan
(Station)
2 men/2 references
Numbers 26:35; 1 Chronicles 7:25

Tahath
(Bottom)
3 men/4 references
1 Chronicles 6:24; 1 Chronicles 7:20;
1 Chronicles 7:20

Tahpenes
1 woman/3 references
Queen of Egypt during the rule
of Solomon and sister-in-law of
Solomon's adversary Hadad the
Edomite.
1 Kings 11:19

Tahrea
(Earth)
1 man/1 reference
1 Chronicles 9:41

Ta lmai
(Ridged)
2 men/6 references
Notably, one of the children of Anak
who was killed after Joshua's death
when Judah battled the Canaanites.
Also, king of Geshur.
Numbers 13:22; 2 Samuel 3:3

Talmon
(Oppressive)
1 man/5 references
1 Chronicles 9:17

Tamah
1 man/1 reference
Nehemiah 7:55

Tamar
(Palm tree)
3 women/22 references
Most notably, daughter of King David
and half sister of Amnon, who raped
her. Her full brother Absalom heard of
it and later had his servants kill Amnon.
Also, daughter-in-law of Jacob. Same
as Thamar. Also, the only daughter of
Absalom, son of King David.
Genesis 38:6; 2 Samuel 13:1; 2 Samuel 14:27

Tanhumeth
(Compassion)
1 man/2 references
2 Kings 25:23

Taphath
(Drop of ointment)
1 woman/1 reference
Daughter of Solomon and the wife of
one of the king's commissary officers.
1 Kings 4:11

Tappuah
(Apple)
1 man/1 reference
1 Chronicles 2:43

Tarea
(Earth)
1 man/1 reference
1 Chronicles 8:35

Tarshish
(Topaz)
2 men/3 references
Notably, one of seven Persian princes
serving under King Ahasuerus.
Genesis 10:4; Esther 1:14

Tartan
1 man/2 references
Assyrian military commander who
conquered the city of Ashdod and
participated in King Sennacherib's
failed attempt to take Jerusalem in
the days of King Hezekiah and the
prophet Isaiah.
2 Kings 18:17

Tatnai
1 man/4 references
Governor who objected to the
rebuilding of Jerusalem's temple and
wrote the Persian king Darius, who
commanded Tatnai to let the work
continue.
Ezra 5:3

Tebah
(Massacre)
1 man/1 reference
Nephew of Abraham.
Genesis 22:24

Tebaliah
(God has dipped)
1 man/1 reference
1 Chronicles 26:11

Tehinnah
(Graciousness)
1 man/1 reference
1 Chronicles 4:12

Tekoa
(Trumpet)
1 man/2 references
1 Chronicles 2:24

Telah
(Breach)
1 man/1 reference
1 Chronicles 7:25

Telem
(Oppression)
1 man/1 reference
Ezra 10:24

Tema
1 man/4 references
Genesis 25:15

Teman
(South)
1 man/5 references
Genesis 36:11

Temeni
(South)
1 man/1 reference
1 Chronicles 4:6

Terah
1 man/11 references
Father of Abram (Abraham), Nahor,
and Haran.
Genesis 11:24

Teresh
1 man/2 references
One of two palace doorkeepers who
conspired to kill their king, Ahasuerus
of Persia. The plot was uncovered by
Mordecai, and both were hanged.
Esther 2:21

Tertius
(Third)
1 man/1 reference
Assistant of Paul who wrote down the apostle's message to the Romans.
Romans 16:22

Tertullus
1 man/2 references
Orator from Jerusalem who accused the apostle Paul before the Roman governor in Caesarea.
Acts 24:1

Thaddaeus
1 man/2 references
One of Jesus' twelve disciples, as listed by Matthew and Mark. Matthew mentions that Thaddaeus's surname was Lebbaeus. Called "Judas, the brother of James" in Luke's Gospel and the book of Acts. Same as Judas and Jude.
Matthew 10:3

Thahash
(Antelope)
1 man/1 reference
Genesis 22:24

Thamah
1 man/1 reference
Ezra 2:53

Thamar
(Palm tree)
1 woman/1 reference
Greek form of the name *Tamar*, used in the New Testament.
Matthew 1:3

Thara
1 man/1 reference
Greek form of the name *Terah*, used in the New Testament.
Luke 3:34

Tharshish
(Topaz)
1 man/1 reference
1 Chronicles 7:10

Theophilus
(Friend of God)
1 man/2 references
Otherwise unknown person for whom Luke wrote his Gospel and the book of Acts.
Luke 1:3

Theudas
1 man/1 reference
False Jewish messiah who attracted four hundred people. They scattered when he was killed.
Acts 5:36

Thomas
(The twin)
1 man/12 references
Jesus' disciple who doubted the other disciples' story of seeing Jesus resurrected, not believing until he saw the Master himself.
Matthew 10:3

Tiberius
(Pertaining to the Tiber River)
1 man/1 reference
Roman emperor who was ruling when John the Baptist and Jesus began their ministries.
Luke 3:1

Tibni
(Strawlike)
1 man/3 references
1 Kings 16:21

Tidal
(Fearfulness)
1 man/2 references
"King of nations" in the days of Abraham.
Genesis 14:1

Tiglath-pileser
1 man/3 references
King of Assyria who conquered the land of Naphtali and Galilee and took the Israelites captive. Same as Tilgath-pilneser and possibly Pul.
2 Kings 15:29

Tikvah
(*Cord*)
2 men/2 references
Same as Tikvath.
2 Kings 22:14; Ezra 10:15

Tikvath
(*Cord*)
1 man/1 reference
Same as Tikvah.
2 Chronicles 34:22

Tilgath-pilneser
1 man/3 references
Variant spelling of the name of the Assyrian king Tiglath-pileser.
1 Chronicles 5:6

Tilon
(*Suspension*)
1 man/1 reference
1 Chronicles 4:20

Timaeus
(*Foul*)
1 man/1 reference
Mark 10:46

Timna
(*Restraint*)
1 man/2 women/4 references
Genesis 36:12; Genesis 36:22; 1 Chronicles 1:36

Timnah
(*Restraint*)
1 man/2 references
Genesis 36:40

Timon
(*Valuable*)
1 man/1 reference
One of seven men selected to serve needy Christians in Jerusalem.
Acts 6:5

Timotheus
(*Dear to God*)
1 man/18 references
Alternative name for Timothy, the apostle Paul's coworker.
Acts 16:1

Timothy
(*Dear to God*)
1 man/8 references
Coworker of the apostle Paul and young pastor who was like a son to him. His name is joined with Paul's in the introductory greetings of 2 Corinthians and Philemon, and Paul also wrote two epistles of guidance to him.
2 Corinthians 1:1

Tiras
(*Fearful*)
1 man/2 references
Genesis 10:2

Tirhakah
1 man/2 references
King of Ethiopia in the time of Judah's king Hezekiah.
2 Kings 19:9

Tirhanah
1 man/1 reference
1 Chronicles 2:48

Tiria
(*Fearful*)
1 man/1 reference
1 Chronicles 4:16

Tirshatha
1 man/5 references
Title of the governor of Judea, used to describe Nehemiah.
Ezra 2:63

Tirzah
(Delightsomeness)
1 woman/4 references
One of five daughters of Zelophehad, who inherited their father's land, a right normally reserved for sons.
Numbers 26:33

Titus
1 man/14 references
The apostle Paul's highly trusted Greek coworker who traveled with him and whom Paul sent to Corinth with a letter of rebuke for the church. When Titus was in Crete, Paul wrote him an epistle on church leadership.
2 Corinthians 2:13

Toah
(To depress)
1 man/1 reference
Same as Tohu.
1 Chronicles 6:34

Tob-adonijah
(Pleasing to Adonijah)
1 man/1 reference
Levite sent by King Jehoshaphat to teach the law of the Lord throughout the nation of Judah.
2 Chronicles 17:8

Tobiah
(Goodness of Jehovah)
2 men/15 references
Notably, Ammonite who resisted the rebuilding of Jerusalem under Governor Nehemiah.
Ezra 2:60; Nehemiah 2:10

Tobijah
(Goodness of Jehovah)
2 men/3 references
Notably, Levite sent by King Jehoshaphat to teach the law of the Lord throughout the nation of Judah.
2 Chronicles 17:8; Zechariah 6:10

Togarmah
1 man/4 references
Genesis 10:3

Tohu
(Abasement)
1 man/1 reference
Same as Toah.
1 Samuel 1:1

Toi
(Error)
1 man/3 references
King of Hamath who sent congratulations and gifts to King David for defeating Toi's enemy Hadadezer. Same as Tou.
2 Samuel 8:9

Tola
(Worm)
2 men/6 references
Notably, seventh judge of Israel who led the nation for twenty-three years.
Genesis 46:13; Judges 10:1

Tou
(Error)
1 man/2 references
Variant spelling of the name of the Assyrian king Toi.
1 Chronicles 18:9

Trophimus
(Nutritive)
1 man/3 references
Gentile believer and coworker of the apostle Paul.
Acts 20:4

Tryphena
(Luxurious)
1 woman/1 reference
Christian woman in Rome
commended by the apostle Paul.
Romans 16:12

Tryphosa
(Luxuriating)
1 woman/1 reference
Christian woman in Rome
commended by the apostle Paul.
Romans 16:12

Tubal
1 man/2 references
Genesis 10:2

Tubal-cain
(Offspring of Cain)
1 man/2 references
First recorded metalworker in the
Bible.
Genesis 4:22

Tychicus
(Fortunate)
1 man/7 references
Asian coworker of Paul who
accompanied him to Macedonia. Also
sent on missions to the Ephesians and
Colossians and perhaps to Crete.
Acts 20:4

Tyrannus
(Tyrant)
1 man/1 reference
Ephesian teacher who allowed the
apostle Paul to debate Christianity in
his school.
Acts 19:9

U

Ucal
(Devoured)
1 man/1 reference
Man to whom Agur spoke the words
of Proverbs 30.
Proverbs 30:1

Uel
(Wish of God)
1 man/1 reference
Ezra 10:34

Ulam
(Solitary)
2 men/4 references
1 Chronicles 7:16; 1 Chronicles 8:39

Ulla
(Burden)
1 man/1 reference
1 Chronicles 7:39

Unni
(Afflicted)
2 men/3 references
Notably, Levite musician who
performed in celebration when
King David brought the ark of the
covenant to Jerusalem.
1 Chronicles 15:18; Nehemiah 12:9

Ur
(Flame)
1 man/1 reference
1 Chronicles 11:35

Urbane
(Of the city)
1 man/1 reference
Christian acquaintance of the apostle
Paul in Rome.
Romans 16:9

Uri
(Fiery)
3 men/8 references
Exodus 31:2; 1 Kings 4:19; Ezra 10:24

Uriah
(Flame of God)
3 men/28 references
Most notably, called Uriah the
Hittite, Bath-sheba's first husband
and a warrior in King David's army.
On King David's orders, he was killed
in battle, to hide the king's sin of
adultery. Same as Urias.
2 Samuel 11:3; Ezra 8:33; Isaiah 8:2

Urias
(Flame of God)
1 man/1 reference
Greek form of the name *Uriah*,
used in the New Testament. Same as
Uriah.
Matthew 1:6

Uriel
(Flame of God)
2 men/4 references
One of a group of Levites appointed
by King David to bring the ark of
the covenant from the house of
Obededom to Jerusalem.
1 Chronicles 6:24; 2 Chronicles 13:2

Urijah
(Flame of God)
4 men/11 references
Priest who followed King Ahaz's
command to build a pagan altar as
a place of worship. Also, priest who
assisted Ezra in reading the book of
the law to the people of Jerusalem.
Also, faithful prophet executed by
King Jehoiakim of Judah.
2 Kings 16:10; Nehemiah 3:4; Nehemiah
8:4; Jeremiah 26:20

Uthai
(Succoring)
2 men/2 references
1 Chronicles 9:4; Ezra 8:14

Uz
(Consultation)
2 men/4 references
Genesis 10:23; Genesis 36:28

Uzai
(Strong)
1 man/1 reference
Nehemiah 3:25

Uzal
1 man/2 references
Genesis 10:27

Uzza
(Strength)
4 men/8 references
Most notably, man who drove the
cart in which the ark of the covenant
was transported. The oxen stumbled,
and Uzza reached out to steady the
ark. God killed him for daring to
touch the holy object. Same as Uzzah.
1 Chronicles 6:29; 1 Chronicles 8:7;
1 Chronicles 13:7; Ezra 2:49

Uzzah
(Strength)
1 man/4 references
A variant spelling of the name *Uzza*.
Same as Uzza.
2 Samuel 6:3

Uzzi
(Forceful)
6 men/11 references
Most notably, overseer of the Levites
after their return from exile. Also, priest
who helped to dedicate the rebuilt walls
of Jerusalem by giving thanks.
1 Chronicles 6:5; 1 Chronicles 7:2;
1 Chronicles 7:7; 1 Chronicles 9:8;
Nehemiah 11:22; Nehemiah 12:19

Uzzia
(Strength of God)
1 man/1 reference
One of King David's valiant warriors.
1 Chronicles 11:44

Uzziah
(Strength of God)
5 men/27 references
Son of Amaziah, king of Judah who obeyed God. In his power, he became proud and wrongly burned incense on the temple's incense altar, resulting in God striking him with leprosy. Same as Azariah.
2 Kings 15:13; 1 Chronicles 6:24;
1 Chronicles 27:25; Ezra 10:21;
Nehemiah 11:4

Uzziel
(Strength of God)
6 men/16 references
Most notably, army captain under King Hezekiah of Judah.
Exodus 6:18; 1 Chronicles 4:42;
1 Chronicles 7:7; 1 Chronicles 25:4;
2 Chronicles 29:14; Nehemiah 3:8

V

Vajezatha
1 man/1 reference
Esther 9:9

Vaniah
(God has answered)
1 man/1 reference
Ezra 10:36

Vashni
(Weak)
1 man/1 reference
Firstborn son of the prophet Samuel who served as a judge in Beersheba. His poor character caused Israel's

leaders to ask Samuel for a king to rule over them. Same as Joel.
1 Chronicles 6:28

Vashti
1 woman/10 references
Queen of the Persian king who refused to appear at his banquet. The king revoked her position and had no more to do with her.
Esther 1:9

Vophsi
(Additional)
1 man/1 reference
Numbers 13:14

Z

Zaavan
(Disquiet)
1 man/1 reference
Genesis 36:27

Zabad
(Giver)
7 men/8 references
Most notably, one of King David's valiant warriors. Also, one of two royal officials who conspired to kill Judah's king Joash.
1 Chronicles 2:36; 1 Chronicles 7:21;
1 Chronicles 11:41; 2 Chronicles 24:26;
Ezra 10:27; Ezra 10:33; Ezra 10:43

Zabbai
(Pure)
2 men/2 references
Ezra 10:28; Nehemiah 3:20

Zabbud
(Given)
1 man/1 reference
Ezra 8:14

Zabdi
(Giving)
4 men/6 references
Most notably, man in charge of the grapes for King David's wine cellars.
Joshua 7:1; 1 Chronicles 8:19; 1 Chronicles 27:27; Nehemiah 11:17

Zabdiel
(Gift of God)
2 men/2 references
Notably, overseer of the priests who served following the exiles' return to Jerusalem.
1 Chronicles 27:2; Nehemiah 11:14

Zabud
(Given)
1 man/1 reference
Principal officer of King Solomon's court and a friend of the king.
1 Kings 4:5

Zaccai
(Pure)
1 man/2 references
Ezra 2:9

Zacchaeus
(Pure)
1 man/3 references
Wealthy chief tax collector who climbed a tree so he could see Jesus, then repented and promised he would give half his goods to the poor and repay fourfold anyone he had wronged.
Luke 19:2

Zacchur
(Mindful)
1 man/1 reference
1 Chronicles 4:26

Zaccur
(Mindful)
6 men/8 references
Most notably, rebuilder of the walls of Jerusalem under Nehemiah. Also, Levite who renewed the covenant under Nehemiah. Also, one of the temple treasurers appointed by Nehemiah.
Numbers 13:4; 1 Chronicles 24:27; 1 Chronicles 25:2; Nehemiah 3:2; Nehemiah 10:12; Nehemiah 13:13

Zachariah
(God has remembered)
2 men/4 references
Notably, son of King Jeroboam of Israel who reigned over Israel for six months before he was killed by the conspirator Shallum.
2 Kings 14:29; 2 Kings 18:2

Zacharias
(God has remembered)
2 men/11 references
Most notably, priest who received a vision that his barren wife would bear a child who would be great before the Lord—John the Baptist. When he doubted, he was struck dumb until the birth of the child. Also, a man, possibly a prophet, mentioned by Jesus. He was killed between the sanctuary and the altar.
Matthew 23:35; Luke 1:5

Zacher
(Memento)
1 man/1 reference
Chief of the tribe of Benjamin who lived in Jerusalem.
1 Chronicles 8:31

Zadok
(Just)
9 men/53 references
Most notably, priest during King David's reign who consecrated Levites to bring the ark of the covenant into

Jerusalem, anointed Solomon king and was later made high priest. Also, young soldier who helped to crown David king of Judah in Hebron. Also, man who repaired Jerusalem's walls under Nehemiah. Also, Jewish leader who renewed the covenant under Nehemiah. Also, priest who resettled Jerusalem following the Babylonian Exile. Also, temple treasurer appointed by Nehemiah.
2 Samuel 8:17; 2 Kings 15:33; 1 Chronicles 6:12; 1 Chronicles 12:28; Nehemiah 3:4; Nehemiah 3:29; Nehemiah 10:21; Nehemiah 11:11; Nehemiah 13:13

Zaham
(Loathing)
1 man/1 reference
Son of Judah's king Rehoboam and a grandson of Solomon.
2 Chronicles 11:19

Zalaph
1 man/1 reference
Nehemiah 3:30

Zalmon
(Shady)
1 man/1 reference
One of King David's mightiest warriors known as "the thirty."
2 Samuel 23:28

Zalmunna
(Shade has been denied)
1 man/12 references
Midianite king whom Gideon pursued and killed after Zalmunna killed Gideon's brothers at Tabor.
Judges 8:5

Zanoah
(Rejected)
1 man/1 reference
1 Chronicles 4:18

Zaphnath-paaneah
1 man/1 reference
Name the Egyptian pharaoh gave to Joseph, the revealer of dreams.
Genesis 41:45

Zara
(Rising)
1 man/1 reference
Greek form of the name *Zarah*, used in the New Testament.
Matthew 1:3

Zarah
(Rising)
1 man/ 2 references
Twin born to Jacob's son Judah and Judah's daughter-in-law Tamar.
Genesis 38:30

Zatthu
1 man/1 reference
Jewish leader who renewed the covenant under Nehemiah.
Nehemiah 10:14

Zattu
1 man/3 references
Ezra 2:8

Zavan
(Disquiet)
1 man/1 reference
1 Chronicles 1:42

Zaza
(Prominent)
1 man/1 reference
1 Chronicles 2:33

Zebadiah
(God has given)
9 men/9 references
Most notably, "mighty man" who supported the future king David during his conflict with Saul. Also,

one of King David's captains of thousands. Also, Levite sent by King Jehoshaphat to teach the law of the Lord throughout the nation of Judah. Also, "ruler of the house of Judah" who was in charge of King Jehoshaphat's household. Also, Jewish exile who returned from Babylon to Judah under Ezra.
1 Chronicles 8:15; 1 Chronicles 8:17; 1 Chronicles 12:7; 1 Chronicles 26:2; 1 Chronicles 27:7; 2 Chronicles 17:8; 2 Chronicles 19:11; Ezra 8:8; Ezra 10:20

Zebah
(Sacrifice)
1 man/12 references
Midianite king whom Gideon pursued—and killed—with three hundred men after Zebah killed Gideon's brothers at Tabor.
Judges 8:5

Zebedee
(Giving)
1 man/12 references
Father of Jesus' disciples James and John and a fisherman on the Sea of Galilee. His sons worked with him until they left to follow Jesus.
Matthew 4:21

Zebina
(Gainfulness)
1 man/1 reference
Ezra 10:43

Zebudah
(Gainfulness)
1 woman/1 reference
Mother of the evil Jehoiakim, the third-to-last king of Judah.
2 Kings 23:36

Zebul
(Dwelling)
1 man/6 references
Ruler of the city of Shechem under King Abimelech.
Judges 9:28

Zebulun
(Habitation)
1 man/6 references
Sixth and last son of Jacob and Leah.
Genesis 30:20

Zechariah
(God has remembered)
27 men/39 references
Most notably, Old Testament minor prophet who ministered in Jerusalem following the return from exile. Also, Levite who was chosen by lot to guard the west side of the house of the Lord. Also, prince of Judah sent by King Jehoshaphat to teach the law of the Lord throughout the nation. Also, prophet who influenced King Uzziah of Judah. Also, temple ruler during the reign of King Josiah of Judah. Also, Jewish exile charged with finding Levites and temple servants to travel to Jerusalem with Ezra.
1 Chronicles 5:7; 1 Chronicles 9:21; 1 Chronicles 9:37; 1 Chronicles 15:18; 1 Chronicles 15:24; 1 Chronicles 24:25; 1 Chronicles 26:11; 1 Chronicles 27:21; 2 Chronicles 17:7; 2 Chronicles 20:14; 2 Chronicles 21:2; 2 Chronicles 24:20; 2 Chronicles 26:5; 2 Chronicles 29:13; 2 Chronicles 34:12; 2 Chronicles 35:8; Ezra 5:1; Ezra 8:3; Ezra 8:11; Ezra 10:26; Nehemiah 8:4; Nehemiah 11:4; Nehemiah 11:5; Nehemiah 11:12; Nehemiah 12:16; Nehemiah 12:35; Isaiah 8:2

Zedekiah
(Right of God)
5 men/62 references
Most notably, originally named

Mattaniah, he was a brother of King Jehoiachin of Judah. Nebuchadnezzar, king of Babylon, conquered Judah, deposed Jehoiachin, renamed Mattaniah as Zedekiah, and made him king. He rebelled against Babylon and did not heed the prophet Jeremiah. Also, false prophet who predicted that King Jehoshaphat of Judah would win over the Syrians. Also, false prophet aganist whom Jeremiah spoke after Judah went into captivity.
1 Kings 22:11; 2 Kings 24:17; 1 Chronicles 3:16; Jeremiah 29:21; Jeremiah 36:12

Zeeb
(Wolf)
1 man/6 references
Midianite prince captured and killed by the men of Ephraim under Gideon's command.
Judges 7:25

Zelek
(Fissure)
1 man/2 references
One of King David's valiant warriors.
2 Samuel 23:37

Zelophehad
(United)
1 man/11 references
Descendant of Joseph through Manasseh who died during the wilderness wanderings. His five daughters asked Moses if they could inherit their father's property in the Promised Land, a right normally reserved for sons. God ruled that they should, since he had no sons.
Numbers 26:33

Zelotes
(Zealot)
1 man/2 references
Surname of Simon, one of Jesus' twelve disciples.
Luke 6:15

Zemira
(Song)
1 man/1 reference
1 Chronicles 7:8

Zenas
(Jove-given)
1 man/1 reference
Lawyer whom the apostle Paul encouraged Titus to help on a journey.
Titus 3:13

Zephaniah
(God has secreted)
4 men/10 references
Most notably, second priest in the temple whom King Zedekiah sent to the prophet Jeremiah, asking him to pray for Israel.
2 Kings 25:18; 1 Chronicles 6:36; Zephaniah 1:1; Zechariah 6:10

Zephi
(Observant)
1 man/1 reference
1 Chronicles 1:36

Zepho
(Observant)
1 man/2 references
Genesis 36:11

Zephon
(Watchtower)
1 man/1 reference
Numbers 26:15

Zerah
(Rising)
7 men/19 references
Most notably, grandson of Jacob, born to Jacob's son Judah and Judah's daughter-in-law Tamar. Also, Ethiopian commander whose army fled before King Asa of Judah.
Genesis 36:13; Genesis 36:33; Numbers 26:13; Numbers 26:20; 1 Chronicles 6:21; 1 Chronicles 6:41; 2 Chronicles 14:9

Zerahiah
(God has risen)
2 men/5 references
Notably, priest through the line of Aaron.
1 Chronicles 6:6; Ezra 8:4

Zeresh
1 woman/4 references
Wife of Haman, the villain of the story of Esther. She and her friends encouraged Haman to build a gallows on which to hang Esther's cousin Mordecai—the gallows that Haman himself would later die on.
Esther 5:10

Zereth
(Splendor)
1 man/1 reference
1 Chronicles 4:7

Zeri
(Distillation)
1 man/1 reference
1 Chronicles 25:3

Zeror
(Parcel)
1 man/1 reference
1 Samuel 9:1

Zeruah
1 woman/1 reference
Widow and the mother of Jeroboam, who became the first king of the northern Jewish nation of Israel.
1 Kings 11:26

Zerubbabel
(Descended of Babylon)
1 man/22 references
Governor of Judah who returned from the Babylonian Exile with many Israelites in his train. He rebuilt an altar so Judah could worship for the Feast of Tabernacles and obeyed the words God spoke through Haggai.
1 Chronicles 3:19

Zeruiah
(Wounded)
1 woman/26 references
Sister of King David and mother of David's battle commander, Joab, and his brothers, Abishai and Asahel.
1 Samuel 26:6

Zetham
(Olive)
1 man/2 references
Chief Levite during King David's reign, in charge of the temple treasures.
1 Chronicles 23:8

Zethan
(Olive)
1 man/1 reference
1 Chronicles 7:10

Zethar
1 man/1 reference
Eunuch serving the Persian king Ahasuerus in Esther's time.
Esther 1:10

Zia
(Agitation)
1 man/1 reference
1 Chronicles 5:13

Ziba
(Station)
1 man/16 references
Servant of King Saul who told King
David where Mephibosheth lived
after David took the throne and also
brought food and the news that his
master sought to take David's throne.
2 Samuel 9:2

Zibeon
(Variegated)
2 men/8 references
Genesis 36:2; Genesis 36:20

Zibia
(Gazelle)
1 man/1 reference
1 Chronicles 8:9

Zibiah
(Gazelle)
1 woman/2 references
Mother of Joash, good king of Judah.
2 Kings 12:1

Zichri
(Memorable)
12 men/12 references
Most notably, brother of Korah, who
rebelled against Moses and was killed
by God. Also, chief of the tribe of
Benjamin who lived in Jerusalem.
Also, mighty man of valor who served
King Jehoshaphat of Judah. Also,
captain of hundreds who made a
covenant with the priest Jehoiada.
Also, "a mighty man of Ephraim."
Exodus 6:21; 1 Chronicles 8:19;
1 Chronicles 8:23; 1 Chronicles 8:27;
1 Chronicles 9:15; 1 Chronicles 26:25;

1 Chronicles 27:16; 2 Chronicles 17:16;
2 Chronicles 23:1; 2 Chronicles 28:7;
Nehemiah 11:9; Nehemiah 12:17

Zidkijah
(Right of God)
1 man/1 reference
Israelite who renewed the covenant
under Nehemiah.
Nehemiah 10:1

Zidon
(Fishery)
1 man/1 reference
1 Chronicles 1:13

Ziha
(Drought)
2 men/3 references
Notably, official over the temple
servants after the Babylonian Exile.
Ezra 2:43; Nehemiah 11:21

Zillah
(Shade)
1 woman/3 references
Second wife of Lamech, a descendant
of Cain. Her son was Tubal-cain.
Genesis 4:19

Zilpah
(Trickle)
1 woman/7 references
Servant of Leah whom Leah gave to
her husband, Jacob, as a wife because
she thought her own childbearing
days were ended. Bore two sons, Gad
and Asher.
Genesis 29:24

Zilthai
(Shady)
2 men/2 references
Notably, one of a group of "mighty
men of valour" who fought for King
David.
1 Chronicles 8:20; 1 Chronicles 12:20

Zimmah
(Lewdness)
3 men/3 references
1 Chronicles 6:20; 1 Chronicles 6:42;
2 Chronicles 29:12

Zimran
(Musical)
1 man/2 references
Son of Abraham by his second wife,
Keturah.
Genesis 25:2

Zimri
(Musical)
4 men/14 references
Notably, king of Israel who conspired
against King Elah and killed him and
his relatives, fulfilling the prophecy
of Jehu. Zimri reigned for seven days.
Also, man killed by Phinehas for
blatant sexual sin.
Numbers 25:14; 1 Kings 16:9; 1 Chronicles
2:6; 1 Chronicles 8:36

Zina
(Well fed)
1 man/1 reference
Levite who was part of David's
reorganization of the Levites. Same as
Zizah.
1 Chronicles 23:10

Ziph
(Flowing)
2 men/2 references
1 Chronicles 2:42; 1 Chronicles 4:16

Ziphah
(Flowing)
1 man/1reference
1 Chronicles 4:16

Ziphion
(Watchtower)
1 man/1 reference
Genesis 46:16

Zippor
(Little bird)
1 man/7 references
Father of the Moabite king Balak,
who consulted the false prophet
Balaam.
Numbers 22:2

Zipporah
(Bird)
1 woman/3 references
Daughter of the Midianite priest
Reuel (also known as Jethro) and wife
of Moses.
Exodus 2:21

Zithri
(Protective)
1 man/1 reference
Exodus 6:22

Ziza
(Prominence)
2 men/2 references
Notably, son of Judah's king
Rehoboam and a grandson of
Solomon.
1 Chronicles 4:37; 2 Chronicles 11:20

Zizah
(Prominence)
1 man/1 reference
Levite who was part of David's
reorganization of the Levites. Same
as Zina.
1 Chronicles 23:11

Zobebah
(Canopy)
1 woman/1 reference
Daughter of Coz, a descendant of
Abraham through Jacob's son Judah.
1 Chronicles 4:8

Zohar
(Whiteness)
2 men/4 references
Father of Ephron, who sold Abraham
a burial place. Also, grandson of Jacob
through his son Simeon.
Genesis 23:8; Genesis 46:10

Zoheth
1 man/1 reference
1 Chronicles 4:20

Zophah
(Breadth)
1 man/2 references
1 Chronicles 7:35

Zophai
(Honeycomb)
1 man/1 reference
1 Chronicles 6:26

Zophar
(Departing)
1 man/4 references
One of three friends of Job who
mourned his losses for a week and
then accused him of wrongdoing. He
was ultimately chastised by God for
criticizing Job.
Job 2:11

Zorobabel
(Descended of Babylon)
1 man/3 references
Matthew 1:12

Zuar
(Small)
1 man/5 references
Numbers 1:8

Zuph
(Honeycomb)
1 man/2 references
1 Samuel 1:1

Zur
(Rock)
2 men/5 references
Notably, Midianite king killed by the
Israelites at God's command.
Numbers 25:15; 1 Chronicles 8:30

Zuriel
(Rock of God)
1 man/1 reference
Chief of the Levites under Eleazar.
Numbers 3:35

Zurishaddai
(Rock of the Almighty)
1 man/5 references
Numbers 1:6

Archaeological Evidences
for the Bible

The Bible describes many ancient cities, peoples, kings, battles, customs, and everyday objects—and archaeology helps bring these past things to light. Archaeology overwhelmingly supports the biblical record, sometimes down to the minutest details. Time and again, when critics have called scripture's statements into question, new discoveries have confirmed the Bible's truth and accuracy. Several finds in recent years, in fact, have been astonishing.

The places mentioned in God's Word are actual, tangible locations that still exist today—often beneath ancient mounds called *tells*—and one after another, forgotten biblical cities have emerged from the deep shadows of antiquity to yield their secrets to archaeologists. While reading these pages, you'll be amazed at the sheer volume of discoveries, both old and new, confirming the veracity of scripture. From Jerusalem to Khirbet Qeiyafa, from Lachish to Gibeah, ancient cities are overflowing with evidence that the Bible is true.

In addition, excavations of sites such as Ras Shamra, Tell Mardikh, Yorghan Tepe, and Amarna have given religious, historical, and cultural context to biblical statements, and clarified the meanings of obscure Hebrew words.

Not every place mentioned in scripture appears here. The fact is that so much evidence has been unearthed we simply don't have space to list it all. Only the most significant or startling archaeological discoveries are mentioned.

When studying a subject, be sure to look up the "See:" suggestions following the entries. These related topics will often add significant details to your understanding of a topic.

Additional information on many of the people and places in the following section can be found in the "Dictionary/Concordance of Key Bible Names, Places, Terms, and Topics" beginning on page 257 and in the "Complete List of Individuals Named in Scripture" beginning on page 379. An extensive section of maps begins on page 591.

A

Abraham: Originally called Abram, Abraham (2166–1991 BC) immigrated from Ur with his father Terah and his wife Sarah, stayed for some time in Haran, then journeyed south into Canaan at age 75. He dwelt most of his time in Hebron and at Beersheba in the Negev. He was the father of Isaac and grandfather of Jacob. Although Abraham made an indelible impression upon the world of the Bible, he left few tracks behind. He is mentioned in Pharaoh Shishak's commemorative stele, however: after his 925 BC raid on Israel, Shishak referred to a place in the Negev known as "the Enclosure of Abram." (See: Amorites; Beersheba; Haran; Hebrews; Hebron; Negev)

Acco: Acco is identified with modern Tell el Fukhkhar, 14.5 miles (23 km) north of Haifa on the coast of Israel; it was called Ptolemais in New Testament times. Paul visited the Christians there when his ship stopped enroute to Rome (Acts 21:7). During the 200s–100s BC, Acco's Hellenistic harbor was the leading port in Israel. Archaeologists are now excavating its ruins.

Achaia: In New Testament times, southern Greece was a Roman province called Achaia. Paul visited its cities of Athens, Corinth, and Nicopolis (Acts 17:15; 18:1; Titus 3:12). Acts 18:12 (NIV) states that "Gallio was proconsul of Achaia," and critics used to say that the Bible was wrong because governors of imperial provinces were called prefects or procurators. Only rare governors of senatorial provinces were called proconsuls. But in the early 1900s an inscription was found at Delphi in Achaia; it was a copy of a letter by Emperor Claudius to "Lucius Junius Gallio, my friend, and the proconsul of Achaia." (See: Athens; Claudius; Corinth; Greece)

Acropolis: The upper part of a Greek city—especially the Acropolis of Athens. (The Greek word *akropolis* comes from *akros*, highest, and *polis*, city.) Athens's Acropolis was filled with temples such as the Parthenon (the temple of Athena) and the Sanctuary of Zeus, as well as many statues and idols. The ruins of the Athenian Acropolis are still visible today. (See: Athens; Idols; Zeus)

Aelia Capitolina: The Romans destroyed Jerusalem in AD 70, and in AD 130 when Emperor Hadrian decided to rebuild it, he made the city a Roman colony with a temple to Jupiter (Zeus), and renamed it Aelia Capitolina. This was the main reason for the Bar Kochba Revolt (AD 132–136). Many Roman archeological finds—such as coins, pottery, bronze figures, as well as tiles and bricks bearing the stamp *Colonia Aelia Capitolina*—have been unearthed in the southwest corner of Jerusalem. (See: Bar Kochba Letters; Jerusalem; Zeus)

Agora: The agora was the center of every Greek city; *agora* means "marketplace," and Luke uses this word in Acts 16:19 and 17:17. The agora was a central square flanked by the city hall, court house, and temples; it served as the civic center. Thus, Luke writes that the Philippians "seized Paul and Silas and dragged them into the marketplace to face the authorities" (Acts 16:19 NIV). The agora also contained shops and booths of every kind—hence it was the "marketplace." Third, it was the social center where people gathered to talk. When Paul was in Athens, "he reasoned. . .in the marketplace day by day with those who happened to be there" (Acts 17:17 NIV). The agora of Athens, where Paul preached, has been extensively excavated since 1931.

Ahab: Omri founded the city of Samaria (1 Kings 16:23–24) and his son Ahab (874–853 BC) expanded it. The Bible describes a "palace. . .adorned with ivory" that Ahab built (1 Kings 22:39 NIV). When excavating this palace area, archaeologists discovered large quantities of ivory plaques and fragments (more than 200 in all) inscribed in Phoenician or Egyptian style; some have Hebrew script on them. (See: Samaria; Samaria Ostraca)

The Kurkh Monolith Inscription, discovered in 1861, a record of the Assyrian king Shalmaneser III, provides extra-biblical information listing "Ahab, the Israelite" as one of twelve kings who fought against the Assyrians in the Battle of Qarqar in 853 BC. Assyrian records state that Ahab supplied 10,000 soldiers and 2,000 chariots—more chariots than any other king contributed. Ahab did have many horses: The large stables in Megiddo, once thought to have been built by Solomon, actually date to Ahab's time. (See: Aram; Shalmaneser)

Ahab sealed a treaty with King Ethbaal of Sidon by marrying Jezebel, his daughter (1 Kings 16:29–33). Ancient Canaanite texts from Ugarit give detailed descriptions of Baal and Asherah, whose worship Jezebel aggressively promoted in Israel (1 Kings 18:18–19). (See: Asherah; Baal; Ugarit)

Ai: In Hebrew, *Ai* means "the Ruin," and thus far it has been an elusive archeological site. The Bible indicates Ai's location, saying that it "is beside Beth Aven, on the east side of Bethel" (Joshua 7:2 NKJV). Though archeologists have excavated sites such as Et-Tell, Beitin, and Bireh, none of these were inhabited at the time of Ai's conquest in 1406 BC. Joshua 7:3 and 10:2 specify that it had few inhabitants. Perhaps it was already in ruins in Joshua's day (as Et-Tell was) and Canaanites simply retreated behind its massive walls in times of trouble. Or perhaps Ai is a yet-undiscovered site. (See: Conquest of Canaan)

Akhenaton: Akhenaton was the Pharaoh (1374–1358 BC) who banned the worship of all other Egyptian gods and enforced sole worship of Aten, the sun-god. He built Akhetaten (modern Amarna), a city dedicated to Aten, and moved Egypt's capitol there. His preoccupation with his religious revolution caused him to ignore turmoil in Canaan, where vassal kings repeatedly begged for help against the attacking Hebrews. Akhetaten was abandoned after Akhenaton's death. (See: Amarna Tablets; Egypt; Habiru)

Akkad: Akkad, mentioned in Genesis 10:10, was a very ancient Mesopotamian city. There are numerous references to it in non-biblical sources, but the city itself has never been found. It could be one of any number of nondescript mounds that dot the landscape of modern Iraq. Although Akkad itself is lost, its language and cuneiform script dominated the ancient world. Akkadian was widely spoken throughout Mesopotamia from 2800 BC till AD 500. Its cuneiform was developed about 2350 BC, and Canaanites were still using it in the 1350s BC. (See: Amarna Tablets; Mesopotamia)

Alexandria: This seaport on the northwest Nile delta was founded by Alexander the Great in 332 BC. It was much praised for its architecture and its famous Pharos lighthouse. Alexandria's large grain-ships carried tons of Egyptian wheat to Rome (Acts 27:6, 38; 28:11). Alexandria was especially celebrated for its great university and its library, which contained more scrolls and books than any other city on earth. The Hebrew scriptures were translated into Greek (in a version called the Septuagint) in Alexandria. Apollos, a Jew from that city was "an eloquent man and mighty in the Scriptures" (Acts 18:24 NKJV). There was a large Jewish population there; they had their own quarter and were ruled by their own ethnarch (governor). According to tradition, Mark carried the Gospel to Alexandria.

The city's ruins have much to tell us, but archaeological excavations have been hindered by the fact that the modern city and the sea completely cover the ancient site. (See: Egypt; Grecian Empire)

Alphabet: The first writing (3100 BC) was pictographic—drawings of objects. For example, a simple ox-head represented an ox. In Mesopotamia, pictographs eventually morphed into cuneiform marks. Beginning around 2500 BC, in the city of Ebla north

of Canaan, scribes converted cuneiform marks into phonetic symbols. In Egypt, hieroglyphic writing remained in use in formal inscriptions for millennia, but scribes invented a cursive script called hieratic, based upon hieroglyphics, for everyday use. (See: Cuneiform Tablets)

The first actual alphabet, the proto-Sinaitic script (discovered written on rocks near Serabit el-Khadem, an Egyptian mine in the Sinai), dates to 1500 BC. By Moses' day it had spread throughout Sinai, Canaan, and Phoenicia, where it developed into the early Phoenician alphabet, the ancient Canaanite alphabet, and the paleo-Hebrew alphabet. (See: Byblos)

The Izbet Sartah Ostracon is an example of proto-Sinaitic script in the process of becoming the paleo-Hebrew alphabet. This later alphabet was in use from 1100–400 BC, and examples of it are the Gezer Calendar, the Siloam Inscription, the Samaria Ostraca, and the Samaritan alphabet. Then, around 400 BC, the Hebrew alphabet changed. The Jews, who had been writing Aramaic correspondence for decades, began writing Hebrew in the same square-lettered alphabet. This is where modern Hebrew gets it distinctive look.

Hebrew, like most other early alphabets, was actually an abjad, consisting only of consonants. Around AD 600, Masoretic scribes added dots to indicate vowels.

The Greek alphabet developed from the Phoenician script about 800 BC, and was in turn the forerunner of the Latin alphabet (500 BC) and modern Western alphabets.

Altars: In almost every Old Testament reference to *altar*, the word is translated from the Hebrew *mizbeah* which means "place of sacrifice." Some altars, however, were used for burning incense. The patriarchs built altars in several places, but after the temple was built at Jerusalem, the Israelites were forbidden to sacrifice on any other altar (Deuteronomy 12:13–14). However, this didn't stop them from doing so (1 Kings 22:43). Archaeologists have dug up some of these illegal altars. (See: Arad; Elephantine Temple)

The altar in Jerusalem had protuberances on its four corners called "horns" (Ezekiel 43:20; Exodus 29:12). In Megiddo, a limestone altar with four horns was unearthed. Similar altars have been found in Beth Shan, Beersheba, Dan, and Lachish. In addition, God told Moses to build an altar of earth or unhewn stones (Exodus 20:24–25), and an altar discovered at Arad, at an illegal temple there, was made of earth and stones. (See: Beth Shan; Beersheba; Dan; Lachish)

Amarna Tablets: The Amarna Tablets are an archive of 382 clay tablets, discovered in Amarna, Egypt, in 1887. (See: Akhenaten) They are written in Akkadian cuneiform and were sent from foreign kings and vassals in Canaan to Pharaoh; some are Pharaoh's messages to them. The letters were written in the 1350s–1330s BC when the Habiru/Hapiru were still conquering Canaan (Judges 1), and many tablets contain desperate appeals for Egyptian troops. In letter 288, for example, Abdi-Heba, king of Jerusalem, wrote Pharaoh that "the Hapiru have taken the very cities of the king," and warned, "If there are no archers this year, all the lands of the king, my lord, are lost." (See Judges 1:8.) (See: Conquest of Canaan; Habiru)

In the early period of the Judges the Israelites formed alliances with the Canaanites (Judges 2:2–3) and even intermarried with them (Judges 3:5–6). They resorted to a mixture of warfare against, and alliances with, the Canaanites. When they gained the upper hand, they made the Canaanites pay tribute (Judges 1:28). This is the kind of complex situation that the Amarna Tablets describe.

Amenhotep II: Pharaoh Amenhotep II (1454–1419 BC) was the Pharaoh of the Exodus. Egyptian records show that he conducted ambitious foreign military campaigns until the ninth year of his reign. That was 1446 BC, the year of the Exodus. After his chariot armies were destroyed (Exodus 14:27–28), Amenhotep had no more great military exploits. (See: Exodus; Ramesses II)

Ammon, Ammonites: The Ammonites were descendants of Lot, Abraham's nephew (Genesis 19:36–38); they lived in modern-day Jordan, along the Jabbok River. They had some cities, including Rabbah their capital, but for the most part were a semi-nomadic people. They were at times foes of Israel, at times allies (Judges 11:13, 32–33; 1 Samuel 11:1–11; 2 Samuel 10:1–19; 12:26–30).

Digs in the citadel (inner fortress) of Rabbah have uncovered pottery dating as early as the Middle Bronze Age. In 1961, the Amman Citadel Inscription, a stone slab containing eight lines of text, dating to about 850 BC, was discovered; it describes a temple of Molech, one of Ammon's gods. In 1972, another inscription was unearthed which describes Amminadab, a king of Ammon about 600 BC. (See: Bronze Age)

Amorites: Amorites have a long history. They began as desert nomads, but by 2600 BC had swept into northern Mesopotamia. By 2000 BC they had conquered the south. They also settled in Syria and Canaan just before Abraham migrated there, and he was allied with them because they weren't yet depraved (Genesis 14:13; 15:16). Four hundred years later, however, they had become as guilty as the Canaanites—and were almost synonymous with them. The first battles Israel fought in Canaan were against Amorite kingdoms (Numbers 21:21–35). (See: Abraham; Mari; Mesopotamia)

Amphitheaters: These were large open-air structures where gladiatorial fights and games were held. Some 230 of them have been found throughout the Roman Empire. Their oval shape distinguished them from semicircular theaters and the longer circuses (hippodromes). The Coliseum of Rome is the most famous amphitheater still standing. Another famous theater has been excavated in Ephesus; it has 25,000 seats. It is here that a massive crowd rioted against Paul's preaching and shouted for hours (Acts 19:28–29). (See: Ephesus; Rome)

Amulets: An amulet is a gem or ornament worn as a magical charm or to ward off evil. Archaeologists have dug up numerous ornaments shaped like crescent moons or sun discs, worn by women or animals to increase fertility (Judges 8:21). They have also found a gold pendant at Tell el-Ajjul (south of Gaza) with an image of Astarte on it. Amulets were widely worn in the ancient world; only the Israelites had prohibitions against them (Ezekiel 13:18; Isaiah 3:18), although they sometimes wore them, too. (See: Ketef Hinnom Amulets)

Antioch: An important Roman city in northwest Syria, it became a major Christian center (Acts 11:20–26). Paul taught in Antioch and launched his missionary journeys from there (Acts 13:1–4). Little archaeological work has been done, since the modern city of Antakya covers the site. However, the Chalice of Antioch was discovered there in 1910; some consider it to be the Holy Grail, the cup that Christ and His disciples drank from at the Last Supper. Though this is unlikely, it is nevertheless a fascinating artifact from the days of the early church.

Antonia, Tower of: Built by Herod the Great, it was the barracks of the Roman garrison. Its location on the northwest corner of the temple courts gave Roman troops quick access to the temple during riots (Acts 21:34; 22:24). It also contained the lavish royal palace of the Roman governor (John 18:28), who occupied it when visiting from Caesarea. Archaeologists have discovered a paved area in the tower area which was likely the "Pavement" (the Gabbatha) where Jesus was brought before Pilate (John 19:13). (See: Caesarea; Herod; Pilate; Temple, Jewish)

Aqueducts: Roman engineers built water systems on elevated stone arches throughout their empire. Large sections of these structures are still standing, from Rome to Caesarea.

Aqueducts supplied Rome with 267,000,000 gallons of fresh water a day. Herod and Pilate built aqueducts that carried water 15 miles (24 km) from the south to Jerusalem. Ruins of this aqueduct can still be seen in Bethlehem. According to Josephus, Pilate used temple funds to pay for this project, a detail that greatly angered the Jews. (See: Pontius Pilate)

Arabia: In the Bible, Arabia didn't refer to the entire Arabian Peninsula, but to the Sinai Peninsula and lands east of Israel. 2 Chronicles 21:16–17 describes Arabs pillaging Jerusalem. Paul went into Arabia after his conversion (Galatians 1:17). (See: Nabateans)

Arad: Arad was a city in the Negev, some 17 miles (28 km) south of Hebron. More than 100 ostraca written in paleo-Hebrew script were found in Tell Arad, including several from about 650 BC—one of which refers to "the house of YHWH." This isn't referring to the temple in Jerusalem, but to the small, illegal temple that Israeli archaeologists unearthed in Arad in 1962. There is a sacrificial altar and two altars of incense in its courtyard. Personal names that appear in the letters include Pashur and Meremoth (Jeremiah 20:1; Ezra 8:33). (See: Altars; Ostraca)

As Moses and the Israelites were heading north, the army of Arad attacked them (Numbers 21:1–3; 33:40). Some 45 years later, the Israelites conquered Arad (Joshua 12:14), and renamed it Hormah which means "devoted to destruction" (Judges 1:16–17). This is not the same Arad that housed a temple, however. Pharaoh Shishak, after his 925 BC raid,

listed *two* Arads (Arad Rabbat and Arad of Yeruham), and the Arad that confronted the Israelites was likely Tell Malhatah, 7.5 miles (12 km) to the southwest of the first Arad. (See: Negev; Shishak)

Aram, Arameans: The Arameans were nomads, mentioned in texts as early as 2300 BC, who settled in northern Mesopotamia called Padan Aram (Genesis 28:5), during the Late Bronze Age. (See: Hebrews) They are called "Syrians" in the KJV. They later created Aramean kingdoms from the Euphrates to Damascus. An Aramean king of Mesopotamia conquered Israel for eight years and was defeated by Othniel (Judges 3:7–8). Later Saul fought the Arameans of Zobah (1 Samuel 14:47), and David conquered them as far north as the Euphrates (2 Samuel 8:3–8).

The Arameans revolted during Solomon's reign, and in the following centuries were a constant threat to Israel. Ahab was forced to repeatedly battle them (1 Kings 20; 22:29–36). Assyrian records confirm the Bible in a key detail: Ben-Hadad was king of Aram, but Elisha anointed Hazael king, and Hazael then assassinated Ben-Hadad and ruled in his place (2 Kings 8:7–15). An inscription by Shalmaneser III of Assyria says, "I fought with Ben-Hadad. I accomplished his defeat. Hazael, son of a nobody, seized his throne." (See: Ahab; Shalmaneser)

Aramaic: Laban, living in Padan Aram, spoke Aramaic instead of Hebrew (Genesis 31:47). Aramaic was understood throughout the Middle East in Hezekiah's day (2 Kings 18:17–18, 26), and during the times of the Assyrian, Babylonian, and Persian Empires. During the Exile, all the Jews learned it. Portions of Daniel and Ezra were written in Aramaic. By New Testament times, the Jews spoke it in addition to Hebrew and Greek; a number of Jesus' words recorded in the Gospels are in Aramaic. (See: Aram; Bar Kokhba Letters; Exile)

Ararat: Mount Ararat is the name of a mountain in modern Turkey, and it's commonly believed that Noah's Ark is preserved under its snows, but the Bible states: "Then the ark rested. . .on the mountains of Ararat" (Genesis 8:4 NKJV). The *mountains* (plural) of "the land of Ararat" (2 Kings 19:37) are an entire range, so the ark could be in a number of locations.

Archelaus: He was a son of Herod the Great who ruled over Judea (4 BC–AD 6) after Herod's death. He was a weak ruler and was soon replaced with a Roman governor. Numerous coins minted during Archelaus's reign have been unearthed. (See: Herod)

Areopagus: When Paul was in Athens, he "saw that the city was given over to idols" (Acts 17:16 NKJV). Mars' Hill (the Areopagus, or the council called the Areopagus that met there) was a rocky spur to the west of the Acropolis. When Paul told the council that God is not represented by idols, the Acropolis with its temples and idols was in full view. (See: Acropolis)

Artemis: Diana was the Roman name for the Greek goddess Artemis. Her temple in Ephesus was one of the Seven Wonders of the ancient world. Silversmiths created shrines of her temple with Artemis inside (Acts 19:24–25), and archaeologists have found many-breasted statues of her. Inscriptions refer to "Artemis the Great," exactly what the mob shouted in Acts 19:28, 34. (See: Ephesus)

Ashdod: Tell Ashdod, covering 53 acres, has been extensively excavated. It was founded by Canaanites about 1625 BC, but evidence of Philistine occupation goes back to the 1100s BC. A Philistine temple has been found, perhaps the very temple where the Ark of the Covenant was placed (1 Samuel 5:1–5). Ashdod rebelled against Sargon, king of Assyria, in 712 BC (Isaiah 20:1), and fragments of his victory stele have been found in the city. Also discovered was a mass grave of 3,000 people dating to this time, many of them decapitated. (See: Philistines; Sargon)

Asherah: The Ugarit texts describe the goddess Asherah as the consort of El and later Baal, and the Canaanites worshipped her in lascivious rites. She was represented by wooden figurines or poles. The Israelites often turned from the true God (Yahweh) to worship Asherah (Judges 3:7; 1 Kings 18:19), and worshipped her even in the temple of Yahweh (2 Kings 21:7). Sometimes they worshipped them together. An inscription found in Khirbet el-Kom, 8 miles (13 km) west of Hebron, dating to the late 700s BC, reads: "Blessed be Uriyahu by Yahweh and by his Asherah." Three inscriptions found in Kuntillet Ajrud in the Sinai also show that many Israelites worshipped her along with God. (See: Ugarit; Ahab; El)

Ashkelon: This was one of the five cities of the Philistines (Joshua 13:3).

The ancient site, lying beneath modern Asqalon, has been only partially excavated. Ashkelon is mentioned in Egyptian Execration Texts of 1900–1800 BC, in the Amarna Letters of the 1350s–1330s BC, and the Israel Stele of 1209 BC. (See: Berlin Fragment; Israel Stele, Philistines)

Ashtoreth: Ashtoreth was a Canaanite mother-goddess, also known as a goddess of love, fertility, and war. The Israelites worshipped her throughout much of their history (Judges 2:13; 10:6; 1 Samuel 7:3–4; 1 Kings 11:5). (See: Canaan)

Ashur: Situated on the Tigris River, Ashur (Numbers 24:22, 24) was the first capitol of Assyria. Its modern name is Qalaat Sherqat. It was excavated over 100 years ago, and huge volumes of tablets, inscriptions, and pottery came to light there. (See: Assyria; Nineveh)

Ashurbanipal: The final great Assyrian ruler (669–627 BC), Ashurbanipal is mentioned in Ezra 4:10. He is called Asnapper in the KJV. He was a lover of learning, and his library of over 22,000 cuneiform tablets has been unearthed; it is our single greatest source of information about Babylonian and Assyrian literature. Ashurbanipal listed Manasseh king of Judah (2 Kings 21:1) as one of his vassals who supported him in quelling Egyptian uprisings. (See: Assyria; Cuneiform Tablets; Manasseh)

Assyria, Assyrians: The Assyrians existed as a kingdom from 2500 BC, and as an empire 1390–1056 BC. After a period of decline, they ruled a new empire from Persia to south Egypt (911–627 BC). Historians refer to this second phase as the Neo-Assyrian Empire, and it is these cruel aggressors that Judah and Israel had to deal with. Their later and most famous capital was Nineveh. (See: Ashurbanipal; Esarhaddon; Nineveh; Sargon; Shalmaneser; Tiglath-Pileser.)

Athens: This was the capital of ancient Greece, and leading city of the Roman province of Achaia. Paul visited Athens about AD 51 (Acts 17:15). Today, it contains a wealth of archaeological sites that Paul witnessed in New Testament times. (See: Acropolis; Areopagus; Idols)

Augustus, Caesar: Octavian (Caesar Augustus), heir of Julius Caesar, founded the Roman Empire in 30 BC and ruled as Caesar from 27 BC to AD 14. He is mentioned in Luke 2:1 (NKJV), which says that "a decree went out from Caesar Augustus that all the world should be registered"—for purposes of taxation. In the Acts of Augustus (written on two bronze plaques), Caesar stated that he had authorized three empire-wide censuses during this reign. They were in 28 BC, 8 BC, and AD 14. Jesus was born about 6 BC, but very likely it took a couple years for the 8 BC census to be organized and enacted in far off Judea. (See: Roman Empire)

Were all people in the Roman Empire required to travel to their town of birth to register? Very likely it varied from province to province, yet as disruptive as this would have been, it was a requirement in some regions. A Roman census document, dating to AD 104, has been found in Egypt, in which all citizens were ordered to return to their original homes for a census.

Avaris: Avaris, the former capitol of the Hyksos, is presently known as Tell el Dab'a, is in the northeast Nile delta of Egypt. Excavations there have yielded much pottery showing a link with Canaan—as well as numerous Minoan articles, indicating trade with Crete. (See: Goshen; Hyksos)

Azekah: A Canaanite city later occupied by Judeans (Joshua 10:10; 15:20, 35). It survives as Tell ez-Zakariyeh, and extensive archaeological work has yielded much evidence of occupation. It is mentioned in the Lachish Letters. (See: Lachish Letters)

B

Baal: According to the Baal Cycle tablets found at Ugarit, Baal (the storm god) was just under El, the high god. Baal's proper name was Hadad (Thunderer). By 1400 BC, Canaanites considered him the most important god in their pantheon because he supposedly had power over rain, crops, and fertility, and El was seen as distant. Baal was extremely immoral: He not only mated with his own sister, but with a heifer. Each part of Canaan had its own Baal, and Israelites often worshipped these local gods (Judges 2:11–13). Idols of Baal have been dug up in Ugarit, Lachish, and Megiddo. (See: Asherah; Canaan; El; Ugarit)

Babel, Tower of: The city of Babel, "a city, with a tower" (Genesis 11:4), has not been discovered, though it's

believed that the tower was a ziggurat—a temple to the gods of Sumer. The most famous ziggurat was excavated by C. Leonard Woolley in 1924, in the ancient city of Ur. (See: Ur)

Babylon: This was an ancient city on the Euphrates River, and the capital of the later Babylonian Empire. Its ruins are 53 miles (83 km) south of Baghdad. Babylon covered 2,100 acres; had high, amazingly thick walls that stretched for 5.5 miles; and was filled with world-famed palaces and temples. The ancient site has been extensively excavated and has yielded such a wealth of cuneiform tablets and objects that much of it has not yet been properly studied. (See: Belshazzar; Nebuchadnezzar)

Babylonians: The Babylonians have a long history, and what we commonly call the Babylonian Empire (620–539 BC) is known to historians as the Neo-Babylonian Empire. The Babylonians were also known as Chaldeans. (See: Babylon; Belshazzar; Nebuchadnezzar)

Babylonian Chronicles: These are a collection of cuneiform tablets describing events in Babylonia (south Mesopotamia) from 2350–500 BC. They include the Babylonian version of 2 Kings 19:36, and Cyrus taking over Babylon. One tablet, called the Chronicle Concerning the Early Years of Nebuchadnezzar II, says that he "besieged the city of Judah and on the second day of the month of Addaru he seized the city and captured the king [Jehoiachin]. He appointed there a king of his own choice [Zedekiah], received its heavy tribute and sent it to Babylon." This matches perfectly the Bible's statements in 2 Kings 24:8–17. (See: Cyrus; Jehoiachin; Nebuchadnezzar)

Balaam Inscription: During a 1967 excavation, an inscription was found written on a plastered wall in Deir Alla, Jordan. It has been dated to 840–760 BC. It refers to the Balaam of the Bible (Numbers 22–24), as it begins with the words, "The sayings of Balaam, son of Beor, the man who was a seer of the gods." However, rather than receiving his visions from God, in this version, Balaam hears from lesser gods and goddesses. This is the oldest piece of Aramaic literature in existence. (See: Succoth)

Bar Kochba Letters: A Jew named Simon Bar Kochba declared himself the Messiah and led a revolt against Roman rule from AD 132–136. When the rebellion was crushed, Bar Kochba retreated to the Judean wilderness by the Dead Sea. In 1961, Israeli archaeologist Yigael Yadin located his caves and discovered a bundle of papyrus documents—much of them relating to the war—written in Aramaic, Hebrew, and Greek. Since all three languages were equally understood in the AD 130s, we know that they were also understood in Jesus' day. (See: Aelia Capitolina)

Beersheba: Abraham dug a well in this area and camped here; later an Israelite city existed nearby. The ancient site of the city of Beersheba is Tell es-Seba, 1.5 miles (3 km) east of the modern city. Excavations there, beginning in 1969, uncovered an Israelite fortress and Hebrew inscriptions. In 1974, a large

horned altar made of stone was discovered there. (See: Abraham; Negev)

Beit Lehi Inscription: Khirbet Beit Lehi is an archeological site some 37.5 miles (60 km) south of Jerusalem, and was discovered in 1961. Among the finds is an inscription with the oldest-known Hebrew writing of the word "Jerusalem," dated to the 600s BC. The inscription, translated, reads: "I am YHWH your Lord. I will accept the cities of Judah and I will redeem Jerusalem" and "Absolve us, O merciful God. Absolve us, O YHWH."

Belshazzar: The "son" (literally grandson) of Nebuchadnezzar (Daniel 5), he ruled Babylon 556–539 BC. Critics once insisted that Belshazzar was merely a literary invention; however, discoveries such as the Nabonidus Chronicle have confirmed that he was a real person. When King Nabonidus went into self-imposed exile at Tema in the Arabian Desert, he left Belshazzar in Babylon as ruler. This is why Belshazzar offered to make Daniel a "third ruler" of Babylon (Daniel 5:7, 29). (See: Babylon; Nebuchadnezzar)

Berlin Fragment: This fragment of an inscription on a gray granite block, housed in the Egyptian Museum of Berlin, has, on the basis of archaic spellings, been dated to the time of Tuthmosis III (1504–1450 BC). It may be the oldest extrabiblical mention of Israel in existence—even older than the Israel Stele. The words "Ashkelon" and "Canaan" (surrounded by name rings) are clearly visible, and two-thirds of the name-ring for what is most probably "Israel" also appears. (See: Israel Stele)

Bethlehem: Bethlehem means "house of bread," so named because a wide valley to the north was filled with grain fields. In the 1350s BC, a complaint appeared in the Amarna Letters that *Bit-Lahmi* had gone over to the Habiru. The Bethlehem Bulla, discovered in excavations at Jerusalem, is a seal impression with three lines of script. It is a record of taxes on goods sent from Bethlehem to Jerusalem. It dates to the 700s–600s BC and is the earliest Hebrew mention of Bethlehem outside of the Bible. Note: Archaeologists say there were only about 300 people living inside Bethlehem when Jesus was born. (See: Bulla; Habiru)

Beth Shan: The mound of Tell el-Husn (Beth Shan), located 16 miles (25.5 km) south of the Sea of Galilee, has yielded ample proof of Canaanite occupation (Joshua 17:16; Judges 1:27). Four temples have been excavated, including "the temple of the Ashtoreths" where Saul's armor was placed (1 Samuel 31:10) and the "temple of Dagon" where his head was displayed (1 Chronicles 10:10). The Amarna Letters mention Beth Shan as well. (See: Ashtoreth; Dagon)

Beth Shemesh: This city was located 13 miles (21 km) west of Bethlehem. Pottery and weapons from Canaanite and Israelite occupations—and a hoard of jewelry—have been dug up here, as well as objects that show that the city was later occupied by Philistines. This dovetails perfectly with the biblical record (Joshua 19:32–38; 1 Samuel 6:12; 2 Chronicles 28:18). In 2012, an ancient seal the size of a penny was discovered at Beth Shemesh. It depicts a man fighting a lion with his bare hands and likely commemorates the story of Samson killing a lion on the road between Zorah and Timnah—a mere 5 miles away (Judges 13:2; 14:5–6). The seal dates to the 1100s BC. (See: Philistines; Timnah 1)

Black Obelisk: This is a black limestone sculpture, 6.5 feet high, found in Calah (modern Nimrud, in Iraq) in 1846, and now in the British Museum. It describes the deeds of King Shalmaneser III of Assyria. It depicts King Jehu of Israel bowing before him, and lists what he gave as tribute around 840 BC: "The tribute of Iaua mar Hu-umrii [Jehu son of Omri]: I have received from him silver, gold, a bowl of gold, chalices of gold, tumblers of gold, buckets of gold, tin, a scepter for the king, and spears." (Jehu was not a descendant of Omri as the Assyrians supposed; however, he had slain Jehoram the grandson of Omri [1 Kings 16:29; 2 Kings 3:1], and became king in his place [2 Kings 9].) (See: Jehu; Shalmaneser)

Board Games: In Jesus' day, people played board games like checkers and an early form of backgammon. Game boards and pegs have been dug up in Debir, Beth Shemesh, Gezer, and many other sites in Israel. Complex, colorful playing boards with intricate game pieces, dating back to 2600 BC, have been excavated in ancient Ur. (See: Ur)

Bronze Age: The Bronze Age began when people learned how to create tools and weapons out of bronze, a mixture of copper and tin; it occurred in Canaan and the Ancient Near East from 3300–1200 BC. Archaeologists divide it into three periods: the Early Bronze Age (3300–2100 BC); the Middle Bronze Age (2100–1550 BC); and the Late Bronze Age (1550–1200 BC). The patriarchs Abraham, Isaac, and Jacob lived during the Middle Bronze Age. The Israelites were oppressed in Egypt, conquered Canaan, and were ruled by judges during the Late Bronze Age. Saul and David ruled at the end of the Late Bronze Age and the beginning of the Iron Age. (See: Iron Age; Swords)

Bulla: A piece of clay stamped with a seal. After the clay dried, the container that it sealed could not be tampered with without damaging the bulla. This ensured that the vase, money container, or sealed document reached its destination intact. King Ahaz's seal of the 700s BC is one of the most famous bullae. It states: "Belonging to Ahaz, son of Yehotam (Jotham), king of Judah." A fingerprint, probably Ahaz's, appears on the edge of the clay. (See: Seal)

Byblos: A city on the coast of Phoenicia, north of Ugarit, and mentioned in Psalm 83:7 and Ezekiel 27:9 ("Gebal" in the KJV). In 1923, the sarcophagus of Ahiram (died 1000 BC), king of Byblos, was discovered there; on it were 38 words, the earliest surviving example of writing in the Phoenician alphabet. (See: Alphabet; Phoenicia)

C

Caesarea: Herod the Great built Caesarea as a seaport on the north coast of Israel, and named it after Caesar Augustus. Later Roman governors were based there. Herod's seawall, built to enclose a harbor, was an engineering marvel of giant limestone blocks and cement that hardened underwater. Both Philip and Peter preached in Caesarea (Acts 8:40; 10:23–24). The Pilate Stone was discovered there in 1961. (See: Herod; Pontius Pilate)

Caesarea Philippi: This was a Roman city at the base of Mount Hermon, a center for the worship of both Caesar and Pan. The Grotto of Pan still exists, marked by a Greek inscription in the carved niche above. It was in the region of this idolatrous city that Jesus confirmed that He was the unique Son of God (Matthew 16:13–17).

Caiaphas: Caiaphas was the high priest who sat in judgment on Jesus (Matthew 26:57–65). In 2011, archaeologists recovered a stolen ossuary (a small stone box) bearing the inscription: "Miriam, daughter of Yeshua, son of Caiaphas, Priest of Ma'aziah." This may well have been the Caiaphas mentioned in the New Testament. In 1990, the tomb of man named Caiaphas was discovered and excavated; however, the ossuary recovered was plain and the inscription makes no mention that this person was the high priest, so it may have just been another person with the same name. (See: Jesus Christ)

Calf Worship: From Egypt to Babylon, bulls symbolized the most powerful gods. In Canaan, El was referred to as "the heavenly bull." The bull was also the symbol of Baal, a god not only of storms, but of fertility. Aaron made a golden calf to represent God and declared "a festival to the LORD" (Exodus 32:4–5 NIV). Jeroboam instituted calf worship in Israel, at Bethel and Dan. Some scholars believe he intended to show that Yahweh was chief of the gods, but the symbol quickly descended into idol worship (1 Kings 12:28–33). Small statues of bulls have been dug up in Samaria. (See: Baal; Dan; El)

Canaan, Canaanites: Canaan was the son of Ham (Genesis 9:18), and his descendants settled in Canaan, north of the Sinai peninsula, west of the Jordan River, and south of Phoenicia (Genesis 10:15–19). Phoenicians were descended from Canaanites, and thousands of urns containing infants' burned bones have been discovered at Carthage, their colony in North Africa—attesting to child sacrifice in Canaanite religion (see 2 Kings 16:3). Considerable artifacts, structures, and writings have been unearthed in Israel and Lebanon which confirm the Bible's statements about the Canaanites. (See: Asherah; Baal; Tell Kabri)

Capernaum: This was a city on the northwest shore of the Sea of Galilee. Jesus often spoke in the synagogue in Capernaum (Mark 1:21). In 1968, under the ruins of a later synagogue, an earlier synagogue was found; it was 60 feet by 79 feet. In 1981 its black basalt floor was uncovered, and pottery on it dated to the first century AD. Jesus likely stood on that very floor when He taught, cast out demons, healed the sick, and declared, "I am the living bread" (John 6:51, 59 NIV).

Carchemish: Carchemish was a city far to the north of Canaan, to the west of Haran, where, in 605 BC, Nebuchadnezzar defeated Pharaoh Neco. Jeremiah wrote about this event in

Jeremiah 46:2 and evidence of the battle has been found in the ancient city mound. The Babylonian Chronicles also describe the battle. (See: Josiah; Nebuchadnezzar; Neco)

Chemosh, Kemosh: The main god of ancient Moab (Numbers 21:29). As his capital was being besieged, Mesha, king of Moab, sacrificed his son to Kemosh (2 Kings 3:4–5, 26–27), and in the Mesha Stele he gives Kemosh credit for helping him to then win the war. (See: Mesha Stele; Moab)

Chorazin: This city was located on the northern shore of the Sea of Galilee, and covered more than 80 acres. Jesus once said, "The scribes and the Pharisees sit in Moses' seat" (Matthew 23:2 KJV), describing a seat in the synagogue where the Law of Moses was read. In 1926, a "Seat of Moses" carved from basalt was found at the ancient synagogue of Chorazin.

Chronology, Old Testament: Dates that are approximations are followed by a period. All other dates are precise, based on 966 BC as the fourth year of King Solomon's reign.

3300 The Early Bronze Age begins

2250 Ebla is attacked and burned; its tablets are baked in the fire and preserved

2166 Abraham is born

2100 The Middle Bronze Age begins

2066 Isaac is born; Abraham is 100

2065 Sodom and Gomorrah are destroyed

2006 Jacob is born; Isaac is 60 (Genesis 25:26)

1876 Jacob (130) and his family enter Egypt (Genesis 47:9); the

430 years begin

1765   The Code of Hammurabi is inscribed on a stele

1500   The Late Bronze Age begins; the proto-Sinaitic script is invented

1446   The Israelites leave Egypt 430 years after 1876 BC (Exodus 12:40)

1406   The Israelite conquest of Canaan begins after 40 years in the desert

1400   After 6 years of war, Joshua divides the land among the 12 tribes

1390   The Danites need land, so migrate north and conquer Laish (Judges 18:27–29)

1375   Joshua dies at age 110 (Joshua 24:29)

1370   The Israelite tribes wage war against the Benjamites (Judges 20)

1365   Israelites renew war against the Canaanites (Judges 1); conquer Bethel (vs. 22)

1355   Canaanite kings write for help during the 1550s–1330s (see: Amarna Letters)

1209   Pharaoh Merneptah makes a punitive raid against Canaan and Israel

1200   The Iron Age begins in the Ancient Near East

1230   Hazor is burned, most likely by Barak after defeating Sisera's army

1201   Midianite raids begin; Israelites retreat to the central mountains 1200 BC

1190   Pharaoh Setnakhte drives Irsu and the pillaging Asiatics out of Egypt

1180   The Hittite empire collapses as Sea Peoples push south by land and sea

1177   Rameses III repulses Sea Peoples (Philistines), who retreat to Canaan

1100   The paleo-Hebrew alphabet comes into being

1050   Saul's reign begins

1022   David kills Goliath

1010   Saul dies in the Battle of Gilboa; David's reign begins in Hebron

970   David dies; Solomon's reign begins

966   Solomon begins building the temple 480 years after the Exodus (1 Kings 6:1)

950   During the 900s, the Gezer Calendar is written in paleo-Hebrew script

930   Solomon dies; the kingdom divides into Judah and Israel

925   Pharaoh Shishak attacks Jerusalem, going as far north as Megiddo in Israel

886   Omri is declared king; he fights and wins a civil war in Israel

880   Omri founds Samaria

853   Ahab and 12 kings fight Shalmaneser III of Assyria in the Battle of Qarqar

850   Mesha of Moab rebels against Israel (see: Mesha Stone)

841   Jehu of Israel kills Joram, Ahaziah, Jezebel, and all the priests of Baal

840   Jehu sends tribute to Shalmaneser III of Assyria (See: Black Obelisk)

800   The Aramean king Hazael boasts of victory over Israel in the Tel Dan Stele

722   Samaria, the capitol of northern Israel, falls to the Assyrians

701   Sennacherib's army besieges Jerusalem; God slays them; the survivors retreat

605 Nebuchadnezzar defeats Pharaoh

Neco at the Battle of Carchemish; he marches south to Judea; he deports some Israelites to Babylon, including Daniel

597   A second deportation: King Jehoiachin, Ezekiel, and others taken to Babylon

586   Jerusalem is destroyed by Nebuchadnezzar; final deportation

539   Cyrus issues a decree that captive peoples can return to their homelands

536   The Jews in Jerusalem start to rebuild God's temple

525   Jews in south Egypt build a temple for God on Elephantine Island

516   The Jews in Jerusalem finish rebuilding their temple for God

458   Ezra the scribe arrives in Jerusalem

445   Nehemiah arrives in Jerusalem as governor; he rebuilds the city walls

332   The Jews open the gates of Jerusalem to Alexander the Great

164   The Maccabees revolt against the Greeks; Israel is independent 164–63 BC

250   Scribes write the earliest Dead Sea Scrolls

37   Herod the Great becomes King of Israel; reigns 37–4 BC

Chronology, New Testament

6   Jesus is born in Bethlehem (BC)

4   Herod the Great dies (BC)

15   Valerius Gratus becomes Roman prefect (AD); deposes Annas the high priest

16   Eleazar ben Ananus, Annas's son, becomes high priest

18   Caiaphas, Annas's son-in-law, becomes high priest

26   Pontius Pilate becomes prefect of Judea

26   Jesus is baptized in late 26 AD, and begins His ministry

30   Jesus is crucified and buried, then resurrects from the dead

35   Saul persecutes Christians, then is converted near Damascus

36   Pilate is deposed; Marcellus becomes overseer of Judea (under Vitellius)

37   Herod Agrippa becomes king of Israel

41   Claudius becomes Roman Emperor

44   Herod Agrippa dies; Cuspius Fadus becomes procurator of Judea

46   Tiberius Alexander becomes procurator of Judea; Paul goes on a first missionary journey

48   Ventidius Camanus becomes procurator of Judea; during his rule uprisings occur; 20,000 Jews die at the temple; the Jews and Samaritans battle

49   Jewish riots in Rome; Claudius Caesar expels all Jews from the capitol

52   M. Antonius Felix becomes procurator of Judea

55   The Sicarii (Jewish assassins) begin killing people; Jews in Egypt revolt; Nero becomes Emperor

59   Porcius Festus becomes procurator of Judea; during his rule Judea is full of robbers, villages are aflame

60   Festus sends Paul as a prisoner to Rome; Luke finishes writing his Gospel

62   Albinus becomes Roman procurator; James (Jesus' brother) is martyred

64   Rome burns and Nero blames the Christians; many are martyred

65   Gessius Florus becomes procurator of Judea

66   The Jewish-Roman War begins

68 Paul is executed in Rome; Peter is crucified there

70 Jerusalem falls to the Roman armies under Titus; the temple is destroyed

73 Masada falls to the Romans

85 John writes his Gospel

96 John writes the book of Revelation

132 The bar-Kokhba Revolt begins (continuing until AD 136), led by a false Messiah

Cisterns: Large, underground reservoirs, cut into the stone and sealed with plaster to hold rainwater for use during the dry season. Both Joseph and Jeremiah were imprisoned in cisterns (Genesis 37:23–24; Jeremiah 38:6). In 2012, a huge cistern dating to the time of Solomon's temple was discovered beneath the Temple Mount; it is capable of holding 66,000 gallons of water and was probably used for temple purification rites, as well as for drinking. (See: Temple, Jewish)

Claudius: Claudius was the fourth Roman Emperor (AD 41–54). In Acts 18:2 (NKJV) Luke wrote that "Claudius had commanded all the Jews to depart from Rome." Roman historian Suetonius said that the AD 49 expulsion of Jews was a result of them rioting over "one Chrestus." Latins often mistook Christus (Christ) for Chrestus. (See: Roman Empire)

Conquest of Canaan: The Exodus from Egypt was in 1446 BC; the conquest of Canaan, which began 40 years later, lasted 1406–1400 BC. Jericho fell in 1406 BC and around1400 BC was one of three dates when Hazor was destroyed. They were just about the only cities Joshua burned, so we shouldn't expect evidence of Canaan-wide destruction. The Israelites' normal practice was to defeat a Canaanite army then move into the intact cities, houses, and lands (Deuteronomy 6:10–11). After the initial war, the Israelites launched new offensives following Joshua's death. (See: Amarna Tablets; Jericho; Hazor; Chronology, Old Testament)

Corinth: Corinth was an important city of Achaia. Paul's enemies took him to Gallio's judgment seat (bema) there (Acts 18:12). This very bema has been excavated. It is a large stone edifice rising 7.5 feet above the side of the public market. Paul also wrote from Corinth, "Erastus, the treasurer of the city, greets you" (Romans 16:23 NKJV). In 1929, archaeologists in Corinth found this inscription on a marble paving stone: "Erastus, commissioner of public works, bore the expense of this pavement." (See: Achaia; Agora)

Crucifixion: The ultimate Roman method of execution, designed both to publicly humiliate and inflict tremendous pain upon the victim. Jesus' hands (wrists) and feet were pierced by nails (Luke 24:39), but skeptics used to doubt that Romans drove nails through victims' feet as well. Then, in 1968 the bones of a crucified Jew named Jehohanan were discovered near Jerusalem with nail marks in both wrists. The seven-inch spike was still lodged in his heels. (See: Jesus Christ)

Cuneiform Tablets: Wedge-shaped writing was created by marking wet clay tablets with a reed; then the tablets were dried in the sun or kiln-dried.

Hundreds of thousands of cuneiform tablets have been unearthed in tells all over the Ancient Near East. Half a million of them have not even been read yet.

Cyrus: The founder of the Persian Empire, Cyrus II—also called Cyrus the Great—conquered much of the Near East and Asia Minor, as well as Babylon. He reigned 559–530 BC. (See: Babylonian Chronicles; Cyrus Cylinder; Persian Empire)

Cyrus Cylinder: A cylinder of baked clay which Cyrus II ordered inscribed in 539/8 BC. It was discovered in the ruins of Babylon in 1879. The cylinder describes Cyrus's belief that the god Marduk chose him as a "righteous ruler." (God said that *He* had raised Cyrus up, even though Cyrus didn't know God; see Isaiah 44:28; 45:1, 4). The cylinder also contains Cyrus's decree to allow captive peoples to return to their homelands. Isaiah had prophesied that Cyrus would do this for the Jews (Isaiah 45:13). This decree also fulfilled a prophecy by Jeremiah (2 Chronicles 36:22–23). (See: Cyrus)

D

Dagon: From 2500 BC on, the god Dagon was worshipped throughout Mesopotamia, especially in Mari. There was a temple of Dagon in Ugarit, and the Philistines worshipped him as well (Judges 16:21–23; 1 Samuel 5:2–7). He was not a fish-god, as is commonly supposed. Dagon was a god of crop fertility and his name is related to the Hebrew word *dagan*, which means "grain." (See: Philistines)

Damascus: Damascus has existed from before Abraham (Genesis 14:15) until this present day. It was the capital of an Aramean kingdom, was conquered by David (2 Samuel 8:5–6), and was ruled by the Nabatean Arabs in Paul's day (2 Corinthians 11:32). Archaeologists have uncovered portions of Straight Street (with its Roman colonnades) where Paul stayed (Acts 9:11), as well as a temple of Jupiter. The city is still inhabited, which inhibits archeological digs. (See: Arameans; Nabateans)

Dan: Dan's ancient city mound (Judges 18:27–29), Tell el-Qadi, covers 50 acres and is in the far north of Israel. It began to be excavated in 1966. Jeroboam set up a golden calf there (1 Kings 12:28–30), and the sanctuary where it was displayed has been uncovered: a huge stairway 27 feet long and 26 feet wide leads up to a stone platform some 10 feet high. Both large and small four-horned altars have been discovered at the base of the sanctuary, and the remains of sheep and goats, as well as numerous religious objects, have been found in the area. (See: Calf Worship; Tel Dan Stele)

David, King: A contemporary of King Hiram of Tyre, David was the second king of Israel and reigned 1010–970 BC. The palace where he sang for King Saul has been unearthed in ancient Gibeah; the foundation walls of David's own palace may have been discovered at Jerusalem, and an administrative palace dating to David's time has been uncovered in Khirbet Qeiyafa.

In addition, the Bible states that Jerusalem was a Canaanite city until David conquered it about 1003 BC. In 2013, a shard from a ceramic jar was discovered beneath the floor of a 10th-century BC building near the southern wall of the Temple Mount. On it were written eight letters in the early Canaanite alphabet, not Hebrew. (See: Gath; Gibeah; Hiram; David's Palace; Tel Dan Stele; Khirbet Qeiyafa)

David's Palace: In August, 2005, Israeli archaeologist Eilat Mazar announced that she had discovered the foundation walls of the Fortress of Zion, the palace of King David, dating to the 900s–800s BC. Secular archaeologists—who deny that David had a kingdom—are skeptical; thus the find is officially called "The Large Stone Structure." Mazar also found fragments of imported luxury goods in the area, and a portion of an elegant jug dating to around David's day. She also found an elegant proto-Aeolic capital (the decorated cap on top of a pillar) at the foot of the scarp. These are exactly the kind of things one would expect to find near a king's palace from the 900s BC. (See: Stepped Stone Structure)

Dead Sea Scrolls: Until 1947, skeptics argued that there were probably so many mistakes in the Hebrew scriptures that there was no way of telling *how* closely the Masoretic Text (AD 600–1000), which makes up our present Old Testament, reflected the original text. That year, however, jars full of ancient scrolls were discovered in caves near the Dead Sea; these 972 texts date back 2,000 years to between 150 BC–AD 70, with some dating to 250 BC. There are at least fragments of every Old Testament book except Esther. The Dead Sea Scrolls have definitively confirmed the accuracy of the Masoretic Text. (See: Essenes; Qumran)

Dothan: Elisha and his servant were staying in Dothan, northeast of Samaria, when an Aramean army surrounded it (2 Kings 6:8–17). Tell Dotha has been excavated and the city of Elisha's day uncovered. It is a typical Israelite city of that time, characterized by small houses, narrow streets, storage pits and bread ovens. (See: Arameans)

E

Ebenezer: An Israelite village 2 miles (3 km) to the west of the Canaanite town of Aphek, in central Israel, 10 miles in from the coast (1 Samuel 4:1; 5:1). Ebenezer is believed to be the small, hilltop settlement of Izbet Sartah. In contrast to the well-watered, fortified Aphek in the valley below, the Israelite village is poor, has only one "Israelite four-room house" in its center, poorer farm buildings around it, storage silos between buildings, and several rough rock-cut cisterns. In 1976, the Izbet Sartah Ostracon was discovered there; it is a small potsherd inscribed with 22 letters of the early Hebrew alphabet. (See: Alphabet)

Ebla: In 1974–75, Italian archaeologist Paolo Matthiae and his team were excavating the mound of Tell Mardikh in Syria, when they discovered nearly 1,800 clay tablets. The tablets date from 2500 BC until 2250 BC when the city was destroyed, and were the records for Ebla, a city and trade empire that flourished and was sacked eight centuries before Moses. Ebla had a complex code of laws, many of them resembling the commandments in the Old Testament written centuries later. Sacrifices for sin, purification rites, and scapegoats were known in Ebla. The tablets contain many Semitic names, such as Adam, Abraham, Esau, Ishmael, David, Saul, etc. The tablets also discuss the Canaanites and Hittites, and refer to ancient Urusalima (Jerusalem), Hazor, Megiddo, and other biblical cities.

Edom, Edomites: A land to the southeast of the Dead Sea, extending south to the Gulf of Aqaba; its people descended from Esau (Genesis 36:8). Till about 1350 BC, Edom was occupied by semi-nomadic tribes; after that, it had a more settled history. A few important sites have been excavated, including Petra. Assyrian records frequently mention Edom, as do ancient Egyptian records. Pharaoh Amenhotep III (1390–1352 BC) built Soleb, and the Soleb Hieroglyph refers to Yahweh (God), saying, "the land of the Shasu of Yhw." A later Egyptian letter of 1192 BC specifies that the Shasu are the "tribes of Edom," Israel's half-Hebrew relatives.

Eglon's Palace: Eglon, king of Moab, oppressed Israel during the time of the judges (Judges 3:12–14), and Eglon's palace was discovered at Jericho in 1933. It is a large structure built during the last half of the 1300s BC, on top of the destroyed city of Jericho ("the City of Palms"). The building was occupied for only a short time, measured 39 feet by 48 feet and was full of expensive pottery. A cuneiform tablet stated that the occupant had been engaged in administrative activities. There are no other buildings from that period in the area. (See: Jericho; Moab)

Egypt: A land in the northeast corner of Africa. The ruins of several cities such as Thebes have been extensively explored, particularly in the more arid south, and many ancient papyrus scrolls have been found in the dry sands. Unfortunately, papyrus doesn't survive in the humid delta where the Hebrews were. Egyptian hieroglyphics frequently mention the Habiru, which, although not exclusively the biblical Hebrews, certainly included them. (See: Akhenaten; Amarna Letters; Amenhotep; Exodus; Habiru; Israel Stele; Neco; Ramesses; Shishak)

Ekron: This Philistine city is mentioned frequently in the Bible (Judges 1:18; 1 Samuel 5:10) as well as in Assyrian cuneiform records. The Assyrian ruler Esarhaddon summoned Ikausu, king of Ekron, to Nineveh. A relief in the palace of Sargon depicts Assyrian armies besieging Ekron. The ancient city is under the ruins of Khirbet el-Muqanna (Tel Miqne). The Ekron Dedicatory Inscription (five lines of writing dating to the 600s BC) was found there in 1996; it is an inscription of King Achish who dedicated a temple, and gives a short list of the previous rulers of Ekron. (See: Esarhaddon; Philistines; Sargon)

El: El, also known as El or El Shaddai to the Hebrews, was also recognized as the Creator God by the Canaanites. They acknowledged El as the original and highest God, but early on began to see Him as distant and uncaring. So they developed a mythology in which He spawned 70 sons and daughters, such as Baal, who were more accessible.

In Exodus 6:2–3 (NKJV), El Shaddai is identified explicitly with the God of Abraham and with Yahweh: "And God spoke to Moses and said to him: 'I am the LORD [Yahweh]. I appeared to Abraham, to Isaac, and to Jacob, as

God Almighty [El Shaddai], but by My name LORD [Yahweh] I was not known to them." Often He was referred to as the LORD God, or Yahweh Elohim in Hebrew. (See Baal; Edom; Ugarit)

Elephantine Papyri: Judea was a province in the Persian Empire and Jewish soldiers manned a garrison in the far south of Egypt, at Elephantine, an island in the Nile on the border of Nubia. Hundreds of papyri letters, mostly in Aramaic, have been found there, and provide great insight into the lives of the Jewish settlers from 499–395 BC. The Passover Letter (written 419 BC and discovered in 1907) gives detailed instructions on how to keep the Passover.

Elephantine Temple: About 525 BC, under the Persian King Cambyses II, Jewish settlers built a temple to Yahweh on Elephantine Island. In 530 BC, the Jew's enemies had forced them to stop building the temple of God in Judea. (They resumed in 520 BC and completed the Jerusalem temple four years later.) In a letter to the Persian governor of Judea, dated 407 BC, the Jews of Egypt requested that their damaged temple be repaired. They also asked help from Sanballat (the governor of Samaria) and Johanan ben Eliashib (the Jewish high priest), both of whom are mentioned in the Bible (Nehemiah 2:19; 12:23). (See: Sanballat; Temple, Jewish)

Ephesus: Paul spent three years in Ephesus, and most of the city he knew has been excavated—including its wide streets, the agora, the foundation of the Temple of Diana/Artemis, and the amphitheater where the riot of Acts 19 took place. Ephesus was, after Rome,

the largest city in the Empire and had a population of about 450,000. It had two agoras, several gymnasiums, and public baths. (See: Amphitheater; Artemis)

Esarhaddon: The son of Sennacherib, king of Assyria, Esarhaddon ruled 681–669 BC. He brought foreign people to Samaria (Ezra 4:2), and during his reign, Judea became a vassal state. Assyrian records tell us that Manasseh king of Judea was forced to supply timber and stone for Esarhaddon's palace. Manasseh also served Esarhaddon's son, Ashurbanipal. (See: Assyria; Manasseh)

Essenes: A Jewish religious sect, they lived in Khirbet Qumran near the Dead Sea. It is largely acknowledged that they were the ones who wrote the Dead Sea Scrolls. They lived during New Testament times, but are not mentioned in the Bible. (See: Dead Sea Scrolls; Qumran)

Ethiopia: (See: Nubia)

Execration Texts, Egyptian: Before a military campaign, the names of enemy cities and peoples (in Canaan and Phoenicia) were written on pottery bowls and figurines then cursed and broken. Such execration (cursing) texts, written 1990–1790 BC, have been discovered and were published in 1926 and 1957. They mention Jerusalem and list cities such as Ashkelon, Shechem, and Lachish. Many chieftains are listed in the earliest texts, because this was when the Amorites had just entered Canaan. Later texts cite more cities and fewer chieftains, showing that they had settled by then. (See: Amorites; Ashkelon; Jerusalem)

Exile, Jewish: In 605, Nebuchadnezzar defeated Pharaoh Neco at the Battle of Carchemish; he marched south to Judea and deported key Israelites to Babylon, including Daniel. In 597, after a Jewish rebellion, there was a second deportation: King Jehoiachin, Ezekiel, and others were then taken to Babylon. In 586, Jerusalem was destroyed by King Nebuchadnezzar, and at this time there was a final deportation. The Exile officially ended in 539 BC with King Cyrus' decree to allow captive peoples to return to their homelands. (See: Cyrus Cylinder; Nebuchadnezzar; Synagogues)

Exodus from Egypt: The Exodus occurred in 1446 BC. There is little archaeological evidence for the exodus of a large group of Hebrews from Egypt, nor have artifacts from millions of nomads been found in the Sinai desert. However, it should also be noted that there is also no evidence for an exodus of another large group of foreigners from Egypt to Canaan during the days of Pharaoh Setnakhte (1189–1186 BC), and those foreigners under Irsu first waged war throughout all Egypt, looted all its temples, etc. Yet no one doubts that this later exodus happened, even though our only source of knowledge about it is the Harris Papyrus.

Regarding the 1446 Exodus, a papyrus called the Admonitions of Ipuwer describes the land of Egypt in chaos, the Nile turning to blood, and slaves plundering their masters. It also describes the breakdown of law and order, as well as famine following natural catastrophes. It is exactly the situation one would expect to see in Egypt after plagues, widespread destruction of trees and crops, and the wiping out of Egypt's army. (See: Amenhotep)

Ezion Geber: This ancient Israelite port on the Gulf of Aqaba (1 Kings 9:26; 22:48), at the junction of sea and land routes, has been identified with Tell el-Kheleifeh. Excavations from 1938–1940 uncovered a Judean fortress, a warehouse, and a trading station. In 1940, a seal was discovered here: It is set on a copper ring and shows a shepherd walking in front of a ram; it bears the name Jotham—very likely King Jotham of Judah (2 Kings 15:32–33). Beneath the Israelite level are signs of earlier Edomite occupation, exactly the situation the Bible describes. (See: Hiram; Seal)

Some archaeologists, however, consider Ezion Geber to be an island named Jezirat Faraun, 7.5 miles (12 km) south of modern Eilat. It had a harbor in Phoenician style and was inhabited during the Iron Age, King Solomon's time.

F

Felix, Governor: According to Roman records, Marcus Antonius Felix was procurator (governor) of Judea and ruled AD 52–58. He was married to a Jewess (Acts 24:24) so the high priest Jonathan requested the emperor to appoint Felix as governor. Unfortunately, Felix was fond of bribes (Acts 24:25–26) and Josephus tells us that during his rule there was a great increase in crime. Paul was imprisoned in Caesarea during Felix's rule. Agrippa's palace in Caesarea, where Paul spoke to the Roman governors, Felix and Festus, has been uncovered.

Festus, Governor: Porcius Festus was procurator (governor) of Judea; he ruled AD 59–62, and was the governor who sent Paul to Rome (Acts 24:27; 25:12). Many bronze coins called *prutah*, minted by Festus, are in existence. Josephus tells us that during his rule, Judea became full of robbers and many villages were afire.

G

Galilee: The Roman province of Galilee was the fertile northern region of Israel, mostly to the west of the Sea of Galilee. Its notable cities were Chorazin, Capernaum, and Tiberias. (See: Chorazin; Capernaum; Tiberias)

Gath: Numerous locations have been suggested for Gath, a key Philistine city (1 Samuel 5:8; 6:17). Tell es-Safi (briefly excavated in 1899) is once again viewed as the most likely site, and a dig is underway. During the 2005 season, the Goliath Shard (also called the Tell es-Safi Potsherd) was found; this is a piece of pottery with two names similar to Goliath inscribed on it. It dates to the time of David and Goliath (1 Samuel 17:4). While this isn't proof that the giant existed, it *is* proof that people in Gath had similar names at the very time that Goliath lived.

In 2008, a seal impression from the 900s BC was discovered, as were two Assyrian destruction layers, and other remains from the Early, Middle, and Late Bronze Ages. In 2010, a Philistine temple was discovered. (See: Philistines)

Gaza: The southernmost of the five Philistine cities, ancient Gaza lies beneath the modern, densely-populated

city of the same name, so little archaeological work has been done. Limited digs show that it was occupied in Old Testament times, and pieces of Philistine pottery have been found. It was at Gaza that Samson pushed apart two pillars, binging a temple down, killing the Philistines seated on its roof (Judges 16:25–30). Excavations of several large Philistine houses show that they were sometimes built around a central hall and that a row of columns supported the upper story and the roof. (See: Philistines)

Gerar: Tell Abu Hureirah, the probable site of ancient Gerar, an early Philistine city, is about 15 miles (9.5 km) northwest of Beersheba. Archaeological work has uncovered much pottery, and showed that the city prospered during the Middle Bronze Age, the time of the patriarchs (Genesis 10:19; 20:1–2). (See: Philistines)

Gethsemane: An olive orchard on the northwest slope of the Mount of Olives, opposite the temple, where Jesus prayed before His arrest (Mark 14:32). Gethsemane is an Aramaic word meaning "oil press." The traditional site is under the care of Franciscan monks; two other nearby sites are also claimed to be the actual location. (See: Jerusalem)

Gezer: Pharaoh conquered Gezer, a city in southwest Canaan, and gave it as a wedding gift to Solomon when he married Pharaoh's daughter. Archaeologists have discovered a layer of debris and ash there, four feet deep in places, dating to the mid 900s BC—at the beginning of Solomon's reign. Solomon rebuilt Gezer's defenses (1 Kings 9:15–17), and archaeologists have excavated this level and uncovered a 216-foot long water tunnel, which, like the city gates and walls, were in the same style as those found in Hazor and Megiddo—which Solomon fortified at this same time. (See: Hazor; Maccabees; Megiddo)

Gezer Calendar: This is an inscription in paleo-Hebrew on a limestone tablet, found in Gezer. It describes the agricultural activities of the calendar year—planting, hoeing, pruning, harvesting, etc. It dates to the 900s BC, shortly after Solomon took over Gezer, and is one of the earliest examples of Hebrew writing. (See: Alphabet; Gezer; Solomon)

Gibeah: Gibeah was a city of Benjamin, now known as Tell el-Ful. Archaeologists reveal that this site was inhabited by Israelites for two centuries before being destroyed in a great fire—undoubtedly the one described in Judges 20:13–19; 37–40. On top of this level, a small fortress (measuring 111.5 feet by 170.6 feet) and a palace were built—dating to 1025–950 BC, the time of Saul. This is the very palace where David played his harp and sang for the troubled king (1 Samuel 15:34; 16:14–23). (See: Bronze Age; David)

Gibeon: Gibeon was a Canaanite city that made a treaty with Israel (Joshua 9). It is now known as el-Jib, 6 miles (9.5 km) north of Jerusalem. The most amazing structure discovered there was the Pool of Gibeon, mentioned in 2 Samuel 2:12–13. It is a huge pit, 82 feet deep, 37 feet in diameter, once containing water; it also has a spiral staircase of 79 steps cut into the stone around its sides. Numerous vases with "Gibeon" stamped on them in

Hebrew were found there. An underground staircase leads from the city to the pool. (See: Conquest of Canaan)

Golgotha: The traditional site of Golgotha (Calvary, where Jesus was crucified) is inside the Church of the Sepulchre. Hebrews 13:12 (NKJV) says that "Jesus. . .suffered outside the gate," but the traditional site was inside the city walls. The earliest mention of Jesus' tomb is found in Onomasticon by Eusebius, who specifies that it was "north of Mount Zion," whereas the traditional site is west-northwest of the city. An alternate site, Gordon's Calvary, *is* north of the old city. In addition, Gordon's Calvary is only 300 feet from the Garden Tomb and John 19:41–42 says that the garden was near Golgotha.

Golgotha means "Place of a Skull" (Mark 15:22 NKJV), and Gordon's Calvary actually *looks* like a skull. Note: Archaeologists state that the Garden Tomb is of a style used hundreds of years before Jesus' day, so may not be His tomb; however, His *actual* tomb will still be north of the city, near Gordon's Calvary. (See: Crucifixion)

Goshen: The fertile, northeast section of the Nile delta, good for grazing and agriculture, was called Goshen. It was the 20th nome (an administrative division) of Egypt and called *Gesem* in Egyptian. It was here that the Hebrews settled (Genesis 45:10), and it was here that they worked as slaves, building the city of Rameses (Exodus 1:11), also known as Zoan, and today called Qantir. Rameses was near Avaris, the former capitol of the Hyksos rulers. (See: Avaris; Egypt; Exodus)

Grecian Empire: The empire founded by Alexander the Great, which lasted from 332–146 BC. It stretched from Greece eastward to the border of India, and spread the Greek language and learning throughout the ancient Near East. Archaeologists have discovered so much architecture and artifacts from the Grecian era throughout the ancient world that they are too numerous to list. (See: Alexandria; Athens)

Greece, Greeks: The Greeks had the earliest great civilization in Europe and the first democracy in the ancient world. By New Testament times, Greece had lost its empire, and the Greek homeland was divided into two Roman provinces, Macedonia in the north and Achaia in the south. (See: Achaia; Artemis; Macedonia; Persians; Zeus)

H

Habiru: In the Amarna Letters, the Habiru are mentioned repeatedly as attacking Canaan. In this context they are recognizable as the Hebrew tribes. However, Habiru (also Hapiru or Apiru) are also mentioned as landless raiders in ancient Hittite, Mari, and Babylonian texts, where the meaning seems to be "wanderers." So while Abraham is mentioned as a Hebrew (Genesis 14:13), it's possibly not because of his descent from Eber (Genesis 11:16–26), but because he was a nomadic shepherd who had wandered into Canaan. (See: Abraham; Amarna Letters; Hebrews)

Hammurabi: He was an Amorite king (1792–1750 BC) who created an empire in Babylonia from Ur in the south to Mari in the north. He is most famous for creating codified laws, some 282 of which are preserved in the Code of Hammurabi, on a stele, 8 feet high, inscribed about 1765 BC. It was found in Susa in 1902, having been carried there by later conquerors. Many of Hammurabi's laws are similar to those in the Old Testament, except that the Hebrew laws are more humane. (See: Amorites; Mesopotamia)

Haran: Abraham settled in this city north of the Euphrates before heading south to Canaan (Genesis 11:31). Haran was just to the east of Carchemish, in the Balikh River valley of what is now Turkey, just 10 miles (16 km) north of the Syrian border. Haran is often mentioned in Babylonian and Assyrian texts, where it is spelled Harran. It has been continuously occupied since 2000 BC, so only limited excavations have been done at the site. Three cities with the name of biblical patriarchs (Nahor, Serug, and Terah) once existed near Haran (See: Carchemish; Mari; Nahor; Serug; Terah; Ur)

Hazor: The ancient city mound of Hazor lies 9 miles (14.5 km) north of the Sea of Galilee; it covers nearly 200 acres, and had a population of some 40,000. It was the royal city of Jabin (Joshua 11:1), and according to archaeologists was destroyed in the late 1400s BC—the time of Joshua (Joshua 11:10–11).

Soon after its destruction, it was rebuilt, then destroyed again in about 1230 BC—the time of Barak (Judges 4:1–2, 23). In 2012, 14 large clay jugs containing burnt wheat were found, dating to a fiery destruction about 1200 BC. Excavations show that Hazor was first occupied by the Canaanites, then by the Israelites. As to why the Bible names Jabin as king for both periods, this was a dynastic title similar to Pharaoh. An 1800s letter from Hazor, an 1800s tablet from Mari, and a text from Egypt in the 1200s *all* list Jabin as king.

In 2010, two fragments written in Akkadian cuneiform, dating from the 1600s–1700s BC, were found at Hazor. They are portions of a law code similar to the Code of Hammurabi. Hopes are high that the entire library of clay tablets—buried beneath the ashes of the city Joshua burned—will yet be uncovered. (See: Alphabet; Conquest of Canaan)

Hebrews: The first mention of Hebrews in the Bible is of "Abram the Hebrew" (Genesis 14:13). *Hebrew* means "to pass over" and this can mean either (a) that this was a generic name applied to any people who had passed over the Euphrates, or (b) that Hebrews were continual nomads, passing over the established boundaries of settled lands (Deuteronomy 26:5).

Some scholars identify the Hebrews of the Bible with the "Habiru," "Khapiru" and "Apiru" that appear in ancient texts from Egypt and other lands (see: Amarna letters; Habiru). If so, the Hebrews were a group of uprooted nomads. There is also a compelling argument which states that the Hebrews ('ebrî) were so called because they were descended from Eber, the direct ancestor of Abraham (Genesis 11:16–24). (See: Habiru)

In addition, Hebrew is not related to any language of the region of Ur, but is a northwest Semitic language, closely related to Eblaite, Aramaic, Ugaritic, and Canaanite dialects. In Deuteronomy 26:5 (NIV) Hebrews are taught to say, "My father was a wandering Aramean." Also, Rebekah's father was called an Aramean (Genesis 25:20). (See: Aramaic; Arameans Ur)

Hebron: An important city in southern Israel, it was already in existence in Abraham's day, and was briefly David's capital (Genesis 13:18; 2 Samuel 2:11). Hebron has been continuously occupied since the earliest times, which has limited archaeological work. However, archaeologist Yosef Garfinkel makes an interesting observation: Hebron was David's first capital, then Jerusalem; these cities are only one day's walk from each other, *and* from Khirbet Qeiyafa, which guarded the east; these three cities were the nucleus of David's kingdom in Judah. (See: Khirbet Qeiyafa; David) The Cave of the Patriarchs in Hebron is the traditional burial site of Abraham and other Patriarchs.

Herod the Great: Herod was king of Israel under the Romans 37–4 BC. He was obsessed with building and among his many projects were the seaport of Caesarea, the fortress of Herodium, the palace at Masada, and the Tower of Antonia. He is remembered for rebuilding and expanding the temple of God in Jerusalem, but he also built a temple to Olympian Zeus. He was a ruthless ruler and tried to kill Jesus when He was an infant (Matthew 2:16). In 2007, archaeologist Ehud Netzer found the tomb of Herod. (See: Antonia, Tower of; Caesarea; Herodion; Idumea; Machaerus; Masada; Temple, Jewish; Zeus)

Herod Antipas: A son of Herod the Great, Herod Antipas was also known as Herod the Tetrarch (Luke 3:19). He ruled over Galilee and Perea 4 BC–AD 39, and built the city of Tiberias on the west shore of the Sea of Galilee. He had John the Baptist executed (Mark 6:17–28). (See: Machaerus; Tiberias)

Hezekiah: Hezekiah was king of Judah (729–686 BC). When Sargon died (705 BC), Hezekiah rebelled against his son, Sennacherib. To show how much this act of defiance irritated Sennacherib, he states in the Bull Inscription, "I laid waste the wide region of Judah and made the overbearing and proud Hezekiah, its king, bow in submission at my feet." Sennacherib was the one making proud boasts, however. While he did conquer Judah temporarily, and while Hezekiah did initially pay tribute (2 Kings 18:14)—as Sennacherib gleefully records in the Taylor Prism—he never took Jerusalem; Hezekiah trusted God to deliver them, and God sent an angel to slay most of Sennacherib's besieging army.

Some 2,000 *LMLK* (Hebrew initials for "in the name of the king") seals have been found stamped on handles of large storage jars from dozens of cities in Judah, some with Hezekiah's full name on them (See: Manasseh; Nubians; Sennacherib; Shebna; Siloam Inscription; Taylor Prism)

Hezekiah's Tunnel: (See: Siloam Inscription)

High Places: The Canaanites had myriad hilltop altars to Baal and Asherah, and though God had commanded the Israelites to destroy such altars (Exodus 34:13–15), they often failed to do so.

In addition, the Israelites often worshipped God on these high places (1 Kings 3:2–3; 22:43). Archaeologists have found hilltop shrines at Megiddo (dating to 3000 BC) and Arad. By the Bronze Age, high places not only had altars, but rooms, platforms, and benches. (See: Altars; Asherah; Baal)

Hiram, King of Tyre: Hiram was the king of Tyre (980–947 BC) who sent cedar wood, carpenters, and stone cutters to build David a palace (2 Samuel 5:11). Hiram later sent Solomon cedar and workmen (1 Kings 5:1–18) to help build God's temple, and helped Solomon build a merchant fleet at Ezion Geber (1 Kings 9:26–28; 10:22). Surviving Phoenician records describe Hiram as a strong ruler who crushed a rebellion in the province of Cyprus, and an inscription on a bronze bowl, discovered in Cyprus refers to "Carthago, servant of Hiram, king of the Sidionians." King Hiram's sarcophagus has been found just south of Tyre. (See: Ezion Geber; Phoenicia; Temple, Jewish; Tyre)

Hittites: The Hittites (Hatti) were a people of what is now Turkey who ruled a kingdom 1850–1550 BC and 1450–1200 BC. Around 1400, God spoke of "all the Hittite country" north by the Euphrates (Joshua 1:4 NIV). The Hittites were later lost to history, and many scholars dismissed the Bible's mentions as myth. Then, in the 1800s, tablets and inscriptions mentioning Hittites were unearthed. In 1906, excavations began at Bogazkoy (Hattusa), the Hittite capital, and soon the trickle of information turned into a flood—and the Bible was once again vindicated.

The Hittite empire collapsed around

1180 BC during the Sea Peoples invasion; it then somewhat recovered and continued to exist as a shadow of its former glory. Solomon and other Israelite kings dealt with these neo-Hittites (1 Kings 10:29; 2 Kings 7:6). (See: Sea Peoples)

The "Hittites" of Canaan with whom Abraham and Esau dealt (Genesis 10:15; 23:3; 26:34) were not ethnic northern Hittites, but "children of Heth," local Canaanites. They are more accurately called Hethites.

Hurrians: Genesis 14:6 (NIV) mentions "the Horites in the hill country of Seir [later Edom]" during the time of the patriarchs. These were Hurrians, a people group that spread throughout the ancient Near East about 2500 BC. They established the Mitanni Empire centered around Haran, and thousands of clay tablets have been dug up at Nuzi, another key Horite city. (See: Edom; Haran; Nuzi)

Hyksos: The Hyksos ("foreign rulers") were most probably Amorites. Around 1800 BC they began emigrating into the Egyptian delta. This was shortly after Jacob and his family moved to Egypt in 1876 BC. By 1650 BC the Hyksos had become so numerous and powerful that they took over all northern Egypt and ruled it from their capital Avaris—until they were driven into Canaan in 1560 BC by native Egyptians. Many scholars believe that the Hebrews were treated well by these fellow-foreigners, and multiplied, but that after the Hyksos were driven out, the Hebrews were oppressed and enslaved (Exodus 1:8–11). (See: Amorites; Avaris; Egypt)

I

Idol: Idols are images of false gods in clay, stone, wood, or metal. The Bible speaks out against idolatry, calling it demon worship (2 Kings 17:12; 1 Corinthians 10:19–20; Revelation 9:20). Not only were idols images of false gods, but they were sometimes lascivious in design. Many homes had their own *teraphim*, or household gods (Genesis 31:19). Idols and engravings of gods and goddesses have been excavated throughout Canaan, Egypt, and the entire Near East. The Greeks and Romans also worshipped idols of their gods. (See: Asherah; Artemis; Baal; Nuzi; Zeus)

Idumea: Idumea comes from the word *Edom*. The Nabatean Arabs drove the Edomites out of their land into southern Judah, which then became known as Idumea. In 125 BC, the Maccabees conquered the Edomites and forced them to convert to Judaism. Herod the Great was from Idumea. (See: Edom; Herod; Maccabees)

Iron Age: The Iron Age began when people switched from creating tools and weapons out of bronze to forging them out of iron; it lasted in Canaan and the ancient Near East from 1200–500 BC. At first, the Philistines held a monopoly on ironworking (1 Samuel 13:19), and iron smelting facilities have been discovered in Ekron. But under David, the Israelites mastered it so well that they were able to carve out an empire from Egypt to the Euphrates. In Gibeah, the capital of Saul, bronze arrowheads have been discovered in a lower level, and an iron plow point in the layer above. (See: Bronze Age; Ekron; Gibeah; Swords)

Israel: Jacob's name was changed to Israel and his descendants were called the "children of Israel," or Israelites. After they conquered Canaan, their land was called Israel. In 930 BC, the kingdom divided into Judah in the south and Israel in the north. Northern Israel lasted for two centuries until its capital Samaria fell to the Assyrians in 722 BC. (See: Berlin Fragment; Israel Stele, Judah; Samaria)

Israel Stele: Early in his reign, Pharaoh Merneptah (1213–1203 BC) led a punitive raid into Canaan. His victory stele, inscribed in 1209 BC and discovered in 1896, names the cities he conquered. It also states, "Israel is laid waste; its seed is no more." This is the earliest confirmed mention of Israel in extrabiblical records. This "seed" likely refers to Israel's crops being burned, a common practice at the time. Israel was just a confederation of tribes during the period of the judges, and Merneptah's stele states this: His hieroglyphics specify that Israel was a "foreign people," not a "country." (See: Berlin Fragment)

J

Jacob's Well: Jacob settled near Shechem and dug a well at the base of Mount Gerizim (Genesis 33:19; John 4:6). This well still exists and is known as Bir Ya'kub. (See: Shechem)

James Ossuary: James was the brother of Jesus; he later became head of the Jerusalem church and wrote an epistle (Mark 6:3; Acts 12:17; 15:12–20; James 1:1). Josephus tells us that he was martyred in AD 62. Then in 2002, the discovery of a limestone ossuary (a box for storing the bones of the dead)

was announced. It dated to the first century AD and inscribed on it were the Aramaic words *Ya'akov bar-Yosef akhui di Yeshua*, which mean, "James, son of Joseph, brother of Jesus."

All scholars acknowledge the early date of the ossuary, since the only time Jews buried in that fashion was AD 20–70; they also concede that the phrase, "James, son of Joseph," is genuine. Many scholars, however, argued that the last words, "brother of Jesus," were a later addition. Because the stakes were high and the skeptics vocal, Oded Golan, the owner of the ossuary, was charged with forgery in 2004.

The world's leading archaeological experts testified in the lengthy court case. Judge Aharon Farkash, who himself has a degree in archaeology, presided; on March 14, 2012, he ruled "that there is no evidence that any of the major artifacts were forged, and that the prosecution failed to prove their accusations beyond a reasonable doubt." Golan was therefore acquitted. The implications of this ruling are enormous: not only is the James Ossuary possibly direct evidence of the historical James, but of Jesus Himself.

Jehoiachin: Jehoiachin was the second-to-last king of Judah; in 597 BC King Nebuchadnezzar took him to Babylon (2 Chronicles 36:9–10). Three clay tablets found in Babylon, dating from the 10th to the 35th year of Nebuchadnezzar have been discovered; they are records of the oil, barley, and other items given to Yaukin (Jehoiachin) and his sons. Jeremiah 52:31–34 adds that in 560 BC, Nebuchadnezzar's son, Awel-Marduk, released Jehoiachin from prison and gave him food from his own table.

Jehu: Jehu was a king of Israel (841–814 BC), and was a contemporary of the prophet Elisha, as well as of Shalmaneser III of Assyria. He is portrayed bowing in submission on the Black Obelisk. (See: Black Obelisk)

Jeremiah: Jeremiah was a prophet during the final days of the kingdom of Judah. Baruch, son of Neriah, was his scribe (Jeremiah 36:4, 26, 32) and two seal impressions have been found which read: "Belonging to Berekyahu, son of Neriyahu, the scribe." Two bullae of Jeremiah's enemies have also come to light. In 2005, Eilat Mazar discovered the bulla of Jucal/Jehucal in Jerusalem (see Jeremiah 37:3; 38:1). It reads: "Belonging to Yehucal, son of Shelemiyahu, son of Shovi." In 2008, she found another bulla that read: "Belonging to Gedaliah, son of Pashur" (Jeremiah 38:1). Gedaliah the son of Ahikam was another contemporary of Jeremiah, and Nebuchadnezzar made him governor of Judah in 586 BC (2 Kings 25:22). (See: Exile; Lachish; Mizpah)

Jericho: Jericho fell in 1406 BC. When archaeologist John Garstang excavated the mound of Jericho, Tell es-Sultan (City IV) from 1930–1936, he found proof that it was the Jericho of Joshua's day—the opinions of archeologists such as Kathleen Kenyon notwithstanding.

Jericho IV was destroyed in early spring after harvest, since grain storage jars were full of wheat, barley, dates, and lentils. This *was* when Joshua besieged Jericho (Joshua 3:15; 5:10). The fact that the storage jars were full shows that the city wasn't besieged long. Joshua's siege lasted one week (Joshua 6:3–5). Houses in Jericho IV were built directly against the city wall, just as the Bible describes (Joshua 2:15). City IV was burned; Garstang found a layer of charcoal, ashes, and fire-reddened bricks over 3 feet thick (Joshua 6:24). The city wall collapsed right down to the base of the Tell (Joshua 6:20).

In nearby tombs, Garstang discovered scarabs of Pharaohs Hatshepsut (1479–1458 BC) and Tuthmosis III (1479–1425 BC). He found the same type of pottery in the tombs as he did in City IV. This dated the pottery of the destroyed city to 1479–1425 BC. Garstang found pottery painted to imitate Cypriot bichrome style; this is a recognized indication for the period 1550–1400 BC. (See: Conquest of Canaan; Eglon's Palace; Scarab)

Jerusalem: Jerusalem is one of the oldest cities in the world. The Ebla Tablets (2500–2250 BC) refer to it as Urusalima, and the Egyptian Execration Texts (1990–1790 BC) mention it as well. It next appears in the Bible in Joshua 10:1 (1406 BC), and shows up in Amarna letter 287 (1350s–1330s BC), where it is under attack by the Habiru. Despite being burned (Judges 1:8), it remained under control of Canaanites called Jebusites until 1003 BC, when David conquered it and made it the capital of Israel (2 Samuel 5:6–9).

In 2010, archaeologist Eilat Mazar announced that she had discovered part of the city walls of David's Jerusalem. It is difficult to conduct archaeological digs because the city is still inhabited; nevertheless, important discoveries are made continually, often by accident. (See: David's Palace; Stepped Stone Structure; Siloam

Inscription; Temple, Jewish; Pool of Siloam; Western Wall)

Jesus Christ: It was popular in the last century to insist that Jesus Christ never existed—that He had been invented by the early church to explain their origins. But all serious historians now acknowledge that Jesus was a historical figure. The earliest non-biblical source to refer to Him is the Samaritan historian, Thallus, who wrote only 20 years after the Crucifixion that in his opinion the darkness over all the earth at Jesus' death had been caused by a solar eclipse.

Josephus, a Jewish historian, also refers to Jesus in *Histories*, Book 18, 3:3 beginning with, "Now there was about this time Jesus, a wise man. . ." While most historians agree that the phrase "He was the Christ" was added by a later Christian scribe, they agree that the core of Josephus's statement is authentic. (See also: Claudius; Crucifixion; James Ossuary)

Jewish-Roman War: This war began in AD 66 as a result of conflicts between the Jews and Greeks, and escalated into armed conflict and a full-blown rebellion against Rome. The Jewish rebels quickly overran the Romans in Judea and Galilee. Roman troops marched south from Syria to crush the rebellion, but were defeated. General Vespasian, with his son Titus, then arrived with four legions and in AD 67 invaded Galilee. By AD 70, Titus's army had surrounded Jerusalem, which fell after a seven-month siege.

In AD 30, Jesus had prophesied about these events (see Luke 19:43–44; 21:20–24). In fulfillment, the Romans dug a trench around the city and built a high wall around that. Josephus, in The Wars of the Jews, described the capture of the city and the slaughter that followed. Jesus had also prophesied: "They will be killed by the sword or sent away as captives to all the nations" (Luke 21:24 NLT). Josephus wrote that 1,100,000 Jews were killed during the siege and 97,000 were sold as slaves throughout the Roman Empire. Some 6,000 prisoners of war ended up in Greece cutting the Corinth Canal.

Joppa: Joppa existed in Joshua's day (Joshua 19:46), and Jonah boarded a ship there (Jonah 1:3). It is most famous as the city where Peter raised Dorcas from the dead, and where he stayed with Simon the tanner (Acts 9:36–43). Much excavation has been done, showing that the city was ruled by the Hyksos, the Philistines, and the Phoenicians. It is referred to in the Amarna Tablets as Ya-Pho, and an inscription found there, dating to the early 1200s BC, mentions Rameses II. A later level was burned, possibly by Merneptah in 1209 BC, and a bronze hinge to the city gate has been unearthed. A Phoenician inscription indicates that there was a temple to a Sidonian god in Joppa around 450 BC. (See: Israel Stele; Phoenicia; Ramesses)

Josiah: Josiah (640–609 BC) was the last great king of Judah. He celebrated the Passover on a huge scale, and he and his officials gave large numbers of sacrificial animals (2 King 23:21–23; 2 Chronicles 35:1–9). One of these officials was Zechariah, and an ostracon reads: "Ashyahu [Josiah] the king has commanded you to give in the hand of

Zakaryahu [Zechariah] silver of Tarshish for the house of Yahweh, three shekels." In 609 BC, when Pharaoh Neco's armies swept through Judah on their way north to Carchemish, Josiah tried to stop the Egyptians, and was killed (2 Chronicles 35:20–24). (See: Carchemish; Judah; Neco)

Judah, Judea: Judah was the southernmost tribe of Israel, living from Jerusalem south to Beersheba. Together with the other tribes, they formed the confederacy of Israel for hundreds of years, and were part of the nation of Israel under its kings, Saul, David, and Solomon. In 930 BC, the kingdom divided into Judah in the south and Israel in the north. Judah's inhabitants were exiled to Babylon in 605, 597, and 586 BC. After Cyrus' proclamation in 539 BC, the Jews returned to Judah, the Persian province of Yehud. It was a Greek and Roman province after that, and the Romans called it Judea. (See: Beersheba; Bethlehem; Exile; Hebron; Israel; Jerusalem)

K

Kadesh Barnea: This was a place in the Negev about 50 miles (80 km) southwest of Beersheba, also known as Kadesh. Abraham camped near its spring (modern 'Ain Qudeirat) for awhile, and the Israelites sent spies from there after coming out of Egypt (Genesis 20:1; Deuteronomy 1:20). No artifacts have been found from these earliest times; however, the remains of several Iron Age fortresses, including a Judean fortress dating to the 800s BC, have been discovered in Kadesh. Two ostraca with Hebrew

writing on them have been found there, as well.

Ketef Hinnom Amulets: In 1979, a burial site was unearthed at Ketef Hinnom, on the edge of the Valley of Hinnom, south of Jerusalem. Two small silver scrolls, which had been used as amulets to ward off evil, were discovered there. A portion of the inscription etched on one reads: "The Lord bless and keep you. The Lord make His face shine upon you, and give you peace." This is from Numbers 6:25–26, and since it dates to the late 600s BC, is the earliest quote of scripture yet discovered. Other quotes echo Deuteronomy 7:9. (See: Amulets)

King's Highway: This ancient north-south route lies east of the Dead Sea and was in use in Abraham's day, as evidenced by the cities lying on its route (Genesis 14:5–6). In 1406 BC the Israelites asked if they could travel north on this highway through Moab, but were refused (Numbers 20:14–21). It later became a Nabatean trade route, then a Roman road; many Roman milestones are still standing. A modern highway in Jordan, which follows part of the old road, still bears the same name in Arabic—Tariq es-Sultani.

Khirbet Qeiyafa: This is one of the most significant new archaeological discoveries in Israel. In 2007, Yosef Garfinkel began digging at this site 20 miles (32 km) west of Jerusalem, on a hill overlooking the Elah Valley, where David killed Goliath. What he discovered has forced skeptics to rethink their doubts about the early kingdom of Judah. Minimalist archaeologists have long argued that there was no evidence for an urban society in David's day, and that the kingdom of Judah only came into being in the 700s BC or later—but a strongly-fortified site at a very early date is evidence of a strong central government at the time. (See: Hebron)

Excavations at Khirbet Qeiyafa show that it was occupied for 80 years by some 500–600 people. Comparing pottery samples, plus carbon-dating two olive pits, places this occupation 1050–980 BC, dating it to the reigns of King Saul (1050–1010 BC) and King David (1010–970 BC). The absence of pig bones shows that this was an Israelite city. (Pig bones typically make up 20 percent of all bones found at Philistine and Canaanite sites.)

A palace covering 1000 square meters was discovered in the center of the city. Around the perimeter were pieces of alabaster vessels imported from Egypt. A building 45 feet long by 18 feet wide was also found; it served as a storeroom for taxes of agricultural goods from surrounding villages. Hundreds of large jars were found at the site, their handles marked with an official seal.

The Qeiyafa Ostracon, discovered in 2008, is a pottery shard containing five lines of text. It is the earliest Hebrew writing ever discovered, and according to epigraphers, describes Saul being chosen as Israel's first king. Three small sacred artifacts (shrines) were discovered in a small room by the city gate. These are miniature models of the temple (with its two pillars and triple-recessed doors) that Solomon would later build in Jerusalem.

Scholars are divided as to whether Khirbet Qeiyafa is biblical Shaaraim, or whether it is Netaim or Adithaim. But they *do* know that it is an impressive Iron Age city dating to David's day. (See: David; David's Palace; Hebron)

L

Lachish: This was a large, fortified city now known as Tell ed-Duweir 26 miles (42 km) southwest of Jerusalem. A number of Canaanite temples have been excavated there, dating between 1550 and 1200 BC. The king of Lachish joined an Amorite coalition in 1406 to fight against Joshua; they were defeated (Joshua 10). Lachish was reoccupied by Canaanites, and messages from two of its kings appear among the Amarna Tablets. (See: Amarna Tablets)

Lachish eventually became an Israelite city. Sennacherib's army besieged it in 701 BC (2 Kings 18:13–15), and arrowheads, sling-stones, a spearhead, the crest of an Assyrian helmet, and scale armor have been discovered near the city gate. Assyrian cuneiform tablets also describe the fall of Lachish. In addition, the Lachish Reliefs, 12 stone panels found in 1850 in a room in Sennacherib's palace, once served as wrap-around wall decorations 8 feet high by 80 feet long. They depict the entire siege of Lachish from beginning to end. (See: Sennacherib)

Lachish Letters: Jeremiah 34:7 states that when the Babylonians were besieging Jerusalem (in 587 BC), only Lachish and Azekah also remained. In 1935 and 1938, 21 messages were found in the gatehouse of the city mound of Lachish, written on ostraca in paleo-Hebrew script. One of them records that the fire signals of Azekah were no longer visible, evidence that it had fallen to the Babylonians. Two letters refer to "the prophet," possibly Jeremiah, and speak of those who "weakened the hands" of the soldiers (Jeremiah 38:4). (See: Azekah; Mizpah; Ostraca)

Large Stone Structure: (See: David's Palace)

M

Maccabees: Ever since Judah came under control of the Grecian Empire in 332 BC, the Jews were subjected to a process of Hellenization—learning the Greek language and conforming to Greek customs and philosophy; many even began to worship Greek gods. In 164 BC, Antiochus Epiphanes, ruler of the Greek Seleucid Empire, forbade circumcision, made possession of the Torah punishable by death, banned the Sabbath and Jewish feasts, and put an idol of Zeus on the Jewish altar.

But Mattathias, a priest of Modiin, rose up and led a rebellion. Under his sons, called the Maccabees ("Hammers"), the Jews battled their Greek rulers and by 143 BC had carved out an independent kingdom of Israel. It lasted till 63 BC.

Archeological digs have been conducted at Beth-zur and large amounts of Maccabean relics, including a fortress, have been found there. Simon Maccabee's fortress at Gezer has also been excavated. At another site, Mareshah (modern Tell Sandahannah), an entire Maccabean town has been uncovered.

Macedonia: In New Testament times, northern Greece was a Roman province called Macedonia. Paul preached the Gospel in cities of Macedonia such as Philippi, Thessalonica, and Berea. (See: Greece; Thessalonica)

Machaerus: Like Herodion and Masada, this stronghold was a hilltop retreat of King Herod. It lay to the east of the Dead Sea. Machaerus was originally built by the Hasmonean king Alexander Jannaeus in 90 BC, but after its destruction by the Romans, was rebuilt by Herod the Great in 30 BC. It was here, according to Josephus, that Herod Agrippa had John the Baptist imprisoned and beheaded (Mark 6:17–27). (See: Masada; Herod; Herod Agrippa; Herodion)

Malta: Malta is a group of three small islands just south of Italy, and Paul was shipwrecked on the main island (Acts 27:39–44; 28:1). Luke called Publius, the Roman ruler of Malta, a *protos*—a "great man" or "chief official" (Acts 28:7). This unusual Greek title appears in Roman records some years earlier as well; in the days of Emperor Claudius, an inscription names Castricius Prudens as *protos* of Malta.

Manasseh: The son of Hezekiah, Manasseh (2 Kings 20:21) reigned over Judah 697–642 BC. Unlike his father, Manasseh submitted to Assyrian rule and paid tribute. Assyrian records—both the Prism of Esarhaddon and the Prism of Ashurbanipal—state that "Manasi king of Yaudi" (Manasseh king of Judah) was one of 22 vassal kings. Manasseh also supplied troops to help Ashurbanipal quell revolts in Egypt. The seal of Manasseh, acquired in Jerusalem in 1974, reads, "Belonging to Manasseh, son of the king," and was likely the seal he used when he was co-regent with his father for his first 10 years.

Mari: In 1933 the remains of the once-thriving Amorite trade center of Mari are found at Tell Hariri near the Euphrates River in eastern Syria. Mari was inhabited as early as 3000 BC and was destroyed by Hammurabi in 1759 BC. Extensive excavations have uncovered a temple complex for Ishtar, a ziggurat, and two royal palaces—as well as over 25,000 tablets written in Akkadian cuneiform. These texts often refer to the Habiru, and mention places near Haran named after the biblical patriarchs, Nahor, Terah, Serug. Even with all the years of digging at Tell Hariri, only half the site has been excavated. (See: Amorites; Cuneiform; Hammurabi; Nahor; Serug; Terah)

Mars' Hill: (See: Areopagus)

Masada: Masada was a fortress atop a small, isolated plateau in southern Judea, west of the Dead Sea. Herod the Great fortified it between 37–31 BC. It was so isolated and impregnable that although Jerusalem fell to the Romans in AD 70, Masada held out till AD 73. Numerous artifacts dating to the siege have been found there—including the very lots (names written on a fragment of pottery) of the ten men chosen to slay their fellow Jews to prevent them from falling into the hands of the Romans. (See: Herod; Jewish-Roman War; Machaerus; Herodion)

Media, Medes: The Medes were an ancient people who lived in what is now Iran, who at one time ruled over the Persians. However, Cyrus the Great rebelled in 553 BC, fought four years of wars, and captured the Median capital Ecbatana in 549 BC. He then made them part of the Persian Empire, and the Medes played a key part in his conquest of the Babylonians (Isaiah 13:1, 17; Jeremiah 51:11, 28). Darius the Mede was, in fact, the first ruler of Babylon (Daniel 5:30–31). (See: Cyrus; Persians)

Megiddo: Megiddo was an ancient hilltop city, presently known as Tell el-Mutesellim. It is in the Plain of Jezreel and controlled the main pass through the Carmel Range. Through this pass merchants traveled (making Megiddo rich) and armies were forced to file. Pharaoh Thutmose III invaded the valley though the pass and defeated a coalition of Canaanite kings about 1470 BC.

Megiddo was burned around 1050 BC, at which time its large Canaanite temple ceased to exist. It was then taken over by the Israelites. King Solomon later highly fortified Megiddo, and the six-chambered city gate and casemate walls he built about 960 BC match the style of those found at Hazor and Gezer (1 Kings 9:15–17). Pharaoh Shishak damaged the city about 925 BC, and part of a stele with Shishak's name inscribed on it was discovered there in 1926.

In 1904 a seal was found in a later level of the city with this inscription: "Belonging to Shema the servant of Jeroboam" (See: 2 Kings 14:23). It dates to the early 700s BC, the time of Jeroboam II. Megiddo has been extensively excavated. (See: Gezer; Hazor; Shishak; Solomon)

Mesopotamia: Mesopotamia consists of two Greek words, *mesos* and *potamos*, which mean "the land between two rivers," the Tigris and Euphrates. It is equivalent to Aram Naharaim (Genesis 24:10 NIV), which means "Aram of the two rivers." The Akkadians and the Babylonians rose in the south of Mesopotamia, and several important kingdoms arose in the north, including the Hurrians, the Amorites, and the Arameans. Haran was a chief city in this area. (See: Akkad; Amorites; Arameans; Babylonia; Haran; Hurrians)

Mesha Stele: The Bible describes how Mesha king of Moab (a vassal state of Israel) rebelled after Ahab died (2 Kings 3:4–6). In 1868, the Mesha Stele was found in Jordan. It was written about 830 BC in the Moabite language in paleo-Hebrew script and is Mesha's account of his rebellion. It states, in part: "I am Mesha, son of Kemosh, king of Moab. And I built this high place to Kemosh to commemorate deliverance from all the kings. . . . Omri was king of Israel, and he oppressed Moab for many days. . . and his son [Ahab] replaced him. . . . But I was victorious over him and his house." The name of Israel's God, Yahweh, appears in line 18. Thirteen Moabite towns, mentioned in the stele, also appear in the Bible. This is one of the most significant archeological discoveries in Bible lands. (See: Ahab; Chemosh; Moab)

Midian, Midianites: Descendants of Keturah, a concubine of Abraham, the Midianites lived in Arabia, near the Gulf of Aqaba, just east of the Sinai Peninsula. Excavations there have unearthed large walled towns and many villages dating to the Late Bronze Age and Early Iron Age. They had a distinctive style of two-colored pottery called Midianite ware.

Midianites living in Sinai gave refuge to Moses, who married a daughter of the priest of Midian (Exodus 2:15–21). Because the people of Midian later tried to corrupt Israel, Moses declared war on them (Numbers 25:1–6, 16–18; 31:1–18). The names of the five kings Israel battled also appear in secular literature of that very era.

Around 1200 BC, the Midianites made a major invasion of the land of Israel (Judges 6:1–2). Research by Israeli archaeologist I. Finkelstein shows that about 1200 BC there was a sudden influx of some 21,000 people into the central hills of Canaan. Almost overnight, 250 new Israelite settlements appeared in these previously-uninhabited highlands. A distinctive Israelite feature of them was the absence of pig bones (Leviticus 11:7).

Mills, Millstones: Stone implements for grinding grain are mentioned frequently in the Bible and have been discovered throughout the Ancient Near East. The mortar and pestle were small hand-mills (Numbers 11:8) for grinding flour for a family. They consisted of an elongated stone for pounding the grain in a stone bowl. Later, the rotary hand mill—with a handle on the upper stone—appeared (Judges 9:53). Two large millstones—the top one turned by a donkey, an ox, or a person—were used for grinding larger quantities of grain (Judges 16:21). Biblical mills were usually made of black basalt found in Galilee and Bashan.

Mizpah: There are several towns named Mizpah in the Bible, but the most famous one is in Benjamin, 8 miles (13 km) north of Jerusalem, where the Israelites met before waging war on Benjamin (Judges 20:1). Saul was declared king in Mizpah (1 Samuel 10:17–24), and after the Babylonian conquest in 586 BC, Gedaliah made Mizpah the new center of Judah (2 Kings 25:22–23). Today it is an abandoned mound known as Tell en-Nasbeh. It has been excavated, and shows long occupation by the Israelites.

Numerous seals have been dug up, including one carved out of onyx that states, "belonging to Jaazniah servant of the king," likely the man who met with Gedaliah at Mizpah (Jeremiah 40:8; 42:1). A seal impression (bulla) of Gedaliah has been found at Lachish, reading: "Belonging to Gedaliah, overseer of the royal house."

Moab, Moabites: The Moabites were descendants of Lot, Abraham's nephew (Genesis 19:36–37); they lived in modern-day Jordan, east of the Dead Sea. The Moabites sometimes oppressed Israel (Judges 3:12–14), and were sometimes subject to Israel (2 Kings 3:4). Ruth, the ancestor of David, was from Moab (Ruth 1:1–4; 4:13–22). In New Testament times, Herod had a fortress called Machaerus in what was once Moab. (See: Machaerus; Mesha Stele)

Mordecai: The cousin of Esther, who started out working in the Persian court ("in the gate"), and became the highest-ranking official under the Persian king, Xerxes I (Esther 2:5–7, 21; 8:1–2). Mordecai is most likely the Hebrew equivalent of a common Babylonian name, Mardukaya or Marduka. A cuneiform text states that a certain Marduka

in Susa was a treasury official of Xerxes I; this is possibly the Mordecai of the Bible. (See: Persians; Xerxes)

Moriah, Mount: Abraham went to the "land of Moriah" to sacrifice Isaac on a mountain there (Genesis 22:2), and 2 Chronicles 3:1 says that the temple at Jerusalem was built on Mount Moriah. Covering this site is the present-day Muslim Dome of the Rock—so-named because of the large rock (58 feet long by 51 feet wide) on top of the hill. The stone appears to have been used for sacrifices in the past, as channels for draining the blood of sacrifices have been cut into it. (See: Abraham; Temple, Jewish)

Muratorian Fragment: The Muratorian fragment is the oldest known canon (list of accepted New Testament books), consisting of 85 surviving lines. It was discovered in a church library in Milan and published in 1840, and was originally written by the church in Rome about AD 170. At this time, Christians had accepted virtually all the books in the New Testament—not only the Gospels and Paul's epistles, but "contested" books such as Jude and Revelation.

Many modern critics argue that Paul never wrote the Pastoral Epistles (1 and 2 Timothy and Titus), but the Muratorian fragment specifies that in addition to his first ten epistles, Paul wrote "one to Titus, and two to Timothy; and these are held sacred in the esteem of the Church." Again, many critics say that John, since Greek wasn't his mother tongue, couldn't have written the polished Greek of the Gospel of John—but the Muratorian fragment states that John had help composing his Gospel, and internal evidence in the Gospel supports this (see John 19:35; 21:24).

N

Nabateans: The Nabateans were Arabs descended from Nebaioth, a son of Ishmael (Genesis 25:13). Just before New Testament times, they drove out the Edomites and created a kingdom stretching from Damascus through the deserts as far south as the Gulf of Aqaba. They straddled the intersections of the main trade routes of their day.

One of their kings, Aretas, is mentioned in 2 Corinthians 11:32. His daughter had married Herod Agrippa, and when Herod divorced her to marry Herodias, Aretas made war against Herod and defeated him. Josephus tells us that many Jews felt that this was God's judgment on Herod for beheading John the Baptist. (See: Damascus; Idumea; Petra)

Nahor: Nahor was the brother of Abraham and a "city of Nahor" existed near Haran (Genesis 11:27; 24:10). It is mentioned in clay tablets (discovered in 1933) in Mari from the 1800s–1700s BC, and in Assyrian inscriptions from the 1300s BC, where it is called Til Nakhiri ("Mound of Nahor"). Several ancient texts place Nahor just south of Haran. (See: Haran; Hebrews)

Nazareth: This is the town in Galilee where Jesus grew up. Archaeologists discovered that in Jesus' day, it was an insignificant village of some 50 houses covering four acres. This is the context for Nathanael's question: "Can anything good come out of Nazareth?" (John 1:46 NKJV).

Nazareth Decree: A decree on a slab of marble found in Nazareth about 1878, states: "Ordinance of Caesar. It is my pleasure that graves and tombs remain undisturbed. . . ." It goes on to warn of capital punishment against anyone who "has in any other way extracted the buried, or has maliciously transferred them to other places. . . or has displaced the sealing of other stones." This decree was likely written in response to Jewish rumors that Jesus' disciples had broken the seal, then stolen His body and taken it someplace else (Matthew 27:66; 28:11–15).

Nebuchadnezzar: Nebuchadnezzar was the son of Nabopolassar, king of the Babylonians (626–605 BC) and founder of the Neo-Babylonian Empire. Nebuchadnezzar reigned 605–561 BC. The prophet Jeremiah warned the Jews to submit to Babylon, but they attempted to rebel with the aid of Egypt—and suffered war and exile as a result. (See: Exile) Archaeological evidence corroborates the Bible's statements, showing that virtually every fortified city in Judah was destroyed in battles at this time. A cuneiform tablet in the British Museum describes events up to the eleventh year of Nebuchadnezzar's reign, including him taking the city of Jerusalem. (See: Babylonia; Babylonian Chronicles; Jehoiachin; Jeremiah; Lachish Letters)

Neco, Pharaoh: Pharaoh Neco II was ruler of Egypt (610–595 BC). When he marched north to help defend the Assyrians from the Babylonians, King

Josiah of Judah tried to stop him—and died in battle as a result (2 Kings 23:29). After battling the Babylonians up north, Neco then deposed the new Judean king, Jehoahaz, and made Jehoiakim king in his place (2 Kings 23:31–35). (See: Carchemish; Josiah)

Negev: This is the dry southlands stretching from Beersheba in the north to the Gulf of Aqaba in the south. Key cities of the Negev are Beersheba, Arad, Ezion Geber, and Kadesh Barnea. Archeologists have discovered that several settlements and forts were established in the Negev in the 900s BC, the very time that King Solomon was consolidating his empire and expanding trade. (See: Abraham; Arad; Beersheba; Ezion Geber; Kadesh Barnea; Solomon)

Nero, Emperor: Nero was the Roman emperor AD 54–68. He was rational during the first years of his reign. When Paul appealed to Caesar for a trial (Acts 25:11), it was to Nero that this request was made—and indications are that he freed Paul from imprisonment in AD 62 (Philemon 22). As time went on, however, Nero became increasingly erratic and violent. When Rome burned in AD 64, the emperor was suspected; Nero blamed the Christians and began an intense persecution. The Roman historian Tacitus described the suffering of the martyrs. It was at this time that Paul was re-arrested and executed. Nero had the apostle Peter crucified. (See: Rome; Roman Empire)

Nineveh: The Assyrians were an oppressive warrior state with a powerful military, unspeakably cruel to conquered nations. (See: Ashdod) Nineveh covered 1,700 acres and was protected by five walls, with the inner wall one hundred feet high and four chariot-widths thick. Its walls were nearly eight miles long. Since Nineveh was at the junction of two rivers, it was guarded on several sides by water.

About 630 BC Nahum declared that Nineveh would be besieged (Nahum 2:1–4; 3:1–3, 14–15). He predicted how the city would fall: "But with an overflowing flood He will make an utter end of its place. . . . The gates of the rivers are opened" (Nahum 1:8; 2:6 nkjv). Less than twenty years later, armies of Babylonians and Medes surrounded Nineveh. They built a dam on the Khoser River; then, in 612 BC, they opened the river gates and the flood washed away part of the wall, allowing them to enter. (See: Babylonians; Nebuchadnezzar)

There used to be no evidence of the existence of Nineveh, so skeptics said the Bible had simply made the city up. Then, in 1842, its ancient city mound was discovered. Today, much of the city has been excavated. (See: Assyria)

Nubia, Nubians: Nubia is called Ethiopia in the kjv, but this is not modern Ethiopia, which didn't yet exist as a kingdom. Rather it refers to Cush. This ancient people lived just south of Egypt in what is now Sudan. During the reign of King Asa, they invaded Judah, but were defeated (2 Chronicles 14:8–13). The Nubians later conquered Egypt, and when Hezekiah was king, Pharaoh Tirhakah attempted to invade Judah, but was driven off by the Assyrians (2 Kings 19:9–10). (See also: Numbers 12:1; Jeremiah 38:7–12).

Nuzi: An ancient city (now Yorghan Tepe) east of the northern Tigris River, where many cuneiform documents have been found that shed light on customs of the patriarchs. For example, in Nuzi, you could adopt a servant as an heir, as Abraham did with Eliezer (Genesis 15:2–4). Also, if a wife was unable to bear a son, she could give her husband a concubine, whose son would be considered the son of the first wife. Sarah did this with Hagar (Genesis 16:1–4).

If a father arranged his daughter's marriage, he did not have to have her consent; a brother could arrange his sister's marriage, as Laban did for Rebekah (Genesis 24:29–60), but required her consent (vs. 58). In Nuzi, a man could sell his birthright—as Esau did (Genesis 25:30–34). Also, possession of the household gods confirmed someone was head of the family, which may be why Rachel took her father's idols for Jacob when they fled Haran (Genesis 31:17–19, 30). There are a number of other striking parallels.

O

Oaths: In the Old Testament, God swore oaths to the patriarchs, and they likewise swore oaths when making a solemn promise (Genesis 14:22–23) or when confirming a treaty with others (Genesis 21:22–32). Frequently Bible characters would declare something like, "May the Lord do this to me and more if I do such-and-such" (see 2 Samuel 3:35). Archaeologists have unearthed many written oaths in the ancient Near East that mirror this practice. For example, in Mesopotamia, people would frequently declare,

"If I do this not, may I be covered with hot asphalt."

Ostraca: Ostraca is the Greek name for pottery shards—broken pieces of clay pots and vases. Often, in the absence of any other writing surfaces, ancient peoples would write letters with ink on these makeshift tablets. A prime example of this is the Lachish Letters. (See: Lachish Letters)

P

Papyrus, Papyrology: Papyrology is the study of ancient writings preserved on papyrus—paper made from papyrus reeds. Papyrus cannot survive for 2,000–3,000 years in moist climates, so most finds related to the Bible have been in the deserts of Egypt and in caves in the dry wilderness of Judea. (See Elephantine Papyri; Dead Sea Scrolls)

Parchment: In ancient times, quality documents were written on parchment, or vellum. These were animal skins that had been specially cured and prepared. This was an expensive process, and only the scriptures and valuable legal documents were written on vellum. We see their value in Paul's statement to Timothy: "Bring the. . .the books, especially the parchments" (2 Timothy 4:13 NKJV). When Constantine requested 50 copies of the Bible in AD 331, he specified that they be written on vellum.

Pergamos: One of the seven churches of Asia, Pergamos has been largely excavated. Apart from having a prominent temple for the cult of emperor-worship, the people of this city worshipped Asklepios, whose symbol was a serpent. Asklepios was described as sitting on a throne with his hand on the head of a serpent, and his image has been found on many coins. There was also an enormous altar to Zeus shaped like a throne—presently in the Berlin Museum—in the city's acropolis. Small wonder that Pergamos was described as the city "where Satan's throne is" (Revelation 2:13 nkjv).

Persians, Persian Empire: The Persians were an ancient people of modern Iran. They were at first subject to the Medes, but Cyrus II, king of the Persians, rebelled in 553 BC and captured the Median capitol Ecbatana in 549 BC. He then created the Persian Empire—also called the Medo-Persian Empire—that stretched from the border of India in the east to Greece in the west. This empire fell to Alexander the Great in 330 BC. Bible characters such as Daniel, Esther, Nehemiah, and Ezra lived under Persian rule. (See: Cyrus; Elephantine Papyri; Medes; Susa; Xerxes)

Peter's House: In 1968, archaeologists were digging in Capernaum beneath a church dating to the AD 400s when they discovered a group of 12 first-century homes; the largest was the house of a fisherman. There were several inscriptions on its walls of "Jesus Christ" and "Peter." It is therefore commonly called "the house of Peter," and while we cannot be certain that this was his actual house, Peter was a fisherman and he lived in Capernaum at this very time. (See: Capernaum)

Petra: The capital of the Nabatean Arab kingdom was the impregnable rock city of Petra in modern-day Jordan. It is an architectural marvel carved out of the rock, and only entered by narrow and easily-defended gorges. It is a major tourist site today. (See: Nabateans)

Philistia, Philistines: In 1177 BC, during the reign of Ramesses III, a massive migration of people from Greece, Crete, and Anatolia launched an attack on Egypt. These invaders, whom historians call Sea Peoples, were repulsed, and they settled on the coast of Canaan. Chief among them were the Peleset (P'listi), so all these peoples were known as Philistines. They had five main cities. (See: Ashdod; Ashkelon; Ekron; Gath; Gaza)

However, according to the Bible, Philistines were already in Canaan around 2066 BC. After Abraham made a covenant with them in Beersheba, "they returned into the land of the Philistines" and "Abraham sojourned in the Philistines' land many days" (Genesis 21:32, 34 kjv). The Philistines were still living in coastal Canaan in1446 BC (Exodus 13:17). (See: Gerar)

Some scholars believe that since Philistines lived there in *his* day, a Hebrew editor called it "the land of the Philistines" to clarify the area referred to. However, the lands and islands of the Sea Peoples were near and had traded with Canaan for centuries already. Doubtless many settled among the Canaanites, especially at Gerar, early on. Since they came from the same lands as the *later* groups called Philistines, the Bible refers to them all by that name. (See: Iron Age; Sea Peoples)

Phoenicia: Phoenicia was the coastal region above Canaan (later Israel), from Acco in the south to Arvad in the north. The Phoenicians were sea-faring traders and once controlled areas as far away as Sicily and Carthage. Their chief cites were Tyre and Sidon, as well as Arvad and Byblos. The "gods of Sidon" were Baal and Ashtoreth (Judges 10:6). The Phoenicians were descended from Canaanites (Genesis 10:15), as was the woman Jesus encountered (Matthew 15:21–22). (See: Acco; Byblos; Canaanites; Hiram; Tyre; Sidon)

Pontius Pilate: Pilate was the prefect (governor) of Judea AD 26–36. He presided over the trial in which Jesus was sentenced to be scourged and crucified. Pilate is mentioned repeatedly in the Gospels, as well as by the Jewish historian Josephus and the Roman historian Tacitus. His historicity was confirmed in 1961 by the discovery of the Pilate Stone in the amphitheater of Caesarea; this inscription is in Latin, and translated reads: "Tiberius Pontius Pilate Prefect of Judea." (See: Antonia Fortress; Aqueducts; Jesus Christ)

Pool of Siloam: Critics in the 20th century contended that John's Gospel wasn't an accurate historical source because it mentioned the "Pool of Siloam" (John 9:7) for which there was no evidence. Further, a site once identified as the Pool of Siloam later proved to be the Pool of Bethesda, which also survives to this day. Then in 2004 Jerusalem city workers were excavating a sewer pipe, when they discovered the actual Pool of Siloam. It was once filled by the waters of the Gihon Spring, and was as large as two football fields. (See: Siloam Inscription)

Pottery: From one end of the Near East to the other, archaeologists dig up literal tons of pottery and pottery shards; these are the most common artifacts uncovered. Pottery is very important in dating sites, since styles changed over the years, and the levels of a dig can be identified by the styles of pottery found in them. At certain points in history clay vessels were elegantly crafted and beautifully painted; other times, vessels were mass-produced with little regard for artistry. For example, during the time of the Judges (Late Bronze Age/Early Iron Age) the Israelites created plain, undecorated pottery; the Canaanites and Philistines of that time produced elaborately-painted wares. Pottery is a factor in the dating of Jericho to Joshua's day. (See: Jericho; Ostraca)

Q

Qumran: This was a religious community atop a plateau near the northwest end of the Dead Sea, 8 miles (12 km) south of Jericho. The inhabitants were a Jewish sect called the Essenes, and they were the ones who copied out the scrolls, found nearby in caves. Indeed, the community had a scriptorium, complete with inkwells and writing benches, dedicated to this purpose. The site was abandoned around AD 68 toward the end of the Jewish-Roman War. (See: Dead Sea Scrolls; Essenes)

R

Ramesses: Ramesses II (1303–1213 BC) was one of the last great pharaohs of Egypt. He is often popularized as the Pharaoh of the Exodus, but Ramesses

II existed some 160 years too late. Amenhotep II is the Pharaoh of the Exodus. Ramesses II is most famous for building the great temple at Abu Simbel in southern Egypt. He also fought an inconclusive battle with the Hittites by the Orontes River in Syria, after which he was forced to sign a treaty with them. (See: Amenhotep; Hittites)

Ras Shamra: (See: Ugarit)

Red Sea: The phrase "Red Sea" in our Bibles is a mistranslation; the Hebrew words are *yam suph* and mean Sea of Reeds. (An Egyptian word similar to *suph* means "papyrus.") Thus, when Exodus 14 says that the escaping Hebrews crossed through the sea, it was most likely referring to papyrus marshes just north of the Bitter Lakes. The digging of the Suez Canal largely drained these marshes.

A "strong east wind" is specifically named as the cause (Exodus 14:21 kjv) of the waters parting. Even today, a phenomena called "wind setdown" (sustained east-west winds) at the Bitter Lakes pushes the waters aside and exposes the lake bottom, allowing Arabs to cross. In Moses' day, God could have stopped the wind abruptly, causing the water to rush back with punishing force upon Pharaoh's chariot army. To date, no remains of buried chariots have been found (See: Exodus)

Roman Empire: The Romans began as a small settlement on the Tiber River, and over time, conquered all Italy. For the first 500 years, Rome was a steadily-growing republic. Julius Caesar brought this era to an end in 49 BC when he initiated a civil war and took over as dictator. Eventually, the Roman Empire spanned from Britain in the west to the Persian Gulf in the east. The Romans laid 54,000 miles of paved roads throughout their empire, many of which still exist.

Julius Caesar's heir, Augustus Caesar, founded the Roman Empire in 30 BC and ruled as Emperor 27 BC–AD 14. After him Tiberius ruled from AD 14–37, then Caligula (AD 37–41), Claudius (AD 41–54), and Nero (AD 54–68). Paul and Peter were martyred under Nero, and most of the New Testament was written by the time of Nero's death.

Later, Vespasian (AD 69–79) and his son Titus (AD 79–81) became emperors; both had been in the Jewish-Roman War. After them, Domitian (AD 81–96) ruled, then Nerva (AD 96–98). Domitian persecuted Christians and exiled the apostle John to the island of Patmos; John was released and allowed to return to Ephesus when Nerva became emperor. (See: Augustus; Claudius; Jewish-Roman War; Nero; Titus; Vespasian)

Rome: Rome was the capital and largest city of the Roman Empire. Both Peter and Paul were martyred in Rome. In the book of Revelation, Rome is described as Babylon the Great, "that great city which reigns over the kings of the earth" (Revelation 17:18 nkjv). The Coliseum, where Nero killed Christians, is still standing, as are many of the giant aqueducts that transported water to the city. (See: Aqueducts; Amphitheaters; Roman Empire)

Rosetta Stone: A damaged basalt slab found in Egypt in 1799, it contained a formal decree in three scripts: hieroglyphic, demotic, and Greek. It was the key to deciphering Egyptian hieroglyphics.

Rylands Papyrus: Skeptics once claimed that the Gospel of John was a late forgery. Then in 1920, the Rylands Library Papyrus P52 was discovered. It is a papyrus fragment containing 14 lines from the Gospel of John, and its strong Hadrianic style dates it to AD 117–138. Tradition says that John's Gospel was written in Ephesus about AD 85, and this date is validated since copies existed in Egypt within just a few years.

S

Samaria: This city was founded by Omri as the new capital of northern Israel around 880 BC (1 Kings 16:23–24). Excavations have uncovered the remains of a substantial palace from the time of Omri and Ahab. Samaria (called Samerina) is mentioned in Assyrian records. Excavations show that the city was repaired in the decades leading up to its final fall to the Assyrians in 722 BC; signs of the destruction in that year have also been discovered.

In the Roman era, a great temple was built to Caesar Augustus over the original Israelite palaces. Samaria was also the name of the Roman province between Judea and Galilee. (See: Ahab; Esarhaddon; Israel; Sargon; Tirzah)

Samaria Ostraca: These 64 ostraca, found in Samaria, were written in cursive paleo-Hebrew characters resembling those found on the Siloam Inscription. The ostraca were found in the treasury of the palace of King Ahab, and date between 850–750 BC. They are dated receipts for quantities and quality of wine, oil, and barley received, as well as the name of the giver and where he was from—such as Shechem. An amazing detail is the listing of clan names: Joshua 17:1–3 names ten clans of Manasseh, and seven of these appear in the Samaria Ostraca. (See: Ostraca; Samaria)

Samaria Papyri: Around 375 BC, a group of prominent citizens of Samaria died in a cave in the Wadi ed-Daliyeh, 9 miles (14 km) north of Jericho. In 1962–63, their remains were discovered, including their personal documents, written on papyri. These mostly dealt with titles and sales of property and slaves. One of the documents was marked with the seal of Samaria's governor from the family of Ballat, indicating that he was the descendant of Sanballat (Nehemiah 2:10; 4:1). (See: Samaria; Sanballat)

Samaritan Temple: The Samaritans worshipped God on Mount Gerizim (John 4:19–21). The Jews rebuilt their temple 536–516 BC—and wouldn't permit the Samaritans to help—so the Samaritans built their own temple on Mount Gerizim around 470–450 BC. Coins and pottery, as well as Carbon-14 in the bones of sacrificial animals, date to this time. The Samaritans built a second temple over that about 200 BC, during the reign of Antiochus III. After the Maccabees threw off their Greek oppressors, John Hyrcanus destroyed this temple in 128 BC. Israeli archaeologist Yitzhak Magen has discovered the remains of both temples. (See: Temple, Jewish; Maccabees)

Sanballat: This was the governor of Samaria who opposed Nehemiah rebuilding the wall of Jerusalem in 445 BC. Sanballat is mentioned by name in Egyptian papyri. (See: Elephantine Temple) The descendants of Tobiah, Sanballat's fellow conspirator from Ammon, are also known from papyrus letters. Geshem the Arab is named in an inscription from Arabia, and his name was also inscribed on a silver bowl found in the Nile delta (Nehemiah 2:19).

Sargon: Sargon II, king of Assyria (722–705 BC), was the father of Sennacherib. Shalmaneser began a three-year siege against Samaria, but died just before it fell (2 Kings 17:1–5). Then the new "king of Assyria [Sargon] took Samaria" (vs. 6) in 722 BC, bringing the northern kingdom to an end. Sargon is mentioned in Isaiah 20:1, when he sent his commander-in-chief against Ashdod in 711 BC. Sargon's inscriptions claim that he conquered Judah; but Judah revolted under his son, Sennacherib. Sargon built a new royal city and palace 10 miles (17 km) northeast of Nineveh, and many descriptions of his reign have been found in the ruins of his palace. (See: Ashdod; Assyria; Ekron; Samaria; Sennacherib)

Scarab: The scarab was the dung beetle of Egypt, revered as a god. Seals of the Pharaohs, in the shape of scarabs, have been found throughout Egypt and Canaan, and help date sites. Scarab seals were worn on rings and as pendants around necks. (See: Jericho; Seals)

Seals: Seals were personal stamps carved out of limestone or gems, or made out of metal, that people used to "sign" documents on clay tablets or bullae (Genesis 38:18, 25). (See: Bulla) They were also used to make an impression on objects—such as jar handles—to mark one's ownership. Originally, seals were shaped like cylinders and an impression was rolled on a clay tablet; later seals were largely signet rings.

More than 200 seals have been found in Israel, bearing the names of key people and officials mentioned in the Bible—such as Azariah, Ahikam, Baalis, Elishama, Ishmael, Jaazniah, Jotham, Gedaliah, Gemariah, Hananiah, Jerahmeel, Menahem, Micaiah, Nathan-Melech, Nehemiah, and Seraiah. The original jasper seal of "Shema, servant of Jeroboam" has been dug up at Megiddo. (See: Ezion Geber; Jeremiah; Megiddo; Mizpah)

Sea Peoples: Shortly after 1200 BC a major migration of people from Greece, the Aegean islands, and Cyprus began. By 1180, these Sea Peoples swept through Asia Minor by land and sea, causing the collapse of the Hittite empire. By 1177 BC they had pushed down the coast through Phoenicia and Canaan/Israel and reached Egypt. They tried to invade, but Rameses III repulsed them; they then retreated to Canaan, settled there, and became known as the Philistines. (See: Hittites; Philistines; Ugarit)

Sennacherib: This Assyrian king (706–681 BC) is most famous for threatening King Hezekiah of Judah, and mocking God, saying that God could not deliver His people just as other gods had failed to deliver theirs (2 Kings 18:13–19:35). In the Taylor Prism, Sennacherib's account of the siege of Jerusalem in 701 BC, he boasted that, "As to Hezekiah the Jew, he did not submit to my yoke. I laid siege to forty-six of his strong cities." The account goes on to say that Sennacherib shut Hezekiah up "like a caged bird within his royal capitol." He did not mention capturing Jerusalem, however, because God killed most of his army, and he was forced to withdraw. As 2 Kings 19:36–37 says, Sennacherib's sons killed him while he was worshipping his god.

The Assyrians under Sennacherib also besieged Lachish in 1701 BC (2 Chronicles 32:9), and a series of gypsum reliefs at Kuyunjik, engraved by the Assyrians, show Sennacherib storming Lachish. (See: Esarhaddon; Lachish; Taylor Prism)

Serug: In Mari, tablets written in Akkadian cuneiform refer to a town near Haran named after the patriarch, Serug (Genesis 11:20). Serug also appears in Assyrian inscriptions of the 600s BC as Sargi and survives today as modern Sürüc, 35 miles (56.5 km) northwest of Haran. Before Abraham's father Terah set foot in Ur, the village of his grandfather Serug existed near Haran. (See: Haran; Hebrews; Mari)

Shalmaneser: Shalmaneser III (858–824 BC) was king of Assyria. He is mentioned in 2 Kings 17:3; 18:9. His exploits are preserved in the Black Obelisk. In the Monolith Inscription, Shalmaneser III lists "Ahab, the Israelite" as part of a coalition fighting against him. (See: Ahab; Black Obelisk; Jehu)

Shebna: This was a wealthy official of Hezekiah's court. Isaiah 22:15 (NKJV) describes him as "Shebna, who is over the house." The prophet Isaiah rebuked him for carving out a fancy tomb for himself (Isaiah 22:16–19). Shebnayahu is a variant of Shebna, and a lintel from a tomb discovered in 1953 reads, "This is the sepulcher of Shebnayahu, who is over the house. There is no silver or gold here but only his bones." (See: Hezekiah)

Shechem: Shechem (modern Tel Balata) lies at the eastern end of the pass between Mount Gerizim and Mount Ebal. Shechem was destroyed about 1550 BC and rebuilt 1450 BC. Shechem and its king Labayu are referred to in the Amarna Letters of the 1350s–1330s BC. About 150 years later, Judges 9:4, 46 mention the temple of Baal-berith in Shechem. It is the largest temple yet found in Canaan, measuring 70 feet by 86 feet; its foundations are 17 feet thick. Abimelech destroyed the temple and its defenses (Judges 9:46–49) during the 1200s BC. Archaeologists have discovered and excavated this highly-fortified, two-towered temple.

Shishak: Pharaoh Shishak (945–924 BC) is known as Sheshonk I in Egyptian annals. In 925 BC, he invaded Judah and Israel; he exacted heavy tribute from Jerusalem—including the gold shields Solomon had made (1 Kings 14:25–26; 2 Chronicles 12:1–9). He ravaged as far north as Megiddo in Israel. Shishak left detailed records of this raid in the Shishak Relief in the Temple of Karnak in Egypt. When his son Osorkon I became Pharaoh the following year he gave 383 tons of gold and silver to Egyptian temples. Much of this treasure had come from the Jewish temple and the royal palace at Jerusalem, as well as from the cities of Judah and Israel. (See: Arad; Megiddo; Taanach)

Sidon: According to tradition, Sidon was the first Phoenician city to be founded. It is often mentioned in conjunction with Tyre. (See: Ahab; Phoenicia; Tyre; Zarephath)

Siloam Inscription: The Bible says, "Hezekiah. . .made a pool and a tunnel and brought water into the city" (2 Kings 20:20 NKJV). (See also 2 Chronicles 32:30; Isaiah 22:9.) Hezekiah's tunnel was cut through solid rock shortly before Sennacherib's attack in 701 BC; it was 1750 feet long. It was rediscovered in 1838. In 1880 an Arab boy discovered six lines of writing on the wall; one of Hezekiah's men had inscribed, in paleo-Hebrew letters, a description of how the workmen—who had been cutting through the stone from both ends—met in the middle.

Sodom and Gomorrah: Sodom and Gomorrah were destroyed about 2065 BC when burning bitumen rained down on them (Genesis 19:24). There are two ruins southeast of the Dead Sea—Bab edh-Dhra and Numeira—whose destruction dates to 2300 BC, 245 years too early to be the biblical Sodom and Gomorrah, but were destroyed by an earthquake and fire that began on the rooftops. Both cities are covered by a layer of ash 4–20 inches deep. A vast cemetery exists near the ancient city of Bab edh-Dhra; about half a million bodies are buried there. The consonants for the Arabic word, *Numeira*, are similar to the consonants for the Hebrew *Gomorrah*.

While the region is now desert, it was once as lush as the Garden of Eden (Genesis 13:10) since traces of wheat, barley, dates, plums, peaches, grapes, figs, pistachio nuts, almonds, olives, lentils, chick peas, and watermelon have been found there. Very likely, Bab edh-Dhra, Numeira, and the other cities in the region were destroyed by the same geological forces that later destroyed Sodom and Gomorrah—which are yet to be discovered.

Solomon: The son of David, Solomon was king of Israel 970–930 BC. He began building the temple of God in 966 BC, the fourth year of his reign. He also fortified cities such as Megiddo, Gezer, and Hazor. His unique casemate (double) walls and trademark gate style (with three chambers on each side) have been unearthed in all three of these cities. In 1966–67, Israeli archaeologist Yigael Yadin discovered two great palatial buildings at Megiddo dating to Solomon's time. More than 40 fortresses, built in Solomon's day, the 900s BC, have been discovered in the southern Negev. (See: Gezer; Hazor; Hiram; Megiddo; Negev; Temple, Jewish)

Stepped Stone Structure: This is a unique archaeological site, 60 feet tall, on the eastern flank of the City of David, the oldest part of Jerusalem. It seems to be a major retaining wall, and is often identified with the Millo (2 Samuel 5:9) which means "Fill." In 2005, Israeli archaeologist Eilat Mazar discovered the Large Stone Structure (the remains of David's palace) directly above the Stepped Stone Structure, and demonstrated that the retaining wall connects with and supports the palace remains above. (See: David's Palace)

Succoth: Jacob built livestock enclosures near Succoth, and in a later century, Gideon attacked the city (Genesis 33:17; Judges 8:13–17). Succoth is believed to be modern Tell Deir Alla. Significant archeological finds have been made here, including a Late Bronze Age temple. The site was destroyed around 1200 BC, the time of Gideon. It was again settled during Iron Age II, at which time the Balaam Inscription was made. (See: Balaam Inscription)

Susa: The ancient capital of the Persians, it is the city where the events mentioned in the book of Esther took place. It was the winter residence of the Persian kings; in summer it was intolerably hot. Extensive archeological work has been done at the site. The stele of Hammurabi's Code was discovered there. (See: Mordecai; Persians)

Swords: During the Bronze Age, the Canaanite sickle-sword (*khopesh* in Egyptian) was the dominant sword make; it went out of use around 1300 BC. A sickle-sword dating to the 1700s BC has been unearthed in Shechem. Around the beginning of the Iron Age, the straight, double-edged sword prevailed. The Philistines introduced these swords to Canaan.

Synagogue: *Synagogue* is the Greek word for "assembly." After the destruction of their temple in 586 BC, the Jews began meeting in houses of assembly. When they returned to Judah after the Exile, they began building synagogues in every city and town. The oldest synagogue, the Wadi Qelt Synagogue, was discovered west of Jericho by Israeli archaeologist Ehud Netzer. It belonged to a Maccabean winter palace complex, and had a small courtyard enclosed by seven rooms. A main hall measuring 53 feet by 37 feet had seating for 70 people. It dates to 70–50 BC. (See: Capernaum; Chorazin)

T

Taanach: A Canaanite city until the times of Solomon, it is 7.5 miles (12 km) southeast of Megiddo in the Plain of Jezreel. It was destroyed during the time of Shishak's invasion. An Arabic village named Ta'annek still exists beside the ancient tell. The most famous find there was a tablet inscribed with cuneiform of a Canaanite alphabet, a receipt for a shipment of grain. (See: Shishak)

Talpioth Tomb: In 1945, a collection of ossuaries were discovered in the Talpioth suburb of Jerusalem. Two containers bear the name *Yeshua* (Jesus), a common name at that time. In 1980, a rock-cut tomb was discovered in East Talpioth containing more ossuaries, including one with an inscription that some interpret to read, *Yeshua bar Yehosef* ("Jesus, son of Joseph"). In 2007, a documentary film was produced, *The Lost Tomb of Jesus*, which claimed that the Talpioth Tomb was the burial place of Jesus and His family members. Many archaeologists, language experts, and Bible scholars dispute these sensational claims.

Taylor Prism: This is a large, intricately-inscribed hexagonal cylinder commemorating the exploits of Sennacherib and describing—among other things—his attack against Samaria and his devastating military advances into Judah. It agrees with the Bible's accounts in many regards and adds additional details, such as Sennacherib's claim that he conquered 46 strong cites in Judah, deported 200,150 people, and carried off much livestock. It also adds proud boasts such as, "As for Hezekiah, the terrifying splendor of my majesty overcame him." The prism is in the British Museum. (See: Sennacherib; Hezekiah)

Tel Dan Stele: The Tel Dan Stele is an inscribed stone (three fragments of an Aramaic inscription) found at the ancient city mound of Dan in northern Israel in 1993/94. Based on the names Joram and Ahaziah on the inscription, it can be dated to 841 BC. In it, an unnamed Aramean king (Hazael, 852–841 BC) boasts of victories over the king of Israel and his ally the "king of the house of David." This is the earliest reference to David outside the Bible. (See: Dan; David)

Tel Kabri: The partially-excavated mound of a hitherto-unknown city, it is on the coast of Israel just north of Haifa. It's the clearest example of a Canaanite city from 2000–1550 BC, since no other city was built over it. Its palace is the only Canaanite palace to ever be fully excavated. Tel Kabri is also unique for its many Minoan-style frescoes. (See: Canaan)

Temple, Jewish: Solomon built the first temple in 966–959 (1 Kings 6:37–38), and it was destroyed by the Babylonians in 586 BC. The second temple was built 536–530 and 520–516 BC. This temple was reworked and enlarged by Herod beginning 20 BC, and destroyed by the Romans in AD 70.

The Bible gives a detailed description of the temple Solomon built, and while little evidence of this temple survives, the Ain Dara temple near Aleppo, built around the same time, is amazingly similar in design and size. (Solomon is known to have employed Phoenician builders.)

In 2008, the stone quarry where rocks were cut for the second temple and the Western Wall was discovered about 1 mile (nearly 2 km) north of Jerusalem in the Sanhedria neighborhood. The site was dated by pottery found there; plus, the stones were the same size as those found in the Western Wall. (See: Western Wall)

Jesus predicted in AD 30 that the temple would be utterly destroyed, saying that "not one stone shall be left here upon another, that shall not be thrown down" (Matthew 24:2 NKJV). When the Romans conquered Jerusalem in AD 70, they set the cedar paneling inside the temple on fire, and the intense heat melted all the gold covering the temple. The Romans then took it apart stone by stone to recover the gold. (See: Jewish-Roman War)

Luke mentions the prohibition against Gentiles entering the temple (Acts 21:27–29). Archaeologists have discovered two stone slabs with warnings to Gentiles, written in Latin and Greek, not to enter the restricted area upon pain of death.

Jesus often taught in the temple courts, and pilgrims ascended stone steps to reach the courts from the south. Teachers often spoke from these steps to crowds in the square below. Archaeologists uncovered the largest of these set of steps, 215 feet wide, in 1968.

Terah: Terah was the father of Abraham. He left Ur to go to Canaan but settled in the region of Haran, in the Balikh River valley of southern Turkey. A town called Til Turahi ("Mound of Terah") is mentioned in Assyrian texts from the 800s BC, as being just north of Haran. (See: Haran; Hebrews)

Thessalonica: This was a Greek city in the Roman province of Macedonia. Because the Greek word *politarch* (city ruler) used in Acts 17:6, 8 for the rulers of Thessalonica, doesn't appear anywhere in Greek literature, scholars doubted Luke's accuracy. But in 1835 the word was found inscribed on the Vardar Gate on the west side of Thessalonica. It listed seven people who had held that very office.

Tiberias: Herod Antipas founded the city of Tiberias on the western shore of the Sea of Galilee in AD 22 but because he built it on top of tombs, pious Jews refused to live there. So Herod populated it with foreigners. Many slaves were freed with the condition that they would settle in Tiberias.

Tiglath-Pileser: Tiglath-Pileser III, also known as Pul to the Israelites (2 Kings 15:29), was king of Assyria (745–727 BC). He was one of the most successful conquerors in history, and is infamous for deporting people from their lands after he defeated them. Menahem, king of Israel (752–742 BC), paid tribute to Tiglath-Pileser (2 Kings 15:13–22) to avoid being invaded. Assyrian records confirm this tribute payment, also stating that Menahem was "overwhelmed like a bird in a snowstorm," and bowed down before the Assyrian king.

Tiglath-Pileser later defeated King Pekah and deported many Israelites (vs. 29).

Timnah 1: This was a Philistine city near Beth-Shemesh (Joshua 15:10–11) to which Samson went and where he fell in love with a Philistine woman (Judges 14:1, 5). Timnah has been identified with Tell Batash. Excavations from 1977–1989 revealed a fortified city covering five acres. A jar was found with writing on the handle, and a bulla was discovered as well. (See: Beth Shemesh; Gaza)

Timnah 2: This was a copper-smelting center 19 miles (30 km) north of the Gulf of Aqaba, first run by Canaanites for some 400 years, then by the Israelites. There were extensive copper mines in the area, and the earliest copper smelting facilities yet discovered anywhere—a stone furnace—was discovered in Timnah. Contrary to popular opinion, these were not King Solomon's mines, as they were not in use during the 900s BC.

Tirzah: Tirzah is modern-day Tell el-Fa'rah, and excavations there confirm the Bible. In 886 BC, Zimri set the royal palace afire (1 Kings 16:18), and archaeologists have found fire destruction dating to the 800s BC. In some areas the debris layer is three feet thick. Omri began rebuilding Tirzah for six years before abandoning it to build Samaria, and the evidence shows that he left behind a well-constructed but unfinished building, 31 feet by 44 feet, atop the destruction level (1 Kings 16:23–24).

Titus, Emperor: Titus, son of Vespasian, was emperor of Rome (AD 79–81). Titus commanded the Roman armies that besieged Jerusalem in AD 70, and destroyed the temple. His victory was commemorated by the Arch of Titus, still standing in Rome. The reliefs on the arch show Roman soldiers carrying the spoils of war—the golden table for the shewbread, the two silver trumpets, and then the golden menorah. (See: Jewish-Roman War; Temple, Jewish; Vespasian)

Tyre: A leading city of Phoenicia, often mentioned together with Sidon. In Ezekiel 26:1–14, God prophesied that Tyre would be conquered, its site scraped bare, and its stones thrown into the sea—and that it would become a place for fishermen to spread their nets. Nebuchadnezzar conquered Tyre but got none of its riches, for the inhabitants fled to a highly-fortified island just off the coast. But years later, Alexander the Great had his army throw the city's stones into the sea to create a causeway out to the island. He then took the island city and gained its wealth. Later, fisherman dried their nets on the causeway. (See: Grecian Empire; Hiram, Phoenicia; Sidon)

U

Ugarit: Ugarit was a city on the coast of Phoenicia, just north of Canaan, and is mentioned in the Amarna Tablets. It disappeared from history after it was sacked by the Sea Peoples about 1180 BC. All that remained was the mound known as Ras Shamra. The world gained a much clearer picture of the Canaanite pantheon when clay tablets (some 1,300 inscriptions) were discovered there in 1928. A temple to Baal has also been found in the ruins. The Ugaritic script turned out to be a Semitic alphabet of a language closely related to Hebrew, and a study of the tablets has helped scholars to better understand some formerly-obscure Hebrew words. (See: Alphabet; Baal; Sea Peoples)

Ur: An ancient city named Ur was 200 miles (322 km) southeast of Baghdad in Iraq, and this is commonly thought of as the Ur mentioned in the Bible. Genesis 11:31 says that Abraham emigrated from Ur. However, many scholars believe that "Ur in Chaldea" was in the north of Mesopotamia and separate from the more famous southern Ur. Terah most probably was from Haran and after spending years in Ur, returned to Haran. This would explain his readiness to settle in Haran even though he had intended to go to Canaan. (See: Abraham; Haran; Hebrews)

V

Vespasian: Vespasian was Roman emperor (AD 69–79). Emperor Nero sent General Vespasian to Israel to crush the Jewish rebellion, and Vespasian (with his son Titus) arrived with four legions, invading Galilee in AD 67. In AD 69, while he was subjugating Judea, civil war broke out in Rome, and Vespasian's troops declared him emperor. He left Titus in charge of the campaign, and became Caesar. (See: Jewish-Roman War; Titus)

W

Western Wall: Jesus said that not one stone of the temple would be left upon another (Mark 13:1–2), and this was fulfilled. The present-day Western Wall—also called the Wailing Wall—wasn't part of the temple, but is the remains of a retaining wall that surrounded the base of the western courtyard of the temple. (See: Temple, Jewish)

X

Xerxes: This was the ruler of the Persian Empire (486–465 BC) who married Esther (Esther 2:17). As Esther 1:1 (NIV) says, "This is what happened during the time of Xerxes, the Xerxes who ruled over 127 provinces stretching from India to Cush." (The KJV and NKJV call him Ahasuerus, the name by which the Jews knew him.) Xerxes attempted to invade Greece, but failed. (See: Persians; Mordecai)

Y

Yehoash Inscription: A controversial artifact said to have been found near the Temple Mount. The inscription describes repairs that Jehoash made to the temple in Jerusalem (2 Kings 12:1–16). Like the James Ossuary, it was declared a fraud, but in the same landmark case Judge Aharon Farkash ruled "that there is no evidence that any of the major artifacts [including this inscription] were forged." Scholars are divided on the issue, and while many experts insist that there is strong, irrefutable evidence that it is genuine, others continue to have reservations. (See: James Ossuary)

Z

Zarephath: This Phoenician town (also known as Sarepta) was in the region of Sidon, and it was here that Elijah lived during the last half of a great famine in Ahab's day (1 Kings 17:8–16). Ruins of the ancient town lie about 8 miles (13 km) south of Sidon. It has been thoroughly excavated. It had pottery workshops and kilns; discoveries include idols and figurines, scores of everyday objects, and several inscriptions, including some in Ugaritic. (See: Ahab; Ugarit)

Zeus: Zeus was the chief god in the Olympian Greek pantheon. The Romans called him Jupiter. The pagans of Lystra thought that Barnabas was Zeus appearing as a man (Acts 14:13). (See: Acropolis; Maccabees; Pergamos)

Maps

of Bible Lands and Events

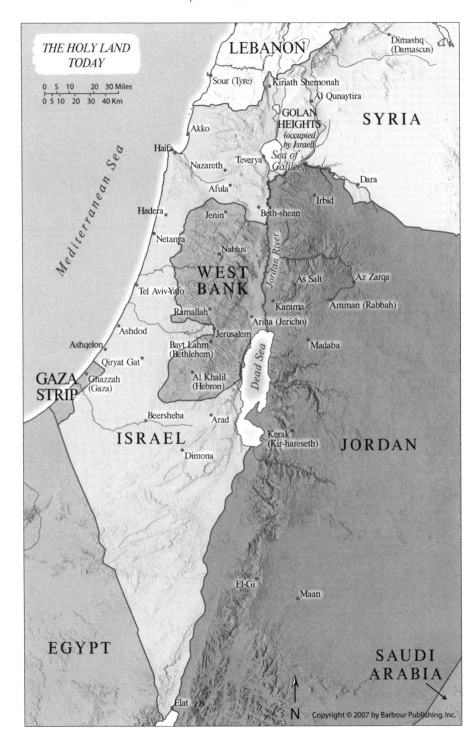

THE HOLY LAND
TODAY

0   5   10   20   30 Miles
0 5 10   20   30   40 Km

Mediterranean Sea

LEBANON

Dimashq
(Damascus)

Sour (Tyre)

Kiriath Shemonah

Al Qunaytira

GOLAN
HEIGHTS
(occupied
by Israel)

SYRIA

Akko

Haifa

Sea of
Galilee

Nazareth

Teverya

Dara

Afula

Irbid

Hadera

Jenin

Beth-shean

Netanya

Nablus

WEST
BANK

Jordan River

As Salt

Az Zarqa

Tel Aviv-Yafo

Ramallah

Karama

Amman (Rabbah)

Ashdod

Jerusalem

Ariha (Jericho)

Ashqelon

Bayt Lahm
(Bethlehem)

Madaba

Qiryat Gat

GAZA
STRIP

Ghazzah
(Gaza)

Al Khalil
(Hebron)

Dead Sea

Beersheba

Arad

Kerak
(Kir-hareseth)

JORDAN

ISRAEL

Dimona

El-Gi

Maan

EGYPT

SAUDI
ARABIA

N

Copyright © 2007 by Barbour Publishing, Inc.

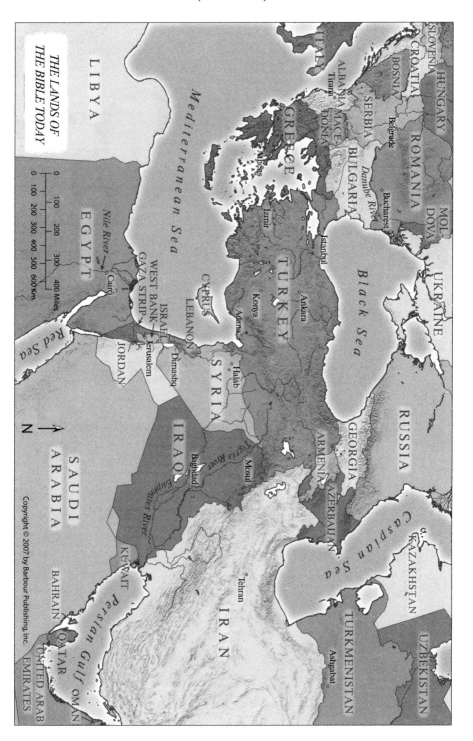

THE LANDS OF
THE BIBLE TODAY

LIBYA

EGYPT

Mediterranean Sea

Nile River

Cairo

Red Sea

N →

SAUDI
ARABIA

Copyright © 2007 by Barbour Publishing, Inc.

ITALY
SLOVENIA
CROATIA
BOSNIA
HUNGARY
ALBANIA
MACE-
DONIA
SERBIA
Tirana
Belgrade
GREECE
Athens
BULGARIA
ROMANIA
Bucharest
Danube River
MOL-
DOVA
Izmir
UKRAINE
Istanbul
TURKEY
Ankara
Konya
Adana
CYPRUS
LEBANON
Halab
SYRIA
Dimashq
Black Sea
RUSSIA
GEORGIA
ARMENIA
AZERBAIJAN
Caspian Sea
KAZAKHSTAN
WEST BANK
GAZA STRIP
ISRAEL
Jerusalem
JORDAN
IRAQ
Baghdad
Mosul
Tigris River
Euphrates River
IRAN
Tehran
KUWAIT
BAHRAIN
QATAR
UNITED ARAB
EMIRATES
Persian Gulf
OMAN
TURKMENISTAN
Ashgabat
UZBEKISTAN

0
100 200 300 400 500 600 Km
0
100 200 300 400 Miles

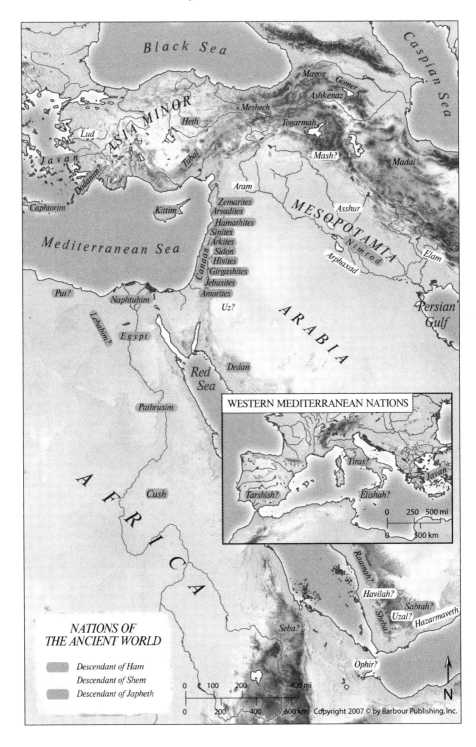

Black Sea

Caspian Sea

Magog
Gomer
Ashkenaz

ASIA MINOR

Meshech

Heth

Togarmah

Lud

Mash?

Madai

Javan

Tubal

Dodanim?

Aram

MESOPOTAMIA

Asshur

Caphtorim

Kittim

Zemarites
Arvadites
Hamathites
Sinites
Arkites
Sidon
Hivites
Girgashites
Jebusites
Amorites

Nimrod

Elam

Mediterranean Sea

Canaan

Arphaxad

Put?

Naphtuhim

Uz?

Persian
Gulf

Lehabim?

ARABIA

Egypt

Red
Sea

Dedan

Pathrusim

WESTERN MEDITERRANEAN NATIONS

AFRICA

Cush

Tiras?

Javan

Tarshish?

Elishah?

0   250   500 mi

0   300 km

Raamah?

Havilah?

Sabtah?
Uzal?   Hazarmaveth
Sheba?

NATIONS OF
THE ANCIENT WORLD

Seba?

Ophir?

Descendant of Ham
Descendant of Shem
Descendant of Japheth

N

0   100   200   400 mi

0   200   400   600 km   Copyright 2007 © by Barbour Publishing, Inc.

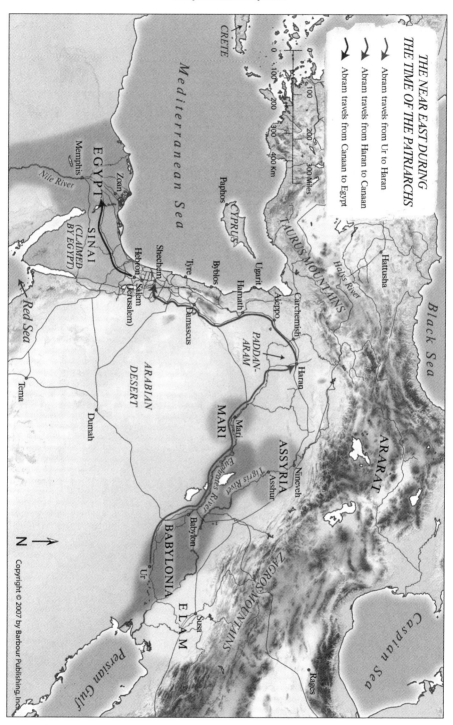

THE NEAR EAST DURING
THE TIME OF THE PATRIARCHS

Abram travels from Ur to Haran
Abram travels from Haran to Canaan
Abram travels from Canaan to Egypt

Black Sea

Caspian Sea

Mediterranean Sea

CRETE

CYPRUS

Paphos

EGYPT

Memphis

Zoan

Nile River

SINAI
(CLAIMED
BY EGYPT)

Red Sea

Tema

Dumah

ARABIAN
DESERT

Shechem
Hebron
Salem
(Jerusalem)
Tyre
Byblos
Damascus
Hamath
Ugarit
Aleppo

TAURUS MOUNTAINS

Halys River

Hattusha

Carchemish

PADDAN-
ARAM

Haran

MARI

Mari

Euphrates River

Tigris River

ASSYRIA

Asshur

Nineveh

ARARAT

ZAGROS MOUNTAINS

Babylon

BABYLONIA

Ur

Susa

ELAM

Rages

Persian Gulf

N →

0   100   200   300   400 Km
0   100   200   300 Miles

Copyright © 2007 by Barbour Publishing, Inc.

596

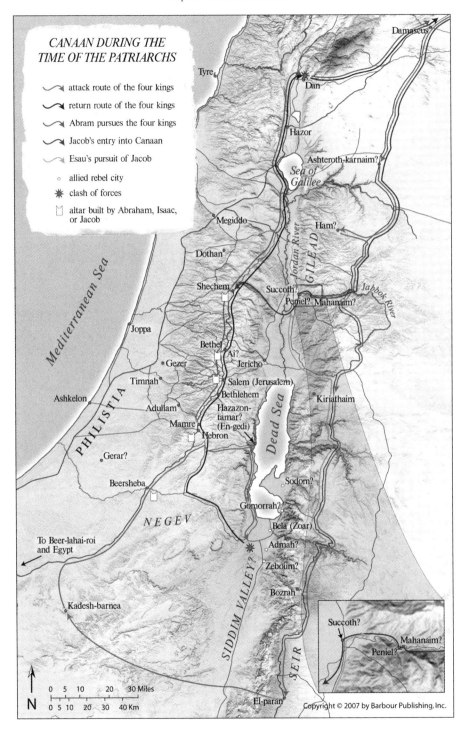

CANAAN DURING THE
TIME OF THE PATRIARCHS

~ attack route of the four kings

~ return route of the four kings

~ Abram pursues the four kings

~ Jacob's entry into Canaan

~ Esau's pursuit of Jacob

○ allied rebel city

✳ clash of forces

⛪ altar built by Abraham, Isaac, or Jacob

Damascus

Tyre

Dan

Hazor

Ashteroth-karnaim?

Sea of Galilee

Megiddo

Ham?

Jordan River

GILEAD

Dothan

Jabbok River

Shechem

Succoth?

Peniel? Mahanaim?

Joppa

Mediterranean Sea

Bethel

Ai?

Gezer

Jericho

Timnah

Salem (Jerusalem)

Ashkelon

PHILISTIA

Bethlehem

Adullam

Kiriathaim

Mamre

Hazazon-
tamar?
(En-gedi)

Hebron

Dead Sea

Gerar?

Sodom?

Beersheba

Gomorrah?

NEGEV

Bela (Zoar)

To Beer-lahai-roi
and Egypt

Admah?

Zeboiim?

SIDDIM VALLEY?

Bozrah

Kadesh-barnea

SEIR

Succoth?

Mahanaim?

Peniel?

0 5 10   20   30 Miles

N

0 5 10   20   30   40 Km

El-paran

Copyright © 2007 by Barbour Publishing, Inc.

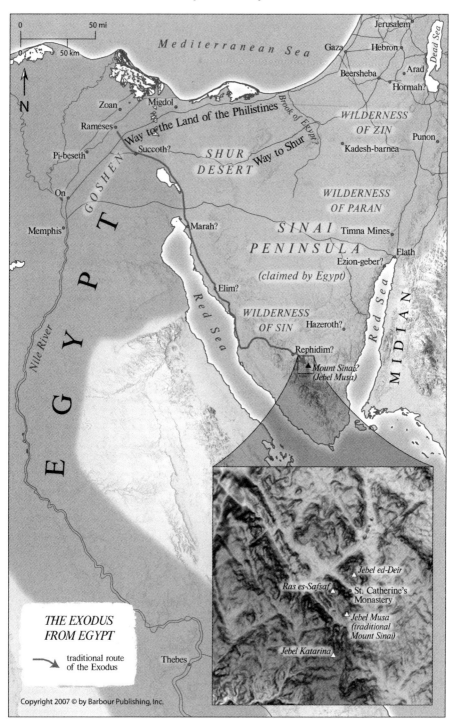

THE EXODUS
FROM EGYPT

→ traditional route
of the Exodus

Copyright 2007 © by Barbour Publishing, Inc.

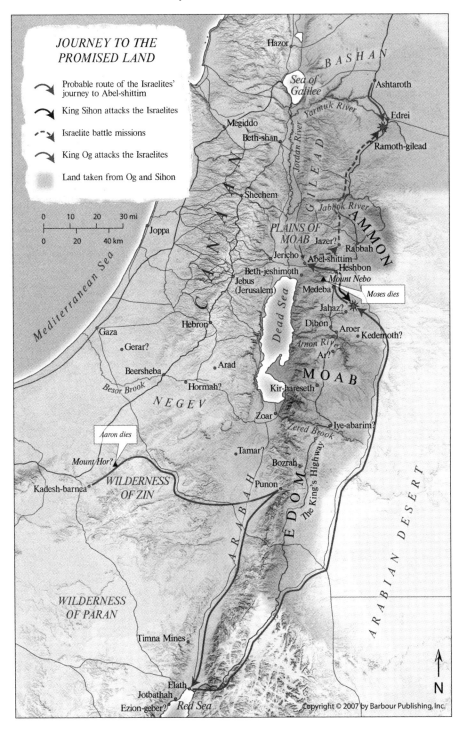

JOURNEY TO THE
PROMISED LAND

Probable route of the Israelites'
journey to Abel-shittim

King Sihon attacks the Israelites

Israelite battle missions

King Og attacks the Israelites

Land taken from Og and Sihon

0   10   20   30 mi

0   20   40 km

BASHAN

Hazor

Sea of
Galilee

Ashtaroth

Edrei

Yarmuk River

Ramoth-gilead

Megiddo

Beth-shan

GILEAD

Jordan River

Shechem

Jabbok River

AMMON

Joppa

PLAINS OF
MOAB   Jazer?

Rabbah

Jericho

Abel-shittim

Heshbon

Beth-jeshimoth

Mount Nebo

Jebus
(Jerusalem)

Medeba

Moses dies

Jahaz?

Hebron

Dibon

Aroer

Kedemoth?

Gaza

Dead Sea

Ar?

Gerar?

Arnon River

Beersheba

Arad

MOAB

Besor Brook

Hormah?

Kir-hareseth

NEGEV

Zoar

Mediterranean Sea

Iye-abarim?

Zered Brook

Tamar?

Aaron dies

Bozrah

Mount Hor?

Punon

WILDERNESS
OF ZIN

The King's Highway

Kadesh-barnea

ARABAH

EDOM

ARABIAN DESERT

WILDERNESS
OF PARAN

Timna Mines

Elath

N

Jotbathah

Red Sea

Ezion-geber?

Copyright © 2007 by Barbour Publishing, Inc.

599

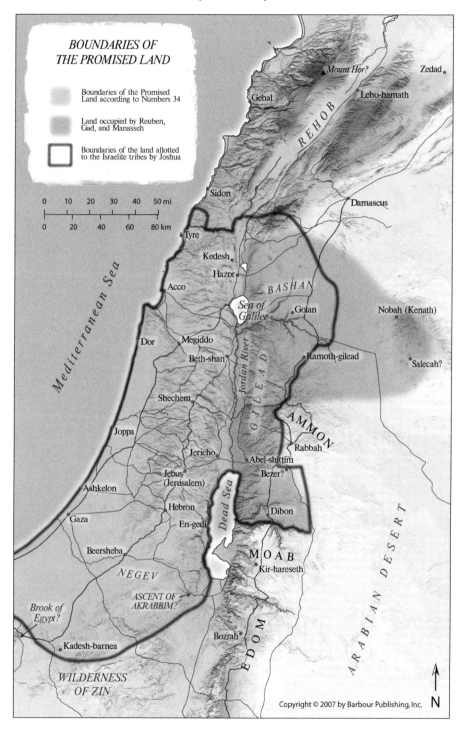

BOUNDARIES OF
THE PROMISED LAND

Boundaries of the Promised
Land according to Numbers 34

Land occupied by Reuben,
Gad, and Manasseh

Boundaries of the land allotted
to the Israelite tribes by Joshua

0   10   20   30   40   50 mi

0   20   40   60   80 km

Mount Hor?

Zedad

Gebal

REHOB

Lebo-hamath

Sidon

Damascus

Tyre

Kedesh

Hazor

BASHAN

Acco

Sea of
Galilee

Golan

Nobah (Kenath)

Mediterranean Sea

Dor

Megiddo

Jordan River

GILEAD

Ramoth-gilead

Salecah?

Beth-shan

Shechem

AMMON

Joppa

Rabbah

Jericho

Abel-shittim

Jebus
(Jerusalem)

Bezer?

Ashkelon

Dead Sea

Hebron

Dibon

Gaza

En-gedi

ARABIAN DESERT

Beersheba

MOAB

NEGEV

Kir-hareseth

ASCENT OF
AKRABBIM?

Brook of
Egypt?

EDOM

Kadesh-barnea

Bozrah

N

WILDERNESS
OF ZIN

Copyright © 2007 by Barbour Publishing, Inc.

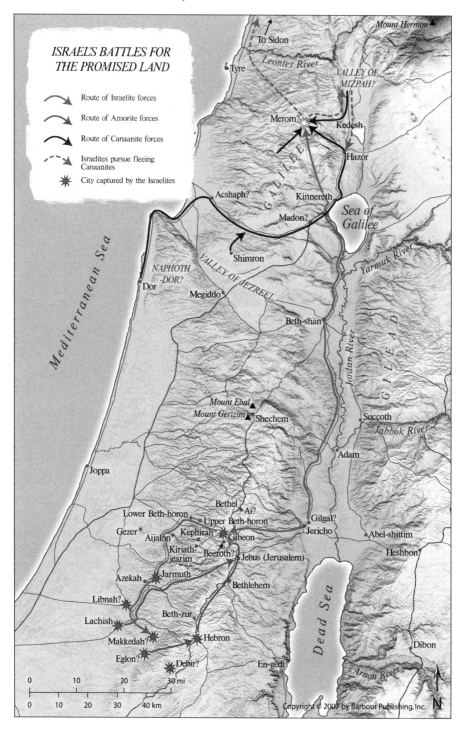

ISRAEL'S BATTLES FOR THE PROMISED LAND

Route of Israelite forces

Route of Amorite forces

Route of Canaanite forces

Israelites pursue fleeing Canaanites

City captured by the Israelites

Mount Hermon ▲

To Sidon

Leontes River

Tyre

VALLEY OF MIZPAH?

Merom? M

Kedesh

Hazor

GALILEE

Acshaph?

Kinnereth

Madon?

Sea of Galilee

Shimron

NAPHOTH -DOR?

VALLEY OF JEZREEL

Yarmuk River

Dor

Megiddo

Beth-shan

GILEAD

Mediterranean Sea

Jordan River

Mount Ebal ▲
Mount Gerizim ▲ Shechem

Succoth

Jabbok River

Adam

Joppa

Bethel
Ai?

Lower Beth-horon
Upper Beth-horon
Gilgal?
Jericho

Gezer
Aijalon
Kephirah
Gibeon

Abel-shittim

Kiriath- jearim
Beeroth?
Jebus (Jerusalem)

Heshbon?

Azekah
Jarmuth

Bethlehem

Libnah?
Beth-zur

Dead Sea

Lachish

Makkedah?
Hebron

Dibon

Eglon?
Debir?

En-gedi

Arnon River

0	10	20	30 mi

0	10	20	30	40 km

Copyright © 2007 by Barbour Publishing, Inc.

N

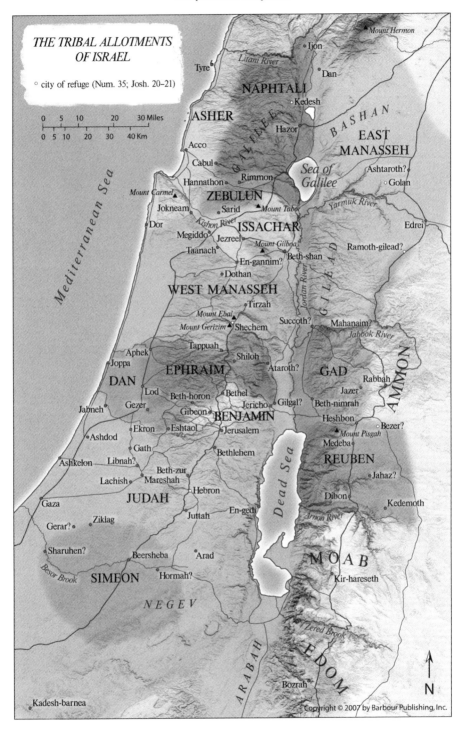

THE TRIBAL ALLOTMENTS
OF ISRAEL

○ city of refuge (Num. 35; Josh. 20–21)

0 5 10   20   30 Miles
0 5 10   20   30   40 Km

Mount Hermon

Ijon

Litani River

Tyre

Dan

NAPHTALI

Kedesh

BASHAN

ASHER

Hazor

EAST
MANASSEH

Acco

GALILEE

Ashtaroth?

Cabul

Sea of
Galilee

Golan

Mount Carmel

Hannathon

Rimmon

ZEBULUN

Yarmuk River

Jokneam

Sarid

Mount Tabor

Kishon River

ISSACHAR

Edrei

Dor

Megiddo

Jezreel

Mount Gilboa

Ramoth-gilead?

Taanach

En-gannim?

Beth-shan

GILEAD

Dothan

WEST MANASSEH

Jordan River

Tirzah

Mount Ebal

Succoth?

Mahanaim?

Mount Gerizim

Shechem

Jabbok River

Tappuah

Shiloh

Aphek

Ataroth?

GAD

AMMON

Joppa

EPHRAIM

DAN

Rabbah

Lod

Beth-horon

Bethel

Jazer

Jabneh

Gezer

Gibeon

Jericho

Gilgal?

Beth-nimrah

Ekron

BENJAMIN

Heshbon

Bezer?

Ashdod

Eshtaol

Jerusalem

Mount Pisgah

Gath

Medeba

Ashkelon

Libnah?

Bethlehem

Dead
Sea

REUBEN

Lachish

Beth-zur

Mareshah

Gaza

Hebron

Jahaz?

Gerar?

Ziklag

Juttah

En-gedi

Dibon

Kedemoth

Arnon River

Sharuhen?

MOAB

Beersheba

Arad

SIMEON

Hormah?

Kir-hareseth

N E G E V

Bezor Brook

ARABAH

Zered Brook

EDOM

Bozrah

N

Kadesh-barnea

Mediterranean Sea

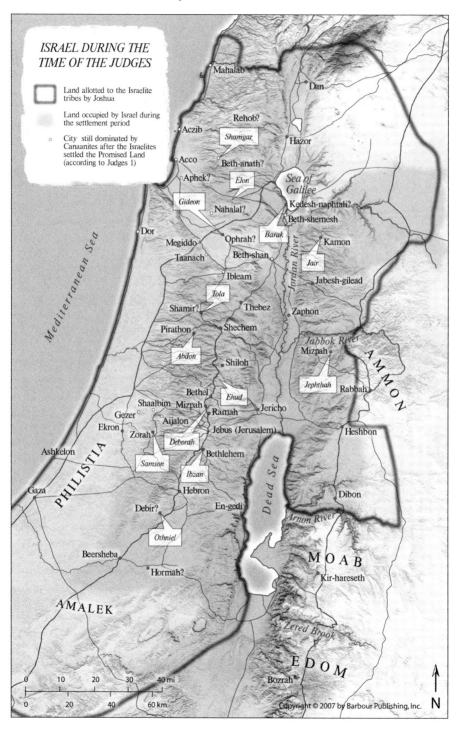

ISRAEL DURING THE
TIME OF THE JUDGES

Land allotted to the Israelite
tribes by Joshua

Land occupied by Israel during
the settlement period

o City still dominated by
Canaanites after the Israelites
settled the Promised Land
(according to Judges 1)

Mahalab

Dan

Rehob?

Aczib

Shamgar

Acco

Hazor

Beth-anath?

Aphek?

Elon

Sea of
Galilee

Gideon

Nahalal?

Kedesh-naphtali?

Dor

Beth-shemesh

Megiddo

Ophrah?

Barak

Kamon

Taanach

Beth-shan

Jordan River

Jair

Ibleam

Jabesh-gilead

Tola

Shamir?

Thebez

Zaphon

Pirathon

Shechem

Jabbok River

Mizpah

AMMON

Abdon

Shiloh

Jephthah

Rabbah

Bethel

Ehud

Shaalbim

Mizpah

Ramah

Jericho

Gezer

Aijalon

Ekron

Zorah?

Jebus (Jerusalem)

Heshbon

Ashkelon

Deborah

Samson

Bethlehem

Dead Sea

Ibzan

Gaza

PHILISTIA

Hebron

Debir?

En-gedi

Dibon

Arnon River

Othniel

Beersheba

MOAB

Hormah?

Kir-hareseth

AMALEK

Mediterranean Sea

Zered Brook

EDOM

0   10   20   30   40 mi

0   20   40   60 km

Bozrah

Copyright © 2007 by Barbour Publishing, Inc.

N

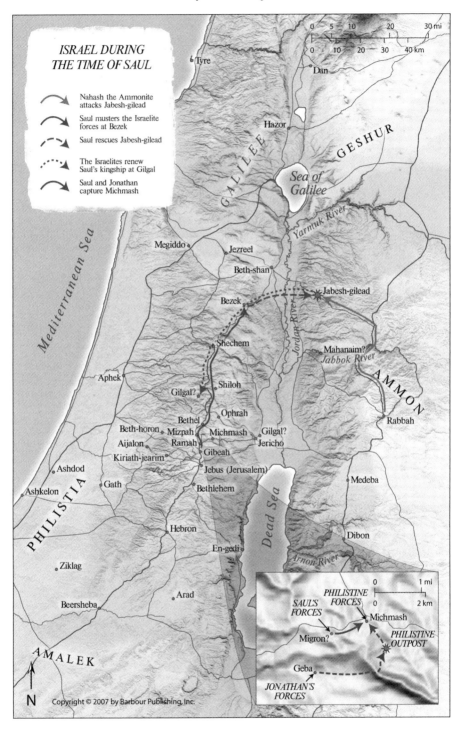

ISRAEL DURING
THE TIME OF SAUL

Nahash the Ammonite
attacks Jabesh-gilead

Saul musters the Israelite
forces at Bezek

Saul rescues Jabesh-gilead

The Israelites renew
Saul's kingship at Gilgal

Saul and Jonathan
capture Michmash

Tyre

Dan

Mediterranean Sea

GALILEE

GESHUR

Hazor

Sea of
Galilee

Yarmuk River

Megiddo

Jezreel

Beth-shan

Bezek

Jabesh-gilead

Shechem

Mahanaim?
Jabbok River

Aphek

Gilgal?

Shiloh

Ophrah

Jordan River

AMMON

Beth-horon

Bethel

Mizpah

Michmash

Gilgal?

Rabbah

Aijalon

Ramah

Gibeah

Jericho

Kiriath-jearim

Jebus (Jerusalem)

Ashdod

Gath

Bethlehem

Medeba

Ashkelon

PHILISTIA

Hebron

Dead Sea

Dibon

En-gedi

Arnon River

Ziklag

Arad

Beersheba

AMALEK

N

Copyright © 2007 by Barbour Publishing, Inc.

SAUL'S
FORCES

PHILISTINE
FORCES

Michmash

PHILISTINE
OUTPOST

Migron?

Geba

JONATHAN'S
FORCES

604

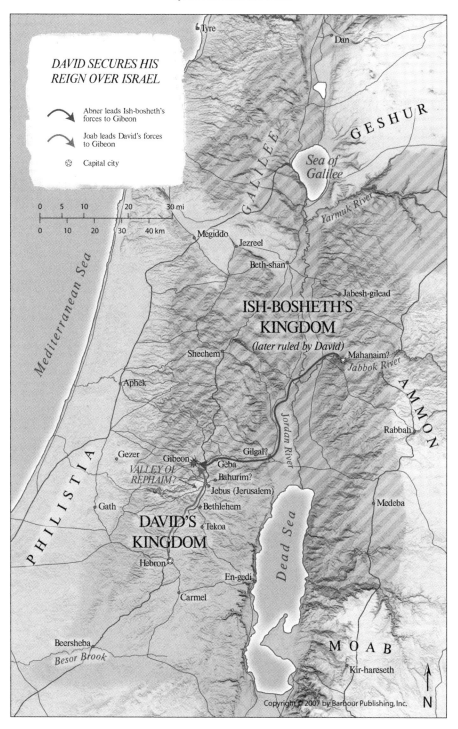

DAVID SECURES HIS
REIGN OVER ISRAEL

Abner leads Ish-bosheth's
forces to Gibeon

Joab leads David's forces
to Gibeon

Capital city

0   5   10   20   30 mi
0   10   20   30   40 km

Tyre

Dan

GESHUR

GALILEE

Sea of
Galilee

Yarmuk River

Mediterranean Sea

Megiddo

Jezreel

Beth-shan

Jabesh-gilead

ISH-BOSHETH'S
KINGDOM

(later ruled by David)

Shechem

Mahanaim?
Jabbok River

Aphek

AMMON

Rabbah

Jordan River

Gezer

Gilgal?

Gibeon

Geba

VALLEY OF
REPHAIM?

Bahurim?

Jebus (Jerusalem)

Gath

Bethlehem

Medeba

DAVID'S
KINGDOM

Tekoa

PHILISTIA

Hebron

Dead Sea

En-gedi

Carmel

Beersheba

Besor Brook

M O A B

Kir-hareseth

Copyright © 2007 by Barnour Publishing, Inc.

N

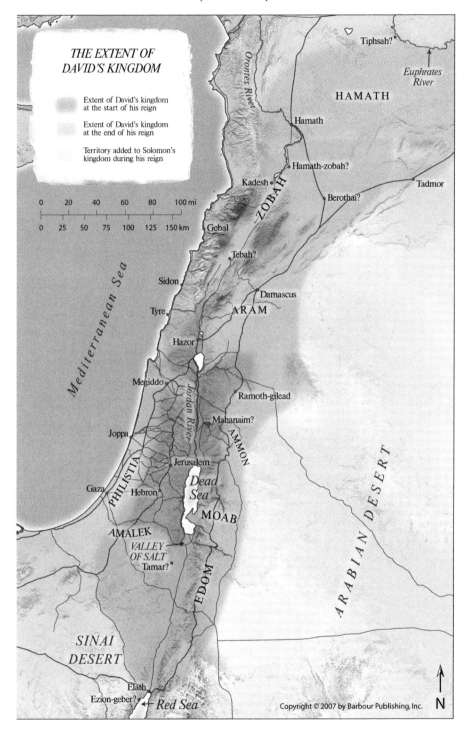

THE EXTENT OF DAVID'S KINGDOM

Extent of David's kingdom at the start of his reign

Extent of David's kingdom at the end of his reign

Territory added to Solomon's kingdom during his reign

0   20   40   60   80   100 mi

0   25   50   75   100   125   150 km

Mediterranean Sea

Orontes River

Euphrates River

Tiphsah?

HAMATH

Hamath

Hamath-zobah?

Kadesh

Berothai?

Tadmor

ZOBAH

Gebal

Tebah?

Sidon

Damascus

Tyre

ARAM

Hazor

Megiddo

Jordan River

Ramoth-gilead

Mahanaim?

AMMON

Joppa

Jerusalem

Gaza

PHILISTIA

Hebron

Dead Sea

MOAB

AMALEK

VALLEY OF SALT

Tamar?

EDOM

ARABIAN DESERT

SINAI DESERT

Elath

Ezion-geber?

Red Sea

Copyright © 2007 by Barbour Publishing, Inc.

N

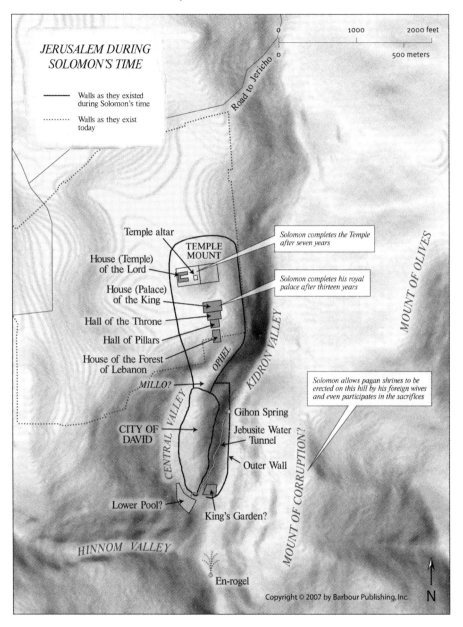

JERUSALEM DURING SOLOMON'S TIME

——— Walls as they existed
during Solomon's time

·········· Walls as they exist
today

Temple altar

TEMPLE MOUNT

House (Temple) of the Lord

Solomon completes the Temple after seven years

House (Palace) of the King

Solomon completes his royal palace after thirteen years

Hall of the Throne

Hall of Pillars

House of the Forest of Lebanon

OPHEL

MILLO?

KIDRON VALLEY

MOUNT OF OLIVES

Solomon allows pagan shrines to be erected on this hill by his foreign wives and even participates in the sacrifices

CENTRAL VALLEY

Gihon Spring

CITY OF DAVID

Jebusite Water Tunnel

Outer Wall

Lower Pool?

King's Garden?

MOUNT OF CORRUPTION?

HINNOM VALLEY

En-rogel

Road to Jericho

0   1000   2000 feet

0   500 meters

Copyright © 2007 by Barbour Publishing, Inc.

N

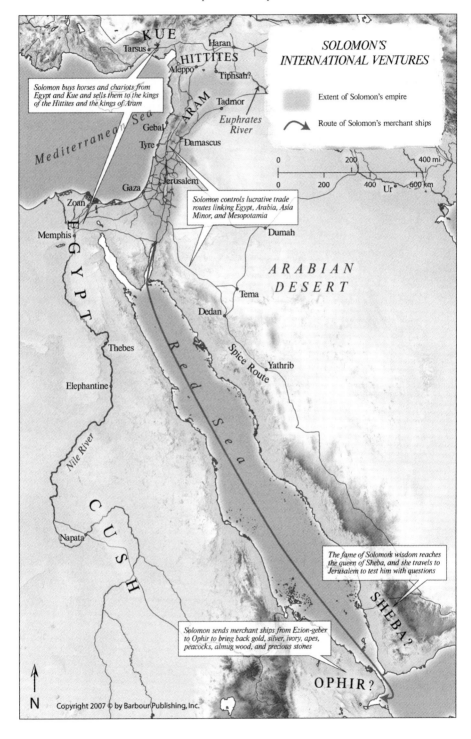

SOLOMON'S
INTERNATIONAL VENTURES

Extent of Solomon's empire

Route of Solomon's merchant ships

KUE

Tarsus

Haran

HITTITES

Aleppo

Tiphsah?

ARAM

Tadmor

Euphrates
River

Gebal

Mediterranean Sea

Damascus

Tyre

Jerusalem

Gaza

Zoan

EGYPT

Memphis

Dumah

ARABIAN
DESERT

Tema

Dedan

Thebes

Spice Route

Yathrib

Elephantine

Red Sea

Nile River

CUSH

Napata

SHEBA?

OPHIR?

0   200   400 mi
0   200   400   600 km
Ur

Solomon buys horses and chariots from
Egypt and Kue and sells them to the kings
of the Hittites and the kings of Aram

Solomon controls lucrative trade
routes linking Egypt, Arabia, Asia
Minor, and Mesopotamia

The fame of Solomon's wisdom reaches
the queen of Sheba, and she travels to
Jerusalem to test him with questions

Solomon sends merchant ships from Ezion-geber
to Ophir to bring back gold, silver, ivory, apes,
peacocks, almug wood, and precious stones

N

Copyright 2007 © by Barbour Publishing, Inc.

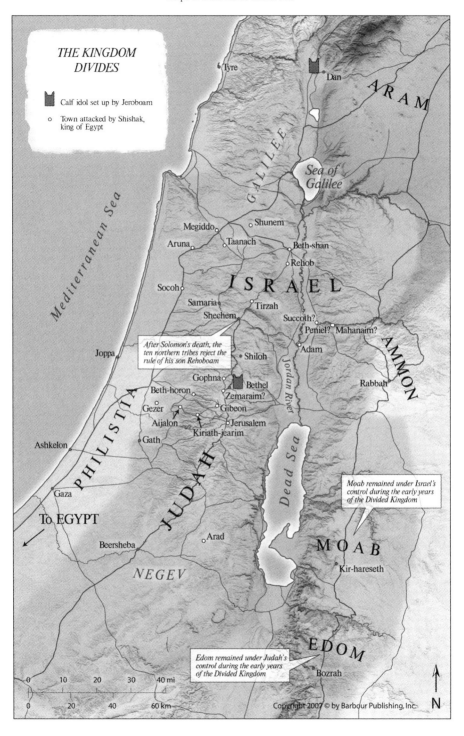

THE KINGDOM DIVIDES

🏛 Calf idol set up by Jeroboam

○ Town attacked by Shishak, king of Egypt

Tyre

Dan

A R A M

GALILEE

Sea of Galilee

Mediterranean Sea

Megiddo

Shunem

Aruna

Taanach

Beth-shan

Rehob

Socoh

I S R A E L

Samaria

Tirzah

Shechem

Succoth?

Peniel? Mahanaim?

Adam

After Solomon's death, the ten northern tribes reject the rule of his son Rehoboam

Joppa

Shiloh

Jordan River

Gophna

Bethel

AMMON

Beth-horon

Zemaraim?

Rabbah

Gezer

Gibeon

Aijalon

Jerusalem

Ashkelon

Kiriath-jearim

Gath

P H I L I S T I A

Dead Sea

Moab remained under Israel's control during the early years of the Divided Kingdom

Gaza

J U D A H

To EGYPT

Arad

M O A B

Beersheba

N E G E V

Kir-hareseth

E D O M

Edom remained under Judah's control during the early years of the Divided Kingdom

Bozrah

0   10   20   30   40 mi

0   20   40   60 km

Copyright 2007 © by Barbour Publishing, Inc.

N

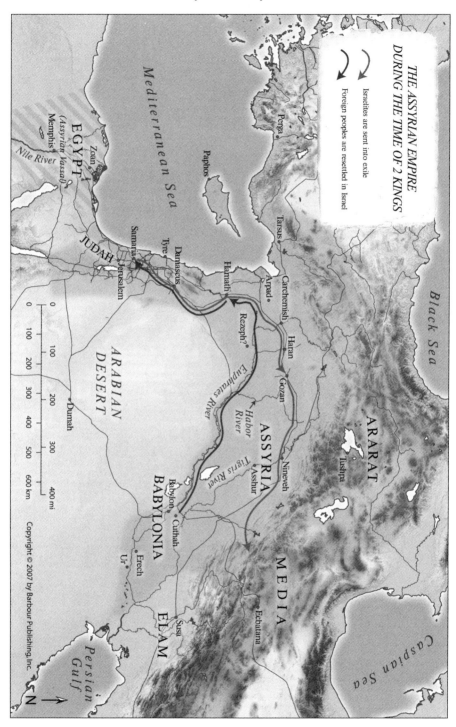

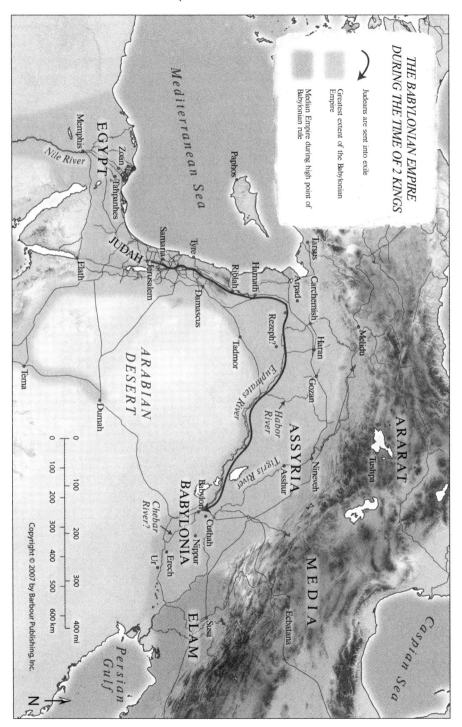

THE BABYLONIAN EMPIRE
DURING THE TIME OF 2 KINGS

Judeans are sent into exile

Greatest extent of the Babylonian
Empire

Median Empire during high point of
Babylonian rule

Mediterranean Sea

Memphis
EGYPT
Nile River
Zoan
Tahpanhes

Paphos

JUDAH
Samaria
Elath
Jerusalem
Tyre
Riblah
Damascus
Hamath
Arpad
Tarsus
Carchemish
Haran
Gozan
Melidi

ARARAT
Tushpa

Rezeph?
Tadmor
Euphrates River
Habor River
Tigris River
ASSYRIA
Asshur
Nineveh

ARABIAN DESERT

Tema

Dumah

BABYLONIA
Babylon
Chebar River?
Cuthah
Nippur
Ur
Erech
ELAM
Susa

MEDIA
Ecbatana

Caspian Sea

Persian Gulf

N

0   0
100   100
200   200
300   300
400   400
500
600 km   400 mi

Copyright © 2007 by Barbour Publishing, Inc.

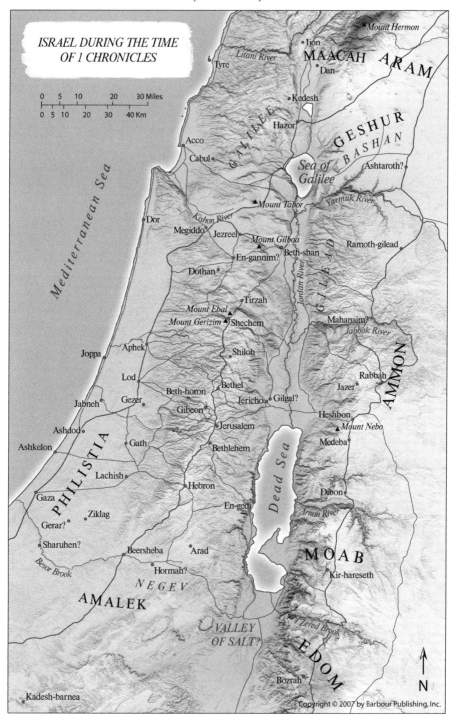

ISRAEL DURING THE TIME
OF 1 CHRONICLES

0   5   10   20   30 Miles
0 5 10   20   30   40 Km

Mediterranean Sea

Mount Hermon

Ijon

MAACAH   ARAM

Tyre

Dan

Litani River

Kedesh

GESHUR

Hazor

BASHAN

Acco

GALILEE

Cabul

Sea of
Galilee

Ashtaroth?

Kishon River

Mount Tabor

Yarmuk River

Dor

Megiddo   Jezreel

Mount Gilboa

Ramoth-gilead

En-gannim?   Beth-shan

GILEAD

Dothan

Jordan River

Tirzah

Mount Ebal

Mahanaim?

Mount Gerizim   Shechem

Jabbok River

Shiloh

Aphek

AMMON

Joppa

Bethel

Rabbah

Lod

Beth-horon

Jericho   Gilgal?

Jazer

Jabneh

Gezer

Gibeon

Heshbon

Ashdod

Jerusalem

Mount Nebo

Ashkelon

Gath

Bethlehem

Medeba

Dead Sea

PHILISTIA

Lachish

Gaza

Hebron

Dibon

Ziklag

En-gedi

Gerar?

Arnon River

Sharuhen?

Beersheba

Arad

MOAB

Hormah?

Kir-hareseth

Bezor Brook

NEGEV

AMALEK

VALLEY
OF SALT?

Zered Brook

EDOM

Bozrah

N

Kadesh-barnea

Copyright © 2007 by Barbour Publishing, Inc.

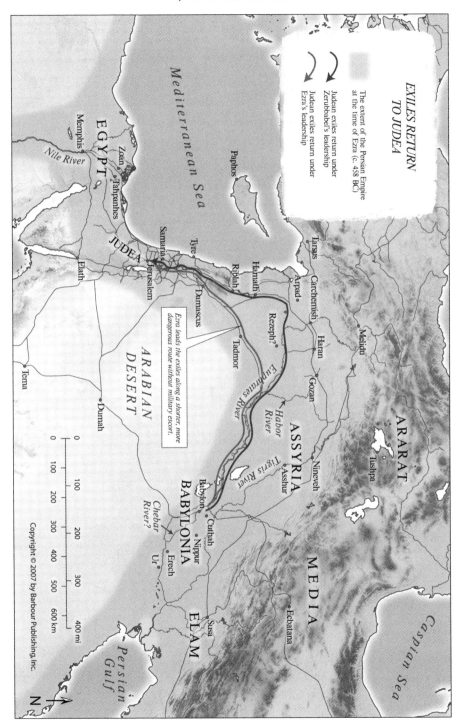

EXILES RETURN
TO JUDEA

The extent of the Persian Empire
at the time of Ezra (c. 458 BC)

Judean exiles return under
Zerubbabel's leadership

Judean exiles return under
Ezra's leadership

*Ezra leads the exiles along a shorter, more
dangerous route without military escort.*

N

Copyright © 2007 by Barbour Publishing, Inc.

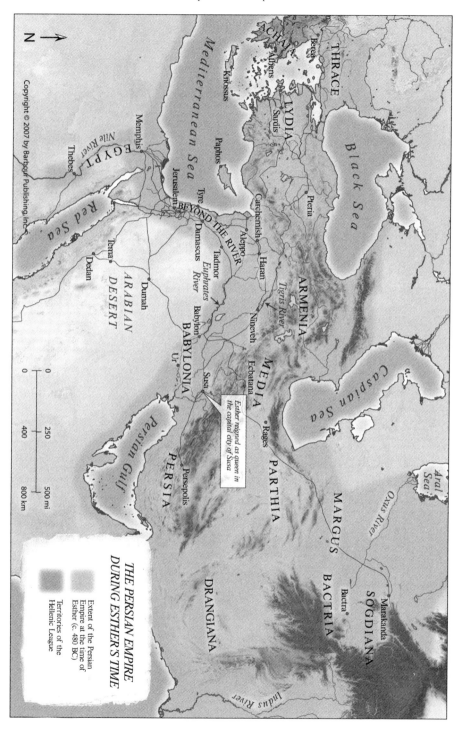

N →

Copyright © 2007 by Barbour Publishing, Inc.

Mediterranean Sea

Nile River

EGYPT

Memphis

Thebes

Red Sea

ACHAIA

Berea

Athens

Knossos

Paphos

Tyre

Jerusalem

BEYOND THE RIVER

Damascus

Tadmor

Euphrates River

Aleppo

Carchemish

Haran

Nineveh

Tigris River

Babylon

BABYLONIA

Ur

Susa

Dedan

Tema

Dumah

ARABIAN DESERT

THRACE

LYDIA

Sardis

Pteria

Black Sea

ARMENIA

MEDIA

Ecbatana

Rages

Caspian Sea

PARTHIA

Aral Sea

Oxus River

MARGUS

BACTRIA

Bactra

Maracanda

SOGDIANA

Persian Gulf

PERSIA

Persepolis

DRANGIANA

Indus River

Esther reigned as queen in the capital city of Susa

0   0
250   400
500 mi 800 km

THE PERSIAN EMPIRE DURING ESTHER'S TIME

Extent of the Persian Empire at the time of Esther (c. 480 BC)

Territories of the Hellenic League

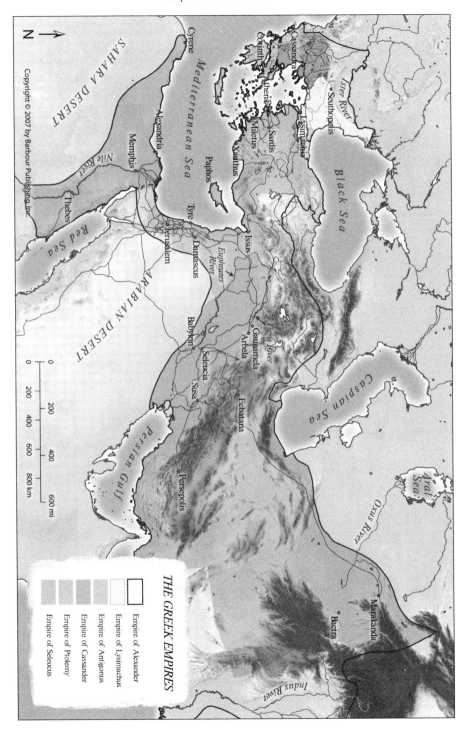

N →

Copyright © 2007 by Barbour Publishing, Inc.

SAHARA DESERT

Cyrene

Mediterranean Sea

Corinth
Cassandra
Athens
Sardis
Miletus
Lysimachia
Xanthus
Paphos

Ister River
Scythopolis

Black Sea

Alexandria

Nile River

Memphis

Thebes

Red Sea

ARABIAN DESERT

Tyre
Jerusalem
Damascus

Euphrates River

Issus

Babylon
Seleucia
Susa

Tigris River

Gaugamela
Arbela
Ecbatana

Caspian Sea

Aral Sea

Oxus River

Persian Gulf

Persepolis

Indus River

Bactra

Marakanda

0
200
400
600
800 km

0
200
400
600 mi

THE GREEK EMPIRES

Empire of Alexander
Empire of Lysimachus
Empire of Antigonus
Empire of Cassander
Empire of Ptolemy
Empire of Seleucus

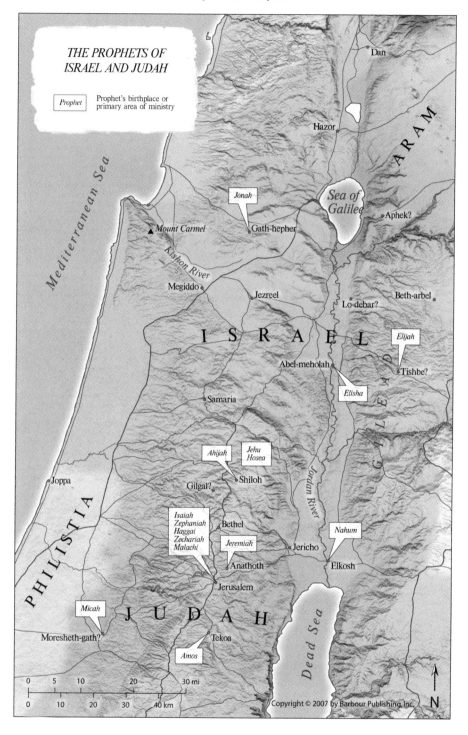

THE PROPHETS OF
ISRAEL AND JUDAH

Prophet — Prophet's birthplace or primary area of ministry

Dan

ARAM

Hazor

Mediterranean Sea

Jonah

Sea of Galilee

Gath-hepher

Aphek?

▲ *Mount Carmel*

Kishon River

Megiddo

Jezreel

Lo-debar?

Beth-arbel

I S R A E L

Elijah

Abel-meholah

Tishbe?

Elisha

Samaria

Ahijah

Jehu Hosea

Joppa

Gilgal?

Shiloh

Jordan River

GILEAD

P H I L I S T I A

Isaiah Zephaniah Haggai Zechariah Malachi

Bethel

Jeremiah

Nahum

Anathoth

Jericho

Elkosh

Jerusalem

Micah

J U D A H

Dead Sea

Moresheth-gath?

Tekoa

Amos

0   5   10   20   30 mi
0   10   20   30   40 km

N

Copyright © 2007 by Barbour Publishing, Inc.

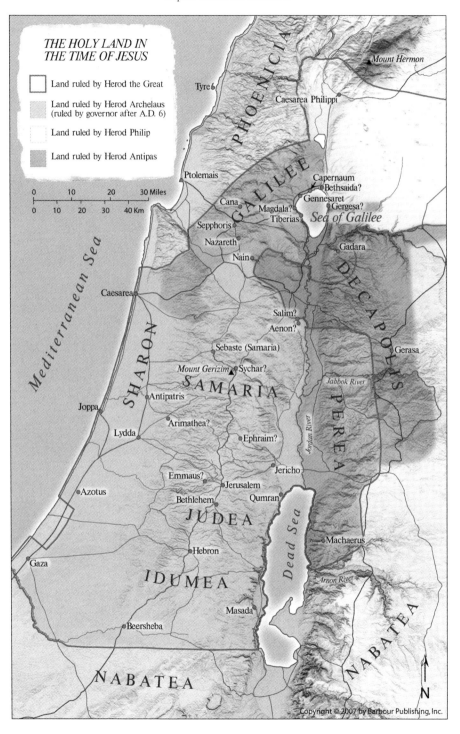

THE HOLY LAND IN
THE TIME OF JESUS

Land ruled by Herod the Great

Land ruled by Herod Archelaus
(ruled by governor after A.D. 6)

Land ruled by Herod Philip

Land ruled by Herod Antipas

0   10   20   30 Miles
0   10   20   30   40 Km

Mount Hermon

Tyre

Caesarea Philippi

PHOENICIA

Ptolemais

GALILEE

Capernaum
Bethsaida?
Cana   Gennesaret
Magdala?   Gergesa?
Tiberias   Sea of Galilee
Sepphoris

Nazareth   Gadara

Nain   DECAPOLIS

Mediterranean Sea

Caesarea

Salim?
Aenon?

Sebaste (Samaria)   Gerasa

SHARON   Mount Gerizim Sychar?

SAMARIA   Jabbok River

Antipatris   PEREA

Joppa   Arimathea?

Lydda   Jordan River

Ephraim?

Emmaus?   Jericho

Azotus   Jerusalem
Bethlehem   Qumran

JUDEA   Dead Sea

Gaza   Hebron

Machaerus

IDUMEA

Arnon River

Masada

Beersheba

NABATEA   NABATEA

N

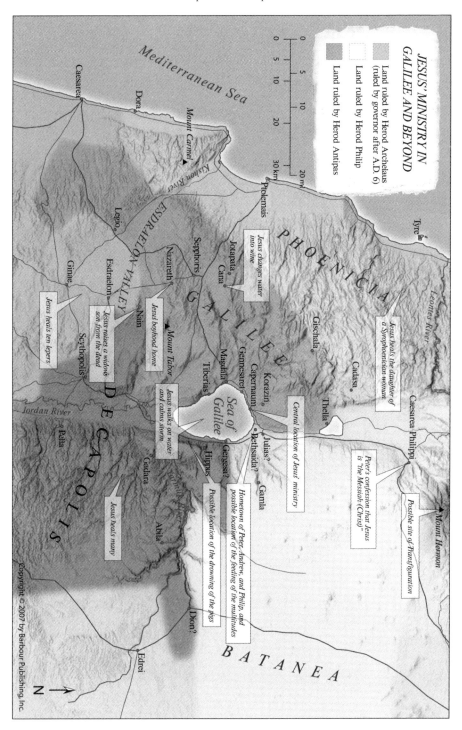

JESUS' MINISTRY IN GALILEE AND BEYOND

Land ruled by Herod Archelaus (ruled by governor after A.D. 6)
Land ruled by Herod Philip
Land ruled by Herod Antipas

Mediterranean Sea

Caesarea
Dora
Mount Carmel
Kishon River
Ptolemais
Tyre
PHOENICIA
Leontes River
Legio
ESDRAELON VALLEY
Sepphoris
Jotapata
Cana
Jesus changes water into wine
Gischala
Cadasa
Nazareth
Jesus heals the daughter of a Syrophoenician woman
GALILEE
Gimae
Esdraelon
Nain
Mount Tabor
Jesus' boyhood home
Magdala
Gennesaret
Capernaum
Korazin
Thella
Caesarea Philippi
Jesus raises a widow's son from the dead
Jesus heals ten lepers
Scythopolis
Tiberias
Sea of Galilee
Central location of Jesus' ministry
Peter's confession that Jesus is "the Messiah (Christ)"
Jesus walks on water and calms storm
Julias?
Bethsaida?
Gamla
Mount Hermon
Possible site of Transfiguration
Jordan River
DECAPOLIS
Hippus
Gergesa?
Hometown of Peter, Andrew, and Philip, and possible location of the feeding of the multitudes
Pella
Gadara
Abila
Jesus heals many
Yarmuk River
Possible location of the drowning of the pigs
Dion?
Edrei
BATANEA
N

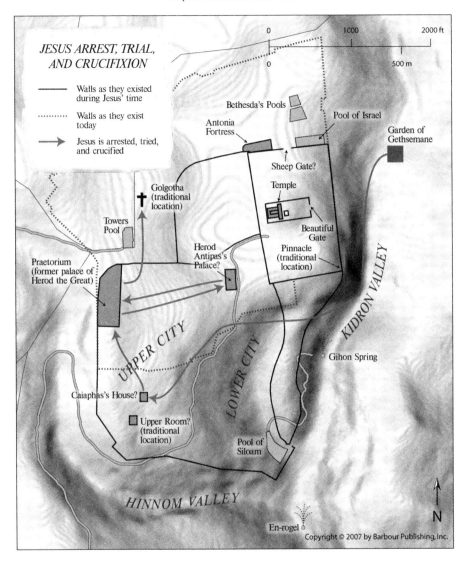

JESUS ARREST, TRIAL,
AND CRUCIFIXION

——— Walls as they existed
during Jesus' time

········· Walls as they exist
today

——→ Jesus is arrested, tried,
and crucified

Bethesda's Pools

Antonia
Fortress

Pool of Israel

Garden of
Gethsemane

Sheep Gate?

Temple

Golgotha
(traditional
location)

Towers
Pool

Beautiful
Gate

Herod
Antipas's
Palace?

Pinnacle
(traditional
location)

Praetorium
(former palace of
Herod the Great)

KIDRON VALLEY

UPPER CITY

Gihon Spring

Caiaphas's House?

LOWER CITY

Upper Room?
(traditional
location)

Pool of
Siloam

HINNOM VALLEY

En-rogel

Copyright © 2007 by Barbour Publishing, Inc.

N

0   1000   2000 ft

0   500 m

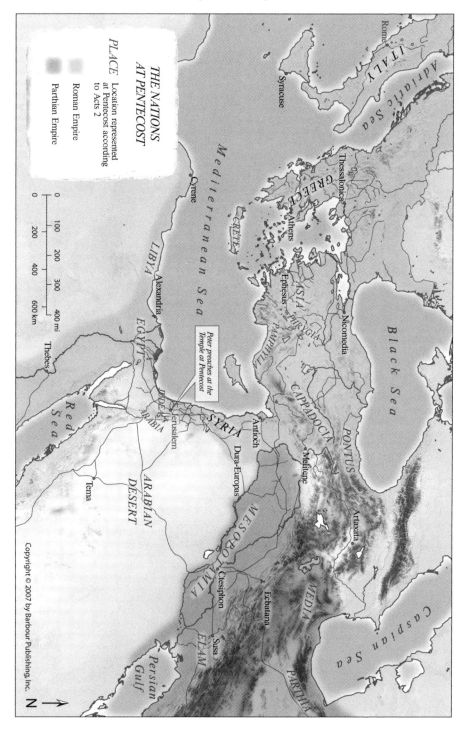

THE NATIONS
AT PENTECOST

PLACE   Location represented
        at Pentecost according
        to Acts 2

        Roman Empire

        Parthian Empire

0
0
100   200
200   400
300
400 mi   600 km

Peter preaches at the
Temple at Pentecost

Copyright © 2007 by Barbour Publishing, Inc.

N →

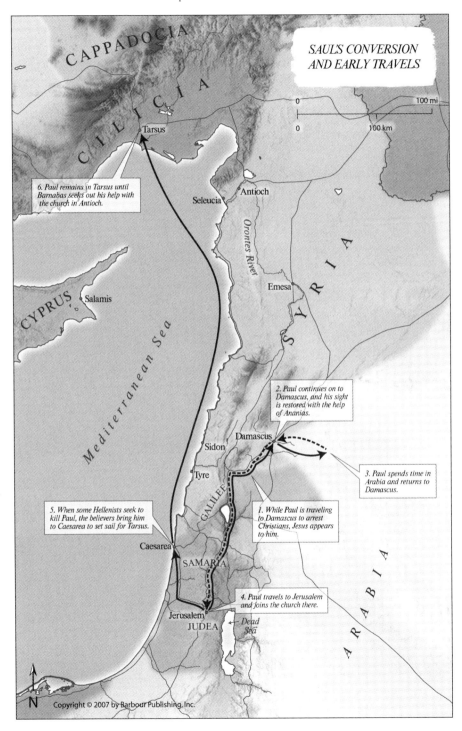

SAUL'S CONVERSION
AND EARLY TRAVELS

100 mi

100 km

CAPPADOCIA

CILICIA

Tarsus

6. Paul remains in Tarsus until
Barnabas seeks out his help with
the church in Antioch.

Seleucia   Antioch

Orontes River

SYRIA

Emesa

CYPRUS   Salamis

Mediterranean Sea

2. Paul continues on to
Damascus, and his sight
is restored with the help
of Ananias.

Sidon   Damascus

Tyre

3. Paul spends time in
Arabia and returns to
Damascus.

GALILEE

5. When some Hellenists seek to
kill Paul, the believers bring him
to Caesarea to set sail for Tarsus.

1. While Paul is traveling
to Damascus to arrest
Christians, Jesus appears
to him.

Caesarea

SAMARIA

ARABIA

4. Paul travels to Jerusalem
and joins the church there.

Jerusalem
JUDEA   Dead
Sea

N

Copyright © 2007 by Barbour Publishing, Inc.

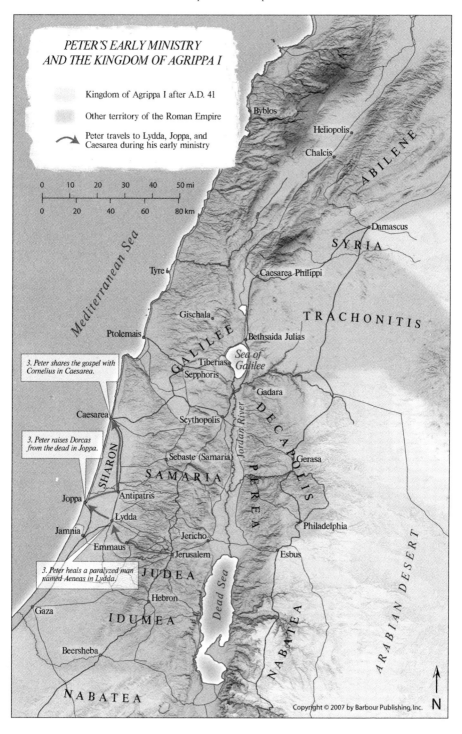

PETER'S EARLY MINISTRY
AND THE KINGDOM OF AGRIPPA I

Kingdom of Agrippa I after A.D. 41

Other territory of the Roman Empire

Peter travels to Lydda, Joppa, and
Caesarea during his early ministry

0   10   20   30   40   50 mi

0   20   40   60   80 km

Byblos

Heliopolis

Chalcis

ABILENE

Damascus

SYRIA

Mediterranean Sea

Tyre

Caesarea Philippi

TRACHONITIS

Gischala

Ptolemais

GALILEE

Bethsaida Julias

Sea of
Galilee

3. Peter shares the gospel with
Cornelius in Caesarea.

Tiberias

Sepphoris

Gadara

DECAPOLIS

Caesarea

Scythopolis

Jordan River

3. Peter raises Dorcas
from the dead in Joppa.

SHARON

Sebaste (Samaria)

Gerasa

SAMARIA

PEREA

Joppa

Antipatris

Lydda

Jamnia

Jericho

Philadelphia

Emmaus

Jerusalem

Esbus

3. Peter heals a paralyzed man
named Aeneas in Lydda.

JUDEA

Dead Sea

Hebron

Gaza

IDUMEA

NABATEA

ARABIAN DESERT

Beersheba

NABATEA

Copyright © 2007 by Barbour Publishing, Inc.

N

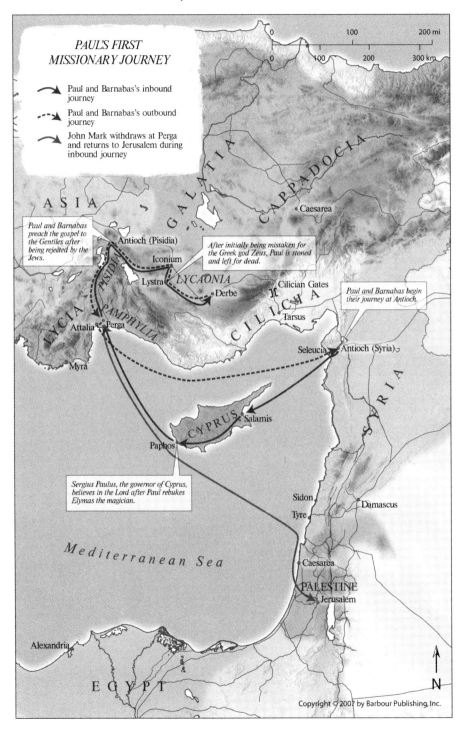

PAUL'S FIRST MISSIONARY JOURNEY

→ Paul and Barnabas's inbound journey

⇢ Paul and Barnabas's outbound journey

↩ John Mark withdraws at Perga and returns to Jerusalem during inbound journey

Paul and Barnabas preach the gospel to the Gentiles after being rejected by the Jews.

After initially being mistaken for the Greek god Zeus, Paul is stoned and left for dead.

Paul and Barnabas begin their journey at Antioch.

Sergius Paulus, the governor of Cyprus, believes in the Lord after Paul rebukes Elymas the magician.

ASIA

GALATIA

CAPPADOCIA

Caesarea

PISIDIA

Antioch (Pisidia)

Iconium

LYCAONIA

LYCIA

Lystra

Derbe

Cilician Gates

PAMPHYLIA

Tarsus

CILICIA

Attalia

Perga

Myra

Seleucia

Antioch (Syria)

SYRIA

CYPRUS

Salamis

Paphos

Sidon

Damascus

Tyre

Mediterranean Sea

Caesarea

PALESTINE

Jerusalem

Alexandria

EGYPT

N

100   200 mi

100   200   300 km

Copyright © 2007 by Barbour Publishing, Inc.

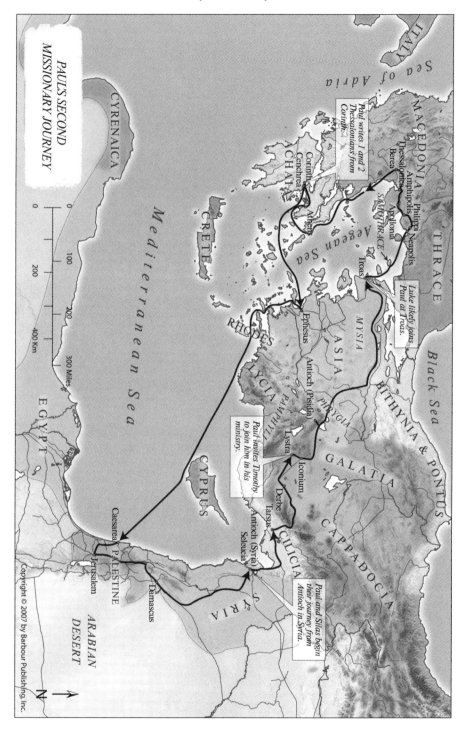

PAUL'S SECOND
MISSIONARY JOURNEY

Paul writes 1 and 2
Thessalonians from
Corinth.

Luke likely joins
Paul at Troas.

Paul invites Timothy
to join him in his
ministry.

Paul and Silas begin
their journey from
Antioch in Syria.

Copyright © 2007 by Barbour Publishing, Inc.

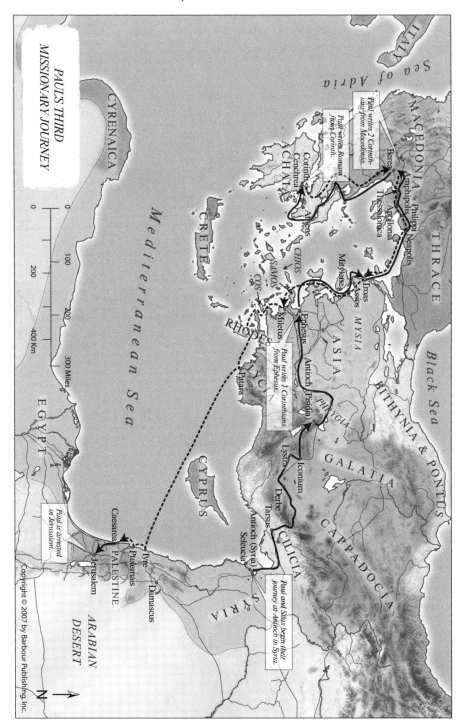

PAUL'S THIRD MISSIONARY JOURNEY

Paul writes 2 Corinthians from Macedonia.

Paul writes Romans from Corinth.

Paul writes 1 Corinthians from Ephesus.

Paul is arrested in Jerusalem.

Paul and Silas begin their journey at Antioch in Syria.

Copyright © 2007 by Barbour Publishing, Inc.

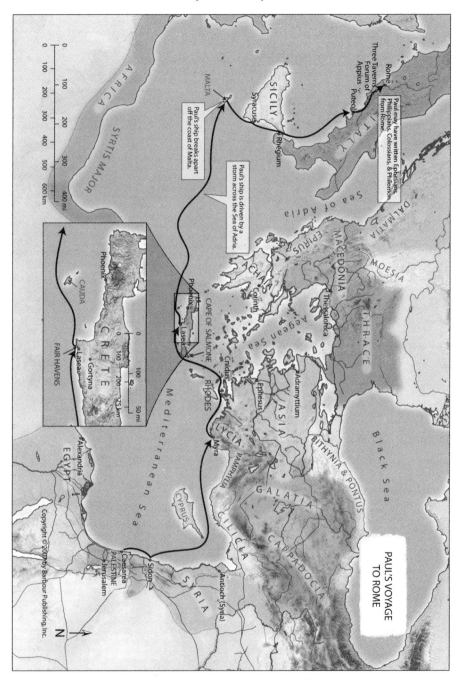

PAUL'S VOYAGE TO ROME

Paul's ship breaks apart off the coast of Malta.

Paul's ship is driven by a storm across the Sea of Adria.

Paul may have written Ephesians, Philippians, Colossians, & Philemon from Rome.

AFRICA

SYRTIS MAJOR

MALTA

SICILY

Syracuse

Rhegium

ITALY

Rome

Three Taverns

Forum of Appius

Puteoli

Sea of Adria

DALMATIA

EPIRUS

MACEDONIA

MOESIA

THRACE

ACHAIA

Corinth

Thessalonica

Aegean Sea

Phoenix

Phoenix

CRETE

CAUDA

FAIR HAVENS

Lasea

Gortyna

CAPE OF SALMONE

Lasea

Cnidus

RHODES

Ephesus

Adramyttium

ASIA

BITHYNIA & PONTUS

Black Sea

LYCIA

Myra

PAMPHILIA

GALATIA

CILICIA

CAPPADOCIA

Mediterranean Sea

CYPRUS

Alexandria

EGYPT

Sidon

Caesarea

PALESTINE

Jerusalem

SYRIA

Antioch (Syria)

N

Copyright © 2007 by Barbour Publishing, Inc.

0   100   200   300   400   500   600 km

0   100   200   300   400 mi

0   100   200 km

0   50   75 mi

100   25 km

50 mi

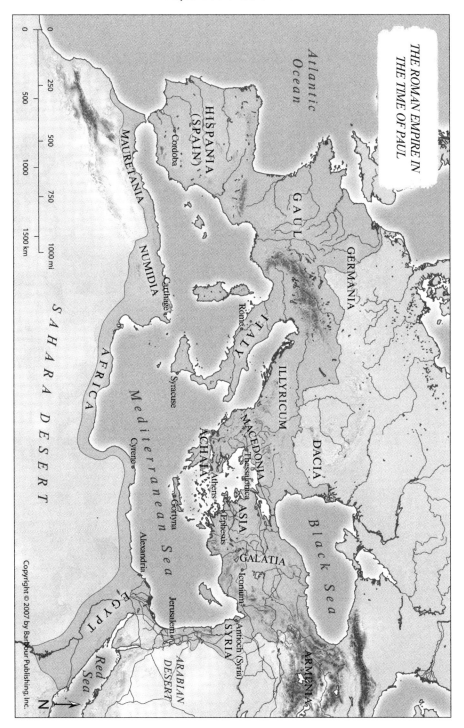

THE ROMAN EMPIRE IN
THE TIME OF PAUL

Atlantic
Ocean

HISPANIA
(SPAIN)

Cordoba

GAUL

GERMANIA

MAURETANIA

NUMIDIA

Carthage

Rome

ITALY

ILLYRICUM

DACIA

Black Sea

AFRICA

Syracuse

Mediterranean Sea

MACEDONIA

Thessalonica

ACHAIA

Athens

ASIA

Ephesus

GALATIA

Iconium

SAHARA DESERT

Cyrene

Gortyna

Alexandria

EGYPT

Jerusalem

Antioch (Syria)

SYRIA

ARMENIA

ARABIAN DESERT

Red Sea

N

0   250   500   1000   1500 km
0   250   500   750   1000 mi

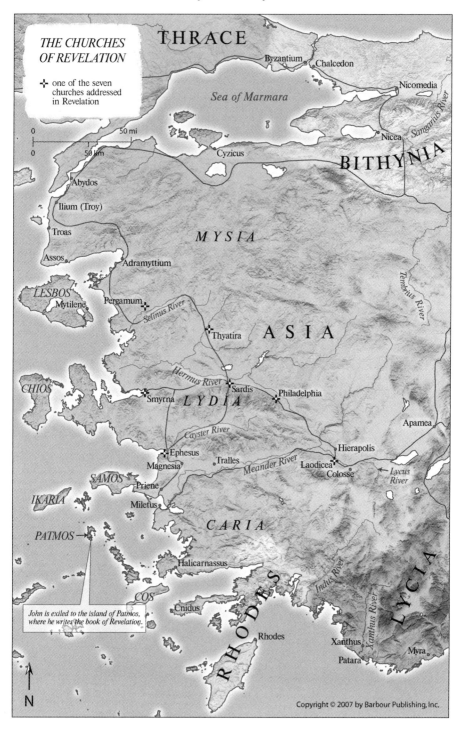

THE CHURCHES
OF REVELATION

✛ one of the seven
churches addressed
in Revelation

THRACE

Byzantium   Chalcedon

Nicomedia

Sea of Marmara

Nicea

BITHYNIA

Cyzicus

Sangarius River

0   50 mi
0   50 km

Abydos

Ilium (Troy)

Troas

Assos

MYSIA

Adramyttium

Tembris River

LESBOS

Mytilene

Pergamum

Selinus River

Thyatira

ASIA

CHIOS

Hermus River

Sardis

Philadelphia

Smyrna   LYDIA

Apamea

Cayster River

Ephesus

Magnesia

Tralles

Meander River

Hierapolis

Laodicea

Colosse

Lycus
River

SAMOS

Priene

Miletus

IKARIA

CARIA

PATMOS →

Halicarnassus

Indus River

Xanthus River

LYCIA

COS

Cnidus

John is exiled to the island of Patmos,
where he writes the book of Revelation.

RHODES

Rhodes

Xanthus

Patara

Myra

N

Copyright © 2007 by Barbour Publishing, Inc.

628

How to
Study the Bible

To the men of God I've known throughout my life
who have taught me how to study the Bible

Introduction

When you study the Bible, you'll discover what millions of people have found throughout the centuries: you're reading the Word of the living God. In times past, He spoke to His special servants audibly, in visions, in dreams; now His main method of revelation to all humanity is His written Word.

Over a period of fifteen hundred years, the Holy Spirit directed forty holy men of God, living on three continents, to write His words into sixty-six books using three different languages. These writings were preserved and collected into the single volume we know as the Bible.

Though people wrote it, the Bible itself says God was its ultimate source. In 2 Timothy 3:16 (KJV), we read, "All scripture is given by inspiration of God," which literally means it was breathed out by God.

The New Testament gives several descriptive titles to the Bible: the Word of God, the oracles of God, the Word of Christ, the holy scriptures, the word of truth, and the word of life. In studying the Bible, we're learning God's Word, holy and true, which contains the knowledge of eternal life.

The people of Thessalonica (who received two letters from the apostle Paul, which became part of the Bible) recognized that the apostle was giving them the Word of God in his preaching and from his pen. First Thessalonians 2:13 (NASB) tells us, "For this reason we also constantly thank God that when you received the word of God which you heard from us, you accepted it not as the word of men, but for what it really is, the word of God."

Years ago, when I was a high school student, my reading skills were poor. I had difficulty understanding and retaining what I read. Later, when I realized that God communicates to us through His written Word, I concluded that if I wanted to know Him and His truth, I must give myself to studying His Word. I've studied the Bible for many years now, encouraged along the way by devoted Christians who love the Bible.

Many Christians have made this same decision, and virtually all will testify to the great spiritual blessings that come from studying God's Word. Having studied and taught the Bible now for more than thirty years, I'll share things I've learned through my own experience as well as what others have taught me.

My hope and prayer is that through reading this book, you'll be encouraged to become one of those believers who is taught by God, learning His Word and receiving the special blessings He's reserved for you.

If you're new to the Christian faith, you'll find helpful recommendations in this book. If you've been a Christian for a while but have struggled in your personal Bible study, you'll be encouraged and challenged to have victory in this area of your life. If you're reading this book as a mature believer established in Bible study, my intention is to stir you up—to remember those things you have already learned and to help others learn how to study God's truth. People in your life need to learn what God has taught you, and you can become an answer to their prayers for a person to help them.

Some may rationalize their lack of Bible study by saying that life is too busy or studying the Bible is too hard. Others, who struggle with sin, as I did early in my Christian life, may honestly admit that it's just too convicting to read. Please don't let excuses stop you from studying God's Word.

Jesus made it clear that learning and living the Bible is God's will for our lives. He said, "'Man shall not live by bread alone, but by every word that proceeds from the mouth of God'" (Matthew 4:4). Bible study isn't just a nice thing to do—it's essential to our lives!

1. Preparation:

Readying Our Hearts for Bible Study

For the word of God is living and active and sharper than any two-edged sword, and piercing as far as the division of soul and spirit, of both joints and marrow, and able to judge the thoughts and intentions of the heart.

HEBREWS 4:12 NASB

People who want to learn how to study the Bible often ask, "Where do I begin?"

It's a good question, but the answer might be surprising. We actually begin with ourselves. We prepare our hearts to study the Bible.

Many activities in life require preparation. If we're going to exercise, we first stretch our muscles to avoid injuries. If we're going to do a job around the house, we first gather the tools and materials the job requires. If we're going on a trip, we first make sure our car is properly maintained, that we've packed everything we need, and that we have a good map.

We might be tempted to think we can just jump in without any kind of preparation, but we've all experienced what happens when we fail to prepare: problems and disappointments.

Studying the Bible also requires some preparation, so we can have a profitable time studying and avoid problems that might discourage us, leading us to give up. I'm talking about personal preparation that focuses on our hearts. This is something we can easily overlook, and if not addressed, contributes to the breakdown of daily Bible study.

Frequently the Bible uses the word *heart* in a figurative sense, referring to the innermost portions of our being—our thoughts, emotions, and will—rather than the physical heart. It's our hearts that interest the Lord. When the prophet Samuel was preparing to anoint the future king of Israel, the Lord told him, "'Man looks at the outward appearance, but the LORD looks at the heart'" (1 Samuel 16:7).

As we think about personal Bible study, we shouldn't view it as another intellectual exercise like the study of math, science, history, or anything else that interests us. When studying these disciplines, the mind is engaged, but not the heart. God wants us to increase our knowledge of His Word with our minds, but He also intends for the power of His Word to affect our hearts and that our lives will be changed to become more like Christ's.

Concern for a change of life was expressed by the Lord Jesus for His disciples when He prayed, "'Sanctify them by Your truth. Your word is truth'" (John 17:17).

Two disciples, who didn't recognize the resurrected Lord Jesus as He walked with them on the Emmaus Road, illustrate the experience of having the heart involved in learning God's Word. As they walked with Jesus, He began to teach them things about Himself from all of the Old Testament scriptures. Later that evening, as they recalled their experience, they said to each other, "'Did not our heart burn within us while He talked with us on the road, and while He opened the Scriptures to us?'" (Luke 24:32).

The hearts of these two disciples had previously been confused and discouraged as they thought the crucifixion of Jesus meant His defeat and end. When they finally recognized Him and He vanished from their presence, they considered how their hearts were warmed with spiritual revival and excitement. The spiritual heartburn they experienced was a good thing!

When our minds and our hearts are prepared and involved in Bible study, our time spent in God's Word is enjoyable and exciting.

People can have a good study Bible, have a few helpful study books, follow numerous recommended procedures, and have a quiet place to concentrate, and still not benefit spiritually from the time spent in the Bible because their hearts aren't prepared to be involved in the process. Their focus may be on only intellectual growth, not spiritual growth.

The religious leaders in Jesus' day, the scribes and Pharisees, made this error. They had a serious heart condition known as hypocrisy. Jesus described them this way: "'These people draw near to Me with their mouth, and honor Me with their lips, but their heart is far from Me'" (Matthew 15:8).

They were the kind of people who go through the motions of religious activity, more concerned about their artificial, external religious rules than about having their hearts right before God through faith and obedience to His Word. The human "heart," described as "deceitful above all things, and desperately wicked" in Jeremiah 17:9, is of major concern to God.

This chapter opened with the words of Hebrews 4:12. The context of this verse reveals that God knows everything about every one of us. As we read His Word, it functions as an X-ray machine or heart monitor, revealing to us what He sees in our hearts. Let's see ourselves as God sees us. His Word exposes our hearts so we can take corrective action (Hebrews 4:13).

Addressing issues of the heart was something that most of the scribes and Pharisees neglected to do, but Ezra, an Old Testament priest, "prepared his heart to seek the Law of the LORD" (Ezra 7:10). That's what we need to do as we begin Bible study.

I suggest that preparing our hearts means three things. First, we need to approach God's Word with reliance. Second, we need to approach God's Word with resolve. And thirdly, with repentance.

RELIANCE

Rely on the Holy Spirit

Many people who begin to study the Bible will soon be saying, "I need help!" That's a good conclusion to come to. We all need help, and the person to help us is God. He gave us His Word and also assists us in understanding it. The technical term for this help is *illumination*. Let's look at a few New Testament verses describing God's work illuminating people's hearts.

On one occasion Jesus was teaching people about His Father's work in the lives of those who would be saved. He quoted the Old Testament when He said, "It is written in the prophets, 'And they shall all be taught by God' " (John 6:45). People who have come to know the Lord have experienced the illuminating work of God in their minds and hearts to understand their own lost, sinful condition and to see that Christ is the solution to their problem.

Paul spoke about illumination when he said, "But the natural man does not receive the things of the Spirit of God, for they are foolishness to him; nor can he know them, because they are spiritually discerned" (1 Corinthians 2:14).

The natural man refers to someone who hasn't been saved and therefore doesn't have the indwelling Holy Spirit. People in this condition reject the Gospel message and view it as foolishness. Subjects such as sin, guilt, forgiveness, grace, and salvation don't make sense to them and don't have personal value. They don't have interest, understanding, trust, or appreciation for Christ and His Word because they haven't had the work of God's Spirit in their hearts. Christ's Word must be understood on a spiritual level, not just an intellectual level.

Even the apostles needed divine help for understanding. Before the risen Lord Jesus returned to heaven, He assisted them in understanding the Old Testament. "And He opened their understanding, that they might comprehend the Scriptures" (Luke 24:45). Even though these men learned the scriptures throughout their lives, they failed to understand all that the Word of God predicted about Jesus. They needed His help to finally see.

John Newton, the author of the beloved hymn "Amazing Grace," wrote in the lyrics of that song, "I once was lost but now am found, was blind but now I see." He was referring to his own experience of not grasping biblical truth as a person who was spiritually lost. When he was saved by God's grace, his spiritual blindness was healed so he could say, "Now I see."

The only person who can make the blind see is God, so He's the One we depend on to give us understanding of His Word. The first thing a person needs, simply put, is to be saved, to be totally dependent on God for all his or her spiritual needs. (See Acts 16:30–31.)

Once we have recognized our need for help from God to understand His Word, we should regularly pray for His assistance. The psalmist realized this and expressed dependence to God: "Open my eyes, that I may see wondrous things from Your law" (Psalm 119:18). This is a great prayer for us as well when we prepare our hearts to study His Word.

We should give great concern to our dependence on the Holy Spirit. Not only does He seek to enlighten us, He also reveals that the enemy of our souls is trying to influence our study of God's Word and lead us astray: "In latter times some will depart from the faith, giving heed to deceiving spirits and doctrines of demons" (1 Timothy 4:1).

Rely on Mature Believers

Not only should we rely on the teaching ministry of the Holy Spirit, but we should also rely on mature believers who have a strong knowledge of God's Word.

According to the apostle Paul, God gives certain people a supernatural ability to teach the Word: "Having then gifts differing according to the grace that is given to us, let us use them. . .he who teaches, in teaching" (Romans 12:6–7). But teaching occurs in many settings, as Moses told the ancient Israelites: "'These words, which I am commanding you today, shall be on your heart. You shall teach them diligently to your sons and shall talk of them when you sit in your house and when you walk by the way and when you lie down and when you rise up'" (Deuteronomy 6:6–7 NASB). The design of God is that mature Christians teach His Word to others.

Just before He ascended into heaven, Jesus gave His apostles their final instructions, telling them, "'Go therefore and make disciples of all the nations, baptizing them in the name of the Father and the Son and the Holy Spirit, *teaching them to observe all that I commanded you*'" (Matthew 28:19–20 NASB, emphasis added). What Jesus commanded is recorded for us in the Bible—and the Holy Spirit and gifted teachers help us to understand and apply those commands to our own lives.

RESOLVE

By saying we must study the Bible with resolve, I mean we should be determined to do this and have clear in our minds why we are spending part of our day studying. This is another part of personal preparation. We'd know why we were studying if we were to give a devotional message or share our thoughts about a biblical topic with a group. We'd be motivated by the specific task before us.

But what we're considering at this point are the reasons we're to be consistent in our everyday study habits. What is it that motivates us to be determined to study like the Berean Christians in Acts 17:11, who "searched the Scriptures daily"?

The best answers come straight from the Bible. The following sections describe what God would have us keep in mind so we'll be motivated to be faithful in our study. Call these the Top Ten Reasons for Personal Bible Study.

1. To settle the issue of our own salvation

Paul reminded Timothy about Timothy's own experience: "From childhood you have known the Holy Scriptures, which are able to make you wise for salvation through faith which is in Christ Jesus" (2 Timothy 3:15). This is the primary issue that needs to be settled in everyone's life.

God uses His Word as a means to save sinners. As we think about our conversion, we may be able to identify Bible verses that God used in our lives to save us—or at least a believer's life-giving words that were based on scripture. God also wants us to have what the hymn writer Fanny Crosby called "blessed assurance." Many Christians experience doubts about their own conversion, and through learning those portions of scripture that address this subject, we can have a deepening confidence about our own salvation.

When people want to start reading the Bible, a good place to begin is the

Gospel of John in the New Testament, because this book was specifically written so people might read about Christ, believe in Him, and receive the gift of eternal life from Him. (See John 20:30–31.) This book of the Bible was written with the purpose of helping those who read it find salvation in Christ.

2. To grow spiritually

New Christians are sometimes described as babes in Christ, and of course, all babies need to grow. Peter gave this instruction to Christians in the early church: "But grow in the grace and knowledge of our Lord and Savior Jesus Christ" (2 Peter 3:18).

He also gave a direct exhortation that they should have the same kind of desire for the basic truths of God's Word that a newborn baby has for milk. "As newborn babes, desire the pure milk of the word, that you may grow thereby" (1 Peter 2:2). This is a picture representing intense hunger for God's Word so that we can grow in our understanding and spiritual strength. The Bible repeatedly refers to itself as food for the soul. Just as our bodies need food to survive, our souls need the spiritual food of the Bible.

In Ephesians 4, Paul expressed the same concern as Peter for the growth of believers. He didn't want them to be tossed about and carried away with every wind of doctrine; he wanted them to be steady and strong. When we neglect to develop our understanding of truth, we can be more easily influenced by the error of false teachers. Spiritual growth through studying the Bible protects us from bad spiritual influence.

3. To receive personal blessing and encouragement

Paul wrote, "For whatever things were written before were written for our learning, that we through the patience and comfort of the Scriptures might have hope" (Romans 15:4). As believers, we often experience discouragement in our Christian walk. A common cause of this discouragement is conflict between believers, which Paul addresses in Romans 15. Difficulties between Christians, which create a lack of unity, can be discouraging. As we all eventually learn, there's no lack of tension and trouble in local churches. But as we study the Bible, we see Christ's example. How He interacted with people is the pattern we're to follow for living and for treating others.

When we study the Bible, we'll also read numerous promises God made to give believers hope, and stories about how God providentially worked in the lives of people. Meditating on all these passages of scripture encourages us to persevere in our own Christian life with comfort and hope. "Great are the works of the LORD; they are studied by all who delight in them" (Psalm 111:2 NASB).

Discouragement can also come from conviction about our sins as we're brought face-to-face with God's holy standards in the Bible. When we're honest about our lives, we have to admit we fall short of His glory. It's frustrating to struggle with the same sins over and over, not being able to break bad habits in our lives. But as we continue to read God's Word, we'll also discover the comfort and hope available to us through God's mercy, grace, and forgiveness in Christ.

We can learn about His power to transform our lives and conquer our sinful habits by the power of His Word. Reading about how He pardoned and delivered others—and then us—gives us hope. The God of patience and comfort wants us to be encouraged. Since the Bible was written for our education, the more we learn, the more we can be encouraged.

4. To receive personal guidance

When faced with many of life's decisions, we often wonder, *What should I do now?* Learning the Bible can be helpful in answering this question. "Your word is a lamp to my feet and a light to my path" (Psalm 119:105). The psalmist pictured the effect of learning God's Word as having a lamp for life that lights the way before us so we can see where we're going.

As the nation of Israel journeyed in the wilderness after their exodus from Egypt, they were led by a pillar of fire at night and pillar of cloud by the day. That was how God worked for that group of people at that time. What God has provided for us in our journey is His written Word, which gives us the light of knowledge and wisdom to follow.

Many times the Bible addresses our specific situation, but when it doesn't, there are principles we can apply to our lives so we have confidence that we're being led by God's Word.

In Psalm 119, the psalmist refers to his daily experience of living in a world filled with spiritual and moral darkness, a world that calls good evil and evil good. As believers concerned with pleasing God and wanting to do His will, we try to make decisions that honor Him, but the influence of a dark world often makes this difficult. Through studying the Bible we learn what the will of God is and experience His direction.

As we seek God's guidance, he'll lead us by His Spirit (Romans 8:14), which always agrees with what God has revealed to us in His Word. His Spirit's leading never contradicts what He's written. If our personal decisions contradict what has been written in the Bible, then we can be sure we aren't being led by God.

5. To defend ourselves against the devil

Soon after we become Christians, we find out that the Christian life involves spiritual warfare. In Ephesians 6, Paul instructs believers with these words, "Put on the whole armor of God, that you may be able to stand against the wiles of the devil" (verse 11). The wiles of the devil are the methods he uses against people, trying to keep them from doing the will of God.

The Christian's defense against this assault is putting on the spiritual armor of God: Christian character and lifestyle empowered by God's Spirit. A vital part of this armor is "the sword of the Spirit, which is the word of God" (verse 17).

When the devil confronted Jesus in Matthew 4:1–10, tempting Him to act independently of God's will and questioning God's provision, protection, and plan, Jesus used God's Word to defend Himself. Three times in this story when the devil tempted him, Jesus responded, "It is written," and then quoted specific verses from Deuteronomy to rebuff the temptations. Jesus was able to draw from His knowledge of the Old Testament to overcome temptation by His knowledge of, trust in, and obedience to the Word. So if you're going to say to the tempter, "Get behind me, Satan!" remember to finish your sentence like Jesus did—with an appropriate text of scripture that counters his temptation.

In the apostle John's first letter, he refers to a group of young men, saying, "You are strong, and the word of God abides in you, and you have overcome the wicked one" (1 John 2:14). These believers withstood the devil's assault through their knowledge and application of scripture.

Through Bible study, we'll also be able to remember specific Bible verses, and by applying them, we'll be able to overcome the devil's temptations.

6. To effectively teach God's truth to the next generation

Deuteronomy 6:4—9 is known to Jews as the *Shema* (Hebrew for *hear*, the first word of the passage), and devout Jews recite it twice daily. It gives instruction about loving God, His Word, and loving our children by teaching them God's Word. "'And these words which I command you today shall be in your heart. You shall teach them diligently to your children, and shall talk of them when you sit in your house, when you walk by the way, when you lie down, and when you rise up'" (Deuteronomy 6:6–7). Parents teaching their children is God's pattern for the Christian home.

Parents aren't simply to teach their children, but to teach them diligently. The text also reveals that the teaching is informal, given throughout the day, inside and outside the home. Parents are the primary teachers of their children, and they can only do this effectively if they first learn God's Word themselves.

Parents are to have answers for their children when questioned about God's Word. Moses confirmed this when he wrote, "When your son asks you in time to come, saying, 'What is the meaning of the testimonies, the statutes, and the judgments which the LORD our God has commanded you?' then you shall say to your son. . ." (Deuteronomy 6:20–21). Parents have only a limited amount of time to teach their children before the children are grown and begin their own lives. I can testify that the time, although it's years long, goes by quickly. So studying the Bible ourselves helps us in this important task.

7. To be able to counsel others

God wants to use us to provide knowledge about what He has said in His Word to others. "Let the word of Christ dwell in you richly in all wisdom, teaching and admonishing one another" (Colossians 3:16). In time, God wants to use you to help others who may be newer to the faith. We might be able to remember with gratitude and fondness older Christians who helped us when we wondered what the Bible said about a particular subject.

We should notice what Colossians 3:16 says about learning the Bible: The

Word of Christ is "to dwell in you." This literally means to be at home in you. The Word of Christ is to take up residence in us, influencing every part of our lives. The text goes on to say that the word should "dwell in you richly in all wisdom," indicating that we're to have a full understanding of the Bible. Then we can be a good friend providing wise counsel.

8. To be ready to speak with unbelievers about Christ

"But sanctify the Lord God in your hearts: and be ready always to give an answer to every man that asketh you a reason of the hope that is in you" (1 Peter 3:15 KJV). The concern of Christians shouldn't be winning arguments but winning people. We should be able to answer questions when we're asked and to give an explanation about our faith. Some people who won't listen to a sermon may want to find out about Christ in a private conversation, and we're told to be ready. The more we learn through studying, the more effective we'll become in sharing God's truth with others.

9. To verify that the teaching of others is the truth of God

One group of early Christians, the Bereans, stood out from the rest. "They received the word with all readiness, and searched the Scriptures daily to find out whether these things were so" (Acts 17:11). They checked in scripture to confirm what Paul taught them was true. They were so committed to this that they did it daily. It's a mistake for us to accept the message of Christian teachers just because they're humorous, dynamic, on television or radio, or have written books. The content of their message must be true, and it's good for us to validate it from our own study. Bible teachers should never be offended that people do this; they should encourage it.

10. To present ourselves approved to God

"Be diligent to present yourself approved to God as a workman who does not need to be ashamed, accurately handling the word of truth" (2 Timothy 2:15 NASB). Learning God's truth involves the work of studying.

Like divers who work to locate pearls in the ocean or miners who labor to find gold in the earth, Christians are workers who study the Bible to discover God's truth. We live our lives before God, and as servants we're to regularly present our lives to Him to be examined. We hope to have a sense of His approval and eventually hear from Him, "Well done, good and faithful servant." Divine approval comes from diligently studying God's Word so we can accurately apply it to our own life and share it with others.

Having examined these ten reasons for studying the Bible, it's now time to ask ourselves, *How many of these reasons are a thoughtful part of my life and motivate me in the study of God's Word?* All ten reasons are very important in the Christian life: Many relate to our personal spiritual growth and whether we experience abundant life. The others relate to how we bless other people.

If you need to improve in this area of "studying the Bible with resolve and purpose," pray and ask God to continue the good work He's begun in your heart of teaching you His truth.

Repentance

Since the beginning of time, sin has brought horrible effects into people's lives. Some of these effects have found their way into our time of studying God's Word.

Two scripture texts specifically describe the necessity of removing our personal sin so that it doesn't hinder our growth in our Bible study time. Repentance is changing our mind about our sin, which should lead us to take action against it. Sad to say, there is no shortage of sin in our lives—so we dare not ignore this aspect of preparing ourselves for Bible study. The comprehensive instruction found in Proverbs 28:13 surely applies here: "He who covers his sins will not prosper, but whoever confesses and forsakes them will have mercy."

The first text specifically related to Bible study speaks about our *desires.* 1 Peter 2:2 states that we should, "as newborn babes, desire the pure milk of the word, that [we] may grow thereby." Please notice that—*before* we can desire the Word in such a way that we can grow spiritually—1 Peter 2:1 states that we must deal with sin in our lives. We're instructed to "lay aside" or rid ourselves of specific sins such as malice, deceit, hypocrisy, envy, and evil speaking. We can imagine this "laying aside" as the taking off of dirty clothes to be replaced by clean ones. The point of 1 Peter 2:1–2 is clear: Sin will cloud our understanding and erode our desire for the Word. When people are sick, their appetite is often affected—they don't feel like eating. The same thing happens in our Bible study: We just won't feel like spending time in God's Word when our sin has not been dealt with.

The second Bible text speaks of personally *receiving and applying* what we study. James 1:21 encourages us to "receive with meekness the implanted word." Once again, notice that the beginning of this verse emphasizes the importance of first dealing with our sin. We're to "lay aside all filthiness and overflow of wickedness." Before there can be *receiving* there must be a *removing*.

Some scholars have noted that the word "filthiness" in verse 21 in the original Greek text, when used in a medical context, has a connection to *ear wax*. When wax builds up in the ears it hinders hearing and must be removed. That meaning illustrates how removing sin can improve our "hearing" of God's Word.

James's letter is addressed to believers called "beloved brethren" who have already had the Word "implanted" in their hearts (verses 18–19) and they must learn this truth about removing sin if they are to become "doers of the word" (verse 22). That's exactly where Bible study should lead us.

When we approach God's Word in reliance on Him and more mature believers, we're progressing toward successful Bible study. When we approach His Word with the resolve of knowing God and His ways better, we're also making strides toward successful study. When we draw near to His Word with repentance, we're removing obstacles that hinder successful Bible study. God's Word is truly "living and active," ready to change us from the inside out.

2. Interpretation:

Discovering What the Bible Means

*Be diligent to present yourself approved to God as a workman who
does not need to be ashamed, accurately handling the word of truth.*
2 TIMOTHY 2:15 NASB

I vividly remember my high school history teacher responding to a student who had just misquoted the Bible in an attempt to prove a point in a classroom discussion. The teacher said, "You can make the Bible mean anything you want it to mean." Even at that young age, I was left with the impression that the Bible should be understood carefully, not carelessly.

Frequently people discussing the meaning of the Bible say, "Oh, that's just your interpretation." Is there a way to figure out what it means? The answer is a resounding yes! In this chapter, I'll share a number of guidelines to help you interpret the Bible properly.

Whether we realize it or not, we all interpret the Bible whenever we try to understand its meaning and make applications to our lives. The fact that we're already doing this shows how important it is that we learn to interpret correctly.

ONE INTERPRETATION, MANY APPLICATIONS

A good thought to begin with is this: Each verse of scripture has only one intended meaning even though there may be many applications. The Bible isn't written to mean different things to different people. Some fast food restaurants tell their customers, "You can have it your way!" That might be true when buying burgers—but it's not true when trying to understand the Bible. The issue in every verse is always what *God* means by it, not what it means to me.

When interpreting a biblical text, there are a number of things to consider. Some texts clearly apply to everyone everywhere, while other texts apply only to people in the Bible who lived in a former time. Some things are to be understood literally, and others figuratively.

Some people bring their personal circumstances to texts of scripture and may wrongly think that God is speaking directly to them in some mysterious and secret way from a particular text.

You may have heard the anecdote about the man who opened his Bible and pointed to a verse hoping God would give him a personal message where his finger landed. He happened to place his finger on Matthew 27:5 and read, "He . . .departed, and went and hanged himself."

Perplexed about what this meant for him, he tried again, turning to another section, and his finger landed on Luke 10:37: "Then Jesus said to him, 'Go and do likewise.'"

Starting to get nervous, he tried again. Turning to John 13, he placed his finger on verse 27: "Then Jesus said to him, 'What you do, do quickly.'"

This funny story illustrates some people's casual and mystical approach to understanding the Bible.

In a personal experience, one day I had a doctor's appointment to get test results on what had the potential to be a serious ailment. That morning, I spent time in prayer and reading my Bible, where I happened to be reading Jeremiah 46. When I came to verse 11, I read these words: "'In vain you will use many medicines; you shall not be cured.'"

Now if I hadn't learned how to interpret the Bible, this would have been a troubling verse. But it wasn't a direct, mystical message from God to me. It was actually addressed to the "daughter of Egypt," and I was glad! Later that day I received good news from the doctor, which confirmed to me that properly interpreting the Bible can save us from unnecessary anxiety.

Poor interpretation comes from preconceived ideas, bad theology, being too hasty in reaching conclusions, and ignoring principles of interpretation. This is why it's so important to learn basic guidelines that help us learn what God means by what He said.

Worth the Investment

You may think you're getting into more work than you want to do, but I encourage you to overcome the temptation to think that it won't be worth it. Some of the best time we spend in our lives will be spent studying the Bible. This isn't just tedious academics, but examining a love letter, the message of a God who loves us. Realizing this makes the time we spend studying enjoyable.

The time and work you invest will be rewarded by great discoveries of precious truth. Miners who search for gold or other precious metals keep their minds fixed on the value of the discovery they hope to make. They know they must devote time to their task.

If you hear about a microwave Bible study plan—that is, a plan that lets you get it done quickly—my advice is to ignore it, because it won't be that beneficial. The Crock-Pot study plan is much better: the one that goes slowly, requiring a greater time commitment, but resulting in greater discoveries.

It's been said that the Bible wasn't written for scholars, but for sinners. It's a book for all of us. Many parts are more difficult than others, but this shouldn't discourage us. Even Peter said that some of the things written by his beloved brother Paul were hard to understand (2 Peter 3:15–16).

A wise pastor once told me as I was beginning to learn God's Word that Bible study is like lifting weights. We start out lifting light weights and eventually work our way up to heavy weights. As we read and study the Bible, we don't have to be overly concerned by those things we don't understand. To switch the metaphor, all we need to do is grab the cookies from the shelf we can reach. As we read God's Word daily, we will grow in understanding and be able to deal with more difficult doctrines later.

Watch Out for False Teachers

As a warning to those who want to understand God's Word, the Bible speaks of false teachers who manipulate what the Bible says and who can be a bad influence if we don't guard ourselves against them. Jesus criticized the Sadducees of

His day, who denied physical resurrection. "'You are mistaken, not knowing the Scriptures'" (Matthew 22:29). These men explained away certain Old Testament texts and spiritualized others, resulting in serious error. Jesus also confronted the scribes, also known as lawyers, who were viewed as experts in the Mosaic law—yet they failed to understand the scriptures correctly themselves, and were guilty of hindering others who were trying to learn God's truth (see Luke 11:52).

Paul spoke of some religious and educated people living in the last days when he said that they are "always learning and never able to come to the knowledge of the truth. . .these also resist the truth" (2 Timothy 3:7–8).

False teachers often redefine biblical words, so we must check to make sure we understand how they are using them or God's intended meaning of verses becomes lost.

Peter described how some people misuse God's Word with horrifying results. He said, "Untaught and unstable people twist [Paul's words] to their own destruction, as they do also the rest of the Scriptures" (2 Peter 3:16). These people play fast and loose with the scriptures, ignoring proper principles of interpretation.

Since we live in the day where there's a battle for the truth, it's important for Christians to be discerning about books, programs, and teachers. I'm glad for all Bible-believing Christians who've had great influence on the world through the media, but we should always be cautious, because it's difficult at times to tell who are wolves in sheep's clothing (Matthew 7:15).

Though there is agreement on the fundamentals of the faith by true believers, there are also in-house debates. Unfortunately, Christians who know the Lord and handle the Bible accurately still have disagreements about what certain passages of the Bible mean. This has resulted in division among Christian individuals and Christian denominations. Differences exist over the nature of the Bible, the age of the earth, divine election, eternal security, gifts of the Spirit, the ritual of baptism, and the timing of the rapture, just to name a few.

Differences between believers will exist until the Lord returns. At that time, He will answer all questions and unify all believers. Until that day comes, we must do our best to love the brethren we disagree with and learn how to interpret the Bible as well as we can. An ancient saying has its place here: "In essentials, unity; in nonessentials, liberty; in all things, charity."

INDUCTIVE BIBLE STUDY

In learning to interpret scripture, we must discuss inductive Bible study, which seeks to discover the facts and details in a text and to draw conclusions about the meaning of a text from those observations. Inductive study has a sequence of three components: observation, interpretation, and application.

- Observation answers the question, What does it say? What is the actual content in the text?
- Interpretation answers the question, What does it mean? Our task is to discover the original intent and meaning of the author.

- Application answers the questions, What does it mean to me? and How does it apply to my life?

When we use this sequence, we'll find information and ideas that might have been overlooked otherwise. When this type of study isn't practiced, the door to interpretive abuses opens.

OBSERVATION

Observation always comes first. Before we consider what a text means, we must ask what it says. This means reading and rereading a text until we become acquainted with it. Occasionally, after I've taught about some part of the Bible, people have asked me with surprise, "How do you get all of that out of one verse?" Part of the answer is learning to be observant.

Most of us have watched television shows where a crime scene is being investigated. The area is taped off, and the authorities begin looking for clues. As clues are found—a footprint or a piece of clothing, perhaps—the detective places a bright marker at the location. A trained eye takes in many clues. Pictures are taken of the scene to be studied later. Evidence is taken to the lab, where even more information is revealed. Many people are involved in a slow process to discover the truth about what happened. This is observation, discovering all that can be found.

As a kid, I grew up watching *Dragnet*, a police show. One of the main characters was Detective Joe Friday. One of his trademark statements was, "Just the facts, ma'am." He wasn't interested in opinions or feelings. All he wanted was factual evidence. During the observation stage, we're also looking for the facts.

In developing our observation skills, we'll find it helpful to ask a series of questions. We can use them for any text. Put your text under a light and interrogate it! We just want the facts. Texts will have answers for most of the following questions.

- Who? Who was writing? To whom was the message originally written? Who are the people involved in the scenario?
- What? What's happening? What's said? Is it a command, an exhortation, a rebuke, a question, an answer, a prayer, a quotation of other scripture, something else? What's the main point? What key words or phrases are used? What's the context? What literary style is being used? Is it narrative, conversation, parable, prophecy, poetry, a letter, or a sermon?
- When? Are there time references? Are there words related to the past, present, or future? Look for words like *after, until, then.*
- Where? Are there locations mentioned—towns, roads, rivers, mountains, regions, or other landmarks?
- Why? Are there any clues about why things are being said or done?
- How? Is there an explanation about how things are done?

These six questions help us gain information to see what a text actually says.

INTERPRETATION

The ultimate interpretation question is, What did God mean by what He said? Interpretation is determining the meaning of a text once all of the facts are in. Compiling evidence from our observation takes some time, and we must guard against jumping to premature conclusions. New evidence can influence our conclusions, so we shouldn't be too hasty in moving to this part of the inductive process. We can see a clear example of this in the judicial system where some verdicts have been overturned when advances in DNA testing provided new evidence.

Some of us have been in Bible study classes where the facilitator asked, What does this passage mean to you? before the group observed the facts and determined what the author intended. This is a good question when asked at the right time because it forces people to think about the Bible, but it's not a good question to ask first because people speak offhandedly before they give thought to the text. In this situation, interpreting the Bible becomes totally subjective, meaning different things to different people.

But every verse in the Bible, generally speaking, means only one thing—what the original author intended—and that's what we're trying to discover. Interpretation of the Bible isn't a matter of personal opinion, feelings, or democratic agreement; it's a matter of gathering evidence from the text and following established principles of interpretation. Some people innocently make the error of reading a text, skipping interpretation altogether, and jumping to application.

John MacArthur tells the story of one of his assistant pastors, who counseled a couple who married as a result of a sermon preached on the destruction of Jericho. The pastor at a previous church had taught that God's people claimed the city, marched around it seven times, and the walls fell down. Then he explained to the young men that if a man believed God had given him a particular single young girl, he could claim her, walk around her seven times, and the walls of her heart would fall down! Of all the lessons to be learned about the fall of Jericho, lessons about marriage aren't among them.

Second Timothy 2:15 (NASB) speaks of "accurately handling the word of truth." In Greek, accurately handling literally means "cutting a straight line." When Paul, a tent maker, wrote to Timothy, he may have had in mind cutting material in a straight line to sew pieces of a tent together. Paul and Timothy needed to be precise and accurate in interpreting and teaching the Bible so it would all fit together without contradiction. They were to cut straight or handle straight the word of truth. Shame waits for those workers who mishandle the word of truth.

When we're trying to discover the meaning of the text, many times it's plain; it's on the surface of what we read. Alistair Begg, of the radio program *Truth for Life*, speaks repeatedly about "the main things and the plain things" when studying the Bible. Focus first on what is clear and obvious.

David Cooper, founder of the Biblical Research Society, established the golden rule of interpretation. The short version is, "If the plain sense makes good sense, seek no other sense or it will result in nonsense." Apply his rule first and work from there. Don't sacrifice plain meaning for unique, mystical, or obscure ideas.

Once we have asked the six observation questions of the text, we then apply six principles of interpretation.

1. The literal principle

The literal principle means interpreting the Bible with the normal meaning of words while recognizing figures of speech like symbolism, allegory, and metaphor. God has communicated with us through written language, so we should understand the words of scripture the way we use them in everyday life. Let a text speak for itself. When Jesus was born, it was a literal virgin birth. The miracles He performed were real. His death and resurrection were actual historical events.

We recognize that many portions of scripture, especially poetry and prophecy, are filled with figurative language. Psalm 91:4 is an example of figurative language in Hebrew poetry: "He shall cover you with His feathers, and under His wings you shall take refuge." This doesn't mean that God has feathers and wings; rather it provides an image of God as our protector the same way a bird protects its young by covering them with its wings.

A prophetic example comes from Revelation 1:16: "He had in His right hand seven stars, out of His mouth went a sharp two-edged sword." Literal interpretation doesn't suggest seven actual stars or a real sword. The symbolic meaning of the stars is explained in Revelation 1:20, while the meaning of the sword is found in Revelation 2:16 and 19:15.

Also in prophetic scripture, the "law of double reference" needs recognition. Bible scholar J. Dwight Pentecost explains the term: "Two events, widely separated as to the time of their fulfillment, may be brought together into the scope of one prophecy. This was done because the prophet had a message for his own day as well as for a future time." An example is Hosea 11:1, which refers to Israel's actual exodus from Egypt—though this same reference is quoted in the New Testament, seven centuries later, to refer to Mary, Joseph, and the baby Jesus fleeing to Egypt to escape the wrath of King Herod (see Matthew 2:14–15). In this text is seen both historical and literal meanings along with the prophetic.

The literal principle—which certainly allows for poetic and prophetic understandings—makes the Bible much easier to understand. There's no need to uncover hidden meanings. Read and study the Bible like you would a letter from a friend—since that's what God has provided for us. Enjoy His Word in its most normal meaning.

2. The historical principle

The Bible must be understood in its historical setting before it can be fully understood in our contemporary setting. Bible students now become historians. We want to discover the original intent of the author by asking, *What did he mean by what he wrote?* Would our interpretation make sense to the first recipients? Before we ask what a text means to us, we must first ask what it meant to the original audience.

It's helpful to investigate the lifestyle and customs of that day, such as foot washing (1 Timothy 5:9–10), praying on a housetop (Acts 10:9), and girding the loins (1 Peter 1:13). Learning about the political and social backgrounds sheds light on certain texts. The Bible study tools mentioned in chapter 4 will prove helpful when studying historical background.

3. The contextual principle

The contextual principle means we should interpret a verse by the verses that surround it. You may have noticed that some verses begin in the middle of a sentence, so it's best to at least go back to the beginning of the sentence to get the flow of the author's thought. Some Bible teachers have said that context is so important that a verse of scripture should never be read by itself; it should always be read in its context to get the author's intended meaning.

The reason for this stance is summarized in this adage: A text out of context becomes a pretext for a proof text! In simpler words, this means a Bible verse standing alone can be misunderstood or misused to prove an error.

When Satan tempted Jesus and suggested that He should throw Himself down from the top of the temple, the devil quoted Bible verses out of context, giving them a wrong meaning. A psalm about trusting God was twisted into meaning that it's all right to test God (Matthew 4:5–6 and Psalm 91:11–12). Jesus corrected the devil's error by quoting another text that rectified the wrong idea (Matthew 4:7 and Deuteronomy 6:16).

The following scriptures provide other examples of verses taken out of context—and therefore misunderstood:

- Matthew 7:1 (NASB) is a commonly quoted passage which says, "'Do not judge so that you will not be judged.'" This is often used to overlook or defend sinful behavior as some say that the Bible teaches we are not allowed to judge other people. Yet, later in the passage, a lot of judging must be done in order to obey what Jesus says in verses 3–6! Matthew 7:1 actually prohibits a sinful judging—questioning of thoughts or motives and judging prematurely or unfairly—rather than true discernment, which Jesus encouraged in John 7:24. In the latter passage, Jesus actually told people to judge—but righteously.
- In an attempt at humor, 1 Corinthians 15:51 has been placed on some church nursery schedules to refer to babies. In part, it reads, "We will not all sleep, but we will all be changed" (NASB)!
- Some have used Jeremiah 10:3–4 to argue against the modern holiday custom of decorating Christmas trees. But the context clearly indicates the prophet was condemning *idolatry* (see verses 8 and 11, and a majority of the book of Jeremiah).

It's best to get the big picture of a text, then zoom in on the context, and finally the details. This is starting with the bird's-eye view and going down to the worm's-eye view.

- Find out the general theme of the book.
- Determine the emphasis of each chapter and how it relates to the book theme.
- Find the paragraph divisions and how they relate to the thrust of each chapter.
- Dig into the verses to get each one's main idea and how they relate to each other.
- Go deeper into verses by doing word studies.

This digging makes our conclusions much more accurate.

4. The compatibility principle

The basic premise of the compatibility principle is to compare verses or passages of scripture with other scripture to see how they fit together. The best commentary on the Bible is the Bible, so we let it interpret itself. Properly understood, the Bible doesn't contradict itself; it complements itself with an amazing harmony. If our interpretations contradict what the Bible says elsewhere, we need to change our conclusions. As we study a text or subject, other portions of scripture shed light on it for fuller understanding. For example, doctrinal truth is spread throughout the Bible.

I remember the first time I seriously read the Gospels, the first four books of the New Testament. I read Matthew, then Mark. By the time I had completed Luke, I knew I had read its stories before—and I had, in Matthew and Mark. I eventually learned that these books all present the life of the Lord Jesus, giving different details to provide a complete picture of His life. The four authors were like a quartet harmonizing. They were singing the same song but hitting different notes. Comparing scripture with scripture is a safeguard against error and contradiction.

5. The grammatical principle

It shouldn't surprise us to learn the grammatical principle has to do with grammar and sentence structure. Recognizing parts of speech and the way they relate to each other can reveal a lot about a biblical text. This is called *syntax*. It's been said that grammar and syntax are a lot like broccoli—you know it's good for you, but you'd rather not eat it. *Every* student of scripture must learn to use the grammatical principle. You'll learn to love it!

Seven easily overlooked but important key words that reveal clues to accurate meaning are *therefore*, *and*, *but*, *that*, *for*, *because*, and *if*. Examples of these are found in Romans 11–12.

In Romans 12:1, Paul writes, "I beseech you *therefore*, brethren, by the mercies of God, that you present your bodies a living sacrifice" (emphasis added). When we see the word *therefore*, we need to find out what it's there for. Find out what thoughts have gone before. In the first eleven chapters of Romans, Paul has laid the great foundation of the mercies of God by describing in detail God's plan of salvation. Paul then draws his thoughts to a practical conclusion in 12:1 and begs the Romans to present themselves to God as dedicated servants. He connects his practical appeal to his lengthy description of God's plan by the word *therefore*.

Verse 2 continues: "*And* do not be conformed to this world, *but* be transformed by the renewing of your mind, *that* you may prove what is that good and acceptable and perfect will of God." *And* introduces an addition, *but* points to a contrast, and *that* is used to begin a conclusion. Paul adds another appeal after his first one in verse 1 by using the word *and* at the beginning of verse 2. Then he presents a contrast with the word *but*. Paul exhorts believers not to succumb to external pressure to live and think like the unbelieving world, *but* to be internally transformed by renewing their thought life. (By the way, the source for renewed thinking is the Bible. See Psalm 1:1–2).

That (along with *for* and *because*) is used to introduce a purpose or reason at the end of verse 2. The reason for having our thinking renewed and our life transformed is so we can have confidence that we know and are doing the will of God.

In verse 19, the word *for* is also used to introduce a reason: Paul has written that Christians shouldn't be vengeful *for* the scriptures say we shouldn't.

An example of the use of *because,* also meaning purpose or reason, is found in Romans 11:20: "*Because* of unbelief they were broken off."

If is used in Romans 12:18: "*If* it is possible, as much as depends on you, live peaceably with all men." This word is used when a condition is present. Paul's point here is that Christians are always to be peacemakers, and if there is a lack of peace between a Christian and another person, it should never be the Christian's fault.

Considering these seven key words helps us better understand the structure and meaning of a text.

6. The Christological principle

Jesus Christ is the main theme of the entire Bible, so keeping an eye out for references to Him as we study is important. The ministry of the Holy Spirit is to point us to Christ. "'But when the Helper comes. . .the Spirit of truth. . .will testify of Me'" (John 15:26).

Jesus said to unbelieving Jews of His day, "'You search the Scriptures, for in them you think you have eternal life; and these are they which testify of Me. . . . For if you believed Moses, you would believe Me; for he wrote about Me'" (John 5:39, 46). Moses wrote the first five books of the Old Testament, so we look for Christ there.

At the end of His earthly ministry, Jesus told His apostles, "'All things must be fulfilled which were written in the Law of Moses and the Prophets and the Psalms concerning Me'" (Luke 24:44). Therefore, we also look for Jesus in the prophetic books and the psalms.

One day, an Ethiopian eunuch was reading the Old Testament text of Isaiah, which contains a prophecy about the Lord Jesus. A believer, Philip, helped him understand what he was reading. "Then Philip opened his mouth, and beginning at this Scripture [Isaiah 53:7–8], preached Jesus to him" (Acts 8:35). We should always be looking for Christ.

Application

Now we come to application, the third component of inductive Bible study. This answers the question, How does this passage apply to me? Bible study doesn't end with interpretation; it continues to the question, So what? The goal of Bible study isn't only gaining information but also experiencing transformation. We're not just trying to get through the Bible; we're letting the Bible get through us. If there's a good example, follow it. If there's a warning, heed it. If there's a command, obey it. If there's a promise, believe it.

Jesus prayed for all believers just before he died: "Sanctify them by Your truth. Your word is truth'" (John 17:17). This is Jesus' request to God the Father that He use His Word to influence believers to live lives set apart for His purposes. Our lifestyle is to be affected by the Bible as well as our beliefs, and this requires a humble response of doing the will of God.

James said that what should characterize believers is being "doers of the word, and not hearers only" (James 1:22). Self-deception is talking ourselves out of obeying the Bible and therefore cheating ourselves out of the blessings of God that accompany obedience. Some people mark their Bibles, but their Bible seldom marks them.

Jesus spoke of the blessing of obedience and the foolishness of self-deception when He ended the Sermon on the Mount. He described two types of people, the obedient and disobedient, as builders. The obedient are like the man who built his house on a rock, which was able to stand when the storm came. The disobedient are like the man who built on a foundation of sand and experienced the destruction of his house when the storm came (Matthew 7:24–27). These two people both heard the truth but responded differently. One only learned it, while the other truly lived it.

Paul states in 2 Timothy 3:16 that scripture is inspired by God and is beneficial for four things, three having a practical emphasis. "All Scripture is given by inspiration of God, and is profitable for doctrine, for reproof, for correction, for instruction in righteousness." Paul is saying scripture is valuable for information to believe, to use as the perfect standard of right and wrong, for being restored after we've sinned, and for remaining restored. These four benefits are to make believers complete so that they can do whatever God has called them to do (verse 17).

Interpreting the Bible then includes the six observation questions, the six interpretation principles, and the necessary application to our lives.

3. Classification:

Examining Bible Study Methods

Now [the Bereans] were more noble-minded than those in
Thessalonica, for they received the word with great eagerness,
examining the Scriptures daily to see whether these things were so.
ACTS 17:11 NASB

As the Berean believers studied the scriptures in an attempt to verify the truthful-ness of Paul's preaching, they were thorough in their approach to God's Word and more than likely using some of study methods that I'll suggest in this chapter. All methods of Bible study have value in learning God's Word, but whatever method we use, the point to remember is that studying the Bible is what's important. It's to our benefit to pursue the habit of daily reading and studying God's Word.

The usefulness of knowing a variety of Bible study methods is that it helps us be flexible in our approach to scripture as we concentrate on a particular text, subject, or even a word. It also contributes to balancing our learning.

BALANCE

Before looking at different methods of Bible study, some thoughts about being balanced in our study are appropriate.

Old Testament/New Testament

I highly recommend balance in Bible study by using a variety of methods. For exam-ple, time spent studying the New Testament should be balanced by study of the Old Testament. It's not surprising that believers living under the new covenant want to spend their time in the New Testament learning about Jesus Christ and His Gospel, but the Old Testament is quoted in the New Testament about 250 times. It's been said, "The new is in the old contained, and the old is in the new explained."

When the Bereans were searching the scriptures, they were studying the Old Testament. The New Testament was in the process of being written at that time. Early Christians had a solid foundation of Old Testament truth, and New Tes-tament truth was added as it gradually became available. This is what's meant by the idea that God's revelation has been progressive.

The amazing preacher Apollos is an example of a person receiving progressive revelation. His preaching from the Old Testament was powerful and accurate as far as it went, but his knowledge was limited. Aquila and Priscilla, believers who heard him teach, shared more of God's revelation with him, and Apollos grew to become more effective in serving Christ (Acts 18:24–28).

Doctrine/Christian Living

Another area is balancing the study of Bible doctrine with the study of practical

Christian living and how to apply doctrinal truth to everyday life.

Paul's preaching did this. He said to the Ephesian elders, "'I have not shunned to declare to you the whole counsel of God'" (Acts 20:27). The "whole counsel of God" is an all-inclusive term related to God's revelation covering both doctrine and duty in the Christian life. There was no subject that he intentionally omitted from his teaching. His preaching was well rounded because, in part, he wanted his hearers to be the same.

This is how our study should be so we gain a wider spectrum of truth and a good foundation of understanding we can build on.

Some Christians seem content to only occasionally study those things that spark their interest, while others have a diet of the latest Christian books that hit the bestseller list. My intention isn't to be critical of popular Christian books, for all pursuit of truth is helpful, but I'm concerned about poor study habits that sometimes neglect using the Bible altogether.

The point needs to be made that we should be involved in a balanced Bible study plan that uses a variety of techniques. In physical health, eating only those foods that we might enjoy—like snacks and sweets—won't contribute to good health. A balanced diet is required. This is equally true when we study the Bible.

Six Important Bible Study Methods

1. The Expositional Method

Expositional Bible study means studying the Bible verse by verse and using the observation, interpretation, and application guidelines from chapter 2. The benefit of this method is that it reveals the flow of the author's thoughts throughout any text of scripture, which contributes to a more accurate understanding of individual verses.

No verse is to be left out as insignificant. Every verse contributes something to the overall idea in every section of scripture—that's why God put it there. It's our mission to discover the meaning.

For example, the verses before and after John 3:16 are not as well-known, but are just as important. The expositional method does require more thinking about how verses relate to each other but also leads to greater understanding in the long run.

In Deuteronomy 12:32, God gave us an important lesson: "Whatever I command you, be careful to observe it; you shall not add to it nor take away from it." In a way, the expositional method of study is like assembling a puzzle—every verse is like a piece of the total picture. If one piece is left out, the picture is incomplete. But when every verse is understood in its proper place, God's marvelous picture can be fully enjoyed.

Bible commentaries are helpful in pursuing the expositional method of Bible study.

2. The Survey Method

The importance of this study method has been well stated by Christian author Merrill Tenney: "Bible survey is fundamental to all Bible study. If a student expects to comprehend any part or doctrine of the scriptures, he must know what they teach as a whole."

When using the survey method, we get a bird's eye view and study entire Bible books to become acquainted with general information rather than the details of each verse. We investigate subjects like the author, when and where he's writing from, his style of writing, a book's theme, important topics contained in the book, who it was written for, and issues or circumstances the recipients might have been facing. Looking at the social, political, and spiritual background—as well as the chronology of events—helps to explain why certain events happened.

We can also survey the entire Old or New Testament so we understand how the books of the Bible are divided and relate to each other. The thirty-nine Old Testament books can be divided into five categories:

- Genesis through Deuteronomy, the first five books, are known as the Law or the Pentateuch (meaning five volumes).
- Joshua through Esther are the twelve historical books.
- Job through Song of Solomon are the five poetic books.
- Isaiah through Daniel are the five major prophets.
- Hosea through Malachi are the twelve minor prophets.

The Old Testament was originally written in Hebrew, with some small sections written in Aramaic. They deal primarily with God's relationship with His chosen nation, Israel.

The twenty-seven New Testament books, originally written in Greek, can be divided into four categories:

- The four Gospels and Acts are the historical books.
- Romans through Philemon, the next thirteen books, are letters of the apostle Paul to churches or individuals.
- Hebrews through Jude, the next eight books, are called the general letters.
- Revelation, a prophetic book, appropriately ends the New Testament.

Bible encyclopedias, Bible dictionaries, and Old and New Testament overviews are all helpful when surveying the Bible.

3. The Topical Method

It is important to develop a good grasp of the major topics and themes in scripture. There are many things for us to learn about the great mysteries of what God has revealed about Himself, His word, and His plan through the ages. He's revealed things about the unseen world of angels and demons, heaven and hell, and life and death.

Directly related to our lives are the subjects of humankind's personal sin and God's only way of salvation through His Son, Jesus Christ. And then there are specific topics from the Bible that interest us—questions relating to finances, prayer, or purpose.

To master these topics it's necessary to accumulate all that the Bible says about them and then organize that information. A Bible concordance and a topical Bible can guide us to specific verses about subjects throughout the Bible. Then we can see how each subject is addressed in the Old Testament and the New Testament, and by individual biblical authors.

This method was especially helpful to me as a young Christian because, like many new believers, I had so many doctrinal questions I wanted answers to. One of the first study books I read was *Major Bible Themes* by Lewis Sperry Chafer (later revised by John Walvoord), explaining fifty-two Bible doctrines. I concentrated on particular subjects to better learn what God had to say about them and in doing this established a strong foundation for my faith. As I continued to study other topics a Bible dictionary provided a nice introduction to each. A Bible encyclopedia also provided more extensive articles for the topics being studied.

Because so many individual verses are examined throughout scripture in the topical Bible study method, we must take care that the verses under consideration are understood in their proper context.

Additional resources that will prove helpful are *Nave's Topical Bible*, containing some twenty-thousand topics, and an online study tool (I recommend The New Topical Textbook by R. A. Torrey at www.bible.topics.com) for finding Bible verses indexed by subject.

4. The Biographical Method

Individual people in the Bible are interesting—and developing character sketches about them will produce many valuable lessons. When you bring together bits and pieces in the Bible about a person's life, amazing pictures can emerge.

The Bible mentions over twenty-nine hundred people, some by name only. A concordance can be used to find every Bible verse in which a name is found, but care must be exercised since many Bible characters shared names. For example, six women in the Bible are named Mary, five men are named John, and five men are named James.

Remember, too, that some people are referred to by more than one name. At times, God assigned a new name to indicate a significant change in a person's circumstances. The elderly and childless couple Abram and Sarai had their names changed to Abraham and Sarah, indicating that they would eventually become the patriarch and matriarch of many nations and believers (Genesis 17:5, 15).

Young Daniel and his three friends Azariah, Mishael, and Azariah, were forcibly abducted by the Babylonians, who changed their Hebrew names to names honoring false gods. Daniel (meaning "God is my judge"), had his name changed to, Belteshazzar (meaning "Bel protect the king." Daniel's friends were renamed

Shadrach, Meshach, and Abednego (Daniel 1:7).

In New Testament times, people were occasionally known more by their Roman than their Hebrew names. Saul was known as Paul (Acts 13:9) while John, who authored the second Gospel, was known as Mark (Acts 12:25). The apostle Peter, meanwhile, was known by three names that all appear together in many translations of John 1:42: Peter (his Greek name), Simon (his Hebrew name), and Cephas (his Aramaic name).

Through faith in God's power, as we see in Hebrews 11, believers have accomplished some amazing things. These Bible characters are examples for us, even in their weaknesses. David, the man after God's own heart, sinned in the matter of Uriah the Hittite (1 Kings 15:5). The apostle Peter denied the Lord (Matthew 26:69–74). Elijah was a man just like us (James 5:17).

This realization should encourage us. Through the experience of the real people of the Bible, we learn that God is forgiving and patient—that He is the God of second chances.

When developing a character sketch, study books such as *All the Men of the Bible* and *All the Women of the Bible* (by Herbert Lockyer) or *Twelve Ordinary Men* and *Twelve Extraordinary Women* (by John MacArthur) may prove helpful.

As you pursue the biographical method of Bible study, honestly ponder the question, "What would God write about *my* life?"

5. The Word Study Method

When a person is new to the Christian faith, some terms may be unfamiliar. Words like *propitiation*, *redemption*, *imputation*, *justification*, and *sanctification* are basic to the "good news" message of God's salvation in scripture. The words of scripture are the words that God inspired, so they become part of our study. God wants us to understand them so that we can believe His truth and experience personal blessing as we apply it to our lives. By using a concordance, you'll be able to locate these words and see how they're used.

Several Greek words might be translated into one English word. Using study tools like *Strong's Exhaustive Concordance* and *Vine's Complete Expository Dictionary* is essential to understanding the variety of meanings. Let's consider a few examples.

The World

Three Greek words all translate into the English word *world*. The Greek word *kosmos* is used in John 3:16: "For God so loved the world that He gave His only begotten Son." This refers to the world order of unsaved people who are opposed to God and controlled by Satan. It is also used in Acts 17:24 describing the orderliness of the material world that was created by God.

The Greek word *aion* is used in Romans 12:2: "And do not be conformed to this world." It refers to the particular age in which we live that's influential with false ideas and evil. J. B. Phillips translates this, "Don't let the world around you squeeze you into its mold," which is a warning against worldliness.

The Greek word *oikoumene* is used in Matthew 24:14: "'And this gospel of the kingdom will be preached in all the world.'" Matthew is referring to the inhabited world of people who hear a worldwide Gospel proclamation.

Love

We use the English word *love* for three Greek words that have slightly different meanings. The conversation that the risen Lord Jesus had with Peter in John 21:15–19 uses two of the Greek words.

Since Peter denied knowing the Lord three times, Jesus asked Peter three times if he really loved Him. In the first two questions, Jesus uses the Greek word *agape,* which refers to self-sacrificing love (also used in John 3:16). In Peter's answer he uses another Greek word for word for love, *phileo,* which emphasizes only fondness, probably because he still feels too much shame to use the word emphasizing a total loving devotion.

When Jesus asks the same question for the third time, He questions even Peter's fondness for Him by also using the word that Peter did, *phileo.* This intentional change of Greek words by Jesus is missed in our English Bible, but it's the reason why Peter was grieved.

Day

Context also has an important bearing on the meaning of words. The word *day*, for example, as used in the Bible, has several meanings that are determined by the context. In Genesis 1:5 there are two meanings: The twelve hours of light are called *day*, and the twenty-four-hour period indicated by the repeated phrase, "the evening and the morning" is also called *day*. When the word *day* appears with a numerical adjective (first day, second day), it consistently refers to a twenty-four-hour period. In Genesis 2:4, *day* also refers to the entire creative week. In Psalm 20:1, *day* refers to an indefinite period of time.

6. The Devotional Method

Many Christians use the phrase "having personal devotions" when referring to the devotional method. This type of study is less technical than the others and is primarily for personal inspiration and encouragement to deepen our relationship with God, drawing near to Him so that He might draw near to us. Bible reading, prayer, and perhaps reading a devotional book with a brief message are normally a part of devotions.

Three popular daily devotional booklets are *Our Daily Bread, Days of Praise*, and *Today in the Word*. Charles Spurgeon's *Morning and Evening* is a classic devotional tool that gives a message for the beginning of the day and one for the end of the day. Another classic is *My Utmost for His Highest* by Oswald Chambers.

Meditation is a normal part of the devotional method. This is the practice of pondering and reflecting on the meaning of God's words and works and their application to our lives. Anyone who has received a letter from a loved one who is far away understands the meaning of meditation. We read and reread the contents and then think about them. The psalmist said, "I will meditate on Your precepts, and contemplate Your ways" (Psalm 119:15).

Our meditation hopefully carries on throughout the day as we consider how God's Word applies to our particular daily activities. Blessing waits for those who delight in the law of the Lord and meditate on it day and night (Psalm 1:2).

Meditation can be greatly aided by memorization of God's Word. Being able to retrieve scripture from memory is useful when we're discouraged; we're able to ponder the uplifting promises of God. "I remembered Your judgments of old, O Lord, and have comforted myself" (Psalm 119:52).

When facing temptation like the Lord Jesus in Matthew 4, we use scripture that we have learned to be able to remain faithful. The psalmist said, "Your word I have hidden in my heart, that I might not sin against You" (Psalm 119:11).

Being a good witness to those who don't know the Lord requires being able to recall appropriate Gospel verses that will be spiritually helpful to them. Many believers have said to themselves following conversations with an unbeliever, "Oh, I wish I would have remembered that particular verse!" They're referring to verses they knew about that would have been helpful in the conversation but that they had never committed to memory.

The devotional method of study prepares us to meet each day with the knowledge that we have been redeemed by Christ and that He'll strengthen us to do His will.

READING THROUGH THE BIBLE

Having recommended six types of Bible study, I want to conclude this chapter by mentioning one more study activity that's advisable: reading through the Bible.

Bible reading should be an ongoing activity in the Christian life. I admire Christians who read through the Bible in one year, something I've never accomplished because I'm easily sidetracked by issues I come across in the text and prefer to investigate at that time. The result is I get behind in my reading schedule. My first attempt to read through the Bible took me five years. That's a lot of rabbit trails! My second time through the Bible took three years. So far, this has been my best attempt. If we have the attitude of Job, we'll stay in God's Word no matter how long it takes us to get through it. He said, "'I have treasured the words of His mouth more than my necessary food'" (Job 23:12).

Remember, the *activity* of Bible study is more important than the *method*, but learning to use these methods opens doors to discovering the great truths of scripture. As they say at Nike, "Just do it!"

4. Collaboration:

Using Bible Study Helps

Bring the cloak that I left with Carpus at Troas when you come—and the books, especially the parchments.

2 TIMOTHY 4:13

Paul, as a Pharisee and as a Christian preacher, was a great student of scripture. No one actually knows what books he was asking Timothy to bring to him when he wrote. But there's a possibility that they were more than books of scripture, that they were books to help him in his own study of scripture.

In this chapter, I'll recommend Bible study tools that are helpful for "a worker" (2 Timothy 2:15). Every worker needs tools of the trade to do his job. The toolbox of Bible students is a personal library, and their tools are study books and helps that aid them in understanding the scriptures. The workshop is that special location where they study.

Study resources produced by Bible scholars give Christians the advantage of reading the insights that these servants of Christ have gained through their own study. Study books are valuable, but they must be kept in their place. They aren't inspired by God as scripture is. They aren't the final word on any biblical text. Our primary source of truth is the Bible. *Sola scriptura* was the Latin saying established during the Protestant Reformation that means "the Bible alone." By using that pronouncement, the Reformers established the Word of God as their only authority for doctrine and practice. God's Word is to be given its rightful place in our lives.

It has been my conviction that when Christians meet to worship and study on the Lord's Day, the Bible should be opened and taught. On rare occasions, I've been in places where a Sunday school manual has been opened in a class and then discussed while Bibles remained closed (though not mine, by the way). This kind of activity doesn't give the Bible its rightful place of priority in a public setting. Whether it's a public or private setting, we shouldn't give our study tools more attention than we give our Bible.

Christians must also beware of becoming *-ites*. These are believers who automatically accept everything that a certain Christian author says or writes. Church history tells the story of an estimated fifty thousand people in the 1840s known as Millerites. They were exclusive followers of the prophetic pronouncements of an influential Bible teacher, William Miller, who had set a date of October 22, 1844, for Christ's return to earth. Many prepared for the exciting day—but were greatly disappointed when it came and went with no sign of Jesus. This kind of sectarianism can lead to troublesome divisions among believers, even when truth is being taught.

This is an old problem addressed by even the apostle Paul when he asked the Corinthian church, "For when one says, 'I am of Paul,' and another, 'I am of Apollos,' are you not carnal?" (1 Corinthians 3:4). We all have our favorite authors and Bible teachers, but they should make this same point—that we should not be isolated followers of only certain individuals. God has blessed the church with many gifted people He wants to use for our blessing. So let's beware of the divisive spirit becoming an -*ite* can produce.

Some Christians have debated whether study books should even be used at all. They believe that only the Bible itself should be studied.

As a young, impressionable believer, I remember listening to a debate between two Christians in the church I attended who took opposing views on this. One said that God speaks only by His Spirit through the Bible and no study books should be used. This sounded very spiritual. The other believed that God could also use study books to be an aid to our better understanding of His Word. Who's right?

My wife and I now own over six hundred study books in our personal library. The Bible-only view is an attractive one economically, but I don't believe it's correct, because as stated earlier, God has gifted certain believers with the gift of teaching. This isn't referring to just a natural ability to teach others. This is a supernatural enablement given by God after salvation (1 Corinthians 12:11, 28).

The gifted teacher can minister through speaking and writing. The mode of getting the information isn't the issue. God uses mature believers to disciple other believers through direct contact in one-to-one or small-group interaction, and indirect contact through the printed page, tapes, CDs, and so on.

None of these resources eliminates the need for spending plenty of time in the Bible. Let's look at some available resources that can help us with our study of the Bible. Please note that the titles I mention are of books that I've used—some may now be out of print or updated under slightly different titles, but all are likely available from libraries, bookstores, or sellers of used books.

BIBLE STUDY HELPS

Study Bibles

As a new believer being invited to a home Bible class, I was amazed to see people with Bibles that had a wealth of additional study notes in them. I had never seen anything like them. I soon purchased a New Scofield Reference Bible. When this wore out years later, my next one was a Ryrie Study Bible. My wife uses a MacArthur Study Bible. Other people I know use the Life Application Study Bible. These are only a few in a long list of study Bibles now available in a variety of English translations.

One thing to remember is that the notes in study Bibles are the explanatory words of people, not the authoritative words of God. The study aids are provided as immediate helps and are not meant to be the end of our investigation. We shouldn't depend too heavily on just the explanations in our study Bibles. They'll have helpful introductions to each book of the Bible and outlines so we can see how books fit together. Explanatory notes about the text, doctrine, and Christian living appear on every page. Some study Bibles have charts, articles, extensive cross-references, a concordance, a topical index, and numerous maps.

Bible Dictionaries and Encyclopedias

Among the first tools we need are Bible dictionaries and encyclopedias. They have more than just the definitions of words. They contain brief articles on major Bible subjects with helpful explanations and scripture references related to the subject. These books cover a spectrum of subjects from A to Z, making them a reference tool that gets used repeatedly. I recommend *The New Unger's Bible Dictionary*, *Zondervan's Pictorial Bible Dictionary*, and *The International Standard Bible Encyclopedia*, a five-volume set.

Exhaustive Concordances

An exhaustive concordance lists every reference where every biblical word is found. When you can remember only a few words of a verse, you can look up one of the words and this book helps you find its reference. Often, in the back, you'll also find an English dictionary for Old Testament Hebrew words and New Testament Greek words. It's important to make sure the concordance you use is keyed to the Bible translation you use. The *Strong's Exhaustive Concordance* is keyed to the King James Version. After my Bible, I use this tool more than any other resource that I have.

Bible Atlases

For those who want a more detailed description of geography in the Bible with explanatory articles, this is the book to use. Atlases contain many more maps than those that appear in the backs of Bibles. This resource won't be used as frequently as others, but it helps to better understand locations and travel in Bible times.

Expository Dictionaries

When studying words of the Bible, use an expository dictionary. A Webster's English dictionary is fine as far as it goes, but it primarily deals with English. We're dealing with English translations of Greek words when we study the New Testament. This study aid examines the original Greek words used in verses and then gives a brief definition and explanation of the word. It also has select references to where the Greek word appears in the New Testament. I recommend *The Expository Dictionary of Old and New Testament Words* by W. E. Vine.

Topical Bibles

Topical Bibles list biblical words alphabetically and give select references to where the word you are looking for is found. Many times the entire verse is written out so you can read the verse in the book. Larger subjects are broken down into subcategories so you can find verses with a particular emphasis. For example, in Nave's Topical Bible, the word *faith* has the following subheadings: faith enjoined; faith exemplified; faith in Christ; the trial of faith. Use this resource when you're doing word studies or character sketches.

661 Complete Bible Companion

Commentaries

This is my favorite category of study helps. Most of the books I own are commentaries. Using these books is like being taught by great men and women of God.

Some are expository in nature, explaining individual verses and analyzing how they fit together. These generally include an outline of the entire book of the Bible.

Other commentaries are more devotional, emphasizing lessons for Christian living.

Some are technical in nature, working closely with the original languages.

After you read several commentaries, you'll soon discover that the books with more pages are normally more helpful because they address more issues. Difficult questions that arise are usually addressed, including possible solutions.

A personal benefit from reading commentaries written by Bible scholars is that you're able to test your own conclusions against what the experts are saying. This obviously requires that you interact with the Bible text yourself before consulting a commentary. Remember, we're learning how to study the Bible, not learning how to study commentaries.

Commentaries aren't the final word about any text. Even Bible scholars disagree at times. My humble experience has been that I find myself not agreeing with any Bible commentator one hundred percent of the time. My guess is that this is the conclusion of most serious students of the Bible.

Books that have been helpful to me are single books that cover the entire Bible like *Jamieson, Fausset, and Brown's Commentary on the Whole Bible* (that's one book!). Sets that cover the entire New Testament or the entire Bible (which provide greater detail) include the six-volume set of Matthew Henry commentaries; *The Bible Knowledge Commentary* by Walvoord and Zuck, a two-volume set; and *The Bible Exposition Commentary* by Warren Wiersbe, a six-volume set. Much larger sets are The New Testament Commentary series by Hendriksen and Kistemaker and the MacArthur New Testament Commentary series.

One of the first things to find out about authors is their theological persuasion. Some write from a dispensational perspective while others write from the Reformed perspective. This is good to know ahead of time because there are doctrinal differences in the content of the books. Your pastor should be able to help with this and make suggestions about what to buy.

Audio Sermons

Sermons are available on CDs and online. Listening to sermons is a way to increase your knowledge by using leisure time. If you spend a lot of time traveling and aren't using the time for other things, you can listen to hours of Bible messages. You can also listen to Bible teachers while you're taking care of projects in your home or yard.

One very helpful website, which allows you to listen to hundreds of sermons, is www.sermonaudio.com. You can search the available recordings by scripture reference, topic, or speaker.

GETTING BIBLE STUDY RESOURCES

I want to say a few things about where to get Bible study tools. Every Christian should own a few basic study books. To develop your personal library, make a wish list of the books you need. I've learned the hard way not to buy books I'm not acquainted with. The money I used to buy ten books that weren't that good could have been used to buy one good book. Add the study tools to your library that are valuable to you. Get recommendations from Christians who you believe can help you with this project and then visit your local Christian bookstore or an Internet bookseller.

You can also borrow Bible study books from your church library or even many public libraries. If the public library lacks a title you're seeking, it might be able to order the book from another library.

The Internet offers a wealth of free Bible study tools. People frequently comment that when they get on the Internet they use up so much time—if this is your case, you might want to use that time for studying the Bible online.

Here's a list of websites in random order with brief descriptions. There is much more on these sites than what's in the descriptions. There are also links to other Bible study sites. When you find a website that's helpful to you, put the link into a Bible study file in your Favorites so you can visit the site repeatedly.

bible.org

You'll find articles by topic or by passage. They have online Bible dictionaries, concordances, encyclopedias, and an extensive question-and-answer section. Under NAVIGATION click on SITE MAP. Then click on LINKS TO OTHER SITES to find a multitude of Christian websites referenced.

crosswalk.com

Under RESOURCES click on BIBLE STUDY TOOLS for commentaries, concordances, dictionaries, and encyclopedias.

studylight.org

Scroll down the left column to STUDY RESOURCES to find daily devotionals, commentaries, concordances, dictionaries, and sermon helps.

preceptaustin.org

Click on SITE INDEX for an alphabetical listing of this entire website. Type any Bible word into the search box to find numerous articles about the word. Bible commentaries with verse-by-verse exposition, dictionaries, and maps are available.

Biblos.com

This Bible study website was formed in 2007 with a mission is to increase the visibility of and accessibility to the scriptures by providing free online access to Bible study tools in many languages and to promote the Gospel of Christ through learning, study, and application of God's word.

Biblestudytools.com

This website is a large Bible study tool box that provides over thirty Bible translations with an amazing "compare translations" tab. Also available are numerous Bible commentaries, encyclopedias, and dictionaries. You'll find an extensive list of daily devotionals that can be searched by topic or author. A topical study tool is also available. A long list of classic sermons is available. The "video" link shows numerous Christian leaders answering Biblical questions.

rbc.org

This is the website of RBC Ministries. At the homepage you'll find the information available in ten languages. Numerous online daily devotionals are available. The strength of this site is the availability of over two hundred Bible-based teachings in easy-to-read, thirty-two page booklets that can be viewed online or requested as printed copies.

e-sword.net

This site provides free, downloadable Bible study software. Numerous Bible translations are available along with Bible commentaries, dictionaries, encyclopedias, topical Bibles, and a concordance. It is so popular, it's been accessed from some 225 countries around the world.

Any of these Bible study resources can be helpful in your personal study.

Getting Organized

My last suggestion is that you save and file your own notes from your study of the scriptures. Get two three-ring binders to hold your study notes. One notebook can be used for study notes by Bible topics, and the other one can be used for study notes by Bible references. It's a blessing to see and read later what God has taught you in your own study of His Word.

5. Motivation:

Putting Thoughts into Action

*You therefore, beloved, knowing this beforehand, be on
your guard so that you are not carried away by the error of
unprincipled men and fall from your own steadfastness, but
grow in the grace and knowledge of our Lord and Savior
Jesus Christ. To Him be the glory, both now and to the day of
eternity. Amen.*

2 Peter 3:17–18 nasb

The following ad appeared in the South Central Telephone Company Yellow Pages: "Born to be battered. . .the loving phone call book. Underline it, circle things, write in the margins, turn down page corners—the more you use it, the more valuable it gets to be."

If that's true of a phone book, think how much truer it is of God's Word!

Many people have made their Bibles "personal" by the comments they've written in them year after year. It's hard for some people to think about replacing their old Bibles with new ones even if they're falling apart—because they've found such wisdom, comfort, and power in the pages they've studied and cherished for years.

Alan Redpath, the pastor of Moody Church in Chicago from 1953 to 1962, advised believers to "wreck" their Bibles every ten years. He meant to wear them out by constant use. I once saw a message on a church sign that read, "A Bible that is falling apart is usually owned by someone who isn't." This is a point well taken.

I imagine most believers would say that reading and studying the Bible is a good thing to do. Virtually all Christian families in the United States own at least one Bible. The Bible is repeatedly the bestselling book every year. . .but perhaps still one of the least read. Why the disconnect? The answer has both a human dimension and a spiritual one.

Hindrances to Bible Study

From a human perspective, the busyness of life can keep us from scripture. Sometimes, we can be lazy when it comes to our spiritual health and responsibilities. And sometimes, we simply don't understand how important Bible study actually is. It needs to be viewed as a personal priority and implemented as part of our daily routine, just like any other activity we see as important.

From a spiritual perspective, sin in our lives can keep us from spending time in the Word. We can lose our spiritual appetite for the knowledge of God. The forces of darkness are doing all they can to keep us from studying God's truth. Any activity that uses up our time will do—it doesn't have to be evil, just something that weighs us down and takes our time.

We might ask, "Isn't going to church enough? Isn't reading and studying the Bible what pastors and Sunday school teachers do?" It's true that this is a large part of what pastors and teachers are to do, but it's also what everyone in a church congregation is supposed to do. Pastor Alistair Begg has said that his job as a pastor isn't just to feed the sheep, but to teach them how to cook!

Learning God's truth through reading and studying the Bible is something He wants for us. Consider these verses, all of which we've already referenced:

> Now these [Bereans] were more noble-minded than those in Thessalonica, for they received the word with great eagerness, examining the Scriptures daily to see whether these things were so.
> ACTS 17:11 NASB

> For whatever was written in earlier times was written for our instruction.
> ROMANS 15:4 NASB

> Study to shew thyself approved unto God, a workman that needeth not to be ashamed, rightly dividing the word of truth.
> 2 TIMOTHY 2:15 KJV

Verses like these should motivate us to be in our Bibles. Believers generally agree that the will of God includes gathering regularly with God's people to worship and pray, living a life of faith and obedience, serving the Lord and spreading His Gospel—but how many add that studying the Bible is also the will of God? Is this optional or essential?

As he ended his second letter, the apostle Peter strongly urged believers to "grow. . .in the knowledge of our Lord and Savior Jesus Christ" (2 Peter 3:18), something that starts with knowing His Word.

Believers who are growing in knowledge of God's truth have made a conscious decision to study the Word. Seek out those people who know a lot about the Bible, and ask them about their own study habits—then imitate their examples. We are all given the same twenty-four hours a day. You might consider rising earlier in the morning or eliminating a television show or two in the evening. Devote even a small amount of time to Bible study, and add to it as the pursuit becomes a regular habit in your life.

Just like eating, studying the Bible is a lifelong activity. We'll never get to the point where we've learned all that there is to know about God's Word, then be able to stop. Our spirit needs God's Word every day just like our bodies need food.

It's wise to make your study time a matter of prayer. We pray about many things, and this subject is important to Him, too. It's no accident that God allowed you to be born at this time with all the advantages we have to learn His Word. Pray about your Bible study every day, because "the prayer of the upright is His delight" (Proverbs 15:8).

Our adversary, the devil, does all he can to keep us from obeying God's will. God wants to bless us, and the devil wants to destroy us. If we as believers fall away from our Bible study, it might seem unimportant to us at the time. But we can be sure that the forces of darkness are celebrating and planning new ways to attack us.

When Jesus defeated Satan's temptation in the wilderness, Luke says, "The devil. . .departed from Him until an opportune time" (Luke 4:13). The devil leaves us for only a brief time. He always returns with different temptations until he finds what's effective against us. Satan knows that Christians, without regular time in the Bible, become weak and ineffective for Christ. But with prayer and the sword of the Spirit—the Word of God—we can overcome this enemy of our souls, enjoying our time with God as we feed on His Word.

God's Goodness

God's goodness should stir us to study His Word. His goodness is revealed in our lives in a variety of ways.

The Roman emperor Diocletian persecuted Christians during his reign. In AD 303 he ordered Bibles to be confiscated and burned. Many were destroyed. Today, in countries hostile to the Christian faith, simply owning a Bible is a crime. In our country we have no obstacles like this. Have you ever pondered the blessing that Bibles are legal in our country and so liberally available to us?

The Bible is also available to us in our language. The International Bible Society says the Bible or parts of it have been translated into about twenty-five hundred of the world's sixty-five hundred languages. The majority of language groups have never read the Bible, and its life-giving words about Jesus Christ, in their own language. It's a sad reality that millions of people still have never heard that blessed name.

In some countries where Bibles are permitted, there aren't enough copies for everyone who wants one. In many places, Bibles are shared by believers so they can each read the Word briefly. In other places, a believer who owns a Bible may be asked to become the pastor of a group simply because no one else has access to the Word.

Imagine the hardship of not having Bibles in our worship services. One of the great joys I have as a Bible teacher is to say, "Let's open our Bibles together." Because of the goodness of God, we don't face the limitations of many fellow Christians around the world. We should acknowledge these blessings by gratefully and faithfully studying the Bible.

Over the years, I've been blessed by numerous men of God, pastors, and missionaries who have exemplified love for and diligent pursuit of the scriptures. I've appreciated people in church congregations who have also had an impact on me. Let me tell you about three of them.

1. The example of Eleanor

A dignified elderly widow, Eleanor, who is now with the Lord, attended multiple church services and home Bible classes each week to hear the Word of the Lord being taught. When it came to scripture, she seemed to have the energy of a young person. The Bible was the book of her life. When we talked, we would always end up discussing God's Word.

I'll never forget visiting her home to drop off a few Bible sermons on cassette tape. She mentioned that she was doing a personal study on the Gospel of Mark and showed me the six Bible commentaries that she was working through. I was amazed that she'd go to so much effort in a personal study, but she was serious about learning God's Word. At the time, I was still learning what it meant to love God's Word, and Eleanor's example made me want the same kind of energy and excitement for the Bible.

2. The example of a man who couldn't read

An older gentleman, who crossed my path only momentarily, left a lasting impression. He was a little man who briefly attended the same home Bible class that I did. He was a quaint, soft-spoken man, always dressed in a suit and tie. During discussions, it was obvious that he knew a lot about the Bible.

One night, the teacher asked him to read a verse aloud. He paused, hung his head, and admitted he didn't know how to read. I was stunned, as I'm sure everyone else was, too. How could someone who lacked reading skills know so much about the Bible? Obviously, he'd listened to other people teach the Bible—a lot.

The fact that this man overcame the obstacle of illiteracy and still learned the Bible is what struck me. When people are determined to learn God's Word, He'll provide the help they need.

3. The example of Amy

The third person is a wife and stay-at-home mom named Amy. Where is the mother of three young children going to find the time to study the Bible?

To add to this challenge, Amy's been legally blind since her teen years. Can a person with obvious time restraints and the obstacle of partial blindness still study the Bible? The answer is yes, though it requires a great amount of determination and love for God's Word.

Using a powerful magnifying glass, Amy studies scripture for an entire hour—and at times an hour and a half—while two of her children are at school and her youngest takes a nap. That is the quiet time God has provided for her. The example of these three believers inspires me. And I'm guessing God has put similar people in your life to serve as examples to you. The apostle Paul once said, "Imitate me, just as I also imitate Christ" (1 Corinthians 11:1). On another occasion he wrote, "Brethren, join in following my example, and note those who so walk, as you have us for a pattern" (Philippians 3:17). Value these kinds of people in your life. Imitate the good that you see in them. Thank God that He has brought them into your life. Pray that you'll be a better Christian for having known them.

MARY AND MARTHA

As we conclude, let's consider the lives of Mary and Martha of Bethany. Mary is a great biblical example of a person whose desire was to be taught by Jesus: Every time she appears in the Bible, she's kneeling before Him. In John 11, she's at His feet in sorrow. In John 12, she's at His feet in adoration. In Luke 10, she's at His feet to learn truth. Mary, the worshiper, wants her soul fed by Jesus—her sister Martha, the worker, wants to feed Jesus.

Mary and Martha had welcomed Jesus into their home. With good intentions,

Martha took steps to prepare a meal for the honored guest. Mary is now introduced into the story: "And she had a sister called Mary, who also sat at Jesus' feet and heard His word" (Luke 10:39). Martha was in the kitchen cooking food, and Mary was in the living room, learning from Jesus. Martha, annoyed that Mary wasn't helping with the work, interrupted the Lord, saying, "'Lord, do You not care that my sister has left me to serve alone? Therefore tell her to help me'" (Luke 10:40).

Jesus, in His divine wisdom, analyzed the situation and told Martha she was filled with unnecessary anxiety that had harmfully affected her priorities. The things she worried about really weren't important. "'One thing is needed,'" Jesus told Martha, "'and Mary has chosen that good part, which will not be taken away from her'" (Luke 10:42).

Jesus commended Mary for having good priorities, namely, learning the Word of God. Bible expositor G. Campbell Morgan calls this "the one supreme necessity."

Mary's experience was that of being taught by the incarnate Christ. Each of us can experience the blessing of being taught by the risen Christ—by the power of His Holy Spirit, through the study of God's amazing Word.

> *Grow in the grace and knowledge of our Lord and Savior*
> *Jesus Christ. To Him be the glory, both now and to the day of*
> *eternity. Amen.*
>
> 2 Peter 3:18 nasb

Appendices

a. Outline for the Expositional Method

Due to its brevity, the New Testament book of Philemon makes for good practice on the expositional method of Bible method.

You'll discover in this personal letter from the apostle Paul to a Christian friend that each individual verse is vitally connected to the others. The book contains the great themes of forgiveness and reconciliation in a historical setting where slavery (an integral part of the story), was an accepted way of life. Onesimus, a runaway slave, had fled from his Christian master, Philemon. Paul shows that through Christian truth the institution of slavery can be transformed from the inside out.

This book study can help people who need to experience forgiveness and reconciliation in their own life.

Below, I will attempt to walk you through an expositional study of Philemon. Practice on this small book, then try other passages by yourself!

STEP 1

Compile your Bible study tools—a Bible, a Bible dictionary, pen or pencil, and paper. I also advise you to commit to a regular time of day to study.

STEP 2

At the tops of blank note pages, write the verse references and the words of the verses in full sentences—that is, if a sentence continues over multiple verses, show an entire sentence on a note page. If a sentence is too long for a single note page, carry it over onto a second or third page. Continue this process until every verse you're studying is accounted for on your note pages, and leave the remainder of each page for your own study notes.

In the case of Philemon, the book's 25 verses actually contain 16 sentences (in the New King James Version), so you'll have 16 pages for study notes, plus one additional page for developing of an outline of the entire book.

In expositional studying you'll want to look beyond the verse numbers and to focus on entire sentences. Study the way you speak—in complete sentences. This helps to overcome our tendency to focus on favorite verses, perhaps out of context, while ignoring less prominent but equally important verses nearby.

Now, read your selected section of scripture repeatedly, acquainting yourself with all the information found in the text. With each reading, slow down and look more closely to discover things that you may have overlooked previously. Reading multiple Bible versions can be helpful in this process.

STEP 3

Write your observations about each verse. Record your findings by asking "who, what, when, where, why, and how." Look for the key words that connect thoughts—and for reoccurring words that emphasize a theme.

Keeping first things first, be careful to write only what is actually stated in the text. Your personal thoughts can be recorded later. (You might want to note the difference by using two headings: "What is stated" and "Additional thoughts and lessons.")

Group sentences together by their most common thought, and give each grouping a title. You should now be able to identify a single theme as the title of the entire portion of scripture you are studying.

Step 4

Try your own study of the book of Philemon as an exercise. Once you're done, compare your notes with the study notes provided below, consulting Bible commentaries and other study resources as well. Keep at it, to refine and improve your own Bible study skills!

Expositional Study Notes
The book of Philemon

(due to limited space, actual scripture text is not shown)

The Theme and Title—Encouraging Forgiveness

vv. 1–3 Paul's greeting
What is stated

v. 1—The letter's authors are named and described as Paul, a prisoner of Christ, and Timothy, a brother to all. The letter's first and main recipient, Philemon, is described two ways, as "our beloved friend and fellow laborer."

v. 2—Three additional recipients are named and described—Apphia the beloved ("our sister" esv), Archippus our fellow soldier, and the congregation that meets in Philemon's house.

v. 3—The first sentence (vv. 1–3) ends with a traditional greeting common in Paul's letters desiring divine blessing on the recipients. In this case, grace and peace have specific reference to the trouble caused by Onesimus.

Additional thoughts

v. 1—Paul begins this letter by immediately referring to his troubling circumstances of imprisonment (Acts 27–28) and connects this to Christ's providence and later as something experienced for His cause—"my chains for the gospel" (v. 13). This letter is called one of Paul's "prison epistles" written while under guard by the Roman authorities. The main characters in this story are obvious by how many times they're referred to. Paul speaks of himself at least twenty-two times, Philemon twenty-six times (though only naming him once), Onesimus the slave eight times, and Christ, the indispensable Person who makes these kinds of forgiveness stories possible, eleven times. This personal letter to Philemon was an open letter for everyone. Philemon's response to Onesimus will eventually affect everyone in his life.

v. 2—Because of their association with Philemon, Apphia (a feminine name), may be Philemon's wife while Archippus may be his son and/or a key church leader. Cross references indicate that Philemon is a wealthy member of the Colossian church and hosts church meetings in his large home (Colossians 4:7–9, 17). Therefore the epistles to the Colossians and Philemon are closely connected.

vv. 4–7 Paul's Praise for Philemon
What is stated

v. 4—This sentence (vv. 4–6) begins with Paul's testimony that he thanks God for Philemon and continually prays for him.

v. 5—Paul gives two reasons for his gratitude: Others told him about Philemon's love toward the saints (i.e. all believers in Christ, Romans 1:5–7), and his faith toward the Lord Jesus.

v. 6—The word "that" begins this verse and finishes the thought of v. 4 by now stating the content of Paul's prayers for Philemon: This difficult verse seems best understood, because of the context, as Paul praying that Philemon's ministry to believers would continue to be fruitful. This is especially true of the impact of Philemon's reconciliation with Onesimus, as the former master realizes that even a one-time slave now possesses the same spiritual blessings that belong to all believers in Christ.

v. 7—Paul testifies that he and Timothy are encouraged because they have heard of the blessing that Philemon has been to the saints. An affectionate touch is added by describing Philemon with the family term "brother" that was also used of Timothy earlier.

Additional thoughts

v. 4—It's good to let people know that we are thankful for them and praying for them. Paul's gratitude for Philemon was given to God rather than to Philemon because it was God who was working in and through him (Philippians 2:12–13).

v. 6—This important prayer request about our service being effective should be on our prayer list for ourselves and our Christian friends.

v. 7—For Philemon to hear that his life has been such a blessing to so many saints should inspire him to do what Paul is about to ask regarding Onesimus, the sinful slave who has also become a saint. As we read vv. 4–7 about what people have said about Philemon, it's good to consider what people may say about our Christian testimony.

vv. 8–21 Paul's plea for Onesimus (6 Things)

vv. 8–9 This plea involves brotherly love
What is stated

v. 8—"Therefore" directs us back to previous words indicating that Paul is making his request to a man who has a reputation for being a blessing to others (vv.

4–7). Paul as an apostle with authority could have commanded that Philemon fulfill his forthcoming request.

v. 9—Paul preferred to make his request based on love. This love would consider Paul's age and all the trials that he has endured over his years and what he's currently going through as a prisoner.

Additional thoughts

vv. 8–9—Some have criticized Paul for being manipulative to get what he wants from Philemon. It's best instead to view his words as wisdom that thoroughly considers all necessary matters to make a proper decision about Onesimus. This is reminiscent of the Lord saying, "Come, let us reason together." Paul is only practicing what he preached—to "speak the truth in love." Too many important decisions end up being wrong because they are not given thorough thought and are made only on the basis of personal emotion and self-interest.

Since this is a book about forgiveness, numerous "forgiveness lessons" can be identified.

Forgiveness lesson #1: Genuine forgiveness is commanded by God and should be motivated by love rather than by mere compulsion (Ephesians 4:32–5:2).

vv. 10–11 This plea involves the conversion of Onesimus
What is stated

v. 10—Onesimus is called Paul's spiritual son. Paul had recently led him to faith in Christ.

v. 11—The conversion of Onesimus produced a significant change in his life. He was formerly detrimental, but is now beneficial.

Additional thoughts

v. 10—It is an act of God's providence that Onesimus traveled hundreds of miles from Colosse to Rome to meet Paul who convinced him to trust in Christ. Since heaven rejoices when a sinner repents (Luke 15:7), Philemon should have the same reaction toward the good news about Onesimus. Timothy is also described as Paul's spiritual son (1 Timothy 1:2).

v. 11—When sinners are saved, they become a new creation in Christ (2 Corinthians 5:17). Through the transforming power of the Gospel Onesimus now lives up to his name (meaning "useful"). The face of Onesimus that was on "wanted posters" is now in the church directory!

Forgiveness lesson #2: If we are to be Christlike, we must learn to forgive others as He did. Since our personal forgiveness comes through Christ's death (Colossians 1:14), we are instructed to forgive others in the same way that He forgave us (Colossians 3:12–13). This includes remembering the Lord's instructions about praying that others would be forgiven (Matthew 6:12) and the example of His dying prayer for His enemies: "Father, forgive them for they know not what they do."

vv. 12–14 This plea involves Philemon's voluntary cooperation
What is stated

v. 12—Paul plans to send Onesimus back to Philemon and asks that Onesimus be received as Paul would be received.

v. 13—Paul wanted Onesimus to stay with him on Philemon's behalf to help him in his ministry.

v. 14—The key word "but" indicates a contrast. Paul didn't want to presume upon Philemon's generosity, but desired his voluntary assistance.

Additional thoughts

v. 12—Onesimus returned to Colosse as a new believer with a penitent spirit and was accompanied by Paul's dependable colaborer, Tychicus, who delivered Paul's prison letters to churches and Onesimus to Philemon (Colossians 4:7–9). Historical background indicates that he could have been severely punished for running away. Reconciliation means that we should accept those who sin against us the way we would accept those who haven't sinned against us.

vv. 13–14—Christians should help each other serve the Lord as the need presents itself.

vv. 15–16 This plea involves God's providence
What is stated

v. 15—In this sentence (vv. 15–16) Paul suggests the possibility that it was God's secret plan that the troubling escape of Onesimus was only temporary so that he could be saved elsewhere and then return permanently.

v. 16—He would return as more than a slave. He would also now be a "beloved" Christian brother in God's family. He is now added to the list of those called "beloved" (vv. 1–2) and those called "brother" (vv. 1, 7). Onesimus would now be especially valuable to Philemon in physical matters related to this life and also in spiritual matters related to Gospel ministry.

Additional thoughts

vv. 15–16—Here is a great example of Romans 8:28. The newfound faith of Onesimus would transform the relationship between this master and slave (Galatians 3:28). While he tried to gain his own freedom by running away, he found true spiritual freedom in Christ (John 8:34–36).

Forgiveness lesson #3: Christians are to be a forgiving people since they worship the sovereign God who is also a God of forgiveness (Psalm 86:5). Philemon needs to see the bigger picture and should be able to say with a forgiving attitude to Onesimus what Joseph said to his brothers: "You meant evil against me, but God meant it for good" (Genesis 50:20).

vv. 17–20 This plea involves Paul's promise
What is stated

v. 17—Paul makes his request based on the partnership that he and Philemon have in the Gospel. He asks that Onesimus be received back as Paul himself would be received if he was standing at the door. This would require Philemon to totally forgive and accept Onesimus. By using himself as a standard, Paul gives an enormous request involving a complete reconciliation between two estranged people.

v. 18—This verse begins with the key words "but if," indicating a strong possibility. In an attempt to remove the obstacle to forgiveness of an unnamed offense, Paul promises to pay back on behalf of Onesimus whatever financial losses Philemon may have experienced because of Onesimus's disappearance and theft.

v. 19—By writing this letter, Paul says that he has put his own signature to Onesimus's bill of indebtedness. To encourage a positive response from Philemon, Paul then reminds him about his own indebtedness to Paul who had also led Philemon to faith in Christ.

v. 20—Paul again appeals to Philemon as a brother asking that he provide him with spiritual blessings once more by meeting his request.

Additional thoughts

v. 18—Paul's gracious offer of restitution on behalf of Onesimus illustrates what Christ's death has done for sinners in paying their entire debt for their sins against God (Isaiah 53:6; 2 Corinthians 5:21). Such an act is called *imputation*—literally, "to put on one's account" (Romans 4:21–24).

v. 18—Like Paul, we should do what we can to help other people be reconciled with each other.

v. 19—This is a reminder that the ground is level at Calvary, as Onesimus—who had nothing—was raised up, while Philemon—who had status and wealth—was made low (James 2:1–5).

Forgiveness lesson #4: Christians must learn to forgive and forget. In v. 17, Paul calls for total forgiveness—which includes reconciliation between Philemon and Onesimus. This would require them to remove any existing grudge or bitterness and not revisit the problem in the future—which is the way God has forgiven us and reconciled us to Himself (Hebrews 10:16–17; Colossians 1:21–22).

Forgiveness lesson #5: Those who have committed an offense in a relationship should take steps to make appropriate acts of restitution that can help restore a broken relationship (Luke 19:8).

Forgiveness lesson #6: Granting or withholding forgiveness affects those around us. When we as peacemakers forgive someone who has sinned against us, those around us are blessed as in v. 20. But if we withhold forgiveness and trouble increases, those around us will be discouraged and saddened. We should strive to make good choices since they affect people in our family and our church (Psalm 119:72–74).

v. 21 — This plea involves Paul's confidence
What is stated

Paul is certain that Philemon will do the right thing in this case and even exceed it, which may include setting Onesimus free from his slavery. Paul believes that he knows how this story will end.

vv. 22–25 Paul's closing
What is stated

v. 22—He requests lodging for his next visit to Colosse since he expects to be released from prison.

v. 23—He sends greetings from Epaphras who is also imprisoned with him and is a member of the Colossian church (Colossians 1:7–8).

v. 24—He sends additional greetings from four other Christians who serve with him and are well-known to the Colossian church.

v. 25—He completes this letter with a benediction which should not be viewed as just a "nice" way to end—instead, he points to the ultimate source of divine strength in granting forgiveness.

Additional thoughts

v. 24—When Paul named Mark in the final greetings, everyone would be reminded of the previous trouble between Paul and Mark that separated them for some time and was documented by Luke in Acts 15:36–41. They eventually experienced forgiveness and reconciliation with each other and once again serve side by side. This final reminder of a happy ending between Paul and Mark would encourage a happy ending between Philemon and Onesimus. For us to know the rest of this story though, we'll have to wait until we get to heaven!

Forgiveness lesson #7: When we think about our own need to forgive others, it's helpful to remember the example of other Christians we know who have forgiven people in their lives. This will encourage us to also have a forgiving spirit.

Forgiveness lesson #8: Paul ends his letter in v. 25 with a specific wish that Philemon experience the empowering grace of Christ, which is a great reminder of Paul's own words of dependence "I can do all things through Christ who strengthens me" (Philippians 4:13)—even granting forgiveness and being reconciled with those who have offended us.

b. Outlines for the Topical Method

The step-by-step methods of topical Bible study are very similar to both the biographical and word-study methods. I'll use a topical study example in the pages following.

What differs is that the topical method of Bible study focuses more on doctrinal issues and important themes, while biographical studies concentrate on people and word studies on particular terms and phrases.

In the following example of topical Bible study, we'll examine the apostle Paul's customary greeting that appears with slight variations at the beginning of each of his thirteen New Testament letters. This greeting, which was common in Paul's day, was deepened with Christian thought.

Paul's salutation in Romans 1:7 reads like this: "Grace to you and peace from God our Father and the Lord Jesus Christ." The two spiritual qualities found in this greeting—grace and peace—will be investigated topically.

The following study will use only selected texts to get you started, leaving many others for your own additional pursuit. God has revealed so much about these two great themes that you will be able to find entire books written on each. For your own topical study, try the following steps.

STEP 1

Compile your Bible study tools—a Bible, a Bible dictionary, a Bible encyclopedia, a topical Bible and/or concordance, and writing materials.

STEP 2

Write the definition of your topic from a Bible dictionary (rather than an English dictionary), since you'll see your topic from the biblical languages and in a biblical context. Later, as you begin to study Bible verses on your topic, your understanding of its definition should blossom.

STEP 3

Compile all the essential scripture texts related to your topic by using a topical Bible and/or concordance. Then, as you read the verses, group texts together into separate categories of emphasis. Select a title that best describes each set of verses that you've grouped together.

STEP 4

Write your observations about what each verse actually says about your topic. Be sure to distinguish between what the verse states and your own personal thoughts. You might want to use headings like "What is stated" and "Additional thoughts."

STEP 5

Try your own study of the topic of grace as an exercise. Once you're done, compare your notes with the study notes provided below, consulting Bible commentaries and other study resources as well. Keep at it, to refine and improve your own Bible study skills!

Topical Study Notes
Grace

The definition: *Baker's Evangelical Dictionary of Biblical Theology* states in part, "An accurate, common definition describes grace as the unmerited favor of God toward man." The *Our Daily Bread* devotional puts it this way: "Grace is everything for nothing to those who don't deserve anything." A suggested acronym for grace is "God's Riches At Christ's Expense," which adds the important thought of God's favor coming through Christ's sacrifice—though that still doesn't fully convey all that grace means.

As seen in the following verses, God's grace is first experienced in salvation. Then it continues to operate throughout our entire Christian life as we "grow in grace." Finally, in heaven, we'll continue to experience "the exceeding riches of His grace" (Ephesians 2:7). Thus, the Christian message is rightly called "the gospel of the grace of God" (Acts 20:24).

The selected verses for this topical study of grace: Numbers 6:25; John 1:14–17; Acts 15:11; Romans 3:24, 6:1–14; 11:5–6; 1 Corinthians 15:9–10; 2 Corinthians 12:7–9; Ephesians 2:8–9, 4:29; 2 Timothy 2:1; Titus 2:11–13; Hebrews 4:15–16; 1 Peter 4:10, 5:10.

Numbers 6:25
What is stated
"The LORD. . .be gracious to you." These words are part of a benediction that Jewish priests were to announce during worship services to the nation of Israel revealing that God was gracious to His people.

Additional thoughts
The words of this benediction surely laid a foundation for Paul's customary New Testament greetings. There were many Old Testament expressions of God's grace and use of this word beginning with Noah (Genesis 6:8), also heard in a self-proclamation by the Lord to Moses (Exodus 34:6–9), and expressed in song by the sons of Korah (Psalm 84:11), while Proverbs 3:34 is quoted in the New Testament in James 4:6.

John 1:14–17
What is stated:
In v. 14, Jesus—the incarnate Word of God—was personally "full of grace and truth" which was visible to His followers. An older edition of the New International Version conveys the truth of v. 16 beautifully: "From the fullness of his grace we have all received one blessing after another." Like waves coming into the shore one after another, a constant flow of blessings was the daily experience of Jesus' followers. Finally, v. 17 contrasts Moses, who gave the law which was to reveal God's righteous standards and show man his sin, with Jesus Christ, through whom came saving "grace and truth" with the fullness of blessings.

Additional thoughts
Saving grace: This aspect of grace is related to the conversion of sinners to Christ

Ephesians 2:8–9
What is stated
"For by grace you have been saved through faith, and that not of yourselves; it is the gift of God, not of works, lest anyone should boast." God's gracious work of saving sinners is described throughout vv. 1–10 and reaches a pinnacle in vv. 5 and 8 with the words "by grace you have been saved."

Additional thoughts
God's method of saving lost sinners makes all boasting worthless by people trying to tally up their good works in an effort to be acceptable to God.

Romans 3:24
What is stated
Paul established everyone's need for salvation by proving the guilt of all sinners in Romans 1:18–3:20 concluding his thoughts with God as our judge announcing a "guilty" verdict against the human race in 3:19. Paul then immediately begins to describe God's salvation which includes sinners "being justified freely by His grace." God as our Savior offers humankind this blessing—guilty sinners can be declared righteous and this is free because of His grace! This is free to sinners because God paid the high cost Himself through His Son's sacrificial death—"redemption that is in Christ Jesus."

Romans 11:5–6
What is stated
As Paul describes God's relationship to His chosen people Israel in Romans 9–11, he clarifies that a system of grace and a separate system of works (moral deeds and religious rituals) cannot be mixed together to secure God's favor. Salvation cannot be by grace plus works, without destroying what grace actually is. The same is true with works: The addition of grace into a system of works will also destroy that system. Paul's point is that, in his day as today, there is a remnant of individual Jews who are Christians by divine grace. They did not obtain this saving blessing through their own good deeds.

Acts 15:11
What is stated
Chapter 15 describes a gathering of Jewish church leaders at a council to define exactly how Gentiles are saved (vv. 1–6). Some believed that in addition to faith in Christ, the Old Testament law of Moses should be observed—with a primary focus on the ceremonial ritual of circumcision. On behalf of the apostles, Peter spoke the clarifying words of v. 11: "But we believe that through the grace of the Lord Jesus Christ we (Jews) shall be saved in the same manner as they (Gentiles)."

Additional thoughts

In a similar way, the New Testament rituals of water baptism and the Lord's table, which have an important place in the Christian life, should be observed by all Christians—but it must be understood that there is no saving merit in these observances.

Sanctifying grace: This aspect of grace is related to our continual growth in the Christian life

Titus 2:11–13
What is stated

v. 11—In the past, God's grace was seen in the appearing of the incarnate Christ at His first coming with a mission to save sinners. In the present, His grace is not only seen in changing our destiny through His salvation, but also in changing our former lifestyle as indicated in the following verses.

v. 12—God's grace continues to function by instructing believers how to live the Christian life. In this instruction two things are to be refused—"ungodliness," which minimizes God's influence on how we live, and "worldly lusts," which pursue a self-centered and sinful lifestyle like unbelievers. Three things are to be developed—we are to "live soberly" or ("sensible," in the English Standard Version) which emphasizes growth in personal wisdom; "righteously," which has to do with our proper treatment of other people; and "godly," which is concerned with always having close fellowship with God.

v. 13—This instruction by grace includes a new positive attitude and outlook for the future as Christ's glorious return is anticipated.

Ephesians 4:29
What is stated

Believers are to be concerned with the effects of their words on other people, thinking about this before they speak. We are not to speak "corrupt" words, since they can be hurtful and destructive. The goal when speaking should be to strengthen people with pleasant words that "impart grace" to them.

Additional thoughts

We are saved by God's grace—and by His grace He changes our lifestyle and speech to become more Christlike. The scripture says of Christ, "all bore witness to Him. . .marveled at the gracious words that proceeded out of His mouth" (Luke 4:22).

Romans 6:1–14
What is stated

Paul anticipates a question from those seeking loopholes to accommodate their practice of sin: "Shall we continue in sin that grace may abound?" The short answer to this question is "Certainly not!" (v. 2). A longer answer is given in vv. 2–14, which state that a sinful lifestyle should never be part of a Christian's life—because the believer's spiritual union with Christ's death and resurrection is designed to free us from sin's dominion and make us alive to do God's will. The section ends with v. 14 stating that—because of the empowering influence of grace—we can live as instruments in God's hands rather than as people dominated by sin, individuals who are simply trying to obey rules (law) by our own strength.

Additional thoughts
Serving grace: This aspect of grace is related to Christian service.

1 Corinthians 15:10
What is stated
Paul humbly credits God's grace for changing his former life of persecuting God's church to one now empowered even to excel others in serving God.

Additional thoughts
Some may attribute their accomplishments in life to their educational achievements, wise financial decisions, or personal abilities. Paul could boast of many such qualities, but ultimately viewed the blessed life only the result of the grace of God.

2 Timothy 2:1
What is stated
Paul encourages Timothy—his son in the Christian faith, to strengthen himself by Christ's grace for the tasks of training qualified men for the ministry and enduring the hardships of spiritual warfare. Timothy should expect grace to help him fight like a soldier (v. 3), compete like an athlete (v. 5), and work like a farmer (v. 6).

1 Peter 4:10
What is stated
Peter exhorts every believer to use their spiritual gifts for the mutual benefit of each other. They should act like diligent stewards who manage other people's assets. In Peter's view, these gifts are "the manifold grace of God"—a variety of different abilities entrusted to believers, along with the distinct purposes that God plans to accomplish through their use. These gifts of grace are then categorized into speaking and serving gifts (v. 11).

Additional thoughts
Spurgeon said "God gives much to you that you may give it to others; it is only meant to run through you as through a pipe."
Sustaining grace: This aspect of grace is related to personal suffering.

2 Corinthians 12:7–9
What is stated
v. 7—Due to his unusual experience of being temporarily transported to heaven, Paul was given a "thorn in the flesh" to keep him humble.

v. 8—Paul prayed repeatedly for relief from this trouble.

v. 9—The Lord's answer to this prayer was no—Paul was denied his requested relief. Instead, he was told the Lord's grace would be sufficient for all that he needed for the moment.

Further explanation stated that Christ's "strength is made perfect in weakness" meaning that the weakness Paul experienced from his trouble should move him to depend more on Christ's sustaining power. Realizing that God uses trouble to stimulate spiritual growth, Paul reevaluated his situation to view it with gladness because he would now be spiritually stronger.

Additional thoughts

It was better for Paul's prayer request to be denied than to be approved. Paul was interested in relief from his trouble while God was interested in developing his strength through humble endurance. For those who always want spectacular answers to their prayers, this aspect of God's grace will take some getting used to!

1 Peter 5:10
What is stated

Peter uses the title "the God of all grace" within the context of Christian suffering. He notes that God provides more grace to those who suffer for His name and receive it through humility (v. 5 quotes Proverbs 3:34). He reminds his readers that they are not alone in suffering, since this is a global reality (v. 9), and he encourages them to have hope since they possess a glorious future. Until then, God's grace limits the duration of suffering—it's for "a while" and He'll use the troubles for His chilren's good to produce maturity, stability, and strength.

Hebrews 4:16
What is stated

When believers recognize their daily need for God's help, they are encouraged to pray with an assurance of being accepted, to "draw near with confidence" (NASB) since they come to God through God's Son, Jesus (vv. 14–15).

What can they expect? God's "mercy"—in other word, not receiving the justice that is really deserved. Instead, God provides "grace"—blessings that are *not* deserved. So to enter this throne room is to approach a sympathetic and benevolent Sovereign who sits on a "throne of grace."

Conclusion

Since Paul is writing each of his letters to Christians who have already experienced God's saving grace, it seems best to view his greetings as a desire for more grace in daily Christian living—grace for our sanctification, our service, and our suffering. And finally, looking forward to God's future expression of grace in heaven.

Since we've only considered a small number of verses about grace, many others await your additional study of the topic.

c. Outlines for the Biographical Method

In the following step-by-step example we'll examine the lives of Aquila and Priscilla, a Christian couple found in the New Testament. It should prove to be an easy study since their names are always listed together—and found in only six verses.

Married believers and single people thinking about marriage will discover great lessons in this study touching on both the marital and spiritual life.

Let's begin with three steps that will always be used in this type of study:

STEP 1

Choose your character for study and assemble the following tools: your Bible, an exhaustive concordance, pens or pencils, and blank paper. A Bible atlas may be helpful in this study due to its frequent geographical references.

STEP 2

Using a concordance, locate all the Bible verses in which the person's name is found. Remember that sometimes a name is common to multiple individuals— or that the same person has different names—so take care that the verses you select are all about the right person.

Write the references on your paper, leaving plenty of space between each so you can record your own observations. You'll want to examine the immediate context of each of your selected verses to locate additional information that may be pertinent to your study. If you discover something interesting, write those references also.

STEP 3

Reread each verse several times to see what is actually stated about the person being studied. Take your time, and ask these questions: "who, what, when, where, why, and how?" Though there may not be an answer to each of the "5 W's," they will assist you in seeing everything that is clearly stated in the verses you've chosen—and may lead to other considerations later in your study.

As always, it is very important to make a clear distinction in your notes between what is actually stated in verses and what may only be implied. Deal primarily on what is actually stated so you read something into the scriptures. (Remember, we cannot improve on what God has said, as Psalm 19:7 states: "The law of the LORD is perfect.") When scripture is silent, it's best to simply accept the fact that God hasn't revealed everything to us.

We will note this difference below by using the headings "What is stated" and "Additional thoughts."

STEP 4

Once you have completed your biographical study notes you'll want to arrange them logically. I have two recommendations:

First, you can use all or parts of the following outline for answering significant questions.

This outline can be adjusted to fit the amount of material that God has revealed in the Bible about the person you're studying:

1. Their calling in life—what is stated about their birth, family, job, community, service for God, etc.?
2. Their communion with God—what was their relationship to God?
3. The chronology of their life—what were the different stages of their life?
4. The character of their life—what kind of person were they?
5. Their companions—who were the other people in their life?
6. The conclusion—what major themes and Bible verse best summarizes their life?

Second, you can organize your material in chronological order—which is the way the selected verses below are arranged.

Step 5

Try your own study of Aquila and Priscilla as an exercise. Once you're done, compare your notes with the study notes provided below, consulting Bible commentaries and other study resources as well. Keep at it, to refine and improve your own Bible study skills!

Biographical Study Notes
Aquila and Priscilla

1. Acts 18:2 (context, 18:1–3)—"Aquila. . . had recently come from Italy with his wife Priscilla."

What is stated
v. 1—Paul was temporarily traveling alone (Acts 17:15–16) from Athens on his second mission trip and met this couple for the first time in the city of Corinth, Greece.

v. 2—Aquila had a Jewish heritage, but both he and his wife are known only by their Roman names. Scripture is silent about Priscilla's ethnic origin. Aquila was born in the Gentile region of Pontus near the Black Sea. They had also traveled to Corinth having recently fled Rome since all Jews had been banished from that city by the Roman emperor.

v. 3—Because they were all experienced tent makers, they did manual labor together in a small business. Paul worked with them and stayed with them as they opened their home to him.

Additional thoughts

vv. 1–2—*Aquila* means "eagle" which was used as a symbol in the Roman military. But because of his Jewish background he could associate his name with favorite Bible verses like Exodus 19:4 and Isaiah 40:31 that describe what God does for His people. The name *Priscilla* has a suggested meaning of "ancient" which she could associate with the nature of God described in Isaiah 46:10 and Daniel 7:9.

Both parties traveled from different cities and ended up in the same place. Their story indicates that God providentially brought them together to work for Him (Proverbs 3:5–6; 16:9). This couple would eventually be able to say that their trial of being forced from their home in Rome turned out to be a blessing in disguise as they eventually became personally acquainted with Paul. God was working all things together for their good (Romans 8:28).

v. 3—The original meeting of these parties was in a business and occupational setting. Paul worked part-time as needed to support himself financially. This was the beginning of a close and lasting friendship between them as Paul not only *worked* with them and *lived* with them, but also *served* the Lord with them. Having the apostle Paul in your home at the end of each day's work would have been an edifying experience as he discussed the scriptures and what God was accomplishing through his Bible teaching ministry in Corinth (18:11).

2. Acts 18:18 (context, 18:18–19)— "Priscilla and Aquila were with him"

What is stated

v. 18—After eighteen months in Corinth, Paul decided that it was time for him to leave the new church he had planted and finish his mission trip, he left by boat and was accompanied by this couple.

v. 19—They had a layover in the seaport city of Ephesus. Paul then left this couple there as he continued his journey to Jerusalem and then back to his sending home church in Antioch, Syria (vv. 21–22).

Additional thoughts

v. 18—This couple packed their bags to move again, but this time for the cause of the Gospel. We are not told when they became Christians, but it's obvious at this point that they are devoted believers who have joined Paul in his mission work.

v. 19—It appears to be a strategic move by Paul to leave this couple in Ephesus. He planned to return there on his next mission trip, and left them behind to establish a Christian testimony in the community through their personal lives, their business, and form a nucleus of new believers which would lay a foundation for the famous Ephesian church described in Acts 19.

3. Acts 18:26 (context, 18:24–28) — "Aquila and Priscilla heard him. . ."

What is stated

vv. 24–25—Apollos, who was Jewish and a gifted itinerant Bible teacher, visited Ephesus.
He was raised in the famous city of Alexandria, Egypt, which was known for its Grecian educational center.

v. 26—While hearing him teach the Old Testament, this couple detects a deficiency in his message that is not stated. They initiate a private meeting with him to explain "the way of God" more accurately. It proved to be a fruitful meeting (vv. 27–28)

v. 27—When Apollos prepared to continue his travels, the brethren—which surely included this well-known couple—gave him a letter of recommendation.

Additional thoughts

v. 26—This couple was diligent in business, which is time consuming—but they maintained a personal priority of always growing together in knowledge of God's Word as they discussed the scriptures together. Their influence reached into the business world and church life—and now, with unified and humble voices, they reached into the theological arena as they were able to respectfully persuade a renowned teacher to improve his Gospel message. In their minds, eloquence and enthusiasm in teaching was no substitute for accuracy.

v. 27—This letter of recommendation was designed to protect churches from false teachers and advance the credentials of Apollos.

4. 1 Corinthians 16:19 — "Aquila and Priscilla greet you"

What is stated:

v. 19—Paul is now on his third foreign mission trip and has returned to Ephesus for a three year stay (Acts 20:17, 31). He sends a letter to the Corinthian church that includes personal greetings from this couple who were former members of that church. The greeting from this couple is made "heartily in the Lord," which describes friendship between Christians who know each other well. Greetings are also given from the Ephesian house-church that meets in their home (1 Corinthians 16:19).

Additional thoughts

v. 19—Upon arriving in Ephesus, this couple began worshipping God in the local synagogue (Acts 18:26). As issues over Jesus became divisive (Acts 19:8–9), a group began to meet in their home. This couple recognized that they were stewards of God entrusted with wealth, and they willingly used their possessions, including their home, to further the cause of Christ. They were living examples to the Corinthians of being "cheerful givers" (2 Corinthians 9:7). Church history indicates that private homes were used for church meetings until the beginning of the fourth century when the Roman Empire recognized Christianity as a legal religion, thus beginning the era of public church buildings.

5. Romans 16:3 (context, 16:3–5)—"Greet Priscilla and Aquila"

What is stated

v. 3—As Paul ends his letter to the Romans with extensive personal greetings, this couple has relocated again, this time from Ephesus back to Rome. They are named and extolled by Paul as his fellow workers.

v. 4—This praise for the couple continues as Paul states that at some point of dangerous persecution they put their own lives in jeopardy for him. He then testifies of his gratitude for them and speaks of the gratitude of every Gentile congregation that had ever come into contact with them.

v. 5—Paul extends greetings to the Roman church also meeting in their home.

Additional thoughts

v. 3—In Paul's letter to the Romans, the valued friendship between Paul and this couple is made clear by the fact that he named them first and gave them the lengthiest description. Occasionally, Priscilla's name is mentioned first, which may be due to her prominent personality—but since scripture is silent on the reason, it's best not to read too much into this.

It is safe to conclude that she was a Proverbs 31 type of woman! Aquila likely encouraged Aquila in reaching her full potential. Though they never had an official title, it was a great honor for them to be called by Paul his "fellow workers in Christ Jesus." They did manual labor in their business, but when they were with Paul they were also active at his side in spiritual work. The couple return to Rome after the death of Claudius.

v. 4—Paul surely remembered the words of Jesus when he thought about this couple's sacrifice for him in dangerous moments, "Greater love has no one than this, than to lay down one's life for his friends." (John 15:13). The fact that every Gentile church that interacted with this Jewish couple was thankful for them is a great testimony to the kind of people they were.

v. 5—Every time this couple moved to a new city, it appears this hospitable couple looked for a home large enough to hold house-church meetings. They opened their home to Paul when they first met him, they opened their home to the Ephesian church, and they opened their home to the Roman church.

6. 2 Timothy 4:19—"Greet Prisca and Aquila"

What is stated

v. 19—This is the third and last time in his letters that Paul mentions this couple. At the end of this letter to a young pastor, Paul asks Timothy to greet them with one final farewell—since Paul now writes from a Roman prison, anticipating his own execution (2 Timothy 1:16–17; 4:6–7). Paul has assigned Timothy the task of leading the Ephesian church (1 Timothy 1:3), so it becomes apparent that Aquila and Priscilla relocated one last time from Rome back to Ephesus. Paul also uses the informal name Prisca for Priscilla, a name that would normally be used only by someone close to the family.

Additional thoughts

v. 19—When a person senses that life will soon end, other important people come to mind. For about fourteen years Paul and this couple had experienced much in the service of Christ. Paul realized that the next place he would likely see them was heaven! As our study ends, we are struck by the oneness and unity of this couple who obviously followed biblical mandates in their Christian home. They were one in marriage, in business, in their giving, in their Bible knowledge, in their faithful service, and in their boldness and courage for Christ. They are a beautiful illustration of what the Bible means when it says two people "shall become one flesh" (Genesis 2:24).

RECOMMENDED BIBLE CHARACTERS TO STUDY

Many diverse people in the Bible are worthy of a closer look. The following list—including both men and women—shows some of the amazing people who by their lives teach great lessons for our Christian lives today.

Old Testament Men

1. Abraham—He became a father in his old age—and the father of all believers.
2. Isaac—He was the miracle child born to Abraham—and offered to God on an altar.
3. Jacob (Israel)—He was born as a twin and lived as a trickster, yet experienced the saving grace of God.
4. Job—He was the man who lost everything but his faith and is remembered for his perseverance.
5. Moses—He was born a Hebrew slave, educated as an Egyptian prince, spoke with God face to face, and led God's people to the promised land.
6. Samson—This warrior-judge was known for his supernatural strength and moral weakness.
7. Samuel—As a young child he was given back to God by his mother to be raised by Eli the priest—and became God's prophet.
8. David—This shepherd boy defeated a giant, served a king, wrote psalms, and later became a king himself.
9. Daniel—He survived abduction to a foreign country and a night in a lion's den, becoming an adviser to kings and a prophet to God's people.
10. Jonah—This missionary prophet ran from God, was swallowed by a great fish, and returned to initiate a revival in a foreign country.

Old Testament Women

1. Sarah—The wife of Abraham miraculously had a child in her old age and became the matriarch of all faithful women.
2. Rebekah—Through God's direction she left her family to become the wife of a man she had never met.
3. Rachel—The woman of a real love story; Jacob worked fourteen years for her

father to be able to marry her.

4. Miriam—She helped save her baby brother, Moses, but he could not save her in Israel's wilderness wanderings.

5. Hannah—God answered the prayer of this barren woman who eventually gave birth to a son that she named Samuel—meaning "God heard."

6. Rahab—This prostitute from the pagan city of Jericho was saved and is listed in the genealogy of the Messiah.

7. Ruth—One book of the Bible tells the story of this proselyte woman who became a widow and was remarried to her kinsman-redeemer.

8. Esther—This Jewish girl became a Persian queen who was used providentially to save her people.

9. Deborah—As a courageous prophetess and judge she was Israel's only female military leader.

10. The good wife—A mother describes to her son the ideal woman to look for as a wife in the poem of Proverbs 31.

New Testament Men

1. James—This half-brother of Jesus grew up as an unbeliever—but later in life followed Jesus and became a church leader.

2. Peter—This man left his family fishing business to became the leader of Jesus' twelve apostles.

3. Nicodemus—This Pharisee is known for his conversation with Jesus about being "born again."

4. Paul—He was a zealous enemy of the Gospel who later became an emissary *for* the Gospel—and authored most of the books of the New Testament.

5. Barnabas—This man was given this nickname because of the encouraging character exemplified when he accepted the recently-converted Paul and introduced him to Jesus' apostles.

6. Luke—He was a physician who accompanied Paul on mission trips—and the only Gentile to write scripture.

7. Silas (Silvanus)—This Jerusalem church leader was selected by Paul as a replacement for John Mark on Paul's second mission trip.

8. Timothy—This young man was trained by Paul and helped write many of his New Testament letters. Two letters from Paul are also addressed to him.

9. Stephen—He was a Christian apologist who became the first church martyr.

10. Philemon—This prominent Christian was encouraged by Paul to take back his now-converted runaway slave as a brother in Christ.

New Testament Women

1. Mary, mother of Jesus—This young virgin was selected by God to miraculously give birth to God's Son.

2. Elizabeth—She miraculously gave birth in her old age to a son later known as John the Baptist.

3. Anna—This widow, who served God for decades in the temple, saw the Christ before her death.

4. Mary Magdalene—This demon-possessed woman was delivered by Christ to become His follower.

5. Mary of Bethany—When this woman is named in scripture, she is always seen at Jesus' feet.

6. The woman at the well—This immoral woman, called by some "the bad Samaritan," had a lengthy conversation with Jesus about living water.

7. The mother of Rufus—This woman's motherly instincts made such an impact on the apostle Paul that he referred to her as his mother.

8. Lydia—This businesswoman became one of the first converts in the new Philippian church.

9. Dorcas (Tabitha)—This charitable woman was miraculously raised from the dead by the apostle Peter.

10–11. Lois and Eunice—Timothy's faithful grandmother and mother together raised him to honor the Lord.

Bible Reading Plan

This plan will help you to read through the whole Bible in a year, by providing an Old Testament passage, a New Testament portion, and an entry from the "Wisdom Books" of Psalms or Proverbs each day. Depending on your personal speed, you can read through the Bible in a year by investing only 20–30 minutes per day.

Day 1	Gen. 1–2	Matt. 1	Ps. 1
Day 2	Gen. 3–4	Matt. 2	Ps. 2
Day 3	Gen. 5–7	Matt. 3	Ps. 3
Day 4	Gen. 8–10	Matt. 4	Ps. 4
Day 5	Gen. 11–13	Matt. 5:1–20	Ps. 5
Day 6	Gen. 14–16	Matt. 5:21–48	Ps. 6
Day 7	Gen. 17–18	Matt. 6:1–18	Ps. 7
Day 8	Gen. 19–20	Matt. 6:19–34	Ps. 8
Day 9	Gen. 21–23	Matt. 7:1–11	Ps. 9:1–8
Day 10	Gen. 24	Matt. 7:12–29	Ps. 9:9–20
Day 11	Gen. 25–26	Matt. 8:1–17	Ps. 10:1–11
Day 12	Gen. 27:1–28:9	Matt. 8:18–34	Ps. 10:12–18
Day 13	Gen. 28:10–29:35	Matt. 9	Ps. 11
Day 14	Gen. 30:1–31:21	Matt. 10:1–15	Ps. 12
Day 15	Gen. 31:22–32:21	Matt. 10:16–36	Ps. 13
Day 16	Gen. 32:22–34:31	Matt. 10:37–11:6	Ps. 14
Day 17	Gen. 35–36	Matt. 11:7–24	Ps. 15
Day 18	Gen. 37–38	Matt. 11:25–30	Ps. 16
Day 19	Gen. 39–40	Matt. 12:1–29	Ps. 17
Day 20	Gen. 41	Matt. 12:30–50	Ps. 18:1–15
Day 21	Gen. 42–43	Matt. 13:1–9	Ps. 18:16–29
Day 22	Gen. 44–45	Matt. 13:10–23	Ps. 18:30–50
Day 23	Gen. 46:1–47:26	Matt. 13:24–43	Ps. 19
Day 24	Gen. 47:27–49:28	Matt. 13:44–58	Ps. 20
Day 25	Gen. 49:29– Exod. 1:22	Matt. 14	Ps. 21
Day 26	Exod. 2–3	Matt. 15:1–28	Ps. 22:1–21
Day 27	Exod. 4:1–5:21	Matt. 15:29–16:12	Ps. 22:22–31
Day 28	Exod. 5:22–7:24	Matt. 16:13–28	Ps. 23
Day 29	Exod. 7:25–9:35	Matt. 17:1–9	Ps. 24
Day 30	Exod. 10–11	Matt. 17:10–27	Ps. 25
Day 31	Exod. 12	Matt. 18:1–20	Ps. 26
Day 32	Exod. 13–14	Matt. 18:21–35	Ps. 27
Day 33	Exod. 15–16	Matt. 19:1–15	Ps. 28
Day 34	Exod. 17–19	Matt. 19:16–30	Ps. 29
Day 35	Exod. 20–21	Matt. 20:1–19	Ps. 30
Day 36	Exod. 22–23	Matt. 20:20–34	Ps. 31:1–8
Day 37	Exod. 24–25	Matt. 21:1–27	Ps. 31:9–18
Day 38	Exod. 26–27	Matt. 21:28–46	Ps. 31:19–24
Day 39	Exod. 28	Matt. 22	Ps. 32
Day 40	Exod. 29	Matt. 23:1–36	Ps. 33:1–12
Day 41	Exod. 30–31	Matt. 23:37–24:28	Ps. 33:13–22
Day 42	Exod. 32–33	Matt. 24:29–51	Ps. 34:1–7
Day 43	Exod. 34:1–35:29	Matt. 25:1–13	Ps. 34:8–22
Day 44	Exod. 35:30–37:29	Matt. 25:14–30	Ps. 35:1–8
Day 45	Exod. 38–39	Matt. 25:31–46	Ps. 35:9–17
Day 46	Exod. 40	Matt. 26:1–35	Ps. 35:18–28
Day 47	Lev. 1–3	Matt. 26:36–68	Ps. 36:1–6
Day 48	Lev. 4:1–5:13	Matt. 26:69–27:26	Ps. 36:7–12
Day 49	Lev. 5:14–7:21	Matt. 27:27–50	Ps. 37:1–6
Day 50	Lev. 7:22–8:36	Matt. 27:51–66	Ps. 37:7–26
Day 51	Lev. 9–10	Matt. 28	Ps. 37:27–40
Day 52	Lev. 11–12	Mark 1:1–28	Ps. 38
Day 53	Lev. 13	Mark 1:29–39	Ps. 39
Day 54	Lev. 14	Mark 1:40–2:12	Ps. 40:1–8

Day 109	Josh. 11:16–13:33	Luke 13:22–35	Ps. 71:7–16
Day 110	Josh. 14–16	Luke 14:1–15	Ps. 71:17–21
Day 111	Josh. 17:1–19:16	Luke 14:16–35	Ps. 71:22–24
Day 112	Josh. 19:17–21:42	Luke 15:1–10	Ps. 72:1–11
Day 113	Josh. 21:43–22:34	Luke 15:11–32	Ps. 72:12–20
Day 114	Josh. 23–24	Luke 16:1–18	Ps. 73:1–9
Day 115	Judg. 1–2	Luke 16:19–17:10	Ps. 73:10–20
Day 116	Judg. 3–4	Luke 17:11–37	Ps. 73:21–28
Day 117	Judg. 5:1–6:24	Luke 18:1–17	Ps. 74:1–3
Day 118	Judg. 6:25–7:25	Luke 18:18–43	Ps. 74:4–11
Day 119	Judg. 8:1–9:23	Luke 19:1–28	Ps. 74:12–17
Day 120	Judg. 9:24–10:18	Luke 19:29–48	Ps. 74:18–23
Day 121	Judg. 11:1–12:7	Luke 20:1–26	Ps. 75:1–7
Day 122	Judg. 12:8–14:20	Luke 20:27–47	Ps. 75:8–10
Day 123	Judg. 15–16	Luke 21:1–19	Ps. 76:1–7
Day 124	Judg. 17–18	Luke 21:20–22:6	Ps. 76:8–12
Day 125	Judg. 19:1–20:23	Luke 22:7–30	Ps. 77:1–11
Day 126	Judg. 20:24–21:25	Luke 22:31–54	Ps. 77:12–20
Day 127	Ruth 1–2	Luke 22:55–23:25	Ps. 78:1–4
Day 128	Ruth 3–4	Luke 23:26–24:12	Ps. 78:5–8
Day 129	1 Sam. 1:1–2:21	Luke 24:13–53	Ps. 78:9–16
Day 130	1 Sam. 2:22–4:22	John 1:1–28	Ps. 78:17–24
Day 131	1 Sam. 5–7	John 1:29–51	Ps. 78:25–33
Day 132	1 Sam. 8:1–9:26	John 2	Ps. 78:34–41
Day 133	1 Sam. 9:27–11:15	John 3:1–22	Ps. 78:42–55
Day 134	1 Sam. 12–13	John 3:23–4:10	Ps. 78:56–66
Day 135	1 Sam. 14	John 4:11–38	Ps. 78:67–72
Day 136	1 Sam. 15–16	John 4:39–54	Ps. 79:1–7
Day 137	1 Sam. 17	John 5:1–24	Ps. 79:8–13
Day 138	1 Sam. 18–19	John 5:25–47	Ps. 80:1–7
Day 139	1 Sam. 20–21	John 6:1–21	Ps. 80:8–19
Day 140	1 Sam. 22–23	John 6:22–42	Ps. 81:1–10
Day 141	1 Sam. 24:1–25:31	John 6:43–71	Ps. 81:11–16
Day 142	1 Sam. 25:32–27:12	John 7:1–24	Ps. 82
Day 143	1 Sam. 28–29	John 7:25–8:11	Ps. 83
Day 144	1 Sam. 30–31	John 8:12–47	Ps. 84:1–4
Day 145	2 Sam. 1–2	John 8:48–9:12	Ps. 84:5–12
Day 146	2 Sam. 3–4	John 9:13–34	Ps. 85:1–7
Day 147	2 Sam. 5:1–7:17	John 9:35–10:10	Ps. 85:8–13
Day 148	2 Sam. 7:18–10:19	John 10:11–30	Ps. 86:1–10
Day 149	2 Sam. 11:1–12:25	John 10:31–11:16	Ps. 86:11–17
Day 150	2 Sam. 12:26–13:39	John 11:17–54	Ps. 87
Day 151	2 Sam. 14:1–15:12	John 11:55–12:19	Ps. 88:1–9
Day 152	2 Sam. 15:13–16:23	John 12:20–43	Ps. 88:10–18
Day 153	2 Sam. 17:1–18:18	John 12:44–13:20	Ps. 89:1–6
Day 154	2 Sam. 18:19–19:39	John 13:21–38	Ps. 89:7–13
Day 155	2 Sam. 19:40–21:22	John 14:1–17	Ps. 89:14–18
Day 156	2 Sam. 22:1–23:7	John 14:18–15:27	Ps. 89:19–29
Day 157	2 Sam. 23:8–24:25	John 16:1–22	Ps. 89:30–37
Day 158	1 Kings 1	John 16:23–17:5	Ps. 89:38–52
Day 159	1 Kings 2	John 17:6–26	Ps. 90:1–12
Day 160	1 Kings 3–4	John 18:1–27	Ps. 90:13–17
Day 161	1 Kings 5–6	John 18:28–19:5	Ps. 91:1–10
Day 162	1 Kings 7	John 19:6–25a	Ps. 91:11–16

Day 217	2 Chron. 34:8–35:19	Rom. 3:1–26	Ps. 118:19–23
Day 218	2 Chron. 35:20–36:23	Rom. 3:27–4:25	Ps. 118:24–29
Day 219	Ezra 1–3	Rom. 5	Ps. 119:1–8
Day 220	Ezra 4–5	Rom. 6:1–7:6	Ps. 119:9–16
Day 221	Ezra 6:1–7:26	Rom. 7:7–25	Ps. 119:17–32
Day 222	Ezra 7:27–9:4	Rom. 8:1–27	Ps. 119:33–40
Day 223	Ezra 9:5–10:44	Rom. 8:28–39	Ps. 119:41–64
Day 224	Neh. 1:1–3:16	Rom. 9:1–18	Ps. 119:65–72
Day 225	Neh. 3:17–5:13	Rom. 9:19–33	Ps. 119:73–80
Day 226	Neh. 5:14–7:73	Rom. 10:1–13	Ps. 119:81–88
Day 227	Neh. 8:1–9:5	Rom. 10:14–11:24	Ps. 119:89–104
Day 228	Neh. 9:6–10:27	Rom. 11:25–12:8	Ps. 119:105–120
Day 229	Neh. 10:28–12:26	Rom. 12:9–13:7	Ps. 119:121–128
Day 230	Neh. 12:27–13:31	Rom. 13:8–14:12	Ps. 119:129–136
Day 231	Esther 1:1–2:18	Rom. 14:13–15:13	Ps. 119:137–152
Day 232	Esther 2:19–5:14	Rom. 15:14–21	Ps. 119:153–168
Day 233	Esther 6–8	Rom. 15:22–33	Ps. 119:169–176
Day 234	Esther 9–10	Rom. 16	Ps. 120–122
Day 235	Job 1–3	1 Cor. 1:1–25	Ps. 123
Day 236	Job 4–6	1 Cor. 1:26–2:16	Ps. 124–125
Day 237	Job 7–9	1 Cor. 3	Ps. 126–127
Day 238	Job 10–13	1 Cor. 4:1–13	Ps. 128–129
Day 239	Job 14–16	1 Cor. 4:14–5:13	Ps. 130
Day 240	Job 17–20	1 Cor. 6	Ps. 131
Day 241	Job 21–23	1 Cor. 7:1–16	Ps. 132
Day 242	Job 24–27	1 Cor. 7:17–40	Ps. 133–134
Day 243	Job 28–30	1 Cor. 8	Ps. 135
Day 244	Job 31–33	1 Cor. 9:1–18	Ps. 136:1–9
Day 245	Job 34–36	1 Cor. 9:19–10:13	Ps. 136:10–26
Day 246	Job 37–39	1 Cor. 10:14–11:1	Ps. 137
Day 247	Job 40–42	1 Cor. 11:2–34	Ps. 138
Day 248	Eccles. 1:1–3:15	1 Cor. 12:1–26	Ps. 139:1–6
Day 249	Eccles. 3:16–6:12	1 Cor. 12:27–13:13	Ps. 139:7–18
Day 250	Eccles. 7:1–9:12	1 Cor. 14:1–22	Ps. 139:19–24
Day 251	Eccles. 9:13–12:14	1 Cor. 14:23–15:11	Ps. 140:1–8
Day 252	SS 1–4	1 Cor. 15:12–34	Ps. 140:9–13
Day 253	SS 5–8	1 Cor. 15:35–58	Ps. 141
Day 254	Isa. 1–2	1 Cor. 16	Ps. 142
Day 255	Isa. 3–5	2 Cor. 1:1–11	Ps. 143:1–6
Day 256	Isa. 6–8	2 Cor. 1:12–2:4	Ps. 143:7–12
Day 257	Isa. 9–10	2 Cor. 2:5–17	Ps. 144
Day 258	Isa. 11–13	2 Cor. 3	Ps. 145
Day 259	Isa. 14–16	2 Cor. 4	Ps. 146
Day 260	Isa. 17–19	2 Cor. 5	Ps. 147:1–11
Day 261	Isa. 20–23	2 Cor. 6	Ps. 147:12–20
Day 262	Isa. 24:1–26:19	2 Cor. 7	Ps. 148
Day 263	Isa. 26:20–28:29	2 Cor. 8	Ps. 149–150
Day 264	Isa. 29–30	2 Cor. 9	Prov. 1:1–9
Day 265	Isa. 31–33	2 Cor. 10	Prov. 1:10–22
Day 266	Isa. 34–36	2 Cor. 11	Prov. 1:23–26
Day 267	Isa. 37–38	2 Cor. 12:1–10	Prov. 1:27–33
Day 268	Isa. 39–40	2 Cor. 12:11–13:14	Prov. 2:1–15
Day 269	Isa. 41–42	Gal. 1	Prov. 2:16–22
Day 270	Isa. 43:1–44:20	Gal. 2	Prov. 3:1–12

Day 271	Isa. 44:21–46:13	Gal. 3:1–18	Prov. 3:13–26
Day 272	Isa. 47:1–49:13	Gal. 3:19–29	Prov. 3:27–35
Day 273	Isa. 49:14–51:23	Gal. 4:1–11	Prov. 4:1–19
Day 274	Isa. 52–54	Gal. 4:12–31	Prov. 4:20–27
Day 275	Isa. 55–57	Gal. 5	Prov. 5:1–14
Day 276	Isa. 58–59	Gal. 6	Prov. 5:15–23
Day 277	Isa. 60–62	Eph. 1	Prov. 6:1–5
Day 278	Isa. 63:1–65:16	Eph. 2	Prov. 6:6–19
Day 279	Isa. 65:17–66:24	Eph. 3:1–4:16	Prov. 6:20–26
Day 280	Jer. 1–2	Eph. 4:17–32	Prov. 6:27–35
Day 281	Jer. 3:1–4:22	Eph. 5	Prov. 7:1–5
Day 282	Jer. 4:23–5:31	Eph. 6	Prov. 7:6–27
Day 283	Jer. 6:1–7:26	Phil. 1:1–26	Prov. 8:1–11
Day 284	Jer. 7:26–9:16	Phil. 1:27–2:18	Prov. 8:12–21
Day 285	Jer. 9:17–11:17	Phil. 2:19–30	Prov. 8:22–36
Day 286	Jer. 11:18–13:27	Phil. 3	Prov. 9:1–6
Day 287	Jer. 14–15	Phil. 4	Prov. 9:7–18
Day 288	Jer. 16–17	Col. 1:1–23	Prov. 10:1–5
Day 289	Jer. 18:1–20:6	Col. 1:24–2:15	Prov. 10:6–14
Day 290	Jer. 20:7–22:19	Col. 2:16–3:4	Prov. 10:15–26
Day 291	Jer. 22:20–23:40	Col. 3:5–4:1	Prov. 10:27–32
Day 292	Jer. 24–25	Col. 4:2–18	Prov. 11:1–11
Day 293	Jer. 26–27	1 Thes. 1:1–2:8	Prov. 11:12–21
Day 294	Jer. 28–29	1 Thes. 2:9–3:13	Prov. 11:22–26
Day 295	Jer. 30:1–31:22	1 Thes. 4:1–5:11	Prov. 11:27–31
Day 296	Jer. 31:23–32:35	1 Thes. 5:12–28	Prov. 12:1–14
Day 297	Jer. 32:36–34:7	2 Thes. 1–2	Prov. 12:15–20
Day 298	Jer. 34:8–36:10	2 Thes. 3	Prov. 12:21–28
Day 299	Jer. 36:11–38:13	1 Tim. 1:1–17	Prov. 13:1–4
Day 300	Jer. 38:14–40:6	1 Tim. 1:18–3:13	Prov. 13:5–13
Day 301	Jer. 40:7–42:22	1 Tim. 3:14–4:10	Prov. 13:14–21
Day 302	Jer. 43–44	1 Tim. 4:11–5:16	Prov. 13:22–25
Day 303	Jer. 45–47	1 Tim. 5:17–6:21	Prov. 14:1–6
Day 304	Jer. 48:1–49:6	2 Tim. 1	Prov. 14:7–22
Day 305	Jer. 49:7–50:16	2 Tim. 2	Prov. 14:23–27
Day 306	Jer. 50:17–51:14	2 Tim. 3	Prov. 14:28–35
Day 307	Jer. 51:15–64	2 Tim. 4	Prov. 15:1–9
Day 308	Jer. 52–Lam. 1	Tit. 1:1–9	Prov. 15:10–17
Day 309	Lam. 2:1–3:38	Tit. 1:10–2:15	Prov. 15:18–26
Day 310	Lam. 3:39–5:22	Tit. 3	Prov. 15:27–33
Day 311	Ezek. 1:1–3:21	Philemon 1	Prov. 16:1–9
Day 312	Ezek. 3:22–5:17	Heb. 1:1–2:4	Prov. 16:10–21
Day 313	Ezek. 6–7	Heb. 2:5–18	Prov. 16:22–33
Day 314	Ezek. 8–10	Heb. 3:1–4:3	Prov. 17:1–5
Day 315	Ezek. 11–12	Heb. 4:4–5:10	Prov. 17:6–12
Day 316	Ezek. 13–14	Heb. 5:11–6:20	Prov. 17:13–22
Day 317	Ezek. 15:1–16:43	Heb. 7:1–28	Prov. 17:23–28
Day 318	Ezek. 16:44–17:24	Heb. 8:1–9:10	Prov. 18:1–7
Day 319	Ezek. 18–19	Heb. 9:11–28	Prov. 18:8–17
Day 320	Ezek. 20	Heb. 10:1–25	Prov. 18:18–24
Day 321	Ezek. 21–22	Heb. 10:26–39	Prov. 19:1–8
Day 322	Ezek. 23	Heb. 11:1–31	Prov. 19:9–14
Day 323	Ezek. 24–26	Heb. 11:32–40	Prov. 19:15–21
Day 324	Ezek. 27–28	Heb. 12:1–13	Prov. 19:22–29

Day 325	Ezek. 29–30	Heb. 12:14–29	Prov. 20:1–18
Day 326	Ezek. 31–32	Heb. 13	Prov. 20:19–24
Day 327	Ezek. 33:1–34:10	Jas. 1	Prov. 20:25–30
Day 328	Ezek. 34:11–36:15	Jas. 2	Prov. 21:1–8
Day 329	Ezek. 36:16–37:28	Jas. 3	Prov. 21:9–18
Day 330	Ezek. 38–39	Jas. 4:1–5:6	Prov. 21:19–24
Day 331	Ezek. 40	Jas. 5:7–20	Prov. 21:25–31
Day 332	Ezek. 41:1–43:12	1 Pet. 1:1–12	Prov. 22:1–9
Day 333	Ezek. 43:13–44:31	1 Pet. 1:13–2:3	Prov. 22:10–23
Day 334	Ezek. 45–46	1 Pet. 2:4–17	Prov. 22:24–29
Day 335	Ezek. 47–48	1 Pet. 2:18–3:7	Prov. 23:1–9
Day 336	Dan. 1:1–2:23	1 Pet. 3:8–4:19	Prov. 23:10–16
Day 337	Dan. 2:24–3:30	1 Pet. 5	Prov. 23:17–25
Day 338	Dan. 4	2 Pet. 1	Prov. 23:26–35
Day 339	Dan. 5	2 Pet. 2	Prov. 24:1–18
Day 340	Dan. 6:1–7:14	2 Pet. 3	Prov. 24:19–27
Day 341	Dan. 7:15–8:27	1 John 1:1–2:17	Prov. 24:28–34
Day 342	Dan. 9–10	1 John 2:18–29	Prov. 25:1–12
Day 343	Dan. 11–12	1 John 3:1–12	Prov. 25:13–17
Day 344	Hos. 1–3	1 John 3:13–4:16	Prov. 25:18–28
Day 345	Hos. 4–6	1 John 4:17–5:21	Prov. 26:1–16
Day 346	Hos. 7–10	2 John	Prov. 26:17–21
Day 347	Hos. 11–14	3 John	Prov. 26:22–27:9
Day 348	Joel 1:1–2:17	Jude	Prov. 27:10–17
Day 349	Joel 2:18–3:21	Rev. 1:1–2:11	Prov. 27:18–27
Day 350	Amos 1:1–4:5	Rev. 2:12–29	Prov. 28:1–8
Day 351	Amos 4:6–6:14	Rev. 3	Prov. 28:9–16
Day 352	Amos 7–9	Rev. 4:1–5:5	Prov. 28:17–24
Day 353	Obad.–Jonah	Rev. 5:6–14	Prov. 28:25–28
Day 354	Mic. 1:1–4:5	Rev. 6:1–7:8	Prov. 29:1–8
Day 355	Mic. 4:6–7:20	Rev. 7:9–8:13	Prov. 29:9–14
Day 356	Nah. 1–3	Rev. 9–10	Prov. 29:15–23
Day 357	Hab. 1–3	Rev. 11	Prov. 29:24–27
Day 358	Zeph. 1–3	Rev. 12	Prov. 30:1–6
Day 359	Hag. 1–2	Rev. 13:1–14:13	Prov. 30:7–16
Day 360	Zech. 1–4	Rev. 14:14–16:3	Prov. 30:17–20
Day 361	Zech. 5–8	Rev. 16:4–21	Prov. 30:21–28
Day 362	Zech. 9–11	Rev. 17:1–18:8	Prov. 30:29–33
Day 363	Zech. 12–14	Rev. 18:9–24	Prov. 31:1–9
Day 364	Mal. 1–2	Rev. 19–20	Prov. 31:10–17
Day 365	Mal. 3–4	Rev. 21–22	Prov. 31:18–31